U0921955

中国城市发展报告

（2015）

主　办

中 国 市 长 协 会

承　办

国际欧亚科学院中国科学中心

《中国城市发展报告》编委会　编

中国城市出版社

·北 京·

图书在版编目（CIP）数据

中国城市发展报告. 2015/《中国城市发展报告》编委会编. —北京：中国城市出版社，2016. 6

ISBN 978 - 7 - 5074 - 3073 - 8

Ⅰ. ①中…　Ⅱ. ①中…　Ⅲ. ①城市经济—经济发展—研究报告—中国—2015　Ⅳ. ①F299. 21

中国版本图书馆 CIP 数据核字（2016）第 114785 号

责任编辑　陈夕涛　孙湛波　徐昌强
装帧设计　美信书籍设计工作室
责任技术编辑　张建军
出版发行　中国城市出版社
地　　址　北京市海淀区三里河路 9 号（邮编　100835）
网　　址　www. citypress. cn
发行部电话　（010）63454857　63289949
发行部传真　（010）63421417
总编室电话　（010）58933140
总编室信箱　citypress@ sina. com
经　　销　新华书店
印　　刷　北京圣夫亚美印刷有限公司
字　　数　628 千字　　印张　28. 5
开　　本　889 × 1194（毫米）　1/16
版　　次　2016 年 6 月第 1 版
印　　次　2016 年 6 月第 1 次印刷
定　　价　398. 00 元

《中国城市发展报告（2015）》机构组成名单

中山大学城市与区域研究中心
中国科学院地理科学与资源研究所
国家遥感应用工程技术研究中心

《中国城市发展报告(2015)》工作委员会

主任委员： 王长远
委　　员： 林家宁　方兆瑞　赵旺华

序　一

蒋正华

（第九届、十届全国人大常委会副委员长，国际欧亚科学院
执行院长，国际欧亚科学院中国科学中心主席）

2015 年 12 月，在时隔 37 年之后，中央召开了城市工作会议，中央政治局的七位常委出席会议。习近平总书记在会上发表重要讲话，分析城市发展面临的形势，明确做好城市工作的指导思想、总体思路、重点任务。李克强总理在讲话中论述了当前城市工作的重点，提出了做好城市工作的具体部署。会议提出，要认识、尊重、顺应城市发展规律，端正城市发展指导思想，推进农民工市民化，加快提高户籍人口城镇化率，增强城市宜居性，改革完善城市规划，提高城市管理水平。同时进一步强调，当前和今后一段时期，我国城市工作应全面贯彻创新、协调、绿色、开放、共享的发展理念，坚持以人为本、科学发展、改革创新、依法治市，转变城市发展方式，完善城市治理体系，提高城市治理能力，着力解决城市病等突出问题，不断提升城市环境质量、人民生活质量、城市竞争力，建设和谐宜居、富有活力、各具特色的现代化城市，提高新型城镇化水平，走出一条中国特色的城市发展道路。

为落实中央城市工作会议精神，2016 年 2 月又出台了《中共中央、国务院关于进一步加强城市规划建设管理工作的若干意见》（以下简称《若干意见》），明确这是为转变城市发展方式、塑造城市特色风貌、提升城市环境质量、创新城市管理服务而制定的法规。其中特别强调创新城市规划理念和创新城市建设与管理模式。

中央城市工作会议精神和中央领导的讲话明确了今后方向，为适应新常态和引领新常态，进一步转变城市发展方式和提升城市发展质量，必须在以下三个方面取得重大突破和创新：

一是正确处理好城市发展的数量与质量、规模与速度、当前与长远发展的关系。按照“框定总量、限定容量、盘活存量、做优增量、提高质量、立足国情、尊重自然、顺应自然、保护自然、改善城市生态环境”的总体思路进行调控，确保城市发展形成适度的体量（户籍人口城镇化率）、适度的节奏（速度）和健康的“体质”，推动城市发展从目前的亚健康状态转变为健康状态。

二是实现城市发展的五个统筹。以《全国主体功能区规划》、《国家新型城镇化规划（2014－2020年）》和《若干意见》为指导，统筹空间、规模、产业三大结构，统筹规划、建设、管理三大环节，统筹改革、科技、文化三大动力，统筹生产、生活、生态三大空间布局，统筹政府、社会、市民三大主体，提升城市建设与治理的全局性、系统性、发展的持续性，实现城市生产空间集约高效、生活空间宜居适度、生态空间山清水秀，努力将城市建成人与自然、人与人和谐相处的美丽家园。

三是推动新型城市建设。要顺应现代城市发展的新理念、新趋势，推动城市绿色发展，提高智能化水平，增强历史文化魅力，全面提升城市的内在品质。重点为：加快绿色城市建设，构建绿色生产方式、生活方式和消费模式，节约集约利用土地、水和能源等资源，推广可再生能源、绿色建筑、绿色交通和绿色出行；推进智慧城市建设，将“互联网＋”、大数据、物联网、云计算等现代化信息技术广泛应用于城市管理服务和居民的生活；注重人文城市建设，通过挖掘城市文化资源、保护历史文化遗产，强化文化传承创新，把城市建成为历史底蕴厚重、时代特色鲜明的人文魅力空间，促进传统文化与现代文化、本土文化与外来文化的交融，形成多元开放的现代城市文化。

《中国城市发展报告（2015）》除坚持“中国城市编年史”的基本定位外，重点围绕智慧城市和幸福城市两大主题，突出新常态特点，内容包括城市建设、城市规划、城市经济、城市管理、城市地理、城市生态环境等方面，仍按综论篇、论坛篇、观察篇、专题篇、案例篇、附录篇六部分编写，力图从不同的视角较全面地反映2015年在新型城镇化方面所取得的新进展以及存在的问题。现在看来，2015年卷还存在一些明显不足之处。例如，针对“一带一路”、“京津冀协同发展”、“长江经济带”等国家战略和“十三五”规划的论文数量较少，反映不够充分；观察篇缺少针砭时弊、切中要害和具有警示作用的论文。在2016年卷中，我们将在这方面认真改进，除邀请权威专家撰写有关稿件外，拟定向放开观察篇与专题篇，在更大范围内征集稿件，全面提升《中国城市发展报告》质量，以期更好地为城市发展的决策者、管理者和研究工作者提供参考。

欢迎广大读者不吝赐教。

序 二

陈政高

（住房和城乡建设部部长，中国市长协会执行会长）

2015年，是中国城市发展史上不平凡的一年。时隔37年之后，中央城市工作会议在北京胜利召开，这是在我国全面建成小康社会、实现第一个百年目标决胜阶段的关键时刻，召开的一次重要会议。习近平总书记、李克强总理在会上作了重要讲话，系统分析了城市发展面临的形势，深刻阐明了做好城市工作的指导思想、总体思路和重点任务，为我国城市未来发展指明了方向。会后正式印发了《中共中央、国务院关于进一步加强城市规划建设管理工作的若干意见》（以下简称《若干意见》），对城市规划建设管理工作做出全面部署，是我们做好城市工作的行动指南。中央城市工作会议和《若干意见》对住房城乡建设工作提出了新的目标、新的要求，为推动住房城乡建设事业的改革发展提供了重大的历史机遇。深入学习贯彻落实会议精神和《若干意见》，是当前和今后一个时期的重大任务。

回顾过去的一年，在党中央、国务院坚强领导下，全国住房城乡建设系统迎难而上，奋力拼搏，全面完成了各项任务：

——实现了房地产市场企稳回升。我们和有关部门研究出台了一系列政策措施，各地加大力度承担了调控主体责任，房地产市场呈现企稳回升态势。保障性安居工程基本建成772万套，棚户区改造开工601万套，创历史新高。棚改货币化安置比例达到29.9%，对去库存发挥了重要作用。

——开拓了城市建设工作新领域。我们启动了城市地下综合管廊和海绵城市建设，推进了城市黑臭水体整治工作。大力开展了“学习中卫经验，清洁城市环境”活动，打响了治理城市违法建筑的攻坚战。继续深入推进了工程质量治理两年行动，开展了老楼危楼安全隐患排查整治工作。

——城乡规划管理工作不断加强。我们稳步推进了城乡规划改革，推动了省域空间规划、市县“多规合一”和城市“双修”三项试点工作，启动了全国城镇体系规划编制工作。

规划编制审批机制和规划督察体制不断完善，重点违法案件监督查处力度加大。

——各项改革任务取得了新进展。我们认真贯彻落实《中共中央、国务院关于深入推进城市执法体制改革 改进城市管理工作的指导意见》，深入推进了城市管理综合执法体制改革。研究起草了住房制度改革方案，认真做好《住房公积金管理条例》修订工作。

2016年是“十三五”开局之年，住房城乡建设系统要全面落实党的十八大和十八届三中、四中、五中全会精神，深入贯彻习近平总书记系列重要讲话精神，按照“五位一体”总体布局和“四个全面”战略布局，牢固树立创新、协调、绿色、开放、共享的发展理念，全面落实中央城市工作会议和《若干意见》提出的各项部署，进一步加强城市规划建设管理工作，努力开创城市现代化建设的新局面。

——贯穿一条工作主线。把学习贯彻中央城市工作会议和《若干意见》精神作为贯穿今年工作的主线。深入学习领会习近平总书记、李克强总理的重要讲话精神，认真贯彻落实会议和《若干意见》提出的各项重大决策部署，各地、各个城市都要绘制任务图，列出时间表，明确责任单位和责任人，真正把每项工作任务落到实处。

——保持房地产市场平稳健康发展。落实地方调控主体责任。完善支持居民住房合理消费的税收、信贷政策，扩大住房需求，促进住房消费，因城施策化解房地产库存。推进以满足新市民住房需求为主的住房制度改革，建立租购并举的住房制度，大力发展住房租赁市场。进一步用足用好住房公积金，支持缴存职工住房消费。加快推进棚户区改造，确保完成新开工600万套棚改任务，大力提高棚改货币化安置比例。

——推动城市规划管理创新。集中力量完成全国城镇体系规划，抓好省级空间规划、“多规合一”、划定城市开发边界等试点并加以推广。完善规划决策机制、审批机制和规划督察体制，提高规划的前瞻性、严肃性、强制性和公开性。继续抓好城市违法建筑治理，加大对规划违法行为的处罚力度。大力推进城市设计，开展城市修补和生态修复，提升城市品质，塑造城市特色风貌。

——大力推进城市基础设施建设。加快城市地下综合管廊建设步伐，2016年开工建设城市地下综合管廊2000公里以上。进一步推进海绵城市建设，抓好16个城市试点工作，总结经验、全面推广。继续抓好城市黑臭水体整治，推动整治工作取得实质性进展。

——全面加强城市管理工作。深入贯彻落实《中共中央、国务院关于深入推进城市执法体制改革改进城市管理工作的指导意见》，理顺管理体制，推进综合执法，加强队伍建设，提高服务水平。

——加快建筑业改革发展步伐。集中精力对建筑业进行全面深入的调研，组织召开全国建筑业大会，深化建筑业改革，推动建筑业可持续发展。大力推广装配式建筑，努力取得突破性进展，推动传统建造方式变革，促进产业转型升级。

中央城市工作会议意义深远，我国城市发展由此掀开了历史性的一页。蓝图已绘就，扬帆正当时。住房城乡建设系统要把思想和行动统一到党中央、国务院决策部署上来，以敢于担当的勇气、坚韧不拔的毅力、雷厉风行的作风、科学务实的精神，奋发有为，开拓进取，乘中央城市工作会议东风，推动住房城乡建设事业再上新台阶。

中国市长协会自2001年开始组织编写《中国城市发展报告》，至今已连续出版14卷。该报告是系统研究探讨有关城市建设、城市管理、城市可持续发展能力等重大问题的综合性年度报告。希望它的出版有助于读者了解我国城市发展的全貌，总结城市发展的经验，思考城市发展的未来。同时，为城市工作的领导者、管理者、研究者提供一个掌握政策、了解信息、更新理念、研究案例的平台。希望中国市长协会以中央城市工作会议精神为指引，发挥自身优势，更好地汇集众智，凝聚共识，为推进我国城市现代化建设贡献力量。

目　录

综论篇

论坛篇

观察篇

专题篇

案例篇

附录篇

综论篇

2015年中国城市发展综述

在中华民族走向复兴的历史坐标系上，2015年是不同寻常的一年，是大有作为的一年。

2015年，中共十八届五中全会针对中国经济转型时期面临的种种问题，提出了“创新、协调、绿色、开放、共享”这五大重要发展理念。习近平总书记在中央财经领导小组第十一次会议上首次提出，在适度扩大总需求的同时，着力加强供给侧结构性改革，着力提高供给体系质量和效率，增强经济持续增长动力，推动我国社会生产力水平实现整体跃升。

2015年，面对错综复杂的国际形势和不断加大的国内外经济下行压力，经过全国人民共同努力，“十二五”规划圆满收官，“一带一路”建设取得实质性进展，亚洲基础设施投资银行正式成立，丝路基金投入运营，人民币纳入国际货币基金组织特别提款权货币篮子，中国经济增长继续居于世界前列。

2015年，中国人民隆重纪念抗日战争暨世界反法西斯战争胜利70周年，北京市与河北省携手获得第24届冬奥会举办权，自主研制的C919大型客机总装下线，中国超级计算机破世界纪录蝉联“六连冠”，我国科学家研制的暗物质探测卫星发射升空，屠呦呦成为国内首位获得诺贝尔奖的科学家。

2015年12月20日至21日，中央城市工作会议在北京举行。会议指出，城市工作是一个系统工程。做好城市工作，要顺应城市工作新形势、改革发展新要求、人民群众新期待，坚持以人民为中心的发展思想，坚持人民城市为人民。这是我们做好城市工作的出发点和落脚点。会议要求，城市工作要把创造优良人居环境作为中心目标，努力把城市建设成为人与人、人与自然和谐共处的美丽家园。

一、新型城镇化进展概况

（一）经济社会持续发展

2015年，党中央、国务院保持战略定力，统筹谋划国际国内两个大局，坚持稳中求进工作总基调，主动适应引领新常态，以新理念指导新实践，以新战略谋求新发展，不断创新宏观调控，国民经济保持在合理区间运行，经济结构进一步优化，转型升级进一步加快，新兴动力进一步积聚，人民生活进一步改善。“大众创业、万众创新”蓬勃兴起，经济保持了总体平稳、稳中有进、稳中有好的发展态势。

初步核算，2015 年国内生产总值676 708亿元，人均49 229元，按可比价格计算，比上年增长6.9%；第一、二、三产业比重为9.0:40.5:50.5。全国居民人均可支配收入21 966元，实际增长7.4%。按常住地分，城镇居民人均可支配收入31 195元，实际增长6.6%；农村居民人均可支配收入11 422元，实际增长7.5%。城乡居民人均收入倍差2.73，比上年缩小0.02。2015 年全国居民收入基尼系数为0.462。全年农民工总量27 747万人，其中外出农民工16 884万人。农民工月均收入水平3 072元，比上年增长7.2%。

2015 年年末中国大陆总人口137 462万人，比上年末增加 680 万人。全年出生人口1 655万人，人口自然增长率为4.96‰。从城乡结构看，城镇常住人口77 116万人，比上年末增加2 200万人，乡村常住人口60 346万人，减少1 520万人，城镇人口占总人口比重为56.10%。全国居住地和户口登记地不在同一个乡镇街道且离开户口登记地半年以上的人口（即人户分离人口）2.94 亿人，其中流动人口为2.47 亿人。年末全国就业人员77 451万人，其中城镇就业人员40 410万人。全年城镇新增就业1 312万人，城镇失业人员再就业 567 万人，就业困难人员就业 173 万人，年末城镇登记失业率4.05%。

2015 年全国房地产开发投资95 979亿元，房屋新开工面积154 454万平方米，商品房销售面积128 495万平方米，商品房销售额87 281亿元，年末全国商品房待售面积71 853万平方米，比上年末增长15.6%。

（二）市级行政区划调整

2015 年年末，全国有设市城市 656 个，其中直辖市 4 个，副省级市 15 个，地级市 276 个，县级市 361 个，县城合计约1 550个，建制镇20 515个。年内全国设市城市建制的调整变动如下：

国务院 2 月 19 日批复海南省人民政府，同意撤销县级儋州市，设立地级儋州市，以原县级儋州市的行政区域为地级儋州市的行政区域。国务院 3 月 16 日批复西藏自治区人民政府，同意撤销林芝地区和林芝县，设立地级林芝市，林芝市设立巴宜区，以原林芝县的行政区域为巴宜区的行政区域。同日，国务院批复新疆维吾尔自治区人民政府，同意撤销吐鲁番地区和县级吐鲁番市，设立地级吐鲁番市，吐鲁番市设立高昌区，以原县级吐鲁番市的行政区域为高昌区的行政区域。

根据国务院批复，江苏省撤销县级金坛市，设立常州市金坛区，撤销县级大丰市，设立盐城市大丰区；广东省撤销县级高要市，设立肇庆市高要区；辽宁省撤销县级普兰店市，设立大连市普兰店区。经国务院批准，四川省撤销康定县设立县级康定市，撤销马尔康县设立县级马尔康市；新疆维吾尔自治区设立县级可克达拉市；广西壮族自治区撤销靖西县设立县级靖西市；云南省撤销腾冲县设立县级腾冲市；黑龙江省撤销东宁县设立县级东宁市。

2015 年，国务院先后批复同意设立贵安综合保税区、中国（杭州）跨境电子商务综合试验区、云南勐腊（磨憨）重点开发开放试验区，设立湖南湘江新区、福州新区、云南滇中新区和哈尔滨新区，同意连云港高新技术产业开发区升级为国家高新技术产业开发区。国务院批复了长江中游城市群发展规划、大别山革命老区振兴发展规划、环渤海地区合作发展纲要、苏州工业园区开展开放创新综合试验总体方案，印发了中国广东、天津、福建的自由贸易试验区总体方案，以及进一步深化中国（上海）自由贸易试验区改革开放方案。

（三）城市（城区）建设

根据住房和城乡建设部统计，2014 年年末，全国设市城市 653 个，城市城区户籍人口 3.86 亿人，暂住人口 0.60 亿人，建成区面积 4.98 万平方公里。

2014 年城市市政公用设施固定资产完成投资16 246.9亿元，占同期全社会固定资产投资总额的 3.17%。主要新增生产能力（或效益）是：供水日综合生产能力 530 万立方米，天然气储气能力 1342 万立方米，集中供热蒸汽能力 0.15 万吨/小时，热水能力 40.6 万兆瓦，道路长度 1.09 万公里，排水管道长度 1.9 万公里，城市污水处理厂日处理能力 443 万立方米，城市生活垃圾无害化日处理能力 2.1 万吨。

2014 年全国城市用水人口 4.35 亿人，人均日生活用水量 173.73 升，用水普及率 97.64%；用气人口 4.21 亿人，燃气普及率 94.56%；集中供热面积 61.1 亿平方米；城市道路长度 35.2 万公里，人均城市道路面积 15.34 平方米；全国城市共有污水处理厂1 808座，污水处理厂集中处理率 85.94%；城市再生水日生产能力2 065万立方米，再生水利用量 36.3 亿立方米；城市共有生活垃圾无害化处理场（厂）819 座，城市生活垃圾无害化处理率达到 91.77%；城市道路清扫保洁（覆盖）面积 67.6 亿平方米，机械清扫率 50.4%；全年清运生活垃圾、粪便 1.94 亿吨；城市建成区绿地率达到 36.24%，人均公园绿地面积 12.95 平方米；2014 年年末，全国共有 225 处国家级风景名胜区，风景名胜区面积 9.9 万平方公里，可游览面积 4.2 万平方公里，全年接待游人 20.4 亿人次。国家投入 56.8 亿元用于风景名胜区的维护和建设。

据交通运输部统计，2014 年年末全国有 22 个城市开通了轨道交通，拥有轨道交通车站 1 829个，其中换乘站 151 个。全国城市及县城拥有公共汽电车 52.88 万辆，其中 BRT 车辆 5 339辆；拥有城市轨道运营车辆17 300辆、41 770标台，出租汽车运营车辆 137.01 万辆，城市客运轮渡 329 艘。全国城市客运拥有公共汽电车运营线路45 052条，运营线路总长度 81.78 万公里，其中 BRT 线路长度2 790.3公里；轨道交通运营线路 92 条，运营线路总长度 2 816.1公里。城市客运轮渡运营航线 126 条，运营航线总长度 497.6 公里。全年城市客运系统运送旅客1 315.66亿人，其中公共汽电车完成 781.88 亿人，BRT 客运量 14.76 亿人次，轨道交通完成 126.66 亿人，出租汽车完成 406.06 亿人，客运轮渡完成 1.07 亿人。城市客运系统完成的客运量构成为：公共汽电车 59.4%、轨道交通 9.6%、出租汽车 30.9%和客运轮渡 0.1%。

（四）县城建设

2014 年年末，全国共有县1 596个，据对1 579个县、10 个新撤销县、14 个特殊区域以及149 个新疆生产建设兵团师团部驻地统计汇总，县城户籍人口14 000万人，暂住人口1 600万人，建成区面积 2. 01 万平方公里。

全国县城市政公用设施固定资产完成投资 3571. 0 亿元，主要新增生产能力（或效益）是：供水日综合生产能力 273 万立方米，天然气储气能力1 308万立方米，集中供热蒸汽能力 397 吨/小时，热水能力 1. 31 万兆瓦，道路长度5 687公里，排水管道长度 1. 0 万公里，污水处理厂日处理能力 206 万立方米，生活垃圾无害化日处理能力7 721吨。

2014 年，全国县城用水人口 1. 39 亿人，用水普及率 88. 89%，人均日生活用水量为118. 22 升；用气人口 1. 15 亿人，燃气普及率达到 73. 23%；集中供热面积 11. 4 亿平方米；县城道路长度 13. 0 万公里，人均城市道路面积 15. 39 平方米；道路清扫保洁面积 22. 9 亿平方米，其中机械清扫面积 7. 9 亿平方米；共有污水处理厂1 554座，污水处理厂集中处理率达到 80. 19%；共有生活垃圾无害化处理场（厂）1 129座，生活垃圾无害化处理率达到71. 58%；全年清运生活垃圾、粪便 0. 72 亿吨；县城建成区绿地率 25. 88%，人均公园绿地面积 9. 91 平方米。

（五）村镇建设

2014 年年末，全国共有建制镇20 401个、乡12 282个。据对17 653个建制镇、11 871个乡、679 个镇乡级特殊区域和 270 万个自然村（其中村民委员会所在地 54. 67 万个）统计汇总，村镇户籍总人口 9. 52 亿人。其中，建制镇建成区人口 1. 56 亿人，乡建成区 0. 30 亿人，镇乡级特殊区域建成区 0. 03 亿人，村庄 7. 63 亿人。全国建制镇建成区面积 379. 5 万公顷，乡建成区 72. 2 万公顷，镇乡级特殊区域建成区 10. 5 万公顷，村庄现状用地面积1 394. 1万公顷。全国已编制总体规划的建制镇16 417个，乡9 060个，镇乡级特殊区域 491 个，行政村32. 2 万个，自然村 76. 6 万个。2014 年，全国村镇规划编制投入达 35. 47 亿元。

2014 年，全国村镇建设总投资16 101亿元，其中房屋建设投资12 559亿元，房屋竣工建筑面积 11. 56 亿平方米。年末村镇实有房屋建筑面积 378. 05 亿平方米，村镇人均住宅建筑面积 33. 37 平方米。

2014 年年末，建制镇建成区用水普及率达到 82. 77%，人均日生活用水量为 98. 68 升，燃气普及率达到 47. 8%，人均道路面积 12. 6 平方米，排水管道暗渠密度 5. 94 公里/平方公里，人均公园绿地面积 2. 39 平方米。乡建成区用水普及率达到 69. 26%，人均日生活用水量为 83. 08 升，燃气普及率达到 20. 3%，人均道路面积 12. 6 平方米，排水管道暗渠密度 3. 83 公里/平方公里，人均公园绿地面积 1. 07 平方米。镇乡级特殊区域建成区用水普及率达到86. 95%，人均日生活用水量为 82. 76 升，燃气普及率达到 50. 3%，人均道路面积 15. 95 平方米，排水管道暗渠密度 5. 25 公里/平方公里，人均公园绿地面积 3. 15 平方米。全国村庄内道路长度 234 万公里，其中硬化路 72 万公里；全国 62. 5% 的行政村有集中供水，村庄内排水管道沟渠长度 54.2 万公里，9.98% 的行政村对生活污水进行了处理，63.98% 的行政村有生活垃圾收集点，48.18% 的行政村对生活垃圾进行了处理。

二、《京津冀协同发展规划纲要》的编制与落实

2014 年 12 月举行的中央经济工作会议部署了 2015 年经济工作的总体要求和主要任务。在优化经济发展空间格局方面，会议明确提出要重点实施“一带一路”、京津冀协同发展、长江经济带三大战略，争取 2015 年的良好开局。

2015 年 3 月 23 日，中央财经领导小组第九次会议审议研究了《京津冀协同发展规划纲要》。中共中央政治局 4 月 30 日召开会议，审议通过《京津冀协同发展规划纲要》。

会议指出，推动京津冀协同发展是一个重大国家战略。战略的核心是有序疏解北京非首都功能，调整经济结构和空间结构，走出一条内涵集约发展的新路子，探索出一种人口经济密集地区优化开发的模式，促进区域协调发展，形成新增长极。

在《中共中央关于制定国民经济和社会发展第十三个五年规划的建议》和之后形成的《国民经济和社会发展第十三个五年规划纲要》中，进一步提出用发展新空间培育发展新动力，用发展新动力开拓发展新空间的思路。要求坚持优势互补、互利共赢、区域一体，推动京津冀协同发展，建设以首都为核心的世界级城市群，辐射带动环渤海地区和北方腹地发展。具体内容包括：

（一）有序疏解北京非首都功能

积极稳妥推进北京非首都功能疏解，降低主城区人口密度。重点疏解高耗能高耗水企业、区域性物流基地和专业市场、部分教育医疗和培训机构、部分行政事业性服务机构和企业总部等。高水平建设北京市行政副中心。规划建设集中承载地和“微中心”。

（二）优化空间格局和功能定位

构建“一核双城三轴四区多节点”的空间格局。优化产业布局，推进建设京津冀协同创新共同体。北京重点发展知识经济、服务经济、绿色经济，加快构建高精尖产业结构。天津优化发展先进制造业、战略性新兴产业和现代服务业，建设全国先进制造研发基地和金融创新运营示范区。河北积极承接北京非首都功能转移和京津科技成果转化，重点建设全国现代商贸物流重要基地、新型工业化基地和产业转型升级试验区。

（三）构建一体化现代交通网络

建设高效密集轨道交通网，强化干线铁路建设，加快建设城际铁路、市域（郊）铁路并逐步成网，充分利用现有能力开行城际、市域（郊）列车，客运专线覆盖所有地级及以上城市。完善高速公路网络，提升国省干线技术等级。构建分工协作的港口群，完善港口集疏运体系，建立海事统筹监管新模式。打造国际一流航空枢纽，构建航空运输协作

机制。

（四）扩大环境容量和生态空间

构建区域生态环境监测网络、预警体系和协调联动机制，削减区域污染物排放总量。加强大气污染联防联控，实施大气污染防治重点地区气化工程，细颗粒物浓度下降25%以上。加强饮用水源地保护，联合开展河流、湖泊、海域污染治理。划定生态保护红线，实施分区管理，建设永定河等生态廊道。加大京津保地区营造林和白洋淀、衡水湖等湖泊湿地恢复力度，共建坝上高原生态防护区、燕山—太行山生态涵养区。

（五）推动公共服务共建共享

建设区域人力资源信息共享与服务平台，衔接区域间劳动用工和人才政策。优化教育资源布局，鼓励高等学校学科共建、资源共享，推动职业教育统筹发展。建立健全区域内双向转诊和检查结果互认制度，支持开展合作办医试点。实现养老保险关系在三省市间的顺利衔接，推动社会保险协同发展。

京津冀三地积极响应中央决策，分别在中共北京市委、天津市委和河北省委的国民经济和社会发展第十三个五年规划建议中提出了落实《京津冀协同发展规划纲要》的具体措施。

北京市提出：京津冀协同发展是具有里程碑意义的大事。北京要紧紧抓住和用好重大历史机遇，紧紧把握北京在京津冀协同发展中的核心地位，继续集中力量落实首都城市战略定位，有序疏解非首都功能，治理“大城市病”。2020年全市常住人口总量控制在2 300万人以内，城六区常住人口比2014年下降15%左右。推动区域性物流基地、专业市场调整退出，部分教育医疗等公共服务机构、行政企事业单位有序疏解迁出，建立与承接地对接机制，积极推进曹妃甸区、新机场临空经济区、张承生态功能区、滨海新区等4个战略合作功能区建设，推动形成“多点一城”疏解格局。要发挥比较优势，发挥示范带动作用，创新合作模式，加快推动错位发展与融合发展，实现区域良性互动，朝着建设国际一流的和谐宜居之都目标奋勇前进。

天津市提出：全力实施京津冀协同发展战略，深化京津冀协同发展，主动融入京津冀城市群建设。要立足大局，坚持目标同向、措施一体、优势互补、互利共赢，积极承接北京非首都功能疏解，强化京津双城联动，加强与河北合作，打造高端产业发展带、城镇聚集轴和核心功能区。加快推进交通一体化发展，构建以海空两港为核心、轨道交通为骨干、公路运输为主体、多种运输方式有效衔接的海陆空立体交通网络，打造京津冀1小时通勤圈，推进交通智能管理、运输服务、安全保障一体化。加强北方国际航运核心区建设，建设国际一流枢纽海港，完善集疏运体系，形成“北集南散”港口功能布局，深化港口群、机场群合作，大力发展航运服务业，强化辐射功能。加强区域生态环境保护，推进生态环保规划、标准、监测、执法一体化。推动产业升级转移，积极对接北京创新资源和优质产业，主动向河北延伸产业链条，推进未来科技城京津合作示范区等对接平台建设，实现产业互补发展、错位发展、共赢发展。

河北省提出：精准推进京津冀协同发展任务落实，积极承接北京非首都功能疏解，用好京津冀协同发展“金字招牌”。推动制造业功能向省级以上产业园区和合作共建园区聚集，教育医疗等社会公共服务功能向资源相对集中、生态环境良好的地区聚集，服务业功能向产业基础好、比较优势明显的地区聚集，行政事业性机构和企业总部功能向首都“一小时通勤圈”内的城镇聚集。精准打造承接平台和载体，谋划建设集中承接非首都功能疏解的载体，支持环京津区域、沿主要交通轴线具备条件的中小城市建成“微中心”，加强产业园区等重点承接平台建设，合作推进京冀曹妃甸协同发展示范区、津冀芦台协同发展示范区、北京新机场临空经济区、京冀中关村（正定）集成电路产业基地等共建园区建设。着力推进交通一体化发展，推动北京平谷线等京津市域铁路和城市轨道交通向我省延伸，积极谋划亦庄至廊坊、房山至涿州、大兴至固安、通州至燕郊轻轨项目建设。完善公路交通网络，打通高速公路“断头路”，拓宽国省干线“瓶颈路”。加强津冀港口协作，携手推进北京新机场建设，基本形成区域一体化交通网络，构建中心城市与卫星城半小时交通圈、京津冀核心区域 1 小时交通圈、相邻城市间 1.5 小时交通圈。科学推进张家口赛区冬奥场馆（地）及残奥设施规划建设，加快京张高铁及崇礼支线、张家口机场改扩建等重大项目建设，进一步完善配套设施，实施“科技冬奥”工程，打造崇礼“低碳奥运专区”，为办成一届精彩、非凡、卓越的冬奥会打下坚实基础。建设京张体育文化旅游带，推动冰雪产业、休闲旅游、会议会展等产业向国际水平迈进。

三、城市基础设施的规划、建设与管理

2015 年，国务院及相关部委先后发布一系列文件，指导各地的城市基础设施规划、建设与管理工作。

（一）“互联网 +”行动发展目标

“互联网 +”是把互联网的创新成果与经济社会各领域深度融合，推动技术进步、效率提升和组织变革，提升实体经济创新力和生产力，形成更广泛的以互联网为基础设施和创新要素的经济社会发展新形态。为加快推动互联网与各领域深入融合和创新发展，国务院于 2015 年提出积极推进“互联网 +”行动的发展目标。

到 2018 年，互联网与经济社会各领域的融合发展将进一步深化，基于互联网的新业态成为新的经济增长动力，互联网支撑大众创业、万众创新的作用进一步增强，互联网成为提供公共服务的重要手段，网络经济与实体经济协同互动的发展格局基本形成。

经济发展进一步提质增效。互联网在促进制造业、农业、能源、环保等产业转型升级方面取得积极成效，劳动生产率进一步提高。基于互联网的新兴业态不断涌现，电子商务、互联网金融快速发展，对经济提质增效的促进作用更加凸显。

社会服务进一步便捷普惠。健康医疗、教育、交通等民生领域互联网应用更加丰富，公

共服务更加多元，线上线下结合更加紧密。社会服务资源配置不断优化，公众享受到更加公平、高效、优质、便捷的服务。

基础支撑进一步夯实提升。网络设施和产业基础得到有效巩固加强，应用支撑和安全保障能力明显增强。固定宽带网络、新一代移动通信网和下一代互联网加快发展，物联网、云计算等新型基础设施更加完备。人工智能等技术及其产业化能力显著增强。

发展环境进一步开放包容。全社会对互联网融合创新的认识不断深入，互联网融合发展面临的体制机制障碍有效破除，公共数据资源开放取得实质性进展，相关标准规范、信用体系和法律法规逐步完善。

到2025年，网络化、智能化、服务化、协同化的“互联网+”产业生态体系基本完善，“互联网+”新经济形态初步形成，“互联网+”成为经济社会创新发展的重要驱动力量。

（二）加强城市停车设施建设

随着城镇化快速发展和居民生活水平不断提升，小汽车保有量大幅提高，城市停车设施供给不足问题日益凸显，挤占非机动车道等公共资源，影响交通通行，制约了城市进一步提升品质和管理服务水平。为此，国家发展改革委等7部门制定了关于加强城市停车设施建设的指导意见。

（1）立足城市交通发展战略，统筹动态交通与静态交通，着眼当前、惠及长远，将停车管理作为交通需求管理的重要手段，适度满足居住区基本停车和从严控制出行停车，以停车产业化为导向，在城市规划、土地供应、金融服务、收费价格、运营管理等方面加大改革力度和政策创新，营造良好的市场化环境，充分调动社会资本积极性，加快推进停车设施建设，有效缓解停车供给不足，加强运营管理，实现停车规范有序，改善城市环境。

（2）坚持市场运作，通过政府规划引导、政策支持，按照市场化经营要求，以企业为主体加快推进停车产业化；坚持改革创新，完善管理体制机制，探索多种合作模式，有效吸引社会资本；坚持集约挖潜，鼓励既有停车资源的开放共享，有效利用、充分发掘城市地上和地下空间资源，建设立体停车设施；坚持建管同步，完善路内停车泊位管理，提升停车信息化水平，加强违法行为治理。

（3）各地依据城市总体规划和综合交通体系规划，以配建停车为主体、路外公共停车为辅助、路内停车为补充，采用差别化的停车供给策略，修订城市建筑物配建停车泊位标准，组织编制停车设施专项规划，并及时纳入城市用地控制性详细规划，做好用地管控。规划需统筹城市功能分区的区位特征、用地属性、公共交通发展等状况，合理测算停车需求，明确阶段性适应目标，优化设施布局，制订近期实施方案，建立项目库，并及时公布。

（4）以居住区、大型综合交通枢纽、城市轨道交通外围站点（P+R）、医院、学校、旅游景区等特殊地区为重点，在内部通过挖潜及改造建设停车设施，并在有条件的周边区域增建公共停车设施。鼓励建设停车楼、地下停车场、机械式立体停车库等集约化的停车设施，并按照一定比例配建电动汽车充电设施，与主体工程同步建设。

（5）通过各种形式广泛吸引社会资本投资建设城市停车设施，大力推广政府和社会资本合作（PPP）模式；鼓励企事业单位、居民小区及个人利用自有土地、地上地下空间建设停车场，允许对外开放并取得相应收益。

2015年，住房城乡建设部等部门还相继发布了一系列相关政策，加强城市停车设施建设，包括《关于加强城市停车设施管理的通知》和《关于进一步完善机动车停放服务收费政策的指导意见》，并先后印发了《城市停车设施规划导则》和《城市停车设施建设指南》。

（三）推进城市地下综合管廊建设

地下综合管廊是指在城市地下用于集中敷设电力、通信、广播电视、给水、排水、热力、燃气等市政管线的公共隧道。国务院办公厅《关于推进城市地下综合管廊建设的指导意见》指出：我国正处在城镇化快速发展时期，地下基础设施建设滞后。推进城市地下综合管廊建设，统筹各类市政管线规划、建设和管理，解决反复开挖路面、架空线网密集、管线事故频发等问题，有利于保障城市安全、完善城市功能、美化城市景观、促进城市集约高效和转型发展，有利于提高城市综合承载能力和城镇化发展质量，有利于增加公共产品有效投资、拉动社会资本投入、打造经济发展新动力。

（1）到2020年，建成一批具有国际先进水平的地下综合管廊并投入运营，反复开挖地面的“马路拉链”问题明显改善，管线安全水平和防灾抗灾能力明显提升，逐步消除主要街道蜘蛛网式架空线，城市地面景观明显好转。

（2）各城市人民政府要按照“先规划、后建设”的原则，在地下管线普查的基础上，统筹各类管线实际发展需要，组织编制地下综合管廊建设规划，规划期限原则上应与城市总体规划相一致。结合地下空间开发利用、各类地下管线、道路交通等专项建设规划，合理确定地下综合管廊建设布局、管线种类、断面形式、平面位置、竖向控制等，明确建设规模和时序，综合考虑城市发展远景，预留和控制有关地下空间。

（3）从2015年起，城市新区、各类园区、成片开发区域的新建道路要根据功能需求，同步建设地下综合管廊；老城区要结合旧城更新、道路改造、河道治理、地下空间开发等，因地制宜、统筹安排地下综合管廊建设。在交通流量较大、地下管线密集的城市道路、轨道交通、地下综合体等地段，城市高强度开发区、重要公共空间、主要道路交叉口、道路与铁路或河流的交叉处，以及道路宽度难以单独敷设多种管线的路段，要优先建设地下综合管廊。

（4）城市规划区范围内的各类管线原则上应敷设于地下空间。已建设地下综合管廊的区域，该区域内的所有管线必须入廊。在地下综合管廊以外的位置新建管线的，规划部门不予许可审批，建设部门不予施工许可审批，市政道路部门不予掘路许可审批。既有管线应根据实际情况逐步有序迁移至地下综合管廊。

（5）入廊管线单位应向地下综合管廊建设运营单位缴纳入廊费和日常维护费，具体收费标准要统筹考虑建设和运营、成本和收益的关系，由地下综合管廊建设运营单位与入廊管线单位根据市场化原则共同协商确定。入廊费主要根据地下综合管廊本体及附属设施建设成本，以及各入廊管线单独敷设和更新改造成本确定。日常维护费主要根据地下综合管廊本体及附属设施维修、更新等维护成本，以及管线占用地下综合管廊空间比例、对附属设施使用强度等因素合理确定。

（6）城市人民政府是地下综合管廊建设管理工作的责任主体，要加强组织领导，明确主管部门，建立协调机制，扎实推进具体工作；要将地下综合管廊建设纳入政府绩效考核体系，建立有效的督查制度，定期对地下综合管廊建设工作进行督促检查。

（四）城镇棚户区和危房改造与基础设施配套建设

近年来，各地区城镇棚户区和城乡危房改造工作取得显著进展。截至2014年年底，全国共改造各类棚户区住房2080万套、农村危房1565万户，其中2013－2014年改造各类棚户区住房820万套、农村危房532万户，有效改善了困难群众的住房条件，发挥了带动消费、扩大投资的积极作用，促进了社会和谐稳定。但与中央政府提出的改造约1亿人居住的城镇棚户区和城中村的目标相比，任务仍然十分艰巨，特别是待改造的棚户区多为基础差、改造难度大的地块，在创新融资机制、完善配套基础设施等方面还存在不少困难和问题。为进一步做好城镇棚户区和城乡危房改造及配套基础设施建设工作，切实解决群众住房困难，有效促进经济增长，国务院于2015年提出关于进一步做好城镇棚户区和城乡危房改造及配套基础设施建设有关工作的意见。

（1）制定城镇棚户区和城乡危房改造及配套基础设施建设三年计划（2015－2017年，以下简称三年计划）。2015－2017年，改造包括城市危房、城中村在内的各类棚户区住房1800万套（其中2015年580万套），农村危房1 060万户（其中2015年432万户），加大棚改配套基础设施建设力度，使城市基础设施更加完备，布局合理、运行安全、服务便捷。

（2）各地区要抓紧编制2015－2017年城镇棚户区改造实施方案并抓好组织落实。一要加快棚改项目建设。依法合规推进棚改，切实做好土地征收、补偿安置等前期工作。建立行政审批快速通道，简化程序，提高效率，对符合相关规定的项目，限期完成立项、规划许可、土地使用、施工许可等审批手续。把城市危房改造纳入棚改政策范围。二要积极推进棚改货币化安置。缩短安置周期，节省过渡费用，让群众尽快住上新房，享有更好的居住环境和物业服务，满足群众多样化居住需求。

（3）各地区要尽快编制2015－2017年棚改配套基础设施建设计划，确定棚改安置住房小区配套基础设施项目，以及与棚改项目直接相关的城市道路和公共交通、通信、供电、供水、供气、供热、停车库（场）、污水与垃圾处理等城市基础设施项目，努力做到配套设施与棚户区改造安置住房同步规划、同步报批、同步建设、同步交付使用。

（4）各地区要抓紧编制2015－2017年农村危房改造实施方案，明确目标任务、资金安排和政策措施，确保年度任务按时完成。落实省级补助资金，将农村危房改造补助资金纳入财政预算，由县级财政直接发放到危房改造农户。

（5）鼓励多种所有制企业作为实施主体承接棚改任务。各地原融资平台公司可通过市场化改制，建立现代企业制度，实现市场化运营，在明确公告今后不再承担政府融资职能的前提下，作为实施主体承接棚改任务。原融资平台公司转型改造后举借的债务实行市场化运作，不纳入政府债务。政府在出资范围内依法履行出资人职责，不对原融资平台公司提供担保。

(6) 住房城乡建设部要会同有关部门督促各地尽快编制和落实三年计划及相关实施方案。发展改革委、财政部要会同有关部门进一步加大中央预算内投资和中央财政支持力度。财政部要会同有关部门安排中央国有资本经营预算资金，对困难中央企业特别是独立工矿区、三线地区和资源枯竭型城市中央企业棚改配套设施建设予以支持。人民银行、财政部、银监会要完善政策措施，支持开发银行、农业发展银行等金融机构加大信贷支持力度。

四、推进生态文明建设

生态文明建设是中国特色社会主义事业的重要内容。但总体上看，我国生态文明建设水平仍滞后于经济社会发展，资源约束趋紧，环境污染严重，生态系统退化，发展与人口资源环境之间的矛盾日益突出，已成为经济社会可持续发展的重大瓶颈制约。

中央政府高度重视生态文明建设，先后出台了一系列重大决策部署。2015 年 4 月 25 日，中共中央、国务院发布《关于加快推进生态文明建设的意见》，提出要牢固树立尊重自然、顺应自然、保护自然的理念，坚持绿水青山就是金山银山，加快形成人与自然和谐发展的现代化建设新格局，开创社会主义生态文明新时代。中共中央办公厅、国务院办公厅印发《党政领导干部生态环境损害责任追究办法（试行）》，从 2015 年 8 月 9 日起施行。

为加快建立系统完整的生态文明制度体系，加快推进生态文明建设，增强生态文明体制改革的系统性、整体性、协同性，2015 年 9 月 21 日，中共中央、国务院印发《生态文明体制改革总体方案》。2015 年 11 月至 12 月，中共中央办公厅、国务院办公厅先后印发《开展领导干部自然资源资产离任审计试点方案》和《生态环境损害赔偿制度改革试点方案》，国务院办公厅印发《编制自然资源资产负债表试点方案》。

（一）生态文明建设的主要目标

到 2020 年，资源节约型和环境友好型社会建设取得重大进展，主体功能区布局基本形成，经济发展质量和效益显著提高，生态文明主流价值观在全社会得到推行，生态文明建设水平与全面建成小康社会目标相适应。

国土空间开发格局进一步优化。经济、人口布局向均衡方向发展，陆海空间开发强度、城市空间规模得到有效控制，城乡结构和空间布局明显优化。

资源利用更加高效。单位国内生产总值二氧化碳排放强度比 2005 年下降 40% ~45%，能源消耗强度持续下降，资源产出率大幅提高，用水总量力争控制在 6700 亿立方米以内，万元工业增加值用水量降低到 65 立方米以下，农田灌溉水有效利用系数提高到 0.55 以上，非化石能源占一次能源消费比重达到15%左右。

生态环境质量总体改善。主要污染物排放总量继续减少，大气环境质量、重点流域和近岸海域水环境质量得到改善，重要江河湖泊水功能区水质达标率提高到80%以上，饮用水安全保障水平持续提升，土壤环境质量总体保持稳定，环境风险得到有效控制。森林覆盖率达到23%以上，草原综合植被覆盖度达到56%，湿地面积不低于8亿亩，50%以上可治理沙化土地得到治理，自然岸线保有率不低于35%，生物多样性丧失速度得到基本控制，全国生态系统稳定性明显增强。

生态文明重大制度基本确立。基本形成源头预防、过程控制、损害赔偿、责任追究的生态文明制度体系，自然资源资产产权和用途管制、生态保护红线、生态保护补偿、生态环境保护管理体制等关键制度建设取得决定性成果。

（二）绿色城镇化和美丽乡村建设

中央提出：要科学合理布局和整治我国城乡的生产空间、生活空间、生态空间。

大力推进绿色城镇化。认真落实《国家新型城镇化规划（2014－2020年）》，根据资源环境承载能力，构建科学合理的城镇化宏观布局，严格控制特大城市规模，增强中小城市承载能力，促进大中小城市和小城镇协调发展。尊重自然格局，依托现有山水脉络、气象条件等，合理布局城镇各类空间，尽量减少对自然的干扰和损害。保护自然景观，传承历史文化，提倡城镇形态多样性，保持特色风貌，防止“千城一面”。科学确定城镇开发强度，提高城镇土地利用效率、建成区人口密度，划定城镇开发边界，从严供给城市建设用地，推动城镇化发展由外延扩张式向内涵提升式转变。严格新城、新区设立条件和程序。强化城镇化过程中的节能理念，大力发展绿色建筑和低碳、便捷的交通体系，推进绿色生态城区建设，提高城镇供排水、防涝、雨水收集利用、供热、供气、环境等基础设施建设水平。所有县城和重点镇都要具备污水、垃圾处理能力，提高建设、运行、管理水平。加强城乡规划“三区四线”（禁建区、限建区和适建区，绿线、蓝线、紫线和黄线）管理，维护城乡规划的权威性、严肃性，杜绝大拆大建。

加快美丽乡村建设。完善县域村庄规划，强化规划的科学性和约束力。加强农村基础设施建设，强化山水林田路综合治理，加快农村危旧房改造，支持农村环境集中连片整治，开展农村垃圾专项治理，加大农村污水处理和改厕力度。加快转变农业发展方式，推进农业结构调整，大力发展农业循环经济，治理农业污染，提升农产品质量安全水平。依托乡村生态资源，在保护生态环境的前提下，加快发展乡村旅游休闲业。引导农民在房前屋后、道路两旁植树护绿。加强农村精神文明建设，以环境整治和民风建设为重点，扎实推进文明村镇创建。

（三）建立空间规划体系

整合目前各部门分头编制的各类空间性规划，编制统一的空间规划，实现规划全覆盖。空间规划是国家空间发展的指南、可持续发展的空间蓝图，是各类开发建设活动的基本依据。空间规划分为国家、省、市县（设区的市空间规划范围为市辖区）三级，要研究建立统一规范的空间规划编制机制。

支持市县推进“多规合一”，统一编制市县空间规划，逐步形成一个市县一个规划、一张蓝图。市县空间规划要统一土地分类标准，根据主体功能定位和省级空间规划要求，划定生产空间、生活空间、生态空间，明确城镇建设区、工业区、农村居民点等的开发边界，以及耕地、林地、草原、河流、湖泊、湿地等的保护边界，加强对城市地下空间的统筹规划。加强对市县“多规合一”试点的指导，研究制定市县空间规划编制指引和技术规范，形成可复制、能推广的经验。

探索规范化的市县空间规划编制程序，扩大社会参与，增强规划的科学性和透明度。鼓励试点地区进行规划编制部门整合，由一个部门负责市县空间规划的编制，可成立由专业人员和有关方面代表组成的规划评议委员会。规划编制前应当进行资源环境承载能力评价，以评价结果作为规划的基本依据。规划编制过程中应当广泛征求各方面意见，全文公布规划草案，充分听取当地居民意见。规划经评议委员会论证通过后，由当地人民代表大会审议通过，并报上级政府部门备案。规划成果应当包括规划文本和较高精度的规划图，并在网络和其他本地媒体公布。鼓励当地居民对规划执行进行监督，对违反规划的开发建设行为进行举报。当地人民代表大会及其常务委员会定期听取空间规划执行情况报告，对当地政府违反规划行为进行问责。

五、城乡统筹、协调发展

“十三五”时期是我国全面建成小康社会、实现“两个一百年”奋斗目标的第一个百年奋斗目标的决胜阶段。“小康不小康，关键看老乡”。如何建成名副其实、惠民富民、以人为本、城乡共荣的全面小康社会，事关经济社会持续健康发展，事关社会主义现代化建设大局。中共中央、国务院在《关于落实发展新理念、加快农业现代化　实现全面小康目标的若干意见》中提出：坚持工业反哺农业、城市支持农村，促进城乡公共资源均衡配置、城乡要素平等交换，稳步提高城乡基本公共服务均等化水平的要求。

（一）加快农村基础设施建设

把国家财政支持的基础设施建设重点放在农村，建好、管好、护好、运营好农村基础设施，实现城乡差距显著缩小。健全农村基础设施投入长效机制，促进城乡基础设施互联互通、共建共享。强化农村饮用水水源保护。实施农村饮水安全巩固提升工程。推动城镇供水设施向周边农村延伸。加快实施农村电网改造升级工程，开展农村“低电压”综合治理，发展绿色小水电。加快实现所有具备条件的乡镇和建制村通硬化路、通班车，推动一定人口规模的自然村通公路。创造条件推进城乡客运一体化。加快国有林区防火应急道路建设。将农村公路养护资金逐步纳入地方财政预算。发展农村规模化沼气。加大农村危房改造力度，统筹搞好农房抗震改造，通过贷款贴息、集中建设公租房等方式，加快解决农村困难家庭的住房安全问题。加强农村防灾减灾体系建设。

（二）提高农村公共服务水平

把社会事业发展的重点放在农村和接纳农业转移人口较多的城镇，加快推动城镇公共服务向农村延伸。加快发展农村学前教育，坚持公办民办并举，扩大农村普惠性学前教育资源。全面改善贫困地区义务教育薄弱学校基本办学条件，改善农村学校寄宿条件，办好乡村小规模学校，推进学校标准化建设。加快普及高中阶段教育，逐步分类推进中等职业教育免除学杂费，率先从建档立卡的家庭经济困难学生实施普通高中免除学杂费，实现家庭经济困难学生资助全覆盖。加强乡村教师队伍建设，拓展教师补充渠道，推动城镇优秀教师向乡村学校流动。整合城乡居民基本医疗保险制度，适当提高政府补助标准、个人缴费和受益水平。建立健全农村留守儿童和妇女、老人关爱服务体系，建立健全农村困境儿童福利保障和未成年人社会保护制度。切实维护农村妇女在财产分配、婚姻生育、政治参与等方面的合法权益，让女性获得公平的教育机会、就业机会、财产性收入、金融资源。加强农村养老服务体系、残疾人康复和供养托养设施建设。全面加强农村公共文化服务体系建设，在农村建设基层综合性文化服务中心，发挥基层文化公共设施整体效应。

（三）开展农村人居环境整治行动和美丽宜居乡村建设

遵循乡村自身发展规律，体现农村特点，注重乡土味道，保留乡村风貌，努力建设农民幸福家园。科学编制县域乡村建设规划和村庄规划，提升民居设计水平，强化乡村建设规划许可管理。继续推进农村环境综合整治，完善以奖促治政策，扩大连片整治范围。实施农村生活垃圾治理5年专项行动。采取城镇管网延伸、集中处理和分散处理等多种方式，加快农村生活污水治理和改厕。开展农村宜居水环境建设，实施农村清洁河道行动，建设生态清洁型小流域。发挥好村级公益事业一事一议财政奖补资金作用，支持改善村内公共设施和人居环境。坚持城乡环境治理并重，逐步把农村环境整治支出纳入地方财政预算，中央财政给予差异化奖补，政策性金融机构提供长期低息贷款，探索政府购买服务、专业公司一体化建设运营机制。加大对传统村落、民居和历史文化名村名镇保护力度，鼓励各地因地制宜探索各具特色的美丽宜居乡村建设模式。

（四）推进农村劳动力转移就业创业和农民工市民化

健全农村劳动力转移就业服务体系，大力促进就地就近转移就业创业，稳定并扩大外出农民工规模，支持农民工返乡创业。大力发展特色县域经济和农村服务业，加快培育中小城市和特色小城镇，增强吸纳农业转移人口能力。加大对农村灵活就业、新就业形态的支持。鼓励各地设立农村妇女就业创业基金，加大妇女小额担保贷款实施力度，加强妇女技能培训，支持农村妇女发展家庭手工业。实施新生代农民工职业技能提升计划，开展农村贫困家庭子女、未升学初高中毕业生、农民工、退役军人免费接受职业培训行动。进一步推进户籍制度改革，落实1亿左右农民工和其他常住人口在城镇定居落户的目标，保障进城落户农民工与城镇居民有同等权利和义务，加快提高户籍人口城镇化率。全面实施居住证制度，建立健全与居住年限等条件相挂钩的基本公共服务提供机制，努力实现基本公共服务常住人口全覆盖。维护进城落户农民土地承包权、宅基地使用权、集体收益分配权，支持引导其依法自愿有偿转让上述权益。

六、可持续城市化的目标与途径

（一）联合国“人居三”大会筹备进程

第三届联合国住房和可持续城市发展大会（人居三）定于2016年10月17日至20日在厄瓜多尔首都基多召开，会议的主题是探讨可持续的城市化和我们现有城市的未来。“人居三”的目的——评估世界人居运动迄今为止的成就，确保世界各国对城市可持续发展的新的政治承诺，建立“新城市议程”来解决贫困和发现和解决新出现的城市挑战。

联合国曾于1976年和1996年分别在加拿大温哥华和土耳其伊斯坦布尔举行了第一和第二届人居会议，就全球面临的城市和住房挑战以及可持续城市发展的未来政策进行了讨论。

“人居三”的筹备工作启动于2014年。在9月17日开幕的筹委会会议上，潘基文秘书长指出，城市化是增长的驱动力和源泉。目前，全世界约一半人口居住在城市之中，预计到21世纪中期，全球城市人口将增至总人口的三分之二，而且新增城市人口几乎全部来自发展中国家。在国际社会致力于制定2015年后全球发展议程之际，城市化在促进可持续发展方面所发挥的作用与日俱增，联合国应当继续致力于推动城市化乡村、城镇以及国家间平等发展。

2015年5月，“人居三”的文件准备工作启动。拟定中的《新城市议程》分为六个领域：社会凝聚力与平等性——宜居城市；城市的构架；空间开发；城市经济；城市生态与环境；城市住房与基本服务。在此基础上，提出了22个议题文件，并最终形成10个政策文件：全民城市和生活权；社会文化城市框架；国家城市政策；城市治理、城市承载力与制度制定；市政财务与地方财政体系；城市空间策略——土地市场与分离；城市经济发展策略；城市经济与抗逆力；城市服务与技术；住房政策。来自世界各国200名专业技术人员参与了上述文件的准备，并提出以行动为导向的《新城市议程》实施建议。

（二）2030年可持续发展议程中的人居目标

2015年9月25日，举世瞩目的“联合国可持续发展峰会”在纽约联合国总部正式拉开帷幕。会议通过了一份由193个会员国共同达成的《改变我们的世界：2030年可持续发展议程》。这一包括17项发展目标和169项具体目标的纲领性文件将推动世界在今后15年内实现三个史无前例的非凡创举：消除极端贫穷、战胜不平等和不公正以及遏制气候变化。

2030年可持续发展议程的第11项发展目标是“建设包容、安全、有抵御灾害能力的可持续城市和人类住区”，其中包括10项具体目标：

（1）到2030年时，所有人都能获得适足、安全和价廉的住房和基本服务，开展贫民窟改造。

（2）到2030年时，为所有人提供安全、无障碍和价廉的可持续交通系统，加强道路安全，特别是扩大公共交通，要特别注意处境脆弱者、妇女、儿童、残疾人和老年人的需要。

（3）到2030年时，在所有国家加强包容和可持续的城市化建设，提高进行参与性可持续人类住区综合规划和管理的能力。

（4）进一步努力保护和捍卫世界文化和自然遗产。

（5）到2030年时，大幅度减少包括水灾在内的各种灾害造成的死亡人数和受影响人数，大幅度减少灾害造成的与全球国内总产值相对的直接经济损失，重点注意保护穷人和处境脆弱群体。

（6）到2030年时，减少对城市环境造成的人均不利影响，包括特别关注空气质量以及城市废物和其他废物的管理。

（7）到2030年时，让所有人，尤其是妇女、儿童、老年人和残疾人，都有安全、包容、无障碍的绿色公共空间。

（8）通过加强国家和区域发展规划，帮助城市、近郊区和农村地区建立积极的经济、社会和环境联系。

（9）到2020年时，大幅度增加有以下特点的城市和人类住区：通过并执行旨在促进包容的统筹政策和计划，提高资源使率，减缓和适应气候变化，建立抗灾能力，并根据《2015-2030年仙台减少灾害风险框架》在各级规划和全面进行灾害风险管理。

（10）通过财务和技术援助等方式，支持最不发达国家就地取材，建造可持续的抗灾建筑。

（三）城市公共空间与设计

2015年10月5日是世界人居日，10月31日是世界城市日。联合国人居署又将每年的10月定为世界城市月，就此敦促各国面对高速城市化的挑战，严肃思考全球人类住区的现况以及所憧憬的未来城市面貌。

2015年世界人居日的主题是“人人享有公共空间”（public space for all）。联合国秘书长指出，公共空间虽然经常被忽视和低估，但仍日趋被视为世界城镇和城市充满活力和不断搏动的心脏，而城镇和城市如今已成为人类一半人口的家园。公共空间对穷人和弱势公民至关重要。如能提高获得公共空间的机会并使之对妇女和女童安全无虞，就能更加公平，促进包容和战胜歧视。优质公共空间有助于人民相互交流，彼此合作，也有助于他们参与公共生活。公共空间也能提供基本服务，提高连通程度，激发经济活力和提高财产价值，从而创造市政收入。但成功的公共空间并非凭空产生；它们需要地方当局、当地居民和其他相关方面共同开展审慎的协作。

2015 年世界城市日的主题是“城市设计、共创宜居”（designed to live together）。联合国人居署执行主任霍安·克洛斯致辞说：城市是人类创造的最复杂的产物之一，是我们设计用来共同生活的地方。2015 年，世界城市日关注的是城市设计在影响我们的生活方式、通行方式、小区的外观、外出安全感等方面的能力。克洛斯指出：

优良的设计有利于社会的融合、平等和多样性。规划居民区，在类型和价格方面提供不同的可能性，能使不同背景和收入水平的居民共同生活，防止贫民窟和门禁社区的滋生，打击隔离和歧视。优良的设计为不同文化、种族和生活方式提供了相互融合和聚会的空间。

优良的设计促进共享资源的可持续使用。规划人口更加稠密的紧凑型城市降低了对自然资源的过度消耗，使所有人平等地享有土地、食品和水，有利于共同生活。

优良的设计激发了小区的活力。设计活动丰富的公共空间、公园、游乐场、街道和广场，有助于为所有居民营造活跃的公共生活。

优良的设计能使城市更加安全。小区夜间活动丰富多彩，提供底层商业活动、照明优良的步行街和公共空间，意味着人身安全更有保障。

优良的设计推动就业和服务的改善。如果有优秀的基础设施和公共交通、更密集的建筑、混合用途的小区，那么工作地、市场、学校和休闲场所都离居民住所更近了，步行、骑行或公共交通都会很便利。

优良的设计有助于创建健康清洁的城市。城市的人口更稠密，靠近工作机会和公用设施，意味着驾车出行的需求降低，交通堵塞和污染减少，土地使用、自然生态区和绿地保护更可持续。

优良的设计预见气候变化，降低灾害影响。在关注周边自然环境的前提下开展规划，避免在风险地带进行开发，在易于遭受洪灾或地震的地带规划自然缓冲区和防御系统，能使建设的住区易于从灾害中恢复，使社区更加安全。

如何保障优良的设计成为城市规划和管理进程的组成部分，对于我们的城市未来具有关键意义。

七、结语

“凡是过去，皆为序章（What’s past is prologue）。”2015 年的中国在经济建设、政治建设、文化建设、社会建设和生态文明建设各方面都取得了新进步。但国际环境仍然错综复杂，国内结构调整转型升级正处在爬坡过坎的关键阶段，全面深化改革任务艰巨。

中共中央总书记国家主席习近平在 2016 年新年贺词中说：“2016 年是我国进入全面建成小康社会决胜阶段的开局之年。中共十八届五中全会明确了未来 5 年我国发展的方向。前景令人鼓舞、催人奋进，但幸福不会从天降。我们要树立必胜信念、继续埋头苦干，贯彻创新、协调、绿色、开放、共享的发展理念，着力推进结构性改革，着力推进改革开放，着力促进社会公平正义，着力营造政治上的绿水青山，为全面建成小康社会决胜阶段开好局、起好步。”

（作者：毛其智，清华大学教授，国际欧亚科学院院士）

An Introduction of Urban Development in China: 2015

2015 is an unusual and significant year on the coordinate system of history showing the great rejuvenation of the Chinese nation.

In 2015, five major development concepts of "innovation, coordination, green, openness and sharing" were put forward on the Fifth Plenary Session of the 18th CPC Central Committee focusing on the various problems in front of Chinese economy in the transition period. On the 11th conference of the Central Leading Group on Financial and Economic Affairs, General Secretary Xi Jinping proposed that, while expanding the total demand moderately, we should make efforts to strengthen the supply-side structural reform, improve the quality and efficiency of the supply system, enhance the momentum of sustainable economic growth, and promote the achievement of overall improvement in the level of Chinese social productivity.

In 2015, in face of the intricate international situation and continually increasing pressure of economic downturn at home and abroad, with the joint efforts of all Chinese people, we have completed the Twelfth Five-year Plan successfully, made substantial progress in the construction of the "One Belt and One Road", formally established the Asian Infrastructure Investment Bank, put the Silk Road Fund into operation, listed RMB into the currency basket with special drawing rights of the International Monetary Fund. Chinese economic growth stood among the first ranks in the world.

2015 we solemnly commemorated the 70th anniversary of the Victory of the Chinese People's War of Resistance Against Japanese Aggression and the World Anti-Fascist War; Beijing and Hebei Province won the bid to host the 24th Winter Olympic Games hand in hand; China's domestically-produced C919 large passenger aircraft rolled off the production line; China's super computer broke the world record for a sixth consecutive year; a satellite developed by Chinese scientists detect "dark matter" was launched; Tu Youyou became China's first scientist to win a Nobel Prize.

The Central Urban Work Conference was held from on December 20 – 21, 2015. The conference noted that the urban work is a systematic project. In order to do well in the urban work, we should conform to the new trend of urbanization, reform and develop new requirements, realize the new expectations of the masses, insist upon the people-centered development thought, and adhere to the idea that the city of people serves the people, which is the starting point and objective of urban work. As required by the conference, we should make efforts to build our cities to a beautiful homeland with the harmonious coexistence between man and man, and between man and nature by adhering to the central objective of creating favorable human settlements.

Ⅰ. Overview of New Urbanization Progress

(Ⅰ) Sustainable development in economy and society

In 2015, the CPC Central Committee and the State Council continued to hold the strategic determinative force to plan the two overall situations respectively at home and abroad as a whole, adhered to the general guideline of making progress while maintaining stability, actively fit in with and led the new normal, used the new concept to guide new practice, pursued new development with new strategies, innovated the macroeconomic regulation and control continually, ensured the operation in a reasonable interval of national economy, and achieved further optimization of economic structure, further acceleration of transformation and upgrading, further accumulation of emerging driving forces and further improvement in people's livelihood. With the prosperous development of "public entrepreneurship and innovation", the economy kept in a favorable development trend of overall steadiness.

According to the preliminary statistics, in 2015, the gross domestic product (GDP) was RMB 67 670.8 billion, or RMB 49 229 per capita, with a year-on-year growth rate of 6.9% calculated by comparable prices; the proportion of three industries (primary industry, secondary industry and tertiary industry) was 9.0:40.5:50.5. The disposable income per capita of residents nationwide was RMB 21 966, up 7.4% actually. By the place of usual residence, per capita disposable income in urban areas was RMB 31 195, up 6.6% actually; per capita in rural areas was RMB 11 422, up 7.5% actually. The income per capita of residents in rural area was 2.73 times lower than that in urban areas, down 0.02 over the previous year. In 2015, the Gini coefficient of resident income in the country was 0.462. The total number of *Nongmingong* (peasant workers) arrived at 277.47 million across the country, including 168.84 million outgoing migrants. The average monthly income of *Nongmingong* reached RMB 3 072, up 7.2% over the previous year.

By the end of 2015, the national population was 1 374.62 million, adding 6.8 million over the end of previous year. The newly-born population all year round was 16.55 million, with a natural population growth rate of 4.96‰. Urban permanent residents numbered 771.16 million, adding 22 million over the end of previous year; rural permanent residents numbered 603. 46 million, a decrease of 15. 20 million; the percentage of urban population accounted for 56. 10% of the total. The population separating from their household register was 294 million, who left the place of household registered for over half a year and whose residence and place of household register were not at the same town and street office, including 247 million floating population. The employed persons in the country reached 774. 51 million at the end of that year, of which the urban employed persons reached 404. 1 million. In the whole year, there were 13. 12 million newly-increased employed persons, 5. 67 million re-employed persons among the previous unemployed persons in cities, and 1. 73 million employed persons with employment difficulties. The urban registered unemployment rate was 4. 05% at the end of that year.

In 2015, the investment in real estate development across the country was RMB 9 597. 9 billion; the newly-build building floor space reaches 1 544. 54 million square meters; the floor space of commercial building sold stood at 1 284. 95 million square meters; the sales of commercial buildings amounted to 8 728. 1 billion yuan; the floor space of commercial building for sale was 718. 53 million square meters, with a year-on-year growth rate of 15. 6%.

(Ⅱ) Adjustment on municipal administrative divisions

By the end of 2015, there have been 656 cities with municipal governments, including 4 municipalities, 15 sub-provincial-level cities, 276 prefecture-level cities and 361 county-level cities, about 1 550 county seats in total and 20 515 designated towns. The changes on the organizational system of cities with municipal governments within this year are as follows.

On February 19, the State Council approved the People's Government of Hainan Province to cancel Danzhou County-level City to set up Danzhou Prefecture-level City, following the administrative regions of former Danzhou County-level City. On March 16, the State Council approved the People's Government of Tibet Autonomous Region to cancel Nyingchi Prefecture and Nyingchi County to set up Nyingchi Prefecture-level City, and set up Bayi District in Nyingchi City, following the administrative regions of former Nyingchi County. On the same day, the State Council approved the People's Government of Xinjiang Uygur Autonomous Region to cancel Turpan Prefecture and Turpan County-level City to set up Turpan Prefecture-level City, and meanwhile, set up Gaochang District in Turpan City, following the administrative regions of former Turpan County-level City.

The State Council approved Jiangsu Province to cancel Jintan County-level City to set up Jintan District in Changzhou City, and cancel Dafeng County-level City to set up Dafeng District in Yancheng City; approved Guangdong Province to cancel Gaoyao County-level City to set up Gaoyao District in Zhaoqing City; and approved Liaoning Province to cancel Pulandian County-level City to set up Pulandian District in Dalian City. The State Council also approved Sichuan Province to cancel

Kangding County to set up Kangding County-level City, and cancel Maerkang County to set up Maerkang County-level City; approved Xinjiang Uygur Autonomous Region to set up Cocodala County-level City; approved Guangxi Zhuang Autonomous Region to cancel Jingxi County to set up Jingxi County-level City; approved Yunnan Province to cancel Tengchong County to set up Tengchong County-level City; and approved Heilongjiang Province to cancel Dongning County to set up Dongning County-level City.

In 2015, the State Council successively approved to set up Guiyang-Anshun Free Trade Zone, China (Hangzhou) International E-commerce Comprehensive Test Area, Yunnan Mengla (Boten) Key Test Area for Development and Opening up; set up Hunan Xiang River New District, Fuzhou New District, Yunnan Central New District and Harbin New District; and agreed to upgrade Lianyungang High-tech Industrial Development Zone to a national high-tech industrial development zone. In addition, the State Council approved the development planning for city clusters along the middle reaches of the Yangtze River, the rejuvenation and development planning for Dabieshan, an old revolutionary base of mountain area, the cooperation and development outline for Circum-Bohai-Sea, and the overall plan for Suzhou Industrial Park to carry out the comprehensive test of opening up and innovation; issued and distributed the overall plan for Pilot Free Trade Zones in Guangdong, Tianjin and Fujian of China; and further deepened the reform and opening-up plan for China (Shanghai) Pilot Free Trade Zone.

(Ⅲ) Construction of cities (districts)

According to statistics of the Ministry of Housing and Urban-Rural Development, by the end of 2014, there have been 653 cities with municipal governments nationwide, urban population numbered 386 million, temporary residents numbered 60 million and total built-up areas amounted to 49 800 square kilometers.

In 2014, the fixed-assets investments in municipal public utilities were RMB 1 624.69 billion, accounting for 3.17% of the total social fixed-assets investments of corresponding period. Major newly-added production capacity (or benefit) included daily water production capacity of 5.3 million cubic meters, natural gas storage capacity of 13.42 million cubic meters, centralized heating capacity of 1 500 tons per hour, hot water supply capacity of 406 000 megawatts, roads of 10 900 kilometers, drain pipes of 19 000 kilometers, daily treatment of municipal sewage of 4.43 million cubic meters and daily harmless treatment of urban domestic garbage of 21 000 tons.

In 2014, the water-using population numbered 435 million, and per capita daily water consumption for residential use was 173.73 liters, with the water-using popularity rate of 97.64%; natural gas-using population numbered 421 million and the popularization rate of natural gas was 94.56%; centralized heating floor area was 6.11 billion square meters; urban roads were 352 000 kilometers and per capita road area was 15.34 square meters; there were 1 808 urban sewage treatment plants all over the country, and the centralized treatment rate of sewage was 85.94%; the daily production capacity of urban recycled water was 20.65 million cubic meters, and the utilization of recycled water was 3.63 billion cubic meters; there were 819 harmless treatment sites (plants) of urban domestic garbage, and harmless treatment rate of urban domestic garbage reached 91.77%; the total surface area of road cleaned and maintained was 6.76 billion square meters, with a mechanical cleaning rate of 50.4%; yearly amount of domestic garbage and night soil cleaned and transported totaled 194 million tons; the green space rate of urban built-up areas reached 36.24%, and per capita park space was 12.95 square meters; as of the end of 2014, there have been 225 national-level scenic spots, and the scenic spots have covered a total area of 99 000 square kilometers, including 42 000 square kilometers available for sightseeing, and accepted tourists for 2.04 billion person times in the year. There was national investment of RMB 5.68 billion in the maintenance and construction of scenic spots.

According to statistics of the Ministry of Transport, by the end of 2014, there have been 22 cities in the country opening up rail transit in urban area and owning 1 829 rail stations, including 151 transfer stations. In all cities and counties across the country, there have been 528 800 public auto and electric buses, including 5 339 BRT buses; 17 300 rail transit vehicles in service or 41 770 operating public vehicles; and 1 370 100 taxis in service and 329 urban passenger ferries. For national urban passenger transportation, there have been 45 052 lines in operation for public auto and electric buses, with a total length of 817 800 kilometers, including BRT lines with a total length of 2 790.3 kilometers; 92 rail transit lines in operation, with a total length of 2 816.1 kilometers. There also have been 126 routes in operation for urban passenger ferries, with a total length of 497.6 kilometers. The urban passenger transport systems carried passengers of 131.566 billion in total in the year, including 78.188 billion passengers carried by public auto and electric buses, 1.476 billion passengers carried by BRT, and 12.666 billion passengers carried by rail transport, 40.606 billion passengers carried by taxis and 107 million passengers carried by passenger ferries. Among total passengers carried by the urban passenger transport systems, public auto and electric buses, rail transport, taxis and passenger ferries accounted for 59.4%, 9.6%, 30.9% and 0.1%, respectively.

(Ⅳ) Construction of county seats

By the end of 2014, there have been 1 596 counties in the country. Based on statistics of 1 579 counties, 10 newly-canceled counties, 14 special areas and 149 Xinjiang Production and Construction Corps-stationed areas, total population numbered 140 million, including 16 million temporary residents, and the build-up area was 20 100 square kilometers.

Fixed-assets investments in municipal public utilities in county seats totally reached RMB 357.10 billion. Major newly-added production capacity (or benefit) included daily water production capacity of 2. 73 million cubic meters, natural gas storage capacity of 13. 08 million cubic meters, centralized heating capacity of 397 tons per hour and hot water supply capacity of 13 100 megawatts, roads of 5 687 kilometers, drain pipes of 10 000 kilometers, daily sewage treatment capacity of 2. 06 million cubic meters and daily harmless treatment capacity of domestic garbage of 7 721 tons.

In 2014, water-using population numbered 139 million over the country, the popularization rate of water hit 88. 89% and per capita daily water consumption for residential use was 118. 22 liters; natural gas using population numbered 115 million, and the popularization rate of natural gas reached 73. 23% ; centralized heating floor area was 1. 14 billion square meters; urban roads were 130 000 kilometers and per capita road space was 15. 39 square meters; the total surface area of road cleaned and maintained was 2. 29 billion square meters, of which mechanically cleaning area was 790 million square meters; there were 1 554 urban sewage treatment plants, and the centralized treatment rate of sewage reached 80. 19% ; there were 1 129 harmless treatment sites (plants) of urban domestic garbage and harmless treatment rate of urban domestic garbage reached 71. 58% ; domestic garbage and night soil cleaned and transported was 72 million tons; the green space rate of county seat built-up areas was 25. 88% , and the area of park space per capita was 9. 91 square meters.

(V) Construction of villages and small towns

By the end of 2014, there have been 20 401 towns and 12 282 townships. Based on data collected from 17 653 towns and 11 871 townships, 679 town-level special areas and 2. 7 million natural villages (among which 546 700 villages accommodated villagers' committees), total residence registered population numbered 952 million, including 156 million in built-up areas of towns, 30 million in built-up areas of townships, 3 million in build-up areas in town-level special areas and 763 million in villages. Built-up area in towns was 3. 795 million hectares; the built-up area in townships was 722 000 hectares; and the build-up area in town-level special areas was 105 000 hectares. Current land area of villages hit 13. 941 million hectares. There have been 16 417 towns, 9 060 townships, 491 town-level special areas, 322 000 administrative villages and 766 000 natural villages under the master plan in the country. In 2014, the investment in the master plan of nationwide villages and towns reached RMB 3. 547 billion.

In 2014, the total investment in the construction of nationwide villages and towns were RMB 1 610. 1 billion, including RMB 1 255. 9 billion invested in housing construction, covering a building floor space of 1. 156 billion square meters. By the end of 2014, the total floor space of building stock in the villages and towns covered 37. 805 billion square meters, with 33. 37 square meters of per capita housing floor space.

By the end of 2014, in the built-up areas of towns, the water coverage rate was 82. 77% ; daily per capita domestic water consumption was 98. 68 liters; gas coverage rate was 47. 8% ; per capita area of paved roads was 12. 6 square meters; drainage pipeline and ducts density was 5. 94 kilometers per square kilometer; and per capita area of pack green space was 2. 39 square meters. In the built-up areas of townships, the water coverage rate was 69. 26% ; daily per capita domestic water consumption was 83. 08 liters; gas coverage rate was 20. 3% ; per capita area of paved roads was 12. 6 square meters; drainage pipeline and ducts density was 3. 83 kilometers per square kilometer; and per capita area of pack green space was 1. 07 square meters. In the built-up areas of town-level special areas, the water coverage rate was 86. 95% ; daily per capita domestic water consumption was 82. 76 liters; gas coverage rate was 50. 3% ; per capita area of paved roads was 15. 95 square meters; drainage pipeline and ducts density was 5. 25 kilometers per square kilometer; and per capita area of pack green space was 3. 15 square meters. Total length of village roads were 2. 34 million kilometers, including hardening roads of 720 000 kilometers; in the administrative villages nationwide, there were 62. 5% had accessed to central water supply; ditches of drainage channel within villages were 542 000 kilometers long; domestic waste water had been treated in 9. 98% of the villages; domestic garbage collection facilities had been set up in 63. 98% of the villages; and domestic garbage had been treated in 48. 18% of the villages.

Ⅱ. Preparation and Implementation of *Beijing-Tianjin-Hebei Coordinated Development Outline*

The Central Economic Working Conference held in December 2014 set out the overall requirements and main tasks of the economic work in 2015. In the aspect of optimizing the spatial pattern of economic development, the conference clearly proposed that we should focus on the implementation of three major strategies including "One Belt and One Road", Beijing-Tianjin-Hebei coordinated development and Yangtze River Economic Zone, so as to strive for a good start of 2015.

The *Beijing-Tianjin-Hebei Coordinated Development Outline* was reviewed and studied on the 11th conference of the Central Leading Group on Financial and Economic Affairs held on March 23, 2015. The *Beijing-Tianjin-Hebei Coordinated Development Outline* was approved on the conference held by the Political Bureau of the CPC on April 30.

It was pointed out on the conference that driving Beijing-Tianjin-Hebei coordinated development is a significant national strategy. The strategy focuses on dispersing the non-capital function of Beijing in order, adjusting economic structure and spatial structure, stepping on a new path of connotative and intensive development, and exploring a mode of optimized development in areas with dense population and economy, so as to promote the coordinated development within the region and create a new growth pole.

The *Recommendations for the 13th Five-year Plan for Economic and Social Development of the*

CPC Central Committee and the follow-up 13th *Five-year Plan for National Economic and Social Development of the People's Republic of China* further put forward the idea of using new development space to cultivate new development force, and using new development force to explore new development space. It is required to adhere to complementary advantages, win-win cooperation and regional integration, promote Beijing-Tianjin-Hebei coordinated development, construct a world-level city cluster cored by the capital which radiates and drives the development of Pan-Bohai Area and the northern hinterland. Specific measures mainly include the follows:

(Ⅰ) Orderly non-capital function dispersal of Beijing

Carry forward the non-capital function dispersal of Beijing actively and steadily, and reduce the population density in the main urban zone. Pay attention to the dispersal of enterprises with high energy consumption and water consumption, regional logistics bases and specialized markets, part of educational, medical and training institutions, part of administrative service institutions, enterprise headquarters, etc. Establish an administrative sub-center of Beijing at a high standard. Planning made for constructing of centralized functional bearing places and "micro-centers" as a whole.

(Ⅱ) Optimization of spatial pattern and functional orientation

Build a spatial pattern featured by "one core, double cities, three axles, four districts and multiple nodes". Optimize the industrial distribution, and boost the construction of Beijing-Tianjin-Hebei coordinated innovation community. Beijing should focus on the development of knowledge economy, service economy and green economy, and accelerate the establishment of high-grade, high-precision and advanced industrial structure. Tianjin should optimize the development of advanced manufacturing industry, strategic emerging industry and modern service industry, and construct the national advanced manufacturing R&D base and the demonstration area for financial innovation in service. Hebei should actively take over the non-capital function transfer of Beijing and the transformation of scientific and technological achievements in Beijing and Tianjin, and focus on the construction of major national bases for modern commercial logistics, new-type industrial bases and test areas for industrial transformation and upgrading.

(Ⅲ) Construction of integrated modern transportation network

Build an efficient and intensive rail transit network, strengthen the construction of trunk railways, accelerate the construction of intercity railways and interurban (suburban) railways and form an integrated network gradually, and make full use of the existing capacity to operate intercity and interurban (suburban) trains, with passenger dedicated lines covering all prefecture-level cities and above. Improve the expressway network, and reinforce the technical level of national and provincial and trunk lines. Build a port cluster based on the division of responsibilities, improve the collecting and distributing system of ports, and establish a new mode of overall maritime administration. Create a world-leading air transport hub, and set up an air transport coordination mechanism.

(Ⅳ) Expansion of environmental capacity and ecological space

Set up the regional monitoring network of ecological environment, the early warning system and the coordinated interaction mechanism, and reduce the total emissions of regional pollutants. Strengthen the joint control and prevention of air pollution, implement the gasification project for the control and prevention of air pollution in major areas, and reduce the concentration of fine particles by at least 25%. Reinforce the protection of drinking water sources, and jointly carry out the pollution regulation of rivers, lakes and seas. Designate the red line of ecological protection, implement divisional management, and construct ecological corridors such as the Yongdinghe River. Enhance the recovery of forests, lakes, and wetlands such as the Baiyangdian Lake and the Hengshuihu Lake within the Beijing-Tianjin-Baoding region, and jointly construct the Bashang Plateau Ecological Protection Zone and the Yan Mountains-Taihang Mountains Ecological Conservation Area.

(Ⅴ) Promotion of co-constructed and shared public service

Construct the regional human resources information sharing and service platform, and fit in with the inter-regional labor and talent policy. Optimize the distribution of educational resources, encourage the discipline co-construction and resource sharing among institutions of higher education, and promote the development of vocational education as a whole. Establish a sound regional system of two-way referral and inter-accreditation, and support to carry out the pilot work of cooperative hospital operation. Achieve the smooth connection of endowment insurance relationships among cities in the three provinces, and promote the coordinated development of social insurance.

Beijing, Tianjin and Hebei have actively responded to the central decision-making, and proposed specific measures for the implementation of the *Beijing-Tianjin-Hebei Coordinated Development Outline* respectively in the recommendations for the 13th five-year plan for national economic and social development of CPC Beijing Municipal Committee, CPC Tianjin Municipal Committee and CPC Hebei Provincial Committee.

Beijing: Beijing-Tianjin-Hebei coordinated development has milestone significance. Beijing should firmly seize and make the best of the great historical opportunity, and hold its core status in Beijing-Tianjin-Hebei coordinated development to continually make efforts to implement the strategic positioning of capital city, and carry out the non-capital function dispersal in order so as to address the city's chronic "urban disease". By 2020, it aims to control the total population of permanent residents within 23 million in the whole city, and reduce the population of permanent residents in the city's six central urban districts by about 15% compared with that of 2014. Beijing should promote the adjustment and withdrawal of regional logistics bases and specialized markets, disperse part of public service agencies such as educational and medical institutions as well as administrative enterprise and public institutions, establish a docking mechanism with the bearing areas, actively carry forward the construction of 4 cooperative function areas including Caofeidian District, Overhead Economic Zone of New Airport, Zhangjiakou-Chengde Ecological Function Zone and Binhai New Area, and promote to form a dispersal pattern featured by "multiple nodes in one city" . Beijing should also give full play to its comparative advantages, play a leading role in demonstration, make innovations in the cooperation mode, accelerate the differential development and the integrated development, achieve the regional positive interaction, and fight for its goal of building a world first-rate harmonious and livable capital.

Tianjin: The city should spare no efforts to implement the strategy of Beijing-Tianjin-Hebei coordinated development, deepen Beijing-Tianjin-Hebei coordinated development and actively participate in the construction of Beijing-Tianjin-Hebei city cluster; keep a foothold in the overall situation, adhere to consistent objectives, integrated measures, complementary advantages and win-win cooperation, actively take over the non-capital function dispersal of Beijing, strengthen the double-city interaction between Beijing and Tianjin, enhance the cooperation with Hebei, and create high-end industry development belts, agglomeration axles of cities and towns and core function areas; accelerate the development of integrated transportation, set up an air-sea-land three-dimensional transportation network which is cored by air and sea ports, based on rail transit, mainly composed of road transportation and effectively connected by multiple transportation modes, create a Beijing-Tianjin-Hebei one-hour commuting circle, and promote the integration of intelligent transport management, transport service and safety guarantee; strengthen the construction of northern international shipping center, build a world first-rate hub harbor, improve the collecting and distributing system, form a layout of port functions featured by "collecting in the north and distributing in the south", deepen the cooperation among port clusters and airport clusters, strive to develop the shipping service industry and enlarge its radiation function; strengthen the regional ecological environmental protection, and carry forward the integration of planning, standard, monitoring and law enforcement of ecological environmental protection; promote the industrial upgrading and transfer, positively take over innovation resources and high quality industries of Beijing, actively extend industrial chains to Hebei, carry forward the construction of docking platforms for the Beijing Future Science City, Beijing-Tianjin Cooperation Demonstration Zone, etc. , and achieve the complementary, differential and win-win development of industries.

Hebei: Hebei should precisely promote the implementation of Beijing-Tianjin-Hebei coordinated development task, actively undertake the non-capital function dispersal of Beijing, and make full use of "gold-lettered signboard" of Beijing-Tianjin-Hebei coordinated development; promote the manufacturing functions to gather to the provincial industrial parks and joint construction park, social service functions like education and health care to gather to regions with relatively concentrated resource and favorable ecological environment, service function to gather to regions with better industrial foundation and obvious advantage, and administrative institutions and corporate headquarter function to gather to towns with feature of arriving Beijing within an hour; precisely create a transitional platform and carrier, plan to construct carriers that undertake non-capital function dispersal; support medium and small cities around Beijing and Tianjin with appropriate conditions to build "micro centers"; reinforce the construction of major transitional platform like industrial park; cooperate to promote co-construction of Beijing-Hebei Caofeidian Coordinated Development Demonstration Area, Tianjin-Hebei Lutai Coordinated Development Demonstration Area, Beijing Overhead Economic Zone of New Airport and Beijing-Hebei Zhongguancun (Zhengding) Integrated Circuit Industry Base; intensify efforts to drive development of traffic integration, promoting Beijing-Tianjin urban rail and urban rail transit like Pinggu line to extend to Hebei province; actively plan for construction of light railway project from Yizhuang to Langfang, Fangshan to Zhuozhou, Daxing to Guan, Tongzhou to Yanjiao; perfect the road traffic network, open up the dead end highway and bottle neck road of provincial and national main roads; strengthen cooperation of Tianjin-Hebei harbor, work together to promote the construction of the new airport in Beijing, basically forming the regional integrated transport network; establish the half-an-hour traffic circle of central city and satellite city, one-hour traffic circle of core regions in Beijing-Tianjin-Hebei, 1.5 hours traffic circle of neighbor cities; promote the scientific planning and construction of Zhangjiakou venues (ground) and Paralympics facilities of Olympic Winter Games; speed up construction of Beijing-Zhangjiakou High-speed Rail and the Chongli branch, reconstruction and expansion of Zhangjiakou Airport; further improve the supporting facilities; carry out Winter Olympic project, making Chongli a "Low carbon Olympic zone", laying a solid foundation for a wonderful, extraordinary and excellent Olympic Winter Games; build Beijing-Zhangjiakou Sports Culture Tourism Zone, promoting development of ice-snow industry, leisure tourism as well as convention and exhibition to the international level.

Ⅲ. Urban Infrastructure Planning, Construction and Management

In 2015, the State Council and relevant ministries and commissions have successively released a series of documents to guide the planning, construction and management of urban infrastructure around China.

(Ⅰ) Goals of "Internet plus" initiative

"Internet plus" is a deep integration of innovative fruits of Internet and all fields of economic society, to promote technological growth, efficiency improvement and organizational reform and to enhance the creativity and productivity of real economy, creating a newer and wider development form of economic society based on Internet and innovative elements. To accelerate the deep integration and innovative progress of Internet and other fields, the State Council set goals for actively promoting the development of "Internet plus" initiative in 2015.

By the year of 2018, the integration of Internet and other fields in economic society should be further deepened. New formats based on Internet should become new driving force for economic growth, thus the Internet's function of supporting public entrepreneurship and mass innovation gets further enhanced and Internet becomes an important mean to provide public service. Consequently, a develop pattern where network economy and real economy coordinate to progress should basically take shape.

Both quality and efficiency have been enhanced in economic development. Positive achievements have been made in Internet's acceleration in transformation and upgrading of manufacturing industry, agriculture, energy, environmental protection and other industries, with a further enhancement in labor productivity. As new formats of Internet are constantly emerging, the facilitation of rapid development of e-commerce and Internet finance on improving economy quality and efficiency becomes more prominent.

Social service gets more convenient and generally preferential. There is a wider application of Internet in people's livelihood like health care, education, traffic, etc., as well as a more diverse category in public service and a closer combination of on-line and off-line service. While social service resource allocation gets more and more optimized, so that people can have access to a more fair, efficient and convenient service of higher quality.

Further enhancement has been made in infrastructure support. Network infrastructure and industrial base have been effectively strengthened, application support and security capabilities significantly enhanced. Fixed broadband network, new generation of mobile communication network and next generation of the Internet develop more rapidly; Internet of things, cloud computing and other new infrastructure become more complete. The technical competence and industrialization capacity of artificial intelligence and other technologies are significantly enhanced.

Development environment becomes more open and inclusive. The whole society constantly deepen their understanding to Internet integration innovation, thus the institutional obstacles in Internet integration innovation can be effectively eliminated.

By the year of 2050, the networked, intelligent, service-oriented and coordinated "Internet plus" industrial ecology system should be basically perfected.

(Ⅱ) Construction of urban parking facility

With the rapid development of urbanization and the improvement of the living standards of residents, quantity of car owners grows significantly. The problem of insufficient supply of urban parking facilities has become increasingly prominent, such as occupying bicycle lanes and other public resources that restrict further improvement of urban living quality and management service level. Therefore, the National Development and Reform Commission with other six ministries established opinions on reinforcing the construction of urban parking facilities.

(1) Based on urban traffic development strategy, make an overall arrangement of dynamic and static traffic with focus on current condition and bringing a long-term benefit to all. Parking management should be regarded as an important mean in traffic demand management, moderately meeting the basic requirement of residential district and strictly controlling daily trip parking. Guided by parking industrialization, intensify reform and policy innovation in urban planning, land supply, financial service, parking price as well as operation and management, creating a favorable market environment and fully mobilize the enthusiasm of the social capital. Accelerate the construction of parking facilities, and effectively alleviate insufficient supply of parking space. Reinforce operations management to achieve the goal of orderly parking and improve urban environment.

(2) Adhere to market operation and accelerate enterprise-oriented parking industrialization through planning guidance and policy support of government in accordance with requirements of market management. Adhere to reform and innovation, improve management system and mechanism and explore various cooperative modes to effectively attract social capital. Adhere to intensive management and exploring potential, encourage open sharing of existing parking space. Effectively make use of and explore urban over-ground and underground space to build three-dimensional parking facilities. Adhere to synchronous construction and management, and improve the on-street parking space management to upgrade the parking information level and strengthening governance of illegal behavior.

(3) On the basis of overall urban planning and comprehensive traffic planning, all regions should regard accessory parking as the main body, off-road public parking as auxiliary, and on-street parking as supplement, adopt strategy of differentiation parking supply to revise the standard for accessory parking space of urban buildings and organize the special planning of parking facilities, then timely incorporate them into detailed planning of urban land control, doing well in management and control of land. When making plan, regions should take into consideration the regional character, property of land and public traffic of urban functional zoning, reasonably estimate the parking demand, make sure the phased adaptive target, optimize the layout of facilities, make near-term implementation plan and establish project library and then release without delay.

(4) With the special areas such as residential districts, large comprehensive traffic hub, peripheral sites of urban rail transit, hospital, school and tourist attractions as the emphasis, all regions should construct parking facilities by means of potential-digging renovation, and build additional public parking facilities in surrounding area with qualified conditions. Encourage the

construction of parking garage, underground parking lots and mechanical spatial parking and other intensive parking facilities. And according to a certain proportion, equip charging facilities for electric vehicles, which should be constructed simultaneously with main parts of the project.

(5) Attract social capital to invest in constructing urban parking facilities in various forms and vigorously promote the model of Public-Private-Partnership (PPP); Encourage enterprises and public institutions, residential communities and individuals to construct parking lots by utilizing self-owned land, over-ground and underground spaces, which should be allowed to open to the public to obtain certain incomes.

In 2015, the Ministry of Housing and Urban-Rural Development and other ministries have successively released a series of relevant policies to strengthen construction of urban-rural parking facilities, including the *Notice on Reinforcing the Management of Urban Parking Facility* and *Opinions on Further Improvement of Charging Policy of Motor Parking Service*, and successively issued the *Guidelines for Planning of Urban Parking Facility* and *Guide for the Construction of Urban Parking Facility.*

(Ⅲ) Construction of urban underground utility tunnel

Underground utility tunnel refers to the urban public pipe gallery which is used for laying municipal pipelines including electricity, communications, radio and television, water supply, drainage, heating, gas, etc. The *Opinions on Promoting Construction of Urban Underground Utility Tunnel* issued by General Office of the State Council points out that China is right in a period of rapid development of urbanization where the construction of underground infrastructure lags behind. Promoting construction of urban underground utility tunnel, making an overall planning, construction and management of various municipal pipelines, and solving problems such as repeated road excavation, intensive overhead wirings and frequent pipelines accidents can be beneficial to ensure urban safety, improve urban functions, beautify urban landscape and stimulate urban intensive, efficient and transformation development; enhance urban comprehensive carrying capacity and urbanization development quality; increase effective investment of public products, stimulate social capital investment, and form new driving force for economic growth.

(1) By the year of 2020, we will complete the construction of underground utility tunnels at international level and put them into operation, significantly improve the situation of "road zipper" caused by repeated road excavation, show a clear boost in the capacity of safety and disaster-resistance of pipelines, eliminate spider web type overhead wirings on the main streets, and markedly turn urban landscape better.

(2) According to the principle of "construction after planning" and on the basis of survey of underground pipelines, all urban governments should give an overall consideration to actual development requirements of various pipelines, and prepare the construction planning of urban

underground utility tunnel which should be generally consistent with overall urban planning in terms of planning duration; take the special planning including underground space utilization, underground pipelines and road traffic into consideration, reasonably confirm the layout, pipeline type, section form, horizontal position and vertical control of underground utility tunnel construction, and define the scale and order of construction; take urban development vision into consideration to reserve and control relevant underground space.

(3) Since 2015, urban new areas, all kinds of parks, new roads in tracts of development zone should simultaneous construct underground utility tunnel in accordance with function demands. Old towns should consider the urban renewal, road renovation, river regulation and underground space exploitation to act according to conditions and plan the arrangement of underground utility tunnel construction as a whole. Underground utility tunnel should be a first priority in sections such as urban roads, rail traffic and underground complex with large traffic flow and intensive underground pipeline in urban development zones with high intensity, important public space, main road intersections and junction of road, rail and river, and in sections where the road width is insufficient to separately lay multiple pipelines.

(4) In principle, various types of pipelines within the scope of urban planning area should be deposited in the underground space. All pipelines in areas that already have underground utility tunnels should be included in the gallery. New pipeline located outside the underground utility tunnel should not obtain approval of planning authorities, approval for construction permits of construction departments, and approval for road excavation permit of the municipal road department. Existing pipelines should be orderly removed to underground utility tunnel according to actual situation.

(5) Who intent to put the pipelines in the tunnel should pay the input charge and daily maintenance expense to the construction and operation units of utility tunnels. The specific charging standards should coordinate the relationship of construction and operation, as well as relationship of costs and benefits, and should be defined by both sides in accordance with market principle. Input charge is mainly defined by construction cost of underground utility tunnel and its accessory facilities, and costs of separate deposition and renovation of each pipeline that needs to be put in. Daily maintenance charge is mainly defined by factors including costs of maintenance and renovation of underground utility tunnel and its accessory facilities, space proportion occupied by pipelines and the intensity of use of accessory facilities.

(6) Urban government serving as the responsibility body of construction and management of underground utility tunnel, should strengthen organizational leadership, make clear the competent department, establish coordinating mechanism and make solid progress in work; include the construction of underground utility tunnel into government performance evaluation system, establish an effective supervision system and regularly push forward the construction supervision.

(Ⅳ) Shantytowns and dilapidated houses renovation and infrastructure complete set service

Recent years, significant progress has been made in renovation of urban shantytowns and urban-rural dilapidated housing. By the end of 2014, there have been totally 20. 8 million units of shantytowns and 15. 65 million dilapidated rural houses renovated nationwide, of which 820 million units of shantytowns and 5. 32 million dilapidated rural houses in 2013–2014, effectively improving the housing conditions of poverty-stricken population, playing a positive role in motivating consumption and expanding investment, and promoting social harmony and stability. However, the task is still arduous compared with the central government's goal of renovating about 100 million urban shantytowns and urban villages, especially the shantytowns to be renovated are poorly based plots with huge difficulty to rebuild. A number of difficulties and problems still exist in the innovation of financing mechanisms and the improvement of supporting infrastructure facilities. In order to put forward the work on urban shantytowns and dilapidated houses renovation and infrastructure construction, solve housing problems of the masses, and effectively stimulate economic growth, the State Council released the notice on further strengthening the work of shantytown and dilapidated houses renovation and infrastructure complete set service.

(1) Make a three-year plan for urban shantytowns and dilapidated houses renovation and infrastructure construction (2015–2017). In 2015–2017, we need to renovate 18 million units of various types of shantytowns housing including urban dilapidated houses and urban village, of which 5. 8 million units need to be renovated in 2015; we need to renovate 10. 6 million rural dilapidated houses, 4. 32 million in 2015. We will work to intensify renovation and construction of shantytowns and infrastructure, so as to make urban infrastructure more perfect, rational, safe, and convenient.

(2) All regions should pay close attention to the preparation and implementation of plan on urban shantytowns renovation of 2015–2017. First, construction of urban shantytowns renovation project should be accelerated. We should push on the urban shantytowns renovation in accordance with the law, and earnestly carry out the preliminary works such as land expropriation, compensation and resettlement. We should establish fast channel for administrative examination and approval to simplify procedure and improve efficiency. As to the project complied with relevant compliance, approval process like project initiation, planning permission, land utilization, and construction permits should be completed within specified time. The urban dilapidated houses reconstruction should be incorporated into policy of shantytowns renovation. Secondly, we should actively promote the monetized resettlement of shantytowns renovation, shorten the settlement cycle and save excessive cost to meet people's diversified living requirements, and provide people

with a fast access to new houses, better living environment, and property service.

(3) The provinces and cities should prepare 2015 – 2017 construction plan of shantytown reconstruction supporting infrastructure as soon as possible, determine the supporting infrastructure of the resettlement housing community of shantytown reconstruction and the supporting infrastructure projects directly related to the shantytown reconstruction projects, such as the urban road and public transportation, communication, power supply, water supply, gas supply, heating supply, parking garage or parking lot, sewage and garbage disposal, etc. , and strive to achieve synchronous approval, construction and delivery between the supporting facilities and the resettlement housing of shantytown reconstruction.

(4) The regions should speed up the preparation of 2015 – 2017 reconstruction plans of dilapidated rural houses, which should clarify the objectives, tasks, funding arrangements and policy measures, so as to ensure the timely completion of the annual task. We should implement the provincial subsidies and include the grant funds for reconstruction of dilapidated rural houses in the fiscal budget, the county finance department should pay directly to the farmer household for the reconstruction of dilapidated rural houses.

(5) We should encourage enterprises of all types of ownership as the implementation subject to undertake the task of shantytown redevelopment. The original financing platform companies in all regions can establish the modern enterprise system by market restructuring to realize the market operation, and under the premise of clear announcement that it will no longer bear the functions of government financing, they should act as the implementation subject undertake the task of shantytown redevelopment. The debt borrowed by the original financing platform companies after the transformation and restructuring should implement the market-oriented operation, which should not be included in the government debt. The government should perform the duties of the investor in the scope of capital contribution, and should not provide guarantee to the original platform companies.

(6) The Ministry of Housing and Urban-Rural Development should work together with relevant ministries to supervise and urge the preparation and implementation of the three-year plan and relevant implementation plan in all regions as soon as possible. The National Development and Reform Commission and the Ministry of Finance should further increase investment in the central budget and the central financial support in conjunction with the relevant ministries. The Ministry of Finance should arrange the central state-owned capital operating budgets jointly with relevant ministries and provide support for the reconstruction of shantytown supporting facilities of central enterprises in the poor central enterprises, especially in the independent industrial and mining areas, three-line areas and resource exhausted cities. The People's Bank of China, the Ministry of Finance and China Banking Regulatory Commission should improve the policies and measures to support the China Development Bank, Agricultural Development Bank of China and other

financial institutions to increase credit support efforts.

Ⅳ. Construction of Ecological Civilization

The construction of ecological civilization is an important part of the cause of socialism with Chinese characteristics. However, on the whole, the construction level of ecological civilization in our country still lags behind in economic and social development, the resource constraint is tight, the environmental pollution is serious, the ecosystem is degrading, the contradiction between development and population, resources and environment have become increasingly prominent, which has been of the major bottleneck of sustainable economic and social development.

The Chinese government attaches great importance to the construction of ecological civilization, which has issued a series of major decisions and arrangements. On April 25, 2015, the CPC Central Committee and the State Council issued the *Opinions on Accelerating the Construction of Ecological Civilization*, which put forward that we should firmly establish the philosophy of respecting nature, complying with nature and protecting the nature, accelerate the formation of a new pattern of modernization construction of harmonious development of man and nature and create a new era of socialist ecological civilization, by adhering to the concept of Green Hills and Clear Waters Being Golden Mountain. The CPC Central Committee General Office and the State Council issued the *Accountability Measures on the Ecological Environment Damage by Party and Government Leading Cadres* (*Trial*), which should be implemented from August 9, 2015.

To accelerate the establishment of a complete ecological civilization system, speed up the construction of ecological civilization and strengthen the systematicness, integrity and synergy of the reform of ecological civilization system, the CPC Central Committee and the State Council issued the *Overall Scheme of the Reform of Ecological Civilization System* on September 21, 2015. From November to December, 2015, the General Office of the CPC Central Committee and the General Office of the State Council have successively issued the *Pilot Scheme on Carrying out Off-office Auditing of Natural Resource Assets to Leading Cadres and Pilot Scheme on the Reform of Compensation System for Damage to the Ecological Environment*, the General Office of the State Council issued the *Pilot Scheme on the Preparation of Natural Resources Assets and Liabilities Table.*

(Ⅰ) Main objectives of the construction of ecological civilization

By 2020, the construction of resource conserving and environment friendly society should obtain great progress, the main function area layout should be basically formed, the quality and efficiency of economic development should have significant improvement, the mainstream value of ecological civilization construction should be promoted in the whole society, and the level of ecological civilization construction should adapt to the goal of building moderately prosperous society.

The land and space development pattern should be further optimized. The economy and population distribution should develop to the direction of equilibrium, the development strength of land and sea and the scale of urban space should be effectively controlled, and the urban-rural structure and space layout should be optimized obviously.

The resource utilization should be more efficient. The carbon dioxide emission intensity per unit of GDP should decrease by 40% ~45% than that of 2005, the energy consumption intensity should continue to decline, and the resource output rate should be greatly improved. The total water use should strive to control in 670 billion cubic meters, the water consumption per 10 000 yuan of value-added by industry should be reduced to 65 cubic meters, the effective utilization coefficient of agricultural irrigation water should be increased to more than 0. 55, and the proportion of non-fossil energy to the primary energy consumption should reach about 15%.

The ecological environment should have an overall improvement. The total discharge of major pollutants should continue to decline, the atmospheric environmental quality and water environment quality in key watersheds and coastal waters should be improved, the compliance rate of water quality in water function areas of important rivers and lakes should be increased to more than 80%, the safety level of drinking water should continue to improve, the soil environment quality should be stable in the whole, and environmental risk should get effective control. The forest coverage rate should reach more than 23%, the comprehensive vegetation coverage in the grassland should reach 56%, the wetland area should not be less than 800 million acres, more than 50% desertificated land can be treated, the retention rate of shoreline rate should not be less than 35%, the loss speed of biodiversity should be under control basically, and the ecosystem stability should be enhanced in the whole country.

The important system of ecological civilization should be basically established. The ecological civilization system featured by prevention in the source, process control, damage compensation and responsibility investigation should be basically formed and the construction of key systems, such as the assets property right of natural resources and use control, ecological protection redline, compensation for ecological protection and ecological environmental protection management system, etc., should have decisive results.

(Ⅱ) Green urbanization and the construction of beautiful countryside

The CPC Central Committee put forward that: We should scientifically plan and improve the production space, living space and ecological space of urban and rural areas.

The green urbanization should be vigorously promoted., We should seriously implement the *National Plan on New Urbanization* (2014 – 2020) and build a scientific and reasonable overall layout for urbanization according to the carrying capacity of resources and environment, strictly control the size of mega cities, enhance the bearing capacity of small and medium-sized cities, and promote the coordinated development of large, medium-sized and small cities and small towns. We should respect for the natural pattern, reasonably plan the various urban spaces by relying on the existing landscape context and meteorological conditions and reduce the interference and damage to the nature as far as possible. We should protect natural landscape, inherit the history and culture, promote the diversity of urban pattern, maintain the characteristic style and prevent "same imagines in the thousand cities" . We should scientifically determine the intensity of urban development, improve the efficiency of urban land use and population density of built-up area, define the urban growth boundary, strictly supply the urban construction land and promote the transformation of urbanization development from external extension and internal improvement. We should strictly implement the set-up conditions and procedures of new towns and new districts, strengthen the energy saving concept in the process of urbanization, vigorously develop the green building and low carbon, convenient traffic system, promote the construction of green ecological city, improve the urban water supply and drainage, water-logging, rainwater collection, heat supply, gas supply and environment and other infrastructure construction standards. All counties and key towns should have the capacity of sewage and garbage disposal, and improve the level of construction, operation and management. We should strengthen the management of "Three Areas and Four Line" (that are prohibited-construction areas, construction restricted area and construction accepted area; as well as the green line, blue line, purple line and yellow line) in urban and rural planning, maintain the authority and seriousness of urban and rural planning and eliminate large demolition and construction.

The construction of beautiful countryside should be accelerated. We should improve the village planning within the county-level, strengthen scientific nature and binding effect of the planning, strengthen rural infrastructure construction, enhance the comprehensive management of mountain, water, forests and farmland, accelerate the transformation of old and dilapidated rural housing, support the contiguous remediation for rural environment, carry out special governance for rural waste, increase rural sewage treatment and latrine improvement efforts, speed up the transformation of agricultural development mode, promote the adjustment of agricultural structure, vigorously develop the agricultural recycling economy, control the agricultural pollution, and improve the quality and safety level of agricultural products. Relying on rural ecological resources and under the premise of protecting the ecological environment, accelerate the development of rural tourism and leisure industry. Guide the farmers to plant trees around their house. Strengthen the construction of spiritual civilization in rural areas, and promote the creation of civilized villages and towns by focusing on the environmental remediation and folk construction.

(Ⅲ) Establish spatial planning system

We should integrate each department to separately compile all kinds of unified spatial planning and achieve full coverage. Spatial planning is a guide to the development of the national space, the space blueprint for sustainable development and the basic basis for all kinds of development and construction activities. Spatial planning is divided into national, provincial, city and county levels (the scope of spatial planning of the city divided into districts is the municipal district), we need to study the establishment of a unified preparation mechanism for standard spatial planning.

We should support the cities and counties to promote plans "more-in-one" and establish a unified spatial planning in cities and counties, and gradually form a planning and a blueprint for one city and one county. The spatial planning of cities and counties should have unified land classification standard, which delimits the production space, living space and ecological space in accordance with the requirements of the main functional orientation and provincial spatial planning, clarify the development boundary of construction area of cities and towns, industrial areas and rural settlements, and the protective boundaries of cultivated land, woodland, grassland, rivers, lakes and wetlands, strengthen the overall planning of the urban underground space. We should strengthen the guidance of plans "more-in-one" in the cities and counties, research and develop the guidelines and technical specifications of spatial planning in the cities and counties, forming the reproducible experience that can be promoted.

We should explore the standardized preparation procedures of spatial planning in the cities and counties, expand public participation, and enhance the scientificity and transparency of planning. Encourage the pilot areas to carry out the integration to planning and preparation departments, one department should be responsible for the preparation of spatial planning in the cities and counties, the planning review committee can be set up by the professional staff and representatives of the relevant aspects. The evaluation to the carrying capacity of resources and environment should be carried out before the planning so that the result of evaluation can be taken as the basic basis for planning. During the preparation of the planning, we should widely solicit opinions from all aspects, publicize the full text of the planning draft and fully listen to the views of local residents. After being demonstrated by the review committee, the planning should be approved by the local People's Congress after consideration and reported to the higher authorities for the record. The planning results should include planning text and a higher accuracy of planning map, and should be published in the network and other local media. Encourage local residents to supervise the implementation of the planning and report the behavior that violates the development and construction of planning. The local People's Congress and its Standing Committee would regularly listen to the report on the implementation of spatial planning and investigate responsibility of the local government for violation of the planning.

V. Urban-rural Master Plan Coordinated Development

The 13th Five Year Plan marks the final stage of the first hundred-year struggling goal of fully completing a well-off society in an all-round way and realizing the two centenary goals. The fellow-villager decides whether we complete the construction of a well-off society in an all-round way. How to actually build a well-off society in an all-round way that benefits people and enriches people and that is featured by people-oriented and urban and rural prosperity concerns the sustainable and healthy development of economy and society as well as the overall situation of the construction of socialist modernization. The CPC Central Committee and the State Council put forward in the *Several Opinions* on the *Implementation of New Ideas of Development and Acceleration of Agricultural Modernization and Realization of the Target of Building a Well-Off Society in an All-Round Way* that: We should continue to encourage industry to support agriculture in return for agriculture's earlier contribution to its development and encourage cities to support rural areas, promote the balanced allocation of urban and rural public resources and equal exchange of urban and rural elements and steadily improve equal level of urban and rural basic public service.

(Ⅰ) Speed up the construction of rural infrastructure

We should focus on the infrastructure construction in rural areas supported by the national finance, build, manage, protect and operate well the rural infrastructure and reduce the gap between the urban and rural areas significantly. Improve the long-term investment mechanism of rural infrastructure and promote the interconnection of urban and rural infrastructure, build and share. Strengthen the protection of drinking water source in rural areas. Implement the consolidation and upgrading project of drinking water safety in rural areas. Promote the extension of urban water supply facilities to the surrounding rural areas. Speed up the implementation of transformation and upgrading projects of rural power grid, carry out the comprehensive management of "low voltage" in rural areas, and develop green small hydropower. Speed up the access to hardened roads and buses for villages and towns equipped with the conditions, promote the access to highway for natural villages with a certain population. Create conditions to promote the integration of urban and rural passenger transport. Speed up the construction of fire emergency road in the state owned forest region. Incorporate the rural road maintenance funds gradually into the local financial budget. Develop rural scale biogas, make more efforts in the reconstruction of dilapidated rural houses, improve earthquake housing reconstruction overall, speed up resolution of the housing security problem of the rural poor families via loan interest and concentrated construction of public rental housing, and strengthen the construction of rural disaster prevention and mitigation system.

(Ⅱ) Improve the level of rural public service

Put the focus of the development of social undertakings on the rural areas and the towns and cities that accept migrant rural population, accelerate the promotion of urban public services to rural areas. Accelerate the development of rural pre-school education, adhere to the development of public and private schools, and expand rural inclusive pre-school education resources. Comprehensively improve the basic conditions of running a school in the schools with weak compulsory education in poor areas, improve the boarding conditions of rural school, run a small school in rural areas, promote the standardization of school construction. Speed up the popularization of high school education and gradually promote the exempt from paying tuition and miscellaneous fees for secondary vocational education step by step, first implement the exempt from tuition and fees of ordinary high schools for students with family economic difficulties, so as to achieve the whole coverage of funding for students having family economic difficulties. Strengthen the construction of rural teachers, expand the channels of teachers, and promote the flow of outstanding teachers in urban areas to rural schools. Integrate the basic medical insurance system of urban and rural residents, appropriately increase government subsidies, individual contributions and benefit levels. Establish and improve the caring service system for leftover children, women and the elderly care service system, establish and improve the welfare guarantee of rural children in plight and the social protection system of juveniles. Earnestly safeguard the legitimate rights and interests of rural women in the distribution of property, marriage, birth, political participation and other aspects so that women can get fair education opportunities, employment opportunities, property income and financial resources. Strengthen the rural old-age service system, the disabled rehabilitation and the construction of supporting and rearing facilities. Comprehensively strengthen the construction of rural public cultural service system, build a cultural service center at the town and village level in rural areas, and play the overall effect of grassroots cultural and public facilities.

(Ⅲ) Carry out remediation action of rural living environment and beautiful and livable rural construction

Following the law of rural development, we should reflect the rural characteristics, pay attention to local tastes, retain rural style, and strive to build a happy home for farmers. Scientifically compile the county-level rural construction planning and village planning, enhance the design level of residential housing, and strengthen the permission management of rural construction planning. Continue to promote the comprehensive improvement of the rural environment, perfect the policy of promoting the treatment by granting award, and expand the contiguous scope of regulation. Implement the "five-year special action" of governance of rural garbage. Take the various methods of extension of urban pipe network, centralized processing and distributed processing, etc. , speed up the rural sewage treatment and latrine improvement. Carry out the construction of livable rural water environment, Implement the rural river cleaning action, construct ecologically clean small watershed. Play the role of "one meeting for one case" financial awards complement funds of village public welfare, and support the improvement of village public facilities and residential environment. Adhere to paying equal attention to the urban and rural environmental governance, and gradually include the rural environment remediation spending into the local financial budget, the central government should give differential premium, the policy financial institutions provide long-term low interest loans, explore the operation mechanism for procurement services of the government and integration construction of professional company. Increase the protection to the traditional villages, houses and historical culture of ancient towns and villages and encourage the regions to explore the distinctive beautiful livable rural construction pattern.

(Ⅳ) Promote transfer employment and entrepreneurship of rural labor force and urbanization of *Nongmingong*

Perfect the service system of transfer employment of rural labor force, vigorously promote local transfer employment and entrepreneurship, stabilize and enlarge the scale of *Nongmingong*, support the *Nongmingong* to start up business in the hometown. Vigorously develop the characteristic county-level economy and rural service industry, accelerate the development of small towns and characteristic small towns, and enhance the ability to absorb agricultural transfer population. Increase the support of rural flexible employment and new employment form. Encourage the establishment of employment and entrepreneurship fund for rural women, increase the implementation of women's small secured loans, strengthen women's skills training, and support the rural women to develop family handicraft industry. Implement the vocational skills promotion plan for new generation of *Nongmingong*, carry out free vocational training action to the children from rural poor families, non-admitted middle and higher school graduates, *Nongmingong* and retired military personnel. Further promote the reform of the household registration system, implement the goal of settling for about 100 million *Nongmingong* and other resident population in cities and towns, guarantee the same rights and obligations of the *Nongmingong* settling in the cities and towns as the urban residents, and accelerate the improvement of urbanization rate of the household population. Fully implement the residence permit system, establish and improve the basic public service provision mechanism linked to the period of resident and other conditions, and strive to achieve the full coverage of the resident population of basic public services. Keep the land contract right and the right to use the homestead and the collective income distribution rights of farmers settling in the cities and towns, and support and guide the transfer of these rights and interests voluntarily in accordance with the law.

Ⅵ. Goal and Approach of Sustainable Urbanization

(Ⅰ) Preparatory process of the third United Nations Conference of Housing and Sustainable Urban Development (Habitat III)

The third United Nations Conference of Housing and Sustainable Urban Development (Habitat III) is scheduled to be held in Quito, the capital of Ecuador from October 17, 2016 to October 20, 2016. The theme of the conference is to discuss the future of sustainable urbanization and our existing city. The purpose of Habitat III is to evaluate the achievement of the world human settlement movement by now, ensure the new political commitment to the sustainable development of city of countries all over the world and establish a New Urban Agenda to tackle poverty and find and solve the emerging urban challenges.

The United Nations held the first Human Settlements Conference (Habitat Ⅰ) and second Human Settlement Conference (Habitat II) in 1976 and 1996 respectively in Vancouver, Canada, and Istanbul, Turkey, in which the global city and housing challenges and future policy of sustainable development of the city are discussed.

The preparatory work of Habitat III started in 2014. In the Preparatory Committee meeting held on September 17th, the General Secretary Ban Ki-moon pointed out that urbanization is a driving force as well as a source of development. A half of the world lives in urban centers. By the middle of this century, more than two-thirds of humanity will be in cities and almost all growth will be in developing countries. As we work to formulate the post-2015 development agenda, the role of urbanization in supporting sustainable development is becoming increasingly important. The United Nations should continue to promote equitable urban development in our human settlements, villages, towns, cities and countries.

In May 2015, the preparation of the documents of Habitat III started. The proposed the New Urban Agenda is divided into six areas: Social Cohesion and Equity - Livable Cities; Urban Frameworks; Spatial Development; Urban Economy; Urban Ecology and Environment; Urban Housing and Basic Services. On the basis of this, the agenda put forward 22 issue papers, and ultimately formed 10 policy papers: Right to the City and Cities for All; Socio Cultural Urban Framework; National Urban Policies; Urban Governance, Capacity and Institutional Development; Municipal Finance and Local Fiscal Systems; Urban Spatial Strategies: Land Market and Segregation; Urban Economic Development Strategies; Urban Ecology Resilience; Urban Services and Technology; Housing Policies. About 200 professional and technical personnel from all countries in the world of participated in the document preparation and put forward the implementation proposal for the action-oriented New Urban Agenda.

(Ⅱ) Habitation goal in the sustainable development agenda in 2030

On September 25, 2015, world-renowned the United Nations Summit for the Adoption of the Post-2015 Development Agenda officially opened the United Nations Headquarters in New York. The meeting passed the document of *Transforming our world: the* 2030 *Agenda for Sustainable Development*, that jointly agreed by the 193 member states. This programmatic document including 17 Sustainable Development Goals and 169 targets will urge the world to achieve three unprecedented extraordinary initiatives within the next 15 years, which include eradicating poverty in all its forms and dimensions, combating inequalities within and among countries, addressing decisively the threat posed by climate change and environmental degradation.

The eleventh development goal of the 2030 Agenda for Sustainable Development is "to make cities and human settlements inclusive, safe, resilient and sustainable", including 10 targets:

(1) By 2030, ensure access for all to adequate, safe and affordable housing and basic services and upgrade slums.

(2) By 2030, provide access to safe, affordable, accessible and sustainable transport systems for all, improving road safety, notably by expanding public transport, with special attention to the needs of those in vulnerable situations, women, children, persons with disabilities and older persons.

(3) By 2030, enhance inclusive and sustainable urbanization and capacity for participatory, integrated and sustainable human settlement planning and management in all countries.

(4) Strengthen efforts to protect and safeguard the world's cultural and natural heritage.

(5) By 2030, significantly reduce the number of deaths and the number of people affected and substantially decrease the direct economic losses relative to global gross domestic product caused by disasters, including water-related disasters, with a focus on protecting the poor and people in vulnerable situations.

(6) By 2030, reduce the adverse per capita environmental impact of cities, including by paying special attention to air quality and municipal and other waste management.

(7) By 2030, provide universal access to safe, inclusive and accessible, green and public spaces, in particular for women and children, older persons and persons with disabilities.

(8) Support positive economic, social and environmental links between urban, peri-urban and rural areas by strengthening national and regional development planning.

(9) By 2020, substantially increase the number of cities and human settlements adopting and implementing integrated policies and plans towards inclusion, resource efficiency, mitigation and adaptation to climate change, resilience to disasters, and develop and implement, in line with the Sendai Framework for Disaster Risk Reduction 2015-2030, holistic disaster risk management at all levels.

(10) Support least developed countries, including through financial and technical assistance, in building sustainable and resilient buildings utilizing local materials.

(Ⅲ) Urban public space and design

October 5, 2015 is World Habitat Day; October 31 is the World City Day. The UN-Habitat defines the October of every year as the World City Month, which has urged countries to seriously reflect on the state of human settlements and on what we want the cities of the future to look like.

The theme of 2015 World Habitat Day is "Public Space for All". The Secretary General of United Nations pointed out that frequently overlooked and undervalued, public spaces are increasingly being recognized as the vibrant, beating hearts of the world's towns and cities, which are today home to half of humanity. Public spaces are crucial for poor and vulnerable citizens. Improving access to them, and making them safe for women and girls, increases equity, promotes inclusion and combats discrimination. High-quality public spaces encourage people to communicate and collaborate with each other, and to participate in public life. Public spaces can also provide basic services, enhance connectivity, spawn economic activity and raise property values while generating municipal revenue. But successful public spaces do not just happen; they require careful collaboration among local authorities, local inhabitants and other actors.

The theme of 2015 World City Day is "Designed to Live Together". Dr. Joan Clos, UN-Habitat Executive Director said: cities are one of the most complex human creations. They are the places we design to live together. This year the World Cities Day focuses on the capacity that urban design has to affect how we live, how we move around, how our neighbourhoods look like and how safe we feel on the streets. Clos pointed out that:

Good design contributes to social integration, equality and diversity. Planning residential areas with different possibilities in terms of typology and price enables residents from different backgrounds and income levels to live together, prevents the creation of isolated ghettos or gated communities, fights segregation and discrimination.

Good design gives space for different cultures, ethnicities and lifestyles to mix and come together.

Good design fosters sustainable use of shared resources. Planning compact, denser cities reduces the overexploitation of natural resources, and facilitates common living by enabling equal access to land, food and water for all.

Good design inspires lively neighborhoods. Designed public spaces, parks, playgrounds, streets and squares filled with activities help create a vibrant public life for all residents.

Good design can make cities safer. Neighbourhoods that remain active and lively at night, with commercial activities on the ground floors, pedestrian friendly well-lit streets and public spaces mean increased personal safety and security.

Good design fosters proximity to jobs and services. With good infrastructure and public transport, higher building density and mixed use neighbourhoods, jobs, markets, schools and recreation are closer to people's homes and are easily accessible by foot, bike or public transport.

Good design helps to create clean, healthy cities. Denser cities and proximity to jobs and services mean reduced need for car use, less congestion and less pollution, as well as more sustainable usage of land and preservation of the natural and green areas.

Good design anticipates climate change and reduces the impacts of disasters. Planning with sensitivity to the surrounding nature, avoiding development in risky zones, planning natural buffers and prevention systems in flood or earthquake prone areas builds resilient settlements and safe communities.

How we all ensure good design is a part of the planning and managing process of a city is key for our urban future.

Ⅶ. Conclusion

"What's past is prologue." In 2015, China has made new progress in economic development, political construction, cultural construction, social construction and ecological civilization construction. However, with the complicated international environment, domestic structural adjustment and transformation and upgrading are at a critical stage of climbing over the ridge at present, indicating that the task of deepening the reform is still very arduous.

General Secretary Xi Jinping pointed out in his 2016 New Year message that "the year 2016 is the first year when China enters the crucial period to build a moderately well-off society in all all-around way. The 5th Plenary Session of the 18th CPC Central Committee has made clear China's development direction for the next five years. The future is encouraging and inspiring. But happiness does not fall from the sky. We shall establish a spirit to prevail, continue to immerse ourselves in hard work, implement the development concepts of innovation, coordination, green, openness and sharing. We shall put forth the efforts in promoting structural reform, and reform and opening up, promoting social fairness and justice, as well as creating a green political eco-system. We shall get off to a good start as we advance in the crucial period for China to build a moderately well-off society in all all-around way."

(Author: Mao Qizhi, professor of Tsinghai University, Academician of International Eurasian Academy of Sciences)

2015年中国城市发展十大事件

2015年，是我国城市发展中具有里程碑意义的一年，中央城市工作会议在时隔37年后再次召开，为当前和今后一个时期城市发展指明了方向。中央城市工作会议指出，要转变城市发展方式，完善城市治理体系，提高城市治理能力，着力解决城市病等突出问题，不断提升城市环境质量、人民生活质量、城市竞争力，建设和谐宜居、富有活力、各具特色的现代化城市，提高新型城镇化水平，走出一条中国特色城市发展道路。会议明确了做好城市工作的指导思想、总体思路、重点任务，并提出了做好城市工作的具体部署。

2015年，是我国城镇化进程中重要的一年，新型城镇化持续深入推进，区域协同发展战略稳步实施。长三角等城镇群规划加快编制，滇中新区等一批国家级新区设立，北京市房山区等59个第二批国家新型城镇化试点出台，撤县设市等行政区划调整加快，各地稳步推进户籍制度改革，城市规划建设管理进一步加强，城市功能进一步完善。《京津冀协同发展规划纲要》批准发布，这是推动京津冀协同发展重大国家战略的纲领性文件，是当前和今后一个时期指导京津冀协同发展工作的基本遵循；纲要提出要努力形成京津冀目标同向、措施一体、优势互补、互利共赢的协同发展新格局，打造中国经济发展新的支撑带。

2015年，是我国转变城市发展方式关键的一年，着力改善城市人居环境，提升城镇化质量。新的《大气污染防治法》修订后实施，以改善大气环境质量为目标，坚持源头治理，从推动转变经济发展方式、优化产业结构、调整能源结构的角度完善了相关制度，体现了中央关于生态文明建设和环境保护的新要求，顺应了公众对改善环境质量的新期待，为加强大气污染防治工作提供了强有力的法律武器。国务院发布《水污染防治行动计划》，以改善水环境质量为核心，系统推进水污染防治、水生态保护和水资源管理，是当前和今后一个时期全国水污染防治工作的行动指南。国务院发布《关于推进海绵城市建设的指导意见》，提出通过海绵城市建设，最大限度地减少城市开发建设对生态环境的影响，切实提高城市排水、防涝、防洪和防灾减灾能力。

2015年，我国在全面实施"一带一路"战略、推动国际区域经济合作方面取得重要成果。中央成立了以张高丽副总理为组长的"一带一路"建设工作领导小组，多次召开会议推进"一带一路"建设的重大事项和重点工作；国家发展改革委等多部门联合发布了《推动共建丝绸之路经济带和21世纪海上丝绸之路的愿景与行动》，提出了"一带一路"的共建原则、框架思路、合作重点、合作机制等内容。中国倡议成立、57国共同筹建的亚洲基础设施投资银行在北京正式开业，将有效增加亚洲地区基础设施投资，推动区域互联互通和经济一体化进程，对亚洲乃至世界经济增长带来积极提振作用，有助于推动全球经济治理体系朝着更加公正合理有效的方向发展。

一、中央城市工作会议在北京召开

城市是我国经济、政治、文化、社会等方面活动的中心，在党和国家工作全局中具有举足轻重的地位。改革开放以来，我国经历了世界历史上规模最大、速度最快的城镇化进程，城市发展波澜壮阔，取得了举世瞩目的成就。城市发展带动了整个经济社会发展，城市建设成为现代化建设的重要引擎。

2015 年 12 月 20 日至 21 日，中央城市工作会议在北京举行。会议分析了我国城市发展面临的形势，明确了做好城市工作的指导思想、总体思路、重点任务，并提出了做好城市工作的具体部署。

会议指出，当前和今后一个时期，我国城市工作的指导思想是：以邓小平理论、“三个代表”重要思想、科学发展观为指导，贯彻创新、协调、绿色、开放、共享的发展理念，坚持以人为本、科学发展、改革创新、依法治市，转变城市发展方式，完善城市治理体系，提高城市治理能力，着力解决城市病等突出问题，不断提升城市环境质量、人民生活质量、城市竞争力，建设和谐宜居、富有活力、各具特色的现代化城市，提高新型城镇化水平，走出一条中国特色城市发展道路。

会议强调，城市工作是一个系统工程。要坚持集约发展，框定总量、限定容量、盘活存量、做优增量、提高质量，立足国情，尊重自然、顺应自然、保护自然，改善城市生态环境，在统筹上下功夫，在重点上求突破，着力提高城市发展持续性、宜居性。

第一，尊重城市发展规律。城市发展是一个自然历史过程，有其自身规律。城市和经济发展两者相辅相成、相互促进。城市发展是农村人口向城市集聚、农业用地按相应规模转化为城市建设用地的过程，人口和用地要匹配，城市规模要同资源环境承载能力相适应。

第二，统筹空间、规模、产业三大结构，提高城市工作全局性。要结合实施“一带一路”建设、京津冀协同发展、长江经济带建设等战略，明确我国城市发展空间布局、功能定位。要以城市群为主体形态，科学规划城市空间布局，实现紧凑集约、高效绿色发展。各城市要结合资源禀赋和区位优势，明确主导产业和特色产业，强化大中小城市和小城镇产业协作协同，逐步形成横向错位发展、纵向分工协作的发展格局。

第三，统筹规划、建设、管理三大环节，提高城市工作的系统性。要综合考虑城市功能定位、文化特色、建设管理等多种因素来制定规划。要加强城市设计，提倡城市修补，加强控制性详细规划的公开性和强制性。要加强对城市的空间立体性、平面协调性、风貌整体性、文脉延续性等方面的规划和管控，留住城市特有的地域环境、文化特色、建筑风格等“基因”。要抓住城市管理和服务这个重点，不断完善城市管理和服务，彻底改变粗放型管理方式，让人民群众在城市生活得更方便、更舒心、更美好。

第四，统筹改革、科技、文化三大动力，提高城市发展持续性。要推进规划、建设、管理、户籍等方面的改革，以主体功能区规划为基础统筹各类空间性规划，推进“多规合一”。要深化城市管理体制改革，确定管理范围、权力清单、责任主体。要推进城市科技、文化等诸多领域改革，优化创新创业生态链，让创新成为城市发展的主动力，释放城市发展新动能。

第五，统筹生产、生活、生态三大布局，提高城市发展的宜居性。城市工作要把创造优良人居环境作为中心目标，努力把城市建设成为人与人、人与自然和谐共处的美丽家园。要深化城镇住房制度改革，继续完善住房保障体系，加快城镇棚户区和危房改造，加快老旧小区改造。要大力开展生态修复，让城市再现绿水青山。要控制城市开发强度，划定水体保护线、绿地系统线、基础设施建设控制线、历史文化保护线、永久基本农田和生态保护红线，防止“摊大饼”式扩张，推动形成绿色低碳的生产生活方式和城市建设运营模式。

第六，统筹政府、社会、市民三大主体，提高各方推动城市发展的积极性。要坚持协调协同，尽最大可能推动政府、社会、市民同心同向行动，使政府有形之手、市场无形之手、市民勤劳之手同向发力。政府要创新城市治理方式，特别是要注意加强城市精细化管理。要提高市民文明素质，尊重市民对城市发展决策的知情权、参与权、监督权，鼓励企业和市民通过各种方式参与城市建设、管理，真正实现城市共治共管、共建共享。

会议指出，城市是我国各类要素资源和经济社会活动最集中的地方，全面建成小康社会、加快实现现代化，必须抓好城市这个“火车头”，把握发展规律，推动以人为核心的新型城镇化，发挥这一扩大内需的最大潜力，有效化解各种“城市病”。要提升规划水平，增强城市规划的科学性和权威性，促进“多规合一”，全面开展城市设计，完善新时期建筑方针，科学谋划城市“成长坐标”。要提升建设水平，加强城市地下和地上基础设施建设，建设海绵城市，加快棚户区和危房改造，有序推进老旧住宅小区综合整治，力争到 2020 年基本完成现有城镇棚户区、城中村和危房改造，推进城市绿色发展，提高建筑标准和工程质量，高度重视做好建筑节能。要提升管理水平，着力打造智慧城市，以实施居住证制度为抓手推动城镇常住人口基本公共服务均等化，加强城市公共管理，全面提升市民素质。推进改革创新，为城市发展提供有力的体制机制保障。

历届中央城市工作会议一览表

会议名称	解决问题	政策措施	政策效果
第一次城市工作会议（1962 年 9 月）	城市失控和环境恶化；城市建设和工业建设比例失调	压缩城市人口，调整市镇建制；确定城市维护资金，加强市政公用设施的养护维修	截至 1963 年 6 月，全国减少职工 2600 万人，到 1964 年年底，建制市由 1961 年年底的 208 个减少到 169 个。截至 1962 年 12 月，64 个大中城市每年增加收入 2.68 亿元，加上工商税附加和公用事业附加，共计 4.5 亿元

续表

会议名称	解决问题	政策措施	政策效果
第二次城市工作会议(1963年9月16日－10月12日)	主要生活必需品供应不足、市政建设落后于生活基本需要;工业调整仍未完成,城市人口过多;如何贯彻执行集中领导和分级管理相结合的原则	加强房屋和市政设施的维修、采取措施强化资金来源;城市废水、废气、废渣的处理和利用,有重点地分期分批安排解决;市政企事业单位改善经营管理;结合"三五"计划,编制城市近期建设规划,并修改现有总体规划;加强城市管理的工作	1963－1965年,城市建设投资占基本建设投资的比例由"二五"时期的2.3%上升到2.9%
第三次城市工作会议(1978年3月6日－3月8日)	城市规划长期废弛,城市建设和管理工作薄弱、混乱,大城市规模控制不住,小城镇的方针贯彻不力,"骨头"与"肉"的关系不协调;城市职工住宅和市政公用设施失修,市容不整、环境差,交通秩序紊乱,副食品供应紧张	控制大城市规模,多搞小城镇;抓好城市规划;狠抓现有设施的维修养护和旧城改造;加速住宅及市政公用设施的建设;大力开展综合利用,防治污染,保护环境;搞好园林绿化、文物保护,积极开展旅游工作;加强城市管理	城市规划工作全面展开(截至1986年,96%的城市和85%县镇编制了总体规划)。加快了住宅建设(1979－1985年,住宅竣工面积每年增速11.2%,新建住宅占新中国成立以来总面积的60%)。大力发展市政公用事业。加强环境卫生管理,绿化美化城市

(参考资料来源:根据历届中央城市工作会议材料整理)

二、《京津冀协同发展规划纲要》批准实施

京津冀地区同属京畿重地,濒临渤海,背靠太岳,携揽"三北",战略地位十分重要,是我国经济最具活力、开放程度最高、创新能力最强、吸纳人口最多的地区之一,也是拉动我国经济发展的重要引擎。推动京津冀协同发展,是党中央、国务院在新的历史条件下做出的重大决策部署,对于协调推进"四个全面"战略布局、实现"两个一百年"奋斗目标和中华民族伟大复兴的中国梦,具有重大现实意义和深远历史意义。

2015年4月30日,中共中央政治局会议审议通过了《京津冀协同发展规划纲要》(以下简称《规划纲要》)。从战略意义、总体要求、定位布局、有序疏解北京非首都功能、推动重点领域率先突破、促进创新驱动发展、统筹协同发展相关任务、深化体制机制改革、开展试点示范、加强组织实施等方面描绘了京津冀协同发展的宏伟蓝图,是推动京津冀协同发展重大国家战略的纲领性文件,是当前和今后一个时期指导京津冀协同发展工作的基本遵循。

推动京津冀协同发展的指导思想是:以有序疏解北京非首都功能、解决北京"大城市病"为基本出发点,以资源环境承载能力为基础,以京津冀城市群建设为载体,以优化区域分工和产业布局为重点,以资源要素空间统筹规划利用为主线,以构建长效体制机制为抓手,着力调整优化经济结构和空间结构,着力构建现代化交通网络系统,着力扩大环境容量生态空间,着力推进产业升级转移,着力推动公共服务共建共享,着力加快市场一体化进程,加快打造现代化新型首都圈,努力形成京津冀目标同向、措施一体、优势互补、互利共赢的协同发展新格局,打造中国经济发展新的支撑带。

京津冀整体功能定位是:以首都为核心的世界级城市群、区域整体协同发展改革引领

区、全国创新驱动经济增长新引擎、生态修复环境改善示范区。三省市定位分别为：北京市“全国政治中心、文化中心、国际交往中心、科技创新中心”；天津市“全国先进制造研发基地、北方国际航运核心区、金融创新运营示范区、改革开放先行区”；河北省“全国现代商贸物流重要基地、产业转型升级试验区、新型城镇化与城乡统筹示范区、京津冀生态环境支撑区”。区域整体定位体现了三省市“一盘棋”的思想，突出了功能互补、错位发展、相辅相成；三省市定位服从和服务于区域整体定位，增强整体性，符合京津冀协同发展的战略需要。

京津冀协同发展的目标是：近期到 2017 年，有序疏解北京非首都功能取得明显进展，在符合协同发展目标且现实急需、具备条件、取得共识的交通一体化、生态环境保护、产业升级转移等重点领域率先取得突破，深化改革、创新驱动、试点示范有序推进，协同发展取得显著成效。中期到 2020 年，北京市常住人口控制在 2300 万人以内，北京“大城市病”等突出问题得到缓解；区域一体化交通网络基本形成，生态环境质量得到有效改善，产业联动发展取得重大进展。公共服务共建共享取得积极成效，协同发展机制有效运转，区域内发展差距趋于缩小，初步形成京津冀协同发展、互利共赢新局面。远期到 2030 年，首都核心功能更加优化，京津冀区域一体化格局基本形成，区域经济结构更加合理，生态环境质量总体良好，公共服务水平趋于均衡，成为具有较强国际竞争力和影响力的重要区域，在引领和支撑全国经济社会发展中发挥更大作用。

《规划纲要》确定了“功能互补、区域联动、轴向集聚、节点支撑”的空间布局思路，明确了以“一核、双城、三轴、四区、多节点”为骨架，推动有序疏解北京非首都功能，构建以重要城市为支点，以战略性功能区平台为载体，以交通干线、生态廊道为纽带的网络型空间格局。“一核”即指北京。把有序疏解北京非首都功能、优化提升首都核心功能、解决北京“大城市病”问题作为京津冀协同发展的首要任务。“双城”是指北京、天津，这是京津冀协同发展的主要引擎，要进一步强化京津联动，全方位拓展合作广度和深度，加快实现同城化发展，共同发挥高端引领和辐射带动作用。“三轴”指的是京津、京保石、京唐秦三个产业发展带和城镇聚集轴，这是支撑京津冀协同发展的主体框架。“四区”分别是中部核心功能区、东部滨海发展区、南部功能拓展区和西北部生态涵养区，每个功能区都有明确的空间范围和发展重点。“多节点”包括石家庄、唐山、保定、邯郸等区域性中心城市和张家口、承德、廊坊、秦皇岛、沧州、邢台、衡水等节点城市，重点是提高其城市综合承载能力和服务能力，有序推动产业和人口聚集。同时，立足于三省市比较优势和现有基础，加快形成定位清晰、分工合理、功能完善、生态宜居的现代城镇体系，走出一条绿色低碳智能的新型城镇化道路。

《规划纲要》提出四类产业和机构确认将被有序疏解，重点是疏解一般性产业特别是高消耗产业，区域性物流基地、区域性专业市场等部分第三产业，部分教育、医疗、培训机构等社会公共服务功能，部分行政性、事业性服务机构和企业总部等四类非首都功能。

《规划纲要》确定了交通一体化、生态环境保护、产业升级转移是三大重点领域。在交通一体化方面，重点是建设高效密集轨道交通网，完善便捷通畅公路交通网，打通国家高速公路“断头路”，全面消除跨区域国省干线“瓶颈路段”，加快构建现代化的津冀港口群，打造国际一流的航空枢纽，加快北京新机场建设，大力发展公交优先的城市交通，提升交通智能化管理水平，提升区域一体化运输服务水平，发展安全绿色可持续交通。在生态环境保护方面，重点是联防联控环境污染，建立一体化的环境准入和退出机制，加强环境污染治理，实施清洁水行动，大力发展循环经济，推进生态保护与建设，谋划建设一批环首都国家公园和森林公园，积极应对气候变化。在推动产业升级转移方面，重点是明确产业定位和方向，加快产业转型升级，推动产业转移对接，加强三省市产业发展规划衔接，制定京津冀产业指导目录，加快津冀承接平台建设，加强京津冀产业协作等。

京津冀协同发展大事记

• 发起阶段（1986－2003 年）

1986 年，环渤海地区 15 个城市共同发起成立了环渤海地区市长联席会。

• 全面启动和实践阶段（2004－2009 年）

2004 年 2 月，国家发改委召集京津冀三省份发改部门在廊坊召开京津冀区域经济发展战略研讨会，达成“廊坊共识”。

2004 年 6 月，环渤海合作机制会议在廊坊举行。会议草拟了《环渤海区域合作框架协议》。这标志着环渤海地区合作机制已从构想、探索进入到全面启动和实践阶段。

2005 年 1 月，国务院常务会议通过《北京城市总体规划（2004－2020）》。规划提出，积极推进环渤海地区的经济合作与协调发展，加强京津冀地区的协调发展，要基本形成以北京、天津为中心的“两小时交通圈”。

2005 年 6 月，国家发改委在唐山市召开“京津冀区域规划工作座谈会”。

2008 年 2 月，“第一次京津冀发改委区域工作联席会”召开。京津冀发改委共同签署了《北京市、天津市、河北省发改委建立“促进京津冀都市圈发展协调沟通机制”的意见》。

• 加速推进（2010 年至今）

2010 年 10 月，河北省政府《关于加快河北省环首都经济圈产业发展的实施意见》正式出台，提出了在规划体系等 6 个方面启动与北京的“对接工程”。

2011 年 3 月，国家“十二五”规划纲要发布，提出“打造首都经济圈”。

2011 年 5 月，首届京津冀区域合作高端会议在河北廊坊召开。

2014 年 1 月，北京市《政府工作报告》提出，落实国家区域发展战略，积极配合编制首都经济圈发展规划，抓紧编制空间布局、基础设施、产业发展和生态保护专项规划，建立健全区域合作发展协调机制，主动融入京津冀城市群发展。

2014 年 2 月，中共中央总书记、国家主席习近平主持召开京津冀三地协同发展座谈会，要求北京、天津、河北三地打破“一亩三分地”的思维定式，强调实现京津冀协同发展是面向未来打造新的首都经济圈、推进区域发展体制机制创新的需要，是一个重大国家战略，并要求抓紧编制首都经济圈一体化发展的相关规划。

2014 年3月，国务院总理李克强作政府工作报告，提出“加强环渤海及京津冀地区经济协作”。

中共中央、国务院印发了《国家新型城镇化规划（2014－2020 年）》，提出将“京津冀”建设成为世界级城市群。

2014 年 8 月，国务院成立京津冀协同发展领导小组，组长由副总理张高丽担任。

2015 年 4 月，《京津冀协同发展规划纲要》获通过，指出推动京津冀协同发展是一个重大国家战略，核心是有序疏解北京非首都功能。作为国家重点战略，京津冀一体将探索出一种人口经济密集地区优化开发的模式。

（参考资料来源：新华网）

三、“一带一路”发展战略推进实施

2013 年 9 月和 10 月，中国国家主席习近平在出访中亚和东南亚国家期间，先后提出共建“丝绸之路经济带”和“21 世纪海上丝绸之路”（简称“一带一路”）的重大倡议，得到国际社会高度关注。中国国务院总理李克强参加 2013 年中国—东盟博览会时强调，铺就面向东盟的海上丝绸之路，打造带动腹地发展的战略支点。初步估算，“一带一路”沿线总人口约 44 亿人，经济总量约 21 万亿美元，分别占全球的 63% 和 29% 。“一带一路”作为中国首倡、高层推动的国家战略，对我国现代化建设和屹立于世界的领导地位具有深远的战略意义。

2015 年 2 月 1 日，推进“一带一路”建设工作会议在北京召开，国务院副总理张高丽主持会议并讲话。会议安排部署 2015 年及今后一段时期推进“一带一路”建设的重大事项和重点工作。

2 月 1 日，中央成立“一带一路”建设工作领导小组，国务院副总理张高丽任组长，中央政策研究室主任王沪宁、国务院副总理汪洋、国务院秘书长杨晶、国务委员杨洁篪任副组长。

3 月 28 日，在博鳌亚洲论坛 2015 年年会开幕式上，国家主席习近平发表主旨演讲时表示：“一带一路”建设秉持的是共商、共建、共享原则，不是封闭的，而是开放包容的；不是中国一家的独奏，而是沿线国家的合唱。“一带一路”建设不是空洞的口号，而是看得见、摸得着的实际举措，将给地区国家带来实实在在的利益。在有关各方共同努力下，“一带一路”建设的愿景与行动文件已经制定，亚洲基础设施投资银行筹建工作迈出实质性步伐，丝路基金已经顺利启动，一批基础设施互联互通项目已经在稳步推进。这些早期收获向我们展现了“一带一路”的广阔前景。

3 月 28 日，国家发展改革委、外交部、商务部联合发布了《推动共建丝绸之路经济带和 21 世纪海上丝绸之路的愿景与行动》，提出：发挥新疆独特的区位优势和向西开放重要窗口作用，深化与中亚、南亚、西亚等国家交流合作，形成丝绸之路经济带上重要的交通枢纽、商贸物流和文化科教中心，打造丝绸之路经济带核心区；发挥广西与东盟国家陆海相邻的独特优势，加快北部湾经济区和珠江—西江经济带开放发展，构建面向东盟区域的国际通道，打造西南、中南地区开放发展新的战略支点，形成21世纪海上丝绸之路与丝绸之路经济带有机衔接的重要门户；利用长三角、珠三角、海峡西岸、环渤海等经济区开放程度高、经济实力强、辐射带动作用大的优势，加快推进中国（上海）自由贸易试验区建设，支持福建建设21世纪海上丝绸之路核心区；充分发挥深圳前海、广州南沙、珠海横琴、福建平潭等开放合作区作用，深化与港澳台合作，打造粤港澳大湾区；利用内陆纵深广阔、人力资源丰富、产业基础较好优势，依托长江中游城市群、成渝城市群、中原城市群、呼包鄂榆城市群、哈长城市群等重点区域，推动区域互动合作和产业集聚发展，打造重庆西部开发开放重要支撑和成都、郑州、武汉、长沙、南昌、合肥等内陆开放型经济高地。

7月21日，“一带一路”建设推进工作会议在北京召开，国务院副总理张高丽主持会议并讲话。会议总结前一段的工作，围绕重点方向、重点国家、重点项目，进一步研究部署下一阶段工作。

12月31日，国家发展和改革委员会发布了《关于进一步加强区域合作工作的指导意见》，提出要大力推进“一带一路”建设。支持各地发挥比较优势，贯彻落实“一带一路”建设顶层设计以及各省（区、市）参与建设“一带一路”实施方案。支持发挥西部地区向西开放前沿阵地、沿海地区龙头引领和内陆腹地战略支撑作用，打造陆海内外联动、东西双向开放的全面开放新格局。重点打造新疆丝绸之路经济带核心区和福建21世纪海上丝绸之路核心区。结合六大国际经济合作走廊建设，支持各地深化与沿线国家（地区）交流合作，共建境外产业集聚区，有针对性地培育打造一批共建走廊试点示范省（区、市）。

“一带一路”战略构想的提出，契合沿线国家的共同需求，为沿线国家优势互补、开放发展开启了新的机遇之窗，是国际合作的新平台。加快“一带一路”建设，有利于促进沿线各国经济繁荣与区域经济合作，加强不同文明交流互鉴，促进世界和平发展，是一项造福世界各国人民的伟大事业。

“一带一路”大事记

2013年9月，国家主席习近平在访问哈萨克斯坦时提出构建“丝绸之路经济带”，逐步形成区域大合作。

2013年10月，国家主席习近平在出席亚太经合组织（APEC）领导人非正式会议期间，在印尼国会发表演讲时，提出中国愿同东盟国家加强海上合作，共同建设“21世纪海上丝绸之路”的倡议。

2013年12月，国家主席习近平在中央经济工作会议上提出，推进“丝绸之路经济带”建设，抓紧制定战略规划，加强基础设施互联互通建设。建设“21世纪海上丝绸之路”，加强海上通道互联互通建设，拉紧相互利益纽带。

2014年3月，国务院总理李克强在政府工作报告中介绍当年重点工作时指出，“抓紧规划建设丝绸之路经济带、21世纪海上丝绸之路”。

2014年5月，作为“丝绸之路经济带”建设的首个实体平台，连云港中哈国际物流基地的启用，标志着中哈两国依托新亚欧大陆桥，共建“丝绸之路经济带”的战略构想进入实质实施阶段。

2014 年 11 月，国家主席习近平在 APEC 峰会上宣布，中国将出资 400 亿美元成立丝路基金。这是专门服务于“一带一路”的营运资金。与此同时，亚洲基础设施投资银行有望成立，中国将是主要股东，亚投行有望成为基础设施建设的重要融资来源。

2014 年 12 月，中央经济工作会议提出“一带一路”是 2015 年区域发展的首要战略，会议提出要重点实施“一带一路”、京津冀协同发展、长江经济带三大战略，争取 2015 年有个良好开局。

2015 年 2 月 1 日，推进“一带一路”建设工作会议在北京召开。中共中央政治局常委、国务院副总理张高丽主持会议并讲话。

2015 年 3 月，2015 年被视为“一带一路”战略落地实施的关键年，国务院总理李克强在政府工作报告中三次提及“一带一路”，“一带一路”成了 2015 年两会出现频率最高的词。

2015 年 3 月 28 日，国家主席习近平在博鳌亚洲论坛开幕式上发表主旨演讲，表示“一带一路”建设不是要替代现有地区合作机制和倡议，而是要在已有基础上，推动沿线各国实现经济战略相互对接、优势互补。

2015 年 3 月 28 日，国家发展改革委、外交部、商务部联合发布了《推动共建丝绸之路经济带和 21 世纪海上丝绸之路的愿景与行动》。

2015 年 5 月 7 日，国家主席习近平开启对欧亚三国的访问，首站抵达哈萨克斯坦。此次访哈可视作是“丝绸之路经济带”的落实之旅，进一步助推“一带一路”的建设。

（参考资料来源：新华网）

四、亚洲基础设施投资银行在北京成立

亚洲基础设施投资银行（简称“亚投行”）是由中国倡议成立、57 国共同筹建的一个政府间性质的亚洲区域多边开发机构，重点支持基础设施建设，成立宗旨是促进亚洲区域的建设互联互通化和经济一体化的进程，并且加强中国及其他亚洲国家和地区的合作。

2013 年 10 月 2 日，习近平主席提出筹建亚洲基础设施投资银行倡议。2014 年 10 月 24 日，包括中国、印度、新加坡等在内 21 个首批意向创始成员国的财政部长和授权代表在北京签约，共同决定成立亚洲基础设施投资银行。

2015 年 3 月 12 日，英国正式申请加入亚投行，成为首个申请加入亚投行的主要西方国家。随后，法国、意大利、卢森堡、瑞士等国表示愿意以创始国的身份加入亚投行。

4 月 15 日，亚投行意向创始成员国确定为 57 个，其中域内国家 37 个、域外国家 20 个。

6 月 29 日，《亚洲基础设施投资银行协定》（以下简称《协定》）签署仪式在北京举行。亚投行 57 个意向创始成员国财长或授权代表出席了签署仪式，其中已通过国内审批程序的 50 个国家正式签署《协定》，其他尚未通过国内审批程序的意向创始成员国见证签署仪式。

11 月 4 日，中国第十二届全国人民代表大会常务委员会第十七次会议批准了《亚洲基

础设施投资银行协定》。

12月25日，中国财政部部长楼继伟在北京宣布，《亚洲基础设施投资银行协定》正式生效，标志着亚洲基础设施投资银行在法律意义上正式成立。亚投行初期投资重点领域包括能源与电力、交通和电信、农村和农业基础设施、供水与污水处理、环境保护、城市发展以及物流等，首批贷款计划在2016年年中左右批准。

截至12月25日，包括缅甸、新加坡、文莱、澳大利亚、中国、蒙古、奥地利、英国、新西兰、卢森堡、韩国、格鲁吉亚、荷兰、德国、挪威、巴基斯坦、约旦在内的17个意向创始成员国（股份总和占比50.1%）已批准《协定》并提交批准书，从而达到《协定》规定的生效条件，即至少有10个签署方批准且签署方初始认缴股本总额不少于总认缴股本的50%，亚洲基础设施投资银行正式成立。

12月31日，菲律宾驻华大使巴西里奥作为政府全权代表在北京签署《亚洲基础设施投资银行协定》。至此，亚洲基础设施投资银行57个意向创始成员国已全部签署《亚洲基础设施投资银行协定》。

2016年1月16日，亚洲基础设施投资银行在北京正式开业，中国国家主席习近平出席开业仪式并致辞，强调通过各成员国携手努力，亚投行一定能成为专业、高效、廉洁的21世纪新型多边开发银行，成为构建人类命运共同体的新平台，为促进亚洲和世界发展繁荣作出新贡献，为改善全球经济治理增添新力量。同日，亚洲基础设施投资银行理事会成立大会在北京举行，会议选举中国财政部部长楼继伟为亚投行理事会主席，选举印尼财长班邦·布罗佐内戈罗和德国财政部国务秘书托马斯·斯蒂芬为理事会副主席；选举金立群先生为亚投行首任行长。会议审议通过了理事会议事规则、总部协定、首届理事会年会时间及地点等决议。

亚投行正式成立并开业，将有效增加亚洲地区基础设施投资，推动区域互联互通和经济一体化进程，也有利于改善亚洲发展中成员国的投资环境，创造就业机会，提升中长期发展潜力，对亚洲乃至世界经济增长带来积极提振作用，对全球经济治理体系改革完善具有重大意义，顺应了世界经济格局调整演变的趋势，有助于推动全球经济治理体系朝着更加公正合理有效的方向发展。

亚投行意向创始成员国列表（截至2015年12月31日）

国家/地区		申请加入时间	批准加入时间	是否签订《亚投行协定》	备　注
亚洲	孟加拉国	2014年10月24日	2014年10月24日	是	
	文莱	2014年10月24日	2014年10月24日	是	
	柬埔寨	2014年10月24日	2014年10月24日	是	
	中国	2014年10月24日	2014年10月24日	是	联合国安理会常任理事国，G20
	印度	2014年10月24日	2014年10月24日	是	G20
	印度尼西亚	2014年11月25日	2014年11月25日	是	G20

续表

国家/地区		申请加入时间	批准加入时间	是否签订《亚投行协定》	备　注
亚洲	约旦		2015年2月7日	是	
	哈萨克斯坦	2014年10月24日	2014年10月24日	是	
	科威特	2014年10月24日	2014年10月24日	是	
	老挝	2014年10月24日	2014年10月24日	是	
	马来西亚	2014年10月24日	2014年10月24日	是	
	马尔代夫		2014年12月31日	是	
	蒙古国	2014年10月24日	2014年10月24日	是	
	缅甸	2014年10月24日	2014年10月24日	是	
	尼泊尔	2014年10月24日	2014年10月24日	是	
	阿曼	2014年10月24日	2014年10月24日	是	
	巴基斯坦	2014年10月24日	2014年10月24日	是	
	菲律宾	2014年10月24日	2014年10月24日	是	
	卡塔尔	2014年10月24日	2014年10月24日	是	
	沙特阿拉伯		2015年1月13日	是	G20
	新加坡	2014年10月24日	2014年10月24日	是	
	韩国	2015年3月26日	2015年4月11日	是	G20
	斯里兰卡	2014年10月24日	2014年10月24日	是	
	塔吉克斯坦		2015年1月13日	是	
	泰国	2014年10月24日	2014年10月24日	是	
	土耳其	2015年3月26日	2015年4月10日	是	G20
	乌兹别克斯坦	2014年10月24日	2014年10月24日	是	
	越南	2014年10月24日	2014年10月24日	是	
	吉尔吉斯斯坦	2015年3月31日	2015年4月9日	是	
	以色列	2015年3月31日	2015年4月15日	是	
	格鲁吉亚	2015年3月28日	2015年4月12日	是	
	阿联酋	2015年3月20日	2015年4月3日	是	
	阿塞拜疆	2015年3月31日	2015年4月15日	是	
	伊朗		2015年4月3日	是	
欧洲	奥地利	2015年3月27日	2015年4月11日	是	
	丹麦	2015年3月28日	2015年4月12日	是	
	法国	2015年3月17日	2015年4月2日	是	联合国安理会常任理事国,G20
	德国	2015年3月17日	2015年4月1日	是	G20
	意大利	2015年3月17日	2015年4月2日	是	G20
	卢森堡	2015年3月18日	2015年3月27日	是	
	荷兰	2015年3月28日	2015年4月12日	是	

续表

国家/地区		申请加入时间	批准加入时间	是否签订《亚投行协定》	备　注
欧洲	西班牙	2015 年 3 月 27 日	2015 年 4 月 11 日	是	
	瑞士	2015 年 3 月 20 日	2015 年 3 月 28 日	是	
	英国	2015 年 3 月 12 日	2015 年 3 月 28 日	是	联合国安理会常任理事国,G20
	瑞典	2015 年 3 月 31 日	2015 年 4 月 15 日	是	
	芬兰	2015 年 3 月 30 日	2015 年 4 月 12 日	是	
	挪威	2015 年 3 月 31 日	2015 年 4 月 14 日	是	
	冰岛	2015 年 3 月 31 日	2015 年 4 月 15 日	是	
	俄罗斯	2015 年 3 月 30 日	2015 年 4 月 14 日	是	联合国安理会常任理事国,G20
	葡萄牙	2015 年 3 月 31 日	2015 年 4 月 15 日	是	
	波兰	2015 年 3 月 31 日	2015 年 4 月 15 日	是	
	马耳他		2015 年 4 月 9 日	是	
大洋洲	新西兰	2014 年 11 月 28 日	2015 年 1 月 4 日	是	
	澳大利亚	2015 年 3 月 29 日	2015 年 4 月 13 日	是	G20
南美洲	巴西	2015 年 3 月 28 日	2015 年 4 月 12 日	是	G20
非洲	埃及	2015 年 3 月 30 日	2015 年 4 月 14 日	是	
	南非	2015 年 3 月 31 日	2015 年 4 月 15 日	是	G20

（参考资料来源：亚洲基础设施开发银行网）

五、《大气污染防治法》修订实施

随着经济社会快速发展，特别是机动车保有量急剧增加，我国大气污染正向煤烟与机动车尾气复合型过渡，区域性大气环境问题日益突出，雾霾等重污染天气频发，现行法已经不能适应新形势的需要。现行的《大气污染防治法》是 1987 年制定的，1995 年、2000 年经历过两次修改。

2015 年 8 月 29 日，《大气污染防治法》由第十二届全国人民代表大会常务委员会第十六次会议修订通过，修订后的《大气污染防治法》自 2016 年 1 月 1 日起施行。这部被称为“史上最严”的大气污染防治法，从修订前的七章 66 条，扩展到现在的八章 129 条，不仅在法条数量大幅度增加，而且几乎对所有现行法条都做出了修改。

修订后的《大气污染防治法》不仅实现了与新修订的《环境保护法》的衔接，也将“大气十条”中的有效政策转化为法律制度，除总则、法律责任和附则外，分别对大气污染防治标准和限期达标规划、大气污染防治的监督管理、大气污染防治措施、重点区域大气污染联合防治、重污染天气应对等内容作了规定。

立法目的：以生态文明建设、保障公众健康、改善大气环境质量及促进经济社会可持续发展为目标，强化了地方政府责任，加强了对地方政府的监督。同时以标本兼治的理念出发，不仅制定严格的治理措施，还坚持源头治理、规划先行，从推动经济发展方式转变、优化产业结构、调整能源结构的角度从根本上解决大气污染的问题。

污染物总量控制和限期达标制度：大气污染的防治，以改善空气质量为目标，实行污染物总量控制制度，推行重点污染物排放权交易，加强对燃煤、工业、机动车、船舶、扬尘、农业等大气污染的综合防治，将挥发性有机物、生活性排放等物质和行为纳入监管范围，鼓励清洁能源的开发和优先并网。实行限制达标制度，限期达标规划向社会公开，政府每年向本级人大报告限期达标规划执行情况，也向社会公开。

对大气进行动态监管：规定国家鼓励和支持大气污染防治科学技术研究，开展对大气污染来源及其变化趋势的分析。

制定系列环境标准：要求制定包括大气环境质量标准、大气污染物排放标准，燃煤、燃油、石油焦、生物质燃料、涂料等含挥发性有机物产品、烟花爆竹及锅炉等产品的质量标准。

重点区域大气污染联防联控机制：由环保部门划定重点防治区域，确定牵头地方政府，定期召开联席会议，统一规划、统一标准、统一监测、统一防治、信息共享和联合执法，对颗粒物、二氧化硫、氮氧化物、挥发性有机物、氨等大气污染物和温室气体实施协同控制。重点区域内的新建、改建及扩建用煤项目，实行煤炭的等量或者减量替代。

重污染天气的应对：对于重污染天气的治理措施，要求建立重污染天气监测预警机制，地方政府制定应急预案，根据预警等级启动应急预案，实施停产、限产、限行、禁燃、停止建筑施工、停止露天燃烧、停止学校户外活动等应急措施，并鼓励燃油机动车驾驶人在不影响道路通行且需停车 3 分钟以上的情况下熄灭发动机。

目标责任制、约谈制和考核评价制度：为实现改善空气质量目标，三种制度齐下，督促地方政府为当地的空气质量负责，并要求将考核结果向社会公开。同时，提高了对大气污染违法行为的处罚力度。对监测数据造假的，不仅要没收违法所得，并处 10 万元以上 50 万元以下罚款，还有可能取消检验资格。

修订后的《大气污染防治法》以改善大气环境质量为目标，强化了地方政府责任，加强了对地方政府的监督；同时，从坚持源头治理，从推动转变经济发展方式、优化产业结构、调整能源结构的角度完善了相关制度。主线更清晰，重点更突出，内容更完备，管控措施更严密，公众参与更畅通，体现了中央关于生态文明建设和环境保护的新要求，顺应了公众对改善环境质量的新期待，为加强大气污染防治工作提供了强有力的法律武器。

六、国务院发布《水污染防治行动计划》

水环境保护事关人民群众切身利益，事关全面建成小康社会，事关实现中华民族伟大复兴中国梦。当前，我国一些地区水环境质量差、水生态受损重、环境隐患多等问题十分突出，影响和损害群众健康，不利于经济社会持续发展。为切实加大水污染防治力度，保障国家水安全，2015 年 4 月 2 日，国务院发布《水污染防治行动计划》，共 10 条、35 款、76 项、238 个具体措施，是当前和今后一个时期全国水污染防治工作的行动指南。

《水污染防治行动计划》提出了工作的总体要求：全面贯彻党的十八大和十八届二中、三中、四中全会精神，大力推进生态文明建设，以改善水环境质量为核心，按照“节水优先、空间均衡、系统治理、两手发力”原则，贯彻“安全、清洁、健康”方针，强化源头控制，水陆统筹、河海兼顾，对江河湖海实施分流域、分区域、分阶段科学治理，系统推进水污染防治、水生态保护和水资源管理。坚持政府市场协同，注重改革创新；坚持全面依法推进，实行最严格环保制度；坚持落实各方责任，严格考核问责；坚持全民参与，推动节水洁水人人有责，形成“政府统领、企业施治、市场驱动、公众参与”的水污染防治新机制，实现环境效益、经济效益与社会效益多赢，为建设“蓝天常在、青山常在、绿水常在”的美丽中国而奋斗。

工作目标：到 2020 年，全国水环境质量得到阶段性改善，污染严重水体较大幅度减少，饮用水安全保障水平持续提升，地下水超采得到严格控制，地下水污染加剧趋势得到初步遏制，近岸海域环境质量稳中趋好，京津冀、长三角、珠三角等区域水生态环境状况有所好转。到 2030 年，力争全国水环境质量总体改善，水生态系统功能初步恢复。到本世纪中叶，生态环境质量全面改善，生态系统实现良性循环。

主要指标：到 2020 年，长江、黄河、珠江、松花江、淮河、海河、辽河等七大重点流域水质优良（达到或优于Ⅲ类）比例总体达到 70% 以上，地级及以上城市建成区黑臭水体均控制在 10% 以内，地级及以上城市集中式饮用水水源水质达到或优于Ⅲ类比例总体高于 93%，全国地下水质量极差的比例控制在 15% 左右，近岸海域水质优良（一、二类）比例达到 70% 左右。京津冀区域丧失使用功能（劣于Ⅴ类）的水体断面比例下降 15 个百分点左右，长三角、珠三角区域力争消除丧失使用功能的水体。到 2030 年，全国七大重点流域水质优良比例总体达到 75% 以上，城市建成区黑臭水体总体得到消除，城市集中式饮用水水源水质达到或优于Ⅲ类比例总体为 95% 左右。

为实现以上目标和指标，行动计划确定了十个方面的措施：一是全面控制污染物排放。针对工业、城镇生活、农业农村和船舶港口等污染来源，提出了相应的减排措施。二是推动经济结构转型升级。加快淘汰落后产能，合理确定产业发展布局、结构和规模，以工业水、再生水和海水利用等推动循环发展。三是着力节约保护水资源。实施最严格水资源管理制度，控制用水总量，提高用水效率，加强水量调度，保证重要河流生态流量。四是强化科技支撑。推广示范先进适用技术，加强基础研究和前瞻技术研发，规范环保产业市场，加快发展环保服务业。五是充分发挥市场机制作用。加快水价改革，完善收费政策，健全税收政策，促进多元投资，建立有利于水环境治理的激励机制。六是严格环境执法监管。严惩各类环境违法行为和违规建设项目，加强行政执法与刑事司法衔接，健全水环境监测网络。七是切实加强水环境管理。强化环境治理目标管理，深化污染物总量控制制度，严格控制各类环境风险，全面推行排污许可。八是全力保障水生态环境安全。保障饮用水水源安全，科学防治地下水污染，深化重点流域水污染防治，加强良好水体和海洋环境保护。整治城市黑臭水体，直辖市、省会城市、计划单列市建成区于2017年年底前基本消除黑臭水体。九是明确和落实各方责任。强化地方政府水环境保护责任，落实排污单位主体责任，国家分流域、分区域、分海域逐年考核计划实施情况，督促各方履责到位。十是强化公众参与和社会监督。国家定期公布水质最差、最好的10个城市名单和各省（自治区、直辖市）水环境状况。加强社会监督，构建全民行动格局。

行动计划238项具体治理措施中，除了136项改进强化措施、12项研究探索性措施外，重点提出了90项改革创新措施。在自然资源用途管制、水节约集约使用、生态保护红线、资源环境承载能力监测预警机制、资源有偿使用、生态补偿、环保市场、社会资本投入、环境信息公开、社会监督等方面体现了改革创新的新要求。

国外城市水体综合治理典型案例

• 英国泰晤士河

19世纪随着工业革命的兴起，河流两岸人口激增，大量的工业废水、生活污水未经处理直排入河，沿岸垃圾随意堆放。1858年，伦敦发生“大恶臭”事件，政府开始治理河流污染。

泰晤士河的治理措施：一是通过立法严格控制污染物排放，规定企业废水必须达标排放，未经许可不得排污；二是修建污水处理厂及配套管网；三是从分散管理到综合管理，自1955年起逐渐施行流域水资源水环境归纳办理；四是加大新技术的研究与利用；五是充分利用市场机制，向排污者收取排污费。

通过综合治理，泰晤士河水质逐渐改善，20世纪70年代重新出现鱼类并逐年增加。目前，泰晤士河水质完全康复到了工业化前的情况。

• 韩国首尔清溪川

20世纪40年代，随着城市化和经济的快速发展，大量的生活污水和工业废水排入河道，致使清溪川的生态功能基本丧失，50年代河道被关闭，70年代河道封盖上建造公路，并建筑了4车道高架桥。

21世纪初，韩国政府下决心开展河道整治和水质康复，主要采取三方面措施：一是疏浚清淤，总投资3900亿韩元的“清溪川复原工程”还原了河流自然面貌；二是全面截污，两岸铺设截污管道，将污水送入处理厂处理；三是保持水量，让河流保持40厘米水深。

现在，清溪川变成主要的生态景观，除生化需氧量和总氮两项目标外，各项水质目标均达到韩国地表水一级标准。

• 德国埃姆舍河

埃姆舍河是莱茵河的一条支流，该流域煤炭挖掘量大，导致地面沉降，致使河床遭到严重破坏，出现河流改道、阻塞乃至河水倒流的情况。19世纪下半叶起，鲁尔工业区的大量工业废水与生活污水直排入河中，河水遭受严重污染，曾是欧洲最脏的河流之一。

德国采纳雨污分流改造和建造污水处理设施，“污水电梯”、绿色堤岸、河道治理等措施修复河道。同时，为了统筹管理水环境和水资源，于1899年建立了德国第一个流域管理机构，即“埃姆舍河治理协会”，独立调配水资源，统筹管理排水、污水处理及相关水质，专职负责干流及支流的污染治理。

埃姆舍河河流治理工程预算为45亿欧元，已实施了部分工程，预计还需几十年时间才能完工。目前，流经多特蒙德市的区域已恢复自然状态。

• 法国塞纳河

塞纳河在20世纪60年代初严峻污染致使河流生态系统溃散。法国采取的工程治理措施主要包括：截污治理，政府规定污水不得直排入河，要求搬迁废水直排的工厂，并新建污水处理设备；完善城市下水道；减少农业污染；河道蓄水补水等。法国还不断修正完善法律制度，严格执法，并多渠道筹集资金用于河道治理。

经过综合治理，塞纳河水生态情况大幅改进，生物品种显著添加，可是沉积物污染与上游农业污染疑问依然存在，说明城市水体整治仅对于河道自身是不行的，需进行全流域归纳办理。

• 奥地利多瑙河

多瑙河的综合治理开发，形成了一套现代化的河流综合治理和开发体系，即在传统治理理念基础上突出“生态治理”概念，并运用到防洪、治污、经济开发等各个领域。主要措施包括：建设生态河堤，恢复河岸植物群落和储水带。基于“亲近自然河流”概念和“自然型护岸”技术，在考虑安全性和耐久性的同时，充分考虑生态效果，把河堤由过去的混凝土人工建筑，改造成适合动植物生长的模拟自然状态，建成无混凝土河堤或混凝土外覆盖植被的生态河堤；优化水资源配置和使用，城市用水99%为地下水和泉水，维持了多瑙河的自然生态流量。奥地利严禁将工业废水和居民生活污水直接排入多瑙河，废污水由紧邻多瑙河的两座大型水处理中心负责处理，出水水质达标后，大部分排入多瑙河，少部分直接渗入地下补充地下水。此外，奥地利严格控制沿岸工业企业数量，并严格监管。

（参考资料来源：《中国环境报》）

七、国家推进海绵城市建设试点

在2013年召开的中央城镇化工作会议上，习近平总书记提出解决城市缺水问题，必须顺应自然。在提升城市排水系统时要优先考虑把有限的雨水留下来，优先考虑更多利用自然力量排水，建设自然积存、自然渗透、自然净化的“海绵城市”。

2014年10月，住房和城乡建设部印发了《海绵城市建设技术指南——低影响开发雨水系统构建（试行）》，提出了海绵城市建设——低影响开发雨水系统构建的基本原则，规划控制目标分解、落实及其构建技术框架，明确了城市规划、工程设计、建设、维护及管理过程中低影响开发雨水系统构建的内容、要求和方法。

2015年1月20日，财政部、住房和城乡建设部、水利部联合发布《关于组织申报2015年海绵城市建设试点城市的通知》，明确2015年海绵城市建设试点城市申报指南。

4月2日，国务院发布《水污染防治行动计划》（国发〔2015〕17号），明确积极推行低影响开发建设模式，建设滞、渗、蓄、用、排相结合的雨水收集利用设施。新建城区硬化地面，可渗透面积要达到 40% 以上。

4 月，财政部、住房和城乡建设部、水利部联合公布 2015 年海绵城市建设试点名单。根据竞争性评审得分，排名在前 16 位的城市进入 2015 年海绵城市建设试点范围，名单如下（按行政区划序列排列）：迁安、白城、镇江、嘉兴、池州、厦门、萍乡、济南、鹤壁、武汉、常德、南宁、重庆、遂宁、贵安新区和西咸新区。

7 月 10 日，住房和城乡建设部办公厅印发《海绵城市建设绩效评价与考核指标（试行）》，明确了海绵城市建设绩效评价与考核指标分为水生态、水环境、水资源、水安全、制度建设及执行情况、显示度 6 个方面 18 项具体考核指标。

8 月 10 日，水利部发布《关于推进海绵城市建设水利工作的指导意见》，提出了海绵城市建设水利工作的总体思路和主要任务，对主要任务进行部署：一要制订海绵城市建设实施方案，二要严格城市河湖水域空间管制，三要因地制宜做好河湖水系连通，四要推进城市水生态治理与修复，五要建设雨水径流调蓄和承泄设施，六要完善城市防洪排涝体系，七要强化城市水资源管理与保护，八要加强城市水源保障和雨洪利用，九要做好城市水土保持与生态清洁小流域治理。

9 月 29 日，国务院总理李克强主持召开国务院常务会议，部署加快雨水蓄排顺畅合理利用的海绵城市建设，有效推进新型城镇化。会议确定：一是海绵城市建设要与棚户区、危房改造和老旧小区更新相结合，加强排水、调蓄等设施建设，加快解决城市内涝、雨水收集利用和黑臭水体治理等问题。二是从今年起在城市新区、各类园区、成片开发区全面推进海绵城市建设，在基础设施规划、施工、竣工等环节都要突出相关要求。三是总结推广试点经验，采取 PPP、政府采购、财政补贴等方式，创新商业模式，吸引社会资本参与项目建设运营。

10 月 11 日，国务院办公厅发布《关于推进海绵城市建设的指导意见》（国办发〔2015〕75 号），意见提出通过海绵城市建设，综合采取“渗、滞、蓄、净、用、排”等措施，最大限度地减少城市开发建设对生态环境的影响，将 70% 的降雨就地消纳和利用。到 2020 年，城市建成区 20% 以上的面积达到目标要求；到 2030 年，城市建成区 80% 以上的面积达到目标要求。

12 月 10 日，住房城乡建设部、国家开发银行联合发布《关于推进开发性金融支持海绵城市建设的通知》，通知要求国家开发银行作为开发性金融机构，要把海绵城市建设作为信贷支持的重点领域，更好地服务国家经济社会发展战略。各级住房和城乡建设部门要把国家开发银行作为重点合作银行，加强合作，增强海绵城市建设项目资金保障，用好用足信贷资金，为海绵城市建设助力。

12 月 20 日至 21 日，中央城市工作会议在北京召开，会议提出，要提升建设水平，加强城市地下和地上基础设施建设，建设海绵城市。城市供排水、污水处理等基础设施，要按照绿色循环低碳的理念进行规划建设。城市建设要以自然为美，把好山好水好风光融入城市。

12 月 30 日，住房城乡建设部、中国农业发展银行联合发布《关于推进政策性金融支持海绵城市建设的通知》，通知要求各级住房和城乡建设部门要高度重视推进政策性金融支持海绵城市建设工作，把中国农业银行作为重点合作银行，加强合作，最大限度发挥政策性金融的支持作用，切实提高信贷资金对海绵城市建设的支撑保障能力。农发行各分行要把海绵城市建设作为信贷支持的重点领域，积极统筹调配信贷规模，优先对海绵城市建设项目给予贷款支持，贷款期限最长可达30年，贷款利率可适当优惠。

通过海绵城市建设，充分发挥建筑、道路和绿地、水系等生态系统对雨水的吸纳、蓄渗和缓释作用，可有效控制雨水径流，实现自然积存、自然渗透、自然净化的城市发展方式，切实提高城市排水、防涝、防洪和防灾减灾能力，对于提高新型城镇化质量、促进人与自然和谐发展具有重要的意义。

国外“海绵城市建设”实践

• 英国：源头入手，一举两用

为解决日益严重的水资源短缺问题和提升伦敦等大城市的市政排水能力，英国政府积极鼓励在居民家中、社区和商业建筑设立雨水收集利用系统，以从根源上解决上述两大问题。

一直以来，英国政府都在采取立法手段，通过《住房建筑管理规定》等法律规定，间接促进家庭雨水回收系统的普及。在2006年至2015年间，英国政府针对新建房屋设立1～6级的评估体系，要求所有的新建房屋至少达到3级以上的可持续利用标准才能获得开工许可，而其中最重要的提升等级方式之一就是建立雨水回收系统。2015年之后，英国政府为更有针对性控制水资源利用效率，直接要求单一住房单元的居民每天设计用水量不超过125升才能获得开工许可。这一规定也要求开发商和居民更加积极地在家中建立雨水回收系统。

在重视家庭雨水回收利用的同时，英国也在大力推动大型市政建筑和商业建筑的雨水利用。当前大伦敦区最为典型的就是伦敦奥林匹克公园。园内主体建筑和林地在建设过程中建立了完善的雨水收集系统。通过回收雨水和废水再利用等方式，这一占地225公顷的公园灌溉用水完全来自于雨水和经过处理的中水。此外，公园还将回收的雨水和中水供给周边居民，使周边街区用水量较其他类似街区下降了40%。公园周边居民的每天人均用水量也下降至105升，远低于伦敦地区的平均水平144升。

法国：形态不一，提升循环

位于欧洲大陆西端的法国受海洋性气候影响明显，全年降水量较为充沛。法国境内不少主要城市的排水、防涝以及雨水循环处理的设计思路各具特色，这些不同的地表水处理体系如同海绵一般，既使得城市免受了内涝之苦，还提升了水循环利用率。

巴黎作为法国首都，其水循环系统堪称世界范围内大都市中的典范。1852年，著名设计师奥斯曼主持改造了被法国人誉为“最无争议”并基本沿用至今的水循环系统。目前，法国正逐步施行雄心勃勃、拟投资额高达1 000亿欧元的“大巴黎改造计划”。巴黎市政府工作人员介绍，在这项宏大的计划中，巴黎会进一步完善维护既有的城市水循环系统，同时还将在巴黎市的多个地点增添蓄水、净水处理中心，提高整个城市对雨水的收集与再利用。

里昂市位于法国的索恩河与罗纳河交汇处，虽然水资源较为丰富，但里昂的水务管理者仍不愿放弃对雨水的利用，并为此做出了极其细致的工作。首先，里昂市区内各个社区收集的雨水被纳入到了城市一体化的水循环体系中，由当地政府负责对水质进行统一监测与管控；其次，里昂政府将本市各处的道路规模、土壤类别与地型走势等信息进行了统一梳理并公示，任何市区内新的建筑项目均需要考虑到这些基本信息，将雨水管理纳入设计规划中，并接受当地政府的查验考核。凭借着这种精细化的城市水循环监管体系，里昂市近年来多次获得国际城市水务管理领域的评比冠军。

• 韩国首尔：提高渗透性，重塑水环境

韩国首都首尔市在过去60年间地表不透水率增长了6倍，降水排水越来越多地依赖人工排水设施，削弱了自然水循环能力。问题的不断升级迫使首尔市政府下决心从制度上保障城市水循环的改善，并于2013年10月底发布了《建设健康的水循环城市综合发展规划》，提出到2050年大气降水地表直接排出比例下降21.9%，地下基底排出增长2.2倍，使年平均降水量的40%成为地下水的推进目标。该规划的实质就是发挥土壤如海绵似的吸水、储水作用。

为此，首尔市提出了五方面的解决方案：一是以政府机关为先导，改善地表透水状况。首先在沥青、花岗岩覆盖的道路两侧修建绿化带，同时使道路地形便于雨水的自然渗入，分阶段地将路边人行道和停车场的不透水地砖更换为透水地砖。特别是从2015年开始，首尔市将确保人行道等设施的透水性列为义务性措施。二是引导城市拆迁改造工程优先考虑水循环恢复。首尔市规定，未来针对老旧小区的拆迁改造工程在设计审核阶段，主管部门必须首先和水循环管理部门对方案进行事先商议，有效降低城市开发对自然水循环的影响。三是扩大雨水利用设施的普及率。首尔市从2013年下半年开始，积极通过媒体宣传雨水的利用价值，引导市民提高水循环意识，提高雨水在城市农业和景观中的使用率。四是引导市民积极参与水循环城市建设。首尔市选定几个生活小区进行水循环改造，包括铺设透水地砖、建造雨水花坛、设置雨水收储设施。五是加强水循环技术研究和制度建设。包括水循环的实地监测体系、水循环技术和改造模型的研究。

• 日本东京：建设储水池，增强再利用

东京的排水系统工程浩大，东京实行雨水和生活污水分流处理，地下的各种排水管道延长总计达1.58万公里。地面上江户川、荒川、隅田川、神田川多条河流纵横，这些水系在美化城市、提供城市水源的同时，发挥着排涝、泄洪的重要作用。20世纪90年代，东京大兴土木，建设了巨型分洪工程——“首都圈外郭放水路”。该工程的主题项目是一条位于地下50米处，全长6.3公里、直径10.6米的隧道。隧道一头连接东京城市下水道，另一头连接入海河流江户川，在发生暴雨时可以用大型抽水机把城市雨水抽入河流，使之排入大海。

东京每年遭遇台风级的大暴雨不过五六次，除这些雨水需要排洪外，一般性的雨水并不造成危害。近年来东京更多考虑的是雨水的利用问题。除新建大楼配套建设雨水储存设施外，各公园、学校周围都建有储水池，所以记者常能看到路旁消防蓄水池的标志。日本注重地面的呼吸性能，很多马路用大粒石子和沥青铺就，便道也普遍使用透水砖，大大提高了其透水性。同时，东京尽量减少地面硬化，多留泥土地面。

（参考资料来源：新华网）

八、国家持续推进新型城镇化建设

2014 年 3 月，中共中央、国务院印发了《国家新型城镇化规划（2014－2020 年）》，这是今后一个时期指导全国城镇化健康发展的宏观性、战略性、基础性规划。在该规划的指导下，2015 年，我国新型城镇化建设持续推进，取得多方面显著成效。

城市群规划加快编制，城市群作为新型城镇化主体形态的地位更加凸显。按照《国家新型城镇化规划（2014－2020 年）》要求，2015 年在城市群规划编制上取得积极成效，以跨省区城市群为重点，开展了长三角、长江中游、成渝、哈长等 4 个跨省区的城市群规划编制，《长江中游城市群发展规划》已于 2015 年 4 月颁布实施。随着规划的颁布和实施，城市群对我国新型城镇化的支撑作用将进一步增强。

一批国家级新区设立，对新型城镇化格局的支点作用进一步增强。2015 年国务院同意设立湖南湘江新区、南京江北新区、福州新区、云南滇中新区、哈尔滨新区。2015 年 4 月，国家发改委等多部门联合发布的《关于促进国家级新区健康发展的指导意见》明确要求新区“要突出体现落实国家重大改革发展任务和创新体制机制的试验示范作用”，并强调新区要“推动产城融合和新型城镇化建设”，这为未来一段时期国家级新区发展指明了方向。

行政区划调整加快，为优化城镇体系结构和做大做强城市提供了支撑。2015 年我国行政区划调整步伐呈加快趋势：一是撤县设市，黑龙江东宁县，广西靖西县，四川康定县、马尔康县，云南腾冲县等县撤销，设立了县级东宁市、靖西市、康定市、马尔康市、腾冲市；二是撤县（市）设区，北京密云县、延庆县，天津宁河县，河北保定满城县、清苑县、徐水县，秦皇岛抚宁县，江苏盐城大丰市，河南三门峡陕县，广东肇庆高要市，广西南宁武鸣县，重庆市潼南县、荣昌县，云南玉溪江川县，陕西榆林横山县，以及青海海东平安县等撤县（市）设区；三是特大城市中心城区有序整合，保定市，设立莲池区；上海市静安区、闸北区撤销，设立新的静安区；常州市武进区和戚墅堰区撤销，设立新的武进区；无锡市崇安区、南长区、北塘区撤销，设立梁溪区；铜陵市铜官山区、狮子山区撤销，设立铜官区。四是新设区。如无锡市设立了新吴区；六安市新设叶集区等。五是撤地设市。新疆哈密地区、吐鲁番地区、西藏林芝地区等撤销，设立地级哈密市、吐鲁番市、林芝市。六是“兵团设市”。新设的可克达拉市（第四师）成为新疆建设兵团的第 8 个市。七是由县级市升为地级市，如海南省县级儋州市撤销，设立地级儋州市。

第二批国家新型城镇化试点出台，在更多领域开展更具针对性的体制机制探索。根据新型城镇化发展新趋势和新要求，在总结梳理第一批试点成效的基础上，2015 年 11 月推出了北京市房山区等 59 个第二批试点，并将北京市大兴区等 14 个农村土地制度改革试点一并纳入。第二批试点优先考虑了改革意愿强，发展潜力大，具体措施实的中小城市、县、建制镇及符合条件的开发区和国家级新区等，并体现了向中西部地区和东北地区适当倾斜，促进京津冀协同发展，以及在长江经济带地区选择若干具备条件的开发区进行城市功能区转型等因素。这样，国家新型城镇化综合试点范围扩大至 135 个城市（镇），地域遍及各省区市及兵团，类型涉及各类大中小城市及小城镇。

城市规划建设管理进一步加强，城市功能进一步完善。2015 年，初步完成了 14 个城市开发边界划定试点工作，开展了永久基本农田、生态保护红线等划定工作，海绵城市、城市综合管廊等工作加快推进，推出了第三批 84 个智慧城市建设试点，“多规合一”工作取得初步成果。7 月，国家发展改革委出台了《关于开展产城融合示范区建设有关工作的通知》，提出“选择 60 个左右条件成熟的地区开展产城融合示范区建设工作”。8 月底，有关地区的建设方案均已上报国家有关部门。12 月，国家发展改革委等七部委出台了《关于促进具备条件的开发区向城市综合功能区转型的指导意见》，提出积极顺应开发区转型升级和政府职能转变背景下的新要求，推动具备条件的开发区城市综合功能改造。2015 年国务院发布《关于进一步做好城镇棚户区和城乡危房改造及配套基础设施建设有关工作的意见》，城镇棚户区改造持续推进。

各地稳步推进户籍制度改革，特大城市在积分落户政策方面积极探索。截至 2015 年 11 月，25 个省份出台了本省深化户籍制度改革的实施意见。概括来看，各省份普遍采用了合法稳定住所（含租赁）、合法稳定就业、参加城镇社会保险三个指标，形成了以城市规模为分类标准的差别化人口迁移和落户政策。一是县城及以下城镇的落户限制全面放开；二是在城区人口 50 万 ~100 万人的城市落户，一般要求合法稳定住所（含租赁）、合法稳定就业两项同时具备，有的省份还规定了年限要求（一般为 1 ~2 年）；三是在城区人口 100 万 ~500 万人的城市落户，一般要求合法稳定住所（含租赁）、合法稳定就业、参加城镇社会保险达到一定年限三项同时具备；四是城区人口 500 万人以上的城市总体态势是要严格控制人口规模。一些特大城市加快公布积分落户政策，北京在通州区探索积分落户政策的基础上，2015 年年底《北京市积分落户管理办法（征求意见稿）》正式公布，向社会公开征集意见。成都已初步制定居住证积分管理办法。

城镇化是现代化的必由之路，是解决农业农村农民问题的重要途径，是推动区域协调发展的有力支撑，是扩大内需和促进产业升级的重要抓手，国家着力推进新型城镇化，努力走出一条以人为本、四化同步、优化布局、生态文明、文化传承的中国特色新型城镇化道路，对全面建成小康社会、加快推进社会主义现代化具有重大现实意义和深远历史意义。

九、天津港发生特别重大火灾爆炸事故

2015 年 8 月 12 日，位于天津市滨海新区天津港的瑞海公司危险品仓库发生火灾爆炸事故，造成 165 人遇难（其中参与救援处置的公安现役消防人员 24 人、天津港消防人员 75 人、公安民警 11 人，事故企业、周边企业员工和居民 55 人），8 人失踪（其中天津消防人员 5 人，周边企业员工、天津港消防人员家属 3 人），798 人受伤（伤情重及较重的伤员 58 人、轻伤员 740 人），304 幢建筑物、12 428辆商品汽车、7 533个集装箱受损。截至 2015 年 12 月 10 日，依据《企业职工伤亡事故经济损失统计标准》等标准和规定统计，已核定的直接经济损失 68. 66 亿元。

事故发生后，党中央、国务院高度重视。习近平总书记两次做出重要批示，并主持召开中央政治局常委会会议，对事故抢险救援和应急处置做出部署、提出明确要求。李克强总理率有关同志亲临事故现场指导救援处置工作，主持召开国务院常务会议进行研究部署。经各方努力，事故救援及现场处置任务于2015年9月13日完成，清运危险化学品1 176吨、汽车7 641辆、集装箱13 834个、货物14 000吨，798名伤员得到妥善医治。

8月16日，国务院总理李克强赶赴天津"8·12"瑞海公司危险品仓库特别重大火灾爆炸事故现场，看望慰问消防队员、救援官兵和伤员及受灾群众，部署下一步救援救治、善后处置和安全生产工作。

8月18日，经国务院批准，成立由公安部、安全监管总局、监察部、交通运输部、环境保护部、全国总工会和天津市等有关方面组成的国务院天津港"8·12"瑞海公司危险品仓库特别重大火灾爆炸事故调查组，邀请最高人民检察院派员参加，并聘请爆炸、消防、刑侦、化工、环保等方面专家参与调查工作。

调查组查明，事故的直接原因是：瑞海公司危险品仓库运抵区南侧集装箱内硝化棉由于湿润剂散失出现局部干燥，在高温（天气）等因素的作用下加速分解放热，积热自燃，引起相邻集装箱内的硝化棉和其他危险化学品长时间大面积燃烧，导致堆放于运抵区的硝酸铵等危险化学品发生爆炸。

调查组认定，瑞海公司严重违反有关法律法规，是造成事故发生的主体责任单位。该公司无视安全生产主体责任，严重违反天津市城市总体规划和滨海新区控制性详细规划，违法建设危险货物堆场，违法经营、违规储存危险货物，安全管理极其混乱，安全隐患长期存在。

调查组同时认定，有关地方党委、政府和部门存在有法不依、执法不严、监管不力、履职不到位等问题。天津交通、港口、海关、安监、规划和国土、市场和质检、海事、公安以及滨海新区环保、行政审批等部门单位，未认真贯彻落实有关法律法规，未认真履行职责，违法违规进行行政许可和项目审查，日常监管严重缺失；有些负责人和工作人员贪赃枉法、滥用职权。天津市委、市政府和滨海新区区委、区政府未全面贯彻落实有关法律法规，对有关部门、单位违反城市规划行为和在安全生产管理方面存在的问题失察失管。交通运输部作为港口危险货物监管主管部门，未依照法定职责对港口危险货物安全管理督促检查，对天津交通运输系统工作指导不到位。海关总署督促指导天津海关工作不到位。有关中介及技术服务机构弄虚作假，违法违规进行安全审查、评价和验收等。

公安机关对24名相关企业人员依法立案侦查并采取刑事强制措施（其中瑞海公司13人，中介和技术服务机构11人）。检察机关对25名行政监察对象依法立案侦查并采取刑事强制措施（其中正厅级2人，副厅级7人，处级16人；包括交通运输部门9人，海关系统5人，天津港（集团）有限公司5人，安全监管部门4人，规划部门2人）。

事故调查组对123名责任人员提出了处理意见。建议对74名责任人员给予党纪政纪处分，其中省部级5人，厅局级22人，县处级22人，科级及以下25人；对其他48名责任人员，建议由天津市纪委及相关部门予以诫勉谈话或批评教育；1名责任人员在调查处理期间病故，不再给予处分。

针对事故暴露出的八个方面的教训与问题，调查组提出了十个方面的防范措施和建议，即坚持安全第一的方针，切实把安全生产工作摆在更加突出的位置；推动生产经营单位落实安全生产主体责任，任何企业均不得违法违规变更经营资质；进一步理顺港口安全管理体制，明确相关部门安全监管职责；完善规章制度，着力提高危险化学品安全监管法治化水平；建立健全危险化学品安全监管体制机制，完善法律法规和标准体系；建立全国统一的监管信息平台，加强危险化学品监控监管；严格执行城市总体规划，严格安全准入条件；大力加强应急救援力量建设和特殊器材装备配备，提升生产安全事故应急处置能力；严格安全评价、环境影响评价等中介机构的监管，规范其从业行为；集中开展危险化学品安全专项整治行动，消除各类安全隐患。

调查组还查明，本次事故对事故中心区及周边局部区域大气环境、水环境和土壤环境造成不同程度的污染。天津渤海湾海洋环境质量未受到影响。没有因环境污染导致的人员中毒与死亡病例。截至 2015 年年底，对大气环境的影响已基本消除，受污染地表水得到有效处置，事故中心区土壤和地下水正在进行分类处置与修复。对事故可能造成的中长期环境和人员健康影响，有关方面正开展持续监测评估，并采取防范措施。

十、深圳发生特别重大滑坡事故

2015 年 12 月 20 日 11 时 40 分，广东省深圳市光明新区凤凰社区恒泰裕工业园发生渣土受纳场滑坡。此次滑坡覆盖面积约 38 万平方米，淤泥渣土厚度达数米至十数米不等，造成附近的恒泰裕、柳溪、德吉成三个工业园 33 栋建筑物被掩埋或不同程度损毁，包括厂房 14 栋、办公楼 2 栋、饭堂 1 间、宿舍楼 3 栋、其他低矮建筑物 13 间，涉及企业 15 家。截至 2016 年 1 月 12 日，已发现 69 名遇难者，另外还有 8 人失联。

灾害发生后，党中央、国务院高度重视。国家主席习近平立即做出重要指示，要求广东省、深圳市迅速组织力量开展抢险救援，第一时间抢救被困人员，尽最大努力减少人员伤亡，做好伤员救治、伤亡人员家属安抚等善后工作；注意科学施救，防止发生次生灾害。国务院总理李克强做出批示，要求抓紧核实情况，全力组织搜救，全力救治受伤人员，尽最大努力减少伤亡；全面排查周边安全隐患，防止发生二次灾害；同时，查清灾害原因，做好善后处置。

深圳市和光明新区灾后立即启动救援应急预案，迅速成立现场救援指挥部，成立现场搜救组、现场监测组、医疗保障组、核查人员组、新闻发布组、自身灾害防范组、外围警戒组、交通疏导组、通信保障组、后勤保障组等 10 个小组，组织公安、消防、特警、卫生、应急、安监以及规划、国土等部门 1 500 多人在现场全面开展救援工作。广东省消防总队还调集东莞、惠州、省特级三个支队共 100 多人参与救援工作。

12 月 25 日，国务院批准成立了深圳市光明新区渣土受纳场“12·20”特别重大滑坡事故调查组，由安全监管总局局长杨焕宁任组长，安全监管总局、公安部、监察部、国土资源部、住房城乡建设部、全国总工会和广东省人民政府有关负责同志任副组长，邀请最高人民检察院派员参加。事故调查组下设技术组、管理组、责任追究组和综合组等四个专项组。

初步查明，深圳光明新区垮塌体为人工堆土，原有山体没有滑动。人工堆土垮塌的地点属于淤泥渣土受纳场，主要堆放渣土和建筑垃圾，由于堆积量大、堆积坡度过陡，导致失稳垮塌，造成多栋楼房倒塌。调查组经调查认定，此次深圳滑坡灾害由受纳场渣土堆填体滑动引起，不是山体滑坡，不属于自然地质灾害，是一起生产安全事故。

深圳光明新区红坳余泥渣土受纳场“12·20”特别重大滑坡事故发生后，最高检及时派员介入事故调查，成立由最高检、广东省检察院和深圳市区两级检察院60余名干警组成的检察调查专案组，制订周密调查方案，全面收集证据材料，依法开展调查工作。现已查明光明新区城市管理局、光明新区查违办、深圳市水土保持监督监测总站等部门的部分工作人员对工作严重不负责任，违法行使职权或不作为，对事故的发生负有重要的责任。截至2016年1月18日，深圳市宝安区人民检察院、福田区人民检察院和龙岗区人民检察院分别对光明新区城市管理局副局长邓志雄、市政服务中心副主任曾科挺、原光明新区光明办事处查违办副主任朱武跃、深圳市水土保持监督检测总站工程师郑存辉等12名犯罪嫌疑人以滥用职权罪、玩忽职守罪立案侦查，并采取了刑事拘留的强制措施。

（作者：邵益生，中国城市规划设计研究院党委书记兼副院长、研究员，国际欧亚科学院院士；周长青，中国城市规划设计研究院水务发展研究所所长，教授级高工）

2015年中国城市市政公用事业建设与发展

城市市政基础设施是城市正常运行和健康发展的物质基础，对于改善城市人居环境、增强城市综合承载能力、提高城市运行效率、确保2020年全面建成小康社会具有重要作用。在中国经济稳步增长和以提高质量为特征的新型城镇化大背景下，城市市政公用事业市场化改革的不断推进，为城市市政公用基础设施建设提供了强大的驱动力量。无论是城市市政基础设施建设，还是市政公用行业供应与保障能力，都得到了快速增长，较好地满足了中国城市发展和人民生活水平提高的需求。

一、城市市政基础设施进展

2014年年末，全国设市城市653个，其中直辖市4个、地级市288个、县级市361个。城市城区户籍人口3.86亿人，暂住人口0.60亿人，建成区面积4.98万平方公里。2014年完成城市市政公用设施固定资产投资16246.9亿元，占同期全社会固定资产投资总额的3.17%。其中，道路桥梁、轨道交通、园林绿化投资分别占城市市政公用设施固定资产投资的47.1%、19.8%和11.2%。

建设水平不断提高，城市综合承载能力稳步提升。城镇供水、排水与污水处理、生活垃圾无害化处理、燃气、集中供热等设施建设进一步加快，运营水平不断提高。预计2015年城市公共供水普及率达到93%，燃气普及率95.3%，集中供热面积64.2亿平方米，污水处理率达到91%，生活垃圾无害化处理率达到92.5%。

城市建设理念创新转变。2015年，住房城乡建设部、财政部等部门在全国范围内组织开展海绵城市和地下综合管廊建设试点。2015年8月，国务院办公厅印发《关于推进城市地下综合管廊建设的指导意见》（国办发〔2015〕61号），对地下综合管廊建设提出明确要求。为了规范和指导城市地下综合管廊工程规划编制工作，提高规划的科学性，避免盲目、无序建设，住房城乡建设部制定了《城市地下综合管廊工程规划编制指引》。2015年10月，国务院办公厅印发《关于推进海绵城市建设的指导意见》（国办发〔2015〕75号），部署加快雨水蓄排顺畅合理利用的海绵城市建设，有效推进新型城镇化。

法规制度进一步完善。国家发展改革委、住房城乡建设部等六部委联合发布《基础设施和公用事业特许经营管理办法》，自2015年6月1日起施行，鼓励和引导社会资本参与基础设施和公用事业建设运营，提高公共服务质量和效率，保护特许经营者合法权益，保障社会公共利益和公共安全。为了加强对污水排入城镇排水管网的管理，保障城镇排水与污水处理设施安全运行，防治城镇水污染，住房城乡建设部发布《城镇污水排入排水管网许可管理办法》，对从事工业、建筑、餐饮、医疗等活动的企业事业单位、个体工商户向城镇排水设施排放污水的活动实施监督管理。

开展城市基础设施建设情况通报。为落实《国务院关于加强城市基础设施建设的意见》（国发〔2013〕36号），加快推进城市基础设施建设，增强城市综合承载能力，改善城市人居环境，2015年，住房城乡建设部决定对设市城市基础设施建设情况实行年度通报，对包括公共供水普及率、自来水漏失率（供水漏失率）、燃气普及率、污水集中处理率、中水回用率（污水再生利用率）、生活垃圾无害化处理率、道路机械化清扫率等指标进行通报。

开展全国城市基础设施建设“十三五”规划编制工作。组织开展全国城镇水务、城镇供水、城市排水（雨水）防涝、城镇生活污水垃圾、城镇燃气、城镇供热、城市园林、风景名胜等基础设施行业和设施建设“十三五”规划，明确“十三五”期间，基础设施建设指导思想、发展目标和主要任务。

二、城市市政基础设施建设

（一）城市供水基础设施建设

城市供水基础设施建设主要是供水管网的建设和自来水厂在取水、净化、送水以及出厂输水干管等环节的基础设施建设。2014年城市供水基础设施（固定资产）投资额达到了475.3亿元，是1978年的4.7亿元的100倍，从固定资产投资来看，城市供水基础设施获得快速的发展。通过固定资产投资的大幅度增加，城市供水基础设施建设规模和供给能力获得大幅度提升，其中，2014年中国城市供水管道总里程达到67.7亿公里，比1978年的3.6亿公里提高了整整19倍之多。通过城市供水管网设施的大幅度增加，提高了城市供水的普及率，增强了城市供水行业的供给能力，大大推动了中国城市供水行业的快速发展。

（二）城市污水处理基础设施建设

近年来，中国在排水和污水处理基础设施方面的投资持续增加，建设稳步推进，取得了显著的建设成就。2014年城市排水与污水处理行业的投资达到900.1亿元，比1980年的2亿元增加了450多倍。在城市排水与污水处理基础设施投资的支撑下，中国在排水、污水处理及再生利用方面的建设稳步推进。2013年建成排水管道长度达到51.1万公里，比1980年的2.19万公里增加了23倍。在污水处理与再生利用方面，2014年污水处理厂达到了1808座，日均处理能力达13088万立方米，分别比1980年的35座污水处理厂增加了52倍，比1980年的日均污水处理能力70万立方米增加了187倍。

（三）城市垃圾处理基础设施建设

随着城市垃圾处理行业基础设施投资的增加，城市垃圾处理行业基础设施的能力和服务水平大幅提高。2014 年全国城市共有生活垃圾无害化处理场（厂）819 座，比上年增加 54 座，日处理能力达到 53.3 万吨，处理量为 1.64 亿吨，城市生活垃圾无害化处理率达到 91.77%，比上年增加 2.47 个百分点。现阶段，卫生填埋为中国最主要的垃圾无害化处理方式，其次为焚烧，应用最少的是堆肥、堆放和简易填埋。全国无害化处理厂总体数目在逐年稳步增长，其主要增长力量为卫生填埋方式的无害化处理厂和垃圾焚烧方式的无害化处理厂。而全国范围内堆肥以及其他方式的无害化处理厂数目呈现总体下降趋势。无论是卫生填埋、焚烧还是堆肥及其他方式的垃圾处理方式，其垃圾处理能力逐年稳步提升。焚烧、卫生填埋以及其他方式的城市生活垃圾无害化年处理量均在逐年提升。由于垃圾填埋厂具有作业难度低、投资运行费用低、管理简单等特点，未来一段时间内仍是无害化处理设施的主流。而中小规模的卫生填埋场主要集中在中西部地区，主要为适应中西部中小城市以及县城的发展需求。大型卫生填满场主要建设在东部发达地区，且以焚烧为主。已建成的生活垃圾焚烧设施主要集中在中国东部地区，浙江、江苏、广东、福建、山东占据了市场化垃圾焚烧发电项目数量的前五位，这五省城市和县城焚烧设施建设项目总数为 117 个，占统计项目总数的 59.7%，焚烧处理能力达 10.32 万吨/天，占总焚烧处理能力的 60.94%。此外，中西部地区如湖北、湖南、重庆、云南等地的焚烧处理设施建设速度加快，垃圾焚烧在县城生活垃圾处理中的应用逐渐得到扩大。

（四）城市燃气基础设施建设

燃气行业发展需要依托传输管网及相关基础设施建设。燃气行业遵循着储量快速增长促进管道建设、管道建设促进市场开拓、市场开拓又促进产量增长的规律。中国天然气资源主要分布在塔里木、柴达木、鄂尔多斯、四川、松辽、渤海湾、东海和南海八个盆地。其中，塔里木、柴达木、鄂尔多斯、四川盆地位于中国新疆、青海、宁夏、甘肃、内蒙古、陕西、四川等西部地区，其天然气资源量占总资源量的 55%；东海和南海盆地位于东部和南部沿海地带。中国天然气市场主要分布在东部经济比较发达的长江三角洲、环渤海和珠江三角洲等地区。从地域分布上看，资源和市场分别处于西部和东部地区，燃气供给地与燃气需求地之间距离较长，需要铺设长距离、大口径的燃气管道，才能连接燃气的供给与需求。为此，城市燃气行业对燃气管道基础设施的需求十分巨大。近几年中国燃气行业基础设施获得快速的发展，但与燃气行业需求仍存一定的差距。中国天然气干线管网仅有西气东输、陕京、涩宁兰、四川环网、海洋到香港地区等几条大型天然气管道，没有形成覆盖全国的长输干线管网。输气管道除在川渝地区形成区域内的环形管网外，其余管道多分散在各油气田内部及邻近地区，尚未形成跨区域的天然气管网。除川渝地区和环渤海地区外，中国的输气管道多是单一气源对单一用户，没有配套的调峰设施及事故应急储备设施，供气可靠性差。

2014 年全国城市人工煤气供气管道长度 2.9 万公里，天然气供气管道长度 43.5 万公里，液化石油气供气管道长度1.1万公里，分别比上年减少4.7%、增长11.9%、减少18.2%。用气人口4.21亿人，燃气普及率94.56%，比上年增加0.31个百分点。

（五）城市供热基础设施建设

供热管道根据管道内流动介质的不同可以分为蒸汽管道和热水管道，中国的供热管道主要以蒸汽管道为主，热水管道为辅。中国气候严寒和寒冷地区的19个省、自治区、直辖市的134个地级以上的大、中城市都有集中供热热力管网设施，并正在向大型化发展，从2005年到2014年供热管道长度以每年1万~2万公里增长，截至2014年年底，中国集中供热主干管长达18.7万公里。热电联产是集中供热行业发展的主流趋势。

三、城市市政基础设施生产与供应

（一）城市供水行业生产与供应

伴随着经济发展和城镇化进程的加快，中国城市常住人口的不断增长也使得对自来水的需求不断增加。城市供水行业在不断完成城市管网建设投资的同时，也在不断加大自来水的生产与供应，以满足不断增长的城市用水需求。城市供水综合生产能力已经从1980年的2 979万立方米/日增加到2014年的2.87亿立方米/日，34年间增长了9.6倍，年平均增长率约为7.07%。从供水情况看，中国城市年供水总量已经从1980年的88.34亿立方米增长到2014年的546.7亿立方米，34年间增长了6倍多，年平均增长率约为5.05%。

（二）城市污水处理行业生产与供应

随着中国城市用水量的不断增长，污水排放量也随着工业生产和居民生活用水量的增加而增加，社会公众对环境以及清洁水的要求推动着污水处理行业产出规模的扩张。在城市污水处理厂运行方面，2014年第四季度，全国36个大中城市（直辖市、省会城市和计划单列市）污水处理厂累计处理污水量45.8亿立方米，同比增长12.0%。2014年，全国城市污水处理厂累计处理污水401.7亿立方米，比2013年增长8.1%。而且，污水处理率显著提高。2003年至2014年，城市污水处理率从42%提升到90%；2003年至2014年全国城市污水日处理量从4 254万立方米/日提升到13 088万立方米/日，增加8 800多立方米，年处理污水总量从不到148亿立方米提升到402多亿立方米，增加250多亿立方米。2014年全国城市污水处理率平均水平为90.18%；除西藏自治区外，其他省份都在60%以上，其中13个省份超过90%。

（三）城市垃圾处理行业的生产和供应

中国对生活垃圾的处理率特别是无害化处理率正在稳步提高。目前，中国城镇人均生活垃圾产生量约1千克/日，且以每年8%~10%的速度逐年快速增加，城市生活垃圾清运量与处理量亦随之不断增长，并且二者的差距在逐年缩小。中国从2006年至2014年城市生活垃圾无害化处理率（=垃圾清运量/无害化垃圾处理量）以平均每年7%左右的增长速度稳步提高，2014年的城市生活垃圾无害化处理率已经达到91.77%。2014年，全国城市生活垃圾总清运量为1.94亿吨。

（四）城市燃气行业生产和供应

城市燃气（包括民用、商业和工业燃气）是由几种气体组成的混合气体，目前主要使用的城市燃气种类包括人工煤气（MG）、液化石油气（LPG）和天然气（NG）。2014年，中国城市人工煤气供气总量为56.0亿立方米，与1980年19.55亿立方米的产量相比，增长了2.86倍；中国城市液化石油气供气总量为1 082.7万吨，与1980年29.05万吨的产量相比，增长了37.3倍；中国城市天然气供气总量为964.4亿立方米，与1980年5.89亿立方米的产量相比，增长了163.7倍，年均增长率为16%。

（五）城市供热行业生产与供应

改革开放以来，中国供热总量不断增加，供热总量总体上呈现不断增长的趋势。全国供热行业蒸汽集中供热总量由1981年的641万吉焦上升到2014年的5.56亿吉焦，2014年是1981年的87倍，1981年到2014年的年均供热增长率为14%。全国供热行业热水集中供热总量由1981年的183万吉焦上升到2014年的27.65亿吉焦，2013年是1981年的1511倍，1981年到2013年的年均供热增长率为24%。随着中国城市化进程的加快，城镇集中供热面积快速增长。2014年全国集中供热面积达61.12亿平方米。

四、城市市政公用事业形势分析

党的十八大首次提出全面建成小康社会，十八届五中全会提出要在已经确定的全面建成小康社会目标要求的基础上，努力实现“人民生活水平和质量普遍提高”“生态环境质量总体改善”等目标。城市市政基础设施作为城市的“骨架”，对于促进城乡、区域协调互动发展，提高人民生活水平和质量，改善城市人居环境、建设城市生态文明等全面建成小康社会目标的实现具有极其重要的支撑作用。

同时，我国正处于城市发展转型和产业发展转型的关键时期，迫切需要城市基础设施提供高质、高效的设置保障，但“政府主导，国有投资”的建设模式已无法支撑城市基础设施的可持续发展。为充分调动社会资本参与城市基础设施投资、建设和运营的积极性，国务院开始推行在城市基础设施建设的PPP模式，推动形成市场化、可持续的投入机制和运营机制。在经济新常态的背景下，加强城市基础设施建设一方面对于经济增长具有明显的拉动作用，同时也为经济和社会的全面发展提供有效的设施保障。

城市基础设施建设也是服务国家重大战略部署的必然要求。我国已处于城镇化深入发展的关键时期，随着内外部环境和条件的深刻变化，城镇化进入以提升质量为主的转型发展新阶段。城市基础设施建设一方面要为新型城镇化的建设以及“一带一路”建设、京津冀协同发展、长江经济带建设、振兴东北老工业基地、中部崛起、西部大开发等国家重大战略的实施提供基础的保障，另一方面也要在国家相关战略的实施过程中不断提高基础设施的质量和服务水平。

（一）城市供水基础设施形势

未来一段时间内，中国城市供水基础设施建设不仅面临着与城镇化进程相匹配的新建管网设施问题，还面临着长期积累下来的老旧管网的更新改造问题。在“十三五”乃至未来一段时间内，城市供水基础设施新建和更新任务仍较重，需要分阶段、有计划地实行城市供水基础设施供给能力与供给质量的提升。为适应新型城镇化进程和老旧设施更新改造的需求，协调好新建设施和更新改造设施的规模，规划好新建和更新改造所需资金规模，探索创新城市供水基础设施投融资渠道，加大各级政府对城市供水行业的投资力度，吸引社会资本参与城市供水基础设施建设，不断提升城市供水基础设施的建设水平和供给能力，从而提升城市供水的供给保障能力，改善当前区域间城市供水基础设施不够均衡的局面。

（二）城市污水处理基础设施形势

由于新型城镇化建设和经济发展致使城市污水排放量快速增加，从而使中国城市污水处理行业处在供不应求的状态，需要不断新增城市污水与排水处理基础设施，不仅包括管网设施建设，也包括污水处理厂设施建设。由于中国城市污水与排水处理设施建成时间较短，相对而言城市排水与污水处理管网设施老化程度较低，因此，未来一段时间内中国城市污水处理行业基础设施建设的重点依然是排水管网、污水处理厂的新建设施，同时需要重视污泥处置和再生水利用设施建设，这样能够实现污泥无害化处理与利用，以及通过再生水的合理使用，提高水资源的利用效率。

（三）城市垃圾处理基础设施形势

从城市垃圾处理基础设施的建设情况来看，仍存在一定的问题，主要表现在：第一，由于处置垃圾渗滤液将会大幅增加企业成本，企业将会直接或间接地将没有得到有效处理的垃圾渗滤液排向河流，造成二次污染。第二，中国填埋气体的利用比率比较低，整体上进展缓慢，存在诸多问题，不能降解废弃物，有效循环利用，这导致垃圾处理行业盈利低，使社会资本不愿进入该行业，无法实现垃圾填埋气体的有效利用。第三，有很多的垃圾焚烧发电厂在垃圾处理的过程中是靠烧煤来实现发电功能的，即它们大多是国家明令禁止的“小火电”发电厂，从而造成垃圾发电与垃圾热值的不相匹配。第四，生活垃圾焚烧厂在中国的选址、建设和运营均会受到较大的社会阻力，邻避效应导致部分垃圾处理厂（场）附近的当地民众的反对，以致城市生活垃圾焚烧厂的数目增长缓慢。因此，在未来一段时间内应该加强宣传教育、创新融资渠道、加强政府监管，提高城市垃圾处理基础设施水平和能力。

从垃圾处理行业的发展趋势来看，未来整个行业的结构将会呈现出以下几点特征：首先，填埋场比例下降乃大势所趋，但近年来仍是主流；其次，垃圾焚烧是必然的选择，但成为主流为时尚早；再次，垃圾分类依然任重道远；最后，餐厨垃圾的单独回收处理市场将加速发展。

（四）城市燃气基础设施形势

城市燃气基础设施建设不足以及设施不完备是制约城市燃气行业发展的瓶颈。下一步应完善已有天然气管道的基础设施，按计划有步骤地建立全国性的长距离输气干线管网，实行跨区域供气，同时通过设备更新改造，建立配套的调峰设施及事故应急储备装置，提高城市燃气基础设施的占有率，改善现有能源使用结构，促进节能减排。

中国这三种气源的未来发展趋势是：液化气仍具有一定的发展潜力，天然气将快速发展，人工煤气由于成本高、污染环境等缺点将会逐渐减少使用。到 2020 年，全国天然气需求量将达到 2221 亿立方米，城市燃气消费将达到占全部消费量的 40% 左右。天然气的消费量目前正以每年 10% 左右的速度增长，而相比之下，管道煤气则出现负增长。

（五）城市供热基础设施形势

热电联产供热和燃煤锅炉供热是主体，同时燃气、燃油锅炉供热面积快速上升。燃煤锅炉供热面积最大的省份为辽宁，燃气锅炉供热面积最大的省份为青海，燃油锅炉供热面积最大的省份为黑龙江和宁夏。在节能减排压力下，使用燃煤锅炉的省市需要在考虑供热成本、本地实际等因素的基础上，适时调整锅炉结构，实现向热电联产、燃气、燃油锅炉转换，这必然要求加快城市供热基础设施建设。

五、城市市政公用事业发展主要任务

（一）大力提升城市供水安全保障能力

加快城市供水设施改造与建设，加强水质监测和应急能力建设，确保城市饮用水安全。城市供水基础设施依照满足需求、适度超前、优质高效的原则，全面推进城镇供水设施建设工程和供水水质安全行动。扩大公共供水管网覆盖范围，提高公共供水有效供给。加强市政和老旧小区供水管网更新改造，对使用超过 50 年、材质落后、漏损严重、影响安全的供水管网实行全面改造，确保 2020 年公共供水管网漏损率控制在 10% 以内。完善城市供水应急预案体系，建立国家、省、市三级应急保障制度，健全应急响应机制，加强应急水源、备用水源建设，增强供水企业应急预案的针对性和可操作性，全面提高应急供水保障能力。健全“两级网三级站”工作机制，推进设市城市供水水质监测预警系统建设。实施城镇供水互联网 + 行动，实行供水水质信息公开制度、水价调整成本公开制度，开展供水企业绩效领跑者引领行动，提升供水服务水平。

（二）加强城市排水与污水处理设施建设

加强城镇污水处理厂及配套管网改造和建设，全面提高管网质量，提升污泥处置水平，推进排水口和截污系统整治，分步实现清污混流、雨污分流，消除河水倒灌、地下水渗入等现象。到2020年，全国地级以上城市建成区力争实现污水全收集、全处理，城市污水处理率达到95%左右，地级及以上城市污泥无害化处理处置率达到90%以上。按照“无害化、资源化”要求，加强污泥处理处置设施建设；在水资源紧缺和水环境质量差的地区，加快推动建筑中水和污水再生利用设施建设。因地制宜、一河一策，采取控源截污、内源治理、生态修复等措施，科学整治城市黑臭水体，到2020年，地级及以上城市建成区黑臭水体均控制在10%以内。加快雨污分流管网改造与排水防涝设施建设，解决城市积水内涝问题。加强海绵型建筑与小区、海绵型道路与广场、海绵型公园与绿地、绿色蓄排与净化利用设施等建设，促进雨水就地蓄积、渗透和利用。到2020年，城市建成区20%以上的面积要将70%的降雨就地消纳和利用。

（三）强化城市垃圾处理设施建设

以大中城市为重点，建设生活垃圾分类示范城市（区）和生活垃圾存量治理示范项目。加大处理设施建设力度，提升生活垃圾处理能力。提高城市生活垃圾处理减量化、资源化和无害化水平。在土地紧缺、人口密度高的城市优先推广焚烧处理技术。力争到2020年，城市生活垃圾焚烧处理能力比“十二五”时期增长26万吨/日，设市城市生活垃圾得到有效处理。加强源头管理，逐步建立餐厨垃圾排放登记制度。在设市城市逐步全面建设餐厨垃圾收集和处理设施。力争到2020年，基本建立城市餐厨垃圾回收和再利用体系。推动建筑垃圾资源化利用，促进再生产品的使用。力争到2020年，基本建立城市建筑垃圾回收和再利用体系。强化城市保洁工作，推进“清洁城市环境”活动，联合金融机构和设备厂家以融资租赁等方式提高城市环卫保洁机械化作业水平，全面提升环卫保洁作业标准。培育环卫龙头骨干企业，实行连锁、专业化经营，实现跨区域综合服务，鼓励从源头收集到处理处置一体化的环卫企业加快发展。

（四）加强城市燃气设施建设和改造

发展城镇燃气设施，更新改造老旧管网，力争到2020年，城镇燃气供气总量达到1600亿立方米，新增城镇燃气管道5万公里，改造完成城镇燃气老旧管道2.5万公里。加大各地老旧管网设施更新改造力度，强化燃气安全管理。拓展燃气应用领域，促进燃气高效利用，不断提高燃气在城镇一次能源利用中的结构比例。以关键技术和标准制定为切入点，从天然气分布式能源、城镇燃气管网设施管理和信息化建设等方面进行技术升级，提高能源利用效率。加强运营监管，预防和化解安全隐患，努力降低安全事故发生率。

（五）加强城市供热设施建设和改造

加快发展北方采暖地区集中供热，扩大集中供热覆盖面积。继续推进北方采暖地区集中供热老旧管网设施改造，“十三五”期间改造完成2.5万公里，增加供热面积5亿立方米。加强供热系统节能，推进供热管网设施节能改造升级和精细化管理，提高供热系统节能水平，降低供热能源消耗。大力推进采暖地区住宅分户计量，完善供热计量收费政策，落实新建住宅必须全部实现供热分户计量、既有住宅要逐步实施供热分户计量改造的要求。健全供热服务质量标准和评估监督办法，研究制定城镇供热管理办法、供热服务评价标准，提高服务水平和供应质量，建立安全、节能、环保、卫生的供热采暖系统。

（作者：王俊豪，中国城市科学研究会公用事业改革与监管委员会主任委员，浙江财经大学原校长）

2015年中国城市交通发展评述

2015年政府工作报告提出，要“坚决治理污染、拥堵等城市病，让出行更方便、环境更宜居”。为了贯彻落实国家新型城镇化发展战略，大力推进绿色城镇化，实现人与自然和谐发展的新格局，优先发展城市公共交通、促进多元交通方式综合协同发展、引导绿色出行等，成为推动城市交通转型发展和构建的重点。2015年，我国城市交通取得了快速发展，在支撑区域协同发展、人居城市建设、方便公众出行等方面发挥了重要作用，但交通拥堵问题依然十分严峻，交通供需生态绿色发展任务艰巨。

一、城市交通发展态势

（一）区域协同发展下的综合交通体系建设

2015年，我国加快了推进区域合作、协同发展和产业结构优化布局调整的力度，城镇群区域综合交通体系规划建设迎来了新的发展机遇。

4月13日，国务院批复了《长江中游城市群发展规划》，规划年限为2015-2020年，规划范围覆盖以武汉城市圈、环长株潭城市群、环鄱阳湖城市群为主体形成的特大型城市群，国土面积约31.7万平方公里。为实现长江中游城市群协同发展目标，规划在交通体系建设方面提出了构筑综合交通运输网络的具体措施，即打造紧密协作的水运网络，完善互联互通的陆运网络，建设高效便捷的空运网络，推进综合交通运输与城市交通发展改革创新。

为推进《国家新型城镇化规划（2014-2020年）》实施，11月24日，国家发展改革委和交通运输部发布了《城镇化地区交通网规划》。规划范围包括21个城镇化地区，涵盖215个城市。到2020年，京津冀、长江三角洲、珠江三角洲三大城市群基本建成城际交通网络，相邻核心城市之间、核心城市与周边节点城市之间实现1小时通达，大部分核心城市之间、核心城市与周边节点城市之间实现1~2小时通达。城际铁路运营里程达到3.6万公里（其中新建城际铁路约8 000公里），覆盖98%的节点城市和近60%的县（市）；新建和改扩建国家高速公路约1.3万公里。对21个城镇化地区的综合交通网布局做出了具体安排，制定了提升运输服务、发展智能交通、创新体制机制、加强规划实施等保障措施。

12月24日，国务院出台了《关于支持沿边重点地区开发开放若干政策措施的意见》，为促进沿边重点地区运输便利化，提升基本公共服务水平，加强旅游支撑能力建设，在铁路、公路、支线机场等交通设施建设方面给出了明确意见。12月28日，国家发展改革委发布了《关于进一步加强区域合作工作的指导意见》，要求积极贯彻落实“一带一路”、京津冀协同发展、长江经济带三大国家战略，加快基础设施互联互通，构建紧密协作、高效便捷、互联互通的综合交通运输网络。

城际铁路建设助力区域协同发展，着力打造1～2小时交通圈。2015年，“轨道上”的京津冀初现端倪，未来京津冀三地未来将以城际铁路互联互通，城际铁路网以北京、天津、石家庄为核心形成“四纵四横一环线”，规划24条城际铁路线，2050年全部建设完成，总规模达3453公里①。福建省海峡西岸城际铁路建设规划（2015－2020年）、成渝地区城际铁路建设规划（2015－2020年）、皖江地区城际铁路建设规划（2015－2020年）、宁夏回族自治区沿黄经济区城际铁路建设规划（2015－2020年）先后获得国家批准。福建省海峡西岸将建设6条城际铁路，总里程583公里。成渝地区规划以成渝双核为中心的“5骨架18辅助”城际铁路网，总里程1008公里。皖江地区以合肥为中心规划6条骨架城际铁路和4条都市区城际铁路，2020年前实施4个项目，总里程310公里。宁夏回族自治区沿黄经济区规划总里程311公里的城际铁路，覆盖区域内80%以上20万人口城镇。

（二）城乡规划建设视野中的城市交通

城市综合交通体系建设已成为城市总体规划的重要内容，在支撑城市可持续发展、城乡区域统筹发展中发挥着越来越关键的作用。2015年，国务院先后批复了珠海、宁波、烟台、安阳、兰州、扬州、呼和浩特、成都、西宁等城市的城市总体规划，批复意见中都明确提出了完善城市基础设施体系，创造良好人居环境的要求；加快完善交通基础设施建设，改善城市与周边地区交通运输条件，加强城市内外交通衔接，建立以公共交通为主体，各种交通方式相结合的多层次、多类型的城市综合交通体系。

完善城市交通设施在城市更新与改造中引起高度重视。5月15日，上海市人民政府印发了《上海市城市更新实施办法》，将完善慢行系统、方便市民生活和低碳出行列入城市更新的重点内容。6月25日，国务院下发了《关于进一步做好城镇棚户区和城乡危房改造及配套基础设施建设有关工作的意见》，要求与棚改项目直接相关的城市道路、公共交通、停车等基础设施要努力做到同步规划、同步报批、同步建设、同步交付使用。

8月3日，国家发展改革委等七部门联合颁发了《关于加强城市停车设施建设的指导意见》，针对城市规划建设中停车设施供给不足的矛盾，提出了将停车管理作为交通需求管理的重要手段，以停车产业化为导向，在城市规划、土地供应、金融服务、收费价格、运营管理等方面加大改革力度和政策创新，制定了14个方面的政策措施。指导意见涵盖了停车设施规划、建设、管理各个方面，对规范停车产业发展，逐步缓解停车供需矛盾，改善城市人居环境等，起到了重要的导向作用。

---

① 新京报讯（记者郭超）http：//news. china. com/domestic/945/20150917/20408907. html.

（三）城市交通转型发展中的城市轨道交通建设

城市轨道交通系统是城市的重大交通基础设施和骨干客运系统，对城市社会经济发展影响重大。针对国家加大简政放权、放管结合改革力度，2015 年 1 月 12 日国家发展改革委发布《关于加强城市轨道交通规划建设管理的通知》，对做好城市轨道交通项目审批权限下放后的落实和衔接工作做了部署。通知指出，要坚持“量力而行、有序发展”的方针，按照统筹衔接、经济适用、便捷高效和安全可靠的原则，科学编制规划，有序发展地铁，鼓励发展轻轨、有轨电车等高架或地面敷设的轨道交通制式。要求把握好建设节奏，确保建设规模和速度与城市交通需求、政府财力和建设管理能力相适应。重申了建设规划审批程序按《国务院办公厅关于加强城市快速轨道交通建设管理的通知》（国办发〔2003〕81 号）有关规定执行。随通知下发了《城市轨道交通规划编制和评审要点》《城市轨道交通工程项目可行性研究报告编制和评估大纲》。

2015 年，随着城市交通转型发展，城市轨道交通建设进展加快，各主要特大城市编制了新的建设规划，或调整了原有的建设规划，北京、天津、成都、大连、深圳等城市的新一轮城市轨道交通建设规划或建设规划调整方案获得批复。

2015 年批复的城市轨道交通建设规划、建设规划调整方案

北京市城市轨道交通第二期建设规划（2015－2021 年）：建设项目 12 个，新建线路长度 262.9 公里，总投资2 122.8亿元。预计到 2021 年形成 27 条运营线路、总长 998.5 公里的轨道交通网络，轨道交通占公共交通出行量比例为 62%。

天津市城市轨道交通第二期建设规划（2015－2020 年）：建设项目 8 个，新建线路长度 228.1 公里，总投资1 794.33亿元，预计到 2020 年形成 14 条运营线路、总长 513 公里的轨道交通网络，轨道交通占公共交通出行量比例达到 40%。

大连市城市轨道交通第二期建设规划（2015－2020 年）：建设项目长度 170.1 公里，总投资 529.04 亿元，预计到 2020 年形成 8 条运营线路、总长 298.6 公里的轨道交通网络，轨道交通占公共交通出行量比例达到 30%。

武汉市城市轨道交通第三期建设规划（2015－2021 年）：建设项目 10 个，线路长度 173.5 公里，总投资1 148.9亿元，预计到 2021 年形成 10 条运营线路、总长 400 公里的轨道交通网络，轨道交通占公共交通出行量比例达到 53%。

呼和浩特市城市轨道交通近期建设规划（2015－2020 年）：建设项目 2 个，线路总长 51.4 公里，总投资 338.81 亿元，预计到 2020 年城市轨道交通占公共交通出行的比例达到 15%。

济南市城市轨道交通近期建设规划（2015－2019 年）：建设 3 条市域快线，线路长 80.6 公里，总投资 437.2 亿元，预期到 2020 年城市轨道交通占公共交通出行的比例达到 15%。

南昌市城市轨道交通第二期建设规划（2015－2021 年）：建设项目 5 个，线路长 82.3 公里，总投资 610.9 亿元，预期到 2021 年形成 4 条运营线路、总长 134.9 公里的轨道交通网络，轨道交通占公共交通出行量比例达到 25%。

南京市城市轨道交通第二期建设规划（2015－2020 年）：建设项目 8 个，线路长 157.2 公里，总投资1 202.2亿元，预期到 2020 年形成 13 条运营线路、总长约 540 公里的轨道交通网络，轨道交通占公共交通出行量比例达到 45%。

南宁市城市轨道交通近期建设规划（2015－2021 年）：近期建设线路长 75.1 公里，总投资 529.37 亿元，预期到 2021 年形成 5 条运营线路、总长 128.2 公里的轨道交通网络，轨道交通占公共交通出行量比例达到 30%。

成都市城市轨道交通近期建设规划（2013－2020 年）调整方案：新增线路 79.1 公里，新增投资 467.2 亿元，预计到 2020 年城市轨道交通运营里程将达到 383 公里。

深圳市城市轨道交通第三期建设规划（2011－2020 年）调整方案：新增新路 85.1 公里，新增投资 730.6 亿元，预计到 2020 年形成 11 条运营线路、总长 434.9 公里的轨道交通网络。

长春市城市轨道交通近期建设规划（2010－2019 年）调整方案：新增线路 28.7 公里，总投资 148.6 亿元，预计到 2019 年形成 5 条运营线路、总长 119.1 公里的轨道交通网络。

广州市轨道交通 7 号线一期工程建设方案调整，为适应广佛同城化并支持顺德地区发展，线路延伸至顺德陈村北滘地区，线路长 13.3 公里，设站 7 座，投资 89.63 亿元。

（参考资料来源：国家发展和改革委网站）

二、生态绿色发展与机制建设

（一）城市成为电动汽车发展的主要市场

2015 年，随着资源约束趋紧、环境污染严重、生态系统退化等矛盾加剧，生态绿色发展需求进一步增强，国家加大了对以电动汽车为主体的新能源汽车发展的支持力度，推动城市交通清洁发展。

4 月 25 日，中共中央、国务院发布《关于加快推进生态文明建设的指导意见》，将发展低碳、便捷的交通体系和节能、新能源汽车列为推进绿色城镇化及绿色产业的重要任务。7 月 26 日，国务院办公厅印发了《生态环境监测网络建设方案》，要求完善生态环境监测网络、实现生态环境监测信息集成共享、科学引导环境管理与风险防范、建立生态环境监测与监管联动机制等，强调了依靠科技创新与技术进步加强监测科研和综合分析。在生态绿色发展的大趋势下，城市交通污染监测正面临着技术与机制的创新，方案为加快实施城市机动车污染联网监测、综合治理指明了方向。

3 月 13 日，交通运输部发布《关于加快推进新能源汽车在交通运输行业推广应用的实施意见》，要求到 2020 年新能源汽车在城市公交、出租汽车和城市物流配送等领域达到 30 万辆，确定了 8 项主要任务和 6 项保障措施，对推动新能源汽车在城市中的推广应用营造了良好的政策环境。财政支持对新阶段新能源汽车产业发展举足轻重，4 月 22 日，财政部等 4 部门发布了《关于 2016－2020 年新能源汽车推广应用财政支持政策的通知》，明确了补助对象、产品和标准，提出了对企业和产品的要求，以及相关工作安排。

为加快实施以纯电驱动为主的新能源汽车发展战略，形成促进电动汽车发展的基础环境，9 月 29 日国务院办公厅出台了《关于加快电动汽车充电基础设施建设的指导意见》，推动充电基础设施建设，要求原则上新建住宅配建停车位应 100% 建设充电设施或预留建设安装条件，大型公共建筑物配建停车场、社会公共停车场建设充电设施或预留建设安装条件的车位比例不低于 10%，每2 000辆电动汽车至少配套建设一座公共充电站。鼓励建设占地少、成本低、见效快的机械式与立体式停车充电一体化设施。10 月 9 日，国家发展改革委、国家能源局、工业和信息化部、住房城乡建设部联合印发了《电动汽车充电基础设施发展指南（2015-2020 年）》，针对制约电动汽车发展的关键问题，部署了加快充电基础设施发展的 5 项重点任务，包括：推动充电基础设施体系建设，加强配套电网保障能力，加快标准完善与技术创新，探索可持续商业模式，开展相关示范工作。

（二）城市综合管理机制改革推动城市交通综合治理

2015 年 12 月 20-21 日，中央召开了城市工作会议，确立了城市管理体制、机制的改革方向，对城市工作提出了具体要求：一要认识、尊重、顺应城市发展规律；二要统筹空间、规模、产业三大结构，提高城市工作全局性；三要统筹规划、建设、管理三大环节，提高城市工作的系统性；四要统筹改革、科技、文化三大动力，提高城市发展持续性；五要统筹生产、生活、生态三大布局，提高城市发展的宜居性，城市交通要按照绿色循环低碳的理念进行规划建设；六要统筹政府、社会、市民三大主体，提高各方推动城市发展的积极性。

为贯彻落实中央城市工作会议精神，12 月 24 日，中共中央、国务院出台《关于深入推进城市执法体制改革改进城市管理工作的指导意见》。意见明确提出，要理顺管理体制，城市管理的主要职责是市政管理、环境管理、交通管理、应急管理和城市规划实施管理等，国务院住房城乡建设主管部门负责对全国城市管理工作的指导。意见将优化城市交通列入完善城市管理的重要内容，强调坚持公交优先战略，着力提升城市公共交通服务水平；加强不同交通工具之间的协调衔接，倡导步行、自行车等绿色出行方式；打造城市交通微循环系统，加大交通需求调控力度，优化交通出行结构，提高路网运行效率；加强城市交通基础设施和智能化交通指挥设施管理维护；整顿机动车交通秩序；加强城市出租客运市场管理；加强静态交通秩序管理，综合治理非法占道停车及非法挪用、占用停车设施，鼓励社会资本投入停车场建设，鼓励单位停车场错时对外开放，逐步缓解停车难问题。

（三）服务市场开放与政府监管“双轮驱动”

2015 年，城市交通设施建设和运营服务的市场化趋势显著，国家和城市政府加大了市场规范和服务监管的力度。

3 月 10 日，国家发展改革委、商务部发布了《外商投资产业指导目录（2015 年修订）》，鼓励外商投资城市封闭型道路建设、经营，城市地铁、轻轨等轨道交通的建设、经营。4 月 25 日，国家发展改革委等 6 部门颁布了《基础设施和公用事业特许经营管理办法》，对包括交通运输、市政工程等基础设施和公用事业领域的特许经营活动做出了具体规定。4 月 30 日，国务院办公厅印发修订后的《国家城市轨道交通运营突发事件应急预案》，进一步完善了城市轨道交通应对突发事件的组织体系、监测预警机制、应急响应、后期处置和保障措施。11 月 3 日，交通运输部、财政部、工业和信息化部联合印发《新能源公交车推广应用考核办法（试行）》，明确了考核工作原则、责任分工、各省市推广应用目标、考核程序等。这些政策的实施，既加大了市场开放的程度，也强化了政府对安全、效率监管的力度。

随着城市汽车数量的快速发展，停车供需矛盾进一步激化。9 月 22 日，住房城乡建设部下发《关于加强城市停车设施管理的通知》，针对城市停车设施“重建设、轻管理”的突出问题，从停车设施规划建设、停车设施经营、信息化与智能化、路内停车泊位、居住区停车、重点地区停车综合治理等 6 个方面，对城市停车设施管理提出了具体的要求，力求优化停车供给、提高停车资源利用效率、缓解停车供需矛盾。

10 月 10 日，交通运输部通过网络公开征集对《关于深化改革进一步推进出租汽车行业健康发展的指导意见》《网络预约出租汽车经营服务管理暂行办法》的意见，鼓励出租汽车服务创新，促进出租汽车多元化服务融合发展，将约租车纳入出租车管理范畴。上海开始规范约租车行业管理，将专车定义为网络预约出租汽车，并列入出租汽车管理框架体系内。9 月向上海奇漾信息技术有限公司（即“滴滴快的”旗下专车运营实体）发放了第一张《上海市出租汽车经营资格证书》，核准经营范围为约租车网络平台，标志着对网络约租车行业发展开始实施准入管理。

11 月 30 日，国务院办公厅转发了公安部、交通运输部《关于推进机动车驾驶人培训考试制度改革的意见》，把基本建立开放有序、公平竞争、服务优质、管理规范的驾驶培训市场体系，基本建立公开透明、权责清晰、运转高效、公正廉洁的驾驶考试管理体制，基本解决培训考试中的不便利、不规范、不经济等问题，列为 2018 年的工作目标，驾驶员培训市场化改革开始启动。

三、城市交通转型发展与技术创新

（一）技术法规的引领作用日益加强

为加强城市停车设施规划编制、科学推进停车设施建设，住房城乡建设部于 9 月 1 日、9 月 22 日分别印发《城市停车设施规划导则》《城市停车设施建设指南》，给出了各项技术要求，从技术层面规范和指导城市停车设施规划与建设。

11 月 18 日住房城乡建设部印发《城市轨道沿线地区规划设计导则》，针对城市总体规划、控制性详细规划及修建性详细规划三个层次，提出了相应的规划原则、控制重点与设计方法，力求进一步加强和改进城市轨道沿线地区规划设计工作，促进轨道交通建设与城市发展相协调。

北京市地方标准《轨道交通接驳设施设计技术指南》(DB11/T123-2015)正式发布，并于2016年1月1日起开始实施。标准规定了轨道交通接驳设施的总体设计要求以及行人、非机动车、公共交通、出租汽车、小汽车等接驳设施的具体设计要求。该标准的颁布，对完善轨道交通接驳系统人性化设计、促进绿色出行，具有重要的指引作用。

11月13日，深圳市规划和国土资源委员会对《深圳市城市规划标准与准则》局部章节条款修订公开征求意见，修订内容涉及中小学校用地、新能源汽车充电设施规划建设、高速公路配套设施等。在新能源汽车推广应用方面，由“鼓励配建停车场设置充电桩，新建停车场应预留设置充电桩的条件”修订为“鼓励配建停车场设置充电桩，其中新建住宅停车场、大型公共建筑物停车场、社会公共停车场须按停车位数量的30%配建充电桩，剩余停车位应全部预留充电设施建设安装条件。商业、工业类项目停车位充电桩配置比例不低于10%”①。

(二) 城市交通多元发展缓解交通拥堵

2015年，各地采取多种措施，构建城市综合交通体系，缓解城市交通拥堵，引导城市交通向“人本、智慧、多元、生态”发展，服务于城市多样化活动需求。

浙江省多个城市人民政府组织编制并发布了治理城市交通拥堵白皮书。《杭州市交通拥堵治理工作白皮书(2016-2020)》，明确了“十三五”杭州市交通拥堵治理工作的目标、举措及重大行动，至2020年，步行、自行车、公共交通等绿色交通出行比例保持75%以上，形成与城市空间结构相协调，以轨道交通和快速路网为骨架，以高品质、多样化的步行、自行车、公共交通为主导的安全、有序、绿色、高效、舒适的城市综合交通系统。宁波、绍兴、温州、金华、湖州、丽水、舟山等城市也出台了2015年治理城市交通拥堵工作白皮书，对2015年的交通治理工作做出了全面系统的安排。

2015年，公共自行车系统发展迅速。据不完全统计，已有123个城市建成公共自行车营运系统，共有51万辆公共自行车，2万多个服务点。公共自行车的普及应用，为短距离出行公众提供了便捷绿色的出行方式，解决了公交出行“最后一公里”的难题。

北京市加大公共自行车投放力度，截至2015年9月，公共自行车服务系统建设规模比去年新增1万辆、站点370个，累计已建成1730个站点、5万辆公共自行车的规模。为让市民更加方便地利用公共自行车出行，2015年8月初，北京市公共自行车部分网点状态实现实时查询，可实时查询周边网点当前的可租车辆和可还空位等信息。

2015年，为改善步行和自行车交通环境，各城市开始重视步行和自行车交通系统建设，逐步还原步行、自行车路权空间，加强了行人过街设施、自行车停车设施、道路林荫绿化、照明等设施建设，全面提升步行和自行车交通系统的安全性、方便性和吸引力。10月11日，国务院办公厅发布《关于推进海绵城市建设的指导意见》，要求推进海绵型道路与广场建设，增强道路绿化带对雨水的消纳功能，在非机动车道、人行道、停车场、广场等扩大使

① 深圳特区报 http://city.shenchuang.com/szyw/20151117/271581.shtml.

用透水铺装。海绵城市建设将促进路面生态铺装材料和施工技术的发展，进一步增强步行、自行车交通的安全性和舒适性。11 月 26 日，住房城乡建设部发文部署了第三批 94 个城市步行和自行车交通系统示范项目验收工作，要求 2016 年 7 月底前全部完成。

为营造更好的绿色出行环境，北京市对“一环八区”，即二环路、三里河、南锣鼓巷、什刹海、奥体中心、中关村西区、青塔、方庄、来广营的步行和自行车系统进行了整治改造，涉及市管道路 82 条、167 公里，区管道路 88 条、81 公里。7 月底启动了北京市步行和自行车交通系统规划编制，谋划步行和自行车交通长远发展蓝图①。上海市政府 11 月 13 日召开“绿色发展”新闻通气会，将“绿色交通”建设作为“十三五”的发展目标。将采用多种措施着力打造公交优先、慢行友好的城市客运交通体系和绿色低碳的城市配送物流体系，推进对外交通低碳绿色发展，着力推进新能源车分时租赁，降低私人小汽车使用强度、缓解交通拥堵和减少交通污染排放。2020 年全市轨道交通运营里程达 800 公里，全市公共交通、步行、自行车出行分担率不低于 80%②。

（三）“互联网 +”和大数据技术推动城市交通规划与管理技术变革

7 月 1 日，国务院颁发了《关于积极推进“互联网 +”行动的指导意见》，明确提出了“互联网 +”高效物流、“互联网 +”便捷交通两大重点行动。要求加快互联网与交通运输领域的深度融合，通过基础设施、运输工具、运行信息等互联网化，推进基于互联网平台的便捷化交通运输服务发展。利用大数据平台挖掘分析人口迁徙规律、公众出行需求、枢纽客流规模、车辆船舶行驶特征等，为优化交通运输设施规划与建设、安全运行控制、交通运输管理决策提供支撑。意见还明确了强化科技驱动、推动数据资源开放等各项保障措施的责任分工。“互联网 +”和大数据技术发展，将加快推动城市交通规划和交通运行管理技术的升级换代与重大变革。

11 月 18 日，以大数据技术为基础的京津冀首个交通节能减排实验室在北京成立。该实验室由北京市交通行业节能减排中心、北京工业大学城市交通学院、北京交通运输职业学院共同建设，包括 7 个子实验室和 1 辆移动监测车，全面覆盖“人、车、路、环境”交通要素。实验室将支撑交通污染规律的研究及环保治理措施的制定，为京津冀区域交通污染联防联控提供支持③。

2015 年，与城市交通、智能交通相关学术活动相继举办。如：5 月 15 日，以“协同发展与交通实践”为主题的 2015 年中国城市交通规划年会暨第 28 次学术研讨会在杭州召开；6 月 27 日，以“大数据背景下的交通小数据研究”为主题的第二届“Open ITS 研究计划联盟大会”在武汉召开；10 月 16 日，第一届交通大数据平台与开放合作国际论坛在深圳召开；10 月 29 日，大数据时代交通调查与交通模型学术研讨会在重庆召开；11 月 4－6 日，

---

① 京郊日报（记者赵语涵）http：//jjrb. bjd. com. cn/html/2015 －09/23/content_ 313882. htm.

② 人民网（记者孙小静）http：//sh. people. com. cn/n/2015/1114/c134768 －27095.

③ 新华网（记者丁静）http：//news. xinhuanet. com/2015 －11/18/c_ 1117186816. htm.

第十届中国智能交通年会在无锡召开；11 月 27－28 日，中国工程院土木水利与建筑工程学部主办的“城市发展与城市交通工程前沿技术研究论坛”在南京召开。这些学术活动交流了最新的研究成果，探讨了交通技术的前沿发展趋势，推动了城市交通规划、交通运行管理技术创新研究与应用实践。

四、结语

2015 年，我国正处在一个社会变革与技术创新高度融合的时代，社会发展和技术换代给城市交通规划建设管理带来极大的挑战和转型发展机遇。在土地、能源、生态等外部条件约束下，加大科技创新驱动，转变城市交通发展模式，推动城市交通向以人为本、绿色、节能、低碳方向发展，依然是 2015 年城市交通发展的主要特征。应用“互联网＋”和大数据技术科学辨识城市交通发展的客观规律，强化优先发展城市公共交通战略实施并引导城市多元交通方式统筹发展，建立完善的政策法规体系，改革城市交通管理模式，融科学规划、理性建设、智慧管理为一体，将是未来城市交通发展的必经之路。

（作者：马林，住房和城乡建设部城市交通工程技术中心副主任，教授级高级工程师）

2015 年中国城市信息化的进展

2015 年是“十二五”规划的收官之年，也是城市信息化重要的转折之年，智慧城市建设仍然是城市信息化的主旋律，在全面深化改革的大环境下，“互联网 +”行动计划和国家大数据战略的出台，使智慧城市发展进入新阶段。“互联网 +”加速推进基于互联网的大众创业和万众创新，以及互联网与经济和社会的深度与跨界融合，从而提升智慧城市建设理念和催化智慧城市新生态；大数据和云计算助力以“简政放权、放管结合和优化服务”为中心的管理体制变革；互联网公司布局智慧城市建设，推进“互联网 + 城市服务”，催生城市生活新体验；智慧城市建设的政府和社会资本合作（PPP）模式得到发展。时隔 37 年中央城市工作会议的重启，彰显城市工作的重要性，会议明确的城市发展主基调与城市信息化的深度融合，将成就智慧城市新理念、新模式、新业态和新生态，并为“十三五”城市信息化的高速发展奠定坚实的基础。

一、“互联网 +”行动促使智慧城市发展进入新阶段

2015 年政府工作报告首次提出“互联网 +”行动和发展智慧城市。作为城市信息化主旋律的智慧城市建设，进入了“互联网 +”的新阶段，“互联网 +”提升智慧城市建设理念，互联网创新成果与城市系统深度融合倒逼信息化体制机制变革以及传统行业变革，催化智慧城市发展新生态。

（一）智慧城市依然是城市信息化的主旋律

2015 年是“十二五”规划的收官之年，智慧城市建设作为一个长期的过程，仍然是城市信息化的主旋律，由国家测绘地理信息局推动的智慧城市时空信息云平台试点以及住房城乡建设部与科技部联合推动的国家智慧试点并行展开。

作为国家第一批智慧城市建设试点城市，徐州市 2015 年 1 月正式启动时空信息云平台建设。该平台作为智慧徐州的数据基础，将汇总地理国情普查、第三次经济普查、地质普查、地址普查等数据，充分拓展天地图 · 徐州服务，向公众提供更加便捷、高效时空信息云服务，重点在智慧国土、税收、地质、矿山等方面进行深入探索，全力建设人口、产业、空间、土地、环境、社会生活和公共服务等领域智能化管理为目标的全新城市形态。2015 年

又有潍坊、柳州、惠州、德清、兰州、吉安等多个城市列入智慧城市时空信息云平台试点。

2015年4月，住房城乡建设部办公厅和科学技术部办公厅联合发布了《关于公布国家智慧城市2014年度试点名单的通知》，确定北京市门头沟区等84个城市（区、县、镇）为新增试点，河北省石家庄市正定县等13个城市（区、县）为扩大范围试点，以及41个项目为专项试点，强调试点要根据《国家新型城镇化规划（2014－2020年）》和发展改革委等8部门联合印发的《关于促进智慧城市健康发展的指导意见》相关要求，以科技创新为支撑，着力解决制约城市发展的现实问题，建设绿色、低碳、智能城市。要从城市发展的战略全局出发，加强顶层设计，促进“多规融合”；推进信息资源共享和社会化开发利用，强化信息安全；创新建设和运营模式，激发市场活力。加上前两批公布的193个城市，住房城乡建设部推进的智慧城市试点已接近300个。

2015年10月，《中共中央关于制定国民经济和社会发展第十三个五年规划的建议》要求支持绿色城市、智慧城市、森林城市建设和城际基础设施互联互通。12月，时隔37年重启的中央城市工作会议强调要提升管理水平，着力打造智慧城市。

智慧城市建设既是2015年城市信息化的主旋律，也是“十三五”期间城市信息化的主线。

（二）“互联网+”提升智慧城市建设理念

经过多年的实践，智慧城市建设逐步从“技术驱动”向“问题驱动”过渡，最终将走向智慧城市建设与城市发展深度融合的城市可持续智慧发展，包括绿色、低碳、智能和宜居。技术驱动强调通过数字城市与物联网、云计算和大数据等技术集成构建智慧城市，问题驱动强调通过智慧城市建设解决环境污染、交通拥堵、管理粗放、应急迟缓等城市病问题，而城市可持续智慧发展则需要技术创新与城市系统的深度与跨界融合及互动，系统性、整体性、协调性、持续性和自适应地解决城市发展问题，“互联网+”为智慧城市建设提供了新的理念。

2015年“互联网+”成为年度热词。7月，国务院发出《关于积极推进“互联网+”行动的指导意见》，明确指出“互联网+”是把互联网的创新成果与经济社会各领域深度融合，推动技术进步、效率提升和组织变革，提升实体经济创新力和生产力，形成更广泛的以互联网为基础设施和创新要素的经济社会发展新形态。互联网创新成果既包括物联网、云计算、大数据和移动互联网及未来的新技术创新，也包括思维模式、体制机制和商业模式的创新，如共享经济、开放理念、体验经济和众包等。从2013年的“互联网思维”到2015年“互联网+”行动计划，反映了以互联网为载体的创新发展对经济与社会的深层次和全方位影响与互动，“互联网+”是新形势下信息化的新模式和新生态。

智慧城市是城市发展的新形态，“互联网+”将从技术、思维模式、体制机制和商业模式等创新多层面全方位为智慧城市提供新的理念、模式和业态，以满足城市可持续智慧发展的需要，进一步催化以互联网为基础设施的智慧城市发展新生态，使智慧城市建设进入“互联网+”的新阶段。

（三）大数据与云计算倒逼城市信息化体制机制变革

“互联网 +”的影响力开始通过大数据与云计算等互联网创新成果发挥作用。

大数据既指一种数据集合，也可以是一种新一代信息技术和服务业态，这种技术或业态主要对数量巨大、来源分散、格式多样的数据进行采集、存储和关联分析，从中发现新知识、创造新价值、提升新能力。2015 年 5 月，贵阳“国际大数据产业博览会暨全球大数据时代贵阳峰会”召开，搭建了大数据领域技术、产品和解决方案的协同创新和展示洽谈平台，国内首个大数据交易所在贵阳市同期成立，面向全国提供数据交易服务。随着大数据概念普及，其价值和重要性逐步被认识，数据已成为国家基础性战略资源，大数据战略成为国家战略。

尽管受人才、技术、数据积累以及数据采集与共享的体制机制等多种因素的制约，大数据在城市信息化中的广泛应用还有很长路程要走，但广州、成都、沈阳等城市开始布局大数据，建立全新的政府职能部门——大数据管理局。以广州为例，大数据管理局为市工信委直属的行政单位，职责包括：研究拟订并组织实施大数据战略、规划和政策措施，引导和推动大数据研究和应用工作；组织制定大数据收集、管理、开放、应用等标准规范；负责统筹规划建设工业大数据库，建立企业能耗、环保、安全生产监测指标等数据库，支撑两化融合公共信息平台的运行；组织建设两化融合公共信息平台和工业大数据平台，统筹协调城市管理智能化视频系统建设，推进视频资源整合共享和综合应用；承担广州超算和云计算技术平台的推广应用等职责。大数据与云计算相生相伴，它们对政府信息化机构、职能和体制机制的影响初见端倪。

结合云计算和大数据应用与发展需要，2015 年 1 月，《国务院关于促进云计算创新发展，培育信息产业新业态的意见》强调：鼓励应用云计算技术整合改造现有电子政务信息系统，实现各领域政务信息系统整体部署和共建共用；探索基于云计算的政务信息化建设运行新机制，推动政务信息资源共享和业务协同，促进简政放权，加强事中事后监管；积极探索地理、人口、知识产权及其他有关管理机构数据资源向社会开放，推动政府部门间数据共享，提升社会管理和公共服务能力。

6 月，《国务院办公厅关于运用大数据加强对市场主体服务和监管的若干意见》指出：要打破信息的地区封锁和部门分割，着力推动信息共享和整合。各地区、各部门已建、在建信息系统要实现互联互通和信息交换共享。除法律法规明确规定外，对申请立项新建的部门信息系统，凡未明确部门间信息共享需求的，一概不予审批；对在建的部门信息系统，凡不能与其他部门互联共享信息的，一概不得通过验收；凡不支持地方信息共享平台建设、不向地方信息共享平台提供信息的部门信息系统，一概不予审批或验收。大数据与云计算通过推进信息共享和整合，倒逼信息化体制和机制变革。

8 月，国务院印发《促进大数据发展行动纲要》，要求加快政府数据开放共享，推动资源整合，提升治理能力；结合信息惠民工程实施和智慧城市建设，推动中央部门与地方政府条块结合、联合试点，实现公共服务的多方数据共享、制度对接和协同配合。

(四)“互联网+”引发传统行业变革

“互联网+”作为信息化的新形态，其深度与跨界融合、开放和共享、体验和众包等禀性，通过打破信息不对称局面和优化信息流程，不仅可提高传统领域和行业的效率，而且可能推动行业变革，甚至颠覆，行业变革最终对智慧城市和城市发展产生影响。

2015年出租车行业便是“互联网+”引发行业改革的样例。2013年下半年以来，手机召车软件平台进入出租车行业，尤其是大量私家车以“专车”和“顺路车”方式进入出租车领域，在性价比、价格、用户体验、服务质量和灵活程度等方面得到了公众认可，创新了基于互联网的出租车新业态，冲击和挑战传统的出租车经营、管理和利润分成机制，2015年有9664万人使用网约出租车，2165万人使用网约专车，同时也触发了传统出租车行业变革。从5月开始，义乌、杭州、北京、上海等地也陆续推出了改革方案。2015年10月，交通部发布《关于深化改革进一步推进出租汽车行业健康发展的指导意见（征求意见稿)》和《网络预约出租汽车经营服务管理暂行办法（征求意见稿)》向社会公开征求意见，使出租车行业改革上升到国家层面。尽管最终的改革还需要一个很长的过程，但它是“互联网+”变革传统行业的充分体现，“互联网+”智慧城市将引发更多、更深入的变革。

二、信息化助推城市行政管理体制改革

随着全面深化改革，行政管理体制改革首当其冲，“简政放权，放管结合、优化服务”成为2015年行政管理体制改革的重点，跨部门信息共享与业务协同是难点和痛点。行政管理体制改革使信息化大有用武之地，同时有利于信息化理顺体制机制，解决难点问题，并促进信息化与行政管理体系的深度融合，助推行政管理体制改革。

(一)信息化助力“三证合一”商事制度改革

“三证合一、一照一码”登记制度从2015年10月1日起在全国范围内全面实施，国内31个省（自治区、直辖市）全部完成了登记业务系统的改造、升级、对接，全部完成了对企业公示系统的改造升级，基本实现了工商、税务、质检等部门的信息共享。

“三证合一、一照一码”登记制度从企业注册登记这一商事制度的源头着手，利用信息化手段，在工商、税务、质检等部门信息共享的基础上实现企业登记过程中政府部门的业务协同，改革了多个部门、多个证件、多个环节的繁琐管理模式，提高政府行政效能和社会运行效率，进一步释放经济发展的内在潜力。

从信息化的维度，“三证合一、一照一码”有利于在政府内部实现企业信息的共享与集成，活化电子政务法人基础数据库，为企业全生命周期监管和信用体系建设奠定坚实基础。

(二)信息化促“多规合一”发挥源头治理关键作用

中央城市工作会议明确指出推进规划、建设、管理、户籍等方面的改革，以主体功能区

规划为基础统筹各类空间性规划，推进“多规合一”。“多规合一”是指推动国民经济和社会发展规划、城乡规划、土地利用规划、生态环境保护规划等多个规划的相互融合，融合到一张可以明确边界线的市县域图上，实现一个市县一本规划、一张蓝图，解决现有的这些规划自成体系、内容冲突、缺乏衔接协调等突出问题。

2015 年，厦门全面试运行“多规合一”，不仅在空间上实现规划“一张图”，并基于全市统一的空间信息业务协同平台，采用并联审批和网上审批，将所有新建、改建和扩建工程等纳入“多规合一”平台，四条主线同步推进、并行开展，减少各方牵制，相对独立又相互配合，解决以往部门责任不清的问题，压缩审批时间，提高审批效率。厦门的“多规合一”工作不仅是规划的协调统一，更是城市管理流程、管理体系的再造。

2015 年 11 月，广州出台“多规合一”工作方案，在“三规合一”成果的基础上，计划到 2016 年年底完成“多规合一”，实现环保、教育、体育、卫生、林业园林、交通、市政、水务、环卫等多个部门的专业规划纳入全市“一张图”平台，进一步构建各类规划定位清晰、功能互补、统一衔接的规划协调机制，强化空间指引。

“多规合一”不仅仅是规划成果的协调统一，更重要的是带动建设过程的多部门“一张图”协同管理，实现“规划一张图”“建设一张图”及“管理一张图”，为城市管理源头治理提供有效的技术手段。

（三）信息化助“不动产统一登记”落地

2015 年是不动产统一登记的关键之年，3 月第一本不动产权证书在徐州颁发，其后泸州也实现不动产权证书发证，拉开了不动产统一登记的大幕。不动产统一登记要实现不动产登记机构、簿册、依据和信息平台“四统一”，2015 年年底前完成不动产职责机构整合，土地、房屋、林地、草原、海域等登记职责整合由一个部门承担，各部门之间可通过数据交换接口、数据抄送等方式，实现土地、房屋、草原、林地、水域滩涂、海域海岛等审批、交易和登记信息实时互通共享，优化工作流程，提高工作效率。根据 10 月中旬的不动产登记第四次部际联席会议的信息，已有 198 个市（州）完成职责整合，1193 个县（区）完成职责机构整合，分别占全国市县总数的 60%、42%。

不动产统一登记涉及基础业务流程梳理、登记资料移交、数据信息对接、登记系统融合、信息平台建设，以及设置统一窗口、颁发统一证书，同时涉及国土资源、公安、民政、财政、税务、工商、金融、审计、统计等部门之间不动产登记有关信息互通共享。信息化发挥着重要作用，而不动产登记数据库的建设可为智慧城市建设提供房地一体化的数据库，为城市管理提供公共基础数据。

（四）网格化城市管理进化为全模式社会管理体系

网格化城市管理是“十一五”期间北京市东城区首创的城市管理新模式。该模式综合运用地理信息、移动通信、导航定位等信息技术，以街道、社区和网格为多层级管控单元，以事件为管理内容，以处置单位为责任人，由监督员利用城管通对责任网格内的部件和事件巡查，以城市网格化管理信息平台为中心，实现从问题主动发现到立案、派遣、处置和结案等环节的全过程闭环数字化管理和量化考核评价，解决了资源共享和多层级多部门条块联动与业务协同的难题。

网络化城市管理以地理空间为基本框架集成和融合各类城市信息、划分多层级管控单元以及全过程闭环数字化管理与量化考核评价等核心机制，使城市网格化管理信息平台具有事件型管理业务的包容性和可扩展性，使网格化管理平台可以持续进化。以北京市朝阳区为例，其城市网格化管理经历了从数量化城市管理向数量化为民服务、数量化文明城区以及现阶段的全模式社会服务管理系统的进化过程。全模式社会服务管理的内容包括应急管理、城市管理、综治维稳、安全生产、社会事业、社会保障、社会服务、经济动态、法律司法、党建工作10大模块，基本涵盖了社会服务管理领域各项工作内容，实现了平战结合、社区内外和城乡一体化管理。

中央城市工作会议强调要加强城市管理数字化平台建设和功能整合，建设综合性城市管理数据库，发展民生服务智慧应用。这也反映出网格化城市管理的发展方向。

三、“互联网+”城市服务新体验

2015年，“互联网+”城市服务在政府和互联网公司的大力推动下，通过移动互联网以智能手机为载体，借助各种APP应用，逐步进入每一个市民的生活，带动信息消费，使市民感受“互联网+”城市新生活。

（一）网络提速降费促进信息消费

政府从网络提速降费着手，推进“互联网+”。2015年5月，《国务院办公厅关于加快高速宽带网络建设　推进网络提速降费的指导意见》要求：加快基础设施建设，大幅提高网络速率，有效降低网络资费，持续提升服务水平。将具备网络条件的4Mbps以下铜缆用户接入速率免费提升到4Mbps~8Mbps，下调百兆光纤接入网费，鼓励电信企业推出流量不清零、流量转赠、套餐匹配等服务。

提速降费要求得到了有效执行，流量不清零、流量转赠、套餐匹配等服务大幅度降低了用户使用移动互联网的成本，达到了信息惠民和促进信息消费效果。

（二）移动互联网应用繁荣惠民便民

据中国互联网络信息中心第37次《中国互联网络发展状况统计报告》，截至2015年12月，全国网民规模达6.88亿，互联网普及率为50.3%，手机网民规模达6.20亿。随着手机终端的大屏化和手机应用体验的不断提升，手机作为网民主要上网终端的趋势明显，移动商务类应用成为拉动网络经济增长的新引擎，2015年手机支付规模达到3.58亿，增长64.5%。

移动互联网的普及，正在改变市民的工作、生活、消费、娱乐、出游的习惯、模式、流程，催生跨区跨境、线上线下、体验分享等多种服务和消费业态兴起。如微信成为一种生活方式，并逐步成为市民城市服务门户，用户可完成朋友圈社交、移动支付、基于公众号的信息与服务获取、城市服务等各种应用，政府也通过微信平台提供服务，如城市服务中社保查询、机动车违法查询、实时路状等。各种专业的 APP 也在为市民提供形式多样服务，如运动 APP 与智能手环结合，带动市民健身运动，促进了智能穿戴设备产业发展；外买 APP 方便市民订餐，同时增加了就业；移动医患交流平台相关的 APP 改变了传统医生和患者的交流和沟通模式，1.52 亿网民使用网络医疗，带动了医疗卫生新生态的发展。

移动互联网应用繁荣，并且惠民和便民的同时，将进一步改变城市信息化乃至智慧城市建设模式，构建“互联网 +”智慧城市新生态。

（三）实时公交与室内定位改变市民出行体验

百度地图推出实时公交服务，结合实时路况、公交路线和大数据挖掘的历史数据，为用户提供更合理的公交乘坐与换乘方案和更准确的方案估时，以方便用户出行，用户可在家中实时掌握公交到站时刻，调整出门时间。百度地图实时公交以广州为起点，迅速覆盖了北京、广州、武汉、重庆、杭州、苏州、成都、南宁、南昌等 9 大城市，2015 年年底将会覆盖更多城市。

2015 年 1 月，高德发布了高德地图室内地图版，为用户提供建筑物内地图、室内定位、室内路线规划等服务，服务已经覆盖全国一、二线城市的建筑2 000余栋，定位精度达到 3 ~ 5 米，楼层定位准确率达到 95% 以上。

四、信息技术与基础设施新发展共促智慧城市建设

海绵城市和地下管廊建设及智慧城市的发展对城市的数字化、动态感知和智能调控以及基础设施的智能化提出了新的要求，而新技术也为智慧城市提供了新的支撑。

（一）民用空间基础设施逐步成为智慧城市重要组成部分

2015 年 10 月，《国家民用空间基础设施中长期发展规划（2015－2025 年）》发布，民用空间基础设施主要包括卫星遥感、通信广播、导航定位三大系统。遥感可为城市地理监测和地理数据更新提供数据源，导航定位是城市定位服务的基础；通信广播可为城市提供新的通信手段，尤其在突发应急条件下。民用空间基础设施将逐步成为智慧城市的重要组成部分。

2015 年国内商用卫星遥感发展迅速。10 月 7 日，“吉林一号”卫星发射成功，构建了一颗全色分辨率为 0.72 米、多光谱 2.88 米的推扫星为主星、两颗地面像元分辨率为 1.12 米的灵巧成像视频星和一颗灵巧成像验证星的第一期星组。灵巧成像视频星，主要开展高分辨率视频成像技术在轨验证，以后将提供热点地区动态影像拍摄服务；灵巧成像验证星将开展多模式成像技术验证。7 月 11 日，由三颗高分辨率卫星组成的“北京二号”民用商业遥感卫星星座（DMC）发射升空，分辨率为全色 1 米、多光谱 4 米。“吉林一号”将为智慧城市

建设提供目前最高分辨率的国产遥感影像，其高分辨率视频影像将成为一种新型实时动态遥感数据源，将带动新的应用模式。

随着无人机的发展，无人机倾斜摄影开始普及，降低了飞行成本，提高了倾斜摄影的灵活度和方便程度。无人机倾斜摄影除用于常规的摄影测量外，还用于应急测绘，所生成的倾斜摄影三维模型可以用于分析和量算，用于应急处置和灾后评估。2015 年 8 月天津港特别重大火灾爆炸事故和 2015 年 12 月深圳山体滑坡事故中，无人机倾斜摄影发挥了重要的作用。

（二）高速宽带网络建设加快三网合一进入推广阶段

《国务院办公厅关于加快高速宽带网络建设推进网络提速降费的指导意见》要求：加快推进全光纤网络城市和第四代移动通信（4G）网络建设。到 2015 年年底，全国设区市城区和部分有条件的非设区市城区 80% 以上家庭具备 100Mbps 光纤接入能力，50% 以上设区市城区实现全光纤网络覆盖；直辖市、省会城市等主要城市宽带用户平均接入速率达到 20Mbps，其他设区市城区和非设区市城区宽带用户平均接入速率达到 10Mbps。建成 4G 基站超过 130 万个，实现乡镇以上地区网络深度覆盖，4G 用户超过 3 亿户。

2015 年 9 月，《国务院办公厅关于印发三网融合推广方案的通知》要求，总结推广试点经验，将广电、电信业务双向进入扩大到全国范围，并实质性开展工作；加快下一代广播电视网建设，加快推动电信宽带网络建设，加强网络统筹规划和共建共享；强化网络信息安全和文化安全监管，切实推动相关产业发展。三网融合进入推广阶段。

（三）城市公用设施正在走向智能化

2015 年 11 月，智慧电杆在上海试点运营。智慧电杆具有智慧照明、汽车充电、联网监控、公共广播、一键求助、移动智能、WiFi 等功能，其每项功能均有独立系统与责任部门联网，并与智慧城市的综合智能系统平台无缝对接，进行远程智能管理。

成都、重庆和银川等一些城市出现了智慧垃圾箱。智慧垃圾箱带有 WiFi 发射器，可同时为多人提供免费上网服务。智慧垃圾箱具有垃圾燃烧自动灭火、臭氧分子智能除臭和紫外线杀菌、雷达监控识别垃圾类型并开启相关的垃圾存放口分类存放、自动短信通知清洁工清理垃圾等多项功能。

智能停车场逐步普及，智能停车场以自动识别车牌号和车辆的图像识别技术为基础，结合网络和自动控制技术，实现进出车辆的自动识别和管理，减少停车场的人工管理成本，提高停车收费管理效率，为城市智能交通体系的建设奠定基础。

五、建设与运营模式多元化加快智慧城市发展进程

（一）大型互联网公司参与智慧城市建设

2015 年 2 月，百度在线网络技术（北京）有限公司与四川省崇州市政府签订战略合作

协议，在智慧城市建设与信息产业发展方面开展战略合作，涉及智慧城市建设、整体区域运营、城市推介宣传、智慧城市标准服务以及智慧旅游、智慧农业、智慧养老等方面，通过百度“翔计划”服务，提升崇州中小企业信息化、智能化程度，扶持和拉动崇州区域内中小企业发展水平，促进崇州经济发展和城市品质提升，促进崇州的智慧化产业、智慧化管理、智慧化生活走在西部前列。崇州市是 2013 年第二批国家智慧城市试点。

腾讯基于“互联网+”的大战略，打造“互联网+”智慧城市。以微信为基础，利用其用户基础和社交网络技术，接入城市的政务服务和生活服务，实现微信平台与城市服务深层需求的紧密结合，构建“互联网+”城市的智慧生态。通过在微信中加入“城市服务”，腾讯已经与海南、河南、上海、重庆、天津、四川、贵州、湖北共 8 个省份以及 31 个城市（包括深圳、长沙、大连等），就城市创新与 IT 服务升级等方面签署了战略合作协议。

阿里巴巴整合旗下资源，推出“智慧城市”一站式解决方案，蚂蚁金服做金融支付，阿里云做大数据和云计算，支付宝、手机淘宝和微博做“城市服务”入口。各地政府通过接入该“城市服务”平台，可以利用手机为用户提供公共服务。上海、广州、深圳、杭州等首批 12 个城市“互联网+”城市服务已同步上线，用户通过支付宝钱包、微博和手机淘宝进入城市服务平台，完成交通违章查询、路况及公交查询、生活缴费、医院挂号等通用服务。该平台 2015 年将在全国 50 个城市上线，惠及 1 亿市民，阿里的“互联网+”城市服务让偏远地区的用户也可以通过手机便利地享受城市公共服务，推进公共服务的均等化。

阿里通过钉钉软件为中小企业打造的沟通和协同的多端平台，推动中小企业内部信息化，全方位提升中小企业沟通和协同效率，为企业员工提供“一种工作方式”。

（二）云计算催生城市间智慧城市建设合作模式

克拉玛依市通过政府采购华为云服务的模式，2015 年先后建成了电子政务云、公共服务云、产业云等应用，实现了资源集中共享，计算资源利用率提高 70%，业务上线周期缩短 18 倍，运维成本减少 99%，使政府、企业和百姓享受到云服务便利。

阿勒泰利用克拉玛依智慧城市建设成果，结合自身实际，基于华为云服务，实现了电子政务云、智慧社区云、智慧医疗云等应用，避免了一次性大笔资金投入，减少了技术人员费用，达到事半功倍的效果。以智慧社区云为例，利用克拉玛依云环境和持续开发集成环境，在满足克拉玛依应用需要的同时，针对阿勒泰的需求进行极少量的软件界面定制就可快速上线运营，通过桌面互联与移动互联结合，实现社区 27 项代办业务，将社区服务延伸到千家万户。

克拉玛依与阿勒泰合作，在全国首次实现一个城市向另一个城市输送信息化能力，催生了基于云计算的智慧城市建设合作模式。

（三）政府和社会资本合作（PPP）模式得到发展

2015 年，山东阳信和云南文山分别与相关企业签订了智慧城市建设 PPP 协议。以山东阳信智慧城市一期项目为例，项目额度 3.2 亿元，其中：非经营性项目 4160 万元，包括云计算中心、城市运行管理中心、智慧城管、肉牛交易中心项目、企业征信平台建设；可经营性项目包括民生服务平台、产业经济平台、能源在线监测系统、居民一卡通等，由阳信县人民政府授予项目企业特许经营权或排他性经营权。项目建设期 3 年，运营期不少于 10 年。合作期内投资收益来源为项目运营收益、政府采购服务和政府运营补贴，共担风险、共享收益。项目中政府采购服务和运营补贴等支出由财政列入年度预算以及中长期财政规划。

PPP 模式有利于解决城市政府资金难题，拓宽社会资本投资渠道；有利于理顺政府与市场关系，加快政府职能转变，充分发挥市场配置资源的决定性作用。但其在智慧建设的有效性有待实践中进一步验证。

六、结语

2015 年城市信息的关键词体现为“互联网 +”、大数据、深度与跨界融合，“互联网 +”和大数据带来的城市信息化和智慧城市的理念提升，强调信息技术尤其是互联网与传统领域和新业态的深度融合，信息技术将在提高传统领域的效能中发挥举足轻重的作用，同时带动跨界发展。以 BAT 为首的互联网公司推进以“互联网 +”城市服务为核心的智慧城市建设为城市信息化开拓新的市场化的发展空间和模式。

尽管大数据技术离实际应用还有较长的路要走，但国家大数据战略的提出，倒逼政府数据开放、共享与业务协同，对城市信息化整体性和协调性发展具有重大的意义。

创新、协调、绿色、开放和共享已经被确立为我国未来一个时期的五大发展理念。可以预计，2015 年出台的《中共中央关于制定国民经济和社会发展第十三个五年规划的建议》《中共中央 国务院关于深入推进城市执法体制改革 改进城市管理工作的指导意见》及其他相关文件将对信息化与城市规划、建设、运行、管理、服务的深度融合带来新的机遇和挑战，“十三五”时期我国城市信息化必将有新的更大的发展。

（作者：梁军，北京超图软件股份有限公司总工程师，教授级高工；王丹，建设综合勘察研究设计院有限公司副院长，研究员；党安荣，清华大学教授；何建邦，中国科学院地理科学与资源研究所研究员，国际欧亚科学院院士）

2015年中国智慧城市建设与试点工作进展

一、中国智慧城市建设的总体情况

（一）中国智慧城市建设的背景

智慧城市是通过大数据、物联网、云计算等现代信息技术的创新应用，实现深层次的信息共享和业务协同，促进城市规划、建设、管理和公共服务的精确化、智能化、便捷化和高效率，进而提升城市综合发展能力和安全与服务水平的城市发展新形态。中国城镇化进程经过几十年努力，已取得世界瞩目的成就，但同时也面临优化城镇化布局和形态、提升基础设施功能和服务水平、增强公共安全和社会治理能力、保护生态环境和传承文化等方面的挑战。党中央提出以集约、智能、绿色、低碳为方针，坚持走以人为本、四化同步、优化布局、生态文明、传承文化的新型城镇化道路。习近平总书记提出要利用新技术建设绿色、低碳、智能城市，解决城市现实问题，用大数据和网格管理技术确保城市安全和公共服务。《国家新型城镇化规划（2014－2020年）》提出了推进智慧城市建设的任务，促进城市规划管理信息化、基础设施智能化、公共服务便捷化、产业发展现代化和社会治理精细化。在这样的背景下，我国开启了以促进新型城镇化建设为目标的智慧城市创建工作。

（二）中国智慧城市建设的特征

从实践上看，国外率先提出的智能城市（Intelligent City）、智慧城市（Smart City）等理念重在对“物”的管理，重在实现城市基础设施的智能化和城市运行管理的综合集成。与发达国家相比，我国城市所承担的功能更多，管理边界更大，在建设智慧城市过程中遇到的问题也更为复杂，所需要解决的问题和发展的重点有很大不同。中国当前最大的国情是全面深化改革，是以经济体制改革为重点，以协同推进经济体制、政治体制、文化体制、社会体制、生态文明体制和党的建设制度改革为主要内容的全面性、系统性、整体性改革，改革涉及的领域之多、范围之广前所未有。将智慧城市理念与中国国情结合，建设具有中国特色的智慧城市，其本质是以系统性、控制性、协同性理念和现代信息技术综合应用来支撑城市管理和服务体制改革和机制创新，解决制约我国城镇化过程中交通拥堵、社会公共服务不畅等瓶颈问题，推动城市功能提升和协调发展，提高城镇化质量。

（三）中国智慧城市建设的必要性

中央制定了“以人为本、四化同步、优化布局、生态文明、文化传承”的新型城镇化道路，促进经济转型升级和社会和谐进步。智慧城市是新型城镇化建设的重要抓手，是智慧地建设城市、智慧地管理和服务城市、智慧地推进城市可持续运行，是贯彻党中央、国务院关于创新驱动发展、推动新型城镇化、全面建成小康社会的重要举措。建设智慧城市可提升城市规划建设管理和服务水平。一是通过实施智慧规划，使城市规划编制逐步从经验化发展到数量化和科学化，并实现“多规合一”；二是通过建筑信息模型等信息化深度应用，实现建筑设计、建造和管理全过程协调性和可控性；三是通过城市市政基础设施智能化，实时了解设施运行状况，保障运行安全；四是通过拓展数字城管的网格化管理思想，实现“多网合一、一网打尽”，实现城市人和物的精细化管理和服务。

建设智慧城市可带动相关领域的投资，是我国扩大内需、启动投资、促进产业升级和转型的新方向之一。通过建设智慧城市，引导社会资本进入城市基础设施和公共服务等领域，可带动就业，实现产业结构调整，促进现代服务业发展。项目建成后，通过运营服务将会产生更高的经济价值和社会价值。

（四）中国智慧城市建设的政策目标

党和国家对建设智慧城市提出了具体要求和工作部署，出台了一系列政策文件。2014年3月党中央、国务院印发《国家新型城镇化规划（2014－2020年）》，明确提出“推进智慧城市建设”，要求统筹城市发展的物质资源、信息资源和智力资源利用，推动物联网、云计算、大数据等新一代信息技术创新应用，实现与城市经济社会发展深度融合，促进城市规划管理信息化、基础设施智能化、公共服务便捷化、产业发展现代化、社会治理精细化。同年8月，国家发展改革委等8部门联合印发《关于促进智慧城市健康发展的指导意见》，进一步对智慧城市建设的指导思想、工作任务、保障措施等提出具体要求，引导智慧城市建设有序推进。2015年3月，国务院发布《关于落实〈政府工作报告〉重点工作部门分工的意见》，提出“发展智慧城市，保护和传承历史、地域文化。加强城市供水供气供电、公交和防洪防涝设施等建设。坚决治理污染、拥堵等城市病，让出行更方便、环境更宜居”，并明确由住房城乡建设部等12个部委局负责落实，智慧城市建设进入了一个新的阶段。中央十八届五中全会通过的《中共中央关于制定国民经济和社会发展第十三个五年规划的建议》提出，实现“十三五”时期发展目标，破解发展难题，厚植发展优势，必须牢固树立创新、协调、绿色、开放、共享的发展理念。并提出要拓展区域发展空间，支持绿色城市、智慧城市、森林城市建设。

在2015年12月召开的中央城市工作会议上，习近平总书记提出要优化创新创业生态链，让创新成为城市发展的主动力，特别是把互联网、云计算等作为城市基础设施加以支持和布局，促进基础设施互联互通，释放城市发展新动能。要加快智慧城市建设，打破信息孤岛和数据分割，促进大数据、物联网、云计算等新一代信息技术与城市管理服务融合，提升城市治理和服务水平。李克强总理提出要推进智慧城市建设，打造维系城市运行的“超级大脑”。建设智慧城市，要破除条条块块间的“信息墙”，要将城市建筑、街道、管网、环境、交通、人口等方面的实时运行状况用数据反映出来，建设综合性城市管理数据库，通过城市大数据开放、信息共享和集成运用，改变传统城市管理中的差不多现象和拍脑袋决策，推动形成“用数据说话、用数据决策、用数据管理、用数据创新”的城市管理新方式。

（五）中国智慧城市建设热潮

根据有关部门 2015 年统计，我国 100% 的副省级以上城市、89% 地级及以上城市、47% 县级及以上城市提出了建设智慧城市的方案。其中东中部地区相对领先，占全国总数的 73%，西部提出或在建智慧城市的地级市 50 个，占西部地级市总量的 56.8%。10 个省份制定省级总体规划，向上延伸形成智慧城市省级、区域群落，向下延伸辐射到城镇（县、乡）。北京、河北、上海、江苏、浙江、福建、山东、河南、广东、陕西、宁夏等 11 个省份制定出台了省级总体规划。部分省份提出构建智慧城市群落，如江苏省提出到 2015 年建成“苏南智慧城市群”，广东省提出打造“珠三角智慧城市群”，陕西省提出到 2017 年基本建成“关中智慧城市群”。

（六）智慧城市协调推进机制初步形成

为落实《关于促进智慧城市健康发展的指导意见》等文件要求，2014 年年底，由国家发展改革委牵头，成立了国务院 25 个部门组成的促进智慧城市健康发展部际协调工作组，初步形成了我国智慧城市建设在中央政府层面的协调推进机制。部际协调工作组 2015 年的重点工作是协调各部门出台相关政策，编制智慧城市评价指标体系总体框架和专项评价指标，完成部分重点指标并开展试评价。

在智慧城市科技创新方面，各部门也形成合力，联合推动智慧城市技术、标准等方面的研究。2015 年，由科技部牵头，住建、工信等多部门共同参与，完成了《智慧城市与城镇功能提升》《物联网与智慧城市》等科技重点专项，提出智慧城市技术支撑体系构建、城市群承载力预警与功能协同、智慧规划与“多规”协调、城市基础设施功能提升与智能管控、城市安全保障与公共智能服务、京津冀协同发展区域示范、综合示范与产业化推广等研究任务，构建国家物联网共性基础、城市网格化管理、城市数据共享与内容管控、“互联网 +”城市公共服务等支撑平台。

二、智慧城市试点工作进展

（一）智慧城市试点背景

住房城乡建设部作为城市规划建设管理的主管部门，一直将推进城镇可持续发展作为部门的重要工作，先后开展了数字化城市管理、“多规合一”、园林城市、绿色生态城区、建筑节能与绿色建筑等试点示范工作，取得了较好的成绩，积累了丰富的经验。从2012年开始，住房城乡建设部在10余年以数字城管为核心的数字城市工作基础上，结合新型城镇化战略部署，开展了国家智慧城市试点工作，把智慧城市创建和市政基础设施建设及安全运行、城市管理、便民服务等结合起来，实现智慧地管理城市和服务公众，探索新型城市建设模式。从2014年开始，住房城乡建设部与科技部联合组织开展试点工作，突出创新驱动发展战略以及科技创新在新型城市建设和加强社会治理中的支撑引领作用。

（二）住房城乡建设部和科技部推进试点的主要思路

在试点推进过程中，两部门坚持“政府引导、市场主导、多元主体、全球参与”方针，坚持部省市联动，政府在政策标准、市场环境等方面进行引导，贯彻“集约、智能、绿色、低碳”的理念，利用先进的科学技术和管理手段，使有限的资源得到充分利用。同时，坚持发挥市场主体作用，鼓励和支持各类市场主体共同参与智慧城市建设发展，鼓励民众参与智慧城市建设，形成政府、企业和民众共同推动的良性循环模式。

鼓励各试点因地制宜，探索具有中国特色的智慧城市发展路径。一是“一城一策、智慧发展”，瞄准城市发展的主要问题和资源禀赋，因地制宜，智慧地推进城市规划、建设、管理、运行和服务的智慧化水平；二是“人为核心、质量关键”，以人为本，以提升城市发展质量为关键，以改革为动力，将城镇真正建设成为人们的安居之处、乐业之地；三是“产城相融、互促共进”，探索大中小城市和小城镇协调发展，增强中西部地区城市发展动力；四是“多元资金、优配资源”，鼓励采用多渠道资金筹措和建设运营模式；五是“体制创新、机制融合”，在城市建设、运行、投融资方面全面探索体制创新、机制融合的解决方案。

（三）试点工作主要进展

国家智慧城市试点得到各地积极响应。截至目前，共发布了2012年度、2013年度、2014年度三批共277个国家智慧城市试点，包含省会城市8个，地级市90个，县级市（县）81个，区和新区85个，乡镇13个，覆盖我国31个省（自治区、直辖市）和新疆生产建设兵团。2014年度还首次开展了以企业为创建主体的专项试点，确定了38个企业的41个专项。

各试点城市从组织保障、顶层设计、项目建设、资金筹措等方面推进试点工作。

组织保障：各试点城市（区、县、镇）均成立了以主要领导为组长的智慧城市工作领导小组，对智慧城市创建进行统筹协调；有9个省成立了省级智慧城市领导小组。在政策扶持方面，13个省级部门、70个试点城市出台了相关扶持政策共90余项，涉及组织管理、财政扶持、产业发展、人才培养以及综合战略等领域。在过程管理方面，各省级部门对辖区内的试点城市开展年度检查和现场交流学习。

顶层设计：据不完全统计，截止到2014年年底，已有65%的试点城市完成智慧城市顶层设计，约 11% 的城市正在开展该项工作。其中江苏省、四川省、湖北省、安徽省、吉林省和北京市等省市的顶层设计工作开展整体较为出色。

城市公共信息平台和公共基础库建设：截止到 2014 年年底，启动公共信息平台建设的试点城市共 89 个，建设内容的总体完成进度为 51.2%；启动城市公共基础数据库建设的试点城市共 149 个，建设内容的总体完成进度为 49.2%。总体看来，公共信息平台和公共基础库建设（部分镇、区试点与上一级联合建设）推进状况良好，总体进度过半。

重点项目建设：总体来看，试点城市重点项目正稳步推进。据不完全统计，2014 年重点项目建设总体进展达到 54%，其中已全部建成项目约占 13.8%；总体进度完成 80% 以上的项目占 28.8%。2012 年度试点在项目推进情况上进展较快。

建设资金筹措：据不完全统计，2014 年度重点项目涉及资金总投入约 1145 亿元。其中涉及财政投入的项目共计 823 个，投入金额总数约 204.7 亿元；涉及社会投入的项目共计 257 个，投入金额总数约 598 亿元；涉及银行贷款的项目为 140 个，贷款金额总数约 216.1 亿元；涉及其他资金投入的项目共 190 个，投入资金总额 125.9 亿元。财政资金从项目数量上看仍是智慧城市项目建设主要资金来源，社会资金重点投向可运营项目且投资总额较大。

（四）2015 年试点主要工作总结

2015 年是试点开展的第三年，住房城乡建设部作为试点主管部门，开展了以下方面的主要工作：

研究起草了《关于深化拓展网格化管理　扎实推进智慧城市试点建设的指导意见》文件，在总结各地数字城管网格化管理经验基础上，提出了深化拓展网格化管理应用领域，建设城市管理、社会治理和公共服务的统一网格化平台，并以此平台为支撑推动智慧城市建设和运行的要求。目前该文件已完成编制，在征求各地意见并完善后发布。

组织开展了城市规划管理信息化、城市网格化管理、城市市政公用设施智能化等领域的应用评价指标研究，提出各领域评价指标项和考核要点。该工作已取得初步成果，将和各部门编制的评价指标一起构成中国完整的智慧城市评价指标体系。

根据行业工作重点和试点推进需求，组织编写了《智慧城市网格化综合管理平台建设指南》《智慧城市多规融合平台建设指南》《智慧城市地下管线综合管理信息平台建设指南》等标准，将在近期完善后发布。

与欧盟合作举办了中欧智慧城市峰会，特邀中欧知名城市市长、业内专家、学者及企业代表交流智慧城市建设的创新理念、技术和成功经验，以智慧城市具体项目为载体，探讨技术与管理方面的合作，并就智慧城市与新能源应用、智慧城市与水务、智慧城市与地下管线及综合管廊建设议题进行深度交流。

2014 年编辑出版了《智慧地推进新型城镇化发展——智慧城市创建案例》。该书发挥了很好的示范指导作用，被中央党校、浦东干部学院、全国市长研修学院选为学习材料。2015 年住房城乡建设部联合科技部、中央党校、北京大学、国务院发展研究中心等单位，对贵阳市、银川市、宜昌市、威海市、北京市东城区等城市（区、镇）的智慧城市创建经验进行总结和评价，相关文字材料已编辑完成，2015年版案例准备近期出版。

通过举办智慧城市建设培训会，邀请专家对智慧城市顶层设计、投融资规划、过程管理、网格化平台建设等内容进行培训，也邀请典型城市介绍经验，并进行现场案例教学，取得不错效果。培训会已经成为试点城市学习交流的重要平台。

三、智慧城市试点成效初步显现

中国智慧城市建设已逐步从理念走向实践，从无序变为有序，从注重形式到追求实效，从单一自建走向合作共赢。国家智慧城市试点城市在公共服务水平、社会治理能力、土地集约利用、生态环境保护、产业融合发展以及资源配置能力等方面开展了积极探索。

（一）加强公共平台建设，促进资源共享

上海市浦东新区充分发挥中国（上海）自由贸易试验区、国家综合配套改革试点、智慧城市试点的多项政策优势，瞄准新型城镇化过程中的新问题和新挑战，以智慧引领模式变革为主线，突出以民为本，在政府平台化创新、城市立体化管理、民生精细化服务、产业融合化发展等方面开展先行先试，快速推进智慧政务服务从“以政府为中心”向“以公众为中心”的服务模式转变，在顶层设计、信息协同共享、政社合作共建、惠民示范引领、产用联动等方面逐步探索和凝练出具有浦东特色的智慧城市发展路径和推进模式。

威海市致力于建立良性的工作机制，加强统筹整合，大力推动智慧城市“市域一体化”建设。以顶层规划增强全市统筹，实现市、区规划统一。推进全市域电子政务云计算资源整合，取消区县级电子政务机房，市级启动的智慧城市项目延伸覆盖到各区县，有效避免了重复建设。推进PPP建设模式，政府购买服务落到实处。充分调动社会力量参与智慧城市建设，缓解财政资金压力，实现共赢。

中新天津生态城充分发挥新建城市包袱小、体制好、技术新等特有优势，在建设过程中不断探索，打造可持续、重体验的智慧城市。重点建设公共平台中的脉动城市数据汇聚平台，通过打通信息和服务的通道，聆听“信息脉动”，使政府与企业深度合作，把握信息脉动带来的机遇，挖掘信息的价值，通过可持续发展的运营模式让智慧化的服务遍及城市的每一个角落。生态城通过脉动城市数据汇聚平台承载了建设、经济、企业、环境、能源、城市管理、城市运维等领域的29类数据，为生态城建设、商务、环境、经济、城管、办公室、投资公司等7个单位14个系统提供了77项数据服务，在经济建设、城市管理与运维、城市数据分析方面初步形成了效果。

（二）优化规划建设，集约资源利用

舞钢市作为河南省城乡一体化试点市，以科学发展为统领，以智慧城市建设为主线，从新型农村社区建设切入，坚持产业为基、就业为本、以城带乡、产城互动，实施土地向规模经营集中、农民向中心镇中心社区集中举措。舞钢市按照“产”“城”一体化定位，高起

点、高标准科学编制新型城镇化建设和经济发展“两个规划”，实现产业发展和城乡一体化建设“一张图”规划，并按规划严格实施，取得明显成效。

无锡市阳山镇针对规划布局、环境污染、农业改革、村庄整治、产业提升等问题，以构建以人为本，生产、生活、生态相协调的智慧小镇为目标，以“规划引领发展，生态决定未来”为理念，以“生态宜居、特色农业、休闲度假和文化养生”为特色，坚持一张好的蓝图干到底，重视并坚持“规划先行”“多规融合”，实施三次产业全面转型，实行土地信托模式下的土地流转，创新多元资金投入模式、空间优化模式。

（三）加强网格化管理服务，提升社会治理能力

北京市朝阳区加强网格化管理服务体系建设，从数量化城市管理到数量化为民服务、数量化文明城区、全模式社会服务管理系统的一系列创新升级活动，逐步健全和完善了以政府为主导、社会为主体，以朝阳社会信用体系为支撑的数量化、智能化、科学化的全模式社会服务管理系统，探索了智慧城市建设的新方向。朝阳区建立涵盖应急管理、城市管理、综治维稳、安全生产、社会事业、社会保障、社会服务、经济动态、法律司法、党建工作等领域的全模式服务管理系统，按照发现问题、案件受理、案件派遣、任务处置、结果反馈、复查核查形成闭环工作流程，通过高位、依法、客观、闭环、公正、全方位的监督，基本解决了朝阳区社会和政府之间、政府内部“条条与条条”之间、“条条与块块”之间责任不清的问题，提升了社会服务管理的常态化、精细化水平。

深圳市坪山新区实施“织网工程”，在“智慧城市”总体框架下，利用大数据来解决人口多、复杂性高、流动性强的城市管理问题，建立了全区统一的公共信息资源库，实现信息充分交换共享；建立了专业的信息采集员队伍，实现统一的信息采集模式；建立事件“采办分离”原则，实现事件处置闭环流转；整合社会管理工作网和数字化城管系统，形成了综合性、开放性、枢纽性的业务平台。

宜昌市通过应用网格化管理的思路理念、方法手段，整合社区人员队伍，创新社会治理体制机制，探索现代城市社会智慧治理新模式，构建了以人为本的网格化管理、信息化支撑、全程化服务的社会服务管理新体系。通过重心下移，关口前移，利用信息技术，把社区作为惠民服务的重要基地，探索出了社区网格化零距离的智慧民生服务体系，解决智慧城市便民服务最后100米不畅通问题，取得了明显成效。

（四）关注民生，提升服务水平

兰州市在创建“智慧城市”过程中，发挥市场配置资源的作用，大力整合资源，创新社会管理，探索社区居家养老服务体系，创立了党委政府与社会力量联动的“民情流水线”和“虚拟养老院”，建成了兰州市三维数字社会服务管理系统平台，提升了民生服务能力，提高了行政管理效能，为广大群众生活提供更多便利。

成都市温江区整合区域人、地、物、事、组织和房屋等信息，统筹公共管理、公共服务和商业服务等资源，构建智慧社区综合信息服务平台，从政务服务、公共服务、商务服务三

方面入手，在平台建设包括智慧医疗、智慧党建、智慧养老、政务服务等多个领域的智慧应用，实现智慧应用与市民生活的深度融合，打造全新的公共服务和便民利民服务和运营模式，实现政务效率全面提升、民生建设全面改善、商务模式转型可复制。

（五）注重生态环境，促进低碳建设

南京市河西新城区（建邺区）以绿色智慧城市建设为目标，突出智能迅捷社会治理导向，突出现代高端智慧产业集聚，以智慧城市理念融贯城市建设、治理和发展，建立了以法定城市规划为主体、低碳生态智慧专项规划为技术支撑的全新规划体系以及9个一级指标和66个二级指标的低碳生态智慧城指标体系。通过建立“指标、规划、技术、管理、市场、政策、行动”七维协同的规划建设管理运行模式，将智慧城市建设理念融贯开发建设管理各个环节。

青岛中德生态园以生态、绿色、低碳为建园目标，构建安全稳定、经济高效、智能低碳、可持续发展的现代新能源体系。以清洁的天然气为主，以风、光、地源热、水源热等可再生能源为辅，融合智能化控制和云计算技术，形成多种能源互补利用、供需互动的区域能源整体解决方案。将信息网、能源网和物质网耦合成智能协同网，通过气、电、热等能源的梯级利用和智能协同，呈现出能源清洁生产、供需互动、互补调峰、高效利用、节能减排的园区能源利用新模式。

（六）推动产业升级，产城融合发展

辽源市以智慧产业作为智慧城市建设突破口，把软件信息产业作为现代服务业发展的主攻方向，吸引了30多家国内外知名软件企业集中落户，并在辽源设立全资子公司，进一步提升了辽源在信息产业领域的核心区位优势。

佛山市乐从镇坚持“产业支撑城市、城市提升产业”的产城融合理念，以产业链为抓手，促进企业转型；以总部经济为核心，助力产业智慧升级；以“三大改革”为契机，转变政府服务方式；以宜居环境为配套，体现以人为本的社会价值取向，致力打造“发展更科学，管理更高效，社会更和谐，生活更美好”的智慧乐从。充分发挥市场配置资源的决定性作用，将智慧城镇项目建设和管理通过服务外包的方式委托乐从智慧城镇发展中心执行；搭建物联天下产业园、高新企业孵化器两个平台，集聚创新要素，提升技术创新能力和国际竞争力。

（七）坚持体制机制创新，智慧解决发展难题

银川市以行政审批为突破，分三个阶段推动智慧政务建设。第一阶段是流程梳理、一站式审批，释放改革红利；第二阶段是数据共享、网上审批，释放信息化红利；第三阶段是数据采集挖掘分析，虚拟审批，释放大数据红利。银川智慧政务取得良好效果，通过智慧政务一站式审批，政务类150多件事项的办理时限由法定的4080个工作日减少到880个工作日，减幅达79%，审批效率平均提高75%。

长沙市湘江新区（大河西先导区）成立长沙先导投资控股有限公司为城市资源综合运营商，以体制机制创新为保障，通过改革释放城镇化发展潜力，通过改革优势、功能优势、区位优势、科教优势和资源优势的叠加聚变，走出一条智慧发展的新路。一是政府引导、企业市场化运营。政府主要负责最终决策和启动资金，其他事务交由先导控股按市场经营与运作。二是构建“一体两翼”的三大运作平台。突出城市产业发展为主体（一体）、强化城市基础设施建设为一个辅翼（一翼）、全面开拓城市发展资金渠道为另一个辅翼（另一翼）的运作平台体系，强化城市产业就业支撑的城市建设基本规律和要求，体现了基础设施在城市建设中的核心地位，抓住了资金和金融在城市建设中的关键作用。三是先导控股全面参与或直接承担城市规划、建设和运营各个阶段和环节的具体事务性工作。

四、下一步主要工作思路

智慧城市建设对经济发展和社会进步都有着巨大而深远的影响，我国才刚起步，还存在着很多不足。面向近期目标和未来发展方向，要着力做好以下几个方面的工作。

一是继续推进公共信息平台和综合性城市管理数据库建设。城市公共信息平台是连接城市政府管理部门和公共服务部门各类信息系统的中枢，城市各类数据资源通过平台进行交换和共享，汇聚成综合性城市管理数据库。公共信息平台和综合性城市管理数据库在智慧城市建设中发挥着至关重要的核心和基础作用，应规避以部门专业信息平台“各自为战”的局面，加快公共信息平台建设步伐，整合和承接各行业信息资源，尽快建立健全涵盖人、地、事、物等要素和城市供水、供电、燃气、供热等生命线运行状态的综合性城市管理数据库，促进跨部门、跨行业、跨层级的业务协同应用。在信息大整合、大集中的同时，做好信息安全保障。

二是提高公共服务智慧化应用水平。以人为本的公共服务是智慧城市建设的首要内容，满足公众需求是智慧城市建设的主要动力所在。随着城市人口的不断增长，城市交通、医疗、教育、社会保障等公共服务水平总体上滞后于公众日益增长的需要，因此，智慧城市建设要突出为民、便民、惠民。要立足不同城市不同发展阶段，结合现有公共服务的实际水平，进行深入的公众调查研究，找出主要需求和主要差距，明确公共服务智慧化发展的主要目标和任务，加快相关系统开发和应用。同时，要注重改进公共服务的基础条件，合理布局、均衡资源、预测容量。

三是进一步加强城市管理、社会治理、公共安全、公共服务等领域网格化综合应用。各地普遍建成的数字化城管网格化管理平台已成为我国城市中贴近百姓、应用广泛、成效显著的公共平台。要在数字化城管网格平台基础上，拓展网格化在社会治理、公共服务、应急管理等民生领域的智慧应用，并逐步实现全面覆盖，打造政务高效、服务便捷、管理睿智、安全运行的城市智慧发展新常态。加强社会治理领域网格化管理，将影响国家安全、社会稳定、治安秩序和群众安全感的各类社会矛盾和问题信息进行综合集成，纳入网格化管理体系，提升城市社会治理水平。加强应急管理领域网格化管理，实现各类应急突发事件和公共安全信息的采集上报、分析研判、协调指挥、处置反馈和考核评价，最大程度地减少灾害损失，保障人民群众生命财产安全。加强公共服务领域网格化管理，在基本公共教育、医疗卫生、社区养老、劳动就业、文化体育等领域开展基于网格化的主动式公共服务，精细划分服务事项，精准定位服务人群，打通服务群众的“最后100米”，推进服务群众“零距离”，切实提高公共服务水平。

四是加快智能化基础设施建设。继续推进城乡一体的宽带网络、视频图像网络和广播电视网建设，加强网络基础设施整合，为智慧城市打下更为广阔的信息化基础。要大范围提高城市供水、供电、燃气、供热、防灾减灾等生命线工程的智能化水平，实时掌握城市基础设施建设运行的基本状态和主要数据变化，及时发现和排除安全隐患。在各地正在建设推进的地下管廊建设中，要运用现代信息技术进行智能化建设和改造，在开展地下管线普查的基础上建立电子档案和专业数据库，建立数据动态更新和维护工作机制，实现基础设施运行的精准化、协同化和一体化。

五是突出产业经济智慧化发展。要发挥市场作用，培育智慧城市相关产业。发挥企业市场主体作用，形成一大批龙头企业和参与企业，从信息网络建设、信息加工处理和信息安全保障的基础建设，到能源、给排水、交通、通信以及城市公共服务等智能化应用系统建设，有效拉动经济，带动就业。要盘活城镇资源，推动智慧城市建设运营模式创新。加强中央、地方财政引导，发挥市场作用，引导和鼓励社会力量开展专业化、个性化的服务，探索多种资金投入方式。

六是完善智慧城市建设体制机制。智慧城市建设是一个复杂的系统工程，要立足国情，充分发挥地方政府在推动智慧城市建设的主导作用，将智慧城市建设作为新型城镇化建设重要抓手，科学编制相关规划，统筹安排城市建设和发展的各项事业。要逐步统一建设标准，实现城市各类信息数据的共享交换，兼顾不同城市、不同区域间数据共享，建立省级层面甚至全国统一的数据共享机制。继续推进智慧城市试点示范，到2020年建成一批特色鲜明的智慧城市，完善评估指标体系，切实发挥试点示范引领作用。要将智慧城市建设与深化改革结合起来，建立健全顶层协调的智慧城市建设规划、信息资源共享使用、业务协同管理等方面的规章制度。

（作者：杨柳忠，住房和城乡建设部城乡规划管理中心研究员）

论坛篇

求解“城乡规划”[①]

加快推进城乡发展一体化，是党的“十八大”提出的战略任务。习近平总书记提出，全面建成小康社会，最艰巨最繁重的任务在农村，特别是农村贫困地区。我们一定要抓紧工作、加大投入，努力在统筹城乡关系上取得重大突破，特别是要在破解城乡二元结构、推进城乡要素平等交换和公共资源均衡配置上取得重大突破。面对中国城乡发展中的复杂的现实问题，城乡规划面临巨大的挑战。

讲到城乡规划，我们要从中国古代城乡一致性与当前的城乡矛盾说起。数千年来，中国社会建立在农村的基础上，农村不仅仅供养城市，而城市的大部分人才都来自农村，本质上城市与乡村并没有真正的文化与制度的差别，经济上也有直接联系，是一元的整体。从秦统一到清末民初，在以郡县制为核心的地方行政制度之下，县成为最基础的治理单元，所谓“郡县治，则天下治”。

鸦片战争之后，城市和乡村之间，沿海和内地之间，渐渐由一体而疏离，但这个时期的社会发展，仍然有一些城乡统筹的实践。例如清末状元张謇，在南通办工厂，经营市政，做了很多事情，所以有人称他建设的南通堪称“中国近代第一城”。张謇的思想和实践，可以说是“城乡并举”。

费孝通先生一直提倡发展现代化小城镇，复兴农村，虽然没有取得成功，但是代表了当时一种重要思潮。

改革开放以后，中国城乡建设取得巨大成就，但也不容忽视，在此过程中长期存在“重城轻乡”的思想，为了发展城市而不惜牺牲农村，为了土地开发简单强调征地，城市化水平不断提高的同时，对乡村发展形成了不可忽视的危害。“三农”问题日益严峻，乡村凋敝令人心焦，现在讨论得很多，但是农村到底怎样发展，似乎还没有一个明确、完整的方向。对此，我有以下两点思考：

---

① 2015年10月17日，中国社会科学院、中国科学院和中国工程院在中国工程院举办2015年度中国城市百人论坛，主题为“新型城镇化进程中的城乡协同发展”。本文系根据作者在论坛上的发言改写而成。

一、要因地制宜采取差别化发展策略

中国幅员辽阔，不同地区有很大差别，东部发达地区和西部欠发达地区的城乡关系就大不相同，因此要因地制宜采取差别化发展战略，建立新型城乡关系。对于特大城市地区，促进生产力要素灵活流动和重组，在区域尺度上对特大城市过分集中的功能进行有机疏解，同时要提高中小城市和城镇人口吸纳和服务功能，使农村富余劳动力在大中小城市均衡分布，有序流动，形成一种协调的城乡统一体。对于欠发达地区，以县域为基本单元，根据各具特色的自然资源、经济基础、文化特色等现实情况，对城镇发展、新农村建设的制度创新进行试点。

例如，江苏是中国经济社会发展的先进地区，也是传统乡村较为富裕、城镇工业迅速发展的省份。即使如此，江苏的城乡二元结构仍然十分明显，城乡人居环境和基础设施水平差距较大。江苏省省委、省政府明确对村庄环境开展整治计划，制定乡村环境建设行动计划，促进面向乡村复兴的村庄环境整治，经过几年的整治，70%实现城乡统筹区域供水，三分之一的县市实现生活垃圾无害处理。

二、以综合系统的方法应对城乡统筹的复杂性

城乡统筹是极具复杂性的问题，政治、经济、文化、社会、生态等各类要素交缠一起，如何统筹非常复杂。研究复杂问题往往有两种方式：一种是从专门问题入手，不断深化，得到结论；另一种是综合整体思考问题，得到结论。后者是比较困难的，也是我们所提倡的“人居环境科学”一直以来的追求。“三规合一”“一张蓝图干到底”就是统筹的具体化。2015年9月份中共中央、国务院印发的《生态文明体制改革总体方案》，提出构建以空间整治、空间结构优化为主要内容，全国统一、相互衔接、分级管理的空间规划体系，即整合目前各部分分头编制的各类空间规划，编制统一的空间规划，实现规划全覆盖。这是将各项建设在空间上融为一体的途径，对规划提出更高的要求，即以统筹之道整合各类规划，建立新的城乡空间体系与秩序。

一般理解城市设计为空间规划。早在1984年，我曾著文《城市设计是提高城市规划与建筑设计质量的重要途径》。当今我国建筑界提倡重视城市设计，从空间规划的角度出发扩充其理念，从邻里、城市、大都市、城市群到整个区域，甚至跨国境，从物质环境扩展到社会空间，这在学术领域可以有进一步的发展。这个概念的扩大可以依据联合国人居署“人居三”文件：“城市和空间规划与设计”（Urban and Spatial Planning and Design）。我个人认为，应将城市空间理论和中国传统设计理论结合起来，根据大自然的环境和人文环境，发展地方文化，扩大城市设计，推进城乡规划。

（作者：吴良镛，中国科学院院士，中国工程院院士，清华大学教授）

智慧城市建设的背景、内容和途径

众所周知，当前智慧城市非常热门，但是也令人迷茫：智慧城市内涵是什么？如何建设智慧城市？这些仍是困扰很多人的问题。本文拟从以下三个方面作些探讨和解答。

一、智慧城市建设的背景

首先谈谈建设的背景。习近平总书记在2012年中央经济工作会议上提出了新型城镇化的“八字方针”：集约、绿色、智能、低碳。李克强总理在2016年3月5日全国人大所作的报告中提出“互联网+”行动计划，并强调要发展“智慧城市”，保护和传承历史、地域文化。其实更重要的是，要通过智慧城市建设，有效治理污染、交通拥堵等城市病，加强城市供水、供气、供电、公交和防洪排涝设施等能效建设，达到让城市生活更便捷、环境更宜居的目的，实现城市的善治。

我们来看看中央近年来提出的一系列规划与战略。智慧城市的战略目标是包含在我国的“五化”之中的：新型工业化是动力，是通过专业化分工与合作来提高生产效率和提供城市就业岗位的主动力；农业现代化是基础，能为经济持续增长提供基础性食品安全保障和生态底板；信息化可融合各种各样的生产要素和治理方式，属协同创新；新型城镇化是机会平台，对于一个民族和一个国家来说，那么多的人口移居到城市里来或重新分布，发展机会很多亦很大；绿色化是方向，是一个可持续发展的战略，这个战略既包含价值观，又具有工具性。

我国为什么要确定一个这样的“五化”同步的发展战略呢？因为我国已经从农业国转向工业国，工业文明刚进行了几十年，但是已经把全球工业文明300年历史的弊端暴露得淋漓尽致，实践已经证明工业文明是不可持续的，文明需要转型，转向生态文明或者后工业文明。在这个过程中，我国又伴随着城镇化和新型工业化，这两大进程是高度相互交织的，使得我国发展机会巨大，但是治理任务非常繁重，挑战也空前巨大。

首先，从问题来看，我国粗放的工业化和城镇化导致“交通拥堵、能源紧张、空气污染、水体污染、垃圾围城、噪声污染、用地矛盾、水资源短缺……”还有贫富不均等一系列社会问题都暴露出来了。这些问题既影响了我国城市健康的发展，又妨碍了社会正义。也就是说，我们要通过善治来应对挑战。

那该如何解决呢？除了从体制上改变，政府效率提高，还需要运用现代科学技术。尤其是信息技术，它是双刃剑，既会带来很多麻烦，也能解决很多问题。通过智慧城市建设来破解城市发展难题、转变经济发展方式就成为必由之路了。这就要求在城市建设过程中，要与善治与绿色化相协调，与智慧城市相同步。从宏观方面看，要实现这么几点：由城市优先发展转变为城乡互补；从高能耗城镇化转变为低能耗城镇化；从大城市扩张转向大中小城市协调发展；从盲目克隆国外建筑转向文化传承；从高环境冲击转向低环境冲击；从放任式机动化转向集约式机动化；从大型、集中式的基础设施建设转向小型、分散循环式；从少数人先富转向社会公平。这些转型都要在城市治理中实现，任务非常繁重。

二、智慧城市的内涵和内容

关于智慧城市内涵，住房城乡建设部的文件说得非常明白：从管理者角度讲，就是促使城市“不得病”“少得病”，或者得了病之后“快治病”，保障城市健康和谐发展；从企业角度讲，利用智慧城市技术手段，提升企业自身运营效力，降低运营成本，提升竞争力；从百姓角度讲，让民众感受到智慧城市带来的“便民”“利民”“惠民”，同时也对政府进行有效监督。

在对智慧城市的理解方面，从手段上说，通过全面感知、信息共享、智能解题，在城市规划、建设、管理、运行过程中采用信息化、智慧化、人性化等手段推进管理创新；从内容上说，智慧城市涵盖城市产业、民生、环境、防灾减灾、行政治理、资本配置等；从理念上看，以智慧系统为“黏合剂”，将集约、低碳、绿色、人文等新理念融入城镇化全过程；从难度上看，智慧城市建设最大的难点是将信息孤岛连接起来，通过信息共享、系统共生来消除部门“信息孤岛”和利益壁垒。

“集约”能够提高城市资源利用和城市的运行效率，而“智能”是城镇化的智慧化与精细化，构建“更为智慧化、百姓生活更便利的城镇”。此外，智慧型城市能够实现“绿色”可持续发展，就是循环利用资源能源、善待和修复生态环境。而“低碳”发展能够降低能源消耗，推广可再生能源，促进民众行为节能减排。我国在 8 年前推行数字城管系统，这个数字城管系统实际上是一种网格化的物理平台，不仅将物联网的感知系统和视频监控系统精确叠加上去，而且又可以发挥现场巡视人员实地拍摄检查并反馈分析的能力。这种系统能够将所有涉及公共服务的事项通过电脑记录下来，然后公之于众，其适应了城市越来越多的专业化发展，因为现代城市管理是多专业协同体系。不管存在多少专业管理部门，网格化平台都可以将其“一网打尽”。

数字城管系统与现在部分地区推行的综合执法有很大区别，综合执法将许多部门的事情集中在一个部门，显然常常是力不从心的，也是与现代城市的复杂性和专业分化趋势是相违背的，因而困难重重。但数字城市网格式管理，不管有多少专业服务机构，系统都可以做出客观评价，有效促进管理效能提高，方便让群众进行绩效监督。由此可见，数字城管系统是一种物理平台，在这个基础之上将其智能化，就可以形成“人—机”复合平台，然后不断地根据问题、现代化进程和人们的要求，来促进这个系统的不断完善。总之，数字城管将让城市发展更加可持续，有效解决现代城市多部门服务和协调复杂性的矛盾。数字城管是城市管治的基础工程，更是每个民众都可享用的“公共品”。因此，可在已有数字化城管系统的基础上进一步优化扩充，作为智慧城市的公共平台。

在对数字城管系统优化扩充的基础之上可引进大数据。大数据和传统的小数据的一个巨大的差别在于：传统小数据必须找出事物之间的因果逻辑性，但大数据完全是方法创新的，它可找出事物之间的相关性而非逻辑性。

此外，大数据与小数据的区别还在于：小数据可用传统办法和工具处理，抽样办法，模型简化；大数据是人们获得新认知、创造新价值的源泉，是改变市场、组织机构以及政府与公民关系的方法。小数据遵循还原论，将事物细分到逻辑原点，找出系统构成要素及内部运行机制、行为、功能，属简单科学；大数据遵循整体论，是由分散的、具体的全部数据集合构成，可全面、完整地把握对象的整体与局部要素的系统行为，属复杂科学。小数据追求统一性、标准化，是关注普遍性规律，能通过理论模型简化结果，是减少错误、保证调查质量的必要途径；大数据容忍多样化、个性化，融合地方性、实践性知识，甚至模糊性（不精确性），强调数据的完整、多样，进一步接近事实。小数据关注因果关系，数据少、精，寻找数据之间线性逻辑关系；大数据关注关联关系，数据海量、混杂非线性，“黑箱方法”，忽略因果细节，只看宏观关联。

通过大数据，我们能捕捉到一些以前难以观察的事物。例如，上海实施了九个新卫星城建设并实行了“职住平衡”，但十几年之后市民还在承受越来越严重的钟摆式交通，始终没有发现多数新增加的就业岗位仍在主城，通过大数据分析，我们马上就能看到新服务业的就业岗位大多数还在主城，所以上海的交通拥堵越来越严重。这只有通过大数据的分析，才能迅速找到相关的症结所在。

数字城管系统正在逐步覆盖。据不完全统计，目前全国已有258个市（区）建设了数字城管系统，其中地级市（含直辖市的区）122个、县区级136个，江苏、浙江、河北三省已实现地级市全覆盖。传统的数字城管基于网格化、精细化，将城市管理涉及的事、部件归类、标准化和传输同步化等使现场管理反应快、准、好。通过数字城管系统的逐级提升，将传统的数字城管从通过因特网、电话受理老百姓投诉，并向百姓反馈处理结果，转变成城市公共信息平台，通过现场拍照、摄像头观察和传感器等，让智慧城管平台主动发现问题、有预见性地应对。此外，数字城管系统还能做到对城管所有部门的实时监督，同步将绩效进行记录公布，接受民众的监督。

智慧城市建设还有一个不断提高的过程，一开始能够找出主要城市病并编类，每一类都尝试用智慧城市的办法去解决，这是“专题性”智慧城市应用的一个重要方面。例如：功能模块类——智慧北京；数据共享类——苏州智慧医疗；虚拟城市类——数字南宁；电子政（商）务类——新加坡电子政务网等。然后将专题性的智慧城市系统叠加，能够解决多个“专题性”问题，同时逐步做到能用信息系统攻克某几个公认的现代城市难题，形成“综合性”智慧方案。

由此可见，那些不能促进城市管治效能提高、节能减排、医治“城市病”的所谓智慧城市方案，都属于“空”“假”“瞎”智慧，是劳民伤财的。

三、智慧城市建设的若干途径

万变不离其宗，智慧城市应该以城市绿色化作为主要的途径，包括：生态城市建设与改造；城市绿色交通规划与“绿道”建设；海绵城市、排水、污水处理、安全供水与防灾；可再生能源与建筑一体化及建筑节能改造；绿色小城镇和宜居村庄建设；城市空气污染系统治理；绿色建筑、绿色社区等。这些都可以智慧化来促进绿色发展，这些是我国进入“城市时代”永恒的社会治理主题。

第一，生态城市建设与改造。城市需要文明转型，如果还停留在工业时代的城市，那两型社会目标就难以实现。什么是生态城市？简单来说就是紧凑混合用地模式：可再生能源占比≥20%；绿色建筑≥80%；生物多样性；绿色交通：步行、自行车、公共交通≥65%；拒绝高耗能、高排放的工业项目。以上六个方面是生态城市 28 项主要指标中的核心指标。

第二，城市交通。上海作为超大城市，上海市市委、市政府定下谁能解决上海的交通问题，都将获得历史性功勋。各种研究机构都应该列专题进行长期攻关。城市交通实际是空间资源的分配问题。中国城市与国外相比有一些差别，例如广泛存在封闭社区，封闭居民区、封闭厂区与机构大院落等，除必须打通交通“毛细管”之外，运用信息化的手段统筹运用多种交通工具，实时感知交通系统的拥堵点等，把城市交通转变成每个驾车者都同步可视的系统是治理的重点。

第三，智慧水务。包括城市排水、污水处理、安全供水、雨水收集与防灾减灾等，这一系列改进只有硬件建设是不够的，还需要软件设施的加强。海绵城市建设就是要尽量使开发前、开发后降雨的径流时间、径流量、径流峰值三大要素保持不变，让城市变为一个巨大的海绵。城市自身能利用雨水、渗透水、净化水、循环用水。这样一来，城市水问题通过智慧水务自身就可解决。

第四，可再生能源、建筑一体化和建筑节能。因为建筑能耗可达到 30% 全社会总能耗。建筑是一个用能大户，但建筑一旦与新能源结合又可以采能，我国如果使用 10% 的屋顶进行太阳能的转换，年发电量相当于一个“三峡”，这方面潜力是非常巨大的。通过推广绿色建筑，达到建筑全生命周期“节能、节地、节水、节材”，这样一种全方位的、全生命周期的“四节”建筑，是我们永恒的、坚定不移的基础性工程。通过历史资料的观察，如能把每幢建筑节能、节水做到可视化，就能产生节约 15% 以上的效果。也就是说，任一个居住单元，一旦能显示自身的节水和节能是同类单元的第几位，居民就会积极自主节省。由此可见，简单地信息化就可以解决节能节水的大问题。

绿色小城镇也非常重要，例如上海“1966”计划，9 个卫星城、60 个小城镇，如都能做到绿色化、智慧化发展，小城镇市民就能享受到和主城同样的各种生活、就业、医疗、教育等方面的优质服务，而空气更洁净，住房更便宜。在智慧城市的建设中，还应突出对城市空气污染系统治理，而城市空气污染系统的管理过程中应通过智能化技术进行管理，具体而言，体现在通过信息技术对污染源头进行分析、现场监测、过程控制、预警预报、系统反应等五大过程。其次，更重要的是，城市是由建筑和社区组成的，通过智慧城市建设，使得建筑和社区更加绿色。对于各类学校而言，也应该建成绿色校区。绿色校区不仅仅能成为技术创新的实验基地，更重要的是绿色环境对学生的良性影响，二者是相互协同发展的。

总之，智慧城市的类型众多，目前概括起来至少可分为三种类型：一是城市管理绩效提高型，通过智慧城市建设使政府服务功能大幅度提高，老百姓能够对政府行为进行监督，帮助各个部门进行绩效考核。二是节能减排（绿色生态）型，城市必须是绿色的，这不仅仅关系这一代人的生活，更关系到下一代人的生活。三是市民生活便捷型，体现为对百姓生活丰富化和优化的关注。前两种是政府必须事先做好顶层设计和实施规划的，并能为第三种以企业为主体参与的“生活优化型智慧城市”奠定基础。而顶层设计的本质是“城市诊断”，首先应该对城市进行系统“会诊”，看准“城市病”，再以智慧手段综合调理（必要时再叠加基础设施完善的方案），从而逐步演进为复合式全功能智慧城市。当前要注意区分那些“挂羊头卖狗肉”的空、假、瞎“智慧”设计方案，确保我国智慧城市有序健康发展。

（作者：仇保兴，国务院参事，中国城市科学研究会理事长）

2015 中国最具幸福感城市

“2015 中国最具幸福感城市”系列榜单于 2015 年 10 月 31 日在北京发布，“小康社会、幸福中国”成为 2015 年新主题。

“中国最具幸福感城市”调查推选活动由新华社《瞭望东方周刊》联合中国市长协会《中国城市发展报告》共同主办，迄今已连续举办 9 年，是目前中国最具影响力和公信力的城市调查推选活动。

本届推选活动从 6 月份启动后，累计8 000多万人次参加了公众调查、抽样调查和大数据采集。经过活动组委会评审，成都、宁波、杭州、南京、西安、长春、长沙、苏州、上海、北京 10 座城市荣获“2015 中国最具幸福感城市”荣誉称号。杭州获得“2015 中国幸福城市政府贡献大奖”。

本届推选活动与“小康社会建设示范城市”评价活动同时进行，集中展示一批在全面建成小康社会进程中有突出贡献的幸福城市形象，推广全面建成小康社会的成就与经验。最终，南京、成都、西安、杭州、宁波、长春、长沙、上海、北京、苏州 10 座城市荣获“2015 中国小康社会建设示范奖”。成都同时荣获“2015 中国小康社会建设政府贡献奖”。

为了突出活动主题，组委会广泛吸取国内外专家学者意见，首次使用大数据采集的调查方式，特别制定了“中国城市幸福感、小康社会建设评价体系”，涵盖教育、医疗卫生、物价、生活环境、社会安全、公共服务、文化生活七大类共 42 个指标。在“世界城市日”发布“中国最具幸福感城市”系列榜单，推广幸福城市小康社会建设成就与经验，有利于进一步提升中国城市形象、打造中国城市世界影响力。

以下是“2015 中国最具幸福感城市”新闻发布会的部分发言稿。

城镇化是实现现代化的必由之路

探讨对中国幸福感城市的评价，必然离不开“中国梦”。习近平总书记指出，实现中华民族伟大复兴是中华民族近代以来最伟大的梦想。这个梦想凝聚了几代中国人的夙愿，体现了中华民族和中国人民的整体利益，是每一个中华儿女的共同期盼。而中国梦的首要目标就是全面建成小康社会。如果说城镇化建设是全面建成小康社会的强大引擎，那么，城市幸福感则是全面建成小康社会的终极目标。

经过多年的不懈努力，我国经济发展和综合国力显著提升，但作为最大的发展中国家的基本国情没有变。中国有 13 亿多人口，截至 2014 年年底，城镇化率还只是 54.77%，不仅远低于发达国家平均水平，也低于人均收入与我国相近的发展中国家的平均水平。

城镇化是实现现代化的必由之路。推进城镇化是解决农业、农村、农民问题的重要途径，是推动区域协调发展的有力支撑，是扩大内需和促进产业升级的重要抓手，是我国经济保持中高速增长、迈向中高端水平、全面建设小康社会的强大引擎，对全面建成小康社会、加快推进社会主义现代化具有重大现实意义和深远历史意义。

新型城镇化是以人为主的城镇化，是宜居宜业的城镇化。2013 年 12 月，中央城镇化工作会议召开，为我国新型城镇化指明了目标和方向。

按照我国的新型城镇化规划，到 2020 年，常住人口城镇化率要达到 60% 左右，户籍人口城镇化率达到 45% 左右，特别是将解决“三个 1 亿人”的问题。

科学规划是保证新型城镇化沿着正确轨道推进的基础。过去的超高速发展，以牺牲环境、突破规划为代价，而新型城镇化规划将着眼于“人”。“让城市融入大自然，让居民望得见山、看得见水、记得住乡愁”，2013 年中央城镇化工作会议上的这句话传达出新型城镇化建设有别于以往城镇化建设的人文情怀。以人为核心的新型城镇化建设，势必要强烈关照城市幸福感。

古希腊哲学家亚里士多德曾言：人们来到城市，是为了生活；人们居住在城市，是为了生活得更好。古代先贤的一句话道出了城市发展的终极目的——城市幸福感。城市幸福感包含了市民对所在城市的认同感、归属感、安定感、满足感，以及外界人群的向往度、赞誉度。这就要求我们在推进以人为核心的新型城镇化建设中，不能满足于速度和数量上的提升，必须从实际出发，实事求是确定城市定位，科学规划、务实行动，避免走弯路。在实施环节要体现尊重自然、顺应自然、天人合一的理念，依托现有山水脉络等独特风光，让城市融入大自然。在建设过程中，既要有现代元素，更要保护和弘扬传统优秀文化，延续城市历史文脉。在促进城乡一体化发展中，要注意保留村庄原始风貌，慎砍树、不填湖、少拆房，尽可能在原有村庄形态上改善居民生活条件，让居住其间的居民自然地、真正地完成由“村民”到“市民”的转变，最大限度地维护人民的尊严，保障人民的身份认同、情感归属、住所安定和人文满足。

在全面推进新型城镇化建设的进程中，城市首当其冲，当然发挥主力军的作用。而城市的市长们则更是关键的群体，责任重大。如何按照中央的大政方针，结合本地的实际，做好新型城镇化这篇大文章，这是摆在各位市长面前的课题，也是此次论坛的研讨主题。通过本次论坛的探讨和交流，大家可以分享各自城市的成就和经验，进一步增进了解和互信，进而开拓新的合作领域，携手推进中国新型城镇化建设和小康社会建设进程，进而对于增强人民幸福感、推动中国城市走向世界，具有积极的历史意义和现实意义。

作为中国最具幸福感城市调查推选活动主办方之一，中国市长协会自成立之初就致力于成为交流城市工作经验的纽带、开展城市合作的桥梁、研究城市问题的论坛和培训城市领导的基地。而作为一个已经连续举办了九届的活动，已成为各城市管理者间交流建设经验、开拓各领域合作、总结展示城市成就的平台。

（作者：齐骥，中国市长协会副会长）

以优质教育不断提升百姓幸福感

在2015年“中国最具幸福感城市”评选中，南京再次被评为“最具幸福感城市”，这也是南京第七次当选“最具幸福感城市”。这是南京市民、全国公众、主办单位及各位专家对南京经济社会发展成就的肯定。

“十二五”初始，创建“幸福都市”就成为南京全局工作的主旋律，并在全国副省级城市中率先建立了幸福都市考核评价指标体系。提高市民的幸福感，保障和改善民生是关键。南京在抓好经济社会发展和城市建设的同时，坚持从民生需求出发，不断优化制度设计，持续加大公共投入，努力让全市人民学有优教、病有良医、住有宜居，“幸福都市”正逐步成为南京的一张亮丽名片。

教育是人生的永恒主题，是城市文明的窗口，更是民族振兴的基石。教育关系个人幸福，也是重要的社会福祉。给孩子们提供“幸福的教育”，让百姓感受到“教育的幸福”，是南京打造幸福都市的重要内容。历史上的南京因崇文重教而闻名，享有“天下文枢”“东南第一学”的美誉。今天的南京是全国重要的科教中心城市，教育资源丰富，学科门类齐全，高学历人群众多，市民受教育程度较高，人民群众对教育的满意度逐年提高。这些年，南京市市委、市政府高度重视教育，以办好人民满意的教育为宗旨，以创建教育名城为目标，不断深化教育综合改革，全面推进教育现代化建设，努力提升教育优质均衡水平，教育正日益成为城市的软实力和竞争力，成为幸福南京的有力支撑。

一是统筹各类教育协调发展。全面启动0~3岁婴幼儿早期发展三年行动计划，重点实施学前教育“增量”“创优”“惠民”三项工程，以及学前一年基本免费教育制度，2011年以来全市新增省、市优质幼儿园130余所，新改造148个农村办园点。按照“学校分布均衡、服务半径适中、服务人口合理”的原则，结合城市发展规划，进一步优化整合幼儿园及中小学校布局结构，组织实施“校安工程”“农村学校提升工程”“薄弱学校改造工程”等一系列扶持项目。整合区域资源，以区为单位提升转型一批职业教育学校。突出地方特色，加强市属高校建设，金陵科技学院转型发展筹建南京软件科技大学，城市职业学院新校区开工建设。目前，南京已基本建立起较为完善的现代国民教育体系和终身教育体系，幼儿教育、基础教育、职业教育、成人教育、高等教育等各类教育齐头并进、协调发展，全市学前教育毛入园率、义务教育巩固率和高中阶段毛入学率分别达98.6%、100%和100%，新增劳动力人均受教育年限达15.5年，各类社会年培训达135万人次，从业人员继续教育年参与率达65%。南京教育基本实现了“四个都能够”：即全市适龄儿童少年都能够接受良好的学前教育和义务教育；完成义务教育的学生，都能够接受多种形式的高中阶段教育；具有深造意愿和学习能力的青少年都能够通过多种途径接受高等教育；广大市民都能够获得多层次继续教育的机会。多层次、多样化、开放式的教育培训，较好地满足了市民的各类教育和学习需求。

二是促进优质教育均衡发展。这是近些年南京教育发展的主导方向和政府部门的基本教育政策。我们通过“名校办分校”“名校办新校”“名校托管弱校”和“名校集团化”等方式推进“名校放大计划”。先后引入十多所品牌学校进驻全市四大保障房片区，在新区开发、旧城改造和新农村建设中配套优质教育资源。积极推动教师“区管校用”试点改革，建立校长与骨干教师交流轮岗制度。义务教育阶段全面实行免试就近入学政策、严格控制公办学校择校比例，中考招生扩大指标生招生数，取消高中招生“三限”政策，实行城乡一体化招生，打通城乡招生限制。通过率先实施免费义务教育、构建15年基础教育政府扶困助学体系、开展特殊少年儿童随班就读试点，确保城乡孩子、残障儿童和外来务工人员子女均享机会公平。这一系列的举措，使更多的孩子能够享受到优质的教育资源。

三是推动素质教育全面发展。实施高质量的素质教育，促进学生全面、个性化发展，是南京教育改革实践的重要经验。在南京，我们倡导学校多层次、多路径、多样化地实现理想目标，努力让不同禀赋、不同个性的学生在一个宽容博大、复杂多样的教育生态中，发现自己的特质，舒展自己的个性，提高自己的本领，最大程度满足社会多样化的人才需求、家庭多样化的教育需求、学生多样化的人生追求。通过把素质教育贯穿于各级各类教育各个环节，贯穿于学校教育、家庭教育和社会教育各个方面，贯穿于青少年成长的全过程，南京教育正努力实现从“全面普及、全面合格”走向“全面优质、全面满足”，从“相对单一的教育供给”到“为学生提供丰富多彩的教育服务”两个转变。目前，南京已基本建立起普教职教双轮驱动、国际国内互通共生、本色特色相辅相成的人才成长的“立交桥”。越来越多的南京学生有更多的机会、更宽松的环境去实现自己的理想和抱负，选择成才的路径和环境。

四是抓好终身教育持续发展。“完善终身教育体系，建设学习型社会”，建设“人人皆学，处处能学，时时可学”的学习型社会，是南京促进教育公平、满足人民群众多样化教育需求，提高全民整体素质、提升城市文明水平的重要任务。近年来，南京着眼于实现人的全面发展，全面实施教育优先、人才优先发展战略，着力提升教育信息化水平、构筑全民终身学习平台，建立完善了开放大学办学体系，开展“名师公益大讲堂”“学分银行”等系列活动，不断增强市民的学习力、创造力和发展力，努力打造“氛围浓厚、人才荟萃、充满活力、富有品位”的学习型城市。

人才决定城市发展，教育点亮城市希望。南京将继续努力，为更多的老百姓提供优质的教育机会、优越的学习条件，为建设“强、富、美、高”的新南京提供坚强的人才支撑、广泛的智力支持和不竭的创新源泉。这是政府部门的重要责任，也是教育工作者的根本追求。

（作者：胡万进，南京市副市长）

提升城乡品质　增进民生福祉

宁波2015年第七次入选“中国最具幸福感城市”，是对宁波最好的激励和鞭策；这里要特别感谢全体宁波人民一直以来对幸福家园的认同和维护，这一荣誉属于生活和创业在宁波的每一位市民，是全体宁波人共同创造了宁波的美丽和幸福。

习近平总书记说，人民对美好生活的向往，就是我们的奋斗目标。城市发展的最终目的，就是要让每一个市民享有更加美好、更有品质、更有尊严的生活。近年来，宁波按照“保基本、抓重点、促均衡、提质量”的思路，大力提高优质公共服务供给能力，积极推进社会保障提标扩面工作，有效推动了改革发展成果更加公平地惠及全体市民。在物质保障方面，2014年宁波66.3%的公共财政用于民生支出，城镇居民人均可支配收入达44 155元，农村居民人均可支配收入达24 283元，连续多年均居全国各大城市前列。在促进就业方面，不断深化国家创业型城市和充分就业县（市）区创建，2014年高校毕业生初次就业率达到95%，城镇登记失业率下降到1.95%，基本实现了劳动者的充分就业。在社会保障体系建设方面，扎实推进被征地人员养老保障、低标准养老保险与基本养老保险制度转换衔接，建立了覆盖城乡居民和所有外来务工人员的社会保障体系。2014年，全市农村五保对象集中供养率为98.3%，城镇“三无”对象集中供养率为99.6%，基本实现老有所依、老有所养。在教育公平方面，据教育部研究报告显示，2014年宁波教育公平指数在全国15个副省级城市中位列第一，11个县（市）区全部通过全国义务教育发展基本均衡评估认定。在社会治理体系方面，我们将社会安全稳定视为底线民生和市民幸福感的重要评价标准，不断深化平安宁波建设，完善矛盾纠纷排查化解机制，人民群众的安全感和基层社会自我服务与治理的能力进一步提升。在城市文明建设方面，宁波再次荣获“全国文明城市”称号，成为全省唯一、全国六个“四连冠”城市之一。

城市发展无止境，幸福追求无极限。我们将以获得“2015中国最具幸福感城市”这一荣誉为新的起点，和1 000万新老宁波人一道，在建设现代化国际港口城市、跻身全国大城市第一方队的征途上砥砺前行，让幸福永驻宁波！我们将进一步加快经济转型发展，大力促进“港口经济圈”与“互联网+”、与高新技术、与城市经济的深度融合，不断增强城市的综合实力和核心竞争力，夯实市民生活品质提升的物质基础和保障；我们将进一步推动社会包容性发展，让宁波人民拥有更加稳定的就业、更加可靠的保障、更加完善的医疗、更加公平的教育、更加优良的环境，推动改革发展成果更加公平地惠及全体市民；我们将进一步提升城乡品质，大力实施“提升城乡品质、建设美丽宁波”三年行动计划，努力把宁波打造成宜居、宜业、宜商、宜游之城，为广大市民建设一个生态优良、环境优质、形象优秀、品质优越的幸福家园；我们将进一步深化文明城市创建，大力弘扬“爱心宁波·尚德甬城”良好风尚，努力推进全域化高水平文明之城建设，使尊道德、讲文明、重礼仪、守秩序成为宁波最美风景。我们相信，只要我们一如既往地顺民意、解民忧、纾民困、促民生，一定会让宁波人民生活得更加幸福、更有尊严。

（作者：万亚伟，中共宁波市市委常委、宣传部部长）

《2015 中国城市幸福感调查报告》的作用

由新华社《瞭望东方周刊》联合中国市长协会《中国城市发展报告》共同主办的“中国最具幸福感城市”调查推选活动，迄今已连续举办 9 年。

这 9 年的时间里，我们坚定不移地调查幸福，坚定不移地寻求城市生活如何更美好的幸福之路。9 年的成长和磨炼，9 年的坚守和承诺，我们的经验越来越丰厚，我们的调查方式越来越丰富，我们的评价体系越来越完善，我们的调查结果越来越厚实。可以说，这项调查活动已成为我国最具影响力和公信力的城市调查品牌活动。

作为这项活动的发起者和主持者，我目睹了她从无到有、从小到大、由大到强、由强到盛的整个历程。我认为，一个能够生存并且连续成功举办 9 年的活动，她的内涵和外延一定是丰富的，她的调查内容一定是顺应时代需要的，她的形式一定是吸引人的，她的结果和影响一定是具有指导意义的。

9 年来，“中国最具幸福感城市调查推选”活动的主题顺应时代，紧随党和政府的步伐，积极宣传和推广不同时期和形势下的中国特色社会主义建设成就与经验，不仅起到了主流媒体应有的舆论导向作用，更重要的是，每年的调查活动为城市管理者在城市民生建设方面起到了示范、指导等智库的作用。

2015 年的主题是“小康社会・幸福中国”。“小康社会建设”是 2015 年调查活动的一大特色。大家知道，2015 年是我国全面建设小康社会的第 15 个年头，为贯彻落实党的十八届三中全会精神，全面推进小康社会建设，集中展示中国城市在小康社会建设过程中的成就与经验，我们新增了小康社会建设成果的评价内容和“小康社会建设评价体系”。该体系涵盖了教育、医疗卫生、物价、生活环境、社会安全、公共服务、文化生活等七大类共 42 个指标。

我们为此新设立了“小康社会建设示范城市”奖项。其目的就是力图集中展示一批在全面建设小康社会过程中有突出贡献的幸福城市，推广城市在小康社会建设中的成就和经验，为如期实现全面建成小康社会的目标提供现实的参考样本。这是区别于往年活动的第一大特色。

2015 年活动的第二大特色，是大数据的运用。大家都知道，近年来，大数据如浪潮般席卷全球，深度改变着人们的生活、工作和思维方式。越来越多的国家开始从战略层面认识大数据，并在城市治理领域融入大数据思维和技术，我国也不例外。2015 年 7 月 1 日，国务院办公厅发布了《关于运用大数据加强对市场主体服务和监管的若干意见》。《意见》中明确提出，提高政府运用大数据的能力，推动政府向社会力量购买大数据资源和技术服务。由此看出，第三方向政府提供的大数据资源和技术服务，将成为社会发展的主潮流。而像新华社这样的主流媒体作为第三方，其公信力和强大资源整合能力势必成为地方政府大数据服务产品的重要来源。

为此，2015 年活动组委会与国内知名门户网站、消费类电商合作，在其数据库中采集与幸福感有关的行为数据，并对此进行专项分析，以便能及时、准确地反映城市发展现状，为城市经济、社会发展提供决策依据，进而促进政府提供更加智能、更加高效的管理和服务，促进城市全面发展。

此次调查活动采用公共调查、抽样调查、大数据采集和材料申报四种方式进行，其中公共调查包含网络调查和微信公众号调查。调查时间为 2015 年 8 月 1 日至 9 月 30 日。其中，2015 年 8 月 1 日至 8 月 30 日为公共调查时间；2015 年 9 月 1 日至 9 月 30 日对公共调查排名前 20 位的城市进行抽样调查和大数据采集。调查对象是中国社会科学院发布的“2014 中国城市综合竞争力百强城市”。

中国最具幸福感城市的评价体系由瞭望东方周刊中国城市评价中心完成。该评价体系分为 22 项主观调查指标和 10 项大数据采集体系，其中主观调查包含了住房现状、物价（含房价）、交通状况、气候、医疗便利程度和质量、环境和污染程度、治安、养老、人情味、餐饮娱乐和文化体育设施、生活节奏、文明程度、执法规范程度、公共服务水平、文化底蕴、购物便利性、赚钱机会、市民个人发展空间、城市发展质量与速度、教育、对外来人的包容度和旅游度假 22 项考核指标；大数据采集体系包含了居民收入、生活品质、城市向往、旅游向往、就业、生态环境、治安、诉讼咨询、交通和教育 10 个大项 51 个小项。

小康社会评价标准依照十六大提出的全面建设小康社会的基本标准。

本次调查中，公共调查回收问卷约8 211万份，其中，有效问卷约7 940万份；抽样调查在 20 个城市发放问卷约 45.4 万份，回收有效问卷约 41.7 万份；大数据采集有效样本数量约 539.7 万份。

本次调查的一些亮点、变化及新发现是：

第一是调查人群的新变化。首先是年轻人增多，被调查者中，25～35 岁的年轻人达 37%；其次，高学历人群增加，这次调查对象中，本科及以上学历的人数占到 83%，调查人群呈现低龄化、高学历化趋势。这说明我们的活动经过 9 年的发展，已经吸引更多的年轻人、高学历人的高度关注，活动在这部分人群中的知名度、关注度大幅提升。

第二是关注内容的变化。和往年相比，2015 年在医疗、治安、养老、教育、就业等民生问题上收获了更高的关注度，这反映了当前形势下社会关注点的新变化、新需求。以医疗满意度为例，2015 年已进入医改的第 6 个年头，5 年的医改历程取得了一定的成效，比如，建立全民覆盖的医保网络，逐步健全基层医疗卫生体系和公共卫生服务体系，以及全面推开的基本药物制度等。2015 年也是全面深化公立医院改革的一年。这一年，100 个地级以上城市推行了公立医院综合改革试点。我们的调查发现，在这个大环境下，城市居民对这些医改新政的感知度比以往更强烈。

第三是城市关注布局的新变化。调查显示，珠三角地区、长三角地区、京津地区等发达地区大型城市的人们对幸福城市的感受度更高，这是此次调查的一个新发现。例如，北京和上海两个城市除物价、交通、生活节奏等指标外，其他指标均排在前列，尤其是在教育、医疗、赚钱机会、公共服务水平等多个指标上均位列前三名，这从一定程度上反映了人们对大城市的向往。

第四是人们对政府公共服务水平的关注度上升。改善公共服务是21世纪公共行政和政府改革的核心理念，也是我国建设服务型政府的主要内容，公共服务直接关系民生幸福。此次调查发现，人们比以往更关注政府公共服务水平。

在中国最具幸福感城市调查活动持续开展的9年历程中，我们很高兴地发现，城市管理者已经意识到经济发展和居民幸福协调发展的重要性。他们对居民幸福感的关注度日益上升，其视角已从单纯追求城市的经济功能转向城市居民的幸福感受度。我们知道，除了市民对所在城市的认同感、归属感、安定感、满足感等，经济发展、社会保障、生活质量也是城市幸福感不可缺少的重要组成。

我们同样意识到，再翔实的调查也不能完全准确描述出对一个城市幸福感的全部含义。但是，我们希望，通过对评价体系、调查手段等孜孜不倦地完善，我们将一步步地靠近理想目标。这是我们坚持9年的动力所在，也是我们脚踏实地的工作指南。

（作者：赵悦，新华社《瞭望东方周刊》常务副总编辑，中国最具幸福感城市调查活动组委会执行主任）

中国城市服务业发展的形势、特点与展望

一、我国服务业发展形势

城市的基本功能是服务，发达国家服务经济已成为城市经济的主体。伴随着我国新型城镇化的推进，服务业在促进城市经济发展、提升城市功能、拓展城市空间、提高城市竞争力等方面发挥着越来越重要的作用，成为新常态下城市经济转型升级的重要引擎。2015 年中国服务业增加值比重达 50.5%。服务业在“稳增长”“促就业”和“扩出口”方面作用突出，已成为支撑中国经济持续健康发展的重要力量。《中华人民共和国国民经济和社会发展第十三个五年规划纲要》提出，要加快推动服务业优质高效发展。开展加快发展现代服务业行动，扩大服务业对外开放，优化服务业发展环境，推动生产性服务业向专业化和价值链高端延伸、生活性服务业向精细化和高品质转变。促进生产性服务业专业化，提高生活性服务业品质，完善服务业发展体制和政策。当前，我国服务业的总体发展形势可归纳为以下五点：

（一）服务业成为新常态下稳增长的新动力

2015 年中国 GDP 达到 67.67 万亿元，经济增长速度为 6.9%。其中，服务业增加值实现 34.16 万亿元，增长 8.3%。得益于金融业、房地产业和新兴服务业的强劲拉动，服务业增加值比重为 50.5%，首次突破 50%。特别是基于大数据、云计算、物联网的服务应用日益活跃，电子商务平台服务、信息技术咨询服务快速发展，2015 年软件和信息技术服务业务收入突破 4 万亿元，同比增长 16.6%，实物商品网上零售额同比增长 31.6%。服务业的贡献率以及对 GDP 的拉动作用日趋明显，成为新常态中国经济发展保持适度增速和迈向中高端水平的新动力。

（二）服务业促就业能力进一步增强

当前，服务业已成为全社会吸纳就业最多的部门。2015 年，我国经济增速下降 0.5 个百分点，但城镇新增就业人数仍达到1 312万人，全面完成全年预期目标，“稳增长”和“保就业”取得“双赢”。其中，服务业就业弹性大，劳动密集、技术密集和知识密集并存。国

家工商总局数据显示，商事制度改革两年来，新增企业中服务业企业占比约80%，2015年年底服务业实有企业占企业总数的74.8%，吸纳就业作用突出。

（三）服务业固定资产投资比重高于工业，信息服务业投资增速最快

2015年服务业固定资产投资311 939亿元，增长10.6%。在服务业各行业中，信息传输、软件和信息技术服务业、批发和零售业、租赁和商务服务业、交通运输仓储和邮政业、科学研究和技术服务业增速最快，分别达34.5%、20.1%、18.6%、14.3%、12.6%。而住宿餐饮业、房地产业、金融业增速变缓，仅为5.1%、2.5%、0.3%。

（四）服务贸易发展加快，成为对外贸易的生力军

在国际市场需求疲软困扰我国制造业发展的同时，服务业在对外贸易方面依然保持强劲势头。2015年我国实现服务贸易进出口7 130亿美元，比上年增长14.6%。其中，服务出口2 882亿美元，增长9.2%；服务进口4 248亿美元，增长18.6%。服务贸易占全球比重和中国外贸比重实现了“双提升”。全年服务业实际使用外资增长17.3%，占全国实际使用外资的比重达到61.1%，融资租赁、科技研发、电子商务等现代服务业向自由贸易试验区集聚态势明显。“走出去”步伐明显加快，2015年服务业对外投资存量首次超过万亿美元大关，已成为服务业领域的净资本输出国。

（五）城市服务业规模不断扩大，效率进一步提高

城市服务业规模不断扩大。2010年，城市服务业增加值为17.6万亿元，2013年达到26.6万亿元，年均增速高达到10.6%。城市服务业吸纳就业能力进一步提升，单位就业规模由2010年的6 449.83万人增至8 653.20万人，平均每年吸纳就业人口超过734.4万人。其中，生产性服务业吸纳就业规模由1 689.45万人增加至2 429.18万人，生活性服务业吸纳就业规模由1 359.49万人增至1 979.9万人。服务业效益进一步提高，城市服务业劳动生产率由2010年的27.3万元/人增加至2013年的30.74万元/人。服务业对经济增长的贡献率，由2010年的39.2%提升到2013年的47.6%。

二、城市服务业发展的主要特点

2013年，全国35个直辖市、省会城市、计划单列市（拉萨数据不全）中，服务业就业人数3 971.1万人，占地级及以上城市的46.4%。结构方面，这些城市服务业增加值占GDP比重为50.69%，高于地级及以上城市平均的36.35%；生产性服务业就业比重为35.0%，远高于地级及以上城市的23.1%。服务业效益方面，人均服务业增加值5.26万元，高于地级及以上城市平均水平的2.06万元；劳动生产率35.14万元/人，高于地级及以上城市的30.74万元/人。鉴于这35个城市服务业发展具有较强的代表性和典型性，同时它们又是服务业提质增效的引领者，本文着重分析这些城市服务业发展的主要特征。

(一) 服务业发展水平空间差异较大

借鉴已有研究成果，遵循系统性、科学性并考虑数据的可获得性，以《中国城市统计年鉴（2015)》数据为基础，从服务业规模（包括服务业增加值、服务业从业人员)、服务业结构（包括服务业增加值占GDP比重、服务业从业人员比重、生产性服务业从业人员比重)、服务业效益（包括人均服务业增加值、服务密度[①]、服务业对城市经济增长贡献率）三个方面构建服务业发展水平评价指标体系，并用熵值法AHP进行综合得分和各子指标测算。将2013年的综合得分用SPSS软件的K值聚类，分成服务业高水平、较高水平、中等水平3类。

在全国35个直辖市、省会城市和计划单列市中，服务业高水平的城市有4个，依次为北京、上海、深圳、广州。这些城市服务业规模大、结构优、效益高。在规模方面，服务业增加值北京1.83万亿元、上海1.69万亿元、广州1.20万亿元、深圳1.03万亿元，均超万亿元大关。在结构方面，北京服务业增加值比重达80%，上海67.8%、广州66.77%、深圳58.8%，率先步入服务经济主导的发展阶段。在效益方面，深圳领先于北京、上海、广州。其中，北京围绕政治中心、文化中心、国际交往中心和科技创新的定位，瞄准科技、互联网和信息、文化教育、金融、商务和旅游、健康医疗六大重点服务领域，持续推动产业结构向高端化、服务化、集聚化方向转型，产业服务化特征更加明显，生产性服务业增加值占地区生产总值的比重已达50%以上；上海围绕国际经济中心、国际金融中心、国际航运中心、国际贸易中心定位，以及自贸区建设、全球科技创新中心建设，金融服务、信息服务以及服务业国际化保持较快的发展势头，2015年实现金融业增加值4 052.23亿元，比上年增长22.9%，金融业成为领跑行业。

服务业较高水平的城市有17个，依次是天津、重庆、成都、杭州、南京、青岛、武汉、宁波、大连、哈尔滨、呼和浩特、济南、长沙、沈阳、厦门、西安、福州。上述城市中，服务业规模、结构、效益水平介于高水平和中等水平之间。各城市间又有所差异，如重庆、成都等服务业规模较大，2015年重庆、成都服务业增加值分别为7 497.75亿元、5 704.5亿元，均达到5 000亿元以上，但服务业效益不高；呼和浩特、厦门等服务业规模相对不大，2015年服务业增加值分别为2 098亿元、1933.1亿元，但结构较优，服务业增加值比重分别达67.9%、55.8%，效益较高；西安服务业结构较优，2015年服务业增加值比重58.9%，但规模相对不大，服务业增加值3427亿元，效益一般。

服务业中等水平的城市有14个，依次是郑州、贵阳、石家庄、乌鲁木齐、太原、昆明、合肥、长春、南昌、海口、南宁、兰州、西宁、银川。这些城市服务业规模较小、结构不够合理、效益较低，但各城市之间也存在差异。例如，服务业效益方面，郑州、贵阳、石家庄、乌鲁木齐、太原等城市甚至高于服务业较高发展水平的成都、重庆；在结构方面，2015年海口、乌鲁木齐服务业增加值比重达75.7%、69.4%；在服务业规模方面，差距较大，

---

① 服务业密度为市辖区服务业增加值/市辖区面积。

如2015年海口服务业增加值879.49亿元，西宁550.1亿元，银川635.2亿元，均小于1 000亿元，继续做大服务业规模，是未来提升服务业综合水平的关键。

从空间分布来看，服务业高水平的城市集中分布在东部沿海地区，中西部没有服务业高水平的城市，今后应重点在中西部地区培育服务业高水平的城市，成为增长极，带动中西部地区服务业的发展。

（二）生产性服务业专业化程度较高，且地域分工明显

从行业来看，科研、技术服务和地质勘查业，文化、体育和娱乐业，交通运输、仓储及邮政业，信息传输、计算机服务和软件业，平均区位熵大于1.3，专业化最强。这些行业以生产性服务业为主，随着制造服务化，城市产业结构从二产向三产演进，这些高端生产性服务业在大都市区率先崛起，承担区域的专业化职能部门。其次是房地产业、居民服务和其他服务业、住宿和餐饮业、租赁和商务服务业、批发零售业，平均区位熵在1.2～1.3之间，专业化较强，这些行业以生活性服务业为主。金融业专业化较弱，平均区位熵仅有1.1。金融业是国家垂直管理的特殊行业，其网点的设置与行政管理系统有较高的一致性，专业化程度低于其他行业。

从2010年到2013年演变来看，专业化水平提高的行业是信息传输、计算机服务和软件业、科研、技术服务和地质勘查业、金融业。居民服务和其他服务业、批发零售业、文化、体育和娱乐业专业化相对稳定。住宿、餐饮业，交通运输、仓储及邮政业，租赁和商务服务业专业化水平有所弱化，呈均衡化发展趋势。

（三）生产性服务业外向服务功能较强，且高度集中在北上广深

生产性服务业外向服务功能较强。在全国35个直辖市、省会城市和计划单列市中的生产性服务业外向服务功能量552.4万人，占服务业外向服务功能量64.6%。生产性服务业外向服务功能量较大的行业为：交通运输、仓储及邮政业150.8万人，信息传输、计算机服务和软件业132.7万人，租赁和商务服务业122.8万人，科研、技术服务和地质勘查业99.1万人，而金融业仅有47万人。生活性服务业外向服务功能量290.9万人，占服务业外向服务功能量的35.4%。生活性服务业外向服务功能量较大的行业是批发和零售业100.8万人，房地产82.8万人，较小的行业是住宿、餐饮业59.4万人，文化、体育和娱乐业27.6万人，居民服务和其他服务业20.9万人。

外向服务分异明显。其中，生产性服务业为主的城市达22个①，包括宁波、南昌、青岛、西宁、乌鲁木齐、哈尔滨、沈阳、上海、西安、石家庄、银川、南宁、长春、大连、呼和浩特、福州、兰州、北京、深圳、太原、南京、广州；生活性服务业为主的城市有8个，包括海口、厦门、天津、武汉、郑州、合肥、成都、贵阳；生产性和生活性服务业并重的城

---

① 以生产性服务业外向功能流量比重大于60%作为生产性服务业主导类型，生活性服务业外向功能流量比重大于60%作为生活性服务业主导类型，介于两者之间的为生产性和生活性服务业并重类型。

市有5个，包括杭州、济南、长沙、重庆、昆明。

外向服务功能高度集中在北上广深。2013年，上述35个城市外向服务功能量843.3万人，占地级以上城市外向服务功能量的85.5%。北京、上海、广州、深圳服务业外向服务功能量达到527.6万人，占35个城市的62.6%。其中，北京和上海外向功能最强，北京占35个城市服务业外向服务功能量的31.6%，上海占17.1%，两者占比接近50%。这4个城市外向服务功能量较大的行业为交通运输、仓储及邮政业，信息传输、计算机服务和软件业，租赁和商务服务业，金融业，批发和零售业，房地产业。

（四）服务业新兴业态不断涌现，已成为区域中心城市服务业发展的重点行业

随着第一、第二、第三产业融合发展，物联网、云计算、大数据、移动互联网、人工智能等新一代信息技术的升级发展，促进互联网加速向各行业渗透，绿色发展方式的兴起，居民对生活质量更高的追求，服务业新业态、新模式、新产业不断涌现。生产性服务业向高端化发展，电子商务、互联网金融、大数据、信息技术咨询、节能环保等服务持续快速发展。生活性服务业方面，更加追求个性化和呈多样化，拓展了文化创意、旅游、休闲养老、远程医疗、远程教育、数字穿戴、数字家庭、智慧社区、智慧城市等与人民生活息息相关的服务新模式，拓展了消费新渠道。

从城市层面的新型业态来看，北京重点发展科学技术服务、互联网和信息服务、文化教育服务、金融服务、商务和旅游服务、健康医疗服务。广州发展方向为健康服务业、互联网金融服务业、产业设计服务业、软件和信息技术服务业、现代物流服务业、电子商务服务业、检验检测服务业、节能环保服务业、融资租赁服务业。西安则以科技服务业为核心，逐步形成科技服务产业集群，建立带动全省、辐射西部的科技服务产业体系。长春市重点培育金融服务业、信息（科技）服务业、文化创意产业、现代物流业、现代商贸服务业、旅游会展业和健康养老等重点行业。长沙市积极发展文化创意、现代物流、电子商务、信息消费、旅游休闲、现代金融业、科技服务、商贸商务、健康服务、养老服务等现代服务业。济南加快发展信息服务、商贸物流、金融服务、文化旅游、商务会展服务业。兰州重点扶持电子商务产业、会展经济、现代物流、文化旅游、科技服务、金融业等服务业新兴业态。

三、城市服务业发展展望

（一）深入推进服务业重点领域的改革开放

服务业领域改革开放进一步深化。近年来，国家出台了多个推动服务业发展和改革相关的文件。2014年8月出台《国务院关于加快发展生产性服务业　促进产业结构调整升级的指导意见》，重点发展研发设计、第三方物流、融资租赁、信息技术服务、节能环保服务、检验检测认证、电子商务、商务咨询、服务外包、售后服务、人力资源服务和品牌建设。2014年8月国务院正式发布《关于促进旅游业改革发展的若干意见》，提出拓展旅游发展空

间，切实落实职工带薪休假制度，旅游业制度红利集中释放。2015 年 2 月出台《关于鼓励民间资本参与养老服务业发展的实施意见》，为养老提供了金融支持，提高养老服务的供给。商务部办公厅 2015 年 4 月印发《电子商务工作要点》通知，要求积极促进城市社区电子商务应用，促进农产品流通和农村电子商务应用，推进服务业应用电子商务创新发展，支持养老家政、健康服务、信息服务、旅游休闲等生活服务业应用电子商务开拓市场，通过线上线下互动结合，满足和带动多样化、个性化的居民服务消费需求。国务院 2015 年 7 月出台《关于积极推进“互联网 +”行动的指导意见》，要求推进信息服务业与其他行业的融合，加大信息资源开发和共享。2015 年 9 月，国务院印发《促进大数据发展行动纲要》，加快政府数据开放共享，推动资源整合，提升治理能力。2015 年 11 月国务院办公厅出台《关于加快发展生活性服务业，促进消费结构升级的指导意见》，要求坚持创新供给，推动新型消费。推动生活消费方式由生存型、传统型、物质型向发展型、现代型、服务型转变，大力发展居民和家庭服务、养老服务、旅游服务、体育服务、文化服务。2015 年 12 月，国际货币基金组织正式宣布人民币加入 SDR，确立了人民币在世界上可以广泛使用的地位；同月，由中国倡议成立的多边金融机构亚洲基础设施投资银行成立，人民币国际化稳步推进。这些文件、意见、政策措施，在市场化、对外开放、新技术应用、产业融合、金融财税、产品结构性等方面实施多项改革，提供多项政策红利，为服务业发展创造良好环境，最大限度地激发企业和市场活力。

（二）生产性服务业向高端化、国际化、专业化方向发展

目前，城市服务业水平的提高主要得益于服务业规模扩大和服务业效益提升，服务业结构优化的贡献较小。发达国家的产业结构中有两个 70% 的现象，即：服务业占 GDP 的 70%，生产性服务业占服务业的 70%。近年来我国服务业整体发展较快，但服务业的比重和生产性服务业占服务业比重依然远低于发达国家水平。生产性服务业竞争力不强，规模偏小、供给水平偏低、产品同质化严重，难以满足制造业高层次需求。未来应积极推动服务业与制造业跨界融合、服务业各部门之间融合，全产业链整合优化，加快构建以现代物流、信息服务、科技服务、金融服务为主的现代服务体系，提高城市生产性服务业高端化、国际化、专业化水平。

（三）生活性服务业向多样化、个性化、品质化方向发展

生活性服务业更加多样化、个性化。基于移动互联网技术的广泛应用，积极运用云计算、物联网、大数据等新一代信息技术，改进服务流程、创新服务方式、精细服务环节，优化服务供给，增加短缺服务。生活性服务业向多样化、个性化的供给改革，如在线旅游、互联网支付、网购、在线教育等。在具体行业上，如国务院在 2014 年 10 月 20 日印发《关于加快发展体育产业 促进体育消费的若干意见》中提出，到 2025 年基本建立布局合理、功能完善、门类齐全的体育产业体系，体育产品和服务更加丰富。高中低不同收入群体、文化、年龄等方面差异客观存在，针对不同人群的服务产品也相应出现和完善，服务产品更加

精细。

生活性服务业品质化发展。一方面，生活性服务业随着居民需求的上升存在明显的供不应求的局面，在教育、医疗、金融、旅游等领域，不能满足消费者需求，大批消费者源源不断到国外消费，这与国内服务业的供给乏力有关。生活性服务业供给侧结构改革已经成为重点发展方向，特别是那些刺激需求作用有限或者有效供给明显不足的领域，包括医疗、家政、养老、教育、旅游、餐饮等生活服务方面。另一方面，随着服务业市场化、法律制度建设的加强，服务业标准的逐步建立，住宿、餐饮、旅游、零售、居民服务等行业服务质量逐步实现标准化，企业和社会公众的标准化意识加强，促进企业规范运营，提高服务品质化发展。北京市 2015 年 7 月出台《提高生活性服务业品质行动计划》，重点实施品牌建设工程、营商环境建设工程、人才培养与岗位技能培训工程等三项重点工程建设。

（四）服务业综合试点将带动城市服务业的创新与升级

服务业综合改革试点。由财政部、商务部、发展改革委、科技部四部委联合启动，以上海、天津、北京、辽宁、重庆、长沙、深圳等城市为试点，要求在完善体制机制和政策环境、创新服务业发展模式等方面进行积极的探索，破解制约服务业发展的瓶颈，加强试点城市对区域服务业发展的辐射带动作用。

服务业区域合作（开放）的试点。2015 年 5 月国务院批复《关于北京市服务业扩大开放综合试点总体方案》，注重制度创新，以促进国际国内要素有序自由流动、资源高效配置、市场深度融合为目的，建立健全服务业扩大开放的体制机制，率先推动科学技术服务、互联网和信息服务、文化教育服务、金融服务、商务和旅游服务、健康医疗服务等六大重点领域扩大开放，同时深化对外投资管理体制改革，带动服务业整体转型升级。2013 年 9 月批复《中国（上海）自由贸易试验区总体方案》，要求发挥上海在服务业领域先行先试的作用，重点是加快服务业开放，推进贸易发展方式转变，深化金融领域的开放创新。2013 年 6 月《海峡两岸服务贸易协议》等文件的出台，要求加强与香港、澳门、台湾地区的服务业合作，加快推进深圳前海、珠海横琴、广州南沙与港澳地区，福建厦门、平潭和江苏昆山与台湾地区的服务业合作试点。

部分服务行业试点。例如，在批发零售业方面，东莞市、义乌市、泉州市等 30 个城市创建国家电子商务示范城市；在金融业方面，上海加强自贸区金融创新试点建设，加快推进资本项目可兑换、人民币跨境使用、金融服务业开放和建设面向国际的金融市场，不断完善金融监管；在信息服务业方面，工业和信息化部启动了国家信息消费试点示范市（区、县）创建工作，2013 年 12 月遴选出首批 68 个国家信息消费试点市（县、区），重点建设宽带和 TD-LTE（4G）等信息基础设施，信息消费试点活动将按照“先试点、后示范”的原则逐步有序展开；在养老服务业方面，2014 年民政部、发展改革委确定温州等全国 42 个地区作为全国首批养老服务业综合改革试点城市，重点围绕健全养老服务体系、引导社会力量参与养老服务、完善养老服务发展政策、强化城市养老服务设施布局、创新养老服务供给方式、培育养老服务产业集群、加强养老服务队伍建设、强化养老服务市场监管开展工作。

（五）服务业正在形成层次有序、错位发展、优势互补的格局

城市服务业发展在空间上很不平衡。东部地区既是我国经济总量最大的地区，也是我国城市服务业增加值总量最大的地区。根据城市服务业发展水平的差异，结合城市发展的功能定位以及比较优势，应促进不同城市、不同区域形成服务业发展层次有序、分工错位、优势互补的格局。

北京、上海、广州、深圳等城市应着力发展金融服务、现代物流、科技服务、信息服务、商务服务等引领未来经济发展的高技术含量、高附加值服务业，强化其国际服务和创新引领功能，形成具有全球影响力和竞争力的增长点及核心节点。天津、重庆、成都、杭州、南京、武汉、济南、西安等服务业较高发展水平的城市应大力推动高新技术产业、先进制造业与金融、物流等生产性服务业的融合发展，促进服务业的分工协作和集聚发展，扩大服务业规模、优化服务业结构、提高服务业效益，形成各具特色的区域性服务中心，成为带动城市群经济发展的重要节点。郑州、贵阳、石家庄、乌鲁木齐、昆明、南宁、兰州等服务业中等发展水平的城市亟须加强经济要素的集聚，优化服务业发展环境，着力发展商贸、物流、文化旅游、科技信息等服务业，加快服务业集聚区和特色功能区建设，形成地区性服务中心。

（作者：申玉铭，首都师范大学资源环境与旅游学院副院长，教授、博士生导师）

参考文献

［1］夏杰长，姚战琪，刘奕等．中国服务业发展报告 2015［M］．北京：经济管理出版社，2015.

［2］申玉铭，柳坤，邱灵．中国城市群核心城市服务业发展的基本特征［J］．地理科学进展，2015，34（8）：957－965.

［3］曾春水，申玉铭．中国城市服务业职能特征研究［J］．地理研究，2015，34（9）：1685－1696.

［4］王海江，苗长虹．我国中心城市对外服务能力的空间格局［J］．地理研究，2009，28（4）：957－967.

［5］许峰，周一星．我国城市职能结构变化和动态特征及趋势．城市发展研究，2008，15（6）：49－55.

观察篇

2015 年中国市长协会舆情观察

一、舆情综述

2015 年，谷尼舆情大数据平台共监测到约 3 亿条相关信息，主要分布在招商旅游、教育、环保、改革、安全维稳、反腐等领域（图 1）。

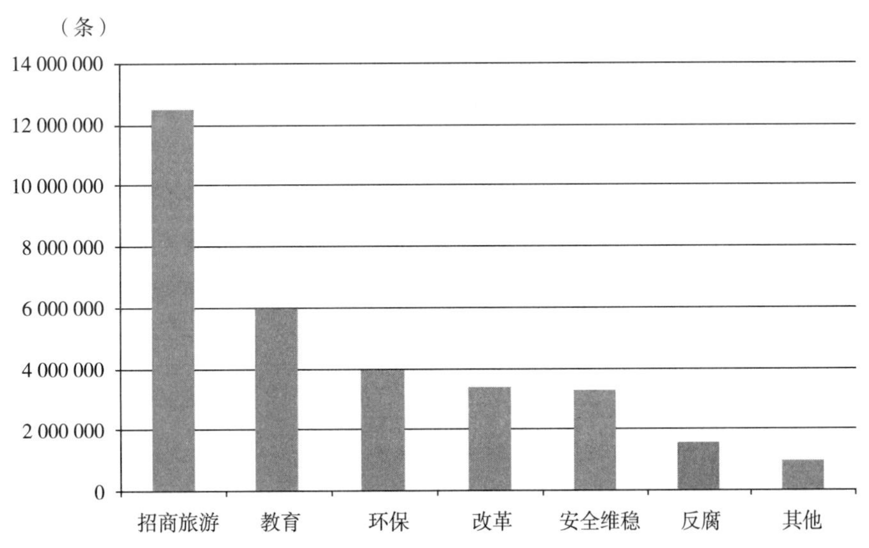

图 1　2015 年谷尼舆情大数据平台监测信息的主要分布领域

“招商旅游”“教育”“环保”等得到最高关注度（图 2）。其中，因国人对旅游的热情越来越高，致使招商旅游话题最高，占比为 39%；教育话题占比 19%，跃居第二位；环保类话题占 13%，因为人们对环境污染的问题，关注度一直较高。

2015 年，关于市长的新闻稿件有 642 500 篇，从媒体关注度舆情趋势图中看，12 月份关注度最高（图 3）。发布新闻量占比较高的是中国日报网（36.25%）、网易网（16.6%）、人民网（8.24%）等媒体。值得关注的事件有：网络媒体“青岛传媒网”发布的《东莞市长袁宝成回应“倒闭潮”：中小企业面临经营压力大》（转载 390 次）；新浪微博“新浪财经”发布的《重庆市长黄奇帆提议将建筑物中的钢材使用量提高两倍》（转载量5 696次，

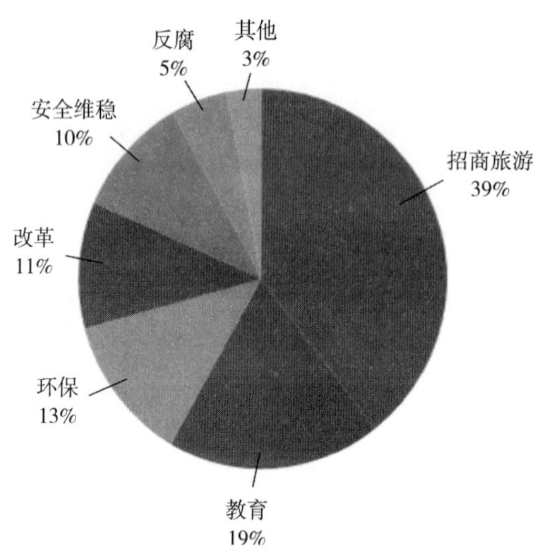

图2　2015年谷尼舆情的关注度分布

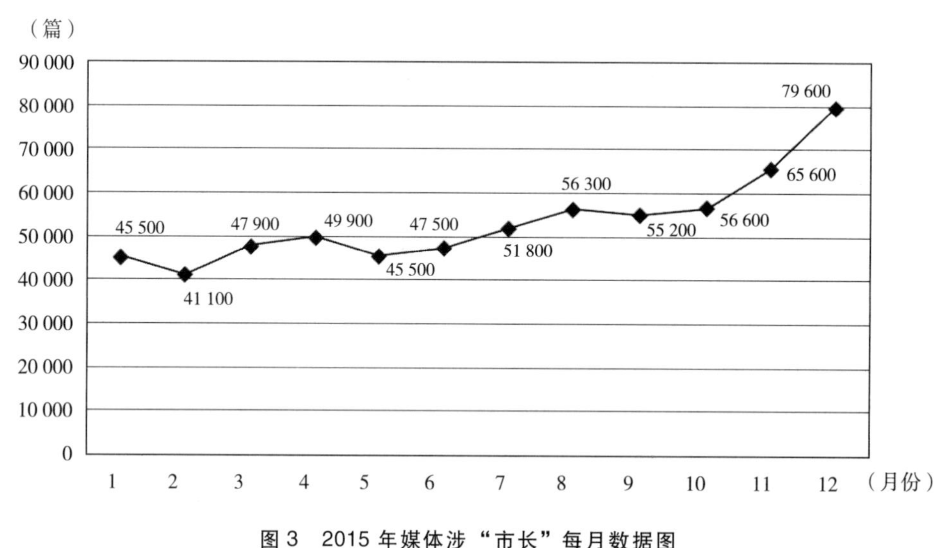

图3　2015年媒体涉“市长”每月数据图

评论3 209条）；微信公号“新晚报”发布的《娄底辞职副市长李向群：不是传奇，我只是回归生活本身》（阅读数100 001，点赞数2 201）。

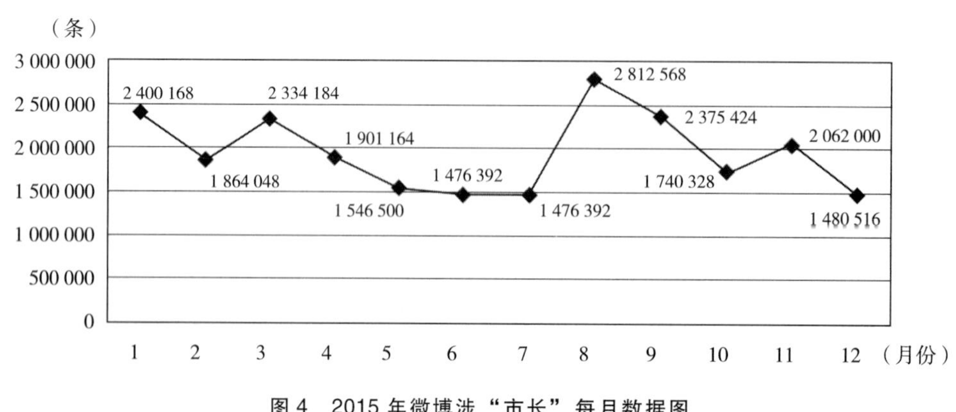

图4　2015年微博涉“市长”每月数据图

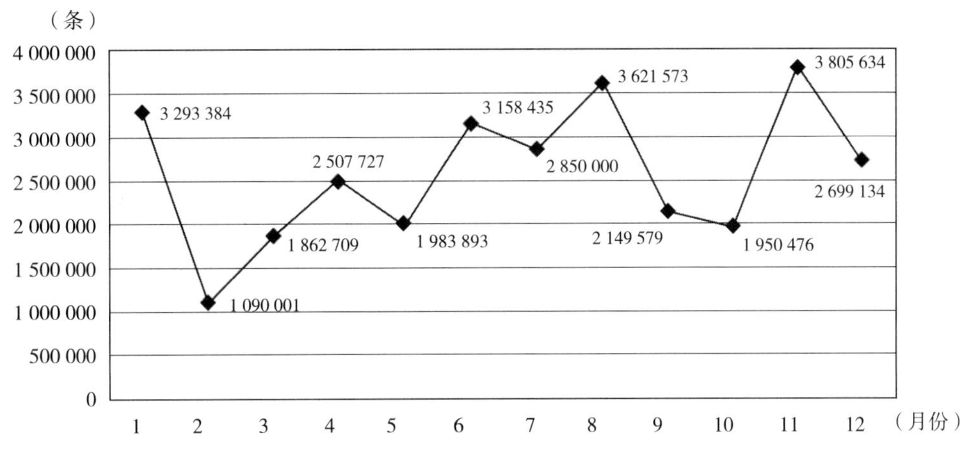

图 5　2015 年微信涉“市长”每月阅读数据图

表 1　网站新闻转载量排序

序号	事　件	来源	转载量(次)
1	东莞市市长袁宝成回应“倒闭潮”:中小企业面临经营压力大	青岛传媒网	390
2	山东菏泽市副市长张毓华辞职　消息称其已投身商海	搜狐网	257
3	甘肃金昌市市长张应华疑在跳楼女生事件现场被打伤	网易新闻	169
4	南昌老市长退休后回江西进贤县创业 5 年建成生态景区	凤凰网	165
5	旺堆当选西藏林芝市首任市长	中国新闻网	159
6	河南南阳市市长程志明因环境污染道歉	张家界在线	144
7	深圳市市长:调集全市消防救援力量　第一时间救人	中国新闻网	141
8	朱立伦县市长执政满意度调查获 4 颗星　表示会加油	中国新闻网	83
9	申亚运会主办权,凌晨一点半,杭州市市长张鸿铭还在陈述演练	网易新闻	78
10	重庆市市长黄奇帆狠批 P2P 一窝蜂:颠覆传统原则会闯祸	搜狐网	43

表 2　微博新闻转载量排序

序号	事　件	来源	转载量(次)	评论(条)
1	重庆市市长黄奇帆提议将建筑物中的钢材使用量提高两倍	新浪微博	5 696	3 209
2	太原市市长耿彦波纪录片《大同》获金马奖	新浪微博	5 072	1 822
3	厦门市副市长臧杰斌说德国上网很困难,而且很贵遭质疑	新浪微博	4 612	987
4	重庆市市长黄奇帆素有“金融市长”之称,被认为是熟谙财经的专家型官员	新浪微博	2 340	484
5	重庆市市长黄奇帆:P2P 金融“像开赌场”	新浪微博	2 305	490
6	深圳滑坡被定性为安全事故　书记市长鞠躬道歉	新浪微博	1 783	813
7	天津市市长黄兴国:十分悲痛自责　我对这次事故负有不可推卸的责任	新浪微博	1 183	1 426
8	郑州市副书记:空气太差,出去招商脸上挂不住	新浪微博	563	726
9	重庆市市长黄奇帆面对诺贝尔经济学奖获得者讲了 5 个精彩的重庆故事	新浪微博	525	119
10	上海市副市长赵雯在监利看望获救上海籍游客	新浪微博	438	2

续表 2

序号	事　件	来源	转载量(次)	评论(条)
11	南昌市原市长李豆罗退休后务农:离开就彻底离开	新浪微博	428	399
12	山东辞职市长梅永红谈下海:吸引我的不是高薪	新浪微博	400	580
13	廖肇羽(阿拉尔市副市长):新疆诸多问题症结,不能简单联想为政治体制与经济模式,而文化背景与宗教信仰的巨大差异才是新疆诸多乱象之源	新浪微博	386	123
14	石家庄市获“国家森林城市”称号　市长邢国辉捧回了牌匾,并在座谈会上发言	新浪微博	364	429
15	山东菏泽市辞职副市长张毓华跳槽深圳一家保险公司	新浪微博	358	319

表 3　微信新闻转载量排序

序号	事　件	公众号	阅读数	点赞数
1	娄底辞职副市长李向群:不是传奇,我只是回归生活本身	人民日报	100 001	2 201
2	山东菏泽市副市长张毓华辞职卖保险	央视新闻	100 001	788
3	济宁市市长梅永红因收入低、压力大辞职下海经商	侠客岛	100 001	656
4	杰人观察就误批贵州毕节市市委书记和市长郑重道歉	杰人观察	91 673	723
5	市长李斌发表电视讲话:“灿鸿”来势凶猛,全市上下紧急投入防台战斗	温岭发布	86 878	690
6	“拆迁市长”耿彦波在任 5 年将大同快速塑造成一个全新的城市	大同老乡俱乐部	70 077	915
7	最大风力 15 级台风“莲花”横穿惠东,副市长黄树正坐镇指挥	惠东西枝江畔	58 816	73
8	杨雄:到 2030 年上海跻身全球重要创新城市行列	上海发布	47 570	296
9	日照市市长刘星泰发话卧龙山街道违建全拆,不获全胜决不收兵	日照大众网	43 682	469
10	浙江为全省民警加保险,天津黄兴国市长带领市委学习保险	保险人百科	41 683	182
11	台风“杜鹃”登陆,莆田再次“沦陷”!市长翁玉耀连夜带头抢修海堤	莆田新城网	40 451	41
12	河南省环保厅约谈了平顶山、新乡、焦作、三门峡四市政府	河南日报	32 611	167
13	太原市市长耿彦波主演的纪录片《大同》获得最佳纪录片奖	太原大小事	32 508	146
14	葛海鹰同志任抚顺市代市长	爱抚顺	28 835	61
15	重庆市市长黄奇帆说金融的本质:一是理财,融资;二、信用、杠杆、风险;三、为实体经济服务	智谷趋势	24 947	34

二、反腐倡廉舆情分析

(一) 舆情走势

2015 年反腐舆情信息量走势较有起伏(图 6)。年初的前三个月信息量较大,排名前三。而后几个月信息量较为平缓。随着 2015 年习近平主席在多个海外场合谈反腐的报道,在 11 月相关信息量又达到一个高点。

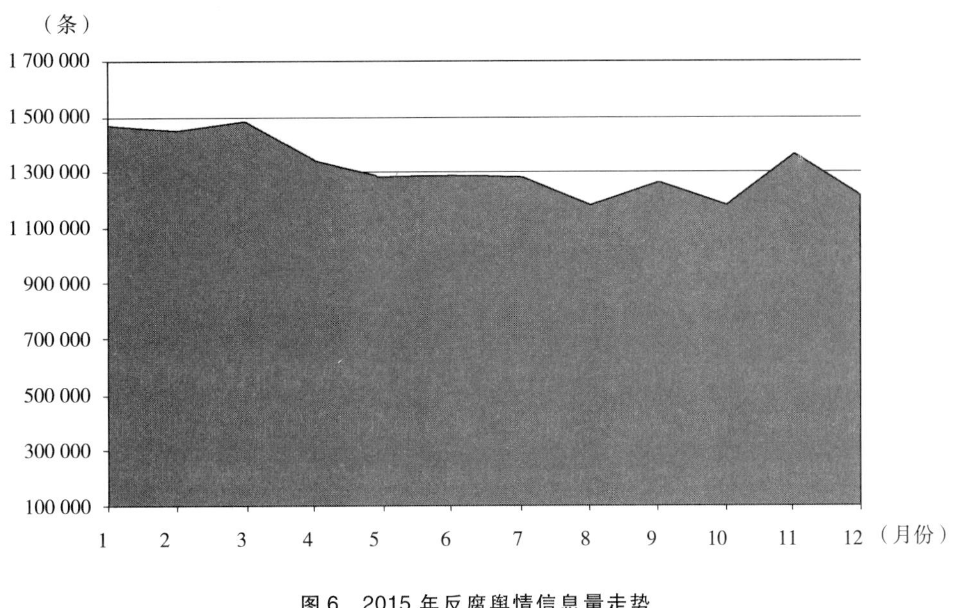

图 6　2015 年反腐舆情信息量走势

（二）2015 年重点话题事件

1. 中美反腐合作

监测数据：共检测到1 650条相关数据。

事件背景：从“猎狐”到“天网”，中国不断加大海外追逃追赃力度，取得成效。美国一方面希望摘除“贪官天堂”的污名，另一方面希望中国协助其实施《海外反腐败法》，重点堵塞美国公民海外逃税漏洞，因此，对中国追逃追赃工作展示了合作态度。

2. 中秋、国庆临近，中纪委严防“四风”反弹

监测数据：共检测到5 660条相关数据。

事件背景：2015 年 8 月 30 日，中央纪委监察部再次公布监督举报窗口，发挥群众和媒体的监督作用，举报反映身边的“四风”问题，特别是违规收送月饼节礼，违规公款吃喝、公款旅游，违规发放津补贴等问题。中纪委强调，持之以恒纠正“四风”事关人心向背，是一项严肃的政治任务、一场输不起的斗争。

3. 制度反腐

监测数据：共检测到1 240条相关数据。

事件背景：2015 年 11 月 30 日，中纪委网站发布《学习贯彻执行廉洁自律准则和党纪处分条例之二：只要方向正确，迈出一步就是胜利》指出，立规修规不能贪大求全、毕其功于一役。制定制度不能过于理想化，不要指望设计出一套至善至美、能管几十年的法规，否则就会旷日持久、议而不决，导致制度迟迟出不来；或者费了很长时间弄出个制度，又把时机错过了，失去了时效性，导致决而不行。此外，文章还指出，制定党内法规是一项严肃的政治工作，既要有理论的储备和支撑，又要有实践的总结与提炼，还要重视历史的回放与梳理。

三、安全维稳舆情分析

（一）舆情走势

安全维稳舆情在2015年信息量起伏较大（图7），5月份最低，其次在10月相关信息数量为倒数第二。相较而言，自7月新《国家安全法》通过和天津港爆炸等事件成为最大的关注焦点后，8月、9月信息量成为全年最高。

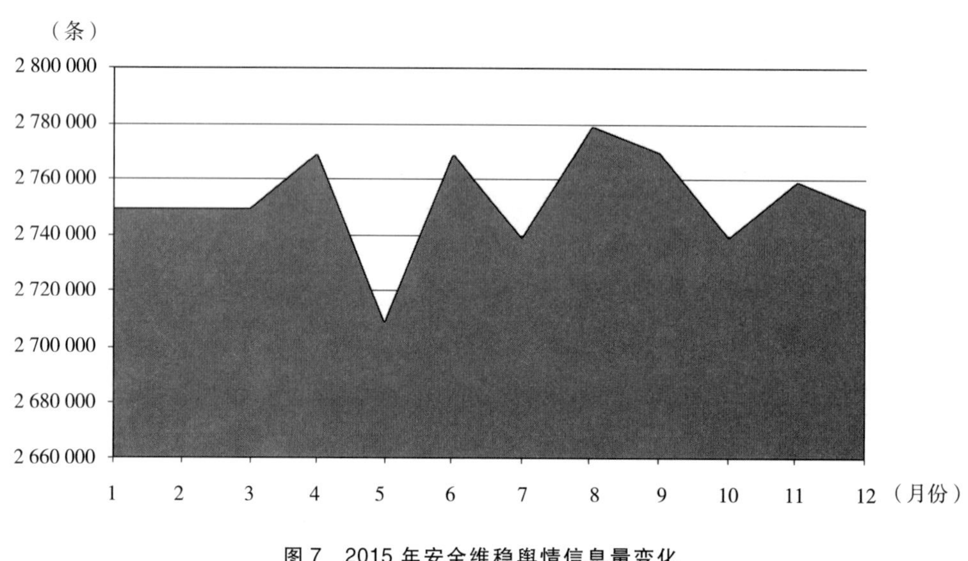

图7 2015年安全维稳舆情信息量变化

（二）2015年重点话题事件

1. 新《国家安全法》以人民安全为宗旨

监测数据：共检测到1 650条相关数据。

事件背景：2015年7月1日上午，全国人大常委会以154票赞成、0票反对、1票弃权表决通过了《国家安全法（草案）》，该法自公布之日起正式生效。法律对政治安全、国土安全、军事安全、文化安全、科技安全等11个领域的国家安全任务进行了界定。这部法的制定以法律的形式确立总体国家安全观的指导地位和国家安全的领导体制，为构建国家安全体系，走出一条中国特色国家安全道路奠定了坚实的法律基础。

2. “东方之星”号客轮翻沉事件

监测数据：共检测到22 800条相关数据。

事件背景：2015年6月1日21时32分，重庆东方轮船公司所属“东方之星”号客轮由南京开往重庆，当航行至湖北省荆州市监利县长江大马洲水道时翻沉，造成442人死亡。经国务院调查组调查认定，此事件是一起由突发罕见的强对流天气——飑线伴有下击暴流——带来的强风暴雨袭击导致的特别重大灾难性事件。

调查组还建议对检查出的在日常管理和监督检查中存在问题负有责任的43名有关人员给予党纪、政纪处分，包括企业7人，行业管理部门、地方党委政府及有关部门36人，其中，副省级干部1人，厅局级干部8人，县处级干部14人。

3. 8·12天津港特大火灾爆炸事故

监测数据：共检测到76 800条相关数据。

事件背景：2015年8月12日23时34分06秒，事故现场发生了第一次大爆炸。距第一次爆炸点约20米处，有多个装有硝酸铵、硝酸钾等氧化剂、易燃固体和腐蚀品集装箱，受到火焰蔓延的作用以及第一次爆炸冲击波影响，23时34分37秒发生了第二次更剧烈的爆炸。据测算，本次事故中爆炸总能量约为450吨TNT当量。

历时三个多月，“8·12”天津港特别重大火灾爆炸事故调查处理进入收尾阶段。追责成为必不可少的内容。天津港（集团）有限公司总裁郑庆跃因疏于管理和把关，对瑞海公司存在的安全隐患和违法违规经营问题未有效督促纠正和处置，被天津市市政府公告免职。

四、改革舆情分析

（一）舆情走势

改革舆情在2015年信息量起伏较大（图8），每次习近平主席主持召开中央全面深化改革会议都引起媒体大量关注。11月、12月，军事改革措施逐步落实，舆情迅速上升并达到全年最高值。

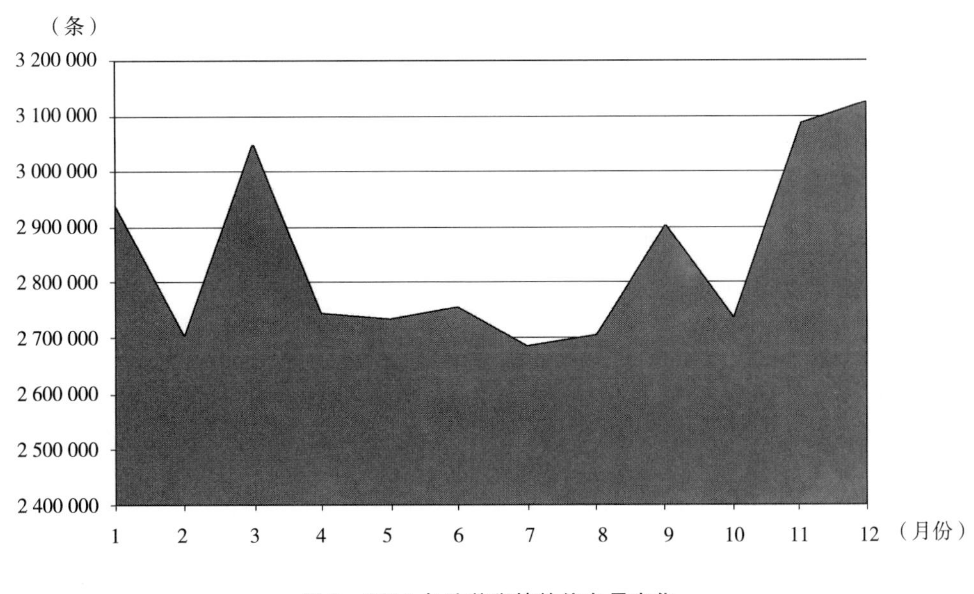

图8　2015年改革舆情的信息量变化

（二）2015年重点话题事件

1. 2015出租车运营改革

监测数据：共检测到1 767条相关数据。

事件背景：2015年10月10日，交通运输部对外发布了《关于深化改革进一步推进出租汽车行业健康发展的指导意见（征求意见稿）》和《网络预约出租汽车经营服务管理暂行办法（征求意见稿）》，进行为期一个月的公开征求意见。

截至10月26日，对半个月时间里的意见汇总显示，相关意见主要集中在10个方面，包括传统出租车改革、专车标准、燃油补贴、驾驶员权益等。其中，网约车条件及专车是否纳入出租车行业管理最受关注，各占两成左右。

2. 央企及事业单位车改方案年内公布

监测数据：共检测到3 590条相关数据。

事件背景：2015年12月7日，中央事业单位和企业车改实施意见分别由国管局和国资委牵头制定，目前已分别形成征求意见稿，正在广泛征求意见。中央车改办将尽快完善两份改革方案，经中央车改领导小组批准后于2015年年内印发并对社会公布，争取到2016年年底基本完成中央企事业单位车改工作。

据统计，中央企事业单位车改涉及一级预算的中央直属事业单位10余家，中央和国家机关部门所属的各级事业单位1万家左右，国资委管理的中央企业100多家，还有数十家中央金融企业及各部委管理的中央企业。

3. 习近平主持召开中央深改组第十八次会议

监测数据：共检测到2 350条相关数据。

事件背景：2015年11月9日，中共中央总书记、国家主席习近平主持召开中央全面深化改革领导小组第十八次会议并发表重要讲话。他强调，党的十八届五中全会通过的《中共中央关于制定国民经济和社会发展第十三个五年规划的建议》是指导我国改革发展的纲领性文件。在全面贯彻党的十八届五中全会精神过程中，要发挥改革的突破性和先导性作用，增强改革创新精神，提高改革行动能力，着力推进国家治理体系和治理能力现代化，着力推进各方面制度更加成熟更加定型，依靠改革为科学发展提供持续动力。

五、招商旅游舆情分析

（一）舆情走势

2015年招商旅游舆情信息波动较大（图9）。因春节来临及国庆节日放长假，使2月份、10月份旅游舆情信息量达到最高。其他时间段相关舆情信息较为平缓。

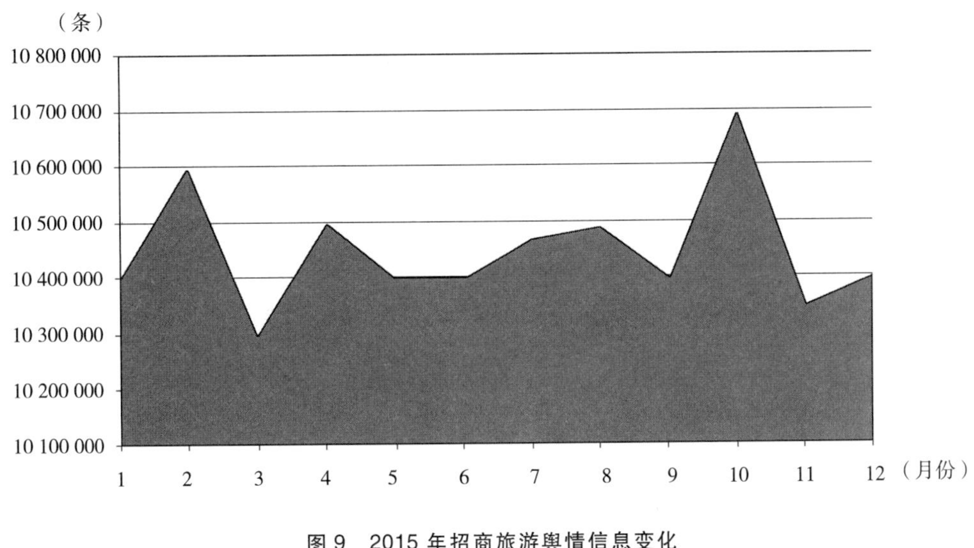

图 9　2015 年招商旅游舆情信息变化

（二）2015 年重点话题事件

1. 青岛“天价虾”事件

监测数据：共检测到 6 410 条相关数据。

事件背景：2015 年 10 月 5 日，一则“青岛一大排档兜售天价大虾”的新闻引发热议。媒体报道称，10 月 4 日，有游客在“善德活海鲜烧烤店”结账时发现，一盘普通的虾要价高达 38 元一只，整盘收费 1 500 余元。6 日晚间，青岛市市北区区委宣传部发布消息称，当地物价局拟对该商铺做出 9 万元的行政处罚。当地网友发布的图片显示，涉事烧烤店已被关停。7 日，青岛市旅游局、工商局、物价局、公安局还联合发布《关于进一步治理规范旅游市场秩序的通告》，要求严厉查处旅游市场中存在的无照经营、不正当竞争、旅游业不公平格式合同条款等违法违规行为。

2. 成立丝绸之路旅游联盟

监测数据：共检测到 1 259 条相关数据。

事件背景：2015 年 6 月 16 日，陕西、甘肃、宁夏等 12 个丝绸之路沿线省区市旅游局以及新疆生产建设兵团旅游局共同发起成立丝绸之路旅游推广联盟。联盟成员通过区域联动与合作，共同开拓境内外旅游市场，携手做大做强丝绸之路旅游品牌。

3. 中美经贸合作

监测数据：共检测到 8 360 条相关数据。

事件背景：2015 年 9 月 23 日，国家主席习近平在西雅图出席中美企业家座谈会。当前，中美两国经济面临着新形势，也面临着新的发展机遇。他强调，中美经贸合作有着巨大潜力。由于发展阶段的差异，中美经济存在很强的互补性，两国经贸合作空间巨大、机遇很多。我们支持美国大公司在华设立地区总部、研发中心，鼓励更多美国中小企业来华拓展业务。

六、教育舆情分析

(一)舆情走势

教育舆情在2015年信息量起伏较大(图10)。有两个主要峰值,一个是高考的6月,一个是新学年开始的9月。其他时间段信息量较为相近。

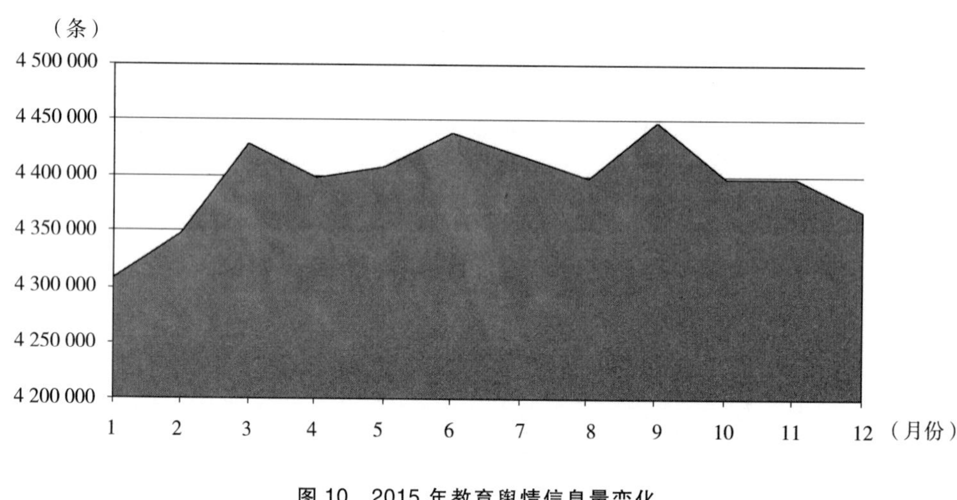

图10 2015年教育舆情信息量变化

(二)2015年重点话题事件

1. 记者卧底替考组织参加江西高考

监测数据:共检测到7 400条相关数据。

事件背景:2015年6月7日上午,《南方都市报》以"记者卧底替考组织参加高考曝光跨省团伙"为题报道了有团伙组织在江西实施高考替考事件。报道称,替考人员中有多人是湖北多所知名高校大学生。

教育部回应称,已责成江西省教育厅和省教育考试院迅速调查核实情况,并请公安部指导有关地方公安机关立案侦查。

2. 教育部调查核实"毒"跑道事件

监测数据:共检测到44 600条相关数据。

事件背景:2015年11月26日,针对多地出现的"毒"跑道伤害学生健康的事件,教育部回应,正在会同有关部门对媒体和群众反映的有毒的塑胶跑道进行调查核实,经过核实后会公布结果。"毒"跑道伤害学生健康事件的主要原因是监管不力。对有质疑的体育场地立即停用,并通过专业机构进行检测,根据检测结果采取相应措施。对正在和即将建设的体育场地,及时提请有关教育部门和学校严格按照国家有关标准建设,主动配合有关监管部门的工作。教育部基础教育一司司长王定华表示,未来对教育行政部门和学校在体育场地建设中因徇私舞弊等行为造成不合格的情况，教育部将加大责任追究力度，对责任人要严肃处理，绝不手软，并通过多种手段加大监管，确保学生的健康安全。

3. 国务院：全面加强和改进学校美育工作

监测数据：共检测到1 180条相关数据。

事件背景：2015年9月29日，国务院办公厅下发《国务院办公厅关于全面加强和改进学校美育工作的意见》，提出2015年起全面加强和改进学校美育工作。到2018年，取得突破性进展，美育资源配置逐步优化，管理机制进一步完善，各级各类学校开齐开足美育课程。到2020年，初步形成大中小幼美育相互衔接、课堂教学和课外活动相互结合、普及教育与专业教育相互促进、学校美育和社会家庭美育相互联系的具有中国特色的现代化美育体系。

七、环保舆情分析

（一）舆情走势

环保舆情在2015年信息量相对平稳，呈上升趋势（图11）。因《环境保护税法（草案）》或年内审议，使11月和12月信息量达到最高。可以看出，影响我们身体健康的环境问题，网络关注度一直较高。

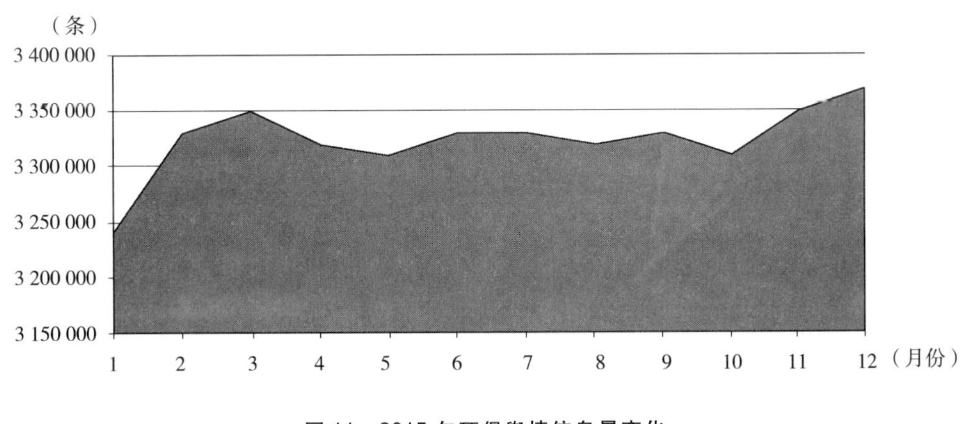

图11　2015年环保舆情信息量变化

（二）2015年重点话题事件

1. 生态环境损害须终身追责

监测数据：共检测到6 570条相关数据。

事件背景：2015年8月17日，中共中央办公厅、国务院办公厅印发了《党政领导干部生态环境损害责任追究办法（试行）》（以下简称《办法》），首次突破了现行法律法规中对地方各级党委领导成员在生态环境保护方面责任规定的缺失。地方发生环境污染和生态破坏事件，不仅政府主要领导成员要担责，党委和相关部门的领导都有可能被追究相应责任。

《办法》规定实行生态环境损害责任终身追究制。对违背科学发展要求、造成生态环境和资源严重破坏的，责任人不论是否已调离、提拔或者退休，都必须严格追责。

2. 《环境保护税法（草案）》或年内审议

监测数据：共检测到 1 027 条相关数据。

事件背景：2015 年 11 月 18 日，媒体报道，目前《环境保护税法（草案）》正在进行最后完善，最快将于 2015 年年底前由国务院审议通过草案。专家称，《环境保护税法（草案）》有望提交全国人大常委会审议，这意味着每年数百亿元规模的环境保护税开征可期。征税对象分为大气污染物、水污染物、固体废物和噪声 4 类，征税标准与现行的排污费收费标准基本持平。对超标、超总量排放污染物的，加倍征收环保税。

3. "十三五"环保战略调整

监测数据：共检测到 887 条相关数据。

事件背景：2015 年 10 月 22 日，环保"十三五"规划从单一目标即总量控制目标、减排目标，变成双目标即环境质量改善和污染物总量控制，内容涉及绿色经济、核安全问题、土壤环境保护、生态环境保护、水环境污染防治等诸多方面。多位专家预计，环保未来 5 年的发展方向和投资重点将上升至国家战略角度，成为政府重点投资领域。围绕着环保领域的十万亿级盛宴或将启动。按照计划，该规划有望 2016 年 3 月上报国务院。

（作者：中国市长协会。技术支持：谷尼舆情智库）

中国海绵城市建设在争论和探索中前行

2015年，是我国海绵城市快速发展的一年。2014年年底，财政部、住房城乡建设部和水利部下发通知，在全国开展中央财政支持一些城市进行海绵城市试点工作，快速带动了地方政府的积极性。之后海绵城市在全国迅速推广，全国16个试点城市加上一些其他没有成为第一批试点的城市在海绵城市理念概念的普及、规划、设计、建设等方面都在进行积极地探索。2015年10月，国务院办公厅下发的国办发〔2015〕75号文件，进一步提出了要全面推广海绵城市，文件从目标、指标、规划、建设、投融资等方面对海绵城市的建设做出了具体的要求。文件下发后，各地也迅速地组织学习，海绵城市的概念进一步得到推广。但是，在全国全面推广普及海绵城市建设的过程中，关于海绵城市的理念、概念、目标、指标等方面的争论从未停止过。本文力图用较短的篇幅，从政策的简要解读、对海绵城市的认知以及海绵城市规划设计等方面对我国2015年的海绵城市建设情况进行简单的回顾和梳理。

一、政策层面

（一）三部委试点文件

2014年年底，财政部、住房城乡建设部和水利部下发《财政部、住房城乡建设部、水利部关于开展中央财政支持海绵城市建设试点工作的通知》（财建〔2014〕838号）。随后，财政部、住房城乡建设部和水利部三部委办公厅又联合下发了《关于组织申报2015年海绵城市建设试点城市的通知》（财办建〔2015〕4号）。两个文件的下发对全国海绵城市的快速启动起到了至关重要的作用。三部委下发的关于海绵城市试点的通知具有以下几个方面的意义：

一是在全国层面，第一次明确了由中央财政拿出专项资金对海绵城市建设试点给予专项资金的补助，而且给予的资金支持力度还比较大，直辖市、省会城市和其他城市中央财政支持的资金分别达到6亿元、5亿元和4亿元。中央财政拿出专项资金支持地方政府海绵城市建设的方式和力度，激发了地方政府的积极性。超过130个城市在2015年海绵城市建设试点申报中编写了海绵城市建设的实施方案。

二是文件明确了海绵城市试点建设的组织形式和试点选择的流程。财建〔2014〕838号文件中明确提出了由省级财政、住房城乡建设和水利部门联合申报，然后财政部、住房城乡建设部、水利部组织资格审查，最后通过竞争性评审的方式，由专家进行现场评审，现场公布评审结果。这种采用公开竞争性评审的方式，有力地保障了海绵城市试点申报的公平性和公正性。

三是文件初步明确了海绵城市建设的要求。财建〔2014〕838号文件对试点城市申报提出了初步的要求，财办建〔2015〕4号又进行了细化说明。两个文件中可以非常明显地看出，海绵城市是关于水资源、水环境、水生态、水安全方面的全面提升。这从一开始就将我国的海绵城市建设的内涵和外延进行了初步的界定，也决定了我国的海绵城市虽然是从美国的低影响开发（Low Impact Development，LID）和绿色基础设施（Green Infrastructure，GI）发展而来的，但是，我国海绵城市是比美国的LID和GI有更加广泛的、更加综合的城市发展理念。

四是试点实施方案的编制大纲初步奠定了海绵城市近期建设规划的编制框架和内容要求。财办建〔2015〕4号文件的附件之一是《海绵城市建设试点城市实施方案编制提纲》，该文件的结构和逻辑顺序比较清晰地表达了我国海绵城市试点建设的内容和要求，具有明显的近期建设规划的色彩，也奠定了今后各地海绵城市近期建设规划的编制框架和内容。当然，这个实施方案也有一些不尽完善的地方，比如，按照2014年住房城乡建设部发布的《海绵城市建设技术指南》中提出的“渗、滞、蓄、净、用、排”六个字对海绵城市建设的工程措施进行分类，在技术逻辑、可操作性和区分的意义方面考虑得不够深。

（二）2015年国办发75号文件

2015年10月16日，国务院办公厅下发了《国务院办公厅关于推进海绵城市建设的指导意见》（国办发〔2015〕75号），从而将海绵城市的建设从试点带动推广到全国，对我国的海绵城市建设乃至城市生态文明建设都具有重要意义。2015年国办发75号文件对我国海绵城市建设的意义主要体现在以下几个方面：

一是首次将海绵城市定义为城市发展方式。文件明确提出：海绵城市是指通过加强城市规划建设管理，充分发挥建筑、道路和绿地、水系等生态系统对雨水的吸纳、蓄渗和缓释作用，有效控制雨水径流，实现自然积存、自然渗透、自然净化的城市发展方式。经过梳理后不难发现，文件将海绵城市定义为一种新的城市发展方式，这对我国海绵城市的发展具有重要意义。该定义弱化了海绵城市的技术属性，更加强调了海绵城市的理念属性和方法学方面的属性，是对海绵城市理解的一次战略性的升华。

二是明确了海绵城市建设的意义。在2015年国办发75号文件中提出的海绵城市建设的意义包括：修复城市水生态、涵养水资源，增强城市防涝能力，扩大公共产品有效投资，提高新型城镇化质量，促进人与自然和谐发展。这里面包括了三个层面的意义：第一个层面明确了海绵城市建设对于我国城市水资源、水环境、水生态、水安全等问题解决的直接意义；第二个层面明确了海绵城市建设对于我国经济发展的有效意义，即有利于扩大公共产品的有效投资；第三个层面明确了海绵城市建设对于生态文明和新型城镇化质量等方面的意义。这三个层面由低到高、由浅入深地全面阐述了我国海绵城市建设的意义。

三是将海绵城市从试点全面推向全国。在此文件下发前，海绵城市主要是在第一批16个试点城市中进行，但是该文件的下发，明确提出全国要全面开展海绵城市建设，这是我国海绵城市建设从试点先行快速地转变为全面启动的重要标志。

四是明确了海绵城市建设的目标和时间节点。文件提出，到2020年，城市建成区20%以上的面积达到目标要求；到2030年，城市建成区80%以上的面积达到目标要求。另外，文件还提出我国海绵城市建设要将70%的降雨就地消纳和利用，关于对这句话的理解，是当前学术界争论的焦点之一，本文稍后会进一步地阐述。

五是提出了各相关规划建设中要将海绵城市建设的关键指标作为项目前置条件。海绵城市规划建设不能自身孤立起来开展，必须和城市规划、设计、建设管理等环节全面结合起来。文件中提出的将海绵城市建设的关键指标作为项目建设前置条件的做法，为各地制订规划建设管理办法，全面落实海绵城市的建设要求提供了有力保障。

六是明确提出了海绵城市建设的目标。2015年国办发75号文件中明确提出了海绵城市的建设目标是“小雨不积水，大雨不内涝，水体不黑臭，热岛有缓解”，这可以进一步看出我国海绵城市建设的内涵不仅包括对小雨的控制，也全面覆盖了城市排水防涝、水环境治理等方面的内容。

七是在国家层面首次提出了防治污水渗漏和合流制污水溢流污染控制的要求。我国的合流制排水管网问题比较多，比较典型的问题是截留倍数比较低，缺乏调蓄和其他合流制污水溢流污染（Combined Sewer Overflows，CSOs）控制的要求和措施，造成雨季合流制管网溢流口频繁溢流，污染了水环境。2015年国办发75号文件中提出了合流制污水溢流污染控制要在国家政策层面，为我国合流制污水管网的改造提供了一个全新的思路。此外，文件还提出了要控制污水管网的渗漏问题，这对我国当前城市黑臭水体的整治乃至城市水环境质量的全面改善，提供了重要的支撑。国务院办公厅在此次文件中明确提出的关于控制污水渗漏的要求，为我国未来解决这类问题指明了方向，也提供了很好的政策接入口。

八是明确提出了PPP模式和开发性、政策性金融在海绵城市建设中的地位。首先，2015年国办发75号文件明确了通过PPP的方式，广泛吸引社会资本参与海绵城市建设，既解决了投融资渠道的问题，又能引入专业的公司来做专业的事情，对于推动海绵城市建设具有重大意义。其次，文件还特别明确提出了要充分发挥开发性、政策性金融作用，这对于降低当前各地海绵城市建设融资成本高、贷款期限长等问题，提供了重要的保障。

九是明确提出了要采用科研设计单位、施工企业、制造企业与金融资本相结合，组建具备综合业务能力的企业集团或联合体，采用总承包等方式统筹组织实施海绵城市建设相关项目，发挥整体效益。海绵城市的建设涉及技术、建设、投资、运营管理等方方面面的问题，通过采用优势企业组建联合体的办法，可以优势互补。此外，海绵城市建设涉及城市雨水的排水区的问题，只有采用连片建设，才能发挥整体效益，而且也只有采用连片建设的模式，才能够和国家当前大力推广的PPP模式的考核和付费机制对应起来。文件提出的这种采用企业联合体进行总体承包的方式，对我国未来的海绵城市建设影响巨大。

十是明确了城市人民政府在海绵城市建设中的主体责任。文件明确提出，城市人民政府是海绵城市建设的责任主体，要完善工作机制，统筹规划建设，抓紧启动实施。同时，文件还明确住房城乡建设部、发展改革委、财政部、水利部和其他各部门在海绵城市建设中的责任分工，这对我国今后海绵城市建设工作的全面和顺利开展提供了有力保障。

（三）住房城乡建设部和国开行、农发行分别下发两个文件

2015 年，住房城乡建设部和国家开发银行联合下发了《住房城乡建设部、国家开发银行关于推进开发性金融支持海绵城市建设的通知（建城〔2015〕208 号)》，和中国农业发展银行联合下发了《住房城乡建设部 中国农业发展银行关于推进政策性金融支持海绵城市建设的通知（建城〔2015〕240 号)》。住房城乡建设部和国开行、农发行分别下发的两个关于支持海绵城市建设的通知是对 2015 年国办发 75 号文件的落实和细化，对于解决海绵城市建设中融资渠道问题提供了重要路径。

两个文件明确了国家开发银行和中国农业发展银行要充分发挥开发性、政策性金融的作用，大力支持海绵城市建设，切实增强信贷资金对海绵城市建设的支撑保障能力。其中，农发行更是明确提出贷款期限最长可达 30 年，贷款利率可适当优惠。

二、对海绵城市的认知

（一）对年径流总量控制率的理解

2015 年，对海绵城市认知中，争论最多的可能是对年径流总量控制率的理解。在住房城乡建设部发布的《海绵城市建设技术指南》中解释说：年径流总量控制率（Volume Capture Ratio of Annual Rainfall）是指根据多年日降雨量统计数据分析计算，通过自然和人工强化的渗透、储存、蒸发（腾）等方式，场地内累计全年得到控制（不外排）的雨量占全年总降雨量的百分比。

当前对于年径流总量控制率的争论主要集中在几个方面：第一个争论是对这个术语本身的叫法。有些人认为，不应该叫年径流总量控制率，应该叫年降雨控制率，这样更加准确，也更加方便理解。实际上，从《海绵城市建设技术指南》中的名词术语的解释中不难看出，我们国家当前所用的年径流总量控制率其实说的是多年平均降雨（Rainfall）总量控制率，但是由于历史原因，采用了径流（Runoff）这个词，因而引起了不少误解和争论，尤其是对于刚开始接触海绵城市的部分专业人士，很容易产生误解。但是鉴于 2015 年国办发 75 号文件也采用了这个词，而且这个词汇当前在不少规划设计人员和政府官员中接受度比较高，如果再换成年降雨总量控制率，也会容易引起新一轮的混乱。

第二个争论是对“控制”两个字的理解。在《海绵城市建设技术指南》中给出的英文术语中，对于“控制”一词用的是“capture”，之后的解释中也清楚地表明，“控制”指的是自然和人工强化的渗透、储存、蒸发（腾）。但是容易引起误解的主要是括号内的“不外

排”三个字。实际上，海绵城市建设中所谓的“控制”指的是不直接外排的那部分降雨，比如对于地下水位较高，或者原土排水能力较弱，或者下部是地下室的生物滞留设施，底部都需要安装渗透盲管（Underdrain），将经过渗透、过滤、净化以后的雨水缓慢排走或者进行收集利用。对于这部分设施处理的雨水，从客观上来说对雨水起到了净化和缓排的作用，显然应该是被“控制”过的，但是这部分很可能是要外排的。随着大家对海绵城市实践的深入和不断的讨论，业内也基本达成共识，年径流总量控制率中所提到的控制，其实指的是“不直接外排”的那部分降雨量占多年平均降雨量的比例。

第三个争论是对年径流总量控制率的计算方式。《海绵城市建设技术指南》中给出的年径流总量控制率的计算方式为控制的雨量占全年总降雨量的比例。而熟悉美国 LID 的人可能更习惯于采用降雨事件频率。这二者的计算方式和表达方式略有不同，但是最后都对应于 24 小时内的一个降雨量，二者并无本质区别。经过业内多次讨论，大家基本达成共识，对采用降雨总量的概念和计算方法已经无需再争论。

（二）对海绵城市建设标准的理解

除了对名词术语本身的理解以外，当前围绕海绵城市建设标准和年径流总量控制率等方面还有几个比较常见的争议：

一是，为什么要采用年径流总量控制率作为海绵城市建设的核心指标。海绵城市是因雨水问题而起的，但是涉及水资源、水环境、水生态、水安全等方面的问题。在《海绵城市建设技术指南》和 2015 年国办发 75 号文件中，均明确强调了年径流总量控制率在海绵城市建设指标中的地位，2015 年国办发 75 号文件更是明确提出了要将年径流总量控制率作为核心控制指标。笔者认为，年径流总量控制率作为核心指标，是基于以下几个方面的考虑：第一，城市降雨的频率分布以小雨和中雨居多，而这部分降雨带来的污染比较严重，控制了这部分降雨，就能在很大程度上控制降雨的径流污染。实际上，在美国常见的五级雨水管理标准中，我国的海绵城市建设中的年径流总量控制率相当于第二级的管理标准，即雨水水质（Water Quality）管理标准。美国的雨水水质管理标准也是通过控制 90% 左右的降雨场次的降雨，从而达到降雨径流污染控制的目的。第二，年径流总量控制率是一个比较综合的指标，可以在一定程度上综合反映雨水管理和控制的水平。比如，通过控制 75% 左右的年径流总量，就可以在一定程度上起到回补地下水，恢复或者接近城市开发前的水文特征，大幅度减少城市降雨径流污染等问题。

二是，涉及年径流总量控制率还有一个核心的争论，那就是该指标的取值问题。2015 年国办发 75 号文件中提出要将 70% 的降雨就地消纳和利用。当然，中国北方、南方城市降雨量、降雨分布特征差异比较大，一刀切都取 70% 显然有不合理的地方。笔者认为，这里说的是 70% 左右的降雨。对于中国大部分地区来说，70% 的年径流总量控制率对应的降雨都不会超过 25mm，这个和美国目前大部分地方在推广 LID 和 GI 中制订的要控制 24 小时内 1~1.2 英寸（25.4~30.8mm）的降雨是基本一致的，而且从目前国内海绵城市试点推行情况和美国西雅图、纽约、华盛顿特区等地的实践来看，这个目标也是基本可以实现的。

（三）对海绵城市作用的理解

2015年，围绕海绵城市到底是起什么作用的讨论也比较多。2015年年初，在各地刚开始接触海绵城市概念的时候，有不少城市将海绵城市简单理解为排水防涝，也有一些城市将海绵城市理解为雨水收集利用。要想准确理解海绵城市的概念及其作用，需要区分海绵城市的语境。我们常说的海绵城市有一个狭义的海绵城市和一个广义的海绵城市之分。比如在建设自然积存、自然渗透、自然净化的海绵城市，以及将70%的降雨就地消纳和利用，此处所说的海绵城市是狭义的海绵城市，其内涵与美国当前提倡的绿色基础设施比较类似。这个狭义的海绵城市的主要作用是改善城市水生态，使城市恢复开发前的水文状态，同时缓解城市降雨径流带来的污染问题。

但是，目前大多数时候说的海绵城市，比如2015年国办发75号文件中提出的海绵城市，其概念包括了绿色基础设施和传统灰色基础设施，这是广义的海绵城市概念。在2015年国办发75号文件中提出了海绵城市建设要将“源头减排、过程控制、系统治理”结合起来，以达到“小雨不积水，大雨不内涝，水体不黑臭，热岛有缓解”的目的。在具体的建设项目安排中，也提到了海绵型道路与广场、海绵型建筑和小区等，这些是属于源头的绿色基础设施部分。文件中也提到了排水防涝问题，污水管网渗漏和合流制溢流污染控制问题，以及黑臭水体治理问题，这些显然都是要通过灰色基础设施与绿色基础设施的配合才能达到的效果。

三、海绵城市规划设计

（一）海绵城市专项规划

2015年全国海绵城市专项规划的编制取得较快进展。在国内较早启动海绵城市专项规划的城市有南宁、遂宁、鹤壁、萍乡、迁安等。目前，各地编制的海绵城市专项规划一般分为两个层次：一个是全市中心城区层面的，有些城市叫海绵城市总体规划，有些城市叫海绵城市专项规划，还有些城市叫海绵城市建设专项规划等。另一个层面是全市海绵城市近期建设区的规划，有些城市叫近期建设区详细规划，有些城市叫近期建设规划等。

这两个层面的规划在城市规划序列中都属于专项规划。前者一般包括分析全市海绵城市建设的基础条件、存在的问题、建设需求，研究确定年径流总量控制率指标，并对其进行分解，分析规划区内的自然山水生态空间格局，进行海绵城市建设分区，划定近期海绵城市建设重点区域等。后者一般在更小的尺度上，对近期海绵城市建设区域进行可行性分析论证，确定近期需要建设的海绵型建筑与小区、海绵型道路与广场、河流湖泊的生态化改造等内容，并分析确定建设指标和建设内容等，有些城市则做到了分图则的深度。

从本质上来说，前者一般对应于城市总体规划范围，其研究的内容是城市总体规划的深化和补充，是对全市海绵城市建设做出的空间和时序上的安排。后者一般对应于城市详细规划，是对详细规划的有力支撑，是对城市近期海绵城市建设内容和建设项目以及具体建设指标的安排。

（二）海绵城市项目设计

海绵城市项目最终要落地，必须依靠科学合理的设计。目前，由于海绵城市对于很多规划院和市政院来说都是相对比较新的课题，也是新的挑战，不少规划院、市政院、园林景观院都在广泛参与海绵城市的规划设计项目。从目前来看，海绵城市的项目设计中也存在一些典型的问题，比如对场地的分析不足，缺乏竖向分析和合理的径流组织，规划设计手段过于单一，过分依赖生物滞留设施、透水铺装和雨水蓄积模块，设计中对土壤的问题关注不足，设计中缺乏方案比选和优化，计算和最终校核过程科学性不足，和景观的结合不足。

（三）海绵城市规划设计导则与标准图集

由于海绵城市的建设技术和本地的降雨、土壤、地下水等密切相关，而之前发布的《海绵城市建设技术指南》为了实现对全国情况的普适性，涉及普遍原理性的东西比较多。各地在 2015 年普遍采用的方式是编制本地的海绵城市规划设计导则和标准图集。南宁在全国率先推出了南宁市海绵城市规划设计导则和标准图集，随后各城市也基本都按照这种模式在快速推进。从本质上来讲，编制本地的海绵城市规划设计导则和标准图集实际是将海绵城市的普遍原理和本地的实际情况相结合，是对全国《海绵城市规划设计导则》深化、细化和本土化的过程，编制这些文件对各地的海绵城市建设提供了有力的支撑。

但是，随之也出现了一些雷同、抄袭和针对性不足等问题，还有一些道路的做法不适合当地的习惯，单项设施的技术参数不太合适等问题，这些问题需要各技术单位在今后的工作中尽力避免。

四、小结

总之，2015 年是我国海绵城市建设的元年。三部委关于海绵城市试点的文件点燃了各地的热情，国办发 75 号文件将海绵城市建设的范围推向全国的设市城市，之后住房城乡建设部和国开行、农发行下发的关于支持海绵城市建设的文件又进一步为海绵城市建设提供了资金保障。

2015 年，围绕海绵城市的争论一直没有停止，集中争论的问题包括年径流总量控制率的概念、指标的确定、对海绵城市内涵的理解、对海绵城市作用的理解等。一年来，业内专业技术人员通过各种论坛、会议、培训、学术期刊和媒体平台，就这些问题展开了激烈的讨论。随着时间的推移，大家对这些问题的理解也越来越趋于一致。总体来说，共识在增加，分歧、海绵城市无用论和海绵城市万能论等极端观点在减少。

同时，在 16 个首批全国海绵城市试点城市的带动下，我国海绵城市的规划、设计、研究、施工、运行、维护等方面的研究和实践也都取得了积极的进展，南宁、济南、镇江、迁安等地海绵城市 PPP 项目也在快速地推进。不少城市都启动了海绵城市专项规划的编制。

总体上来说，2015 年是中国海绵城市建设在争论和探索中快速前进的一年。通过争论，业界统一了认识；通过探索，各地积累了经验。虽然当前各地海绵城市建设也都不同程度地存在人才、技术、资金、体制机制等方面的困难和制约，但是海绵城市建设是国务院近期部署的一项重大工作，对于统筹解决我国水资源、水环境、水生态、水安全等方面的问题都有重要意义，各地在接下来还需加强交流，加强探索，以便更好地推进海绵城市建设。

（作者：王家卓，中国城市规划设计研究院水务与工程专业院资源能源研究所所长）

珠三角产业发展空间布局新态势

一、引言

改革开放以来，珠三角产业经济获得了极大的发展，形成了以先进制造业、高新技术产业、现代服务业为主的二、三产业齐头并进的态势。但随着我国经济进入“新常态”，珠三角原有的依赖低成本人力、土地资源的传统发展方式和遍地开花的空间布局模式已经不可持续，亟须进行产业结构的转型升级和空间布局上的统筹规划。本文在对珠三角产业发展演变历程进行总结分析的基础上，应对目前珠三角面临的机遇和挑战，结合2014年编制完成的《珠江三角洲全域规划（2014－2020年）》，对新常态下珠三角产业发展的趋势和重点，及其空间布局的新态势做出分析和解读，以期以珠三角为例，对其他地区的产业发展提供借鉴参考。

二、珠三角产业发展演变历程

改革开放以来，珠三角产业发展获得了长足进步，根据其在区域产业格局中的地位、产业主导类型和空间布局模式，可以分为以下三个阶段：

（一）改革开放到20世纪90年代中期：承接产业转移为主的经济探索起飞阶段

从20世纪70年代末期改革开放到90年代中期，珠三角地区凭借毗邻港澳、靠近东南亚的区位优势，抓住港澳制造业转移和改革开放试点的有利条件，以“三来一补”“大进大出”的加工贸易起步，通过吸引我国香港和台湾、东南亚以及欧美企业投资，迅速成为中国外向度最高、经济发展最快的地区，GDP从1980年的132亿元迅速增长至1995年的4 076亿元，年平均增长率达25.7%。

这一阶段珠三角产业发展主要是借助我国香港和台湾以及东南亚地区制造业的产业转移实现的。产业类型上，20世纪80年代初期以承接香港食品饮料、纺织服装等轻工业为主；20世纪80年代末到90年代初期，以承接台湾地区传统制造业和电子产业为主；20世纪90年代中期，日本、韩国和欧美制造业向珠三角的转移逐步推动重化工业的发展，兴起了以汽车、石化、钢铁和装备制造业为重点的重工业浪潮（图1）。

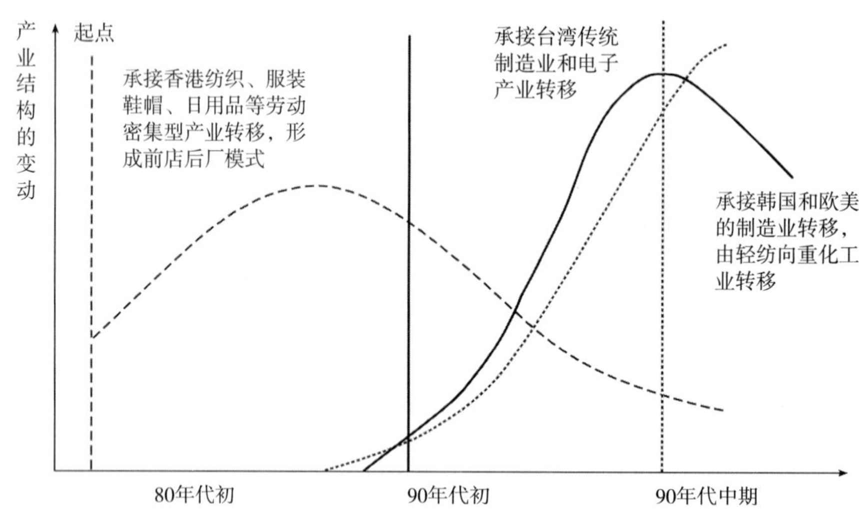

图1 珠三角承接产业转移过程（路红艳，2009）

空间布局上，这一阶段产业发展大量集中于村镇工业园区，“村村点火、户户冒烟”的现象普遍，并出现了具有专门化职能的新兴工业化城镇，成为产业快速发展的重点载体。

（二）90年代中期到21世纪初期：以高新技术产业、房地产业支撑的经济高速发展阶段

这一时期，承接产业转移的重点发生了变化，即由承接简单加工装配、贴牌生产（OEM）的劳动密集型产业逐渐向承接高加工度、自主设计（ODM）的资本、技术密集型产业转变，电子信息制造等高新技术迅猛发展，工业经济素质和实力得到了明显提升。1995年至2002年，珠三角地区工业总产值平均每年递增13.3%，家用电器、机械、建材、食品、电子、石油加工、精细化工等成为支柱行业。2003年，珠三角的电子及通信设备制造业占全省的比重达98.54%，初步形成了现代的IT产业群和家电产业群。珠三角各城市基本上都将高新技术产业作为今后经济发展的重点，兴建了各类工业园区。同时第三产业也进入快速发展阶段，珠三角逐渐开始承接香港的部分生产性服务功能；受到土地及住房制度改革影响，珠三角房地产市场掀起热潮，并开启了以广州华南板块为代表的郊区“大盘”时代。

空间布局上，通过“工业进园”等措施，该阶段的产业发展主要集中于各类经济开发区、高新区以及新城、新区，初步形成了集聚态势。但经统计，珠三角各类国家级开发区就有21个（图2），规划或建设的新城新区更是多达52个（图3），整体上仍处于遍地开花、缺乏重点的状态。

（三）21世纪初至今：产业结构转型升级阶段

随着珠三角经济的高速发展和产业集聚程度的提高，土地、资源、能源和劳动力等生产要素成本不断攀升，加上2007年以来原材料和劳动力价格上涨、人民币持续升值等因素，珠三角的要素成本优势逐渐丧失。不论是从产业结构优化的内在要求，还是从要素成本上升

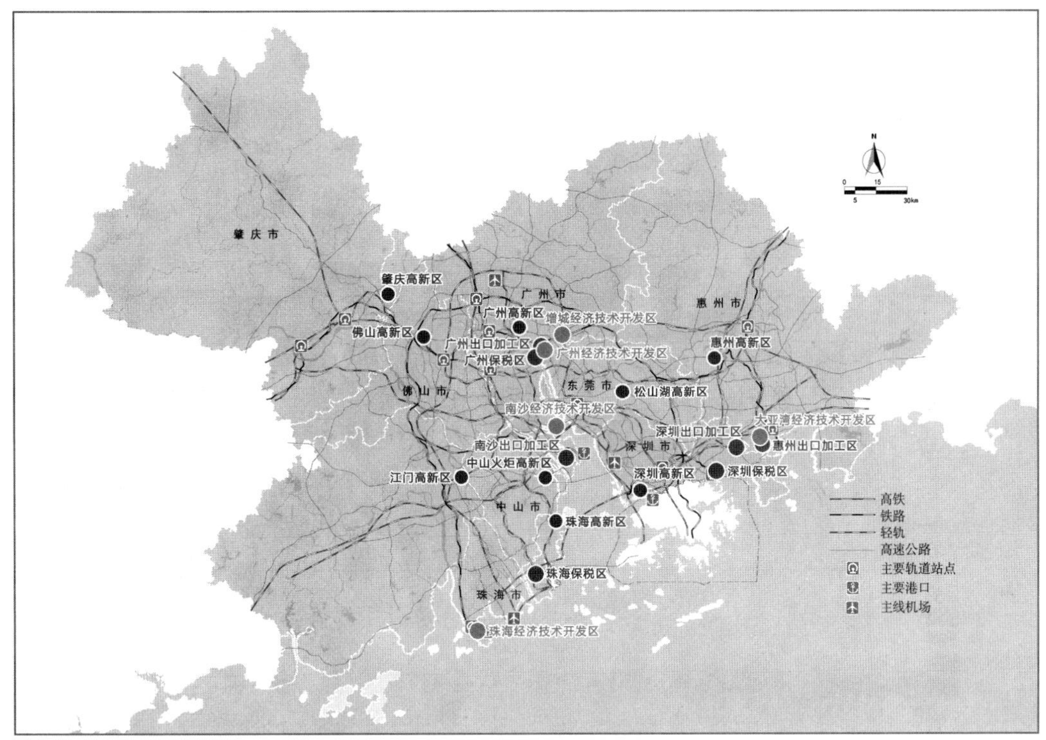

图 2　珠三角各类国家级开发区分布示意图

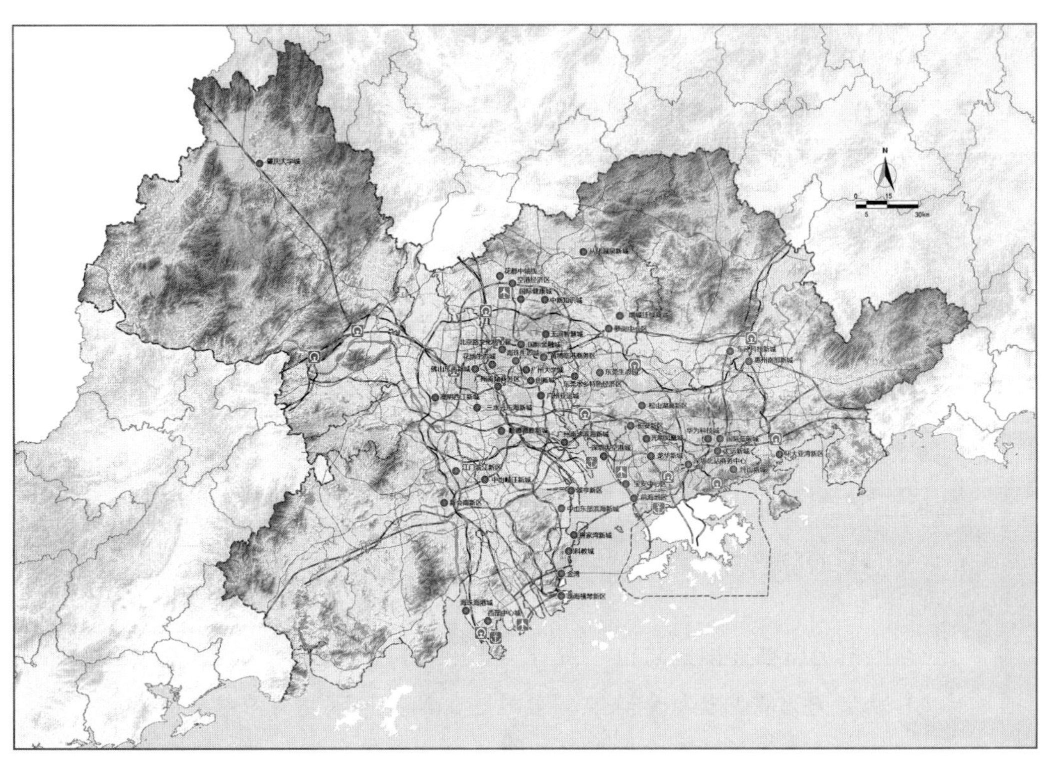

图 3　珠三角各市主要新城、新区分布示意图

的外在压力来看，珠三角转变经济发展方式、实现产业结构转换升级势在必行。

这一阶段，高新技术产业和先进制造业产值不断增加。2012 年，高技术制造业产值约占规模以上工业总产值的 28%，先进制造业增加值占规模以上工业增加值比重达 52%。以批发零售、金融、房地产、商务服务等为主的第三产业也得到快速发展，一直处于与第二产业齐头并进的态势，其中现代服务业占第三产业增加值比重达 60%（图 4）。

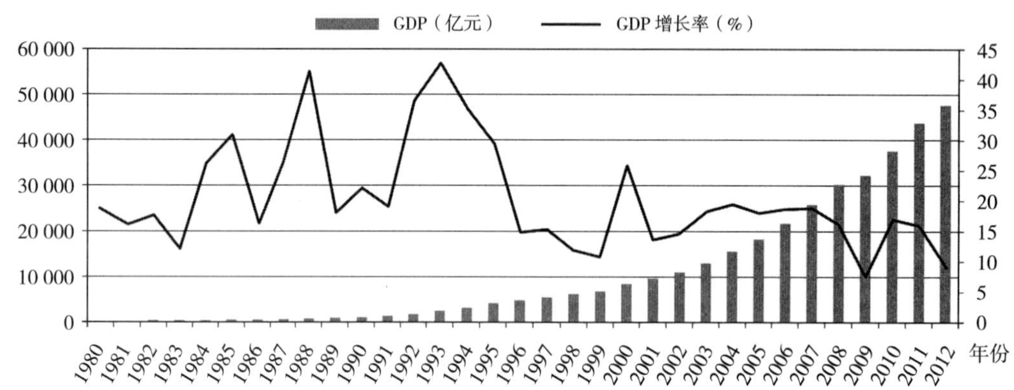

图 4　珠三角 GDP 及增长率变化

数据来源：《珠江三角洲全域规划（2014—2020 年）》。

总的来说，经过以上三个阶段的发展，珠三角产业总量极大提升，形成了“二、三产业并进”的产业体系，取得了较好的成绩（图 5）。但仍在发展动力、产业结构、空间布局上存在一定的问题，如：偏于依赖外向型经济，应对风险的能力不足；经济发展较为粗放，对低成本人力、土地资源的依赖性强；传统制造业等低端产业仍占较大比例，产业结构不佳；产业散乱布局于村镇工业园、各市开发区等，集聚度差，缺乏统筹。

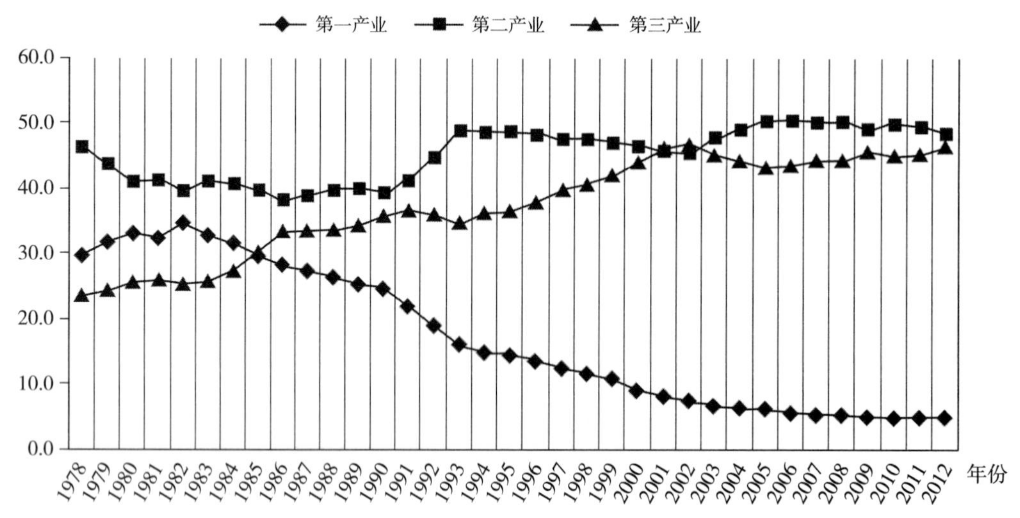

图 5　改革开放以来珠三角三次产业变化

数据来源：《珠江三角洲全域规划（2014—2020 年）》。

三、珠三角产业发展的机遇与挑战

（一）发展机遇

1. “新常态”战略为珠三角产业发展提出新的思路

“新常态”战略提出加快从要素驱动、投资驱动转向创新驱动转变的要求，这与“十二五”以来，以智能化、数字化、信息化、融合化为特征的物联网、云计算、大数据等新一代信息技术加速崛起是相适应的。珠三角在电子信息产业发展方面具有较好基础和突出优势，“新常态”创新驱动思路将加快珠三角将实现传统制造向“先进智造”的转型，并重新掌握制造业的竞争地位。

同时“新常态”对于新兴产业、服务业的重视，使得以体育休闲、文化创意为主的现代服务业新兴业态不断涌现并得到了快速发展。珠三角向来在文化传媒、体育休闲、品牌广告、会议展览等方面有良好的基础，未来将更多地发挥该方面的优势。

2. “一带一路”战略为珠三角产业发展提出新的要求

珠三角作为海上丝绸之路的起点和重要枢纽，作为全球重要的制造业基地之一，是我国与亚非拉新兴经济体经贸合作最重要的载体。亚非拉等新兴市场国家具有巨大的基础设施建设需求，这与珠三角经济实用装备的制造能力具有较好的契合性。加强与海上丝绸之路沿线国家的经贸交流，将有利于珠三角拓展新的海外市场，继续保持较高速度经济增长。

另一方面，在“一带一路”战略下，珠三角要建成世界级城市群，必须具备相应的高端产业功能，如金融、贸易、文化、管理等，在高端功能的服务拓展、产业功能的转型升级以及新兴功能的培育发展等方面都应发挥全国性、区域性的驱动引领与辐射带动作用。这将是珠三角未来产业发展的主要方向之一。

3. 珠江—西江经济带对珠三角产业发展提供新的方向

珠江—西江经济带发展上升为国家战略，一是在有利于促进珠三角产业向西南省份转移的同时，强化珠三角城市、港口对生产组织、货物运输的服务功能，推进珠三角从承接外来产业向辐射内陆发展的产业地位转变；二是加强了珠三角与桂、滇、湘、黔等资源富集区之间的经济合作，推动珠江西岸装备制造业发展。

（二）面临挑战

1. 以往传统发展方式难以为继的挑战

珠三角以往产业快速发展的比较优势主要体现在劳动力成本、管理成本、环境成本、土地成本等比较低廉（图6）。但随着经济形势和城镇化进程的变化，以往资源依赖性、粗放式的发展方式已经难以为继。一是劳动力、土地等生产要素成本持续上升，珠三角的传统优势已经逐渐丧失；二是对土地扩张的过度依赖，导致了城镇化发展质量、土地使用效率及生态环境水平的降低，以往发展模式导致的低端产业、低效用地和低层次人力资源的相互依附共生的问题日益凸显，各种发展矛盾亟须破解。

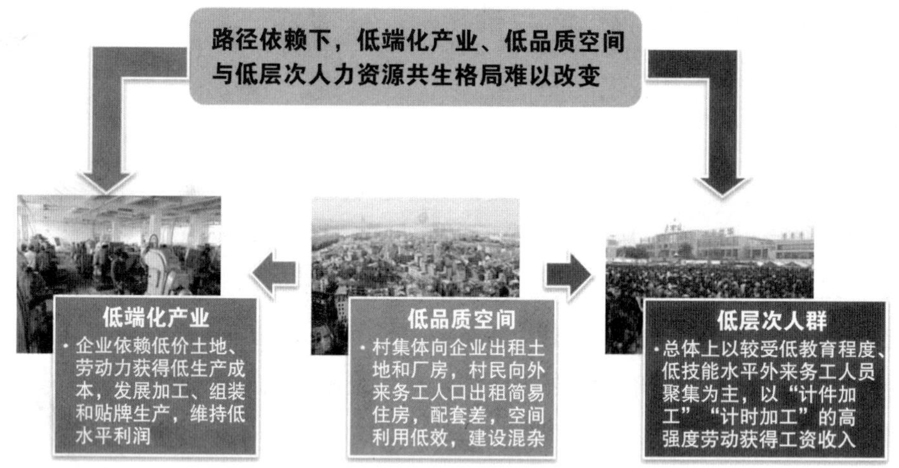

图6　珠三角传统发展路径依赖下的低端共生格局

2. 以往传统产业行业产能过剩的挑战

我国目前生产能力已经由过去的供给不足向供给大幅过剩的阶段转变，钢铁、水泥、汽车、风电、LED、光伏等行业都出现了此种情形。在此背景下，珠三角需要进一步明确产业转型升级和结构优化调整的方向，积极发展以装备制造为主体的先进制造业，带动钢铁、汽车、石化等行业消耗过剩产能，并扩大与装备制造出口相关的生产性服务业出口。

3. 以往产业空间布局缺乏统筹、用地低效的挑战

过去30多年的产业发展历程中，不管是村镇工业“村村点火”的铺开布局，还是各市都推行“工业进园”而建设的各类开发区、高新园区等，珠三角产业空间在一定程度上都存在缺乏统筹整合的问题。这种空间布局方式除了是对产业用地的一种浪费，难以充分发挥产业用地的集聚效应外，也很难体现出珠三角内部区域的产业分工和联系。

四、新常态下珠三角产业发展趋势及重点

（一）产业发展趋势

1. 从要素驱动、投资驱动转向创新驱动转变

在全球金融危机、珠三角外向型加工业受挫、土地资源日益稀缺的背景下，依赖廉价劳动力和土地等资源的发展模式面临巨大挑战，“创新驱动”是引领珠三角转型升级的必然选择。珠三角将逐渐形成以技术创新、产业化创新为主体的创新格局，区域创新能力逐渐增强；产业创新服务体系也将得到进一步完善，将大力发展科技研发、金融服务等服务职能，提高知识创新和原发创新能力。

2. 从传统低端产业向重型化、高新化、高端化产业转变

依托政府大项目或现有产业发展的基础，区域产业重型化、高新化、高端化趋势明显，

重工业和高新技术行业的发展置换了部分低价值区段的制造业发展，工业结构不断优化，整体竞争力不断提高。同时珠三角的产业转型呈现一定的空间差异，已进入后工业化发展阶段的东岸以“创新发展，服务驱动”为主，服务化趋势明显，发展相对滞后的西岸则是工业化和城镇化双轮驱动，呈现再工业化的发展模式。

3. 从“外向主导”向“内外兼顾”转变

由于国际国内发展形势的变化，未来珠三角产业发展一方面应进一步加大对外开放、技术创新的力度，另一方面应更加重视泛珠三角及珠三角内部之间合作与协调。泛珠地区的崛起和深化开放，将进一步推动内贸和对内运输快速增长，珠三角产业的内向转型也将推动中国产业发展由外部市场向内生市场带动的转换，其在全球产业体系中的地位和角色更有可能由制造中心向区域生产组织和服务中心转变。

4. 从无序产业空间向区域化、集中化布局转变

一方面，产业布局的区域分工逐渐凸显。核心圈层城市二产比重下降，总部、营销、服务等高端环节则留在核心地区，外围圈层成为制造业主要增长区域，内外圈层之间形成高度的产业分工和联系，实现区域内完成整条产业价值链体系。另一方面，工业进园发展趋势明显，产业空间得到有效整合，产业用地破碎化得到一定改善。产业园区和重大战略地区成为珠三角产业发展的重要平台，产业发展的规模效应和集聚效应不断强化，用地效益提高。

总体而言，珠三角产业规模已进入平稳增长阶段，但在发展动力、产业结构、空间布局等方面仍面临一定的困境。如何应对当前国际及区域发展形势，破解产业动力不可持续、空间布局零散低效等难题，进一步提高产业发展效益和产业创新能力，加快现代服务业和先进制造业的发展等问题，都是珠三角建设世界级城市群的重大考验。

（二）产业发展重点

《珠江三角洲全域规划（2014－2020年）》结合国内外产业发展形势和珠三角实际情况，提出构建“11＋7＋7”现代产业体系的发展目标，规划推动先进制造业和现代服务业协同发展并形成两大重点产业双轮驱动，培育发展战略性新兴产业形成新兴主导产业，改造提升优势传统产业焕发新的竞争优势（图7）。

对《珠江三角洲全域规划（2014－2020年）》提出的产业发展目标进行分析，可以看出其产业发展重点很好地反映了前述发展趋势：

（1）突出创新产业体系：《珠江三角洲全域规划（2014－2020年）》中科技信息、文化创意及各类战略新兴产业都是对“创新驱动”战略的响应。《广东省十三五规划纲要》中也特别提出应推进工业化与信息化深度融合，加快培育发展信息化新业态；广州、深圳等市也将电子商务、科技服务等作为“十三五”的发展重点。

（2）强化高端服务功能：金融保险、总部经济等现代服务业作为珠三角建设世界级城市群必备高端职能的地位被强化。《广东省十三五规划纲要》提出支持广州、深圳开展国家服务业综合改革试点；广州市“十三五”更提出要重点发展7大服务业，其中金融业到2020年增加值占GDP比重达12%，物流业到2020年增加值占GDP比重达8%。

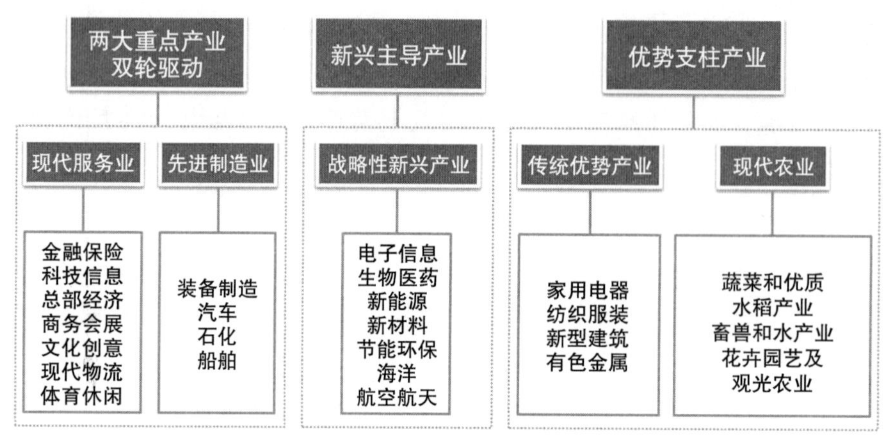

图7　珠三角“11+7+7”现代产业体系

数据来源:《珠江三角洲全域规划(2014－2020年)》。

(3)体现重化工业优势:珠三角目前拥有良好的重化工业基础和港口区位条件,在“一带一路”和珠江—西江经济带战略支撑下,资金技术密集、关联度高、带动性强的装备制造、汽车、石化、船舶等优势产业是拉动珠三角外圈层经济快速发展、带动泛珠地区产业联动的重要抓手。

(4)推进传统产业转型:家电、纺织服装、农业等传统产业仍在珠三角多数地区占据较大的比例,对该类产业应以改造提升为主,积极引入新技术,通过政策支持和市场的自发培育塑造,提升价值链加工环节。

五、珠三角产业空间布局新态势

珠三角产业空间布局态势可以概括为“区域化”“集聚化”,《珠江三角洲全域规划(2014－2020年)》中关于产业空间布局的规划内容很好地体现了该发展态势。

(一)区域化:“两环一带”的产业空间布局结构

受区位条件、产业基础、政策因素等影响,广州、深圳、佛山、东莞等内圈层城市的GDP总量、人均GDP增速等方面普遍快于外圈层城市,内外圈层发展差距逐渐加大,珠江东西两岸产业分工也逐渐明显,产业发展的“区域化”分工态势日益凸显。总体上,未来珠三角生产服务业将高度集中在内圈层的核心城市,其中金融服务、科技研发服务主要集中在广、深两个核心城市;技术密集型产业向内圈层的中心城区集聚;外圈层承接劳动密集型产业的扩散。珠江东西两岸也呈现出东岸以电子信息为主导的高新技术产业、西岸以重型化为特征的装备制造产业的发展格局。《珠江三角洲全域规划(2014－2020年)》将这种空间布局态势总结为“两环一带”的产业空间布局结构(图8)。

1. 湾区创新服务环

以广州和深圳为两大核心,以环湾区的国家级新区及重大平台为依托,大力发展现代金

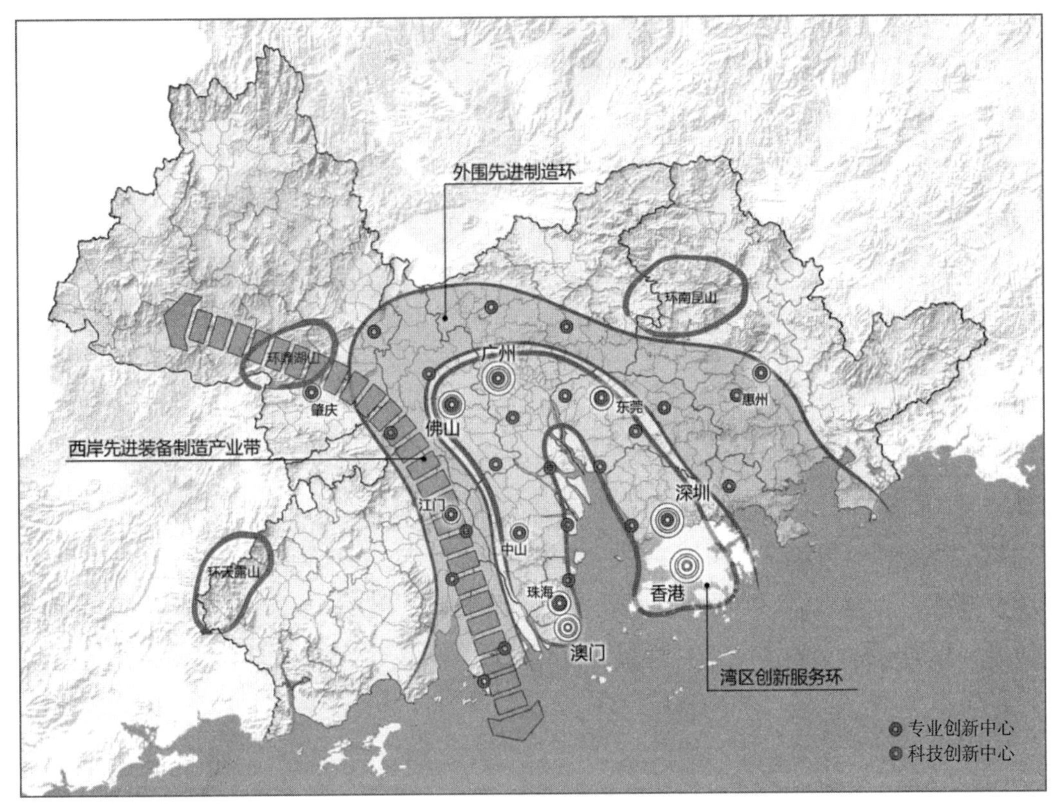

图8　珠三角“两环一带”的产业空间布局结构

融、现代物流、现代商贸、科技服务、总部经济等现代服务业，构筑珠三角世界级城市群的高端服务和科技研发等功能高度密集核心湾区。

2. 外围先进制造环

珠江西岸地区依托各市园区重点发展生物医药、节能环保、新能源、新材料等战略性新兴产业，并强化传统优势制造业的技术升级和改造。珠江东岸地区以信息技术、生物制造业、新能源、新材料、新能源汽车为主要发展方向，引导形成一批具有较强创新自主性和技术引领性的骨干企业，形成一批特色鲜明的产业链和产业集聚区，打造东岸战略新兴产业发展走廊。

3. 西岸先进装备制造产业带

珠江西岸依托已有的制造业基础，大力发展先进装备制造业，培育本土创新能力，逐步完善产业链，推动西岸形成以大型企业和优势产品为龙头、中小企业和配套产品为基础、产业链完整、产业集群发达的先进装备制造业发展走廊。

（二）集聚化：产业发展的新兴战略地区

珠三角各市在以往经济发展过程中，均规划建设了多个开发区、新城、新区等战略地区，作为本市产业发展的重要空间载体。根据统计，各市规划或建设的新城新区多达52个。这种“遍地开花”的开发模式一方面分散了产业资源投入，不利于产业的高效集聚；另一方面其规划建设更多立足于各市自身利益，竞争往往大于合作。在珠三角建设世界级城市群的背景及区域一体化的要求下，出于区域统筹考虑的产业集聚化日益成为产业发展的新态势。立足区域发展视角，面向建设世界级城市群的目标，对各市发展重点平台进行筛选，以下几类地区将成为珠三角产业发展的新兴战略地区。建立新型战略地区的目标是：

（1）承担突破性职能，参与国际竞争：包括承担高端生产性服务业、先进制造业、“二、三产业融合”职能的战略地区，如南沙新区、前海深港现代服务业合作区、惠州大亚湾新区等。

（2）依托综合性枢纽，促进要素流动：包括依托国际化空港、海港等促进世界级要素集聚和交换的核心地区，依托城际轨道、高铁站点等加强区内联系、拓展区域腹地的关键节点，如广州空港经济区、深圳大空港城、广州南站商务区等。

（3）创新体制示范，引领区域转型：包括国家级新区、区域体制创新示范试点、中外合作创新试点等，如珠海横琴新区、东莞水乡经济区、广州中新知识城等。

（4）多方参与共建，深化区域合作：包括加强珠三角内部合作的地区、深化粤港澳合作的地区、拓展泛珠地区合作的地区、引领全球合作的地区，如中山翠亨新区等。

根据以上原则，筛选出17个新兴战略地区（表1），作为珠三角最重要的产业发展空间载体，承担高端现代服务业、先进制造业和战略新兴产业功能，引领区域转型创新。根据职能等级划分，又可分为国际级职能与区域级职能两类。其中国际级职能新兴战略地区5个，包括深圳前海深港现代服务业合作区、广州南沙新区、珠海横琴新区、广州空港经济区、深圳大空港城，面向全球发展国际级别高端生产性服务业，承担国际枢纽网络功能。其他地区为区域级职能新兴战略地区，共12个（图9），重点为各类现代服务业、装备制造业等，以加强粤港澳合作、拓展泛珠腹地、深化珠三角内部联系、区域转型示范为主要任务，是提升珠三角整体实力的支撑地区。

表1　珠三角重点地区产业发展指引表

序号	新兴战略地区	重点产业功能
1	深圳前海深港现代服务业合作区	世界级金融、科技和信息服务业
2	广州南沙新区	商贸会展、生态疗养、体育旅游、离岸数据、文化创意等高端服务业
3	珠海横琴新区	信息服务、外包服务、商贸服务等区域性商务服务产业，高端疗养，研发设计
4	广州空港经济区	航空核心产业、现代物流、综合服务、商务会展、保税制造
5	深圳大空港城	商务会展与创意服务产业、科技服务与高端制造产业
6	广州南站商务区	交通服务、生产服务、城市服务等现代服务业
7	中新（广州）知识城	知识密集型服务业、高附加值制造业
8	佛山中德工业服务区	工业服务、研发创新
9	广东省金融科技产业融合创新综合实验区	金融后台服务、金融研发、金融信息咨询
10	肇庆新区	居住、商业、文化休闲等现代服务业

续表 1

序号	新兴战略地区	重点产业功能
11	深圳国际低碳城	节能环保、生命健康、智慧低碳信息、高端低碳装备制造等新兴低碳产业
12	东莞水乡特色发展经济区	休闲旅游、文化创意、居住等现代服务业
13	东莞松山湖高新技术产业开发区	生物技术、电子信息、科技研发
14	惠州环大亚湾新区	石油化工、海洋经济、生态旅游
15	珠海高栏港经济区	船舶和海洋工程装备制造产业、清洁能源产业、石油化工产业和港口物流
16	中山翠亨新区	文化服务业、创意产业和电子商务等现代服务业，风电新能源产业
17	江门大广海湾经济区	先进装备制造业，海洋生物、海水综合利用、海洋可再生能源等海洋新兴产业，滨海旅游、健康服务等现代服务业

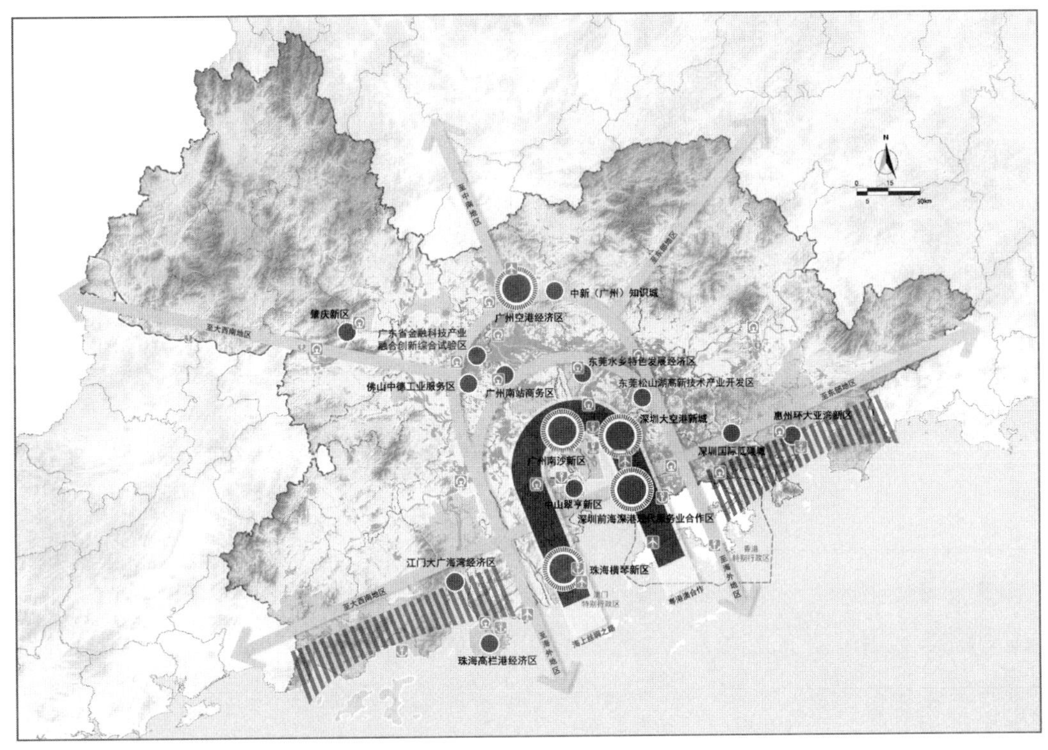

图 9　珠三角新兴战略地区空间分布图

六、结论

改革开放以来，珠三角依靠其区位及人力、土地优势，在产业发展上取得了长足的进步。但在“新常态”及“一带一路”战略背景下，珠三角以往依赖低成本资源的传统发展方式及缺乏统筹、粗放低效的空间布局已经不能满足新时代的要求。珠三角近年来出台的各类政策、规划，包括最近编制完成的《珠三角全域规划》，都对该问题提出了相应的解决思路和策略。本文在相关的研究、规划基础上，对珠三角产业发展及空间的新态势进行了总结，认为珠三角未来产业发展应突出创新产业体系，强化高端服务功能，体现重化工业优势，推进传统产业转型。在空间布局上应实现“区域化”“集聚化”，在区域产业分工的基础上，重点发展若干承载区域产业功能的战略地区。

（作者：李亚洲，广州市城市规划勘测设计研究院；闫永涛，高级工程师，广州市城市规划勘测设计研究院政府规划编制部总工程师）

参考文献

［1］中国城市规划设计研究院编制．珠三角产业发展的空间布局及政策应对，2014 年 12 月．www. gdupi. com/prd2014/productshow. asp? id =114.

［2］周艳群．长三角和珠三角经济发展历程的回顾与比较．www. stats-sh. gov. cn/tjqt/201103/88781. html.

［3］广东省住房和城乡建设厅．珠江三角洲全域规划（2014－2020 年），2014 年．

［4］路红艳，珠三角地区产业演进与金融危机背景下结构调整趋势研究［J］．经济前沿，2009（9）.

［5］广东省十三五规划纲要，2016 年 1 月．

［6］广州市十三五规划纲要，2016 年 2 月．

珠三角城市群的产业转型与变革

一、珠三角城市群：东亚最大的巨型城市区域

改革开放以来，珠三角依托邻近港澳的区位优势，借助香港国际金融中心、商贸中心和航运中心的特殊功能，积极参与全球生产分工，迅速成长为具有世界影响力的制造业基地，取得了举世瞩目的成绩。在工业化的带动下，珠三角城市化进程快速推进，已成为中国最具世界影响的三大城市群之一。2015 年世界银行发布的《东亚变化中的城市图景：度量十年的空间增长》报告也因此指出，珠三角已取代东京大都市区成为东亚地区规模最大的“巨型城市区域”（World Bank，2015）。自 2007 年以来，珠三角的发展进入了调整转型期，城市群的发展呈现出新特征。2014 年 5 月，广东省政府决定开展珠三角全域规划，项目的展开让我们对珠三角城市群的发展现状和未来的转型变革有了更清晰的认识和思考。

（一）经济与人口增长呈现新常态特征

2014 年，珠三角地区生产总值达到 5.8 万亿元，占全国约 9.1% 的经济总量，是我国经济增长的三大引擎之一；常住人口达到5 763.38万人，其中非户籍常住人口约为2 555.44万人，约占全国流动人口的 10.84%，是我国人口密度最高、吸纳外来人口就业创业最为集中的地区之一。但从经济增长层面的变化来看（图 1），2000－2010 年期间，珠三角的 GDP 增速基本在 12% 以上，2010 年后逐步回落到 8% ~10% 的增长区间。从人口增长方面的变化来看（图 2），2006－2010 年是珠三角人口高速增长阶段，常住人口每年增长 180 万 ~250 万人，特别是非户籍常住人口增长率高达 7% 以上；2011 年以来，人口增长逐步趋缓，常住人口每年仅增长 30 万 ~50 万人，而非户籍常住人口则出现回流现象。中国经济发展的新常态在珠三角反应明显。

（二）巨型城市连绵地区

珠三角是我国城镇建设连绵化程度最高的地区之一，在约 5.6 万平方公里的地域空间上分布了广州、深圳 2 座超大城市，佛山、东莞 2 座特大城市，人口密度已超过1 000人/平方公里。根据国土资源部的有关统计，2012 年珠三角现状城乡居民点建设用地达到7 408.79平

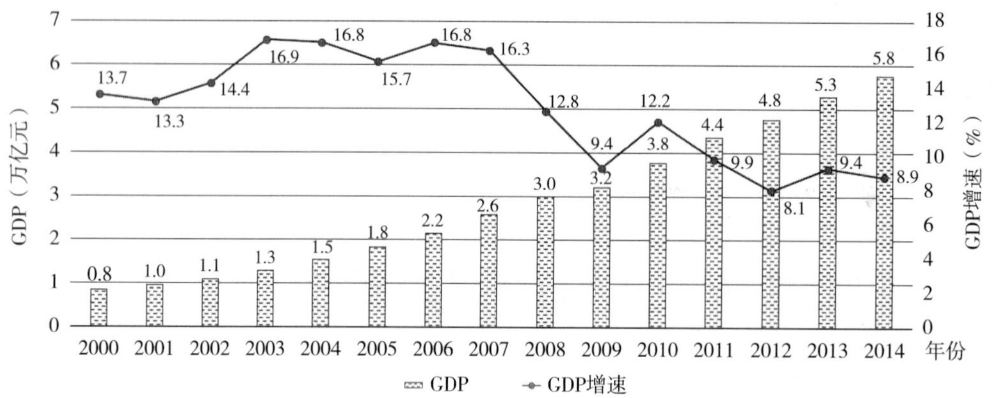

图1　2000年以来珠三角地区生产总值（GDP）及其增速变化

数据来源：广东统计年鉴（2001－2015）。

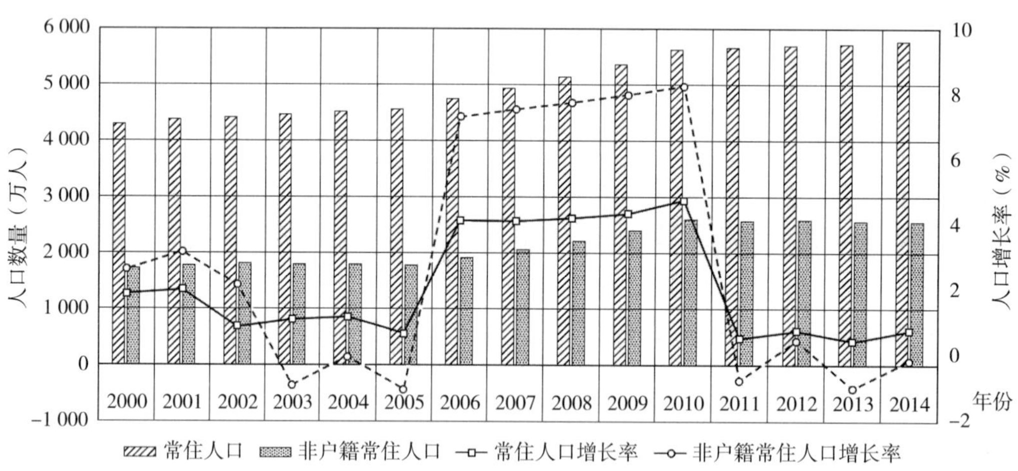

图2　2000年以来珠三角人口及其增速变化

数据来源：广东统计年鉴（2001－2015）。

方公里（图3）。在珠三角的核心地区，城市边界、城乡边界逐渐趋于模糊，都市连绵区的面积达到了1.5万平方公里。

（三）形成“双中心、三梯队、网络型”的城市群结构

近十几年来，珠三角城市通过各自的发展路径实现了规模和量能的提升，城市群功能网络逐步从过去的以广深为核心、其他城市同属下一层级的扁平结构，优化为以广深为核心、佛莞为第二梯队、其他城市为第三梯队的层级式结构（表1）。特别是在全球化的影响下，广州作为国家中心城市、深圳作为国家经济中心城市的作用日益显现，其集聚发展要素、组织资源配置的功能得到了进一步的强化，带动珠三角城市群的国际影响和全球地位逐步提高。同时，在区域对内对外交通、信息网络和生产网络日益完善的条件下，网络型城镇群也逐步形成。

图3 珠三角城乡建成空间高度连绵

表1 珠三角城市形成的三大梯队结构

单位：万亿；万人

城市梯队	量　级	各城市情况(2014)	占珠三角比重
第一梯队	GDP≥1.5 万亿	广州(1.67)、深圳(1.60)	56.74%
	常住人口≥1 000 万人	广州(1 308.1)、深圳(1 077.9)	41.40%
第二梯队	0.5 万亿≤GDP≤1.0 万亿	佛山(0.74)、东莞(0.59)	23.11%
	500 万人≤常住人口≤1 000 万人	佛山(735.1)、东莞(834.3)	27.23%
第三梯队	0.1 万亿≤GDP≤0.5 万亿	珠海(0.19)、惠州(0.30)、中山(0.28)、江门(0.21)、肇庆(0.18)	20.15%
	100 万人≤常住人口≤500 万人	珠海(161.4)、惠州(472.7)、中山(319.3)、江门(451.1)、肇庆(403.9)	31.37%

数据来源：广东统计年鉴（2015）。

（四）区域性产业集群初步形成

珠三角产业的起步和发展呈现出两种不同路径：珠江东岸地区依托香港发展纺织服装、电子、玩具等外源型的“三来一补”加工业（薛凤旋、杨春，1998）；珠江西岸地区则从传统工业和乡镇企业起步，形成了以纺织、陶瓷、五金、灯饰、家用电器等为代表的内源型经济（许学强，1988；李立勋，1997）。经过30多年的集聚发展以及近年来的转型升级，珠三角制造业依托主要园区和专业镇，在内圈层逐步形成了板块式的簇群发展，并呈现分别以广佛和深莞为中心向外辐射的两个集聚扇面。根据对2014年珠三角183万家注册企业的地址和业务类别的空间解析（图4），总体上看，珠三角改革开放初期的“诸侯经济”形态，经过长期的竞合过程，现在已形成了鲜明的区域性产业集群，即东岸以电子信息、医药等知识密集型产业为主，西岸以机械装备制造等技术密集型产业为主的产业差异化发展格局。

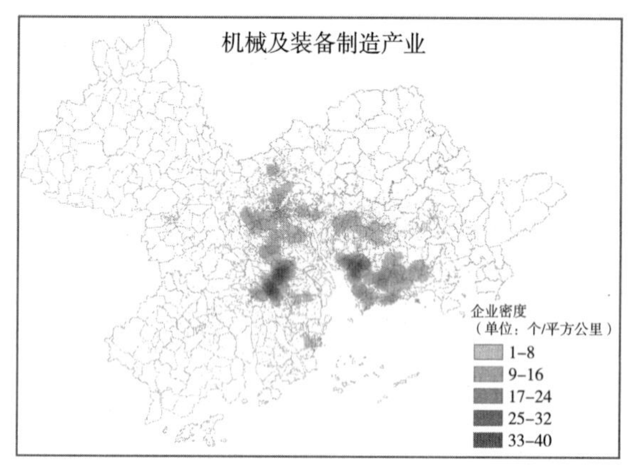

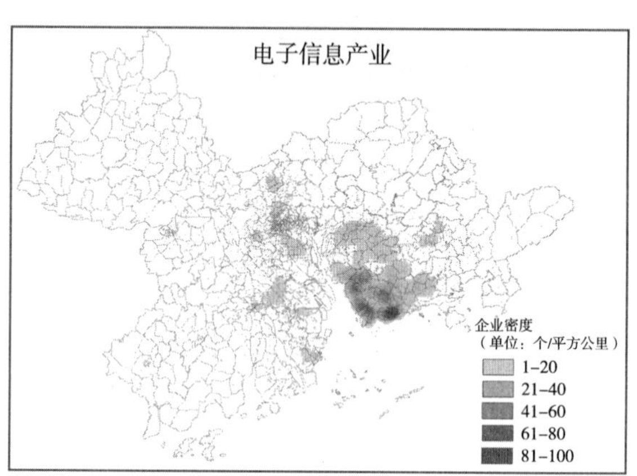

图4 珠三角西岸装备制造产业集群与东岸电子信息产业集群

数据来源：广东省工商局，2014年广东省企业名录数据（包含约183万家珠三角企业）。

（五）关键廊道交通流量聚集

随着珠三角区域一体化的推进，广深等中心城市在区域发展中的组织服务功能得到强化，城市之间分工协作逐步深入，带动区域交通客货流量也进一步向关键走廊聚集。根据路网交通流量的监测（图5），目前，珠三角已经形成以广深（港）、广珠（澳）、广佛三大交

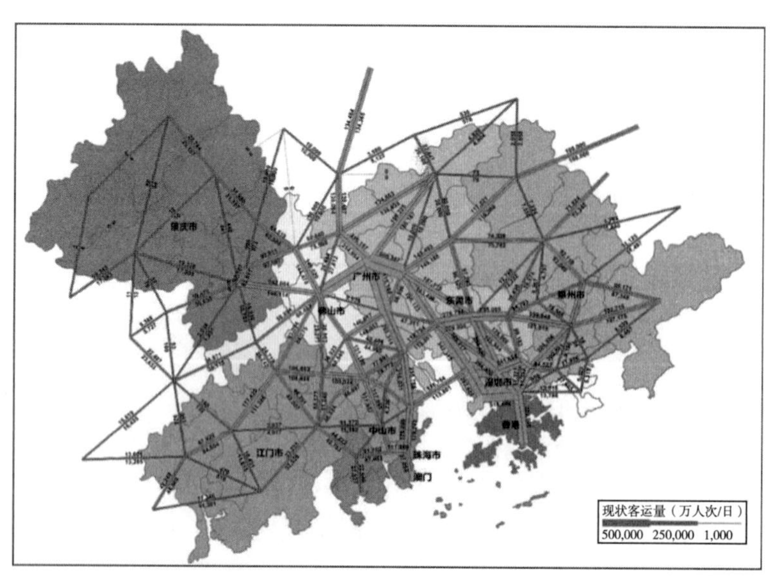

图5 2013年珠三角区县级客流蛛网图（人次/日）

通走廊为骨干的区域交通格局，广州—佛山、深圳—东莞中心区之间主要通道的日客流量单向已超过30万人次（含过境交通）。同时，随着珠三角城际轨道交通建设的推进，广深通道、广珠通道客运量增长也远高于区域客运量增长的平均水平，表明珠三角交通流量向关键走廊聚集的趋势仍将进一步加剧。

（六）环境污染跨越峰值，局部恶化

2000年以来，珠三角工业化快速发展，特别是工业重型化的政策导向，导致大气、水等环境污染逐步加剧，灰霾天气频频出现。2008年开始，随着“双转移”战略实施以及全省迎接2010年广州亚运会的顺利举行，珠三角各市开始大力推进产业转型升级、节能减排、河涌整治，并严格执行国家和省关于大气污染防治的法律法规和标准要求，建立健全区域大气污染联防联控制度，环境污染治理取得突出成效。目前，珠三角城市灰霾日数、单位GDP碳排放量等指标已跨越峰值，并开始进入下降通道。但值得注意的是，伴随产业转移，珠三角大气环境污染由内圈层向外围地区扩散的迹象较为明显，而在季风作用下，冬季外围产生的大气污染又回流到珠三角（图6）；城市内部河涌得到有效治理，水质状况呈好转趋势的同时，跨界河流污染情况仍然严峻。

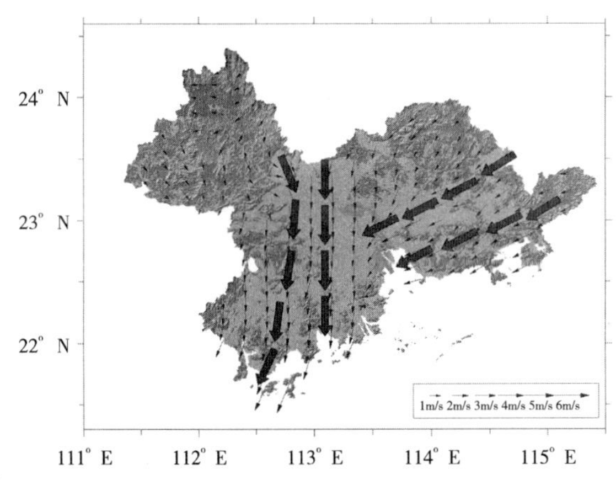

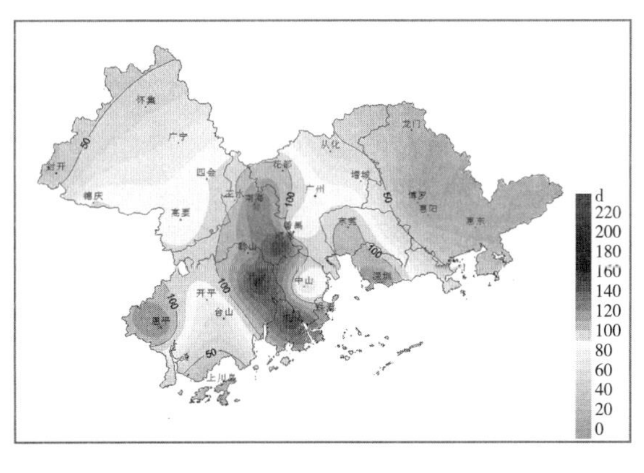

图6 珠三角常年主导风向与灰霾日数分布

资料来源：广东省气象局，珠三角区域气象站站点统计资料。

二、问题与挑战

（一）“躯干型”经济面临外部市场环境变化的冲击

改革开放以来，珠三角采取了基于比较优势的出口导向型发展模式，凭借劳动力丰裕和土地、资源等价格低廉的优势，承接发达国家产业梯度转移，发展加工、组装等产业链低端环节嵌入全球生产网络，承担着低端加工制造的“躯干”角色（李坤等，2011）。这种发展

模式有利于在工业化初期以较低成本迅速积累财富，但实际上低成本的背后是高度依赖外商直接投资（FDI）以及对本地自主创新、自有品牌、人力资本、知识网络等方面的忽视（肖金成，2010）。全球经济网络由创造知识、组织生产的“大脑”和实施生产加工环节的“躯干”构成，“大脑”具有门槛，而“躯干”则具有可替代性。当“躯干型”经济在发展到一定规模后，对外部经济环境的依附所带来的制约将愈发凸显。2008 年国际金融危机后珠三角经济所遭受的冲击恰恰反映了这种“躯干型”经济的脆弱性，在国内劳动力成本上涨、资源环境约束趋紧的背景下，珠三角原本的竞争优势逐步弱化，跨国企业的生产环节开始向东南亚、南美等成本更低的国家和地区转移。一方面，在发达国家“再工业化”和东南亚国家“低成本竞争”的双重夹击下，珠三角原有的发展模式已不可持续。另一方面，国家“一带一路”战略实施并赋予珠三角“21 世纪海上丝绸之路”建设主力军和排头兵的使命，也要求珠三角具有服务于中国企业走出去的强大总部功能。因此，珠三角需要加快“躯干经济”向“大脑经济”转型升级，大力培育发展创新功能，建立与境外紧密的社会联系网络，提供金融、法律、会计、咨询、评估等专业服务。

（二）连绵区城乡混杂品质不高，亟须转型提质

改革开放以来，珠三角地区出现了以农业快速增长、乡镇企业快速发展、外商直接投资迅速增多以及吸引大量农村剩余劳动力的农村城镇化现象。在自下而上城镇化和工业化模式作用下，珠三角村镇地区非农产业迅速发展，非农建设用地快速扩张蔓延，由原先的高人口密度农业区转化成了一种城乡土地利用混杂交错、农业活动和非农业活动高度混合、社会经济结构急剧变化的过渡性地域类型。进入 2000 年后，随着大城市主导的城市化快速扩张，城市建设用地与村镇地区犬牙交错，又进一步加剧了这种“半城半乡”空间景观特征的显化。在多方面的要素的复合作用下，使珠三角内圈层形成了约 1.5 万平方公里的城乡建设连绵区，除了城市和个别镇中心区建设面貌、空间品质较高外，大部分区域城乡空间均质无序、功能混合严重、设施配套滞后、生态斑块破碎、景观风貌单一（图 7）。当前，珠三角建设世界级城市群的背景下，需要对现有产业升级、培育发展和引入具有引领作用和创新力的高端功能，而高端产业和功能的注入则需要提供与之相匹配的高品质优质空间场所。从此种意义上看，珠三角大量存在的低效、低品质的城乡混杂空间已经难以适应珠三角转型升级的需要，亟须转型提质。

三、面向可持续发展的转变思考

（一）珠三角的功能发展

珠三角在国家和区域中所承担的核心功能，需要置于历史进程中加以观察。从历史变迁中，可以理解珠三角的角色功能其实是不断演进的过程，在这个过程中，存在着贯穿始终的规律。

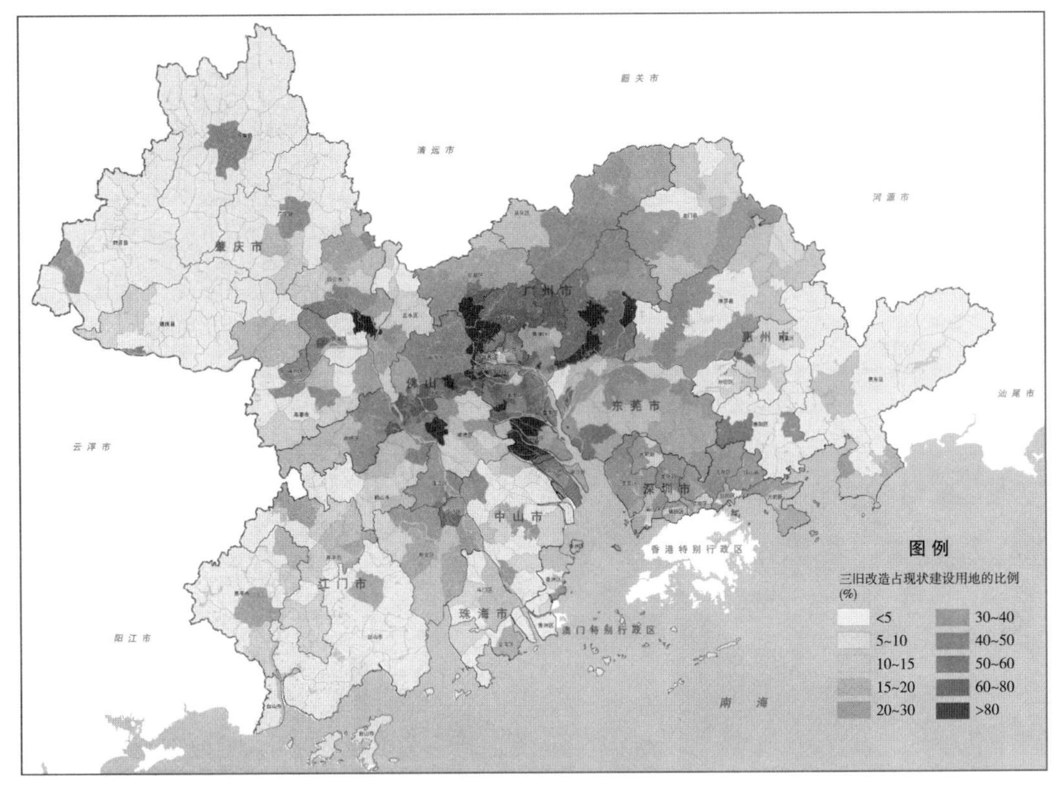

图 7　珠三角城镇连绵区存在大量的低效、低品质“三旧”用地

1. *历史回顾：国家视角与全球视角*

珠三角的开发进程，可追溯到先秦时期。秦朝建立大一统王朝，出于管理运输需要，在岭南开灵渠，并沿西江设南海郡、桂林郡、象郡三郡。公元前 110 年左右的汉武帝时期，珠三角西侧的徐闻合浦成为海上丝绸之路的始发港。随后的历史中，帝国都城不断东移，中原进入岭南的通道也自西向东不断开辟，同时岭南地区政治军事中心也由梧州向东移，最后至广州（图 8），并带动岭南经济中心和海上丝路出发港也迁至广州，至宋朝则在广州设立市舶司。

随着 16 世纪全球地理大发现的推进，东西方文明开始发生大规模的正面接触。明初（1523 年）因“争贡之役”开始海禁，广州“一口通商”使珠江口成为外国人从海上进入中国的唯一通道，葡萄牙人也因此在 1553 年选择珠江口畔的澳门作为落脚地。正因为澳门的存在，清乾隆二十二年（1757 年）再次海禁时依然保留了广州“一口通商”。鸦片战争以后，香港成为殖民者的新驻地，渐渐被开发经营为东方转口贸易基地和国际性商业都会，珠三角被卷入资本主义世界体系（图 9）。

从珠三角发展的历史脉络中可以看出，尽管珠三角远离国家政治经济中心，但由于地处大陆南端海滨这一独特的位置，使它日益受国家力量与全球化力量相互交织作用的影响。一方面，国家始终需要通过国家功能的在这个地区的设置实现对外的管控，并随着国家经济重心的转移，珠三角与中原之间新的联系通道不断开辟；另一方面，由于地处偏远，珠三角的开放在有利于国家对外交往的同时，不会对国家安全构成根本性威胁，从而得以保留足够的

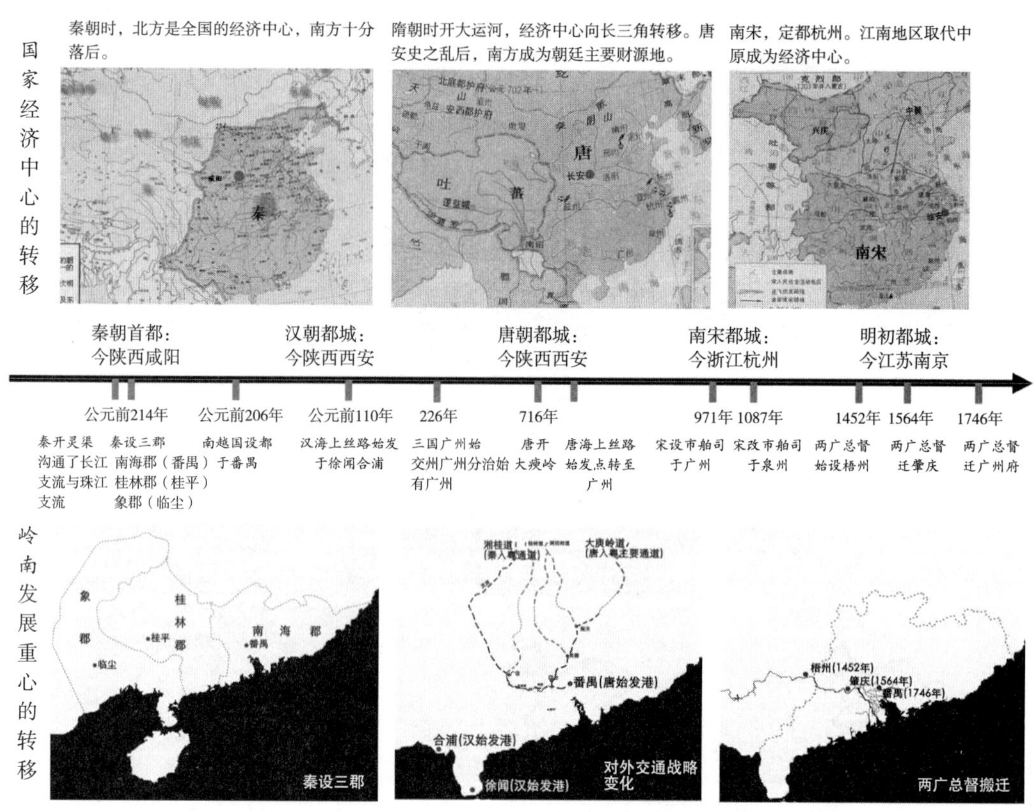

图8 历史上珠三角发展与国家经济的关系

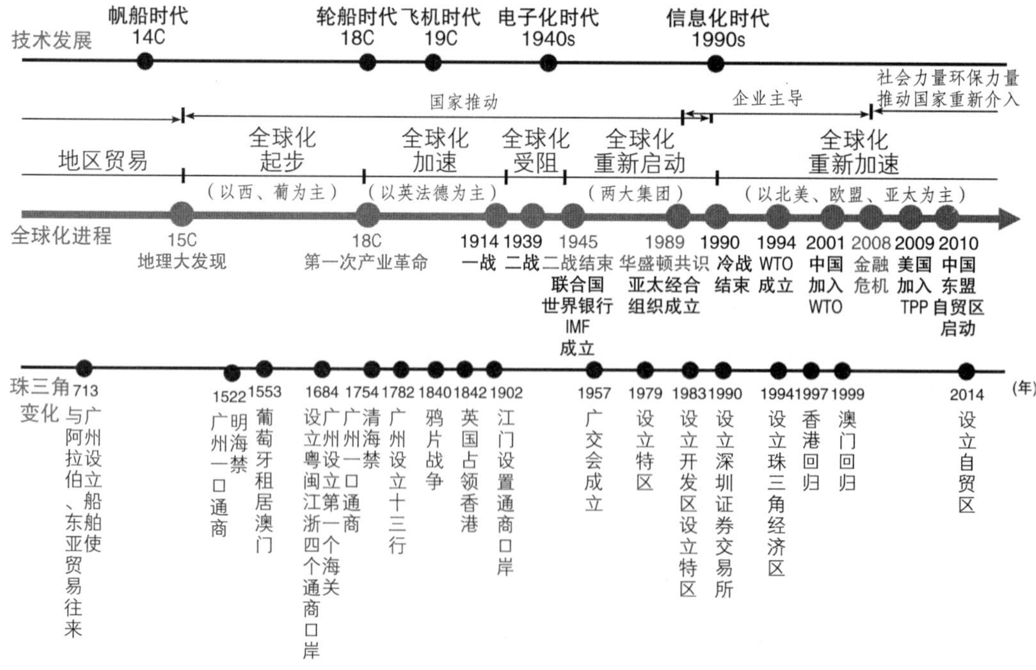

图9 全球化历程及其对珠三角的影响

经济自由度，长期得益于海外贸易的繁荣。两次海禁均保留广州“一口通商”，使珠三角成为西方文明进入中国的最重要的据点，也由此不断提升珠三角在全国经济体系中的地位。

而在新中国成立后，这一角色也一直未曾改变：在国际国内环境变化中，珠三角一直承担先行、探路、试验等重要角色。1957 年，国家在广州设立“中国出口商品交易会”；1980 年在深圳、珠海设立经济特区；1990 年，国家在深圳设立“深圳证券交易所”；1996 年，珠海设立“中国国际航空航天博览会”。这些国家功能的设置，与港澳的国际性功能相互作用，引领了珠三角世界制造业基地的进程。

2. 新时期珠三角的功能演进

从历史脉络分析来看，珠三角的发展始终不能脱离国家体系与全球化进程的框架。那么，在当前国家“一带一路”战略和全球市场格局调整的背景下，珠三角的功能演进将可能出现何种新动向？

“一带一路”是中国在全新的国际国内新形势下推动的全球化新战略，也给对珠三角带来全新机遇与巨大挑战。珠三角传统的外贸企业需要面对新的选择。一方面，大量企业需要从为欧美企业贴牌代工转向建立自己的总部并形成独立自主的品牌；另一方面，企业需要主动走出国门，开辟陌生的国际新兴市场。

当中国企业走出国门在外投资时，中国企业就成了跨国企业。萨森（2011）对跨国企业的研究指出，跨国企业的分散化程度越高（如跨国设立分支机构），对企业的核心管理和服务职能的要求就越高，对所在城市的专业服务功能也要求越高。那么，“走出去”的中国跨国企业给珠三角带来的挑战是，珠三角的核心城市如何为企业提供强有力的管理与服务支持，这种支持有赖于本地强大的金融、法律、风险评估等专业服务机构以及利于国际交往的公共服务环境所共同结成的社会基础网络。社会基础网络是否强大，决定了区域核心城市在全球竞争中是否足够专业。

珠三角在长期的对外贸易中培育了良好的专业化的社会基础网络环境，但在面临国际市场的转换时，需要与国家战略紧紧绑定，同时，要在“躯干经济”基础上培育新的“大脑经济”功能，也需要国家力量的支撑。当前环境下，对珠三角转型发展将产生关键作用的国家功能包括以下几个方面：

面向新兴市场的国家级门户枢纽。珠三角作为我国向南开放的桥头堡，需要培育更加专业的面向东南亚市场的枢纽服务功能，包括国际机场、海港航线与服务功能的升级，以及建立基于枢纽港口的政府间通关、边检、关税等方面的互惠互信。

展示中国和平崛起的国家级窗口。近代中国连年战乱，珠三角首当其冲见证了战争带来的苦难。新中国重新打开国门，珠三角成为改革开放的试验田与先锋队，亲历了中国从被压迫迅速走向繁荣的光辉历程。改革开放所带来的中国和平崛起的经验对众多发展中国家具有极高的样板示范价值，珠三角则将成为展示中国和平崛起的最佳窗口，向更多发展中国家和地区输出改革开放、和平崛起的价值观与经验。

开展“南南合作”的国家级平台。以广州为代表的珠三角城市拥有悠久的外贸历史和相关服务资源，也已成为来自非洲、中东地区等新兴市场国家人口的聚集地，一方面带来了严峻的管理难题，另一方面也逐渐形成了巨大的社会关系与信息网络，这为珠三角面向这些地区市场的服务及开展“南南合作”提供了丰富的信息环境。发挥文化的影响力，讲好“中国故事”，传播“中国声音”，既是战略需要，也有坚实的社会网络基础。

（二）空间开发策略的转变

在新时期的空间开发中，应当如何尊重自然，使人类活动与自然本底和谐共处？对珠三角全域规划而言，荷兰在1998年第五次国家空间规划中使用的层次分析法是很好的借鉴（图10），空间开发策略的制定首先需要对区域空间资源要素进行全面的解析，从而建立更具智慧的空间开发模型。

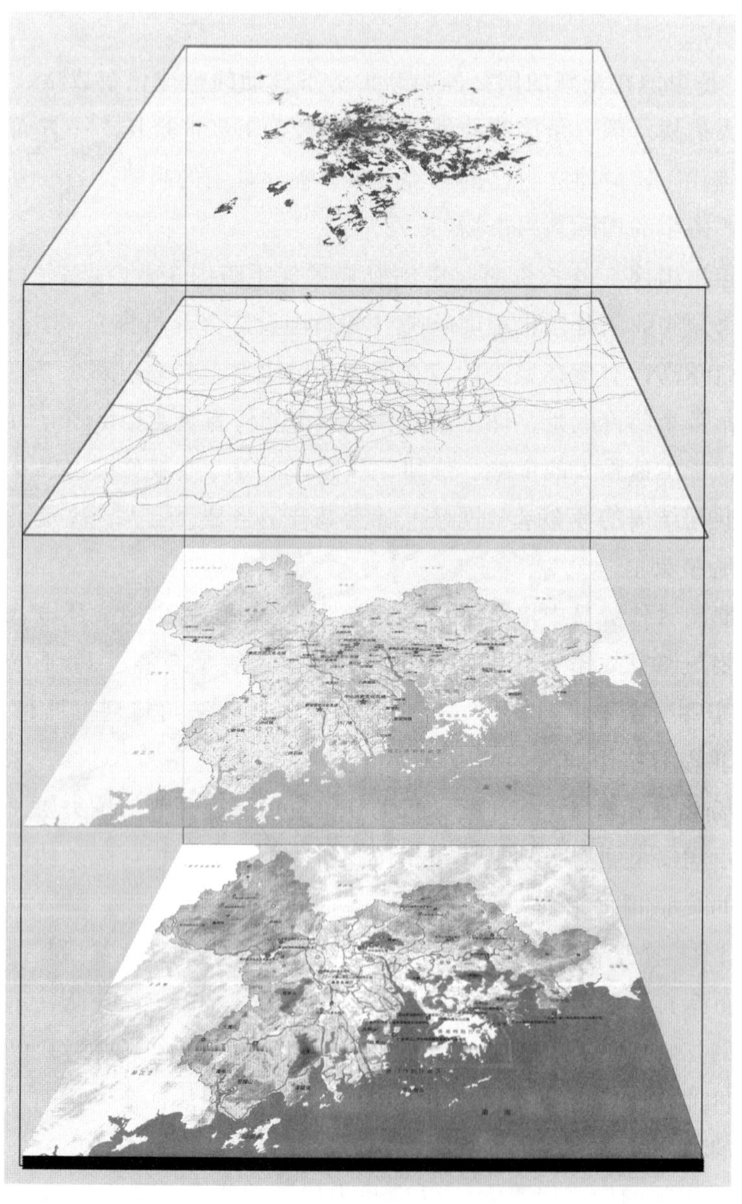

图10 珠三角空间要素叠加分析示意

1. 珠三角的自然基底

珠三角由西江、北江和东江三角洲组成，是一个十分独特的三角洲。古珠江河口湾不断接受河流沉积物的填充，但由于复杂边界对河流与海洋动力的重塑和改造，三角洲的沉积发育在不同区域表现出不同特征，形成了三种不同类型的沉积地貌特征，大致可划分为东岸地区的台地型地区（以山地、台地为主，人类活动选择在海拔较高的台地上进行）、广佛河网地区（没有大山间隔，河网密集，人类往往选择在河口、河岸位置发展）和西岸的江河及丘陵地带（人类活动在山河谷地带开展，因自然分隔形成团块状形态）。特定的地形地貌孕育了与之相适应的土地利用方式，形成了不同的人类聚落形态，其中，西岸水网地区在农耕文明时期承载了更加丰富的功能，也孕育了更深厚的传统城镇文化，相对而言，东岸台地相对贫瘠，然而却更加契合工业化与现代化发展需求，在改革开放以来形成了巨大的城镇连绵地区（图 11）。

图 11　珠三角东西两岸城镇空间发展形态示意图

2. 珠三角的环境资源分布格局

珠三角的资源、环境承载能力分配并不均匀，部分地区逐步接近或已达到上限，相比过去资源环境的约束趋紧，亟须按照可持续发展要求，探索绿色、低碳的社会经济发展新方式。

（1）空气质量：外圈层优于内圈层，东岸优于西岸。自 2000 年以来，珠三角灰霾天气经历了从快速增加到不断减少的变化过程。2007 年为广东省霾日最多的年份，2008 年后迎接广州亚运会等生态建设工程的推进，使珠三角灰霾日数整体出现大幅下降。空间分布方面，珠三角灰霾天气严重的地区主要集中在中部经济较为发达的地区，尤其是珠江口西岸地区沿南海—顺德—鹤山—新会—斗门一带的灰霾天气最为严重，明显高于东岸地区；珠三角东、西北两翼的灰霾天气相对较轻（图12）。

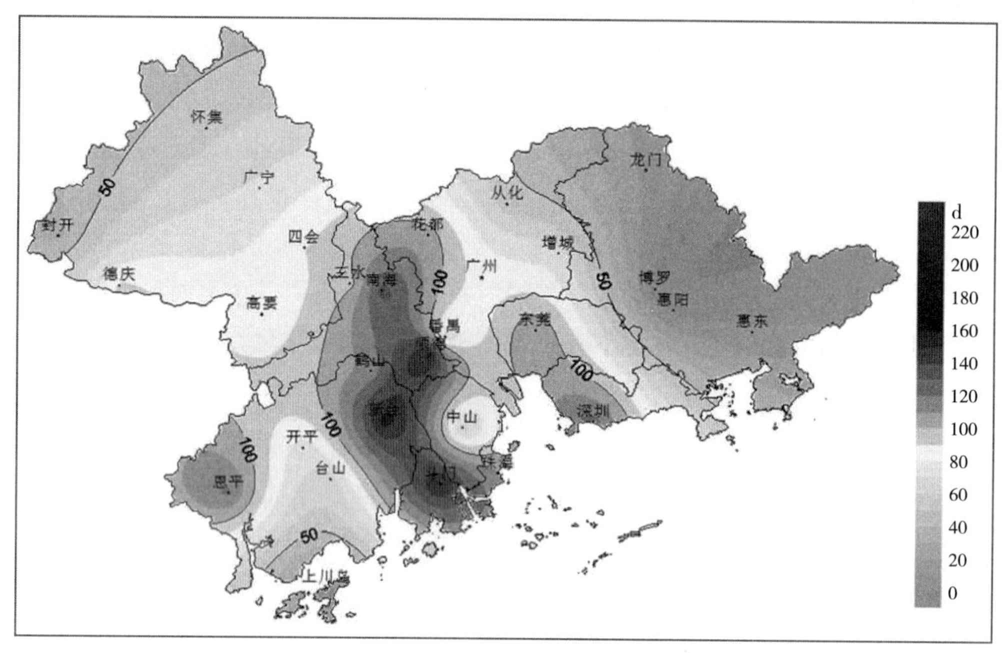

图12　2000—2013年珠三角年平均灰霾日数分布

（2）水资源分布：与区域经济发展格局不协调，总体呈现为西江富余、东江紧缺、潭江波动大。珠三角区域水资源总量丰沛，但人均年水资源量仅为998立方米，属于重度缺水区域（低于1 000立方米/人）（图13）。珠三角经济和人口重心在东部，而水资源重心在西部，造成西江流域水资源丰富但开发利用程度低（仅1.3%左右），而东江流域水资源开发利用程度过高（接近30%），正在实施已经满负荷的分水方案，难以支撑该流域各市不断增长的用水需求。

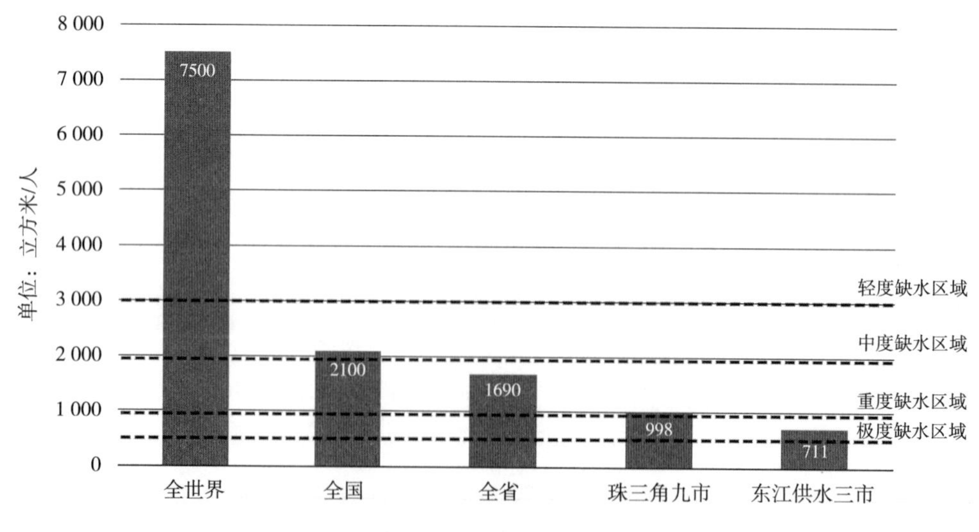

图13　珠三角人均水资源状况分析

3. 差异化的区域空间开发策略

对珠三角自然本底与环境资源分布情况的分析，使我们意识到区域发展无法脱离其所在的自然本底，区域中的人类活动也在持续影响干扰着环境。概括而言，由于环境和资源禀赋的差异，珠三角的东岸地区和西岸地区，珠三角内圈层和外圈层，应根据当地的自然本底和环境承载力，采取不同的空间开发策略。

首先，在东西岸开发策略上，应通过创新与内生资源发掘创造新经济成长空间。东岸地区是巨大的城镇连绵地带，地势平坦，交通网络密集而成熟，然而，水资源的约束已成为现实的发展障碍。一方面，区域调水工程势在必行；另一方面，积极推进创新发展战略，促进产业转型升级，尤其是耗水量大的重型工业淘汰或转移，将有助于缓解这一地区的用水矛盾。西岸地区应充分发挥水网环境优势，一方面，重新发掘水岸的生态、景观与文化价值，修复水岸自然生境，并创造吸引人的水岸户外休闲活动场所；另一方面，发掘西江航道运输与水利价值，在严格控制污染的前提下，推动西岸产业适度重型化，避免劳动密集型产业的粗放蔓延。

其次，在内外圈层开发策略上，应积极推动生态、生产双扩容。珠三角的环境污染问题高度集中在核心圈层的城镇密集地区，但环境问题的解决之道却必须在更大的区域范围内考虑。因此，珠三角全域规划将外围城市辖区内的生态空间纳入珠三角统筹管治范围，通过跨区域水环境与大气环境合作治理，在更大区域范围内控制污染，实现生态扩容；同时，加强珠三角对外围城市产业辐射力度，在更大范围内布局产业，从而使核心圈层产业向低排放低污染的方向转型，实现产业扩容。

最后，在整体空间开发模式上，应从沿路扩张模式向组团集聚模式开发的转变。沿路扩张模式形成于工业化初期，在很长一段时间主导了珠三角的空间拓展，形成了大量沿路“一层皮”的“马路经济”。从生态基底的视角来看，沿路扩张模式对生态斑块、生物迁徙路径都产生了极大的割裂性破坏。随着轨道交通等技术的成熟以及工业化时代“马路经济”效益的不断下降，以公共服务节点引领的组团式集聚发展模式应成为未来珠三角空间拓展的主要形式。

（三）产业转型与城市提升

珠三角的产业经济正在经历深刻转型，无论是受到全球经济短周期波动的影响，还是因为传统行业旧有的生产方式已难以为继，珠三角的曾引以为傲的外向型劳动密集型产业面临大规模衰落淘汰，各市也在积极思考促进转型升级的对策。产业的转型升级不仅意味着行业门类的兴替和企业的关停并转，更意味着空间增长逻辑的改变，尤其是大量新兴的创新活动正在寻找新的空间载体。因此，珠三角全域规划希望响应产业转型趋势，从空间环境营造的角度为创新发展提供有力的支持。

1. 城市中心地区：从 CBD 到 CAZ

传统的城市中心区倾向于打造中央商务区（CBD）。从功能上看，CBD 是城市及区域经济活动的核心组织功能的聚集，包括企业总部、金融等生产性服务业以及大量的相关服务业；从空间形态上看，CBD 通常以大型高层办公建筑和高密度路网为主要特征，我国的 CBD 还通常规划有大尺度纪念性公共空间。这种较为纯粹的商务办公空间正在发生改变。

城市经济的转型其实包括产业价值链的上移或产业结构的调整两个路向。价值链上移会指向科技、研发等技术创新的发展；而产业结构调整则会指向金融等专业创新服务和文化创意产业的发展。科技创新活动衍生出了硅谷等大都市外围地区的创新带；但是专业创新和文化创意产业的发展则指向了城市中心区，因为这类产业首先会依托奥登伯格的“第三场所”而存在：城市中心大量的图书馆、博物馆、歌剧院、画廊和咖啡馆等“第三场所”成为此类产业发展的沃土；同时，创新企业的成长还会追寻波特的“竞争优势”而产生聚集分布。于是，城市中心区便在新经济的孕育和发展中起到引领作用。由此，围绕“第三场所”展开的城市中心区将逐渐从服务于经济组织的 CBD 形态转变为集时尚、体验、休闲为一体的，更加满足人本化丰富体验需求的中央活动区（CAZ）。

要推动城市中心区从 CBD 形态向 CAZ 形态转变，势必对当前城市中心区的城市更新工作提出更高的要求。城市更新的目标不仅在于空间改造与设施更新，更在于培育城市新兴产业。传统上将大型工程或城市大事件作为城市更新催化剂的做法，确实有助于改善更新地区的“硬”环境（设施）与“软”环境（形象），但从培育城市新产业的角度看则仍然不够，必须注入能够引导关联行业衍生的“内容”，如艺术学院、科技创意园地等带有科技、文化元素的设施，从而引发一系列产业链条的更替，在根本上改变地区的产业生态。

2. 外围工业化地区：从“园城分置”到“集合城市”

珠三角巨型城市区域是在多种因素的作用下，在改革开放后的近 30 年时间迅速成型的，其中，最重要的因素是珠三角长期所依赖的外源型经济，引发了一种“外源型空间”的出现。

在外源型经济的驱动下，无论是 90 年代的经开区、高新区，还是 2000 年以来的各类综合性产业园区，通常通过招商引资引入外来企业，本地根植性不强，依赖外部市场，因此这类产业园区通常被置于城市辖区边缘的交通干道附近，距离原城市中心远，如广州黄埔经开区等离城区达 30 多公里；另一方面，这种外源型扩张几乎与珠三角改革开放以来的城镇化同步发生，城市发展框架被过早拉大，而大部分城市中心地区的功能并不成熟。在土地财政影响下，政府通过在靠近中心城区的区位规划新城，配置高标准服务与设施以尽快聚集人气。远郊的产业园区与城区的新城在空间上的离异，导致了一种生产空间与生活空间的分离的“园城分置”现象，并伴随着一系列城市与区域问题，如潮汐交通、“马路经济”与城乡混杂、环境破坏以及乡村衰败等。

显然，这种扩张型发展模式本身已难以为继，而当前珠三角的产业转型趋势也正在对过去形成的“外源型空间”造成冲击，劳动密集型产业的逐步退出虽然为新兴产业的进驻提供空间，但缺乏服务配套的单一产业空间显然无法适应创新型产业的需求。为了消解当前广泛存在的“园城分置”现象，推动“外向型空间”的转型，核心手段是重建工业化地区的空间秩序。因此，借鉴法国“市镇联合体”的经验，珠三角可以用“集合城市”的概念来系统性地应对“园城分置”下的各类问题。

所谓“集合城市”，是采取“集中发展下有机重构”的理念，以公共引导的方式，将空间毗邻的传统工业化城镇联合组成组团式的城镇集合体，在每个“集合城市”中，建设串联集合内部各城镇节点的公共交通；围绕公交枢纽开辟公共开敞空间，提升环境品质；围绕公交枢纽及城镇中心，建设集合公共服务中心，为集合内居民提供优质便利的服务。集合中倡导采用共享式的公共服务中心建设模式，即围绕各城镇中的公交枢纽站点，配置具有一定差异的共享式公共服务设施，依托公交网络与集合内其他城镇共享使用。通过这种集合方式，一方面解决城镇自身公共服务配套不足的问题，另一方面缓解传统工业化城镇对中心城市核心地区的畸形依赖，从而在整体上建立良性的城镇网络。

3. *水岸地区的活化：从防洪堤围到堤岸公园*

珠三角巨型城市区域的形成过程，也是不断将大自然推离都市人群的过程。而当珠三角地区居民的财富不断累积，人们对健康生活的向往越来越强烈，同时，在产业转型的背景下，科技创新企业与人才对环境的要求也越来越高。由此，如何让都市人群更易接触优质的生态开敞空间，也成为产业转型与城市提升过程中不可忽视的课题。

珠三角地区作为典型的河网型地区，密集的河流一直以来都承载了丰富的功能，如运输、灌溉、水利等，人们逐水而居，临水而商，形成了最早的城镇聚落文化。线性的河流并不像大型的生态斑块那样远离城市，而是穿城而过，河流水岸成为人与自然接触的最佳界面，同时，河流还是天然的低温廊道和通风廊道，有利于改善沿岸的风热环境，促进空气交换，改善灰霾与热岛现象。基于以上考虑，规划将水系作为珠三角生态开敞空间建设的“纲”，通过管控、整治、设计，赋予河岸地带高可达性、宜人环境并注入文化、体育等丰富元素，引导珠三角水岸健康生活（图 14）。

珠三角河网沿线建设了大量堤围，从最初以单一的防洪为主，到农业时期的围垦造田造地，到围垦与防洪相结合，以及工业发展需求，堤围不断加强，目前已形成超过6 000公里的堤围岸线。通过适当的工程或设计手段，将这些堤围连接，使步行或骑单车的人们可轻松通过，从而使其具备开展线性活动的良好条件，把堤岸沿线设置带状绿地形成“堤岸公园”，同时还可与珠三角已建成的绿道网有机结合，作为城乡慢行休息的载体，从而创造新的绿道形式，打造“绿道升级版”。这样，未来的珠三角将形成有轨道交通连接的功能网络，由水岸绿道连接的休闲网络，在提高城市群功能效率的同时确保居民生活的品质。

四、结论

（一）国家功能的注入将有助于珠三角转型服务于国家新战略

珠三角的产业经济转型并非无根之木，转型过程仍然深深扎根于地方的产业基础和社会文化网络中，而这种基础网络是在漫长的历史中逐渐累积形成的。从历史视角看珠三角的转型，我们可以看到国家力量与市场力量一直以来都是交织扭结在一起，共同推动了珠三角城镇密集连绵带、全球重要制造业基地的形成。历史上，广州市舶司的设置和两次“一口通

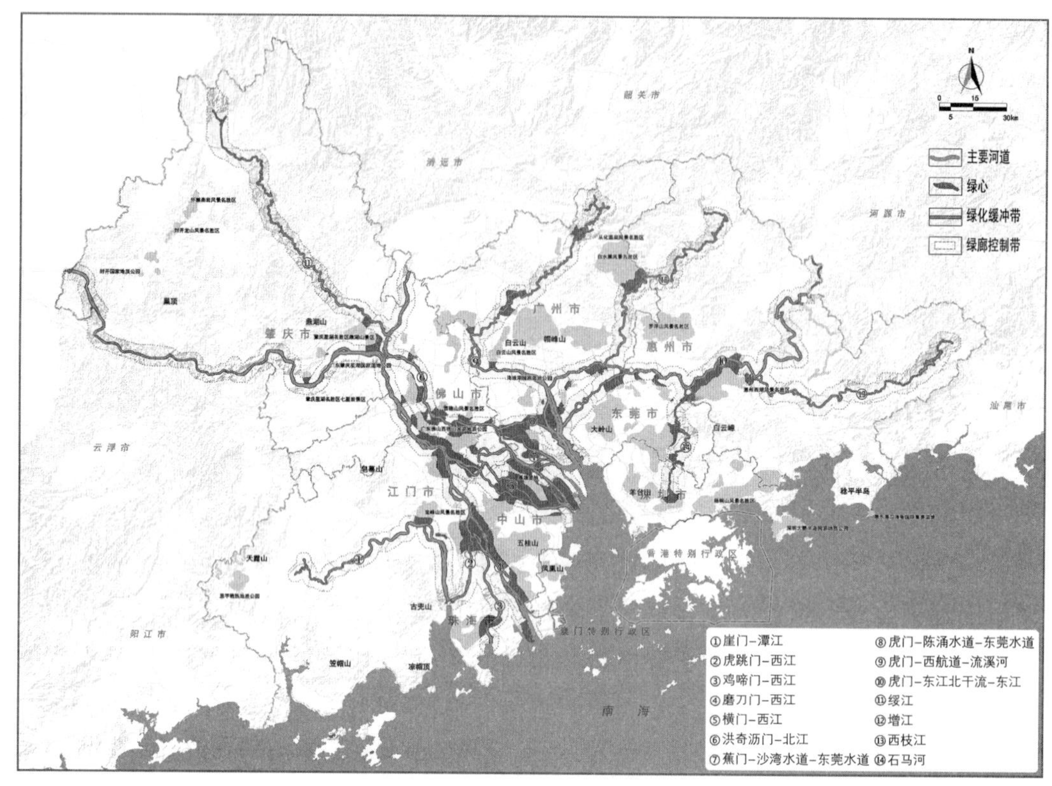

图 14 依托珠三角河网水系形成的连续且功能复合的区域绿廊

商”都赋予了广州在整个国家无可取代的商业地位，也深刻影响了近代的地缘政治格局；改革开放以来，广交会、深圳证券交易所等国家级设施的设置，同样发挥了巨大的影响力，赋予了广州、深圳各自领域独特的引领地位。

因此，在新一轮的转型过程中，市场力量的倒逼是一个方面，但同时不可忽视国家机构力量的再次注入。在国家“一带一路”战略框架下，“南南合作”“东盟交流”“南海问题”等都是具有鲜明区域特色的关键性议题，珠三角拥有处理这些议题的地缘优势与专业能力，如能注入相应的国家功能，将有助于国家透过珠三角扩大大国影响力，并将珠三角的发展推向新的高度。

（二）空间开发策略要做出转变

由于环境和资源禀赋的差异，珠三角的东岸地区和西岸地区，珠三角内圈层和外圈层，应根据当地的自然本底和环境承载力，采取不同的空间开发策略。

珠三角应充分发挥水网环境优势，重新发掘水岸的生态、景观与文化价值，修复水岸自然生境，并创造吸引人的水岸户外休闲活动场所。在整体空间开发模式上，应从沿路扩张模式向组团集聚模式开发的转变。沿路扩张模式形成于工业化初期，在很长一段时间主导了珠三角的空间拓展，形成了大量沿路“一层皮”的“马路经济”。从生态基底的视角来看，沿路扩张模式对生态斑块、生物迁徙路径都产生了极大的割裂性破坏。随着轨道交通等技术的成熟，以及工业化时代“马路经济”效益的不断下降，以公共服务节点引领的组团式集聚发展模式应成为未来珠三角空间拓展的主要形式。

（三）空间的转型须与功能转型相匹配

功能是特定生产关系的反映，而空间既是这种生产关系的载体，同时也是生产关系的实体表现，如珠三角普遍存在的“外源型空间”就是与外源型经济相匹配的，体现了高度依赖区域货运交通、低成本、粗放发展等产业经济特征。当城市和区域的功能发生转变时，原有的空间模式难以适应新兴产业的需求，从而在新的需求下催生出新的空间形态模式。

因此，珠三角全域规划作为一个区域性的空间规划，特别重视观察这种功能转型引起的空间转型趋势，尤其针对城市中心区、外围工业化地区等转型趋势强烈的地区提出了一系列空间建设措施，以期为新时期的转型与变革创造良好的空间支撑。

（作者：马向明，广东省城乡规划设计研究院总工程师，城市规划教授级高级工程师；陈洋，广东省城乡规划设计研究院高级规划师；明立波，广东省城乡规划设计研究院高级规划师）

参考文献

[1] World Bank. *East Asia's Changing Urban Landscape: Measuring a Decade of Spatial Growth* [M]. Washington, DC: World Bank. 2015, 21-25.

[2] 薛凤旋，杨春．外资：发展中国家城市化的新动力——珠江三角洲个案研究［J］．经济地理，1997（3）：193-206.

[3] 许学强．珠江三角洲的发展与城市化［M］．广州：中山大学出版社，1988：17-20.

[4] 李立勋．珠江三角洲乡镇企业发展的地域特征［J］．热带地理，1997（1）：47-52.

[5] 李坤，于渤，李清均．“躯干国家”制造向“头脑国家”制造转型的路径选择——基于高端装备制造产业成长路径选择的视角［J］．管理世界，2011（1）：1-11.

[6] 肖金成．珠三角城市群产业结构调整策略研究［J］．开放导报，2010（6）：77-79.

[7] 萨斯基娅，萨森．新型空间形式：巨型区域和全球城市［J］．国际城市规划，2011（2）：36.

海南省海澄文一体化的路径与保障机制

进入21世纪以来，我国中西部地区的许多省会城市和计划单列城市，为提升其综合竞争力，增强中心城市的辐射带动功能，纷纷同周边地域上相连的城市一起实行一体化发展。例如，河南省的郑（州）汴（开封）一体化（后又扩展至郑汴洛一体化）、湖南省的长（沙）株（洲）潭（湘潭）一体化、陕西省的西（安）咸（阳）一体化、黑龙江省的哈（尔滨）大（庆）一体化、吉林省的长（春）吉（林）一体化、新疆维吾尔自治区的乌（鲁木齐）昌（吉）一体化等。实践证明，这类中心城市与周边城市一体化的发展模式，对加快区域城镇化的进程，特别是促进要素集聚、壮大经济实力、拓展新的发展空间、打造新的经济增长极，以及实现集约发展、联动发展、互补发展，进而推动省会都市圈和省内城市群的形成发展，发挥了重要的核心作用。

2015年6月，海南省省委、省政府提出加快推进海口、澄迈、文昌三市县一体化发展，并将其作为推动全省“多规合一”改革、助推区域经济一体化、形成海南经济增长极、打造国际旅游岛升级版的重要举措。2016年1月海南省五届四次人大会议通过的《海南省国民经济和社会发展第十三个五年规划纲要》明确提出，要着力推进海澄文功能协作、产业互补、交通一体、设施高效一体化发展，到2020年其经济总量占全省50%以上。

一、海澄文一体化的背景分析

（一）三市县概况

海澄文三市县位于海南省北部沿海，北临北部湾琼州海峡，最近处距雷州半岛仅18海里，土地总面积6 868平方公里，占全省土地总面积的19.3%。2014年，海澄文三市县常住总人口为323.1万人，占全省常住人口的35.8%。海澄文一体化区域基本情况见表1。

区位交通、资源与生态环境是海澄文地区突出的比较优势。在区位交通方面，海澄文不仅地处中国沿海港口与北部湾各港口航运的咽喉，而且也是海南岛对外联系（尤其是通往珠三角地区）的重要门户，区位十分重要。近年来，随着环岛高速公路、环岛高铁、海南中线高速和琼文高速的相继建成通车，以及海口美兰国际机场二期、海口新海港客货滚装码头一期、澄迈马村港区二期竣工交付使用，海口—澄迈已成为全省陆海空综合交通枢纽，为三市一体化发展奠定了基础。

表1 海澄文一体化区域基本情况表

市县名	土地面积（km^2）	常住人口（万人）	地区生产总值（亿元）	固定资产投入（亿元）	社会消费品零售总额（亿元）	地方一般公共财政收入（亿元）	城镇化率（%）
海口	2 304	220	1 091.7	824.6	541.3	100.1	76.6
澄迈	2 076	48	226.8	263.7	27.0	20.5	44.1
文昌	2 488	55	159.8	141.9	54.6	13.0	49.5
合计	6 868	323	1 478.3	1 230.2	622.9	133.6	67.2

在自然资源方面，海澄文地处热带北缘沿海地带，属热带海洋性季风气候，冬季不冷，夏季高温多雨，光热与降水资源充足。以海口市为例，年平均气温24.2℃，1月平均气温17.7℃，年均降水量1 664毫米，全年无霜期346天，有利于发展热带特色高效农业。另外，海澄文具有得天独厚的海洋资源优势。三市县海岸线总长约500公里，海域面积7 276平方公里，沿海有滩涂约180平方公里，-10米等深线以内浅海面积超过1 000平方公里，适合于发展海水养殖；近海海洋鱼类等生物资源丰富；沿海港湾众多，仅文昌市就有大小港湾40多处，不仅建港条件良好，而且又是优质的滨海休闲旅游资源。

在生态环境方面，海澄文地区空气质量优良率98%以上，水环境质量总体良好，地表水大部为Ⅲ类水质，近岸海域水质优良，森林覆盖率达44.67%，各类自然保护区和生态功能区均有效地得到了保护。

在经济社会发展方面，海澄文三市县在海南省占有十分重要的地位。2014年，三市县地区生产总值1 478.3亿元，占全省地区生产总值的42.2%；人均地区生产总值45 749元，为全省平均值的1.18倍；常住人口城镇化率为67.2%，高出全省平均水平13.5个百分点；三次产业增加值结构为12.3%∶24.7%∶63%。但与发达地区相比，海澄文三市县经济总体发展水平不高，不仅经济总量规模较小，而且人均地区生产总值（2014年为45 754元/人）还略低于全国平均水平（4.66万元/人）。

（二）一体化发展的重要意义

（1）落实“21世纪海上丝绸之路”国家战略的需要。“21世纪海上丝绸之路”作为“一带一路”国家战略的重要组成部分，而海澄文独特的区位交通优势，使其不仅是联结中国与东南亚和南亚地区黄金航道的交通枢纽，也是经贸联系的重要枢纽与文化交流的枢纽，起着重要战略支点作用。为此，需要通过海澄文一体化发展，提升其综合竞争力，并增强辐射影响力。

（2）南海常态维权和开发海洋资源的需要。南海诸岛自古以来就是中国的领土，为应对近年来美、日等域外国家在南海制造紧张局势、妄图使南海问题国际化，以及周边一些国家非法侵占我国岛礁和大规模掠夺海洋油气资源的行径，南海维权将成为一项常态化任务。特别是随着2012年6月三沙市的成立，南海岛礁建设及海洋资源开发步伐加快，后勤保障服务的重要性日益凸显。海澄文作为海南省经济技术实力相对较强、港口转运条件较好的城市，不仅在南海维权的后勤保障和海上救援任务方面，而且在海洋资源大规模开发所需的海洋工程装备修造方面，将承担基地的重任。目前，国家已明确将文昌市的木兰湾和清澜港作为三沙市的后勤保障基地和应急救援基地，海口及澄迈也将承担海洋工程配套装备制造及舰船修造与物资供应等保障服务功能。

（3）海南省加快对外开放与发展的需要。海南省虽具有经济特区、国际旅游岛等政策优势，但由于历史和原有经济基础较差等原因，目前对外开放水平仍不高。2014 年，全省经济外向度仅 27.4%，远低于全国平均水平（41.5%）。今后，海澄文一体化将依托其港口、机场、综合保税区、航空及港口物流园等开放平台优势而成为海南省下一轮对外开放的重点区域，并有可能成为未来海南自由贸易区的核心区。

（三）一体化发展中存在的问题

（1）核心城市（海口）辐射带动能力较弱。海口作为海南省的省会、海澄文一体化的核心城市，2014 年地区生产总值总量 1 091.7 亿元，仅相当于“长三角”和“珠三角”地区一个较发达的县级市水平，在全国 36 个省会城市和计划单列市中居倒数第三位；加之产业结构不合理，特别是工业基础薄弱（工业占 GDP 的 13.5%），先进制造业和高技术产业规模较小、竞争力不强，服务业中生产性服务业占比不到 30%，因而对要素的集聚作用不强，对包括澄迈、文昌在内的周边地区辐射带动能力较弱。

（2）三市县经济社会发展差距较大。海澄文三市县由于目前所处的经济发展阶段不同，因而产业结构和经济发展水平差异明显。根据国际上通行的 H · 钱纳里判别地区经济发展阶段的 9 项指标，海口市三次产业增加值结构为 5.2∶19.9∶74.8（%），人均 GDP 为49 943元（折合8 033美元），城镇化率为 76.6%，总体上处于工业化中后期阶段；澄迈县三次产业增加值结构为 26.8∶47.6∶25.6（%），人均 GDP 为47 421元（折合7 628美元），城镇化率为 44.1%，总体上为工业化中期阶段；文昌市三次产业增加值结构为 40.3∶25∶34.7（%），人均 GDP 为29 055元（折合4 674美元），城镇化率为 49.5%，处于工业化中期初始阶段。三市县经济社会发展水平的显著差异，导致基础设施与基本公共服务水平的落差较大，给海澄文一体化发展带来巨大挑战。

（3）空间结构松散。海澄文三市县在长期发展过程中，由于缺少统筹规划，导致空间开发相对分散，建设用地利用粗放。人口与产业主要集中于北部滨海地区，而包括东部沿海在内的中、南部广大地区开发利用程度均不高。即使在北部滨海地区的海口主城区，位于南渡江以东、包括美兰国际机场在内的江东组团开发利用也明显不足。迄今，海口市主城区与同位于北部滨海的澄迈县老城和文昌市的铺前尚未连成一片。在产业布局上，也存在园区数量多（合计 48 个）、布局分散、占地面积过大、开发利用程度低、经济效益不高等问题，其中 11 个省级产业园区用地总规模达 189 平方公里，但实际已开发利用不足三成。

（4）体制机制障碍。在海澄文三市县一体化进程中，还存在一些亟待解决的问题。例如，如何逐步消除行政壁垒、市场分割，促进资金、资源、技术、信息等生产要素自由流动与优化配置；如何协调三市县的财税政策与利益分配等体制机制等，都需要通过深化改革和体制机制创新逐步解决。

二、海澄文一体化的发展思路

海澄文一体化发展应坚持“市场主导、政府引导”，“资源共享、互利共赢”，“分工协作、优势互补”，“统一规划、统筹推进”，“生态优先、绿色发展”的原则，打破行政分割，着力解决同质化竞争问题，提高资源配置效率和基础设施效能，合力推进经济转型升级，共同提升产业综合实力、开放合作水平和科技创新能力，协同保护区域生态环境，实现公共服务均等化，提升公共服务品质；构建充满活力、富有效率、具有更加开放体制机制的省会都市圈（省会经济圈）。为此，必须重点推进“五个一体化”。

（一）基础设施一体化——推进一体化的基础

立足于加强海澄文地区人流、物流、信息流联系，以实现快捷、安全、高效为目标，通过路网同城化、公共交通同城化、信息服务和市政设施同城化，促进海澄文三大组团间一体化发展。为此，近期要进一步加强三市县道路、城际公交、旅游车辆、港口等方面的对接及互联互通。例如，加快文昌—海口—澄迈滨海旅游公路、海文高速+海口绕城高速、文昌—定安—澄迈—临高高等级公路三大通道建设；整合区内港口岸线资源，形成功能清晰、特色鲜明、进出便利的一体化港口群等。同时，还要抓紧建立一体化的交通运输管理机制，实现市民公交“一卡通”、游客客运联程联运一票到底，旅游车辆、出租车统一管理。此外，还应加强同城化地区的能源、环保、通信、市政等基础设施的同标准建设与共建共享。

（二）产业发展与布局一体化——推进一体化的核心

立足于海澄文三地产业发展的原有基础、资源优势、市场需求与科技创新能力，按照“优势互补、错位发展”的原则，优化三地产业结构与产业布局，促进产业的合理分工协作，形成特色鲜明，优势互补的产业分工协作体系。其中，海口应依托教育、医疗、信息等优质资源，发展省会经济，重点发展以旅游、金融、会展、商务、购物、医疗健康、科技教育为主体的现代服务业，加快发展高新技术产业，打造成为全省现代服务业发展中心区和高技术产业基地。澄迈重点发展先进制造业、互联网信息产业和现代物流业，打造成为琼北的新型工业区。文昌重点建成以滨海旅游、航天科普、侨乡及乡村文化为特色的海南国际旅游岛的重要休闲度假旅游目的地，以及热带高效特色农业基地。

（三）城镇空间布局与城乡发展一体化——推进一体化的平台

以城镇合理布局和统筹城乡发展为出发点，优化城镇空间布局，加快广大农村地区的城镇化步伐，重点推进城镇空间的同城化和城乡融合发展。着力将海口主城区、澄迈老城、文昌铺前—木兰湾打造成滨海同城化地区，形成“滨海同城化地区+卫星城+特色小镇+美丽乡村”的城乡一体化格局。

（四）公共服务与社会保障一体化——推进一体化的归宿

以基本公共服务均等化为目标，建立一体化的基础教育体系，逐步实现三市县城镇常住人口和农村户籍子女享有义务教育的同等待遇，并有序推进义务教育均衡发展，努力缩小城乡义务教育发展差距；建立覆盖城乡居民一体化的基本卫生医疗体系，加快发展涵盖卫生、医疗、康复、养老在内的健康产业，使三地市城乡居民享有均等化的医疗服务。

在社会保障方面，重点建立和完善城乡一体的劳动就业保障体系、基本住房保障体系、社会救助保障体系、居民健康保障体系及公共安全保障体系五大体系。

（五）生态文明建设一体化——推进一体化的保障

以主体功能区规划为依据，统筹三市县生态功能区的一体化建设、生态敏感区的一体化保护，以及环境污染的一体化联防联治；统筹三市县海陆及岸线资源一体化的开发利用，对近岸海域的生态保护和开发进行严格地管控，实行最严格的环境准入制度，提高产业项目准入门槛，严守生态环保红线和环境质量底线，构建一体化的环境质量检测体系；强化对跨区域的东寨港红树林自然保护区、雷琼世界地质公园、海南岛北部滨海岸线等生态资源的保护；统筹推进南渡江、五源河以及其他城市内河水系治理，严控同城化地区的点源污染和卫星城镇周边的面源污染。

三、海澄文一体化的空间结构

点—轴系统是区域发展与区域规划中最常用的空间结构模式，其基本原理为：以人口与产业集聚的不同规模城镇为节点，以线状的交通基础设施为轴线，通过轴线对人口、产业、资金、技术、信息的吸引，导致原有节点的不断壮大和新节点的形成，并随着交通线的不断延伸与拓展，最终发展成网络状空间结构。海澄文地区按照“壮大极核、轴向集聚、节点支撑、功能互补、海陆统筹”的发展思路，构建“一核、四城、五轴、五区”的空间结构，实现人口有序集中和产业有效集聚（图1）。

（一）一核：做大做强海口主城区发展极核

海口市主城区是海澄文一体化发展核心，主要位于海口市区外环路以北地区，包括中心城区组团、长流组团和江东组团（图2），为全市人口及产业的集中分布区。其功能定位：区域性旅游目的地和集散中心，金融、会展、物流、房地产、教育、文化体育、科技等服务业以及先进制造业与高新技术产业的集聚区。当前发展中存在的主要问题为经济总量规模小、产业结构不合理。今后应充分发挥其区位、交通、生态、人文、地缘和省会等优势，突出转型、提质、增效，加快发展现代服务业和高技术产业，引导城镇人口集中和高端产业集聚，不断增强综合经济实力和竞争力，建成为引领海南省、辐射北部湾和东南亚地区的现代服务业中心与绿色制造业基

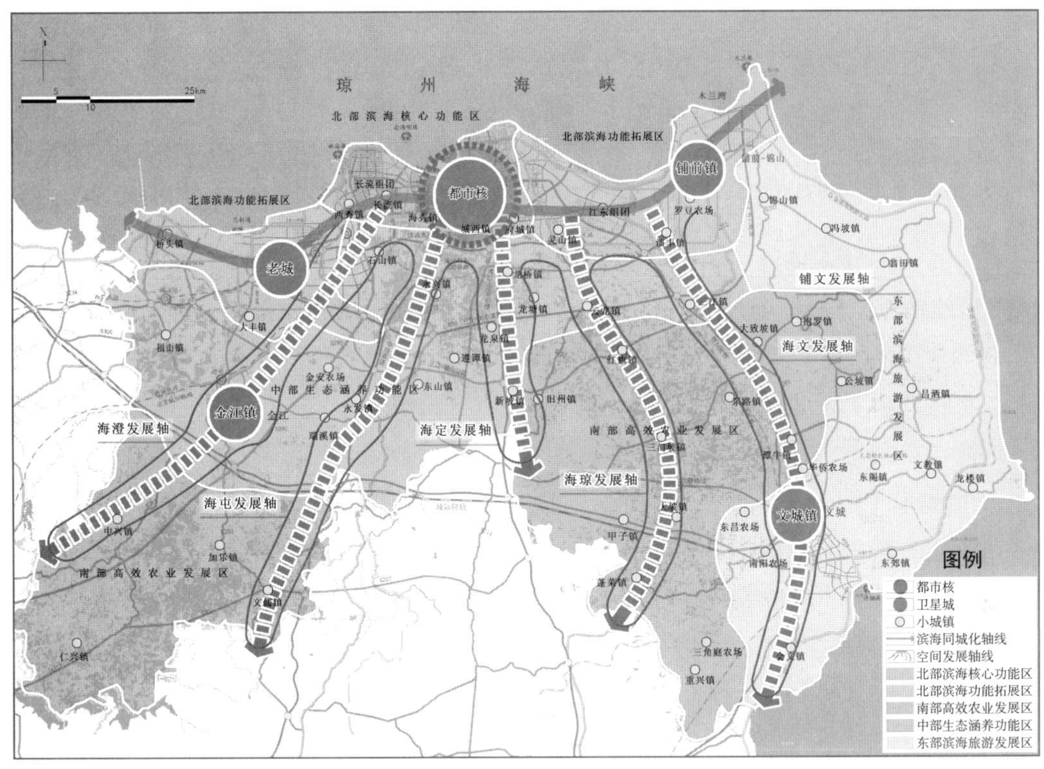

图1　海澄文一体化空间总体格局

图2　中心城区与长流组团、江东组团

地、经贸文化交流中心、南海开放开发的前沿核心区和南海维权与后勤保障服务基地。

（二）四城：实现四城联动发展

澄迈的金江与老城、文昌市的文城和木兰新城是海澄文一体化发展的四个重要支点。其中，老城是海澄文地区的先进制造业、信息与互联网等新兴产业、港口物流中心；金江为澄迈县的县城、综合服务中心、休闲旅游目的地；文城为文昌市中心城区及全市经济、文化、商贸中心和旅游服务中心；位于文昌市西北部木兰湾沿岸的木兰新城为重要的旅游服务休闲基地及三沙市的后勤保障服务基地。今后要通过加快交通基础设施与产业一体化发展，加强海口主城区与四城的联动发展，实现海口主城区与老城、铺前—锦山在空间上的对接，形成滨海城市化连绵区，增强滨海发展极核的竞争力和辐射带动功能。

（三）五轴：推动海陆统筹发展主轴

（1）海文发展轴。以海文高速公路、海南环岛高铁东线以及省道201为复合轴，重点发展该轴沿线的美兰国际机场临空经济区、三江镇、大致坡镇、咸来镇、潭牛镇、新桥镇等重点镇和产业园区，打造海澄文一体化地区的科技研发转化、综合保税物流、电子信息及先进制造业发展带和主要城镇集聚轴。

（2）海琼发展轴。以海榆东线公路（原国道233线）为主轴，重点发展沿线的云龙镇、旧州镇、红旗镇和三门坡镇，打造乡村休闲旅游发展带和主要城镇集聚轴。

（3）海定发展轴。以海南岛东线高速公路和南渡江西岸沿江公路为复合轴，发展沿线的龙桥、龙塘、龙泉、新坡等镇，打造南渡江滨水休闲旅游和主要城镇集聚轴。

（4）海屯发展轴。以海榆中线高等级公路（原国道224线）为主轴，重点发展沿线的永兴、罗京、永发、京山等重点镇，打造乡村休闲旅游、汽车零部件产业发展带和主要城镇集聚轴。

（5）海澄发展轴。以海南环岛铁路西线和国道225线为复合轴，重点发展北部的老城—马村和南部的金江，辐射带动沿线的仁兴、中兴和加乐等重点镇，打造海澄文地区的港口物流、信息与互联网产业、装备制造业发展带和主要城镇集聚轴。

（四）五区：因地制宜划分五大功能区

（1）北部滨海核心功能区。该区位于海口市主城区的北部。东西界于南渡江与海口新海港间，南界为南海大道，包括中心城区与长流两个组团，为海澄文一体化核心区中的核心。其中，中心城区应重点强化政治、金融、商贸、医疗、教育、文化、旅游、服务与管理功能；长流组团承担中心城市和国际旅游岛双重功能，并通过建设美安科技新城，加快发展电子信息、生物医药、高端装备制造等新兴产业，打造成为海口市的新增长极。

（2）北部滨海功能拓展区。在合理开发利用岸线资源的基础上，将北部滨海核心功能区向东西侧拓展。向西延伸至澄迈县的老城——马村和桥头镇，依托马村港口和原有产业基础，做大做强新型工业、软件与互联网产业、港口与临港物流业、滨海休闲旅游业四大支柱产业，建成为国家级软件产业基地、海南省先进制造业基地、临港工业基地和生产性服务业基地；向东延伸至海口市南渡江以东的江东组团、文昌市西北部的铺前—木兰湾滨海地带。其中，江东组团重点建设海南岛门户枢纽（美兰国际空港），培育旅游与科教等现代综合服务功能，发展航空产业和保税物流业，建设海南省教育培训与科技研发基地；文昌市西北部依托“两桥一路”，建成与海口市同城化发展区域，并通过建设规划总面积为83平方公里的木兰新城，重点发展滨海旅游、体育、文化娱乐等休闲产业，同时为三沙市提供后勤保障服务。

(3) 东部滨海旅游发展区。该区包括文昌市东北部、东部和东南部滨海地区。岸线资源丰富，发展空间广阔，自然环境优美，特别是文昌市东部北起潮滩湾，串联月亮湾、铜鼓岭、淇水湾、八门湾、东郊椰林高隆湾等在内滨海黄金旅游带，不仅拥有洁净的海水、沙滩、阳光、椰林等旅游资源，而且在东南部的龙楼还建有全国第四个航天发射基地，是海澄文一体化地区开展包括航天文化旅游在内的滨海休闲度假旅游的最佳区域。

(4) 中部生态休闲功能区。该区包括澄迈县的中部和海口市的中部区域。生态系统较为完整，环境质量相对较好，水资源较丰富，是支撑海澄文一体化发展的生态功能区域。重点发挥生态保障、水源涵养、休闲旅游等功能。依托南渡江滨水资源和周边生态旅游资源，通过改善对外交通和基础设施，逐步形成山水特色鲜明、城镇与旅游区散落分布的生态休闲功能区。

(5) 南部高效农业功能区。该区包括澄迈县的南部、海口市的南部和文昌市的西部地区。水、土和热量资源丰富，生态环境良好，十分有利于发展热带特色农业，是推动海澄文一体化发展的战略腹地与农产品主产区。重点发展冬季瓜菜、热带水果、橡胶等热带经济作物，以及优质畜禽养殖、水产品等特色农副产品生产和乡村旅游休闲产业。

四、海澄文一体化的保障机制

（一）做好一体化的顶层设计

做好一体化的顶层设计是确保海澄文一体化顺利实施的重要条件。而《海澄文一体化规划》（以下简称《规划》）是顶层设计的集中体现。《规划》以党的十八届五中全会提出的“创新、协调、绿色、开放、共享”发展理念为指导，按照《国家新型城镇化规划(2014-2020)》《海南省总体规划纲要（2015—2030)》和《海南省国民经济和社会发展第十三个五年规划纲要》的要求，不仅要提出推进海澄文一体化的总体战略、发展定位和空间布局，而且还要明确构建功能协作、产业互补、交通一体、设施共享的一体化发展路径，以及实施《规划》的保障机制和重大项目建设，提高其科学性和可操作性。

（二）深化要素市场一体化改革

改革是推动发展的强大动力，也是推进体制机制创新的重要基础。海澄文一体化发展应以要素市场一体化改革为切入点，探索建立一体化的财政税收、金融、土地、技术和信息等要素市场体系。

一是财税体制改革。以建立一体化的财税制度和投融资方式为目标，逐步消除三市县共享税种分成比例差异，建立健全的财政转移支付办法，对省级重点产业园区和跨市县的重点基础设施建设给予财政资金倾斜。

二是金融市场一体化改革。除积极吸引国内外投资者并利用债券市场多渠道募集资金外，鼓励三市县共同出资设立海澄文一体化发展基金，推动投融资统一平台建设；建立股份交易平台，为战略性新兴产业和低碳制造业提供创新股权基金；深化三市县票据市场、保险市场、产权市场、柜台交易市场等各类资本市场的分工协作；推动建立支付清算、异地存储、信用担保等业务同城化。

三是土地要素市场一体化改革。重点深化城镇国有土地有偿使用制度改革，扩大土地有偿使用范围；慎重稳妥推进农村土地制度改革，建立城乡统一的建设用地市场，并开展农村空心村整治宅基地进入市场试点。

四是技术和信息市场一体化改革。以网络互联为平台、信息互通为纽带，建设一体化的网络基础设施为目标，大力推进下一代互联网建设，推进三网融合；同时，整合区域信息资源，建设区域大数据中心。

（三）推进体制机制创新

一是建立行政协调机制。由省政府牵头，建立海澄文一体化领导小组，研究、协调和决策空间规划、产业布局、重点项目、政策制定等重大事项；同时，建立三市县职能部门（发改、环保、国土、规划、交通、港务、旅游、林业等）的对口协调机制，通过建立联席会议，加强部门对口衔接，打破行政区划分割，推进区域一体化管理。

二是建立利益分成机制。建立科学合理的跨市县投资、产业转移对接、园区共建、科技成果落地等项目分配体制。对跨行政区的项目和税源，按照“利益共享、权责对等、友好协商、互利共赢”原则，综合考虑资本、资源、技术、人力等的投入，由一体化领导小组协商确定分配比例。

三是构建协同发展机制。主要包括：

——建立基础设施互联互通机制。统筹规划建设区域路网及水电气管网等基础设施，建立三市县公路、铁路及港口协作机制，推进区域综合交通运输信息互联互通共享开放，形成区域统一开放的运输市场。

——建立生态环境保护联动机制。以大气污染联防联治、流域治理、海陆水资源保护及生态安全为重点，统一三市县生态环境规划、标准、监测、执法体系、搭建区域循环经济技术市场、产品服务平台，加快建立海口与澄迈、文昌之间的横向生态补偿机制。

——建立产业发展协同机制。统一三市县的招商条件和产业政策，协商制定产业园区准入条件、准入门槛和负面清单；统筹税收、人才引进、用地、用工、水电气等优惠政策，避免相互间不必要竞争。要根据海澄文的产业发展条件实行差异化的招商，同一产业按产业链（如研发、加工制造、销售）实行差异化布局。

（四）开展一体化发展试点示范

要从实际出发，选择有条件的区域率先推进，积极推动交通及基础设施、生态环境保护、产业合作、公共服务、对外开放等领域先行先试，通过试点带动其他地区发展。

一要打造先行先试平台。配合海南申报国际自由贸易试验区和建设海口国家级新区需要，将美兰临空经济区、海口综合保税区、美安科技新城、澄迈老城经济开发区、文昌市木兰湾新城作为产业协同发展、开展投资和贸易便利化改革、创新管理体制机制等一体化发展的试点地区；探索海口与澄迈共建海口港协同发展示范区，打造国际自由贸易港。

二是推进重点领域率先试点。例如，交通一体化方面，推进海澄文城市公交“一卡通”互联互通试点，开展货物多式联运试点；生态环境保护一体化方面，推进南渡江生态环境共同治理，探索开展跨区域的 SO_2、NO_2 及挥发性有机物等排污权有偿使用与交易试点；产业发展与布局一体化方面，鼓励国家级和省级经济开发区共建跨区域合作园区或产业联盟，积极推动海口市部分产业或生产加工环节向澄迈和文昌转移，加快两地承接平台建设。

三是推动社会与公共服务一体化试点。例如，推进农民工进城落户政策先行先试，建立区域内统一的人力资源市场及公共就业服务平台，完善医疗保险转移接续和异地就医服务试点，开展跨地区购买养老服务试点，探索建立统一的质量安全监管、重大动植物疫情防控体系。

（作者：毛汉英，中国科学院地理科学与资源研究所研究员、国际欧亚科学院院士；黄金川，中国科学院地理科学与资源研究所副研究员）

参考文献

[1] 海南省统计局．海南省统计年鉴 2015［M］．北京：中国统计出版社，2015.

[2] 海口市统计局．海口市统计年鉴 2015［M］．北京：中国统计出版社，2015.

[3] 中共海南省委关于制定海南“十三五”规划的建议［N］．海南日报，2015－12－16.

[4] 海南省“十三五”规划纲要（草案摘要）［N］．海南日报，2016－01－27.

[5] 甘露．以海澄文一体化打造海南经济增长极［J］．新东方，2015（5）：38－42.

[6] 孙旭东，慕野．后开发区时代下的“营城”战略探讨——以海南省澄迈老城工业开发区为例［J］．规划师，2015（9）：110－117.

[7] 陈玮，慕野，孙旭东．海南省文昌市城乡总体规划（2011－2030）［J］．城市规划通讯，2013（13）：15－16.

运用建筑能效公示降低经济成本①

一、建筑能耗公示的运用

中国目前的建筑能耗约占全世界终端能耗的三分之一，并且还在继续上升[1]。中国的建筑面积每年都在以20亿平方米（相当于美国建筑总量的四分之一）的速度快速增长[2]，导致了大规模的能源消耗和碳排放，建筑节能已成为中国政府优先考虑的重点领域之一。中国正在通过推广新技术、提升建筑规范和标准并制定融资激励等措施，鼓励提高建筑能效。然而，仅靠行政手段和政府经费并不能满足投资需求。要在建筑行业成功地实现减排，中国应当让市场在节能方面发挥更大的作用。

建筑能效公示是一项低成本的市场工具，有助于中国以最经济的方式实现建筑节能改善。建筑规范和标准能确立基准能效要求，而能效比对和能效公示可以向业主提供所需工具和信息，帮助他们更好地了解建筑的能源效率，实现业主、买主、投资者和租户之间的信息共享，从而提高整个市场的节能意识。建筑能效数据一旦为公众掌握，就可以大大促进对建筑节能的需求。具体而言，有了公开的建筑能效数据，客户就可以根据建筑的预计运营成本，做出明智的购买或租赁决定。

本文着重讨论推广能效公示如何有助于建设一个更强大的建筑能效市场。信息公示与有效的执法、针对性的激励措施、充分的技术服务和融资渠道相结合，有助于推动市场对建筑能效的投资。中美两国的信息公示经验都说明公示政策有可能推动市场变革。例如，美国按《有毒物质排放清单》披露排放信息[3]，导致污染企业资产价格下降，对投资者行为产生了

① 本文为保尔森基金会气候变化与空气质量（CCAQ）项目组2015年度系列报告之一。报告就如何利用市场机制减少引起气候变化的常规污染物及温室气体排放，为政府决策机构和政策影响机构提供参考性政策建议，所涵盖的主题包括电力行业改革、电力需求响应、碳排放权交易体系和建筑能效公示。

保尔森基金会由亨利·保尔森先生在2011年创立，是一家以“知行合一”为宗旨的非党派智库。基金会的使命是推动全球环境保护及中美两国的可持续发展，促进及拓宽两国间的相互了解。基金会秉承以下原则：只有中美两国互补协作，才能应对当今最紧迫的经济和环境挑战。基金会总部位于芝加哥大学，同时在北京和华盛顿设有工作团队。基金会的工作主要是通过项目、倡导和研究，推动经济增长，创造就业机会，促进智慧城市建设和推行负责任的环境政策。智库与领先的学者和实践工作者携手，针对中国当前面临的公共政策挑战、环境问题，以及中美经济关系的机遇等，研究、编写及发表一流的报告。基金会网站为 www. paulsoninstitute. org. cn。

影响，也促使企业做出减排及低排放投资的决策。中国自2012年起实时公布大气PM2.5数据，公众能使用移动设备随时随地查看污染数据，促使室内空气净化器和口罩的需求上升，也推动了类似的市场变革。建筑能效领域也可以借鉴同样的公示模式。

通过对大型公共建筑能耗监测信息系统的投资，以及利用各城市的机构职能落实公示工作，中国已在建筑能效公示方面取得了初步成果，但还可以有更大的作为。

建筑能效公示方面的国际经验可以为中国推动建筑节能提供重要借鉴。在过去10年中，纽约等美国大城市和欧洲多国都制定了新的建筑能效公示法律，以鼓励建筑节能。本文回顾这些节能成就，并就建筑公示可能产生的影响，评价这些早期经验对中国有以下借鉴意义：

（1）建筑能效公示为建筑业主和运营商提高建筑能效提供了一个虽小却意义重大的激励手段。自2010年起，纽约市使用美国环保署的能源之星建筑集群管家比对工具，对超过1.3万栋物业实行了强制报告和比对[4]。经过3年的努力，全市的建筑能耗普遍下降。目前所掌握的数据仍然有限，未来几年将出现更多的证据。

（2）美国的建筑能效比对将大数据分析与房地产以及公用事业公司、节能服务承包商等能源供应商结合在一起，形成了一种新型商业模式。随着公众越来越容易通过网络平台获取各种数据，建筑规范日益提高，业主、潜在买家和开发商也会有越来越大的动力投资节能建筑。能效比对的影响可能大大超过早期节能服务公司模式或者旨在改变行为模式、促进节能投资的努力。

（3）建筑能效比对和能效公示有可能帮助决策者、公用事业和节能服务公司识别需要服务和财务激励的街区和建筑。

①建筑能效公示公开建筑能耗数据的过程，业主和电力公司通过在线平台将每年的能源使用数据录入集中数据库。一旦业主通过中央数据库上报数据，相关政府机构就会对数据进行评估验证并以用户友好的方式公示，潜在买家、租户和投资者就可以在交易时考虑建筑的能源效能。公示还可以帮助服务供应商更容易寻找到和联系上需要能效服务的团体和业主。（本文中提到的能效公示不包含能效标识概念）

②建筑能效标识以颁发证书或在网络公布的形式，通过节能等级或评分，用可视化形式公开披露建筑能效信息。

节能建筑的价值远远超出了节约成本和减少碳排放的范畴。越来越多的研究表明，能效较高的建筑很可能质量更高，更有利于住户的健康。例如，《建筑与环境》杂志发表的一项研究结果认为[5]，降低能耗与提高住户舒适度相关。低能耗建筑“在住户满意度的某些方面可以达到最高水平”。同样，劳伦斯伯克利国家实验室在2000年进行的一项研究表明，室内环境的改善可以大幅度提高员工的工作效率和健康水平。论文列举了热能回收和节能光源等几种节能措施，不但能够改善室内环境质量和住户健康，甚至能提升员工业绩。

随着中国城市化的快速发展，更积极地追求建筑能效，发展未来的智慧城市，必能使中国获益匪浅。而建筑能效公示可以成为实现这一目标的重要的市场工具。

二、建筑能效比对和公示对中国加速减排的作用

建筑能效比对和公示有助于促进中国现有建筑提高能效和减少排放。经验表明，如果业主和运营商实施建筑能效比对，即根据标准计量和跟踪能耗情况，并与类似建筑比对以评估能效，他们就更有可能投资于能效。部分原因是，比对可以帮助建筑业主更容易地找出最经济的节能措施。而通过网络平台有效地公示比对结果及使用建筑标识等工具又为市场带来了竞争，从而促进了对节能技术和能效实践的投资。

在能效投资方面，除了建筑规范松弛之外，能效技术和旧房改造的成本居高不下，缺乏对节能的激励，也是建筑能效投资不足的原因之一。对能效项目普遍缺乏积极性，产生了一种被欧盟委员会称之为恶性“归咎循环”的现象。在这个“归咎循环”中，监管机构因政策不力而受到批评，建筑业则被指责为执行能效措施的障碍，而消费者声称缺乏必要的能效信息来做出明智的购买决策。结果，承包商、开发商和建筑商都强调没有投资节能建筑或改造项目的动力。

在这个循环的每个环节，各方面都在等待其他方面先做出改变，然后再决定购买、建造、委托或投资于可持续建筑。挪威的一项建筑能效研究认为，能效措施发展缓慢的原因是公共能效政策有缺陷，政府没有积极推广，建筑业的创新或研发投资太少。研究人员认为，开发商过于注重降低短期成本，对最新设计改进成果重视不足，结果就是重复使用老旧、低能效的设计，包括在新项目中使用过时设备、材料和建筑管理系统。

能效比对和公示可以克服某些障碍，用良性循环取代“归咎循环”，提高对建筑能效及相关节能的认识，促进物业开发商和建筑业主共同采取行动。就像家用电器的能效标识一样，以消费者能够理解的方式提供更多建筑能效信息，帮助他们在购买或租赁时做出明智的选择。能效公示在直接鼓励建筑业主投资于能效改造的同时，也给科技企业提供了创新的动力。因此，能源效能的汇报工作与数据收集及分析工作同样重要。如果建筑能源效能数据对市场参与者有用，那么公示将很有效。按照最乐观的长期设想方案，建筑能效比对和公示可以改变客户在租赁或购买时的期望值，使建筑市场发生显著转变。例如，客户有可能将能效看作物业整体质量的关键指标。加强能效公示还可以提升高能效物业的相对价值，刺激对能效产品、材料和服务的需求，但目前买家缺乏评估物业能效的方法。尽管建筑能效政策将继续依赖于建筑规范和标准等传统法规，但能效公示在鼓励住户和业主做出更好选择的同时，也有助于解决市场失灵问题。建筑能效和运营数据相结合可以促进对能效改造和实践的投资。短期内，向住户和业主提供简单的能效数据时，也可以提供更多运营数据，这样可以极大地促进能效投资。

三、建筑能效数据助力新兴产业发展

在欧美，建筑能效比对和公示已经加大了能效服务相关市场的力量。例如，美国的能效

比对和公示正在创建一个全新的可以利用数据帮助业主改善能源利用效率的行业。这类公示及其鼓励的市场行为已经超越了节能的范畴，可以加快在能效审计、数据分析、需求响应和清洁能源调度等领域创造新的就业机会。

在配套政策的支持下，美国建筑能效公示的早期成果之一是催生了能源服务市场。目前，美国已成为世界上最成熟的能源服务市场之一，美国节能服务公司加快开发绿色建筑，帮助业主为新楼建设和旧楼改造争取能效投资资金，以最少的前期投资实现长期节能目标。按照这一模式，业主和节能服务公司签订节能绩效合同，服务公司提供节能咨询服务，从节能产生的利润中提取一定比例的投资回报。自 20 世纪 70 年代以来，尤其是 90 年代开始，世界各地节能服务公司的数量急剧增加，说明能效服务需求不断增长。

节能服务公司模式已在其他国家获得成功，也同样有可能为中国做出重大贡献。目前在中国注册的节能服务公司有2 000多家，但大多数仅承接相对简单的技术项目，而不是提供范围更广也更全面的节能解决方案（这也是美国面临的一项挑战）。美国的节能服务公司涵盖工业和各个建筑部门，而中国的节能服务公司从工业节能开始起步，近些年才开始涉足建筑领域。中国可以在此基础上让节能服务公司在市场中发挥更大的作用。公共建筑能效公示可以为节能服务公司提供新的商机，为这些公司参与建筑能效市场开辟新渠道，催生新的商业模式。

在过去 10 年中，一些新创公司开发了更具创意的办法来收集和发布楼宇能效信息，促进智能决策和能效投资。Opower 等新创建的私营公用事业公司发现[6]，让楼宇业主和能源经理与他们的临近楼宇或商业竞争对手进行能效对比，可以显著地推动楼宇运营改革。Opower 在 2014 年年初给楼宇业主和公用事业用户寄送信函和电邮，使用柱状图和简单的表情符传递能效对比信息，估计由此节省的电力超过了 40 亿千瓦时。Opower 的经验与其他公用事业公司相仿，它们都发现了信息具有“推动”用户采用低能耗模式的力量。

另一家新创公司 Retroficiency 使用公共和私人数据来促进楼宇节能。该公司展示了如何运用数据使城市居民区与能效投资相匹配。例如，Retroficiency 发现[7]，纽约的居民区如果使用更好的隔热材料，要比使用更好的窗户获益更多。该公司绘制的地图是一款功能强大的工具，可以帮助决策者和私营公司寻找降低城市和楼宇能耗的机会。随着这些新型商业模式的涌现，一个新兴行业正初露端倪，有可能改变业主、运营商和投资者对待能效的态度。

麻省理工学院最近的一项研究强调，建筑能效标识和新数据结合在一起可以协助地方政府和规划者搭建更强大的能效政策平台。“眼下，各州、市政府和公用事业公司可以获得多项数据：物业评估报告、家庭用能账单、红外成像和先进计量数据。建筑标识，特别是通过现场住宅评估所产生的标识，可以为市、州政府及公用事业公司提供一项新数据，方便用户掌握现有住宅评级、建筑系统架构以及改建需求。将现有数据和这一丰富的数据集相结合，能够使利益相关方更好地发掘住宅能效潜力，创建更节能的建筑模式，并为住宅升级制定有的放矢的激励措施。”[8]

社交媒体也积极参与。纽约的新创公司 Honest Buildings 在 2012 年开始收集和发布纽约逾 25 万栋建筑的数据[9]，在网上公开商用物业数据，鼓励在楼宇建设、维修和改建决策过程中提高能效意识。公司成立的第一年，Honest Buildings 即与企业及非政府组织一起公布建筑能效数据，推动在新楼建设和旧楼改造中提高能效。不过，尽管做出了这些初步努力，市场发展依旧缓慢，客户对建筑能效数据的需求依然低迷。即便如此，节能服务公司和承包商仍然可以借助 Honest Buildings 的平台锁定客户，客户也可以借此通过招标来降低项目价格。

新创公司并不是唯一的参与者。随着可用的数据越来越多，IBM、霍尼韦尔、西门子和通用电气等科技巨头也开始加入能源公司和公用事业公司的行列，将公共和私有建筑的能效数据结合到各自的服务中。需求侧管理、能源存储、屋顶太阳能光伏发电、家庭能源管理——所有这些技术与大量数据相结合，正在为迅速提高建筑能效开辟新途径。这些发展对中国有着非常重要的意义。2015 年 1 月，国家发改委和中国银监会共同发布了《能效信贷指引》[10]，为金融机构在能效类项目融资上提供指导。该指引的第 5 条规定，能效信贷业务的重点服务领域包括既有和新建居住建筑、国家机关办公建筑和其他公共建筑。该指引还指出，要优先支持达到先进能效标准的建筑融资项目。建筑能效公示是一个有助于确保金融资源合理分配的工具，可以帮助银行更好地识别应优先考虑的项目，帮助节能服务公司扩大市场，改造不达标建筑。金融机构加大参与将有助于新型商业模式在中国的发展。

四、中国在建筑能效公示方面取得的进展

中国正在拟定大型公共建筑能效公示制度。事实上，中国的公共建筑节能和公示工作始于“十一五”期间。到 2008 年，中国制定了多项政策支持建筑能效公示，国务院在 2008 年公布了《民用建筑节能条例》和《公共机构节能条例》。前者第 32 条规定，国家机关办公建筑和大型公共建筑的能源消耗情况应当依照有关规定向社会公布。到目前为止，政策重点一直是大型公共建筑。在公共建筑中，大型公共建筑面积仅占 8.3%，但用能却占公共建筑的 38%。

2014 年，自然资源保护协会和能源基金会开展联合研究，总结了中国在提高大型公共建筑能效方面的进步，指出通过向潜在买主、租户、建筑运营商及投资者等群体公示建筑能效信息，可以更好地发挥市场力量推动建筑能效提升。自 2007 年住房和城乡建设部建立大型公共建筑能耗监测系统以来，已经分五个批次（截至 2014 年 4 月）收集了 20 个城市的 3 680栋建筑的用能信息。与 2012 年相比，目前的公示系统有了很大的进步，当时中国并不要求公示，无论对内对外都不需要。

中国最新的进展是 2014 年 7 月由住房和城乡建设部推出的能效比对和公示计划，这是一项由世界银行和全球环境基金共同倡议并资助的项目。该计划使用网络比对工具来测量建筑运营能效，前身是已经在北京的医院、酒店和办公建筑内应用的“中国建筑能效比对工具”。该网络工具借鉴美国的能源之星建筑集群管家，并吸收了纽约市的建筑能效比对和公示政策的经验。中国在 2015 年发布了网络比对工具新版本。这个计划的目标是，比对面积在 2017 年前达到 2 900 万平方米，在 2025 年达到 1.71 亿平方米[11]。

北京和宁波是第一批试点城市，将在 2015 年至 2017 年期间试用这个新平台收集市级数

据。该项目将在2018年向全国推广。宁波和北京的试点还将把建筑能效与北京、上海、深圳等几个城市的排放权交易试点整合在一起。

设计者、投资者、开发商、业主、住户、运营商、创业者和监管机构之间要扩大信息共享，才能最大程度地发挥能效投资的效益。如果不能获取可靠的建筑能效信息，就会限制对公示平台和其他有效工具的上游投资。目前，公众访问相关数据和机构信息共享仍然有限。

建筑能效公示要取得预期效果，政府的表率作用至关重要，特别是公共建筑，是显示政府以身作则的一个良机。政府部门带头推动能效公示并提高能效，最显著的收益就是节约资金，降低政府开支，公共资金可以投资于其他可持续性服务和项目。根据世界银行2012年的一份报告，中国可以通过荣誉性鼓励（比如向政府机构颁奖和分享节能收益），来鼓励公共机构提高能源效率，明确问责制度，建立节能服务专业技术能力和开发多元化融资渠道。

五、美国政府机构在创建建筑能效市场中发挥了表率作用

美国是家电节能标识的先行者，在1992年就启动了能源之星计划。“能源之星”是由美国环保署和能源部共同开发的项目，自1995年起在自愿的基础上应用于新建住房，希望复制能源之星成功培育出新的能效家电供应链的成绩。（虽然能源之星是自愿参加的项目，但电冰箱等产品申请能源之星评级说明这类家电大多数都符合能源之星的要求）美国做法的一个重要方面是许多标识计划都着重于提高建筑的运营能效，并以能效比对为支持。能源之星和LEED（能源和环境设计领导计划，这是美国另一项主要的绿色建筑自愿计划）等普及较广的项目都要求有运营标识。可惜目前仅有一小部分建筑和住宅参与了这些项目。例如，截至2013年10月，美国有超过1.7万个LEED认证项目，涉及总建筑面积约2.34亿平方米，仅相当于当年全国商用楼面面积的3%。到2013年年底，超过150万栋新住宅和2.5万栋建筑及厂房获得了能源之星评级，但也只占新住宅和新楼宇总数的一小部分。

近年来，许多州和市（比如加利福尼亚州和纽约市）都开始在建筑市场某些领域执行强制性能效标识和公示政策。在许多情况下，这些强制性的法律法规都起源于销售或租赁等与建筑交易相关的规则。2011年，华盛顿州颁布了一项基于交易信息披露的法律，要求在出售或出租楼宇时必须公示能效信息。西雅图后来通过年度报告法强化了这项要求。初步报告显示，这两部法律推动了当地的能效和建筑管理比对服务。

对于美国许多决策者来说，相对于提高建筑规范和标准，能效公示法律的优点是为改善能源效率提供了一个更加市场化的方法。除了建筑规范和标准以外，信息越多，市场效率就越高。

目前，一些城市的建筑比对信息已经上网，创造出大量的新数据和商机。《纽约市法84》法令规定在全市强制性实施建筑能效比对。2012年，纽约市在美国率先通过网络公示所有大型私有建筑的能效信息。三年来，相关数据不断积累。从2010年5月开始，所有市属建筑都要进行年度能效比对。从2011年5月1日起，大型私有建筑也要披露相关数据。

具体来说，《纽约市法84》要求面积超过929平方米的公共建筑和超过4 645平方米的

私有建筑（或由多栋建筑组成、总面积超过 9 290 平方米的私有建筑）每年提交用能报告。2012 年，总共有 20 320 栋大型私有建筑和 3 097 栋公共建筑通过美国环保署的能源之星建筑集群管家比对工具报告了用能数据，涉及面积共计 2.39 亿平方米，约占 2012 年全市房屋总面积的 45%。2013 年，纽约市的合规率达到了 84%。在两到三年内，楼宇业主的合规率将达到 92%。

《纽约市法 84》还包括审计相关条款，要求楼宇业主将用能账单的副本至少保存三年。美国全国建筑能效分析也采用了纽约市的数据，数据匿名输入能源部的建筑能效数据库，以可视化的方式对类似建筑进行能效比对。

纽约市对能源数据的利用很有创意。除了计算建筑的能源之星评级外，还计算物业和楼宇的用能强度（EUI）分数，根据天气和入住率进行标准化调整。分数按 1～100 显示，使业主和潜在住户更好地了解同类建筑的能耗和可能节省的成本。纽约市的数据显示，不同部门的建筑能效有相当大的差异。

美国其他城市纷纷效仿纽约。奥斯汀、波士顿、芝加哥、华盛顿特区、明尼阿波利斯、费城、旧金山、西雅图和马里兰州的蒙哥马利县也通过了类似的比对法规。这些地区开始逐步获得比对数据，无论是公开发布还是仅供业主使用，当地都将开始按能效划分建筑类别。可信而易懂的数据对于刺激市场响应至关重要，易于获取的可靠数据也为监管法规提供了信息基础，这些法规涉及建筑能效、逐步加强的能效规范、促进能效投资的绿色信贷，也涉及向客户提供一揽子节能措施的商业模式。最后，城市规划者和设计者也通过数据了解各种城市形态及塑造城市形态的城市规划法规对建筑能效的影响，这是最终设计出更具能效、更宜居城市的关键因素。

纽约的经验显示，即使建筑和所有权情况很复杂，也能找到适当的能效公示解决方案。纽约市高层建筑林立，楼龄和建筑质量各异。许多建筑内业主和租户混杂。住户和潜在住户可以利用能效比对来识别能效最高的楼宇。此外，比对可以帮助决策者明确业主应当努力争取达到的标准和目标，并要求业主实现这些目标。

最近，美国联邦机构在推动“可持续性和能源计分卡计划”下的建筑能效公示中起到了表率作用。该计划于 2011 年 4 月启动，除其他指标之外，该计划还根据能源强度、温室气体污染和绿色建筑实践对联邦机构做出评估。计划自推出以来，已有 24 个联邦机构和部门公布了年度计分卡，公示多个领域的可持续性表现，包括建筑能效。计分卡计划要求联邦机构负责实现节能目标，并帮助联邦机构识别机会和改进能源效率。例如，2015 年 1 月，美国国防部和内政部的计分卡显示建筑可持续性仍有改善空间，这两个部的可持续性建筑分别只有 0.8% 和 3.1%。另一方面，国务院对取得高可持续性发展评级的 18.5% 的楼宇进行追踪。

建筑的能源资产评分是能源部开发的另一项工具，按 1～10 评分，给商用和多家庭住宅建筑评定能效分数。该工具帮助楼宇业主寻找能效升级机会，包括对楼宇外围结构、采暖、通风和空调系统或照明进行改进。

各方面的建筑节能意识和对节能的承诺日益增长，正在推动能效投资增长。除了联邦机构带头之外，私营部门也不断革新技术，为方便获取建筑能效信息搭建新的平台。这带动了能效审计、计量表安装、照明升级和电器设备更新等服务市场的成长。由于强制性公示法律迫使业主披露与建筑的结构性低效相关的潜在运营成本，而买家也认识到高能效建筑的水电费支出要低于低能效建筑，对能效服务的需求将随之增长。这将对经济产生显著的积极影响。马萨诸塞大学安姆斯特分校和市场转型研究所共同进行的一项研究显示，美国现有的建筑公示政策有可能在2020年前创造出5.9万个新的工作机会，为消费者节省38亿美元。

美国的经验：美国大量的公共和私营比对数据，特别是商用和住宅建筑的比对数据，促进了一个行业的蓬勃发展，该行业以新颖的方式将数据分析和建筑能效相结合。美国的建筑能效比对计划培养了创新商业模式，使业主甚至承包商更容易通过网络平台获取能效数据。美国的经验教训可以在以下几方面供中国借鉴：

（1）政府的带头作用有助于推动建筑能效公示和节能努力。

（2）网络公示建筑比对信息可以创造出丰富的新数据和新商机，促进能效市场的发展。

六、欧盟的经验表明，数据准入推动了能效提高

欧盟也有根据当地情况实施能效公示的案例。自20世纪90年代起，欧盟的国家、州或地方政府所属公共建筑已成为建筑能效公示的试验平台。早在1997年，丹麦就要求开展建筑能源认证计划。在欧盟，公共建筑是一个理想的能效公示试验场，因为这些建筑的所有者和使用者通常是同一个政府机构。利益冲突较少使得认证过程比较简单，更容易实施。

欧盟2002年颁布的《建筑能效指令》（EPBD）彻底改变了建筑公示规则。该指令建立了一个能效认证框架，要求欧盟成员国在2006年以前通过相关立法，这是欧盟27个成员国首次采取集体行动。实际上，第一批成员国在2009年开始落实能效公示要求。《建筑能效指令》的创新之处在于，要求新楼在建设时申请认证，旧楼在出售或出租时公示能效证书（EPC）。指令还要求大型公共建筑在显著位置张贴能效证书。2010年，欧盟修订了《建筑能效指令》，要求增加公示内容。根据修订的版本，业主在物业出租或购买等交易之前要公示该建筑的能效信息。能效认证的成本一般不超过几百欧元。

欧盟国家使用资产标识和运营标识这两个数据来告诉买家一栋建筑的用能特征。多数欧盟国家仅要求公共建筑提供运营标识，私有建筑只需提供资产标识，以保护私有建筑的隐私。这些标准通常需要进行独立评估，给出能效认证评级。能效认证参考现行法规等多种因素，便于用户比较和评估能效。评估还就如何提高建筑能效和评级，提出最经济的改进建议。

迄今为止，建筑能效指令的实施进展缓慢。究其原因，首先是能效标识可能设计不当，过于看轻对用户来说最重要的能源成本。例如，德国的能效认证用颜色和千瓦时/平方米来显示一栋建筑的能源效率，用户或买家要具备相应的专业知识才能据此估算应付的水电费。如果直接显示能源消费量并按字母相应分级将更有效。其次，消费者对能效认证结果的认知和理解不足，不同国家的能效认证显示方式又不同，消费者难以比较。最后，或许也是最重

要的一点，各个国家和地区在实施和遵守的程度上有天壤之别。

中国应注意欧盟在推动和实施建筑能效比对时遇到的挑战，在设计国内公示方案时汲取这些经验教训。

欧盟的经验教训：在有配套政策支持的情况下，建筑标识和能效公示是一个非常有用的工具。欧盟经验表明，有三类配套政策有助于通过公示促进建筑改造：

（1）法规要求：在优质比对数据的基础上制定良好的法规，可以鼓励楼宇改造。

（2）融资激励：政府制定激励措施，方便用户获得商业融资和项目服务。

（3）市场开发：加强供应链的培养和能力建设，增强需求侧的公众意识，可以提高建筑能效需求。

尽管在建筑能源效能的测量和公示方面有丰富的国际经验，但迄今为止，很少有研究评估建筑能效公示法规对建筑能耗的影响，因为这些法规确实太新了。多数已实施公示指令的欧盟成员国在2009年前后才开始颁发能效证书。美国的强制性建筑能效比对政策也是最近才制定的。

但是，针对公示对物业价值影响的研究揭示了能效指令的效果。例如，欧盟委员会发现，只有在购房者愿意为节能建筑支付更高价格的前提下，节能建筑实践才能进一步普及。委员会对物业价值研究的评估发现，在许多城市和国家，建筑能效评分和物业的售价及租金密切相关，不分地区，不分种类的物业都是如此。就办公楼而言，能效得分最低，租金也最低。尽管这些研究提供了有益的启示，但到目前为止这些研究并不一定找到了这其中的因果关系。

根据调查所做的购房分析显示，迄今为止欧盟指令的实施结果参差不齐，部分原因是买家在评估物业时并不特别重视能效。购房者表示，即使有能效标识，也很少在买房时加以考虑。不过，购房者普遍认为能效是节省成本的直接途径，也是住宅舒适度的一个标志。显然，建筑能效已经和房屋质量一样，成为购房决策的影响因素之一。

欧盟对建筑改造的调研结果同样莫衷一是。欧盟用建筑能效标识来鼓励业主进行能效相关的改造和投资。然而，受访者往往羞于承认能效认证在改造决定中起到了作用。

欧盟业主研究的一个缺陷在于侧重于个人住宅，而不是大型建筑或全体现有建筑。大量涌现的美国建筑比对数据可能会对大型建筑的相关能效决策提供令人信服的证据，这些大型建筑包括大型办公楼和公寓楼，与曼哈顿和中国常见的楼宇类似。

有些地区已经披露类似数据。根据能源之星计划报告，2008－2012年期间，有3.5万栋建筑参加了比对计划，剔除天气和气候因素，修正后的建筑用能强度平均降低了7%。[12]初始得分最低的建筑，在节能的绝对值和百分比方面升幅最大。美国环保署指出，若照此发展，这些建筑的总体能耗将在2020年减少25%。纽约目前受强制性比对约束的建筑面积最大，三年来的数据显示，办公楼和公寓楼的用能强度都有所下降，但还不足以被称为一种趋势。

然而，随着人们越来越认识到建筑在碳排放和常规污染物排放中的作用，比对活动就越来越有望加快新建和改建项目中的绿色建筑投资和能效升级。对建筑能效公示的投资有望推动中国的节能发展，建筑能效与需求侧管理和分布式能源相结合时效果可能会更显著。随着市场的发展，率先提供数据、能效服务发展更快的地区将获得先发优势。

七、保尔森对话会认为，能效公示有助于创建能效市场

中国在能效公示方面已经积累了多年的经验，包括三星计划和 LEED 等强制性或自愿性计划。中国在制定更严格的建筑规范的同时，也迅速提高了建筑规范的合规比率。现有公示平台仍有改进的空间，以确保及时有效地比较类似建筑及后续建筑标准并提高效率。此外，加强实施力度也会产生更有意义的效果。

中国的决策层可以借鉴欧美的经验，并根据国内实践，不断强化现有公示平台。基于中国已经取得的进展，保尔森基金会在 2015 年 6 月组织了一场专家对话会，讨论如何改进目前的数据收集方法、报告流程和公示平台，以推动能效投资。专家小组肯定了能效公示对建立建筑能效服务市场的价值，讨论了投资的主要障碍。专家们就能效公示如何加快中国的建筑节能发展提出了 5 点建议：

（1）公共建筑以身作则。几位与会者强调，在提供数据收集和报告框架以及数据公示方面，公共建筑都应该起到表率作用。目前的公示制度就是针对公共建筑而定，但可以采取更多措施，每年连续一贯地收集和报告同一建筑的能效数据，便于有效地对比。根据专家们的意见，政府应当在建立数据报告框架中起表率作用，以确保各级政府机构实施良好行为规范，并产生深远影响。

（2）公众参与，推动市场发展。要进一步推动公众参与，通过数据普及，促进建筑能效服务需求。数据普及可以带动市场，因为包括节能服务公司在内的民营企业能够利用大数据技术，帮助业主和运营商找到低成本改进潜力最大的楼宇。如果公众可以获得的数据仍然有限，那么能效投资就会更多依赖于行政措施，或依赖个别业主及运营商的积极性，能效领域的进展就会放慢。

（3）为业主提供全面指引。随着建筑能效公示平台的成熟，必须建立相关系统，让业主定期了解本建筑与类似建筑的比对数据，了解改进设计和运营的可用资源，并了解整改时限的明确指令。有了清晰、全面的指引，业主就可以对物业做出必要的改进，确保市场从公示投资中充分获益。

（4）收集多元化建筑数据。数据不应仅限于总能耗，还应包括面积、所用电器、隔热材料、入住率以及气候等外部因素。收集多种数据有助于确保精确比对和做出必要改进。

（5）加强业主对公示的信心和参与。确保公示不会泄露商业机密或个人信息。业主和企业相信数据公示不会威胁其商业竞争力时，就会更愿意公示数据。此外，肯定业主在公示中的带头作用能促进他们继续参与，并鼓励其他相关者参与。

对话会的结果肯定了能效公示在创建建筑能效市场中的价值。这次对话会最重要的成果之一是，与会专家普遍认同建筑能效公示可以带来的经济效益，部分专家认为建筑能效公示的经济效益会远远超过实施成本。

八、建议和结论

（一）建议

根据保尔森基金会2015年6月建筑能效公示对话会的成果，以及中国公共政策专家和节能建筑领域商界领袖的建议，结合欧美大规模实施建筑能效公示的经验教训，保尔森基金会谨就中国建筑能效公示提出以下建议：

（1）扩大数据收集种类。除了收集总能耗的数据，还应包括面积、所用电器、隔热材料、入住率以及气候等多元数据。收集多元化数据有助于确保精确比对和后续必要的能效改造。通过分类、分板块、分气候区、分项等方式将收集好的数据进行格式化，提高数据公示后的比对性。

（2）建立坚实的法律法规基础，实施建筑（尤其是公共建筑）能效公示制度并严格执行。虽然2008年以来颁布了多项法规鼓励公共建筑进行能效公示，但据业主和运营商反映，公开建筑能效数据或与有关政府机构和平台共享数据仍缺乏坚实的法律基础。出席对话会的部分专家特别指出了这一点，认为这是推广能效数据公示的主要障碍。法律基础可以包括关于公示时间的具体指导，也可以包括公共建筑能效公示的标准化模板，比如应公示哪些数据、公示频率、公示对象、公示平台以及便于比较的公示格式。

（3）建立推广时间表，以公共建筑为起点，逐步将更多建筑纳入公示范围，并同时开展强大的公示培训计划及项目。数名与会专家一致认为，公共建筑能效公示可以加快培育目前尚不存在的建筑能效服务市场。政府大楼、学校、医院和其他公共建筑是启动公示计划的良好起点。但是，让尚未积极行动起来的政府负责人了解公示的好处以及采取行动提高建筑能源效能的重要性往往需要时间。美国开发、规范和实施公共建筑能效计分卡制度就花费了数年时间。推动政府机构参与各种类型的能效数据公示，培训建筑运营商收集和格式化数据，让政府机构在数据公示前采取初步措施改善突出的能效问题，这些都需要时间。在某些情况下，积极的激励措施可以加速计划实施，例如以公用事业数据公示为条件提供改造经费的做法就是一个很好的例子。目前，加利福尼亚州正在根据2012年通过的《加利福尼亚州清洁能源就业法》进行尝试，主要是为公立学校的节能改造提供资金。这些都是很重要的步骤，花费了数年时间才完成。伴随着中国的快速城镇化步伐，中国需要加快在建筑能源效能比对及公示法律与实践方面的发展，为市场上数十亿平方米的节能建筑的建设提供条件，帮助中国实现降低碳强度和能源强度的目标。

（二）结论

（1）在中国某些地方，实时公示公共建筑能效数据仍然比较敏感，但保尔森基金会倡导中国政府应在数据公示上采取措施，包括建立坚实的法律基础，解决数据公开的法律问题。大量经验表明，中国政府已经在这方面采取了协调一致、循序渐进的措施，但仍有努力的空间。越早解决数据分享与公示的法律问题，市场就能越早在节能方面发挥核心作用。在尚不能实现公示的情况下，可以从开展内部评级系统开始，对类似的公共建筑进行比对，奖励优秀，为能效欠佳的建筑制订改进计划。随着时间的推移，这些做法可以逐步建立起对公示的信心。

（2）有了可信的数据，市场就可以在推进建筑节能改造方面发挥作用，并加快新物业在开发过程中采纳节能设计的速度。比对工作还可以强化政府办公楼能源管理政策，支持中国实现低碳城市的目标。我们认为，基于以上建议，并辅之以日益增强的建筑规范和执行力度，有助于中国实现建筑节能目标。大幅度降低建筑能耗将减少建筑行业的常规气体污染物排放和温室气体排放，有助于中国实现改善空气质量、应对气候变化的长远目标。除了环境效益外，建筑能效需求的上升还将在服务领域创造出新的就业机会，包括能效审计、旧楼改造和设备升级。通过加强信息公示和配套政策，在市场和建筑能效二者之间建立关联管理，这对企业和社会来说无疑是双赢的结果。

致谢：衷心感谢保尔森基金会的工作团队成员 Elle Carberry（柯凯丽）、Chelsea Eakin（艾巧思）、Dinda Elliott（艾鼎德）、付莉霓、Kate Gordon（成可黛）、Hortense Halle-Yang（海棠）、姜新燕、娄雪莲和万婧的辛勤工作；衷心感谢中国企业管理科学基金会及中国企业联合会的尹援平、王菲菲和于武；衷心感谢能源基金会的莫争春及劳伦斯伯克利国家实验室的 Carolyn Szum 和冯威在协调报告审阅方面提供的帮助。

（作者：Anders Hove（侯安德），保尔森基金会研究部副主任；Gailius J. Draugelis（卓力石），世界银行中国及蒙古局贷款和咨询服务国别业务协调人、首席能源专家；Merisha Enoe（尹美霞），保尔森基金会研究部经理）

参考文献

[1] J. Eon et al., "China's Building Energy Use: A Long-Term Perspective based on a Detailed Assessment," Pacific Northwest National Laboratory, PNNL - 21073, January 2012, accessed at http://www.pnnl.gov/main/publications/external/technical_reports/PNNL - 21073. pdf. "In 2007, China's buildings sector consumed 31% of China's total final energy..."; Wei Feng et al., Evaluation of Energy Savings of the New Chinese Commercial Building Energy Standard, Lawrence Berkeley National Lab and China Academy of Building Research, 2014, accessed at http://aceee.org/files/proceedings/2014/data/papers/4 - 761. pdf.

[2] "Cleantech in China Building a green future," PWC, September 2013, accessed at http://www.pwc.com/en_US/us/technology/publications/cleantech-perspectives/pdfs/pwc-cleantech-perspectives-china-greenfuture. pdf. "China currently has approximately 40 billion square meters of building space, which is about five times as much as the U.S. Each year, more than two billion square meters are added..."; Gong, Ming, Changsha Meixi Green Residential Design, 2013, Volume 11, accessed at http://d.wanfangdata.com.cn/Periodical_csjsllyj201311778. aspx. "According to statistics, carbon emissions from buildings account for about 46% of China's total carbon emissions."

[3] Madhu Khanna et al., "Toxics Release Information: A Policy Tool for Environmental Protection," PERE Working Paper No. 7, May 1997, accessed at http://ssrn.com/abstract=45557.

[4] PlaNYC, New York City Local Law 84 Benchmarking Report, September 2014, The City of New York Office of the Mayor, accessed at http: // www. nyc. gov/html/planyc/downloads/pdf/publications/2014_ nyc_ ll84_ benchmarking_ report. pdf; According to New York City Local Law 84, public properties over 10, 000 square feet, single private sector properties over 50, 000 square feet, and multiple private sector properties over 100 000 square feet must report and benchmark data on an annual basis through the EPA's Energy Star Portfolio Manager benchmarking tool. Failure to benchmark results in a US $ 500. 00 fine on a quarterly basis until the property owner is in compliance. Reporting energy use on an annual basis allows building owners, tenants and property managers to compare their buildings' energy performance in to similar properties (benchmark). Publically disclosed energy data is available online at: www. nyc. gov/ ll84data; Benchmarking Data Disclosure and Reports, 2013 Energy and Water Data Disclosure for Local Law 84, April 28, 2015, NYC's Mayor's Office of Sustainability, accessed at http: //www. nyc. gov/html/gbee/ html/plan/ll84_ scores. shtml. Data disclosed includes information on total greenhouse gas emissions, property floor area, energy consumption per square foot, and Energy Star scores.

[5] Koen Steemers and Shweta Manchanda, "Energy efficiency design and occupant well-being: Case studies in the UK and India," Building and Environment, Volume 45, Issue 2, pages 270 ~ 278, February 2010, (www. sciencedirect. com/science/article/pii/S0360132309002431)

[6] Stephen Lacey, "Who Will Emerge as the Opower of Commercial Building Efficiency?" Greentech Media, March 17, 2014, (www. greentechmedia. com/articles/read/Will-There-Ever-Be-an-Opowerof-Commercial-Building-Efficiency)

[7] Katherine Tweed, "Building Genome Project: Retroficiency Takes a CityWide Approach to Efficiency," Greentech Media, April 16, 2014, accessed at (www. greentechmedia. com/articles/read/retroficiency-buildinggenome-project)

[8] Nikhil Nadkarni and Harvey Michaels, "A New Model for Disclosing the Energy Performance of Residential Buildings," March 2012, accessed at http: //web. mit. edu/energ y-efficiency/docs/EESP_ Nadkarni_ BuildingPerformanceDisclosure. pdf. "Building labeling can create a new data resource for states, cities, and utilities as they work to identify efficiency needs. Under the current conditions, states, cities, and utilities have access to a few data streams: property assessor reports (covering home size, age, etc.), home energy bills, infrared imagery (being piloted), and advanced metering data (where applicable). Building labels, especially if generated through on-site home assessments, can provide a new datastream to cities, states, and utilities that captures the housing stock's ratings, shape of building systems, and retrofit needs. Using this rich dataset in conjunction with the existing data enables these stakeholders to better identify residential efficiency potential, create more powerful building models, and develop targeted incentives for home upgrades."

[9] Jeff St. John, "Honest Buildings: 250, 000 New York City Buildings Online," Greentech Media, May 9, 2012, (www. greentechmedia. com/articles/read/honest-buildings - 250 000 - new-yorkcity-buildings-online)

[10] "能效信贷指引" [Energy Efficiency Credit Guidelines], NDRC and China Banking Regulatory Commission, January 19, 2015 (www. cbrc. gov. cn/chinese/home/docView/9B09B258DCCF4E439A9DE3520 51885E8. html)

[11] Carolyn Szum, "Research on Very Low-Energy Building Operations andManagement Methods," Lawrence Berkeley National Laboratory, August 25, 2014, (https: //cercbee. lbl. gov/sites/all/files/attachments/Day% 201 - Panel% 204 - LowE-ICF-Carolyn. FINAL_ . pdf)

[12] "Energy Star Portfolio Manager Data Trends," U. S. Environmental Protection Agency, October 2012, (www. energystar. gov/ sites/default/files/buildings/tools/DataTrends_ Savings_ 20121002. pdf)

专题篇

我国城市创新发展的模式

城市是经济社会发展的重要载体，是国家和区域综合竞争力的关键支撑。我国70%以上的GDP、80%以上的国家税收来自城市，90%以上的大学和科研力量等创新资源分布在城市，城市在一个地区经济发展和创新驱动中起着重要的推动和支撑作用。党的十八大提出实施创新驱动发展战略、建设创新型国家的战略决策，创新型城市建设已成为创新型国家建设的重要组成部分。自2010年开始，国家科技部启动创新型城市试点建设工作，印发了《关于进一步推进创新型城市试点工作的指导意见》，目前全国已有57个城市进入试点或建设阶段，各地也在探索出了各具特色的城市创新发展模式，城市创新正成为我国区域创新的重要载体。对于城市创新发展模式的分类可以从多种角度进行，本文在梳理全国主要城市创新发展路径基础上，探索性地将城市创新模式划分为五类，即：以高端研发实现创新引领型、“外引内生”相结合双重推动型、构建产业集群式创新网络辐射型、依靠政府科技体制机制创新推动型、承接大都市技术转移发展型五大类创新模式，以期对培育创新增长极、推动创新驱动的新型城镇化发展提供借鉴。

一、我国城市创新发展的主要模式

（一）以高端研发实现创新引领型

1. 基本内涵

在这类发展模式中，一般都会有一个在科技方面具有引领作用的核心城市：科技资源丰富，且经济基础好，能通过强化和提升自主创新与研发服务能力，将自身打造成原始创新策源地、技术创新总部集聚地、科技成果交易核心区、高端创新型人才集聚区和高端产业示范引领区，在周边城市群中居于稳定的创新中心地位，并辐射带动周边区域的协同发展，与周边卫星城市形成上下游高度融合的产业协作链与创新链，如北京与京津冀城市群、上海与长三角城市群、武汉与武汉城市圈等。

2. 运行机制

该类模式以高新科技产业园区为抓手，注重发挥政府引导作用，围绕创新主体的合作需求，通过与各地政府建立战略合作关系，选择相应的地市建立高新科技园区（分园），两地或三地共同搭建科技合作服务平台，促进各地企业合作需求对接，服务企业跨区域布局发展，推动科技创新和区域经济协同发展。支持企业跨区域布局，开展技术研发合作，组织项目对接，设立分支机构等，促成先进适用技术成果的及时落地转化和应用推广。

3. 典型特征

该类模式中，有高端研发引领辐射作用的城市通常具有优越的地理区位，信息较为发达，城市科技条件好，科教资源丰富，特别是具有高校和科研机构集聚的优势，有高素质的研究人员，具有依靠科技要素禀赋和原始创新驱动经济发展的相对优势；同时要求城市经济发达，能为创新活动提供丰富的资本、技术、人力等创新性因素，又具有良好的创新环境和产业基础。因此，该类城市往往是一个国家或区域的经济中心、创新中心。我国的北京、上海、南京、合肥、武汉等城市是该类模式的典型代表。

这类城市具有研发资源的中心效应，可集聚大量的劳动力和知识组织所提供的外部环境，如大学和企业中的实验室、专业生产服务、大量的顾问等；通过高新技术企业和孵化器、中介机构、金融机构等将科教资源直接转化为生产力。企业作为创新成果转化和应用的主体在促进科研成果的应用方面具有不可替代的优势，需要高校和科研机构加强与企业合作，通过共建研发基地、孵化器、技术研发中心等推动研发成果的转化和应用。除研发资源的集聚效应外，该类城市还发挥着科技创新扩散的作用，新技术的发明和自主创新成果在该类城市产生并随着与其他城市之间的创新要素的互动而扩散到其他地区。

4. 优劣势分析

该模式的优势在于以原始创新和知识创新为引擎，以高校和科研机构创新的原始创新为主，创新引致的良好效应的独享程度比较高，使得整个经济体的自组织能力和抵御外部联动风险的能力较强，不仅会大大提高城市经济的发展速度，而且可能会给城市经济和产业形态带来根本性的变革。劣势在于：在既定的条件下推动创新的成本过高，创新成果从科研机构诞生到应用于经济社会领域需要复杂的转化过程和漫长的周期，包含的技术风险、市场风险、管理风险等在内的综合风险会比较高。未来的发展方向在于：完善推进科技成果转化的体制机制，加强科技成果转化与推广应用。

（二）“外引内生”集成创新型

1. 基本内涵

“外引内生”相结合的集成创新式发展模式，一般适用于自身科技资源较为缺乏，但区位条件和经济、产业基础较好，有集聚和吸引外部资源优势的城市。它们能通过引进外部科技资源与本土企业的技术创新进行融合，增强企业的自主创新能力，优化产业结构。这类城市一般是区域性的中心城市，作为创新源头，带动辐射周边地区的科技创新发展。

2. 运行机制

该类模式以产学研为突破口，通过体制机制创新，将外部科技资源与本土企业有效嫁接，研发和生产新的应用导向型技术和产品，进而推动城市在产业、社会民生、管理等方面发展的创新模式，即“外部引进”和“内部集成”的模式对这类城市具有较好的适用性。

采取这种发展模式的城市往往具有较好的区域比较优势，市场意识比较成熟，经济体制比较完善，产业基础好，民营经济活跃，有创新创业的文化环境，政策制度比较宽松且政府的推动力强，外部性科技资源流入的成本较低，能够迅速地形成良好的利益展示机制以便进一步吸引和留住外部创新性资源。深圳和常州是这一模式的典型代表。值得注意的是，对于一些科教资源缺乏人才也缺乏的城市，并不能简单地复制区域中心城市整合本地创新资源的创新路径。

3. 典型特征

“外引内生”集成创新型发展模式必须具备的两大关键性要素：外部创新性要素的聚集效果和本土企业、产业的发展基础。城市内部宽松的制度环境和较好的产业发展基础不断吸引外部的科教资源流向城市，而科教资源聚集又为本土企业开展创新活动提供了智力和技术支撑，有效地促进了高校和科研院所的科研成果转化，促进了企业的自主创新能力。具体而言，城市经济在市场化竞争的压力下，通过本土企业与外部高校、科研院所开展项目合作、共建孵化器、研发中心、示范基地等形式的合作，来弥补城市内部创新资源的不足和提高城市自身研究能力和研究人员的业务和创新能力。在这一过程中，外部环境系统的支撑对创新资源的流入起着非常重要的作用，如投资环境营造、科技公共服务体系构建等。

4. 优劣势分析

这类模式的优势在于：全开放式的吸引外部资源的方式使得创新性资源的供给比较充足，既有效弥补了创新要素缺口，又降低了创新成本和风险。在当前开放经济的背景条件下，这种以市场需求为导向、本土企业为主体、产学研相结合的创新模式，提高了科技成果的转化效率。劣势在于：由于缺乏内部科教资源，且外部的科教资源创新活动基本围绕企业创新能力的提升，容易导致城市内部自身原始创新、知识创新和基础创新能力的不足，影响了城市持续创新能力的提升。因此，要在进一步探索和完善吸引留住外部创新资源的制度机制基础上，加强城市知识创新的能力建设，提高城市创新的自主性，增强城市经济自我完善、自我发展的能力。

（三）产业集群式创新网络驱动型

1. 基本内涵

城市基于本地区比较优势和资源优势，选择优势要素形成某种优势产业，并在市场机制作用下逐步形成具有分工协作关联的生产、服务企业和科研、信息、培训等社会服务机构在空间上的集中，进而通过各主体间设施资源共享、知识信息流动、创新分工合作等规模范围效应的发挥，增强要素创新的强度和频率，促进城市经济的全面创新。这类城市往往基于特殊的资源禀赋能形成一定的优势产业，并通过产业集群式发展集聚与整合科技资源，构建集群式创新网络，推动产业向高端化水平迈进。这类城市如深圳、常州、昆山等。

2. 典型特征

该类模式的特点是城市经济发达，市场基础好，特色产业优势明显，并集聚了大量的相关产业，企业间创新网络密集。与传统的线性创新机制不同，集群式创新机制不再强调企业是创新活动的唯一源泉，而是认为创新是一个由多个经济活动主体分工、协作构成的网络系统。各个主体根据自身职能发挥不同作用，交换信息、知识，实施合作创新和跟随创新。因此，该模式的实质是通过产业的集群化发展，形成集群创新网络，通过各网络节点主体协同创新，进而带动城市全要素创新。

3. 运行机制

该模式在产业集群内部，创新活动由企业、政府、社会机构等多个创新主体参与，并由核心企业、机构和外部支持系统组成。其中，生产企业以市场需求为导向直接从事创新，零部件或原材料供应商、服务企业进行跟随关联创新，大学、科研机构与企业合作提供先进知识和技术；教育培训、金融等中介机构分别提供创新所需的专业人才、资金和信息；地方政府、行业协会、社区网络等社会机构为集群提供创新所需的政策扶持、公共平台、制度规范和文化环境等。企业与企业之间，企业与其他行为主体之间，通过产业联系、制度以及政策等积极参与到创新过程中，形成区域协同的创新网络。在这一过程中，各创新行为主体不断地利用集体学习的力量进行创新，城市的创新氛围和创新体系逐步形成。与此同时，由于产业集群在发展壮大的过程中，吸收了大量周边的生产要素，这些要素的质量将随着产业集群的不断优化升级而得到提高，进而推动城市经济的全要素创新。需要强调的是，在集群创新网络中，各节点主体自身功能发挥、分工合作及要素交流的频率和稳定程度，直接影响着集群创新系统的作用范围和强度，制约着产业集群式创新的运行状况，因而也就影响了城市创新能力的提升。

4. 优劣势分析

这类创新模式的优势主要体现在要素共享优势、创新协作优势和知识扩散优势三个方面。一是通过创新资源的共享降低企业创新成本，并产生规模效应，促进集群创新能力的可持续发展，优化企业的创新环境；二是集群内的上下游企业通过相互合作、相互学习，增强集体学习能力和合作创新能力；三是在产业集群内部，企业之间、企业与科研机构之间通过研究成果转移、人员溢出、企业衍生、社会交流网络等途径，促使集群内的知识技术迅速扩散。但由于实际运行中企业协作外部配套服务体系不完善等原因，作为产业集群核心竞争力源泉的专业化分工和创新协作优势等并未得到充分发挥。当前，产业价值链在经济全球化和信息化的进程中正发生着重大变化，产品和产业分工的界限越来越模糊，形成了生产环节中的分工和产业交叉融合的新型分工模式。

（四）政府科技体制机制创新推动型

1. 基本内涵

该类创新模式的主要特点是：城市政府制定明确的创新的发展战略，制定和颁布促进城市创新的政策措施，不断加大创新基础设施投资，推动国际、国内的创新资源要素向城市集聚，支持和鼓励创新主体之间形成互动和网络关系，营造有利于创新的文化氛围，引导全社会参与城市创新。这类城市如萍乡、兰州等。

2. 典型特征

该类城市一般经济发展总体水平不高，市场机制落后，科教资源较缺乏，科技基础条件较差，企业自主创新能力较弱，以发展传统产业为主。受制于经济和环境的约束，市场在该阶段难以体现出主导作用，政府在城市创新中通过科技体制机制创新来集聚科技资源，提升城市创新能力，推动经济社会发展。

3. 运行机制

该类模式中，政府依靠自身在政策法规、资金支持、公共服务等方面的职能发挥，通过政策引导、人才引进、科技创新服务体系建设等方式服务于创新主体的培育，进而为增强城市创新能力提供有效的保障。首先，该类城市总体经济发展水平不高的基本特征决定了在创新的过程中，对资金的大规模需求，需要政府不断强化对高新技术企业和高新技术产品的金融支持。资金支持的形式主要包括：政府对科技研发费用的直接投资、财政补贴、设置技术创新引导基金、采取科技创新研究开发活动的创新税收优惠政策、建立金融支持平台等。其次，科技进步与创新的关键取决于创新人才，政府通过实施一系列创新人才政策，加强与大专院校、科研单位、大型企业的联系等方式培养和开发人才，对技术创新人才进行技术培训等措施加强对科技创新人才的引进、培育和提升。再次，政府构建的科技创新服务体系的好坏，直接影响到创新活动的成败。一方面，政府组织、制定相关政策，探索建立官、产、学、研联合机制，搭建企业或行业公共研发平台，促使高校、科研机构与企业形成利益共同体，引导发挥各自比较优势，联合进行研究开发，共同生产销售；另一方面，政府通过组织并规范创新服务中介组织，提供资金融通、创业直达、技术支持、管理咨询、项目评估、市场开拓等多项中介服务，加速科技创新成果的商品化和市场化。因此，该模式对政府的功能要求较高，政府通过制定创新战略、政策法规、培育创新主体等完善城市了科技创新环境，为城市创新提供一系列制度保障。

4. 优劣势分析

该类创新模式是一种典型的自上而下的强制性制度变迁。其优势在于：对城市市场经济发展水平要求相对不高，在政府相关制度供给高效率的前提下起步发展速度较快，由政府出面解决经济社会发展中面临的突出矛盾，经济发展相对平稳，较少出现大起大落的局面。劣势在于：创新本身就是根植于市场，但该模式由于过于依赖政府力量，不仅容易出现政府经济对于民间经济的挤出效应，而且不利于市场经济主体的培育和发展。

（五）承接大都市技术转移型

1. 基本内涵

当前，我国不少大中城市周围县（市）充分利用紧邻区域中心城市的区位优势，积极融入中心城市都市圈，利用产业梯次转移、配套中心城市的上游产业等方式，提升自身创新能力。这类城市自身科技资源较为缺乏，但由于具有靠近大都市，可通过融入大都市产业链或承接大都市产业转移而接受其知识、技术、资本、人才等科技资源的辐射，进而推动城市经济社会的发展。这类城市如廊坊、嘉兴、南通等。

2. 典型特征

该类创新模式的特点为：由于区域产业专业化程度低，基于专业化分工协作的产业集群（产业链）和支撑性组织不完善；大学、公共研究机构等知识创新资源和知识转移机构相对缺乏，教育培训机构只能满足低水平的职业培训需求，知识生成与扩散能力无法满足企业的需求；区内企业规模较小，科研投入强度、创新活动数量和对外部知识的吸收能力均低于周边地区平均水平，创新网络亟待完善。该模式在接受中心城市的辐射方面具有得天独厚的优势，具备良好的基础建设条件、便利的交通及良好的生活环境、完备的劳动力市场以及良好的治安环境及便利的投资政策，能够主动有效地接受中心城市在人才、技术、资本以及关联产业等方面的辐射。

3. 运行机制

围绕在大城市周边的中小城市，根据自身邻近大城市的地缘优势及劳动力、土地等要素成本的比较优势，采取多种形式开展创新活动，不断接受中心城市的资金、项目、人才、技术等扩散转移，并加快推进基础设施建设和融资平台等创业环境建设，服务于本地社会经济发展。一般而言，为解决好大城市的科技资源扩散，该类地区吸引大城市的科技资源的形式有以下几种：一是通过土地、税收、资金等政策优惠吸引大城市的科技创新型企业，建设科技水平高端化、产学研体系完备的研发机构或产业基地，提升企业科技创新的能力和水平；二是加强与大城市合作的研发层次，如技术转让、合作共建科技园区、产业基地，合作共建企业技术研发中心等；三是通过加快提升科技创新配套能力和科技创新外部环境等建设，如基础设施、软硬件条件、政策与体制机制等。

4. 优劣势分析

该创新模式的优势是区位优势明显，容易受到多种外力的拉动；劣势是对于无法复制的区位优势要求较高，限制了其适应范围，难以形成自主发展机制。这类城市未来发展方向为：通过大力推进制度创新改善创新环境，学习和吸取发达地区经验和知识，吸引发达地区的资源为我所用，促进知识和技术的流动、传播和运用，逐步形成能支撑与发达地区产业体系对接的地方创新体系。因此，这类地区的科技工作需注重采取多种形式吸引、组织中心城市的科技创新资源向本地区的辐射和转移，从而提升自身的创新能力。

总之，城市的科技创新发展模式植根于城镇经济基础、资源禀赋条件以及创新文化要素条件等多种因素，每种模式有其发展的独特性和适用性。创新路径既要基于城镇自身的要素禀赋条件基础，又要遵循科技创新体系建设的一般特征与规律。

二、未来我国城市创新的发展方向

1. 分类推进城市创新发展

按照我国各个城市在经济发展特点、区域资源禀赋、科技发展基础、科教创新资源布局、区域功能定位的不同，实施特色化、个性化的差别政策，分阶段、分批次、分梯级推进各个城市的科技创新工作，鼓励各个城镇针对自身条件和基础开展不同形式、不同方向的创新模式试点，形成各具特色的多元化创新发展路径。

2. 引导和支持企业加大创新投入，提高企业的整体创新能力

企业是城市经济活动的基本单元，城市的科技创新只有以企业作为技术创新的主体，才能敏锐地把握市场需求，有效整合产学研力量，加快创新成果的转化应用，推进科技与经济的有效结合。新时期，国家宜采用财政补贴、税收优惠、信贷支持、股权激烈等多种方式加大对企业技术创新的金融支持；建立和完善促进城市科技型企业，特别是科技型中小微企业发展的财税激励政策；支持企业建立研发机构，如对企业建立技术中心和工程中心分别给予财政补助；促进企业之间、企业与高等院校和科研院所之间的知识流动和技术转移，深化产学研合作。

3. 加强城市多层次的公共服务平台建设

要注重围绕解决城市发展中关键技术问题的能力建设搭建公共创新服务平台。鼓励和支持城镇企业和高校、科研院所联合共建公共研发平台或者借助高校与科研机构的研发资源，专门针对城市产业的共性关键技术开展研发和创新活动。积极鼓励和支持企业与外部研发机构建立技术研究中心，以及与成果转化、人才培训、信息服务相结合的“四位一体”的产业集群公共技术研发平台。

4. 以高新技术产业开发区和大学科技园为载体，构建产业集群创新网络

高新技术产业是城镇经济竞争的焦点，是城镇创新的源泉。经济发展水平较高的城市，对于已有的高新技术产业开发区和科技园，要重视建立园区内相关产业的网络体系，努力形成大中小企业密切配合、专业分工和协作完善的产业集群网络体系。要充分发挥高新技术产业开发区和大学科技园对创新资源和要素的集聚作用。

（作者：胡志坚，中国科学技术发展战略研究院院长；王书华，博士，研究员，中国科学技术发展战略研究院农村与区域发展研究所所长）

我国城市建设用地的变化与调控对策

城市建设用地总量及其用地结构动态变化的合理性是衡量一个国家和地区城镇化进程是否健康、城镇化发展质量是否高效的重要标志。适度的城市建设用地总量和城市用地结构优化是推动城市保持集约高效的城市生产空间、宜居适度的城市生活空间和山清水秀的城市生态空间的重要保障，也是永葆城市成长活力、旺盛发展动力、激发发展潜力、实现城市可持续发展的必由之路。中国是全球城市建设用地总量最大、变化最为剧烈、诱发的用地矛盾最为突出的国家之一，采取综合手段调控城市建设用地总量与速度、优化城市建设用地结构，提高城市建设用地集约利用效率，是关系到国家现代化大局的重要任务。为此，需要深刻分析改革开放以来中国城市化过程中城市建设用地的动态变化特征与存在问题，进而有针对性地提出城市建设用地总量调控与结构优化的对策建议。

一、中国城市建设用地的动态变化特征

（一）城市建设用地总量与人均建设用地成倍增加

改革开放以来，中国城市建设用地在数量、人均面积和用地扩张弹性系数上均经历了巨大变化。

1. 34 年城市建设用地增加了 6.44 倍，年均净增 1 311 平方公里

《中国城市建设统计年鉴（2014 年）》数据显示：中国设市城市建设用地面积 1981－2014 年从 6 720 平方公里增至 49 982.7 平方公里，增长了 6.44 倍，年均增长率达 6.27%，呈显著的指数增长和快速扩张的趋势（图 1A）。同时，年均净增加面积也呈整体上升趋势，1981－2014 年净增长 43 262.7 平方公里，年均净增加面积约为 1 311 平方公里，其中 2000 年以来年均净增长量更是高达 1 940 平方公里。

2. 34 年人均城市建设用地增加了 2.78 倍，年均净增 2.37 平方米

从人均城市建设用地面积看，34 年来中国人均城市建设用地面积从 1981 年的 46.67 平方米增至 2014 年的 129.57 平方米，年均净增 2.37 平方米。人均建设用地需求不断增加，导致城市扩张压力逐步加大，同时也暴露出用地浪费严重、用地效率低下和利用不集约等问题。

3. 34 年城市建设用地扩张速度明显高于人口增长速度

从表征城区人口变化速度与城市建设用地变化速度关系的城市建设用地扩张弹性系数（城市建设用地变化速度/城区人口变化速度）来看，1981－2014 年中国城市建设用地扩张弹性系数均值为 1.71（剔除奇异值后），城市建设用地扩张速度明显高于人口增长速度，两者并不同步，而且近年来这种不同步更为明显。

（二）城市建设用地增长速度呈现出大快大慢的波浪状起伏变化态势

从城市建设用地增长速度来看，中国城市建设用地增长呈现波状变化趋势，整体与经济发展的阶段性和城市用地政策以及耕地保护变化相对应（图 1B）。根据增速的形态变化特征可将整体时间段划分为 6 个明显的变化阶段。以东南亚金融危机的 1998 年为界，可划分为

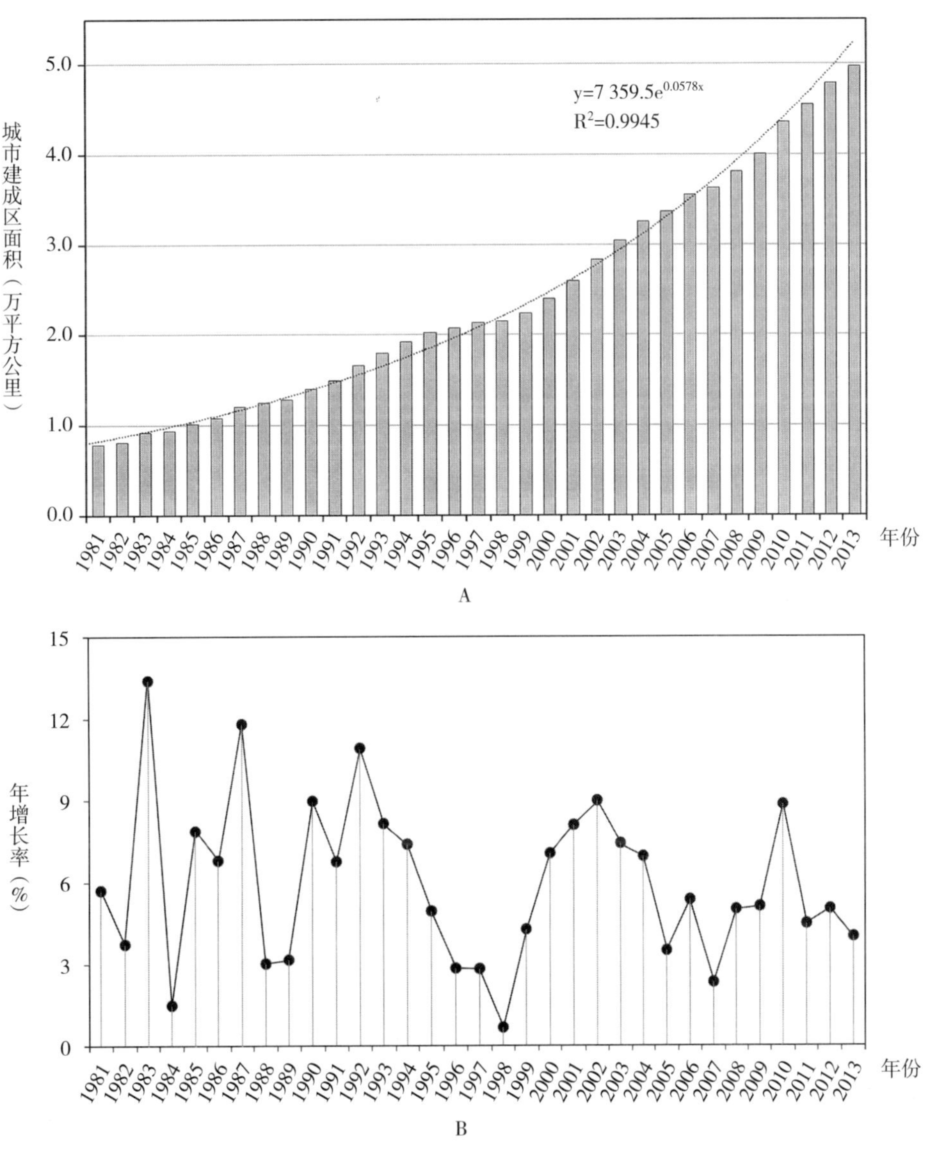

图 1　中国城市建设用地（建成区）增长趋势与年均增长率变化情况

前后两个大的时间段：1981－1998年增速波动更为频繁而且振幅较大；1998－2013年增速波动变小，增速振幅缩小。而1981－1998年又可细分为2个子阶段：其中1981－1992年处于耕地保护制度和房地产制度改革的探索期，其间的年际波动最大，可视为频繁波动的阶段；1992－1998年增速逐年降低，可视为增速减缓阶段；由于1992年国办发文《关于严禁开发区和城镇建设占用耕地撂荒的通知》，耕地保护力度加大。1998－2013年也可细分为以下4个子阶段：1998－2002年为快速扩张增长阶段（过热增长阶段）；2002－2007年为增速减缓阶段（耕地保护政策初步建立）；2007－2010年为增速复苏式升高阶段（为刺激经济中央政府实施“四万亿投资”计划）；2010－2013年为增速调整式减缓阶段。

（三）城市建设用地结构总体处在稳定变化的合理区间

近年来，中国城市建设用地的内部结构同样出现变化，但从不同用地的比例来看这种变化并不显著（图2和表1）。其中，从全国来看，2000－2011年[①]居住用地比例一直保持在30% ~33%，工业用地比例维持在20% ~23%，两者占建设用地总面积的50% ~54%，而且均处于规划城市建设用地结构标准之内（GBJ 137 －90）。道路广场用地的变化幅度较大，占比从2000年的8.21%增至2006年的10.63%和2011年的11.33%，但仍处于合理区间范围内（GBJ 137 －90设定的道路广场用地比例为8% ~15%）。绿地占比也有较大幅度提高，11年间提高了2个百分点左右（8.36%增至10.66%），但也处于合理区间范围内（GBJ 137 －90设定的绿地比例为8% ~15%）。居住、工业、道路广场和绿地四大类用地总和占建设用地比例从2000年的70.81%增至2006年的72.94%和2011年的74.38%，已经处于合理区间范围的边缘。未来四类用地比例极有可能突破城市用地分类与规划建设用地标准设定的适宜比例范围（60% ~75%）。

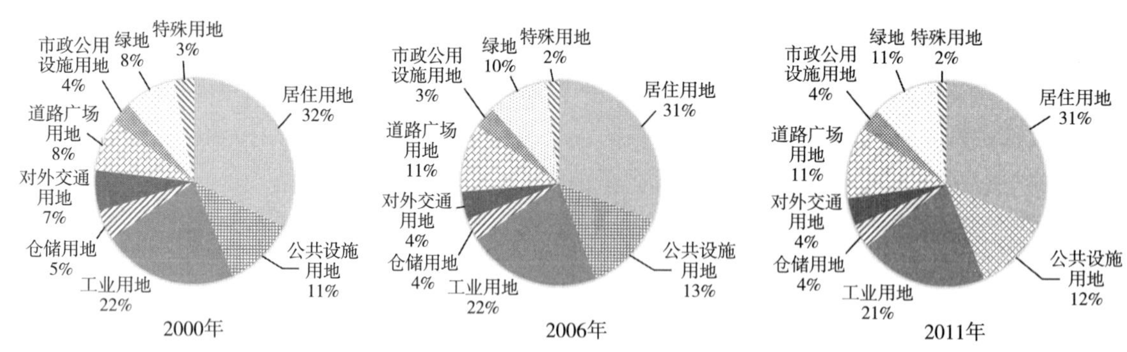

图2 中国城市建设用地结构的动态变化示意图

其他不同用地类型的变化差别较为显著，其中，公共设施用地占比在2000－2011年先增后减，总体比例维持在11% ~13%；仓储用地比例先减后增，总体比例保持在3.5% ~5%；对外交通用地占比有所降低，从6.40%减至2011年的4.45%；市政公用设施用地整

① 由于2012年城市建设用地分类标准发生变化，因此选择2000－2011作为城市建设用地结构演化的研究时间段。

体占比呈增长趋势，11 年间从 3.41% 增至 3.55%；特殊用地占比降低显著，从 2000 年的 3.28% 降至 2011 年的 1.67%。

表 1　2000－2011 年中国城市建设用地结构变化

单位:平方公里

	建设用地面积	居住用地	公共设施用地	工业用地	仓储用地	对外交通用地	道路广场用地	市政公用设施用地	绿地	特殊用地	本年征用面积
2000 年用地面积	22 113.66	7 121.90	2 512.24	4 874.45	1 046.52	1 414.95	1 814.48	754.91	1 848.33	725.88	447.25
2000 年用地比重（%）	100	32.21	11.36	22.04	4.73	6.40	8.21	3.41	8.36	3.28	—
2006 年用地面积	31 765.70	9 772.15	4 228.54	6 867.07	1 130.78	1 407.39	3 377.53	1 119.83	3 154.69	707.72	1 396.48
2006 年用地比重（%）	100	30.76	13.31	21.62	3.56	4.43	10.63	3.53	9.93	2.23	—
2011 年用地面积	41 805.25	13 181.70	5 086.55	8 721.20	1 581.42	1 861.26	4 734.86	1 483.23	4 455.47	699.56	1 841.72
2011 年用地比重（%）	100	31.53	12.17	20.86	3.78	4.45	11.33	3.55	10.66	1.67	—

总体来看，随着城市发展对绿地空间、交通出行和公共服务的需求增加，中国城市建设用地的结构也出现明显的转型。其中，居住用地占比基本稳定，工业用地占比出现下降趋势，说明随着节地产业的不断发展，城市工业用地扩张势头得到抑制。同时，为满足上述的其他城市功能发展，绿地、道路广场用地以及市政公用设施用地等出现明显的增长趋势。

（四）东中西部地区和省域城市建设用地变化的区域差异显著

1. 东部地区各类城市建设用地总量占全国 50% 以上，近年呈微降趋势

从区域差异来看，2000－2011 年东部地区城市建设用地占全国总量的 50% ~56%，中部地区占比 29% ~34%，西部地区占比 15% ~17%，区域差异性显著（表 2）。同时，从具体用地结构来看，仍大体保持着类似的比例关系。但值得注意的是：2006－2011 年东部地区耕地占比减少了约 11 个百分点，而中西部地区则出现明显的增长趋势，尤其是中部地区。

表 2　2000－2011 年中国城市建设用地的区域差异

单位:平方公里;%

用地类型	2000 年			2006 年			2011 年		
	东部	中部	西部	东部	中部	西部	东部	中部	西部
城市建设用地总面积及占比	1 1143.6 (50.4)	7 524.5 (34.0)	3 445.6 (15.6)	19 131.4 (56.0)	9 891.3 (29.0)	5 144.0 (15.1)	21 909.4 (52.4)	13 066.2 (31.3)	6 829.6 (16.3)
居住用地及占比	3 557.7 (50.0)	2 459.2 (34.5)	1 105.1 (15.5)	4 963.6 (50.8)	3 165.0 (32.4)	1 643.6 (16.8)	6 707.1 (50.9)	4 178.6 (31.7)	2 296.1 (17.4)
公共设施用地及占比	1 183.8 (47.1)	897.3 (35.7)	431.2 (17.2)	2 171.9 (51.4)	1 310.1 (31.0)	746.6 (17.7)	2 624.1 (51.6)	1 603.3 (31.5)	859.1 (16.9)

续表 2

用地类型	2000 年			2006 年			2011 年		
	东部	中部	西部	东部	中部	西部	东部	中部	西部
工业用地及占比	2 507. 1 (51. 4)	1 657. 3 (34. 0)	710. 0 (14. 6)	3 912. 7 (57. 0)	2 033. 0 (29. 6)	921. 4 (13. 4)	4 914. 3 (56. 3)	2 580. 8 (29. 6)	1 226. 1 (14. 1)
仓储用地及占比	519. 5 (49. 6)	370. 7 (35. 4)	156. 3 (14. 9)	578. 6 (51. 2)	374. 3 (33. 1)	177. 9 (15. 7)	863. 6 (54. 6)	474. 8 (30. 0)	243. 0 (15. 4)
对外交通用地及占比	741. 7 (52. 4)	451. 4 (31. 9)	221. 9 (15. 7)	690. 8 (49. 1)	487. 1 (34. 6)	229. 5 (16. 3)	926. 3 (49. 8)	666. 7 (35. 8)	268. 3 (14. 4)
道路广场用地及占比	889. 9 (49. 0)	638. 9 (35. 2)	285. 7 (15. 7)	1 801. 8 (53. 3)	995. 4 (29. 5)	580. 4 (17. 2)	2 523. 1 (53. 3)	1 427. 0 (30. 1)	784. 8 (16. 6)
市政公用设施用地及占比	346. 0 (45. 8)	281. 7 (37. 3)	127. 3 (16. 9)	548. 0 (48. 9)	381. 1 (34. 0)	190. 7 (17. 0)	665. 3 (44. 9)	541. 7 (36. 5)	276. 2 (18. 6)
绿地及占比	974. 4 (52. 7)	598. 5 (32. 4)	275. 5 (14. 9)	1 693. 9 (53. 7)	940. 6 (29. 8)	520. 2 (16. 5)	2 319. 5 (52. 1)	1 409. 1 (31. 6)	726. 9 (16. 3)
特殊用地及占比	423. 6 (58. 3)	169. 6 (23. 4)	132. 7 (18. 3)	369. 3 (52. 2)	204. 5 (28. 9)	133. 9 (18. 9)	366. 1 (52. 3)	184. 3 (26. 3)	149. 2 (21. 3)
本年征用土地面积及占比	198. 5 (44. 4)	156. 7 (35. 0)	92. 0 (20. 6)	862. 6 (61. 8)	332. 7 (23. 8)	201. 1 (14. 4)	997. 9 (54. 2)	551. 8 (30. 0)	292. 1 (15. 9)
耕地及占比				431. 0 (63. 3)	133. 2 (19. 6)	116. 3 (17. 1)	406. 0 (52. 4)	228. 0 (29. 4)	141. 4 (18. 2)

注：括号内为全国占比。

2. 经济发达的广东、江苏、山东等省建设用地总量长期位居全国前列

从省域差异来看，城市建设用地的省域差别更为明显。城市建设用地总量上，广东、山东和上海一直处于全国前列（表 3）。在全国排序上，近年来东南沿海的江苏、浙江、福建以及首都北京和直辖市重庆均出现大幅提升。因此，从城市扩张的总量控制而言，重点区域将是这些省份。相对而言，黑龙江和山西的排序降低最为明显。

表 3　2000－2011 年中国城市建设用地面积的省域差异

单位:平方公里

位次	省(自治区、直辖市)名称	2000 年城市建设用地面积	省(自治区、直辖市)名称	2006 年城市建设用地面积	省(自治区、直辖市)名称	2011 年城市建设用地面积
1	广东	1 589. 06	广东	2 932. 09	广东	4 125. 59
2	山东	1 519. 72	山东	2 848. 46	山东	3 680. 66
3	上海	1 457. 14	江苏	2 483. 91	江苏	3 552. 61
4	辽宁	1 432. 37	上海	2 401. 00	上海	2 904. 25
5	湖北	1 284. 41	辽宁	1 847. 43	浙江	2 263. 41
6	黑龙江	1 262. 83	浙江	1 735. 05	辽宁	2 249. 09
7	江苏	1 246. 27	河南	1 517. 65	湖北	2 042. 57
8	河南	983. 68	黑龙江	1 494. 78	河南	2 019. 26
9	四川	947. 36	湖北	1 351. 44	四川	1 745. 51
10	河北	925. 33	河北	1 314. 94	黑龙江	1 722. 14

续表 3

位次	省(自治区、直辖市)名称	2000 年城市建设用地面积	省(自治区、直辖市)名称	2006 年城市建设用地面积	省(自治区、直辖市)名称	2011 年城市建设用地面积
11	浙江	870.14	北京	1 254.23	河北	1 625.16
12	安徽	845.35	四川	1 210.03	安徽	1 565.01
13	湖南	795.41	湖南	1 191.89	湖南	1 474.90
14	吉林	706.06	安徽	1 147.65	北京	1 425.87
15	山西	568.45	吉林	915.32	吉林	1 197.97
16	内蒙古	558.90	内蒙古	778.64	内蒙古	1 179.53
17	广西	541.30	江西	758.99	福建	1 076.98
18	江西	519.38	广西	744.57	江西	986.44
19	新疆	496.99	山西	734.90	重庆	945.48
20	北京	490.11	福建	717.95	新疆	932.95
21	陕西	433.98	新疆	703.73	广西	931.56
22	福建	433.70	陕西	653.31	云南	884.74
23	天津	385.86	重庆	620.44	山西	878.41
24	甘肃	363.16	天津	539.98	天津	710.60
25	云南	315.26	云南	535.99	陕西	706.48
26	贵州	300.05	甘肃	505.03	甘肃	615.37
27	重庆	289.40	贵州	465.30	贵州	524.22
28	海南	252.63	海南	311.81	宁夏	312.95
29	宁夏	115.69	宁夏	264.63	海南	267.91
30	青海	91.23	青海	107.76	青海	121.68
31	西藏	66.32	西藏	77.80	西藏	80.20

3. 城市建设用地增长重点区域逐步从东部省份向中西部省份转移

从省域城市建设用地增速来看，有 25 个省份在 2000－2006 年的增速高于 2006－2011 年的平均增速（图 3）。表 3 数据显示：城市建设用地的增长重点逐步从东部省份向中西部省份转移。其中，2000－2006 年，北京、宁夏、重庆、江苏、浙江、山东、广东、上海和云南的年均增速均超过 8%；而 2006－2011 年，云南、重庆、内蒙古、湖北、福建、四川、江苏和西藏的年均增速超过 6%。2006－2011 年，内蒙古、吉林、安徽、湖北、四川和西藏的增速均高于 2000－2006 年的平均增速。

（五）大中小城市建设用地比例基本保持在 5:2:3

以城区人口为基础数据，参照新颁布的《关于调整城市规模划分标准的通知》（国发〔2014〕51 号），分别将 2006 年、2011 年和 2014 年的城市建设用地情况总结见表 4[①]。

① 仅选择 2006 年和 2011 年进行对比分析是因为 2000 年中国城市建设统计年鉴中并未统计城区人口数据。

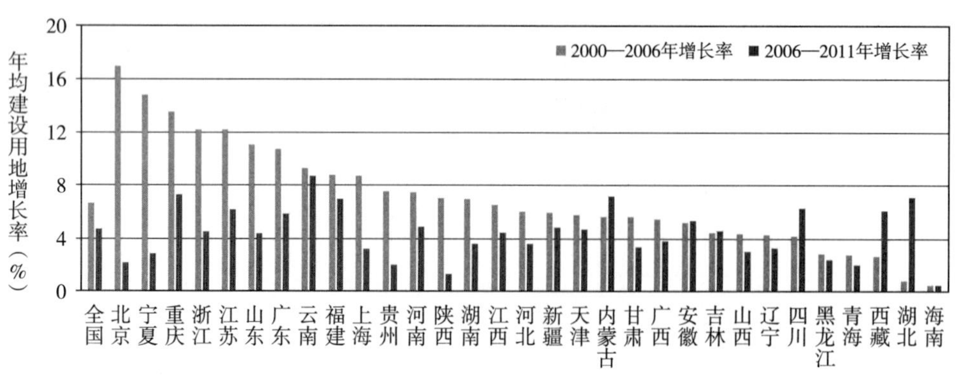

图3 2000－2011年中国城市建设用地年均增速的省域差异示意图

2006–2014年，中国城市规模等级和城市建设用地占比呈现出显著变化。其中，城区常住人口1 000万以上的超大城市数量由2个变为3个，其建设用地占比呈“U”形变化趋势；城区常住人口500万～1 000万的特大城市数量由4个变为5个，其建设用地占比呈逐步降低的趋势；城区常住人口300万～500万的Ⅰ型大城市数量由6个增为11个，建设用地占比增加5%左右；城区常住人口100万～300万的Ⅱ型大城市数量从46个变为50个，但城市建设用地占比仅提高了1个百分点左右；城区常住人口50万～100万的中等城市数量有明显增加，从85个增至96个，但建设用地占比保持不变；城区常住人口50万以下的小城市数量略有减少，其中，城区常住人口20万以下的Ⅱ型小城市数量减少52个，城区常住人口20万～50万的Ⅰ型小城市增加34个，致使Ⅰ型小城市建设用地占比基本不变，Ⅱ型小城市建设用地占比降低5%左右。总体来看，大（大城市及以上）中小城市建设用地的总体占比基本保持在5:2:3的比例。大城市数量最少，却消耗了最大的城市建设用地面积。从城市建设用地平均面积来看，超大城市建设用地平均面积是Ⅱ型小城市的90多倍。

表4 2006－2014年中国不同规模等级城市建设用地变化情况

城市规模等级分类	2006年			2011年			2014年		
	城市数量（个）	建设用地总面积（平方公里）	面积占比（%）	城市数量（个）	建设用地总面积（平方公里）	面积占比（%）	城市数量（个）	建设用地总面积（平方公里）	面积占比（%）
超大城市	2	3 655.23	10.41	2	4 330.12	9.51	3	5 390.84	10.57
特大城市	5	2 968.58	8.46	5	3 734.66	8.20	4	3 577.03	7.01
大城市	52	9 663.33	27.55	56	14 441.64	31.72	62	17 184.43	33.68
Ⅰ型大城市	6	2 092.79	5.97	5	1 880.03	4.12	12	5 498.79	10.78
Ⅱ型大城市	46	7 570.54	21.58	51	12 561.61	27.60	50	11 685.64	22.91
中等城市	85	6 355.36	18.12	87	8 046.32	17.46	96	9 247.1	18.13
小城市	511	12 450.42	35.45	506	15 065.57	33.10	493	15 617.9	30.61
Ⅰ型小城市	218	7 588.88	21.64	251	10 241.64	22.50	252	10 885.95	21.34
Ⅱ型小城市	293	4 861.54	13.86	255	4 823.93	10.60	241	4 731.95	9.28

（六）省会城市和计划单列市建设用地占全国的1/3以上，且呈增加趋势

省会城市和计划单列市处于中国城市体系的顶端，对建设用地的整体变化具有极为重要的影响。表5数据显示：2000年31个省会城市和5个计划单列市的建成区面积分别占全国城市建成区总面积的27.4%和34.0%，2014年分别提升到34.0%和34.1%，总体占比高并呈增长的趋势。从建成区面积的平均增速来看，2000-2006年是高速增长期，年均增长高达10.15%；2006-2011年增速有所下滑，年均增速降至5.69%；但2011-2014年又提高到6.27%。上述增速均明显高于同期的全国平均水平，表明省会城市和计划单列市的快速城市扩张势头虽有所减弱但仍需有效遏制。从净增加面积来看，31个省会城市和5个计划单列市的年均净增加面积在3个时间段也是先减后增：2000-2006年净增面积为5 280平方公里，年均净增加880平方公里；2006-2011年净增面积为3 394平方公里，年均净增679平方公里；2011-2014年净增面积为2 258平方公里，年均净增753平方公里。因此，不论从总量、增速还是净增加面积来看，省会城市和计划单列市城市建设用地的扩张相比其他城市都更为严重，也应该受到更多的关注。

表5 省会城市和计划单列市建设用地变化情况

城市名称	建成区面积（平方公里）				年均用地增速（%）			年均净增加面积（平方公里）		
	2000年	2006年	2011年	2014年	2000-2006年	2006-2011年	2011-2014年	2000-2006年	2006-2011年	2011-2014年
北京	490.1	1 254.2	1 319.9	1 385.6	16.95	1.03	1.63	764.1	65.7	65.7
重庆	249.5	631.4	1 034.9	1 231.4	5.76	5.65	3.90	154.1	170.6	86.5
广州	430.7	779.9	990.1	1 035.0	7.72	3.76	7.85	63.0	35.5	53.5
上海	549.6	860.2	998.8	998.8	1.80	8.78	3.23	20.0	103.0	30.0
深圳	136.5	719.9	841.7	890.0	10.36	2.96	9.83	67.0	23.6	56.4
天津	385.9	540.0	710.6	797.1	7.40	5.76	2.64	113.3	105.0	35.0
南京	201.4	574.9	637.7	734.3	1.64	8.61	0.47	24.0	132.0	5.5
成都	207.8	396.9	483.4	604.1	9.05	9.36	3.95	108.4	150.9	51.5
武汉	210.0	222.3	506.4	552.6	12.02	2.08	2.95	163.6	35.9	33.4
青岛	119.1	227.5	291.5	490.7	7.75	3.03	0.00	310.6	138.5	100.0
杭州	177.2	327.5	433.0	470.0	19.10	2.09	4.82	373.5	62.8	96.6
长春	159.0	267.4	418.2	469.7	10.78	5.75	2.77	150.3	105.5	37.0
沈阳	211.7	325.0	430.0	465.0	21.02	5.77	2.69	146.7	69.7	23.7
西安	187.0	261.4	342.6	440.0	10.27	8.57	5.84	99.7	114.4	62.9
昆明	147.7	232.8	314.7	418.5	11.64	5.55	3.02	85.7	54.9	21.7
郑州	133.2	282.0	354.7	412.7	11.58	9.29	6.91	76.1	88.3	54.7
乌鲁木齐	139.6	235.9	383.8	412.3	12.25	4.36	8.00	84.0	40.0	54.0
合肥	125.0	224.7	339.1	402.0	16.89	3.10	2.56	185.4	50.4	27.9

续表 5

城市名称	建成区面积(平方公里)				年均用地增速(%)			年均净增加面积(平方公里)		
	2000 年	2006 年	2011 年	2014 年	2000—2006 年	2006—2011 年	2011—2014 年	2000—2006 年	2006—2011 年	2011—2014 年
哈尔滨	167.6	331.2	367.1	400.6	11.39	5.09	18.95	108.4	64.0	199.2
大连	234.0	258.0	390.0	395.5	13.31	4.69	5.18	148.8	72.7	58.0
济南	119.6	305.0	355.4	383.3	0.95	17.90	2.95	12.3	284.1	46.2
太原	177.0	197.0	300.0	330.0	4.53	12.30	2.07	36.2	121.9	17.5
宁波	68.5	215.2	284.9	308.6	10.40	4.89	1.49	349.2	210.3	44.9
厦门	81.9	158.0	246.3	301.0	31.94	3.18	1.88	583.4	121.8	48.4
贵阳	98.4	132.0	162.0	299.0	7.49	5.83	8.11	59.8	55.7	59.5
长沙	118.8	155.0	276.9	294.4	18.13	1.30	15.85	57.8	6.1	54.1
南宁	110.2	170.0	225.7	285.1	16.73	10.39	5.97	381.8	403.6	196.5
兰州	146.6	154.0	197.0	269.1	11.39	4.02	7.72	189.1	86.4	120.7
石家庄	112.0	175.0	210.5	264.0	5.02	4.18	22.66	33.6	30.0	137.0
南昌	84.0	168.0	208.0	262.0	7.87	6.22	9.97	85.0	81.9	103.8
福州	91.5	177.2	232.1	253.8	2.03	1.63	13.25	6.6	4.9	28.5
呼和浩特	83.0	150.0	173.6	230.0	5.74	5.56	8.70	74.4	81.2	97.5
银川	52.1	105.7	126.4	160.8	0.83	5.05	10.96	7.4	43.0	72.1
海口	33.6	91.4	97.5	151.6	1.88	3.24	6.27	6.8	11.1	15.0
拉萨	51.4	58.0	62.9	91.3	12.52	3.65	8.36	53.6	20.7	34.4
西宁	57.2	63.9	75.0	90.0	9.14	10.23	2.41	96.3	147.9	28.5
合计或均值	6 148.3	11 428.4	14 822.1	16 979.8	10.1	5.7	6.3	5 280.0	3 393.7	2 257.7

注：由于 2000－2014 年多个城市建设用地面积数据缺失，故用城市建成面积代替。

二、中国城市建设用地扩张存在的主要问题

（一）城市建设用地无序蔓延问题严重，人均建设用地居高不下

20 世纪 80 年代以来，中国城市建设用地与经济社会的快速发展相一致，经历了快速甚至超高速的扩张过程。不论是城市建设用地总量变化，还是净增加量、人均城市建设用地面积变化和增长速度都是全球罕见的。尤其是新城新区的无序扩张蔓延，动辄几百平方公里甚至上千平方公里，进一步助长了城市蔓延。不可否认，这种快速扩张为支撑经济快速发展、满足城市居民的社会需求提供了保障。但同时也带来了相应的社会经济和生态环境问题，加剧了城市病（人口膨胀、交通拥堵、环境恶化、住房紧张、就业困难等）的发生。例如，城市快速扩张对大量的自然和半自然生态系统的破坏和侵占，导致城市发展的资源环境承载力趋紧（大气污染、水污染和土壤污染等）。在城市快速扩张的同时，人均城市建设用地仍

存在不集约和浪费问题。2014 年中国城市人均建设用地面积为 129.57 平方米，大大超出国家标准（85.1～105.0 平方米/人），也明显高于发达国家的人均 84.4 平方米和其他发展中国家人均 83.3 平方米的水平。此外，还存在已有建设用地利用强度偏低、容积率不高和土地经济效益产出偏低等一系列问题。就目前的趋势来看，虽然近几年城市建设用地的增长速度有所下降，但是净增加量仍然巨大，人均用地量仍居高不下，加之城市化的快速推进和大量的农村人口转移，未来仍不排除在局部区域甚至全国出现城市蔓延的可能。因此，防范和遏制城市蔓延仍是城市建设用地管理的核心任务之一。

（二）城市建设用地结构不尽合理，降低了城市用地集约利用效率

虽然近年来中国城市建设用地结构并未发生显著变化，但其整体结构仍需不够合理。突出地反映在居住、工业、道路广场和绿地四大类用地总和占建设用地比例已经处于合理区间的边缘；用地结构存在“两低两高”现象，即：绿地和道路广场占比偏低，居住和工业用地占比较高。尽管从增速和占比来看近几年上述现象已有所缓解，但仍然导致居住和工业用地供过于求，并且加剧了土地的闲置、低效利用，而其他用地则供不应求，无法满足正常的社会经济发展需求。特别是近年随着房价的猛涨，不少城市住宅用地面积出现了冒进式的增长趋势；而相关基础设施和公共服务设施配套则明显滞后，不仅制约了交通、供水、供电、信息、污水和垃圾处理等基础设施的建设，而且也不利于商业、教育、医疗、餐饮、娱乐等服务设施和功能的发挥，从而导致各地不断出现“鬼城”和“睡城”现象。用地结构和用地空间配置不合理以及产城发展的不融合已经演化为城市运行效率低下的重要诱因，为此，需要对城市建设用地结构加以调整优化。

（三）城镇化和经济增长过于依赖建设用地，短期难以扭转

近期，人口变化和经济发展仍是驱动城市扩张最重要的社会经济因素。经济增长和建设用地扩展间仍存在较强的耦合关系。同时，基于政绩的考虑和对土地财政的依赖，短期内地方发展经济对建设用地仍将保持大量的需求，且管控难度较大。因此，随着城镇化的推进，城市建设用地快速增加的趋势不仅在短期内无法避免，而且长期也难以得到有效遏制。虽然近年来，产业结构转型和节地产业发展已取得了一定进展，但是转型发展仍处于初始阶段，无法从根本上扭转城市建设用地过快和非集约增长的基本态势。

（四）新城新区建设过多过大，加剧了城市建设用地的过度扩张

自 1992 年浦东新区开发建设以来，我国新城新区建设取得了举世瞩目的成就，对加快工业化和城镇化进程做出了重大贡献，但不少地方政府把新城新区建设作为推动城镇化的主要手段，由此暴露出一系列亟待解决的现实问题。据不完全统计，至 2016 年 2 月，全国已建在建的各类新城新区达 106 个，其中国家级 17 个，省级 38 个，市级 64 个；按照规划面积划分，超过1 000平方公里的新城新区达 19 个，500～1 000平方公里 10 个，100～500 平方公里约 41 个。新城新区规划总面积达到 7.35 万平方公里，远远超过了 2014 年全国城市建

成区面积（约5万平方公里）。不仅直辖市、计划单列市和省会城市建设了新城新区，而且多数地级城市和部分县级市甚至县城也在规划和建设新城新区。新城新区建设过快过大，不仅加大了地方政府严重的负债风险，而且被部分地方政府作为又一次圈地的“良机”，以新城新区建设的名义，行大规模圈地、卖地之事，导致大量优质耕地被侵占，大批农民被赶进城而沦为新一批“三无”农民。

三、中国城市建设用地调控的对策建议

（一）综合防范城市用地无序扩张蔓延，提高土地集约利用水平

针对当前的城市无序扩张蔓延问题，必须综合运用多种调控手段和措施。2015年12月中央城市工作会议指出，在城市集约发展中正确处理好城市发展的数量与质量、规模与速度、快变量与慢变量之间的辩证关系，框定总量，限定容量，盘活存量，做优增量，提高质量，立足国情，尊重自然、顺应自然、保护自然，改善城市生态环境。通过五大变量的优化调控，确保城市发展形成适度的“体量”，适速的“节奏”和健康的“体质”，推动城市由亚健康状态转变为经常性的健康状态。在具体做法上，首先，应科学地划定城市增长边界。为防止城市周边的大量自然和半自然生态系统被“蚕食”，应对城市增长科学设限划定增长红线，并将城市规划由扩张性规划向限定城市增长边界规划转变是调控的重心之一。其次，应充分发掘建设用地的内部潜力，鼓励进行旧城改造，鼓励进行土地置换，合理运用土地增减挂钩机制，为城市建设提供适度的用地保障；并在地价政策、税收政策、信贷政策上对利用存量土地进行建设给予优惠，降低其建设成本，形成“优惠挖潜”“高价外延”的机制；要坚决查处土地闲置行为，突出解决“圈而不用”等现象，提高土地利用效率。最后，城市内部还应合理利用城市地上空间和地下空间，提高三维空间利用效率。同时，还需要积极推进产业结构转型和节地产业发展，实现城市建设用地集约高效发展。

（二）优化城市建设用地结构和功能，实现城市精明集约增长

在城市发展科学规律的指引下，全面贯彻创新、协调、绿色、开放、共享的城市发展理念，创新城市发展新模式，不断转变城市发展方式，优化城市建设用地结构和功能，不断提升城市人居环境质量和人民生活质量，将城市建设成为精明增长城市、创新城市、紧凑城市、低碳城市、智慧城市、平安城市和法治城市，建成和谐宜居、富有活力、各具特色的现代化城市，提高新型城镇化水平，走出一条中国特色的城市现代化发展道路。

为应对城市建设用地结构和功能问题，应进一步提升城市规划的科学性，突出强制性和控制性指标内容，有效配置城市各类土地资源，强调土地的混合使用和密集开发策略，集中紧凑规划城市建设用地，形成精明增长的城市发展模式。随着城市发展对城市功能多样化需求的不断增加，城市用地也需逐步增加其多样化水平。新城新区建设需积极推进产城融合发展、增加基础设施和公共服务设施配套，实现用地功能的均衡协调，逐步缓解大城市病。旧

城改造需增加绿地、广场等公共空间，实现用地功能的总体均衡，满足居民生活需求。对于一些大型公共服务设施如医院和学校等的布局应综合考量交通、人流等因素，以免引发交通拥堵。对少数超大城市，应逐步推进非核心功能由中心城区向外围的有序疏解。

（三）因地制宜制订差别化的建设用地调控措施

通过对中国近34年来城市建设用地动态变化特征的分析发现，不同区域和不同等级城市建设用地在面积、结构和增速上都存在较大的差异。因此，建议针对不同区域和不同规模等级的城市，量身制作差别化的城市扩张管治与用地调控措施。例如，针对中西部地区（尤其是中部地区）在耕地占比上出现明显的增加趋势，应设计更为严格的耕地保护和管治措施。从城市扩张的总量控制而言，东南沿海的江苏、浙江、福建以及北京和重庆应作为重点防范省（市）域。从城市扩张速度而言，城市建设用地的增长重点逐步从东部省（市）向中西部省区转移。因此，增速控制的重点应该是中西部地区。同时，城市规模等级也是城市扩张管治需要考虑的问题之一。中国的超大城市和特大城市消耗了最多的城市建设用地，因此对这些城市应制订出最严格的控制总量措施，倒逼其盘活存量，更新现量，推动城市有机更新和精明增长。总之，要实现更为有效的城市建设用地调控和管理目标，必须针对不同区域和不同规模等级的城市，因地因城制宜，因类优化，合理地制定差异化的调控政策措施，确保每个城市的建设用地保持一个合理的总量和速度增长指标。

（四）科学引导我国新城新区的适度理性建设

新城新区建设是推动新型城镇化的一种重要手段，但不是唯一手段。对于新城新区建设要从国家战略层面做好顶层设计、科学引导和合理布局。新城新区建设既要禁止搞“一刀切”，也要禁止放任自流，随报即批。为此，一是建议建立新城新区建设的国家综合评估审查机制，从国家经济社会发展的战略安全角度，做好统一的国家新城新区建设规划和顶层设计，严把新城新区审批关；二是制定切实可行措施，规范在建和规划建设的各类新城新区，将其纳入城市土地利用规划和城市总体规划，确保新城新区建设范围与城市总体规划的建成控制区面积精准衔接，对已经超标建设的新城新区建议限期整改，对脱离实际在规划建设的新城新区和正在超标建设的新城新区立即停止建设；三是做好新城新区建设的科学规划，量需而动，量力而行，量地而置，正确处理好新城新区与旧城在产业外溢对接、功能疏解互补、交通对接、人员分流、基础设施和公共服务设施配套等方面的相互依存关系，协调好新城新区与主城及原有行政区划存在的错综复杂关系，防止出现“建了新城空老城，建了新城变空城”等不良现象发生，不断提高新城新区建设的产业集中度和用地集约度。

（作者：方创琳，中国科学院地理科学与资源研究所研究员、长江学者特聘教授、博士生导师，区域与城市规划设计研究中心主任，中国地理学会人文地理专业委员会主任；李广东，博士，中国科学院地理科学与资源研究所助理研究员）

参考文献

[1] 中华人民共和国住宅与城乡建设部．中国城市建设统计年鉴（2014 年）［M］．北京：中国统计出版社，2015：23－165.

[2] 方创琳，马海涛．新型城镇化背景下的中国新区建设与土地集约利用［J］．中国土地科学，2013，27（7）：4－10.

[3] 王婧，方创琳，李裕瑞．中国城乡人口与建设用地的时空变化及其耦合特征研究［J］．自然资源学报，2014，29（8）：1271－1281.

[4] 李广东，方创琳．中国县域国土空间集约利用计量测度与影响机理［J］．地理学报，2014，69（12）：1739－1752.

[5] 方创琳．中国新型城镇化发展报告［M］．北京：科学出版社，2014：35－98.

[6] 方创琳，马海涛．新城新区，如何让城市更美好？［N］．光明日报，2014－07－01（11）．

新型城镇化背景下户籍制度改革及面临的挑战

一、新型城镇化对户籍制度改革的总体要求

改革开放以来，我国城镇化经历了快速的发展过程。1978－2014年，城镇常住人口从1.7亿人增加到7.5亿人，城镇化率从17.9%提升到54.8%，年均提高约1个百分点。在城镇化快速发展过程中，城镇化与现有户籍制度之间的矛盾日益凸显。受城乡分割的户籍制度影响，大量农业转移人口虽然被统计为城镇人口，但并未拥有城镇户口，未能与城镇居民享受同等的教育、就业、医疗、养老、保障性住房等方面的基本公共服务，造成农业转移人口难以融入城市社会，市民化进程严重滞后于城镇化。

中央政府于2014年制定并颁布了《国家新型城镇化规划（2014－2020年）》（以下简称《规划》），在“指导思想”上，要求“紧紧围绕全面提高城镇化质量，加快转变城镇化发展方式，以人的城镇化为核心，有序推进农业转移人口市民化”；在“发展目标”上，明确提出，到2020年，“努力实现1亿左右农业转移人口和其他常住人口在城镇落户”；在“规划内容”上，编制了“有序推进农业转移人口市民化”专篇，对“推进符合条件农业转移人口落户城镇”“推进农业转移人口享有城镇基本公共服务”和“建立健全农业转移人口市民化推进机制”等内容进行了具体规划。此外，中央政府还于2014年发布了《国务院关于进一步推进户籍制度改革的意见》（以下简称《意见》）和《国务院关于调整城市规模划分标准的通知》，并于2015年11月以国务院令形式颁布了《居住证暂行条例》。这些重要文件均旨在促进新型城镇化的健康发展、有序推进农业转移人口市民化，并要求对我国户籍管理制度进行改革。综合来看，主要包括以下几个方面：

一是要取消农业户口与非农业户口性质区分，建立城乡统一的户口登记制度和实际居住人口登记制度。取消城乡二元户口登记制度，统一登记为居民户口。建立健全实际居住人口登记制度，加强和完善人口统计调查，全面、准确掌握人口规模、人员结构、地区分布等情况，建设和完善覆盖全国人口、以公民身份号码为唯一标识、以人口基础信息为基准的国家人口基础信息库。

二是要建立居住证制度，并为居住证持有人提供城镇基本公共服务和便利。公民离开常住户口所在地，到其他城市居住半年以上，符合有合法稳定就业、合法稳定住所、连续就读

条件之一的，可以依规申领居住证。居住证持有人在居住地依法享受劳动就业，参加社会保险，缴存、提取和使用住房公积金的权利。县级以上人民政府应当建立健全为居住证持有人提供基本公共服务和便利的机制，包括义务教育、基本公共就业服务、基本公共卫生服务和计划生育服务、公共文化体育服务、法律援助和其他法律服务以及国家规定的其他基本公共服务。

三是要实施差别化落户政策，健全农业转移人口落户制度。以合法稳定就业和合法稳定住所（含租赁）等为前置条件，全面放开建制镇和小城市落户限制，有序放开城区人口50万~100万人的城市落户限制，合理放开城区人口100万~300万人的大城市落户限制，合理确定城区人口300万~500万人的大城市落户条件，严格控制城区人口500万人以上的特大城市人口规模。逐步使符合条件的农业转移人口落户城镇，融入城镇社区。

四是配套推进农村土地、产权等制度改革，切实保障农业转移人口的合法权益。加快推进农村土地确权、登记、颁证，依法保障农民的土地承包经营权、宅基地使用权。坚持依法、自愿、有偿的原则，引导农业转移人口有序流转土地承包经营权。现阶段，不得以退出土地承包经营权、宅基地使用权、集体收益分配权作为农民进城落户的条件。

二、各省（自治区、直辖市）户籍制度改革落实情况

从目前的情况来看，各地对中央精神的贯彻落实情况总体良好。自国家《规划》和《意见》出台以来，已有26个省份出台了具体方案，包括新疆、黑龙江、河南、河北、四川、山东、安徽、贵州、山西、陕西、江西、湖南、吉林、江苏、福建、广西、青海、甘肃、广东、重庆、云南、辽宁、湖北、内蒙古、北京、浙江。截至2015年12月，我国中部的省份均已出台方案，西部的省份除宁夏和西藏外也均已出台方案；东部的省份相对较为迟缓，北京和浙江都是在2015年年底才出台方案，而天津、上海、海南等省份还暂未出台正式方案，但天津和上海对积分落户的细则出台了相关方案。

从各省（自治区、直辖市）出台方案的具体内容来看，各省（自治区、直辖市）对改革目标，具体措施等方面与《意见》的精神一致，但也根据各省（自治区、直辖市）的实际情况制定了更加细化、更加适合本地实情的方案。下面主要从改革的总体目标和具体措施方面对各省（自治区、直辖市）的方案进行总结和比较。

（一）总体目标的落实情况

根据国家《规划》和《意见》制定的改革目标，22个省份制定了本地改革的总体目标，大多数省份明确提出，到2020年，基本建立与全面建成小康社会相适应，有效支撑社会管理和公共服务，依法保障公民权利，以人为本、科学高效、规范有序的新型户籍制度。还有部分省份并未列出改革的目标，仅对改革的措施进行了规定，如黑龙江省、福建省等。

在22个省份中，有15个省份提出了到2020年农业转移人口落户的目标以及户籍人口城镇化率的目标（表1)。11个省份提出了到2020年农业转移人口落户的目标。如果进行汇

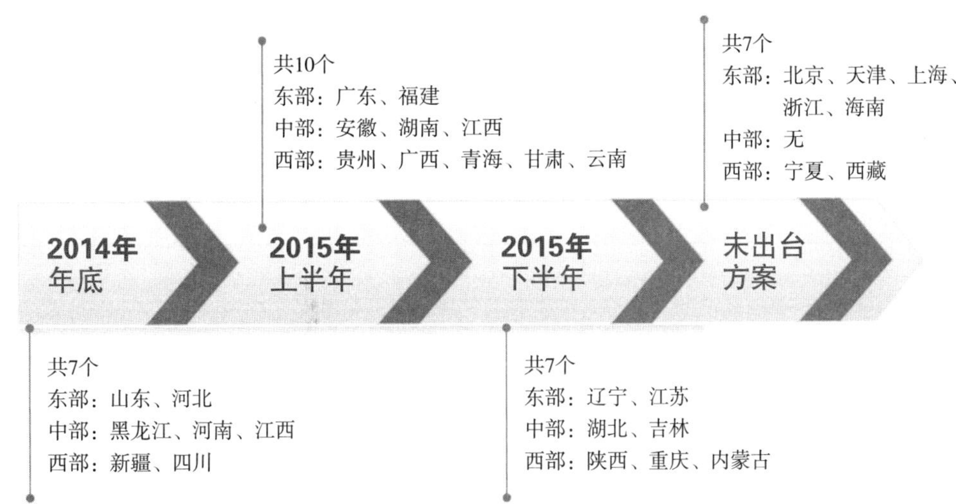

图1　各省（自治区、直辖市）户籍制度改革实施方案出台时间

总，这些省份将实现6 625.5万人的农村转移人口落户城镇，剩余的省份仅需完成不到4 000万人的目标就可保证《意见》中实现1亿左右农业转移人口和其他常住人口在城镇落户目标的完成。其中，广东省、河北省、河南省、陕西省等省份农村转移人口目标都超过1 000万人，总计4 400万人。部分省份虽然没有制定农村转移人口落户目标，但对城镇化率目标做出要求。江苏省提出到2020年常住人口城镇化率目标为72%，而户籍人口城镇化率目标要与常住人口城镇化率缩小到5个点以内，也就是至少要达到67%，这一水平将远远高于全国户籍城镇化率的平均水平。重庆市提出到2020年常住人口城镇化率目标达到65%，而户籍人口城镇化率达到50%。安徽省提出到2020年常住人口城镇化率目标达到58%。

表1　各省份农村转移人口目标

省份	农村转移人口目标(人)	城镇化率目标
广东	1 300万	
河北省	1 000万(600万城中村居民和400万农业转移人口)	45%(户籍人口)
安徽省		58%(常住人口)
河南省	1 100万	56%(常住人口)
湖北	500万	61%(常住人口)
山西省	360万	
贵州省	300万	
广西	600万	
青海	40万	50%(户籍人口)
甘肃	25.5万	
重庆市		65%(常住人口)以及50%(户籍人口)
云南省		50%(常住人口)以及38%(户籍人口)
陕西省	1 000万	62%(常住人口)

续表 1

省份	农村转移人口目标(人)	城镇化率目标
江苏省		72%(常住人口)以及 67%(户籍人口)
内蒙古	400 万	
小计	6 625.5 万	

(二)差别化落户政策的落实情况

1. 特大城市

《意见》要求严格控制特大城市人口规模。具体要求如下:改进城区人口 500 万以上的城市现行落户政策,建立、完善积分落户制度。根据综合承载能力和经济社会发展需要,以具有合法稳定的就业和合法稳定住所(含租赁)、参加城镇社会保险年限、连续居住年限等为主要指标,合理设置积分分值。可以看出,《意见》要求通过积分落户的手段对特大城市的人口规模进行限制,而且对积分的条件做出了要求。

表 2 特大城市控制人口实施方案及要求

省份	特大城市	政策	积分指标
北京		积分落户制度	合法稳定的就业及住所、教育背景、居住区域、职业、纳税、诚信记录等(征求意见稿)
辽宁	沈阳(大连)	积分落户制度	具有合法稳定的就业和合法稳定的住所(含租赁)、参加城镇社会保险年限、连续居住年限
湖北	武汉	积分落户制度	合法稳定的就业、合法稳定的住所(含租赁)、参加城镇社会保险年限、连续居住年限、文化程度、专业职称(职业技能)、个人诚信记录
黑龙江	哈尔滨	实行"双轨制"落户政策(主城区与非主城区),建立积分落户制度	合法稳定的就业和合法稳定的住所(含租赁)、参加城镇社会保险年限、连续居住年限、为经济发展所做贡献
陕西	西安	积分落户制度	该市自行确定
四川	成都	积分落户制度	该市自行确定
江苏	南京、苏州	积分落户制度	
重庆	重庆	条件准入	调整优化都市功能核心区与都市功能拓展区落户条件:务工经商 5 年,具有合法稳定住所的,对与战略性新兴产业企业签订劳动合同的,务工经商年限可放宽至 3 年
广东	广州、深圳	条件准入	重点吸纳本地经济社会发展急需的各类型专业人才落户
浙江	杭州(宁波、温州)	积分落户制度	具体政策由各市人民政府研究制定

从各地出台的方案来看(表 2),各地均要求要严格控制特大城市的规模,但在具体的控制措施上主要有两种方式:一是积分落户制度。这是大多数特大城市所采取的方式,在积分的指标上,除了《意见》里提到的四条指标外,各地还设定了其他指标进行积分。如武汉市加入了文化程度、专业职称(职业技能)、个人诚信记录等指标;哈尔滨市则加入了为

经济发展做贡献的指标。

在具体的积分方案上，目前北京市出台了《北京市积分落户管理办法（征求意见稿）》（表3），该征求意见稿对积分的指标及分值都做出了较为详细的要求。北京市政府将根据年度人口调控情况，每年向社会公布落户分数线。市有关部门根据申请人积分情况和落户分数线，初步确定年度积分落户人员，并对积分情况向社会公示。通过公示后，申请人可按相关规定办理常住户口。

表3　北京市积分落户指标及分值（征求意见稿）

	积分指标	积分值
合法稳定的就业		3分/年
合法稳定的居所		0.5分/年
教育背景	博士	39分
	硕士	27分
	本科	15分
	专科	9分
居住区域	居住转移到城六区外	2分/年(最高6分)
	工作就业均转移到城六区外	4分/年(最高12分)
	居住转移到城六区内	减2分/年(最高减6分)
	工作就业均转移到城六区内	减4分/年(最高减12分)
疏解行业就业指标		减6分/年
创新企业指标	创业企业	2分/年(最高6分)
	相关服务机构	1分/年(最高3分)
	高新技术企业	1分/年(最高3分)
专业技术职务	中级	2分
	高级	5分
纳税指标	连续3年纳税且满足要求条件	6分
不良信用记录		每条减12分
不良违法记录		每条减30分

二是条件准入机制，也就是满足要求的条件就可以落户，不必达到一定的积分值。“条件准入”中的条件往往与城市发展需求等有密切联系。如广东省提出广州、深圳要重点吸纳本地经济社会发展急需的各类型专业人才落户；重庆市则是放宽与战略性新兴产业企业签订劳动合同的人群落户的条件。

另外，不论是积分落户还是条件准入，部分特大城市还根据城区发展水平的差异，设置双重标准。如哈尔滨市实行“双轨制”落户政策，对综合承载能力压力相对较大的四个主城区适当控制，而对人口相对较少的非主城区适当放宽落户条件。

2. 大城市

《意见》要求要合理确定大城市人口规模。具体要求如下：在城区人口100万～300万人的城市合法稳定就业达到一定年限并有合法稳定住所（含租赁），城区人口300万～500万人的城市，要适度控制落户规模和节奏，可以对合法稳定就业的范围、年限和合法稳定住所（含租赁）的范围、条件等做出较严格的规定，也可结合本地实际，建立积分落户制度。大城市对参加城镇社会保险年限的要求不得超过5年。

从各省出台的方案来看各省份对大城市落户条件要求不同，基本上可以分为三类：合理确定落户条件、有序放开、全面放开等（表4）。提出合理确定条件的省份数量最多，辽宁省、河北省、安徽省、黑龙江、湖南省、吉林省、云南省、内蒙古自治区等。在这些条件里，有合法稳定就业和稳定居所几乎是必备条件，只有陕西省、青海省比较特殊：陕西省要求具有稳定住所或合法产权住所或工作且缴纳社保；青海省要求具有合法房产或合法工作、有稳定居所缴纳社保。其他条件的差异主要是对社保及其年限的要求。对社保年限要求最高的是广东省，社保年限必须达到5年，但实际上佛山、东莞等城市已经迈入特大城市的行列，广东省将这些城市列入第二梯队，因此其落户要求也相对严格。其他大城市大部分没有对社保年限做出具体的要求，只注明要满足一定年限，或者设置了社保年限的上限。

提出有序放开大城市落户的省份有河南省、湖北省、江西省、山西省、陕西省等。尽管提出要有序放开大城市落户，但目前其要求的条件实际上与提出合理确定落户条件的大城市并没有本质不同，都从合法稳定就业、合法稳定居所以及社保年限等方面做出了要求。

西部地区的甘肃省和四川省提出要全面放开大城市落户，但同样也从合法稳定就业、合法稳定居所以及社保年限等方面做出了要求。

部分省份对省会城市单独制定标准。如河南省提出有序放开大城市落户，而对于省会城市则实行积分制；山东省的济南市和青岛市实行阶梯式落户通道和差别化落户标准。

表4 各省份大城市控制人口实施方案及要求

省份	大城市	政策	稳定就业	稳定居所	社保年限
广东	珠海、佛山、东莞、中山		是	是	5年
福建	厦门	积分落户制度			
山东	济南、青岛	合理确定条件	是	是	
江苏	无锡、常州等	确定条件	是	是	一定年限
辽宁	鞍山、抚顺、本溪	合理确定条件	是	是	无要求
河北	石家庄	合理确定条件	是	是	无要求
安徽		合理确定条件	是	是	一定年限
黑龙江		合理确定条件	是	是	2年
湖南		合理确定条件	是	是	不超3年
吉林	长春、吉林	合理确定条件	是	是	2年以上
云南	昆明	合理确定条件	是	是	一定年限

续表4

份	大城市	政策	稳定就业	稳定居所	社保年限
内蒙古	呼和浩特、包头	合理确定条件	是	是	一定年限
贵州		合理确定条件	是(3年)	是(3年)	5年
河南		有序放开大城市落户,省会实行积分制	是	是	不超过2年
湖北		有序放开大中城市落户	是	是	不超3年
江西	南昌	有序放开南昌市中心城区落户限制			
山西	太原	有序放开大城市落户限制			
陕西		有序放开	稳定住所或合法产权住所或工作且缴纳社保		
新疆		控制乌鲁木齐市人口			
广西	南宁、柳州		是	是	一定年限
青海	西宁	进一步放开西宁市落户限制	合法房产或合法工作、有稳定居所缴纳社保		
甘肃		全面放开全市城市和城镇落户	是	是	一定年限
四川		全面放开大中小城市和建制镇落户	是	是	一定年限

3. 中小城市和建制镇

《意见》要求要有序放开中等城市落户限制。合法稳定就业并有合法稳定住所（含租赁），同时按照国家规定参加城镇社会保险达到一定年限的人员。城市综合承载能力压力大的地方，可以对合法稳定就业的范围、年限和合法稳定住所（含租赁）的范围、条件等做出具体规定，但对合法稳定住所（含租赁）不得设置住房面积、金额等要求，对参加城镇社会保险年限的要求不得超过3年。

《意见》要求要全面放开建制镇和小城市落户限制。具体要求：在县级市市区、县人民政府驻地镇和其他建制镇有合法稳定住所（含租赁）的人员，本人及其共同居住生活的配偶、未成年子女、父母等，可以在当地申请登记常住户口。

从各个省份的方案来看，各省份对中等城市的落户要求与《意见》基本一致，但各个省份要求的严格程度不同，其中广东省比较严格，要求合法稳定就业满3年并有合法稳定住所，同时按照有关规定参加社会保险满3年的人员可以落户；其他省份的要求对社会保险的要求基本为1年。对于小城镇，各省份全部要求全面放开小城镇落户，条件为有合法稳定居所，与《意见》一致。

4. 总体特征

1）落户条件从特大城市到中小城市依次降低

从《意见》中对不同规模等级城市的落户要求以及各省实际的贯彻落实情况来看，落户条件从特大城市到中小城市依次降低。特大城市落户的条件不论是从数量上还是从严格程度上都要远远高于其他规模的城市。特大城市除了稳定合法就业、合法稳定居所、社保缴纳年限等条件外，对连续居住年限也做出了要求，以及一些其他的根据城市自身的特点制定的其他落户条件要求。另外，同样是社保，在缴纳的年限上，特大城市、大城市等都比中小城市要长。到小城镇，落户条件则极为放松，几乎是只要有合法稳定的居所便可以实现落户。

表5　不同规模等级城市落户要求

城市规模	稳定合法就业	合法稳定居所	社保缴纳年限	连续居住年限	其他条件
特大城市	是	是	高(不超过5年)	是	是
大城市	是	是	中(不超过3年)	否	否
中等城市	是	是	低(0~1年)	否	否
小城市	否	是	否	否	否

2）特大城市、大城市落户条件在很大程度上了考虑了城市自身的发展需要，高学历人才在落户的竞争中占据优势

广东省提出广州、深圳要重点吸纳本地经济社会发展急需的各类型专业人才落户；重庆市则是放宽与战略性新兴产业企业签订劳动合同的人群落户的条件。而部分省份明确提出要提高高学历、专业人才的城镇落户率，如吉林省、江西省、河北省等，山东省的济南市、青岛市则全面放开本科学历人才落户。有些省份更是全面放开专业人口的落户限制，如吉林省、江西省、河北省等。另外，特殊人才、急缺的专业人才即使是中专学历也成为青睐的对象。总之，高学历的人才、掌握一定技能的专业人才在落户上占据优势。

表6　部分省份对高学历及专业人才的落户意见

省份	高校毕业生	大专	中专	其他专业人才
吉林	放开	放开	放开	放开
江西	放开	放开	放开	放开
河北	放开	放开	放开	放开
山东	放开	不断提高	不断提高	不断提高
青海	放宽	放宽	放宽	放宽
广东	放宽	放宽	特殊专业	特殊专业
辽宁	放宽	放宽	放宽	放宽
江苏	不断提高	不断提高	不断提高	不断提高
安徽	不断提高	不断提高	不断提高	不断提高
河南	不断提高	不断提高	不断提高	不断提高
湖北	不断提高	不断提高	不断提高	不断提高
山西	不断提高	不断提高	不断提高	不断提高

3）全面落实居住证制度，逐步推进公共服务常住人口全覆盖

从各省份落实方案来看，居住证制度得到广泛响应。公民离开常住户口所在地到其他设区的市级以上城市居住半年以上的，在居住地申领居住证，并以居住证为载体，建立健全与居住年限等条件相挂钩的基本公共服务提供机制。居住证持有人享有与当地户籍人口同等的

劳动就业、基本公共教育、基本医疗卫生服务、计划生育服务、公共文化服务、证照办理服务等权利；以连续居住年限和参加社会保险年限等为条件，逐步享有与当地户籍人口同等的中等职业教育资助、就业扶持、住房保障、养老服务、社会福利、社会救助等权利，同时结合随迁子女在当地连续就学年限等情况，逐步享有随迁子女在当地参加中考和高考的资格。

4）重视保障农村转移人口权利，开展农业转移人口的市民化成本分担机制与农村权益自愿退出机制的探索与试点

在保障农业转移人口及其他常住人口合法权益方面，各省份均出台了条目不等的措施来贯彻落实《意见》的精神，而提到较多的主要有两方面：完善农村产权制度以及加强基本公共服务财政保障能力。

在完善农村产权制度方面，各省份从农村土地确权、登记、颁证、农村集体经济组织产权制度改革、建立农村产权流转交易市场等方面进行了相关规定，并且大多数省份也紧随《意见》的精神，明确提出进城落户农民是否有偿退出“三权”应在尊重农民意愿前提下开展试点，不得以退出土地承包经营权、宅基地使用权、集体收益分配权作为农民进城落户的条件。

在加强基本公共服务财政保障能力方面，在积极探索建立财政转移支付同农业转移人口市民化挂钩机制的同时，部分省份已经提出探讨市民化成本分担机制以及减少用地挂钩制度。例如，河南省提出“建立健全农业转移人口市民化成本分担机制，明确政府、企业、个人的支出责任”；安徽省提出“各级政府承担基本公共服务成本投入。企业社会保险费用和住房公积金，提供多种形式的住房保障。农民工承担社会保险以及住房公积金、就业培训成本中的个人支出部分”。另外，重庆市率先提出建立建设用地与吸纳转移人口挂钩制度，体现“建设用地计划指标跟着产业和人口走”的政策导向。

另外，国家新型城镇化试点方案中选择了江苏、安徽两省和宁波等62个城市（镇）列为国家新型城镇化综合试点地区，其重点任务之一就是探索建立农业转移人口市民化成本分担机制，以及探索建立多元化可持续的城镇化投融资机制，鼓励政府和社会资本进行合作。

三、新型户籍改革面临的挑战

最新的户籍改革是对户籍制度的一次总体调整，对合理布局大中小城市和小城镇、合理引导人口分布，对保障农村转移人口平等享受基本公共服务等意义将产生十分重要的作用，这将对我国的城镇化、经济发展、社会公平等方面产生深远的影响。在城镇化方面，户籍改革将进一步提升城镇化的质量。农业转移人口的市民化将提高我国的户籍城镇化率，解决进城农民“进不去的城，回不去的乡”的尴尬困境，促使进城农民更好地融入城市社会。另外，新型的户籍制度将引导人口在不同规模等级城市之间的流动，在优化大中小城市和小城镇布局方面发挥作用。在社会公平方面，新型户籍制度的实施将在保障农村转移人口的权利方面发挥作用，解决农村转移人口无法在就业、教育、医疗、养老、住房保障等方面与城镇居民享受同等的基本公共服务的问题。公共服务覆盖全部常住人口的目标将使更多城乡居民

享受日益均等化的基本公共服务，更好地分享经济社会发展成果，拥有更好的社会保障和发展机会，促进社会公平。在经济发展方面，推进户籍制度改革，将有利于劳动力的自由流动，化解劳动力就业的结构性矛盾，提高劳动力资源配置效率，促进我国加快从人口大国转变为人力资源强国，进一步释放人口红利和改革红利。

当然，我们也应该注意到，目前的户籍改革还面临一些严峻挑战：

一是农村转移人口的落户意愿与政府的户籍改革政策趋向存在较大偏差。受区位经济发展优势的，大量的农村转移人口流向经济发达、就业机会较多、收入水平较高的东部地区特大城市以及大城市，而数量众多的中小城市对农村转移人口的吸引力并不大。据国家人口计划生育委员会调查，希望在城镇落户的流动人口中，约70%青睐于大城市。因此，国家严格限制特大城市、大城市落户与农村转移人口希望在特大城市、大城市落户的现实之间必将产生较大的矛盾，而由于中小城市对农村转移人口吸引力不大，即使逐步放开中小城市落户，是否能起到引导农村转移人口落户的效果也存在很大的不确定性。同时，农村转移人口的空间分布集中在特大城市、大城市的现状也与政策的引导趋向存在一定的矛盾，这都使目前的户籍改革效果面临严峻的挑战。

二是城镇原有居民与农村转移人口在城镇基本公共服务享受资格与范围方面存在一定的利益冲突。不少城镇居民担心农村转移人口的加入会降低当地公共服务的水平与质量，增加他们的税负成本，特别是对那些需要当地政府财政补贴的公共服务与社会福利，如廉租房、保障房等。尤其是在那些流动人口集聚社区，有些城镇居民担心流动人口会因人数的优势而逐步取代他们对当地公共事务的主导权。因此，如何既能保障落户农村转移人口享受平等的城市公共服务的权利，又能协调好同原有城镇居民的利益关系，是需要解决的一大难点。

三是地方政府与中央政府在责任主体与成本分摊方面仍需协调。解决农村转移人口落户问题的关键还是财政保障问题，这直接关系到落户人口能否享受到城市的公共服务。尽管目前政策中提出了中央财政转移支付、多方分担机制等措施，但中央、地方政府、城镇居民和流动人口等各方利益群体在提供与享受城镇基本公共服务中的责任、义务和权益仍需进一步明确，同时在具体的实施细则以及实施过程可能遇到的问题等方面还需要进一步探索。

四是不同规模城市落户标准的差异将进一步导致高端人才向高规模、高等级的城市集中，中小城镇发展面临较严峻的人才流失问题。可以看到，尽管规模等级高的城市在落户方面的条件严格，但不论是积分落户还是条件准入等机制都对高学历、专业人口有利，有的城市更是明确向高学历人才敞开大门。由于特大城市、大城市较之中小城市有强大的吸引力，高端人才必然向特大城市、大城市集聚，中小城市在吸引人才方面仍然处于劣势，这对中小城市的发展会造成一定的影响。

五是无专业技能的普通农民工群体在市民化进程中仍处于被排斥、受歧视的劣势地位。尽管新型户籍制度改革在很多方面降低了落户的门槛，但是很多条件对农民工群体而言，仍然具有一定的难度。例如，很多农村转移人口在城市没有稳定的就业，或者就业但无法正常缴纳社保，这些硬性条件仍将很大一部分农村转移人口排除在落户的人群之外。而且，无专业技能或比较低级的劳动力在面对其他的群体竞争时也常常处于劣势地位。

总之，尽管目前的户籍改革已经迈出了非常重要的一步，但户籍制度改革任重而道远，仍然需要通过不断地探索和实践来逐渐完善提升。

（作者：刘盛和，中国科学院地理科学与资源研究所，博士，研究员，刘振博士生）

参考文献

［1］姚士谋，张平宇，余成，李广宇，王成新．中国新型城镇化理论与实践问题［J］．地理科学，2014，6（6）：641-647.

［2］陆大道，陈明星．关于“国家新型城镇化规划（2014—2020）”编制大背景的几点认识［J］．地理学报，2015，70（2）．

［3］孙文凯，白重恩，谢沛初．户籍制度改革对中国农村劳动力流动的影响［J］．经济研究，2011，1：28-41.

［4］刘涛，齐元静，曹广忠，刘慧．中国流动人口空间格局的演变特征、形成机制及城镇化效应——基于2000年和2010年人口普查分县数据的分析［J］．Journal of Geographical Sciences，2015，2：008.

［5］蔡建明，王国霞，杨振山．我国人口迁移趋势及空间格局演变［J］．人口研究，2007，31（5）：9-19.

［6］戚伟，刘盛和．中国城市流动人口位序规模分布研究［J］．地理研究，2015，34（10）．

我国城市养老服务现状及发展趋势

一、我国城市人口老龄化的总体态势

人口老龄化加速已经成为我国社会经济发展的重要社会背景。根据国家统计局数字，2014 年年底，我国 60 周岁及以上的人口已达到 2.12 亿人，占总人口的 15.5%。根据有关方面预测，到 2030 年，我国老年人口将达到 3.71 亿人，占总人口的 25.3%；2050 年达到 4.83 亿人，占总人口的 34.1%，每三个人当中就有一个老年人。当前，我国 80 岁以上的高龄老年人口已经达到2 500万人，失能老年人口规模庞大，突破4 000万人。患有慢性病的老年人持续增多，这些老年人口内部变动将进一步加剧人口老龄化的严峻性。

与此同时，我国的城镇化仍在不断推进，城市人口规模不断增加。在城镇化的推动下，青壮年人口由农村向城市大规模转移，客观上降低了大城市和发达地区城镇的老龄化水平，但是，由于农村剩余劳动力资源的逐渐减少，城市的老龄化速度将不断加快。2014 年，城市老年人口的总量为 0.92 亿人，占全国老年人口比重为 43.6%。据预测，未来城市老年人口将一直增长，2020 年、2030 年、2050 年城市老年人口占全国老年人口比重将分别增长至 48.6%、55.4%、71%。因此，从老年人口增长的空间分布趋势来看，城市将成为未来养老服务开发的战略重点。我国城镇化与老龄化并行，在此过程中，城市人口压力、交通压力、住房压力、环境压力、发展的不均衡、制度转型等问题复杂交错，将会使养老问题更为复杂、棘手。

不同规模的城市由于人口结构、经济基础、公共服务等方面差异，城市老龄化现状与养老服务中的问题不尽相同，但总体空间分布具有一些普遍特点。第一，特大城市的人口老龄化水平继续提高。按常住人口统计，2010 年我国人口超过千万的特大城市有 6 个，分别为北京、上海、重庆、广州、天津、深圳。截至 2014 年年底，六大城市户籍人口总量中 60 岁以上人口比例分别为 22.6%、28.8%、19.4%、16.7%、21.2%、6%（表 1）。其中深圳的户籍人口统计基数远低于常住人口，因此老龄人口的比例偏低。除此以外的特大城市中，尽管外来流动人口的大量进入对老龄化程度进行了稀释，但由于发达地区人口平均预期寿命延长，育龄妇女生育年龄推后、生育率下降，对外来人口或多或少进行控制等因素的影响，户籍人口的老龄化率依然处于较高水平。一方面，特大城市的养老问题与人口过密、空间蔓延、交通拥堵、住房紧缺等城市问题相叠加，影响因素错综复杂。与中小城市相比，特大城市的社会关系网络相对稀薄，传统的家庭和社会网络对老年人口的养老支撑能力较弱，助推了人们对社会化养老的需求。另一方面，由于特大城市经济实力雄厚，政府提供公共服务能力较强，社会力量介入养老服务体系建设的积极性高。因此，解决特大城市养老服务问题具有高度的紧迫性和现实可行性。

第二，我国老龄化最为严重的城市主要集中分布在经济较为发达地区的周边，特别是浙江省、江苏省及辽宁省的二、三线城市，如苏州、无锡、嘉兴、沈阳、大连、鞍山等城市老龄化率普遍超过20%。中西部省区城市的老年人口比重相对较低，如银川、昆明、乌鲁木齐等。

表1　2015 年我国部分主要城市户籍人口中老年人口的比例

城市	60 岁以上人口数(万人)	户籍人口比例(%)
上海	413.98	28.8
北京	301.00	22.6
广州	140.65	16.7
深圳*	17.00	6.0
天津	215.42	21.2
杭州	144.91	20.3
苏州	159.20	24.1
无锡	114.57	24.1
嘉兴	81.26	23.4
沈阳	152.02	20.8
鞍山	76.78	22.1
大连	129.58	21.8
长沙	119.40	16.3
赣州	124.50	13.1
重庆	656.17	19.4
成都	249.28	20.6
银川	23.75	13.8
昆明	91.90	16.8
乌鲁木齐	38.48	14.9

数据来源：国家统计局2015 全国统计年鉴及各省市统计年鉴，其中深圳市为2014 统计年鉴。

*因深圳市户籍人口远低于常住人口，所以60 岁以上人口比例偏低。

2015 年国家及地方紧锣密鼓地出台养老服务的相关政策措施，政策涉及金融、养老机构、社区、居家、行政审批、管理、外资介入、医养结合、社会力量介入、政府购买服务，标准化等方面，政策行政法规效力更强，更具有操作性。其中，2015 年2 月25 日，民政部、发展改革委等十部委联合发布了《关于鼓励民间资本参与养老服务业发展的实施意见》，鼓励民间资本在城镇社区举办或运营老年人日间照料中心、老年人活动中心等养老服务设施，为有需求的老年人，特别是高龄、空巢、独居、生活困难的老年人，提供集中就餐、托养、助浴、健康、休闲和上门照护等服务，并协助做好老年人信息登记、身体状况评估等工作；同时，对落实税费优惠政策、加强人才保障、保障用地需求等做出了相关规定。2015 年 5 月 1 日，全国首部居家养老服务法规《北京市居家养老服务条例》（以下简称《条例》）正式实施。《条例》明确了政府责任，标志着居家养老服务开始走向正轨，养老政策开始从机构养老向居家养老倾斜。2015 年 7 月 1 日，京津冀地区共同实施协同地方标准《老年护理常见风险防控要求》，这是我国首个关于老年护理常见风险防控的标准，填补了我国老年护理常见风险防控标准的空白。2015 年 8 月 23 日，《基本养老保险基金投资管理办法》（以下简称《办法》）正式发布，养老金入市成为未来趋势。《办法》明确了养老金目前只在境内投资，投资股票、股票基金、混合基金、股票型养老金产品的比例，合计不得高于养老基金资产净值的 30%，参与股指期货、国债期货交易，只能以套期保值为目的。2015 年 11 月，国务院常务会议决定，要推进医疗卫生与养老服务结合，更好地保障人们老有所医、老有所养。一是促进医养融合对接。医疗机构为养老机构开通预约就诊绿色通道，养老机构内设的医疗机构可作为医院康复护理场所；支持养老机构按规定开办老年病、康复、中医医院和临终关怀机构等；推进基层医疗机构与社区、居家养老结合，为老年人家庭提供签约医疗服务。二是鼓励社会力量兴办医养结合机构，支持医疗资源丰富地区将公立医院转为康复、老年护理等机构。三是强化投融资、用地等支持，扩大政府购买基本健康养老服务，创新长期护理保险等产品。会议决定，在全国每个省份至少选择一个地区开展医养结合试点示范。

人口学家认为，随着老年人口的快速增加，中国应对老龄化社会的人口调整最佳时期不到 20 年，而中国已经成为世界上生育率最低的国家之一，因此，必须适度调整人口计划生育政策。2015 年 12 月 27 日，全国人大常委会审议通过了修订后的《人口与计划生育法》。“全面放开二孩”政策将于 2016 年 1 月 1 日起正式实施，未来育龄夫妇将自主决定生育子女的数量和生育间隔。这一调整预期将会促使生育率回升到世代更替水平，使年轻人口比重得以迅速增加，从而缓解中国的人口老龄化水平。从全面放开二孩政策实施以来各地生育意愿的有限调查结果来看，受文化观念转变、子女教育负担等因素的影响，满足条件的家庭中只有一小部分希望生育二孩，因此，政策调整的预期目标能否实现仍需通过时间加以检验。

二、城市养老的主要形式由传统的居家/家庭型向社会型转变

面对日渐加剧的城市人口老龄化趋势，传统的居家/家庭型养老模式受到强烈冲击。随着我国 30 多年来实施的独生子女政策的效果已经开始显现，户均人口减少，城市居民 4 – 2 – 1 家庭逐渐增多，传统家庭赡养的支撑能力日益下降。同时，子女在城市的生活、购房、就业等压力下，对单独生活的父母所给予的关注降低，城市老年的空巢化现象明显。空巢化已经成为驱动城市老年人养老模式转型的重要因素。根据高晓路等（2014）的调查结果，北京所有老人家庭中，老年人家庭中单身和只有老人的比重高达 52.3%，空巢化趋势十分明显。

城市高龄老人、失能老人数量庞大，对专业化医疗和照护服务的需求提高。目前我国高龄老年人口已经达到2 500万人，失能老年人口规模突破了4 000万人。随着城市人口预期寿命延长，将会有越来越多的城市高龄老人。然而，尽管我国国民预期寿命有所增加，但健康

预期寿命增加缓慢。糖尿病所致健康损失急速增加，近23年来糖尿病导致的健康损失增幅超过100%；社会人口学状况（包括人均收入、人口年龄、生育率和平均受教育年限）对健康损失的影响显著。2013年的一项研究发现，我国男女合计健康预期寿命为67.9岁。而第六次全国人口普查显示，我国人口的平均预期寿命是75岁，也就是说，我国老年人平均在68岁到75岁的7年时间内处于“失能”期，这与西方许多发达国家相比，时间要漫长得多。而老年人一旦“失能”，不仅给其个人造成生活上的痛苦，而且常常由于尊严的丧失造成心灵的伤痛，给家庭、子女和社会带来各种负担。因此，失能老人的养老服务成为老龄化社会中最为严峻的问题。

城市老年人口的消费能力逐年提高。尽管我国经济发展水平总体还不高、人均GDP水平还不高，仅有5.2万元，约为8 016美元，但随着收入倍增计划的实施，人均收入将大幅增加。而且当前，我国东部地区，特别是一线城市的人均收入水平已经较高，接近中等发达国家水平，人均年收入超过6万元的老年人口相对较多。2015年全国企业退休人员平均养老金达2200元/月。同时，城市老年人口的其他财富积累较多，如储蓄、住房等。相关调查表明，目前全国拥有2套及以上住房的老年人占老年总人口的75%。受发达国家养老观念影响，老年人在衡量自身消费能力基础上，将有大批老年人接受社会化的养老服务产品。

我国正处于快速城镇化过程中，过去几年的城镇化发展中，人口、产业和各种经济要素不断向特大城市集聚，对于人口结构的老龄化问题考虑有限，使得城市养老服务体系建设滞后、相关服务设施严重不足。未来在新型城镇化建设过程中，人口将进一步向城市快速集中，城市养老需求也将迅速扩大。因此，近年来，加强城市社会养老服务体系建设，已成为政府关心、社会关注、群众关切的重大民生问题。社会化力量参与养老，也使养老服务更加趋于层次化、多元化、个性化，促进老年人口的养老模式选择从依靠家庭养老转向社会化养老。

人口老龄化和养老服务问题受到国家的高度重视。2012年我国出台《中华人民共和国老年人权益保障法》修订版，新法将“积极应对人口老龄化”提到国家战略层面。2013年开始，与养老服务相关的政策措施密集出台，因此，社会上将2013年称为中国的“养老元年”。国家层面的政策主要贯彻了“养老服务社会化”的理念，明确了对社会力量进入养老领域的扶持与规范化的态度。在国家政策的指导下，各大城市相继出台了养老服务建设的详细法规及规划。例如，北京将进一步强化“9064”（即90%的老年人在社会化服务协助下通过家庭照顾养老，6%的老年人通过政府购买社区照顾服务养老，4%的老年人入住养老服务机构集中养老）的社会养老服务体系建设规划，侧重发展护养型养老机构，养老机构要医养结合，要与居家养老相结合。

三、城市养老服务设施的建设与产业发展

（一）城市养老服务设施建设步伐加快

随着老龄化日益加剧，城市养老服务设施建设发展迅速，“十二五”期间养老服务设施

和养老服务产业的发展尤其迅猛，在数量、规模和人均设施拥有量方面都有大幅提高。根据民政部社会服务发展统计公报和全国老龄工作委员会的统计，2012 年年底，全国拥有养老床位 416.5 万张，比上年增长 12.8%，每千名老年人拥有养老床位 21.5 张；2013 年年底，全国拥有养老床位 493.7 万张，比上年增长 18.9%，每千名老年人拥有养老床位 24.4 张；2014 年年底，全国有各类养老床位 577.8 万张，比上年增长 17.0%（其中社区留宿和日间照料床位 187.5 万张），每千名老年人拥有养老床位 27.2 张；2015 年年底，全国养老机构床位数已达到 669.8 万张，每千名老人拥有养老床位数达到 30.2 张。

据民政部 2015 年发布的数字，2014 年年底，全国各类养老服务机构和设施（提供住宿的养老服务）94 110个，其中：养老服务机构33 043个，社区养老服务机构和设施18 927个，互助型的养老设施40 357个，军队离退休干部休养所1 783个；年末收留抚养老年人 318.4 万人，比上年增长 4.2%。其中民办养老机构的比例也逐年提高。

尽管发展迅速，但是总体来看，我国人均拥有的养老机构床位数仍然不足，与发达国家千名老年人拥有 50~70 张的床位数相比仍有较大差距。由于养老观念和生活方式的转型，我国有更多的老年人、特别是城市老年人转向社会养老。与这样的社会需求相比，目前养老服务机构的数量和规模还有较大缺口，未来一方面要增加养老机构床位数的供给，另一方面也需要对需求合理地进行引导。

同时，城乡养老服务的发展不均衡的状况较为明显。目前，全国居家养老服务设施基本覆盖城镇社区和50%以上的农村社区。2014 年年末，我国城市养老服务机构（提供住宿的社会服务机构）共计7 642个，较上年增长 8%；与此相对，农村养老服务机构（提供住宿的社会服务机构）2014 年共计 20 261 个，比 2013 年大幅减少 33%（民政部，2015）。其中一个原因可能是城镇化使更多的农村纳入城市，但是从一定程度上仍可看出农村养老服务的严重萎缩。

民政部地级以上行政单元的城市养老服务机构（与农村养老服务机构分开统计）数据显示，2014 年年末，城市养老服务机构个数最多的是上海，已达 410 个，重庆、天津、北京的城市养老服务机构也较多[①]，大连、南京、苏州、青岛、淄博、武汉等城市养老机构分布也较多，这与前文所述的我国老龄化程度最高的地区或城市相对应。

另外，从养老机构的规模来看，我国城市的养老机构规模以 300 人以下的中型、小型机构比例最高，养老机构的比重随机构规模的增加而变小。然而，内陆欠发达地区的城市养老服务机构规模一般都较大，如朔州、六安、韶关、遂宁、昭通、银川等城市。其中原因，首先是这些地区的财政支持力度较小，社会力量举办养老机构的情况较多，为了保证正常运营，只能选择扩大规模来获得维持运营的利润。其次，养老服务的劳动力资源也是重要的影响因素，内陆欠发达地区人口大量外迁，当地养老服务人员反而相对欠缺，特大城市或发达地区的二、三线城市，由于工资水平较高，养老服务教育培训的机会较多，人力资源相对充

① 由于城市养老机构与农村养老机构分开统计，此处的北京、天津、重庆等城市的养老机构总量低于城市实际拥有的养老机构数。

沛。考虑到未来我国城市化的趋势，农村和中西部地区城市的劳动力依然会向特大城市或发达地区城市转移，其结果是后者的机构养老服务人员或居家养老服务人员供给保持充足，大中小型城市养老服务设施的规模结构分布较为合理。然而，西部地区城市的养老服务机构的人才不足现象会更加突出，养老服务机构的规模较合理规模来说依然偏大。

（二）主要城市老年医疗护理服务得到提升

随着我国高龄、失能老年人数量的大幅增加，城市老年医疗护理服务需求量巨大。失能老人照护是技术性、复杂性、连续性很强的工作。失能老人一般都患有两种或两种以上的慢性病，因此，失能老人长期照护的对象既是身体失能而生活不能自理，同时还是需要长期的医疗、康复和护理的老年患者。他们不但需要日常生活护理，同时还需要正常的经济保障、健康维护和精神慰藉以及医疗、康复、护理和临终关怀等服务。以上种种都不是由一个家庭内部即可解决的问题，护理失能老人所涉及的服务包括医疗、保健、护理、社工、康复、心理、营养、药事、管理等非常复杂的专业技术领域，因此，近年城市介助、介护的床位不断提高。可以说这部分服务是养老服务产业的“刚性需求”。

截至2014年年底，全国一线特大城市中，上海的介护床位和介助床位数最多，分别达到20 969个和11 209个，其次是天津和北京，其介护床位分别是6 967个、6 177个，天津介助床位数也较多，达5 717个。广州的介护床位数相对较多，达到5 356个。可以看出，一线城市养老服务内容的调整和满足老年人对于医疗、护理、康复等需求方面，已经开始加强。

与此同时，我国城市的其他与老年人健康、医疗相关的措施得以实施。近年，北京、上海、沈阳等城市还积极兴办老年医院，2006年北京市完成了市、区（县）两级老年医院建设任务，实际开放床位2 665张。2013年，床位增加到3 409张。2006北京市建立家庭病床5 000余张，2007年社区卫生服务机构近7300名老年人建立家庭病床，2008年新增床位2 493张。近年，北京家庭病床建设进入平稳发展期，每年兴建的床位保持在500张左右。

（三）城市社区居家养老服务逐渐兴起

我国《社会养老服务体系建设规划（2011－2015年）》提出，社会养老服务体系建设的目标是建成以居家为基础、社区为依托、机构为支撑的养老服务格局。城市的社区居家养老服务与居家养老、社区养老密切相关，日益受到政府与市场的重视。目前，养老服务成为社区服务中的重点内容，社区中的生活照料、家政服务更加侧重于老年人；社区的老年人康复护理、医疗保健、精神慰藉等服务逐渐加强，更加突出上门服务的形式。对于家庭日间暂时无人或者无力照护的社区老年人，结合社区服务设施建设，城市社区集中建立了日间照料中心，增强了社区养老服务能力，居家养老服务平台建设也得到稳步推进。

另外，城市着力建设老年宜居社区，从老年人居住环境的角度提升社区居家养老的品质。如，加强交通出行便利性，无障碍设施改造，加强社区医疗设施建设等。同时，城市逐步提高城市困难老年人住房质量，老年人是城市保障性住房的主要居住人群之一。

(四) 城市养老服务逐步形成养老产业体系

近年来，随着社会养老需求的逐年增长，养老产业市场逐渐细分，出现了老年用品、老年住宅、老年服务、老年医护、老年教育、老年文化、老年娱乐等多种多样的老龄服务及其配套服务。一些新的服务业态如老年金融、老年旅游、智能化养老等也正在快速兴起。

养老产业的投资主体也越来越多元化。政府按照“兜底”原则，将有限财政资金重点投向中低收入的失能老年群体。其他的健康老年人、半失能老年人的养老服务需求问题将更多地交给市场去解决。在相关政策的引导和扶持下，国有、民营资本争相进入市场，养老产业正在向市场化、产业化的方向快速发展。

然而一方面，随着产业化的推进，养老产业发展也呈现出一些突出问题。老年住宅、综合性养老社区的开发方兴未艾，但目前总体上还处在无序发展的阶段，以养老、异地养老以及养老养生等为名，实则圈地开发房地产的项目众多。另一方面，养老产业的产业结构尚未清晰，如何将原有的年轻社会的产业形式与养老服务产业结合，产业结构与产业链条如何构建，都是未来需求解决的问题。同时，老年人的服务需求是多元化的、多层次的、动态化的。目前，我国城市的老龄产业的终端产品和服务，种类单一、不足、缺乏预见性，无法满足老年人巨大的养老服务需求。

四、当前城市养老服务需求与供给亟须解决的几个问题

与老龄化进程相伴，城市社会养老服务体系的建设和发展将是一个较长的发展过程，其间难免出现各种问题。从当前的实际来看，存在的问题主要有以下方面：

(一) 老年人自身的过渡期问题

养老问题和老年人的行为心理取向与社会经济发展阶段高度相关。我国的老人处在人口和家庭结构转型、社会养老服务体系尚未完善的冲突期，随着社会收入差距加大向社会底层沉淀，导致生活方式和养老观念都发生剧烈的变化。在特殊的经济社会和制度背景下，相当多的老年人对于如何养老处于茫然阶段，一方面不想给子女带来更大压力，另一方面又不知道如何才能让自己幸福地度过晚年。目前，值得特别关注的一个现象是，城市中比较年轻和健康的老人似乎认为，近年来社会上出现的众多的老年社区、养老公寓可以帮助他们解决养老问题，但实际上他们对养老的阶段性考虑不足，并没有考虑这些设施能否提供充分的长期照护，同时，对自己的经济能力和对养老服务品质的控制能力也存在疑虑。目前，囿于信息以及其他一些客观条件的限制，老年人对社区提供的服务认知程度还不够高。总之，人们普遍缺乏养老的家庭规划和个人规划，具有很大的盲目性。

(二) 居家养老的常态化和标准化服务的问题

居家养老服务涵盖生活照料、家政服务、康复护理、医疗保健、精神慰藉等众多方面。

其中，老年人的康复护理、医疗保健、精神慰藉等的专业性、技术性极强。而当前，我国城市居家养老的专业人才、护理人才、管理人才严重缺失。目前，城市中的护理人员90%来自农村，护理人员的信息也主要由家政公司带发，护理人员还没有系统、统一的教育背景评估、专业知识技能有限，服务意识差，人员流动性很大，无法长期提供优质的服务。政府应对于护理行业人员的教育培训给予优惠、灵活的政策。同时，政府需制定各类护理服务的标准，规范行业管理。

（三）养老机构空置率问题

与城市的养老设施数量不足相比，养老服务不到位的矛盾更加突出，表现为结构失衡和空间失衡两个方面。城市老年人群体在年龄、经济能力、身心状况、社会和家庭环境等方面高度分化，其应对外部变化和风险的能力都远低于年轻人群，这种群体分化对老年人的需求特征和消费行为造成很大的影响。然而目前，城市老年服务的功能过于单一，大部分养老机构只能提供日常生活性服务，而针对高龄老人、失能老人的医疗、康复、护理和临终关怀等服务普遍缺失。其结果就是，可提供专业护理服务的护养型机构“一床难求”，而一些疗养型的养老院大量空置，经营欠佳。另外，很多新建的城市郊区养老机构，尽管环境较好，价位也比较合适，但老年人或因感到不便或因离家人和子女太远而不愿入住；在城市中心区，养老机构的新扩建则由于找不到用地或其他各种原因难以实现。例如，广州约有六成的养老院由于证照不齐或日照、消防不符合规范无法通过验收。国家统计局公布的数据显示，2014年年末全国各类提供住宿的养老服务机构3.4万个、床位551.4万张，入住的老人却只有288.7万人，空置率高达48%。其中，上海市的床位空置率超过30%，北京市为40%～50%，南京市目前有一半在建或已建好的养老床位处于空置状态。不仅如此，近年来各地民办养老机构关门停业的现象也十分普遍。

机构的空置意味着养老服务业投资的失败，不仅浪费了大量宝贵的土地资源和财政资源，扭曲了养老服务业的正常发展，更是直接损害了政府的公信力：政府对养老服务业的土地、财政投入不断增加，养老机构床位数量超速增长，然而老年人却并没有因此受惠，有效供给不足，这种反差引发的不安和焦虑情绪正在蔓延。可见，养老服务建设和规划政策的合理性和有效性是民生保障和基层社会治理中的一个重要问题，直接影响健康老龄化社会目标的实现。

五、我国城市养老服务建设的未来走向

（一）深入调研并动态追踪不同城市老年人口结构的变化趋势

不同城市的养老服务建设需要与城市各自的老年人口年龄、健康、经济、教育结构等众多因素相匹配，城市老年人口结构的预测是政府部门规划与监督市场合理科学建设的基础。

国际社会对老年服务进行市场细分时，首先根据年龄及健康状况将老年人分为三类：健

康老年人、半失能老年人、失能老年人。通过这样的分类，各城市明确了老龄服务的轻重缓急，对于制度安排、政策重点、财政投入、发展导向都将十分明晰。欧洲国家在“精细化照护”理念的指导下，实施科学的需求评估标准体系 InterRAI，在一些国家，长期照护病床的需求总量降低了 1/4 左右。通过对老年人经济、教育文化等估算与预测，社区与机构的服务规模、档次、品质以及未来的规划安排等具体问题也都将迎刃而解。美国的相关研究表明，过去 10 年间，相当多的私人养老机构关闭，具有较高收入和素质的白人居民越来越转向居家养老，这一现象符合人类的社会环境心理学特征，反映了养老需求的长期发展趋势。

（二）结合各地区各城市不同的环境、产业基础，未来将形成各具特色的养老产业区

上海、北京、广州、天津等特大城市将形成老年综合产业带，居家养老服务与机构养老服务建设与当地老年人口相适应，老年金融、老年文化、智能化老年产品等多种养老服务将集中分布于这些城市。海南、黑龙江、云南等省份的城市将形成以旅游带动的老年产业带。

我国幅员辽阔，不同地区、城乡之间，乃至城市的不同空间单元，在自然环境、人文经济社会条件方面都存在显著的差异，要特别注意识别这些因素对社会养老服务的影响，因地制宜选择不同的模式，设置不同的标准。

（三）城市老年服务的专业型、技术型人才是未来养老服务产业健康发展的基础

当前老年服务的护理人才、管理人才严重缺失。未来可通过以下途径来解决：一是城市政府对护理行业从业人员的政策优惠及补贴，参照发达国家吸引国外护理人才的方式，在户口积分、子女随迁或就学等方面对外来护理人员给予优惠，给在岗职工补贴等激励措施；二是重视并给予老年服务的职业技术技能教育相应的灵活及优惠政策，如城市办学的土地优惠政策、城市社会财政对教育的支持等；三是通过确定各类管理服务标准，保障服务品质和水准，推进护理人员的专业定级，提高老年服务人员的社会地位。

（四）加强城市老年宜居环境建设，最大程度地保障老年人就地养老的可能性

城市中应保障老年人的基本住房需求，逐步提高城市贫困老年人的住房质量。如在城市保障性安居工程建设中，明确老年人是保障性住房的主要居住人群，并优先保障。促进城市老旧社区的电梯改造，改善城市无障碍环境，积极拓展老年人游览健身活动空间，加强人口高度集中区域内的公园、绿地建设等。加大中小城市，特别是中西部地区的中小城市老年宜居环境的建设。重视城市新城区、远郊区县的无障碍环境、老年配套设施和服务设施建设。

（作者：高晓路，中国科学院地理科学与资源研究所，研究员，博士生导师，Email：gaoxl@ igsnrr. ac. cn；颜秉秋，中国科学院地理科学与资源研究所，博士后，Email：yanbingqiu@ aliyun. com. cn）

低碳城市的评价体系与空间格局

一、引言

低碳城市是新时期中国城市转型发展的重要方向。2009年中国政府承诺，到2020年碳排放强度比2005年下降40%～45%。为实现预期减排目标、应对快速城镇化过程中农村人口转移与资源消耗的压力，低碳城市成为一种自上而下的政策在全国推广。国家发展改革委、环境保护部、住房城乡建设部分别开展低碳城市、生态城市、低碳生态城市的授予或评价活动。迄今为止，国家发展改革委确立了6个省、36个城市作为低碳省或低碳城市试点，环境保护部授予了38个城市/县为国家级生态市/县，住房城乡建设部批准了6个城市为第一批中德低碳生态试点示范城市。此外，全国97%的地级以上城市亦将生态城市、低碳城市或低碳生态城市作为其发展战略。然而，对低碳城市、生态城市、低碳生态城市的概念界定、评价标准至今尚未定论，不仅造成相关示范性城市的生态与环境绩效难以评估，也会导致其他城市的低碳建设停留于概念规划。实质上，低碳城市是生态城市的一种特殊类型，发展生态城市的最终目标是实现人地系统之间的生态平衡，低碳城市作为应对气候变化的一种区域响应，其发展目标是减少碳排放，实现人地系统之间的碳平衡。在生态文明导向的中国新型城镇化建设时期，低碳城市评价体系的构建是可持续城市理论拓展与深化亟须解决的问题。

中国的低碳城市或低碳生态城市评价引起了国内外学者的广泛关注。已有研究主要从两个方面进行低碳评价：第一类为碳排放导向的低碳评价，以碳排放为核心指标构建评价体系。由于人均碳排放或单位GDP碳排放等指标太综合而难以有效地确定城市或区域是否低碳，因而Price等基于能源终端使用部门（工业、商业、交通、电力、居民）碳排放构建了一个低碳城市或区域评价指标体系。陈飞等认为脱钩指数可从宏观层面评价城市低碳发展水平，建筑、交通、生产等则构成了城市层面的碳排放。林剑艺等认为考虑国家碳减排目标才能有效指导低碳城市发展实践，因而，基于分解分析与情景分析方法提出了一个包括能源利用、产业过程、农业、林业、废物处理的低碳指标体系。然而，因地方减排目标不明、能源统计资料可信度低，以能源或碳排放强度表征的国家节能目标在地方实施不力，某些政策甚至被扭曲。

第二类为综合性低碳评价，主要包括基于集成指标、基准指标、因果联系指标的评价。基于集成指标的评价主要考虑低碳城市评价的全面性与综合性，例如，Su等人从经济发展与社会进步、能源结构与利用效率、生活水平、发展环境等方面构建了低碳发展评价体系。Yu 从资源高效利用、环境友好、经济持续、社会和谐等方面评价低碳生态城市，并给出不同指标在 2015 年与 2020 年的基准值。Zhou 等人研发了城市生态与低碳指标评价工具（ELITE），确立了涵盖 33 个评价基准的指标体系。然而，在低碳转向过程中存在区域差异，通用的标准可能会造成碳减排的区域不公平。基于因果联系的评价在全面性、综合性评价基础上还考虑指标之间的因果联系，驱动力—压力—状态—影响—响应（DPSIR）框架是常用的功能分析方法。如 Zhou 等人基于该框架从技术、制度和认知视角评价低碳响应，以确保低碳响应从根本上减少碳排放及其带来的环境变化与气候影响。

综合来看，基于因果联系的综合评价更有利于从动力学视角揭示社会经济活动、碳排放、自然环境之间相互作用的机制。中国城市社会经济水平各异，城镇化与工业化进程并不同步，碳排放及其驱动因素呈现明显的空间异质性，有必要对全国城市低碳发展格局进行评估，为全面推进低碳城市建设提供基础。本文在综合前人研究成果的基础上构建低碳城市 DPSIR 概念分析框架，借鉴碳排放导向的低碳评价及其他综合评价体系，完善碳排放驱动机制分析、压力测度、状态评估、影响分析、响应评判，结合社会经济统计数据与气象数据，运用层次分析与熵值分析方法，借助 GIS 平台，完成了全国 288 个地级以上城市的低碳评价，以期为全国范围内城市尺度更有针对性的碳减排管理提供指导。

二、分析框架、评价指标与数据处理

（一）DPSIR 分析框架

DPSIR 框架是一个理解社会经济与环境系统之间复杂相互作用的概念模型。该框架在经济合作发展组织提出的 P－S－R 框架和联合国可持续发展委员会提出的 D－P－R 框架上演化而来，最先被欧洲环境署用于环境管理与政策评估，现被广泛用于提供决策支持的研究项目。从系统分析的视角看，社会经济发展等驱动力（D）对环境施加压力（P），结果造成环境状态（S）变化，进而对人类健康与生态系统产生影响（I），随之人类社会作出响应（R），通过适应或治理措施，这些响应（R）直接反馈到驱动力（D）、压力（P）、状态（S）和影响（I）。该框架全面涵盖经济、社会、环境、政策四大要素，结构化了揭示环境问题的指标，展示了人类活动与环境影响的因果联系及反馈机制，因而广泛应用于环境评估与管理。本文通过构建低碳城市评价的 DPSIR 框架（图 1），阐明碳排放的社会经济动力学机制、造成的资源环境压力、导致的环境状态变化、引起的环境影响以及为减少碳排放而做出的社会响应。

具体而言，驱动力（D）指标反映了推动碳排放增长的城市人类活动，已有研究表明社会经济因素、空间形态因素、气候/区位因素是影响碳排放的主要因素。压力（P）指标反映了城市人类经济活动对环境施加的压力，如城市各部门（交通、建筑、工业、土地利用、农业、林业与废弃物）的温室气体排放。状态（S）指标反映了环境的物理、生物与化学状

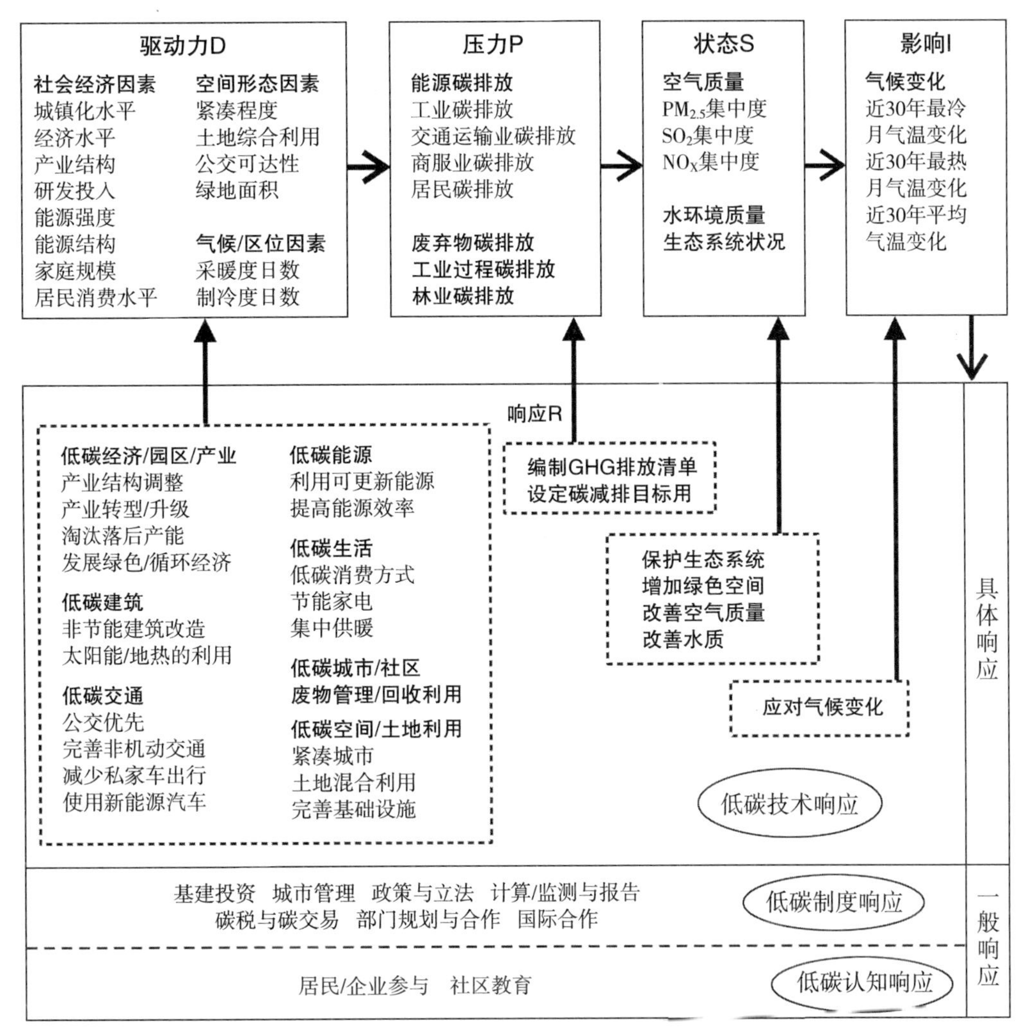

图 1　低碳城市评价的 DPSIR 框架

况，如因温室气体排放引起的空气、水、生态系统质量问题。影响（I）指标反映了因环境状态变化而对生态系统、人类健康与建成区等造成的影响，如气候变化。响应（R）指标反映了环境问题的社会响应，如减少温室气体的政策与战略等。

（二）低碳城市评价的指标体系

以中国 288 个地级及以上城市为研究对象，基于低碳城市评价的 DPSIR 分析框架，遵循科学性、系统性、完整性、有效性、可操作性等原则，构建低碳城市评价的指标体系（表 1）。根据熵值法与德尔菲层次分析法对中国 288 个城市 27 项指标进行处理，城市低碳水平评价的指标权重值见表 1。为综合考虑指标权重赋值时的主观、客观因素，本文的指标权重（w_{ij}）取基于熵值计算的权重（w_{ij1}）与基于德尔菲层次分析法计算的权重（w_{ij2}）的平均值，即 $w_{ij}=1/2\times(w_{ij1}+w_{ij2})$。城市低碳发展水平采用低碳指数（*LCI*）表征，由低碳驱动力指数（*DI*）、低碳压力指数（*PI*）、低碳状态指数（*SI*）、低碳影响指数（*II*）、低碳响应指数（*RI*）构成。低碳驱动力与响应是促进低碳城市发展的重要因素，低碳认知响应、低碳制度响应与低碳技术响应三个响应指标的权重位居前三位，研发投入、人均 GDP、城镇化水平、人口密度的权重紧随其后。表征能源消费碳排放结构的压力指标、表征生态和环境质量的状态指标以及表征气候变化的温度变化率指标权重相对较小。对低碳城市管理而言，驱动力与响应是关注的重点对象。

表 1　低碳城市评价的指标体系及权重

准则层		指标层	作用方向	w_{ij1}	w_{ij2}	w_{ij}
驱动力(0.454)	社会经济因素(0.321)	城镇化水平(%)	+	0.086	0.066	0.076
		人均 GDP(元)	+	0.060	0.098	0.079
		第二产业比重(%)	-	0.017	0.017	0.017
		研发投入比重(%)	+	0.112	0.073	0.092
		万元 GDP 能耗(tce/万元)	-	0.033	0.006	0.020
		煤炭消费比重(%)	-	0.025	0.050	0.037
	空间形态因素(0.102)	建成区人口密度(人/km^2)	+	0.041	0.081	0.061
		居住用地比重(%)	+	0.023	0.014	0.019
		500m 范围内公交覆盖率(%)	+	0.015	0.014	0.014
		绿化率(%)	+	0.007	0.009	0.008
	区位因素(0.031)	采暖度日数	-	0.018	0.011	0.015
		制冷度日数	-	0.018	0.014	0.016
压力(0.069)	能源消费碳排放(0.069)	工业碳排放(万吨)	-	0.008	0.003	0.006
		建筑业碳排放(万吨)	-	0.052	0.004	0.028
		交通运输业碳排放(万吨)	-	0.012	0.001	0.007
		商服业碳排放(万吨)	-	0.033	0.003	0.018
		居民碳排放(万吨)	-	0.020	0.002	0.011
状态(0.053)	大气质量(0.029)	$PM_{2.5}$ 年平均浓度	-	0.010	0.001	0.005
		工业烟尘排放量(万吨)	-	0.016	0.001	0.009
		工业 SO_2 排放量(万吨)	-	0.028	0.002	0.015
	水质量	废水排放量(万吨)	-	0.047	0.002	0.025
影响(0.045)	气候变化(0.045)	近 30 年最冷月气温变化率(%)	-	0.018	0.015	0.016
		近 30 年最热月气温变化率(%)	-	0.018	0.005	0.012
		近 30 年平均气温变化率(%)	-	0.018	0.015	0.017
响应(0.379)		低碳技术响应	+	0.166	0.067	0.116
		低碳制度响应	+	0.063	0.185	0.124
		低碳认知响应	+	0.036	0.240	0.138

（三）数据来源与处理

低碳城市评价中，城镇化水平（市辖区年末总人口/全市年末总人口）、人均 GDP、第二产业比重、研发投入比重、建成区人口密度、居住用地比重、绿化率、工业烟尘与 SO_2 排放量、废水排放量等指标来自于2014年中国城市统计年鉴。500m 范围内公交覆盖率数据来自北京城市实验室共享的数据，PM2.5 平均浓度数据来自中国大气网发布的数据。借鉴已有研究，能源消费碳排放根据估算而得，工业、建筑业、交通运输业、商服业、居民等部门的碳排放计算公式及数据来源见表2。基于城市部门能源估算值计算万元GDP能耗、煤炭消费比重。根据中国气象科学数据共享服务网提供的1982－2012年中国国家824个气象站气温观测资料，经整理、建模、校正后计算得出288个地级以上城市的采暖度日数、制冷度日数、近30年最冷月与最热月气温变化率，以及近30年平均气温变化率。借鉴 Zhou 等人的研究，采用内容分析方法计算低碳技术响应、低碳制度响应、低碳认知响应的分值。

表2　城市部门能源消费碳排放

碳排放部门		计算公式	变量说明	数据来源
居民碳排放 C_{res}	用电碳排放 C_{elec}	$C_{elec}=E_{elec}\times EF_{elec}$	E_{elec} 为城镇居民用电量；EF_{elec} 为电力碳排放系数，根据所致基准电网而定	《中国城市统计年鉴(2014)》；中国区域电网基准线排放因子
	用气碳排放 C_{gas}	$C_{gas}=E_{ng}\times EF_{ng}+E_{lpg}\times EF_{lpg}$	E_{ng}、E_{lpg} 分别为城镇居民消费的天然气、液化气量；EF_{ng}、EF_{lpg} 分别为天然气、液化气的碳排放系数	《中国城市统计年鉴(2014)》
	供暖碳排放 C_{heat}	$C_{heat}=S_{heat}\times N\times EF_{tce}$	S_{heat} 为供暖面积；N 为单位面积供暖耗煤量，EF_{tce} 为标煤碳排放系数	《中国城市建设统计年鉴(2014)》；《严寒和寒冷地区居住建筑节能设计标准(JGJ26－2010)》
	出行碳排放 C_{travel}	$C_{travel}=Q_{bus}\times L_{bus}\times E_{diesel}\times EF_{diesel}+Q_{taxi}\times L_{taxi}\times E_{gasoline}\times EF_{gasoline}+Q_{car}\times E'_{gasoline}\times EF_{gasoline}/Q'_{car}$	Q_{bus}、Q_{taxi}、Q_{car} 分别为城镇公交车、出租车与私家车的数量，Q'_{car} 为城镇所在省的私家车的数量；L_{bus}、L_{taxi} 分别为公交车、出租车的年行驶里程；E_{diesel}、$E_{gasoline}$ 分别为公交车、出租车的百公里油耗；EF_{diesel}、$EF_{gasoline}$ 分别为柴油、汽油的碳排放系数；$E'_{gasoline}$ 为全省城镇居民汽油消费量	《中国城市统计年鉴(2014)》；《中国区域经济统计年鉴(2014)》
交通运输业 C_{trans}		$C_{trans}=\sum(E'_{trans,fuel}\times EF_{fuel})\times Q_{c-car}/Q'_{c-car}$	Q_{c-car}、Q'_{c-car} 分别为城镇及所在省民用车数量；$E'_{trans,fuel}$ 为城镇所在省交通运输业能源消费量，为能源碳排放系数	《中国城市统计年鉴(2014)》；《中国区域经济统计年鉴(2014)》；《中国能源统计年鉴(2014)》
工业碳排放 C_{ins}		$C_{ins}=\sum(E'_{ins,fuel}EF_{fuel})\times V_{ins}/V'_{ins}$	$E'_{ins,fuel}$、$E'_{com,fuel}$、$E'_{cons,fuel}$ 分别为城镇所在省工业、商服业、建筑业能源消费量，V'_{ins}、V'_{com} 分别为城镇所在省工业、商服业增加值；V_{ins}、V_{com} 分别为城镇工业、商服业增加值；S'_{cons}、S_{cons} 分别为城镇及所在省建筑业施工面积	
商服业碳排放 C_{com}		$C_{com}=\sum(E'_{com,fuel}EF_{fuel})\times V_{com}/V'_{com}$		
建筑业碳排放 C_{cons}		$C_{cons}=\sum(E'_{cons,fuel}\times EF_{fuel})\times S_{cons}/S'_{cons}$		

三、中国低碳城市的总体评价与空间格局

（一）中国城市低碳发展水平的总体评价

通过计算中国288个地级及以上城市的低碳指数 LCI，根据自然断裂点法将其分为四级

（图 2a），高碳城市（$LCI<0.3$）、相对高碳城市（$0.3\leqslant LCI\leqslant 0.369$）、相对低碳城市（$0.369\leqslant LCI\leqslant 0.465$）、低碳城市（$LCI>0.465$）。四类城市所占的比重分别是 44%、24%、

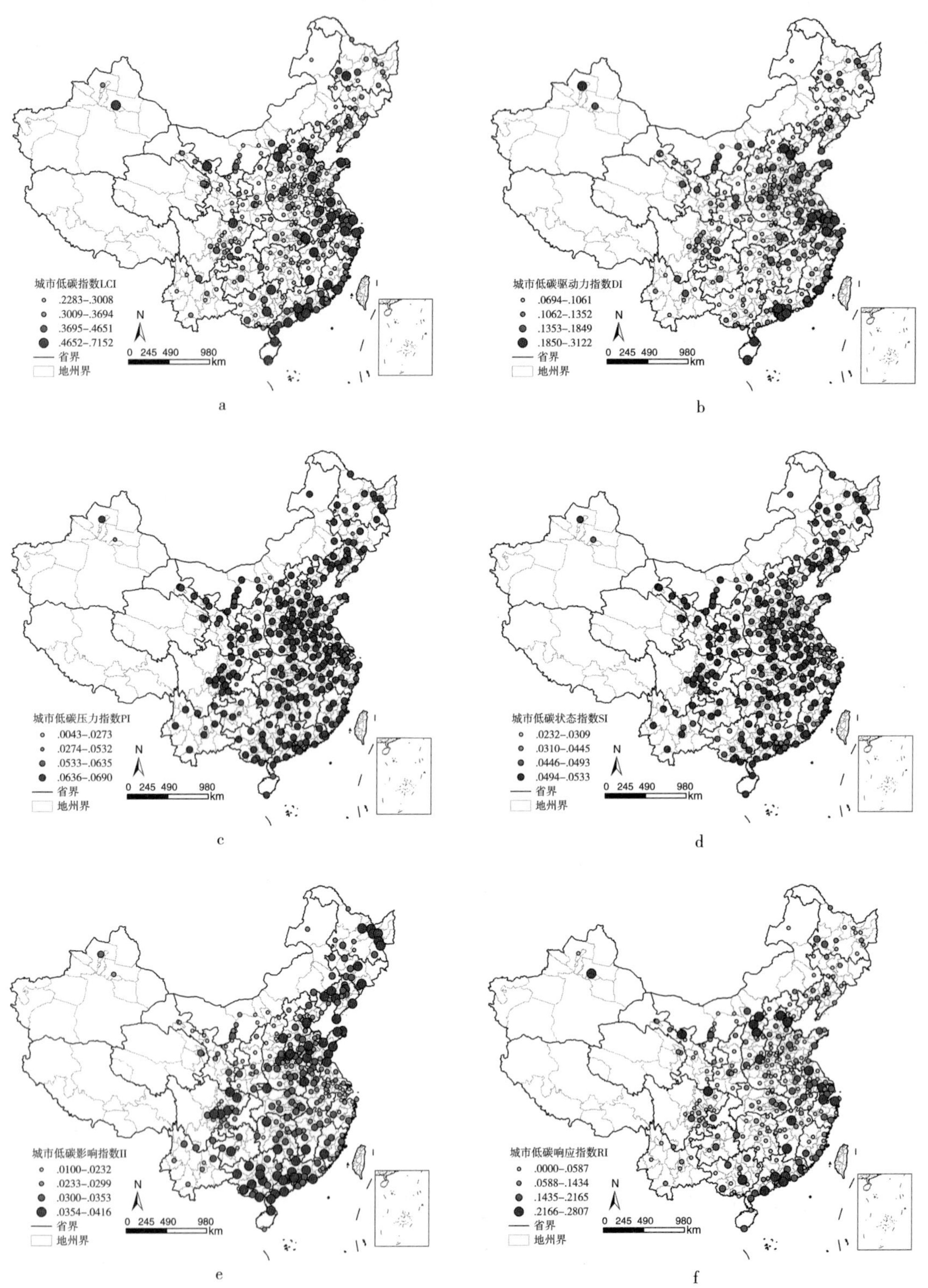

图 2　中国低碳城市空间格局

19%、13%，高碳城市比重较大。城市四个等级的平均低碳指数从低到高依次为0.271、0.331、0.413、0.522，低碳城市平均低碳指数是高碳城市平均低碳指数的1.9倍。288个地级以上城市的平均低碳指数为0.345，处于相对高碳水平。城市低碳指数在各城市间具有一定差距，低碳指数最高的深圳市（0.715）得分为低碳指数最低的中卫市（0.228）得分的3倍多。中国过去30年“唯GDP论”的政绩考核模式在推动城镇化与工业化快速推进的同时，也造成过半城市走上高能耗、高排放之路，且碳减排压力巨大。

中国288个地级及以上城市低碳发展水平的区域差异较大（图3）。东部、中部、西部低碳发展呈“梯度化”分异，低碳城市与高碳城市比重自东向西分别减少与增加。东部地区城市的低碳发展水平最高，低碳城市所占比重为24%，是中部地区的2.4倍、西部地区的4倍。西部地区城市低碳发展的后发优势高于中部地区，相对低碳城市所占比重比中部地区多6%，相对高碳城市比中部少6%。从空间分布看，低碳城市主要集中在东部沿海（图2a），零星分布于西部地区，以胡焕庸线为底边形成倒“V”型的空间格局，“V”型包围的中间区域形成中部低碳发展塌陷区。珠三角、海西、长三角、长江中游城市群以及京津地区的低碳城市构成了“V”型的两翼，这些城市城镇化与工业化水平较高，自身的升级、转型发展需求促使其低碳驱动力与响应力均比较强。河南、湖北、湖南、河北等中部及东部内陆边缘地区省份的城市低碳发展进程滞后，这些城市面对产业转移的诱惑与经济发展的压力，造成低碳驱动力与响应力均比较弱。而乌鲁木齐、金昌、攀枝花、咸阳等西部资源型城市，面临资源枯竭的挑战，主动响应低碳发展，因而低碳发展进程推动较快。

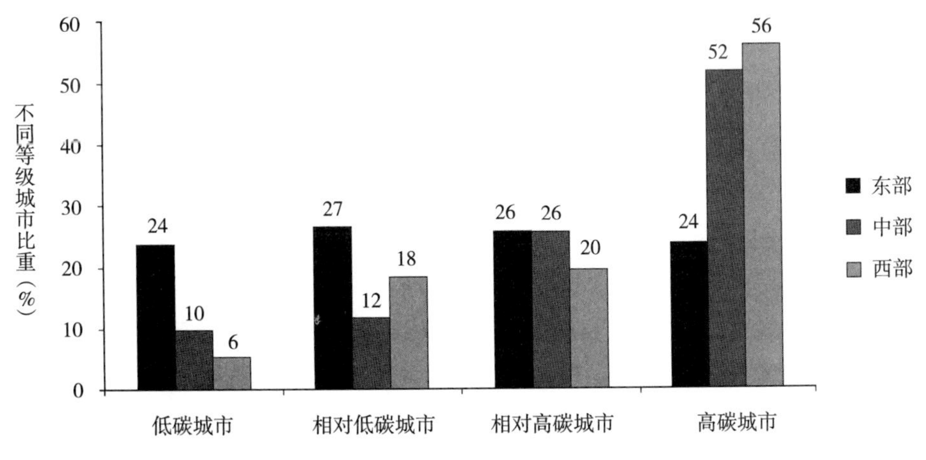

图3 东中西部地区各级低碳城市比重

（二）中国城市低碳发展结构的空间分异

根据自然断裂点法将低碳驱动力指数（*DI*）、低碳压力指数（*PI*）、低碳状态指数（*SI*）、低碳影响指数（*II*）、低碳响应指数（*RI*）分为四个等级（图2b-f）。人地系统中短期社会经济活动较快的变化导致低碳驱动力指数与低碳响应指数整体水平较高、空间分异较大。较慢的资源环境累计变化以及气候要素的长期变化造成低碳压力指数、低碳状态指数、低碳影响指数整体水平较低，三者的权重之和为0.17，远小于低碳驱动力与响应力对低碳发展的影响。低碳驱动力与低碳响应力是决定城市低碳发展水平的重要因素，也是造成低碳城市空间分异的关键所在，因而将重点分析低碳驱动力指数与低碳响应指数的空间分异。

中国288个地级及以上城市的低碳驱动力总体处于相对较低的驱动水平，平均低碳驱动力指数为0.124。低驱动力城市（$DI<0.106$）、相对较低驱动力城市（$0.106\leqslant DI<0.135$）、相对较高驱动力城市（$0.135\leqslant DI\leqslant0.185$）、高驱动力城市（$DI>0.185$）的比重分别为35%、37%、21%、7%，其平均低碳驱动力指数分别为0.093、0.118、0.154、0.221。低碳驱动力最强的深圳市（0.312）得分为低碳驱动力最弱的衡水市（0.069）得分的4倍多。影响城市低碳驱动力的因素中，作用程度较高的四大因素依次为研发投入、人均GDP、城镇化水平、人口密度（表1）。21个高驱动力城市主要分布于珠三角、长三角、海西城市群与京津地区，除无锡、苏州、芜湖的研发投入驱动强度位于首位外，其他城市城镇化的驱动强度位于首位。其中，珠三角的城市人均GDP对低碳发展作用较大，如深圳、东莞、珠海、广州、中山、佛山等城市。海口、杭州、中山、厦门、三亚、上海、北京等城市的清洁能源对低碳发展推动较大，汕头、郑州等城市紧凑型城市格局对低碳发展的影响较强。低驱动力城市广泛分布于中西部地区，万元GDP能耗高、第二产业比重大、公交覆盖率低是限制其低碳发展的重要因素。

中国288个地级及以上城市的低碳响应力总体处于相对较低水平，平均低碳响应指数为0.078。低响应力城市（$RI<0.059$）、相对较低响应力城市（$0.059\leqslant RI<0.143$）、相对较高响应力城市（$0.143\leqslant RI\leqslant0.216$）、高响应力城市（$RI>0.216$）的比重分别为58%、21%、14%、7%，其平均低碳驱动力指数分别为0.022、0.104、0.185、0.251。低碳认知、低碳制度、低碳技术是影响城市低碳响应力三大因素。21个高响应力城市主要分布于珠三角、长三角城市群，京津地区，以及西部资源型城市，且低碳认知、低碳技术的响应力远高于低碳制度的响应力。虽然高响应力城市的低碳认知的总体影响程度均大于低碳技术的影响程度，但排名较前的城市低碳技术响应指数均比较高，如杭州、深圳、广元、淮安等城市。低响应力城市主要分布于中部地区，特别是河南省的部分城市如郑州、新乡、焦作等。

（三）中国低碳城市的纵横对比分析

本文划定的低碳城市（即中国低碳城市）与国家低碳试点城市的低碳指数及排名见表3，其中本文评价得出的38个低碳城市涵盖了17个低碳试点城市。其他国家低碳试点城市中，青岛、镇江、贵阳、重庆、苏州、景德镇、昆明低碳城市指数相对较高，属于相对低碳城市。池州、秦皇岛、南平、延安、呼伦贝尔低碳指数比较低，属于高碳城市。低碳城市在全国大范围推广暂有难度，低碳试点城市率先开展社会经济与空间的低碳发展，具有一定现实意义。低碳试点城市涵盖现有低碳城市评价体系下低碳、相对低碳与高碳三种类别的城市，试点城市的空间覆盖度与低碳发展等级覆盖度比较全面。现有评价体系下的低碳城市集聚性较强，30个省（市）中河北省、河南省、湖南省、辽宁省、吉林省等12个省份没有低碳城市，而仅广东一省就有7个低碳城市。

表3　中国低碳城市与低碳试点城市低碳指数及排名

类型	城市	LCI	排名	城市	LCI	排名	城市	LCI	排名
中国低碳城市与国家低碳试点	深圳市	0.715	1	天津市	0.559	10	赣州市	0.496	21
	北京市	0.618	2	乌鲁木齐市	0.554	11	温州市	0.495	22
	杭州市	0.59	3	厦门市	0.544	12	桂林市	0.475	34
	广州市	0.574	6	广元市	0.542	13	上海市	0.472	36
	南昌市	0.567	7	晋城市	0.533	14	金昌市	0.472	37
	淮安市	0.565	8	宁波市	0.515	17			
其他中国低碳城市	无锡市	0.576	4	蚌埠市	0.496	20	贵港市	0.486	29
	三亚市	0.576	5	龙岩市	0.493	23	湛江市	0.484	30
	惠州市	0.563	9	珠海市	0.493	24	揭阳市	0.483	31
	铜陵市	0.525	15	海口市	0.488	25	济南市	0.482	32
	鄂州市	0.516	16	大庆市	0.488	26	中山市	0.478	33
	南京市	0.512	18	烟台市	0.488	27	大同市	0.474	35
	阳江市	0.503	19	朔州市	0.487	28	黄石市	0.47	38
其他低碳试点城市	青岛市	0.465	39	昆明市	0.369	94	池州市	0.296	168
	镇江市	0.461	41	石家庄市	0.367	95	秦皇岛市	0.294	174
	贵阳市	0.428	57	保定市	0.354	103	南平市	0.291	178
	重庆市	0.407	66	吉林市	0.346	115	延安市	0.29	180
	苏州市	0.407	68	武汉市	0.345	117	呼伦贝尔市	0.258	259
	景德镇市	0.389	77	遵义市	0.335	121			

四种不同低碳水平的城市以及全国288个地级及以上城市的低碳相关性分析见表4。在5%的显著性水平下，与全国及另外三种低碳水平的城市相比，低碳城市的社会经济驱动力与低碳发展正相关性较强，碳排放压力与低碳发展负相关性最强。可以说，低碳城市的社会经济发展对低碳发展驱动力较强，碳排放压力对低碳发展的影响最小。与相对低碳城市、相对高碳城市、高碳城市相比，低碳城市的环境状况与低碳发展呈负相关，说明碳排放造成的环境压力对低碳城市的低碳水平影响较小。全面对比其他类型城市的低碳发展水平，可以看出，相对低碳城市、相对高碳城市社会经济的驱动力与低碳发展水平相关性较弱，这在一定程度上表明这两类城市的社会经济结构有待进一步调整与优化。另外，相对高碳城市的碳排放压力与低碳发展水平相关性较弱，说明该类城市的碳减排压力较大，减排潜力有待提升。高碳城市与其他城市相比，长期气候变化下的温度变化对低碳发展影响较大，说明该类城市供暖与制冷效率有待进一步提升。

表 4　不同类别城市的低碳相关性系数

LCI	DI	PI	SI	II	RI
低碳城市	0. 601	-0. 392	-0. 111	-0. 063	0. 570
相对低碳城市	0. 035	-0. 114	0. 060	-0. 182	0. 680
相对高碳城市	-0. 016	-0. 013	0. 049	-0. 174	0. 689
高碳城市	0. 629	-0. 159	0. 071	0. 165	0. 445

四、结论

本文构建了低碳城市评价的动力学分析框架（DPSIR 框架），结合社会经济统计数据、气象数据、自下而上的碳排放估算数据，全面评价了全国 288 个地级以上城市的低碳发展水平，分析了各城市低碳发展的总体格局与结构分异，评估了现有低碳试点城市的低碳绩效，阐释了不同低碳等级下城市低碳发展的影响因素。研究结果表明：

（1）低碳城市评价的 DPSIR 分析框架有助于全面分析人地系统相互作用的动力学机制。DPSIR 框架将人类社会经济要素与自然要素综合在一起进行研究，发挥了地理学综合性优势，能从多方面进行交叉研究。整合了短期社会经济活动、长期气候变化与资源环境变化的低碳城市评价体系，更能从根本上探寻低碳发展的驱动因素，阐释低碳城市的内涵。

（2）中国 288 个地级及以上城市总体处于相对高碳水平，以胡焕庸线为底边形成的倒“V”型结构塑造了低碳城市的基本空间格局。中国城市低碳发展水平存在“级差化”分异特征，不同等级城市的低碳发展水平表征了不同的社会经济发展模式。以胡焕庸线为底边的倒“V”型低碳格局从另一侧面证实了“中部塌陷”的存在，在新的经济发展常态与新的国家发展战略格局下，中部地区，特别是河南、湖北、湖南等省，若不抓住生态文明转向中低碳发展的机遇，“中部崛起”必将延期。而积极地进行社会经济结构调整与空间优化、积极地进行低碳响应，则可能打破胡焕庸线对社会经济要素的锁定作用，使低碳城市在东中西部同步进行。

（3）低碳驱动力与低碳响应力决定了城市低碳发展水平及空间分异。在低碳驱动力与低碳响应力的共同作用下，高驱动力城市与高响应度城市的“集聚性”空间分异格局造成低碳城市呈现“集聚性”与“梯度化”的分布态势。低碳城市主要集中于东部沿海城市群地带，低碳城市比重自东向西依次减少。高低碳驱动力城市主要有研发驱动型、基于城镇化的社会经济发展驱动型、基于城镇化的清洁能源发展驱动型、基于城镇化的紧凑城市发展驱动型。低碳技术与低碳认知响应力远高于低碳制度响应力对城市低碳发展的作用。

（4）中国的低碳试点城市具有多等级性，不同低碳等级城市的低碳水平影响因素各异。低碳试点城市涵盖低碳、相对低碳、高碳三种等级的城市，高碳水平下的低碳试点城市转型尤为重要。不同等级城市的低碳发展水平在社会经济驱动力、碳排放压力、生态环境状况、长期温度变化、低碳城市响应力的作用下呈现结构分异，较高的社会经济驱动力、较低的碳排放压力、相对稳定的生态环境变化与较强的低碳城市响应力促进低碳城市的发展。

（5）不同低碳等级的城市应根据 DPSIR 框架提供的低碳发展结构化清单，结合地方特性，选择因地制宜的低碳发展路径。低碳驱动力与低碳响应力是造成城市低碳发展水平变化的快变量，是城市低碳发展短期规划应重点关注的内容。城镇化推进过程中的研发投入、社会经济发展、清洁能源利用、空间结构优化调整是低碳驱动力与响应力作用的重点方向。

（作者：秦耀辰，教授，博士生导师，河南大学环境与规划学院院长，黄河中下游数字地理技术教育部重点实验室主任；张丽君，博士，河南大学低碳发展模拟研究中心副教授）

参考文献

[1] Yu L. *Low carbon eco-city: New approach for Chinese urbanisation* [J]. Habitat International, 2014, 44 (10): 102-110.

[2] De Jong M, Joss S, Schraven D, et al. *Sustainable - smart - resilient - low carbon - eco - knowledge cities; making sense of a multitude of concepts promoting sustainable urbanization* [J]. Journal of Cleaner Production, 2015, 109 (12): 25-38.

[3] Price L, Zhou N, Fridley D, Ohshita S, Lu H, Zheng N. *Development of a low-carbon indicator system for China* [J]. Habitat International, 2013, 37 (1): 4-21.

[4] Chen F, Zhu D. *Theoretical research on low-carbon city and empirical study of Shanghai* [J]. Habitat International, 2013, 37 (1): 33-42.

[5] Lin J, Jacoby J, Cui S, et al. *A model for developing a target integrated low carbon city indicator system: The case of Xiamen, China* [J]. Ecological Indicators, 2014, 40 (5): 51-57.

[6] Lo K. *China's low-carbon city initiatives: the implementation gap and the limits of the target responsibility system* [J]. Habitat International, 2014, 42 (4): 236-244.

[7] Su M, Li R, Lu W, et al. *Evaluation of a low-carbon city: method and application* [J]. Entropy, 2013, 15 (4): 1171-1185.

[8] Zhou N, He G, Williams C, et al. *ELITE cities: A low-carbon eco-city evaluation tool for China* [J]. Ecological Indicators, 2015, 48 (1): 448-456.

[9] Balta-Ozkan N, Watson T, Mocca E. *Spatially uneven development and low carbon transitions: Insights from urban and regional planning* [J]. Energy Policy, 2015, 85 (10): 500-510.

[10] Zhou G, Singh J, Wu J, et al. *Evaluating low-carbon city initiatives from the DPSIR framework perspective* [J]. Habitat International, 2015, 50 (12): 289-299.

[11] OECD. *OECD core set of indicators for environmental performance reviews* [R]. 1994, In: OECD Environment Monographs No. 83. OECD, Paris, <http://www.oecd.org/env/indicators-modelling-outlooks/31558547.pdf>.

[12] EEA Report. *Environmental Indicators: Typology and Overview. 1999* [R]. <http://reports.eea.europa.eu/TEC25/en/tech_25_text.pdf>.

[13] Tscherning K, Helming K, Krippner B, et al. *Does research applying the DPSIR framework support decision making?* [J]. Land Use Policy, 2012, 29 (1): 102-110.

[14] Ness B, Anderberg S, Olsson L. *Structuring problems in sustainability science: The multi-level DPSIR framework*

[J] . Geoforum, 2010, 41 (3): 479-488.

[15] Lewison R L, Rudd M A, Al-Hayek W, et al. *How the DPSIR framework can be used for structuring problems and facilitating empirical research in coastal systems* [J] . Environmental Science & Policy, 2016, 56 (2): 110-119.

[16] Yang L, Li Y. *Low-carbon city in China* [J] . Sustainable Cities and Society, 2013, 9 (12): 62-66.

[17] Zhang J, Xie Y, Luan B, et al. *Urban macro-level impact factors on Direct CO_2 Emissions of urban residents in China* [J] . Energy and Buildings, 2015, 107 (11): 131-143.

[18] Ko Y. *Urban form and residential energy use a review of design principles and research findings* [J] . Journal of planning literature, 2013, 28 (4): 327-351.

[19] 张金萍, 闫卫阳, 孙玮, 等. 中国低碳发展的类型及空间分异 [J] . 资源科学, 2014, 36 (12): 2491-2499.

[20] 陈明星, 陆大道, 张华. 中国城市化水平的综合测度及其动力因子分析 [J] . 地理学报, 2009, 64 (4): 387-398.

[21] 徐建华. 计量地理学 [M] . 北京: 高等教育出版社, 2006.

[22] 中国大气网. 2015 年空气质量排行榜 [EB/OL] . http: //www. chndaqi. com. 2016-01-15.

[23] Long Y, Li M Y, Liu X J. *Bus coverage of Chinese cities* [DB/OL] . Ranking at Beijing City Lab, http: // www. beijingcity lab. com. 2014.

[24] Fridley D, Zheng N, Qin Y. *Inventoryof China's energy-related CO2 emissions in* 2008 [R] . Berkeley, CA: Lawrence Berkeley National Laboratory (LBNL-4600E) . http: //china. lbl. gov/sites/china. lbl. gov/files/ China_ Emissions_ Inventory_ 2008. pdf.

[25] 宁晓菊, 张丽君, 杨群涛, 等. 1951 年以来中国无霜期的变化趋势 [J] . 地理学报, 2015, 70 (11): 1811-1822.

我国循环城市的发展途径与建议

一、循环城市理念及其发展现状

（一）国际背景

今天，全球50%以上的人口已经居住在城市。预测到2030年，近60%的世界人口（约50亿人）将聚居在城镇地区。作为商业、文化、科技、生产生活、社会发展的枢纽，城市在带给人们空前丰富的物质和精神财富的同时，也遇到了前所未有的挑战。快速的城市化导致人口膨胀、交通拥挤、环境污染、资源紧缺、贫富差距、文化冲突等日益严峻的城市问题。可持续的城市繁荣与发展已成为21世纪全球社会面临的最紧迫挑战。

因此，国际社会越来越多地致力于倡导新型城市化，并赋予城市在这一转型过程中的引领作用。2015年9月联合国大会批准了17个可持续发展目标（SDGs）。这是政府间协议设置的一系列发展目标之一，替代2015年年底到期的千年发展目标（MDGs）。新的可持续发展目标不仅涉及最贫穷国家，还包括更广泛更全面的目标群，涵盖了更多样化的议题。这17个SDGs目标中的第11个，也被称为城市SDG，特别强调了“使城市和人类居住区具有包容性，安全，自我恢复能力，可持续”。此外，联合国全球峰会——第三届人类居住大会将于2016年10月在厄瓜多尔首都基多（Quito）举行。在这次会议上，近200个联合国成员国将共聚一堂，共同发布一个“新城市议程”。该议程将提供协议性不具约束力的准则和策略，为未来20年全球城市居住区的发展提供指导。

全球许多城市以前所未有的规模消耗乃至浪费着各种资源，并正在遭受着水污染、空气污染等诸多严峻的环境威胁，显然，维持现在的发展状态是不行的。无论是新城市的规划管理还是旧城区的更新改造，其现有发展模式都需要进行深刻的转变。城市可持续发展目标的批准，以及即将到来的全球新城市议程将毫无疑问地为世界各地的城市带来广泛的发展机会。这意味着要探讨更为广泛的城市发展模式。其中，建设循环再生型城市（Regenerative City）是在经济、社会和技术上最具可操作性的发展模式。这就要求不局限于维持城市的资源环境系统，更强调促进城市生态系统的循环再生，真正满足城市发展和环境改善同步的要求。

（二）循环城市的基本理念与目标要求

循环城市可定义为：能够循环利用资源并持续地恢复和改善与其所依赖的生态系统之间的关系的城市。具体来说，循环城市理念就是要重建城市与自然之间的循环与互动关系。循环城市发展理念使城市从线性的“消耗资源—破坏生态”的系统转型为与周围生态环境互惠共生的系统。传统的可持续理念要求尽可能减少对生态环境的破坏，而循环再生理念则追求促进生态环境的良性循环发展。循环城市的发展具有以下三种基本的循环特点：

一是资源循环利用。主要包括：①循环化。向垃圾要资源，要求大力提升垃圾回收、处理和再利用率。②服务化。要求注重资源的实用性，将资源配置在最能发挥其功效的地方，而不是低效或闲置于拥有者手中，让资源功能性超越所有权发挥作用。③高效化。减少资源消耗，要求大力提高资源利用效率，从源头上减少消耗，节约资源使用量。

二是自然资产和生态系统的循环再生。主要包括：①城市是生态系统循环再生的中心，激励城市扮演资源—经济—社会—环境系统循环发展的引领者和推动者。②城市是生产系统的枢纽，将城市从单纯的自然资源消费者转变为同时也是自然资源生产者。③分散化管理和政策支持，支持基层组织或个人积极参与循环发展。

三是城市空间再利用。主要包括：①紧凑结构。更新升级现有的布局而不是大规模扩张。②以人为本。建设包容性、安全性、韧性和可持续性的城市社区。③鼓励绿色建筑和绿化区域的规划建设。

循环再生愿景的核心在于建立和促进城市与其周边区域之间互惠互利的共生关系。通过将废弃物资源化利用，循环城市可以不断提高自身健康状态，进而提升其所依赖的生态系统的健康状况。体现在将营养物质返回到土壤中，植树造林，农作物轮作耕种，补充流域水资源，增加城市生物多样性和在市内大力发展生态型基础设施，等等。这些措施有助于在本地、区域以及全球范围内增强生态系统的可再生能力。

循环城市发展就是希望模仿自然界的循环代谢系统，闭合城市资源循环系统。比如，循环城市将处理后的水重新引入到自然水系统中，提高对当地（周边）粮食的需求比例，处理并提取城市污水和废弃物中的肥料物质应用于周边农田，极大地降低对石油产品的依赖，并加大可再生能源的使用。同时，积极探索回收再利用废弃的资源和物质，使循环城市成为一个生产中心，促进城市与其周边区域之间的和谐互惠发展。

二、循环城市理念符合中国新型城镇化建设要求

（一）中国新型城镇化要解决的问题

经济增长和快速城镇化虽然让中国在减贫和提高人们生活水平方面受益匪浅，同时中国也正遭受由此带来的环境压力，如空气污染和水污染都对人们生活造成不利影响，并危害经济的长期繁荣稳定。当前，我国城镇化发展进程中面临的问题有：人口城镇化不彻底，农民

工不能市民化，城乡二元社会结构矛盾加剧；土地城镇化快于人口城镇化，城镇建设占用土地过多，对土地、能源和生态环境的承载能力提出严峻挑战；城镇体系不合理，大城市和一线城市人口过于集中，中小城市发展机会不均等；服务业发展滞后，公共服务供给严重不足。

上述问题，只有通过推进新型城镇化，加快转变城镇化发展方式，全面提高城镇化的发展质量，才能逐步解决。

（二）新型城镇化背景下循环城市的作用

中国新型城镇化的主要目标是为了提高城镇化的质量，强调以人的城镇化为核心，有序推进农业人口市民化；以综合承载力为支撑，提升城市可持续发展水平；推动大中小城市和小城镇协调发展。具体来说，循环城市在新型城镇化以下一些方面可发挥积极的作用：

（1）积极推进农业转移人口市民化和城乡一体化

循环城市强调城市与周边郊区在生产生活多方面紧密联系，通过增加从周边区域获取资源来满足发展需求，将带动城郊农业生产能力以及粮食供应能力的提升，相应地促进水资源和肥料利用效率的提高，并可降低能源需求。通过加强这种城市—周边的紧密联系，城乡互动更加频繁，互惠互利，有利于城乡统筹，实现城乡经济一体化发展。循环城市鼓励积极发展中小城市和小城镇，以吸纳农业人口，为此建议放宽中小城镇的落户条件。循环城市的发展不是要把农村都变成城市，更不是追求城乡一体化，而是按照城乡各自发展规律，走城乡差别化互补性的协调发展道路。

（2）完善土地利用机制，创新投融资机制

循环城市要求城市空间集约型开发，以提升资源利用效率、改善交通通达性和创造便利的人员交流空间，这种集约型开发有利于遏制城市扩张的冲动。同时，循环城市极力提倡可再生能源利用、智能科技创新和投融资创新。循环城市建设所激励的创新型土地、财政、投融资等政策，充分释放新型城镇化蕴藏的巨大内需潜力，为经济持续健康发展提供持久强劲的动力。

（3）加快培育中小城市和特色小城镇，辐射带动新农村建设

循环城市强调大中小城镇的互补性协调发展，比如城市中心发展高科技和服务业，郊区开发利用新能源，农村发展新型农业等。循环城市的区域性差别化发展导向引导人口均匀有序分布，合理优化城市体系和格局，实现以大带小，以小促大，把大中城市和小城镇连接起来共同发展。

（4）全面提升城市多功能性，尤其是服务功能

循环城市具有生活、生产、休闲、服务等多方面的功能。在城市及郊区开发新能源，如屋顶太阳能和风电场建设，规划城市立体农业，建设雨水公园，设计海绵城市铺装透水性地面等，使城市自身成为能源、粮食、水资源的生产者，而不仅仅是消费者。同时，这些新型设计设施和空间还具有休闲娱乐功能，为市民提供休憩、健身以及交流互动场所。循环城市所强调的加强垃圾处理、回收和再生利用体系也有利于建设和维护清洁健康的城市环境。在

循环城市整理规划下，各种生产生活设施配套建设，合力提升城市公共服务水平，包括医疗、教育、体育、公园绿地、消防防灾等，优化城镇功能，改善人居环境和完善公共服务。

(5) 健全新型城镇化工作推进机制

循环城市理念旨在将城市多部门多产业联合在一个资源循环利用的大系统中，因此，它非常强调协调不同行政级别之间以及城市不同部门之间的工作。过去的城镇化，除了创新不够、绿色不够、共享不够，就是协调不够。除了创新发展之外，循环城市提倡的多层级协调和多部门协调对于新型城镇化而言具有极强的针对性。

新型城镇化的核心在于不以牺牲农业和粮食、生态和环境为代价，着眼农民，涵盖农村，实现城乡基础设施一体化和公共服务均等化，促进经济社会发展，实现共同富裕。新型城镇化的“新”就是要由过去片面注重追求城市规模扩大、空间扩张，改变为以提升城市的文化、公共服务等内涵为中心，真正使我们的城镇成为具有较高品质的适宜人居之所。循环城市以城乡互动、产城一体、节约集约、生态宜居、和谐发展为基本特征，高度契合新型城镇化发展要求。

(三) 新型城镇化建设与循环城市的结合——海绵城市

循环城市是能够对其所依赖的生态系统产生积极影响的城市。但循环城市在现实中应该是什么样的？比如在水资源保护方面，如何做到既能降低水耗又能循环利用和保护水资源？习近平总书记针对中国城镇化发展，提出了建设自然积存、自然渗透、自然净化的“海绵城市”。为此，近两年来，国务院、财政部、住房城乡建设部、水利部多次发文，明确海绵城市建设工作目标和基本原则，成为推进我国新型城镇化建设的一个行动纲领。

从概念上来说，海绵城市表示一类具有高渗水性的城市，能像海绵一样把雨水吸收并经过土壤层过滤存储于地下水中。它不同于那种由大面积不透水地面组成的城市系统。海绵城市补充了城市地区及其周边地下水资源并可供抽取利用。这些地下水更容易净化处理从而作为城市供水来源。

海绵城市建设应按照“生态为本、自然循环；规划引领、统筹推进；政府引导，社会参与”的原则，其建设方法为是从传统“快排”模式转化为“渗、滞、蓄、净、用、排”等工程技术措施。在具体规划建设中，海绵城市必须具有丰富的可渗水区域，为此要求：

一是在城市街区之间有连片开放式绿地，互连互通的水道、沟渠和池塘等，可以自然地蓄留和过滤雨水以及改善城市生态系统，增加生物多样性，并同时创造文化和娱乐空间。

二是绿色屋顶，在雨水被收集或排放到地下之前可以蓄留并净化一部分。

三是设计建造多孔隙地面，包括建设生物洼地和生物滞留系统，蓄留地表雨水并进一步渗入到地下水中；公路和人行道也采用多孔隙铺路材料，在方便安全驾驶和舒适步行的同时让水能顺利下渗；排水系统应方便水的缓慢渗透，或能直接将雨水导入到绿地或水域以便自然下渗。

四是节约用水和循环利用，包括推广社区规模的中水循环利用系统，通过阶梯水价政策激励用户节约用水，开展节约用水活动增强节约意识，引进或改进智能供水监控系统以及时查找漏水或低效用水的地方。

据此，海绵城市建设可以在城市新区、各类园区、成片开发区全面推进。在老城区可以结合棚户区与危房改造区和老旧小区有机更新等，统一规划，综合解决防洪安全、雨水收集利用、黑臭水体治理等问题。同时，海绵城市建设还应加强海绵型建筑与小区、海绵型道路与广场、海绵型公园与绿地、绿色蓄排与净化利用设施等建设，加强自然水系保护与生态修复，切实保护良好水体和饮用水源。

在推进海绵城市建设进程中，应鼓励社会资本参与投资建设和运营管理，鼓励有实力的科研设计单位、施工企业、制造企业与金融资本相组合，统筹组织实施海绵城市建设相关项目。

三、循环城市发展的路径

世界各地的许多案例研究表明，循环再生城市发展有各种各样的好处，例如，能闭合其资源循环系统并主要从邻近区域获取发展资源；可为当地创造社会、经济和环境等多方面的价值等。具体而言，循环城市建设可从以下三个方面进行试点。

（一）资源再生

循环城市发展希望模仿自然界中的循环代谢系统。这就需要发展模式上的转变，从旧的线性代谢（城市系统独立于资源循环系统）转变为新的循环代谢。这也意味着要闭合城市资源循环系统，发掘城市废弃物的价值并投入到本地其他部门的再生产中。比如，城市消耗的全部能源都需要通过自然过程循环再生。因此，只有可再生能源才是循环城市唯一可行的能源来源。作为向可更新能源转型的一种适应性措施，发展分布式可更新能源技术将实现在城市和周边区域能源生产企业的分散化布局，并可大大减少能源供应风险。此外，相比常规发电而言，大多数可更新能源的生产需要消耗更少的冷却用水。

类似地，城市发展所用过的所有原材料都不需要被丢到垃圾填埋场，而是通过回收、升级、再利用或者投入到其他行业/部门的生产中，从而使这些原材料保留在资源利用的循环系统之中。

通过大力开发可再生能源和推动废弃物回收再利用，可作为开展循环城市建设的成功试点，并将带动其他行业和部门的循环式发展。

（二）生态循环

受损生态系统的恢复、自然资产的保护和城市资源自给能力的提升是循环城市的基本特征。因此，循环城市不仅是消费者，而且还积极参与生产所需资源，并促进它所依赖的自然生态系统的恢复。其主要作用为：

一是城市的粮食供应可以由都市农业（包括立体农业）补充。城市对本地资源需求的增加将带动城郊农业生产能力以及粮食供应能力的提升，相应地促进水资源和肥料利用效率的提高，并通过减少粮食储存和包装而降低能源需求。增加对都市农业和近郊农业的投入将显著提高城市粮食自给率。

二是保护河流、湿地等城市水生态系统。水资源可以通过区域性雨水收集存储或通过大量城市绿地设施促进雨水下渗到地下水中以便存储利用。

三是要形成水资源的循环利用。城市需要一个多级联动的水资源利用体系，回收和再利用废水，并从中提取有价值的营养物质，再将处理过的水排放到河流和海洋。从废水中提取的营养物质回填到土壤中有利于维持土壤肥力。加拿大的卡尔加里市就是一个成功的例子。卡尔加里市的一个市政项目受到省级层面政策的支持，将城市污水中的有机物质转变为有机肥料并供应给郊区农业生产。

四是通过人工植树造林提供木材等原材料，不仅可以保证木材的持续供应，同时也产生生态效益。增加的林地可以保持表层土壤的整体性，并可改善土壤肥力，防止水土流失。森林同时还可吸收二氧化碳以增加土壤固碳能力，从而增加大量碳汇。

五是大量绿色基础设施，如屋顶花园、园林建筑，有益于减少污染物，固定二氧化碳，调蓄水量，净化地下水源和缓解洪涝灾害，等等。

循环城市由于可增加从周边区域获取资源来满足发展需求，因而可减少从区外及世界各地的资源进口，并减少资源运输需求从而降低交通领域的能源消耗。此外，城市生态系统自身生产能力的循环更新会引导城市与其周边区域乃至城乡之间，建立新型更紧密的互动关系。

（三）空间优化

城市空间的再利用也是建设循环城市的路径之一。相比较于大量扩充新建设用地而言，城市化进程的重点更应放在改造现有的城市结构和更新升级当前的布局，以提升城市发展密度。增加密度可带来多方面有好处，如高效利用能源、资源、物质、基础设施和交通工具。同时，循环城市还强调要让城市以人为中心，增加交流便利性、交通通达性、社会包容性以积极提升城市及其周边区域的自然生态系统功能。在优先考虑城市改造更新项目的同时，也要保护好历史文化古迹并赋予新的价值。城市生态环境系统建设也是空间优化的主要方面之一。比如要确保城市有丰富的绿地和植被，以有利于减少短波辐射、冷却环境、创造更舒适的城市微气候；改善城市生态，促进退化土地的植被再生以及生物修复项目也应受到优先考虑，这些项目不仅对环境有益，同时还能增加城市的宜居性和审美价值。在城市空间规划的大背景下，绿地不能只向市外扩张，也应该向市内发展。由于市内空间有限，可考虑建设绿色廊道而不是绿色片区。廊道规划可以像血脉一样连通城市现有的结构。

此外，循环城市的发展还能促进本地区社会经济的整体发展，为本地创造更多的就业机会，增加居民的收入和促进消费。因而，这种循环模式不仅维护了当地税收水平，从而使经济发展的财富在当地循环积累，而且由于分布式资源供应方式可促进城市治理的多方参与，也有利于城市社会保持均衡发展。

与此同时，循环再生的城市发展对企业也是极具吸引力的。一个具有长期活力的、低风险的、更能承受外部冲击的城市能够为企业提供良好的经营环境，使企业保持长期繁荣。一个清晰的循环发展政策框架也更能创造出投资者所喜爱的那种稳定的投资环境。

四、中国循环城市发展的政策建议

虽然循环城市的理论与实践均已取得了蓬勃发展，但迄今为止，全球尚未有一个公认的循环城市，甚至对于循环城市也没有一个完整而清晰的概念。纵观国内城市编制的循环城市建设规划，其所依据的思维观念、基本原理和采用的模型方法多有缺失和弊端，此中更不乏生态环境规划或社会经济规划的翻版。因此，完善循环城市的概念内涵，探究规划编制的基本理论和适宜的模型方法体系，乃是当前循环城市建设规划中亟待解决的关键问题。

（一）设立愿景目标，并加强政策引导

尽管循环城市发展存在多种好处，但在执行实践中仍存在障碍。克服这些困难需要强有力的领导和政治勇气。阻碍改革的最大因素是人们无法勾勒出一个不同于现状的未来，同时人们也缺乏对这种未来必定会实现的信心。这一障碍表现为缺乏强烈意愿以及决策中的短视行为。

从仅有的循环城市探索案例中，我们已经可以感受到一个鼓舞人心的愿景和强有力的领导在引领着城市发展走上循环再生的道路。比如，旧金山市前市长积极参与制订全市100%可再生能源发电的目标和计划，德国法兰克福也以100%可再生能源为发展目标。类似的这些城市的市长们设想了一个完全不同的更优于现状的未来，并正采取一系列措施付诸实践。未来设想的良好生活环境就是我们努力的目标，也是指导行动的纲领。具体到一个城市，第一步就是要设立定性或定量的目标。设定目标能够显示并传达政治意愿、政治承诺、领导能力和远见。目标的设定直接为行动提供了动力，将能够促进变革。同时，设定目标还可激励更多的参与者参加进来，因为明确而直接的政策导向让人感觉到投资的安全性，更能吸引投资者。

为确保设定的目标落实到位，必须有相应的发展路线图、分阶段发展策略及阶段性评估指标作为保障，使得总目标的设定更加行之有效。

可持续发展目标和联合国第三届人类居住大会要求城市参与并承担更大的责任。中国应积极响应这一号召，率先推动转型发展。更为重要的是，我们不能再被动地等待来自国际同行与国家立法方面的推动，而应在国际规则的起草工作中积极发挥作用，并在国际舞台上彰显自己的重要性。尽管各国政府是制定总体政策框架的关键，但城市和地方政府才是真正要落实具体解决方案的主体。

（二）鼓励城市积极创新

目前城市工作的重心仍然是经济发展，缺乏催生城市生态环保创新的有效机制。生态环境建设融资难的根源也类似——并不是缺资本，而是难以吸引资本。要解决目前这些挑战，

必须有创新的政策、技术手段和解决方案。而要催生这种创新，必须采取有力的激励机制——让生态环保创新能够有利可图。为此要求：

一是建立政府官员评估的新机制和新标准。这些机制包括新的官员奖惩措施，比如摒弃“经济增长作为政府绩效评估的唯一标准”，建立“终身问责制”。一个正式的评估体系的建立不仅能够评估地方官员在各自管辖范围内的环境绩效，并可能成为他们优先推动环境表现的动力。这也将有助于明确责任问题和建立问责制。另外，应该建立面向过程的考核指标，而不仅仅是以结果为导向的考核指标。考虑到环境保育的积极影响主要在于长期效应，面向过程的考核指标将允许既评估政府官员的短期工作成果，又考虑其工作对长期可持续发展的有效性。

二是加强能力建设和体制创新。虽然中国一直在努力提高政府工作人员的各项能力，但快速变化的环境不断给政府工作提出新的要求和挑战，需要政府官员不断提高技能，以解决中国城市化中的各种挑战。投资于公共行政工作人员的能力建设可以保证业务主管人员具有合适的技能和工具来应对当前的新挑战。

三是建立跨部门协调机构。大部分的创新和创造性的想法来自于一个可以自由思考和跨界合作的环境。构建部门之间的伙伴关系以及采用更综合的办法来解决问题将是至关重要的。为此，我们建议创建正式的、制度化的平台以促进和协调跨部门的合作。

四是引进新的和替代性的融资机制，以便在局部范围内调动金融资源。包括公私合作伙伴关系（PPP）、私人主动融资（PFI）和民间集资。同时建议改进公共资金分配方法（例如参与式预算方案）。适当条件下，也可以在市域范围内采用创新性和地方性的税收制度，如碳税、垃圾税或污染税以及其他财政或税收为基础的机制，以保证相对于资源密集型的项目来说污染较少的项目能够更加受到青睐。从长远看，应建立稳定的、长期的国家和区域政策框架支持可持续经济发展，鼓励私人投资者投资于受政府扶持的技术和行业中。

五是大力支持绿色科技研发，其中围绕智能和高科技解决方案而发展的城市经济将是循环城市的重要组成部分。一些急需发展和扩张的重要技术领域有：可更新能源、能源效率提升、水资源管理、固体废弃物管理、交通运输管理、IT 智能系统应用、都市农业、生物修复、可持续绿色建筑等。

（三）加强城市资源环境标准、准则的制定

首先，要建立操作性强的城市资源环境建设标准或指南，在指南中明确实施资源环境规划和建设的具体工作细则、范围、内容、职责分工、评价标准、程序和方法等，使资源环境的规划和建设更加制度化、规范化，提高城市环境建设工作质量。

其次，不断完善城市环境建设法规，完善评价指标体系。应尽快完善城市环境建设立法，使环境建设有法可依。依据我国现行的法律法规与制度准则，借鉴西方发达国家的成功做法，制定与国际标准趋同的、有中国特色的资源环境规划建设准则，使城市环境的标准规定全面、操作性强、应用广泛，避免随意性、片面性和局限性。

再次，建立环境审计。可参考最高审计机关国际组织资源环境审计委员会的《从环境

视角进行审计活动的指南》等资料，建立适合于我国的资源环境操作规程与作业方法，其内容应考虑资源环境审计的基本技术标准和评价指标，并考虑环境财务审计、环境合规性审计、环境绩效审计、环境风险评估等方面。其中的评价指标应从不同的审计对象与审计目标出发，分别建立水污染、大气污染、噪声污染、固体废弃物污染等审计评价指标体系。

最后，敦促并规范企业环境信息披露。提高环境信息披露必须加快实施环境审计，尽快建立起有关环境污染的审计记录、计量、计价、成本费用、报告等一系列要素的统一环境审计制度。同时，发展环境会计，节省审计成本，降低审计风险，可从环境会计和环境审计两方面着手，共同促进我国城市环境可持续发展。

（四）吸引全社会积极参与

一方面，有力的领导和强烈的发展愿景还需要辅以宣传、教育和良好的沟通才能促进城市发展。另一方面，当地民众不应只是循环城市发展的受益者，他们也应参与到规划管理过程中。民众参与决策会使决策更具有群众基础，得到更多人的支持，增强认可度和合法性。同时，广泛的民众支持也会让循环城市发展的宏大目标更容易实现。

吸收所有主要利益相关者参与规划过程有利于考虑多样化的诉求，这已被证明是有利于公平发展的。在旧金山100%可再生能源战略中，不同利益的代表与当地政府工作人员一同出席讨论会，商量制定一个规划策略，而这种公私合作的讨论最终确定在低收入社区建立太阳能发电站。在多伦多，成立了一个关于粮食的多边政策理事会。在日本，一直将公众参与纳入到制定垃圾处理政策的过程中，从而更容易成功地执行。

除让那些积极主动的群体参与进来外，循环城市发展的领导者们还应该有意识地接触那些通常被忽视的弱势和边缘化群体。例如，在德国汉堡市Altona区的重建过程中，残障人士也被列为利益相关方参与了社区规划过程，他们的特别需求和权利也在最终的方案中得到体现。同样在汉堡的Wilhelmsburg区，由于那里移民群体比重较大而成为典型的代表性不足的地区，导致居民很少参与到公众决策活动中。汉堡IBA（国际建筑展）带着翻译人员到这些街区去逐户地访问，消除语言和文化隔阂，重新制定推广策略，这一明智的决定成功争取到这些居民参与到规划过程中。

公众参与城市改造与发展形成了一个正反馈系统。那些对自己城市感到自豪的居民会感受到更强的主人翁地位。有了这种情感上的“收获”，当地居民会更加投入地参与到改善自身生活环境的过程中来。

闭合式资源循环系统在社区层面提供了更多的人际交往机会。居民们寻求互惠互利的方式来发现邻居们的废弃物品所存在的对其他人的有益价值，并且人们会高兴地看到其废弃用品对其他人有用。这就可以帮助建立当地的社会联系，并提升全市范围内的文化价值。同样，都市农业已经被证明可以让当地居民感到自豪，感受到其在邻里社区的主人翁地位，这种生活感受可以提高社会凝聚力并降低犯罪率。这在贫困和边缘化的社区里尤为重要，由于人们在同一个项目中共同合作，他们更容易与邻居产生较紧密的联系。

（五）加强城市部门间的协调

生态系统是个多要素相互交织的网络，某一点的改变可能会影响整个网络的变化。资源问题已超越城市边界，其与外界的广泛联系更涉及很多个城市部门，而在单一部门范围内考虑任何问题都会是低效的或者远远不够的。比如说，要闭合城市水循环系统意味着要级联式地回收利用水资源，但污水中存在的营养物质可能是其他资源循环系统中所需要的。循环城市就是要放弃封闭单一的方法，综合考虑多种资源循环系统，跨部门寻找资源利用的最佳方式。因此，要在循环城市建设上取得显著进展必须要加强政府部门之间在纵向与横向上的沟通协调。良好的政府管理体系有助于推广好的实践经验，并将分散的活动连为一体。

一个有效的方法是建立专门的机构或办公室来协调不同部门之间的利益冲突并寻求综合性发展战略。哥本哈根就是一个积极的例子，为执行其气候保护计划，让科技与环境管理部协调总体活动。所有部门都参与环境管理工作，也都在其部门内部安排相应的协调人，而科技与环境管理部则监督总体进展，并及时发布定期更新的环境信息，让公众和利益相关方及时便捷地了解到相关信息。这种专门的办事机构，负责协调当地政府部门间的工作，促进跨部门的规划、实施和协同增效，是建设循环城市的一个有效的方法。

城市的资源来源一般都会超出其行政范围，循环城市特点就是与其周边的资源供应地有着融洽的治理关系。比如在水资源的管理与供应中，如果要把城市内外作为一个整体考虑，就必须要考虑整个流域的情况。这就要求城市当局与周边更大区域的管理机构进行沟通。多层次的对话与协商对于实现统一行动至关重要。地方、区域以及中央政府之间的沟通与协调有利于推动从国家层面出台激励性城市发展政策，来鼓励更多的地方机构采取大胆的行动或实施改革措施。

尽管国家层面的管理在城市发展中的重要作用值得肯定，但同时适当地推动分散化管理，会让地方政府有更大的权力做出影响本地区的决定，并能够根据当地情况及时调整政策措施。循环城市发展中的高效治理遵循辅助性原则，即提倡政府将权力和职责下放至能够有效履行此种权力和职责的最小管辖层次。

（六）进一步加强国际合作

在全球化日益深入发展的背景下，进一步加强建设循环城市的国际合作尤为重要。当前全球的城市都在以日趋开放的心态，与其他城市分享他们的问题、挑战与解决方案。已有的促进城市之间合作交流的平台已经很多，各地政府部门应该多支持这种平台的建设。例如，许多中国城市和世界其他城市结成的姐妹城市联系可以用于加强知识交流或者是促进建设性的竞争。前文提到的联合国的平台与倡议，包括即将举行的联合国第三届人类居住大会，都可以作为中国城市展示形象、分享经验和交流学习的机会。

城市间互相交流好的政策措施对于促进彼此的成功转型都非常重要。新的解决措施也需要进行测试，如果有效，就要与其他城市共享，以促进成果的推广。

五、结论与展望

中国城市正面临着严峻的环境压力，中国城市必须走转型发展的路子。这意味着要跨越通用的可持续发展思维，探索更广更全面的城市发展模式，即把重点放在不仅仅是维持城市生态环境系统的稳定，而且要积极促进资源的循环利用和再生。

循环城市的愿景是让城市持续为所有人提供改善生活质量的机会，使人们的潜能得到充分发挥。循环城市发展之路始于我们思维的转变。尽管还没有完美的循环城市的案例，但世界很多城市和地区的经验已证明，循环城市发展在某些行业和领域已经成为现实。城市迫切需要实现循环再生发展，这既能确保其所依赖的地球系统处于长期繁荣，更能使城市在多方面受益。城市如果能提高对本地资源的利用（减少对长距离的外地资源的消耗）并闭合其自身资源循环系统（减少废弃物排放），将会在其地域范围内创造显著的社会、经济和环境效益。

循环城市建设规划的理念、内容设计、研究方法能够充分贯彻中央提出的科学发展观，有助于在定性定量定位紧密结合的基础上系统而深层次地认知其发展的现状、障碍、潜力，正确地把握未来的发展目标与对策，以利科学决策和实践。同时，这种新型城市化也反映了一种新型的发展模式，即在经济社会“新常态”发展模式下，走出以人为本、稳定发展、鼓励创新、协调环境等新型特色城镇化道路。

（作者：陈波平，世界未来委员会（WFC）中国区总监；杨亮，德国基尔大学景观—人类发展学院博士后研究员，世界未来委员会（WFC）中国循环城市项目研究员；郑明媚，中国城市和小城镇改革发展中心，智慧城市发展联盟执行秘书长）

参考文献

[1] 仇保兴．城市生态化改造的必由之路——重建微循环［J］．城市观察，2012，6：5－20.

[2] 格林斯坦，等．循环城市：城市土地利用与再利用［M］．丁成日，等译．商务印书馆有限公司，2007.

[3] 国家发改委城市和小城镇改革发展中心课题组．中国特色新型城镇化建设路径．行政管理改革，2014－04－23. http：//theory. people. com. cn/n/2014/0423/c207270－24933042. html.

[4] 国务院．国务院关于深入推进新型城镇化建设的若干意见（国发〔2016〕8号），2016－02－06.

[5] 国务院办公厅．国务院办公厅关于推进海绵城市建设的指导意见（国办发〔2015〕75号），2015－10－11.

[6] 李伯华，何清华，刘沛林．循环城市建设的动态测度及实证研究——以衡阳市为例［J］．生态经济，2010，12：24－27.

[7] 李树华．共生、循环——低碳经济社会背景下城市园林绿地建设的基本思路［J］．中国园林，2010，6：19－22.

[8] 世界未来委员会（WFC）. 循环城市——通向理想城市之路，2015.
[9] 唐双成，罗纨，贾忠华，袁黄春. 西安市雨水花园蓄渗雨水径流的试验研究［J］. 水土保持学报，2012，6：75-79.
[10] 王雯雯，赵智杰，秦华鹏. 基于SWMM的低冲击开发模式水文效应模拟评估［J］. 北京大学学报（自然科学版），2012，48（2）：303-309.
[11] 邢薇，赵冬泉，陈吉宁，王浩正. 基于低影响开发（LID）的可持续城市雨水系统［J］. 中国给水排水，2011，20：13-16.
[12] 张彪，谢高地，薛康，王金增，肖玉，张灿强. 北京城市绿地调蓄雨水径流功能及其价值评估. 生态学报，2011，31（13）：3839-3845.
[13] 章林伟. 海绵城市建设是中国城镇化转型发展的助推器［N］. 中国建设报，2015-11-12.
[14] 住房城乡建设部. 海绵城市建设技术指南——低影响开发雨水系统构建（试行），2014-10.

案例篇

2015中国城市幸福感调查报告

一、调查概述

城市幸福感是指市民对所在城市的认同感、归属感、安定感、满足感，以及外界人群的向往度、赞誉度。对于城市幸福感来说，影响它的因素是多方面的，包括经济发展、社会保障、生活质量等。党的十八大以来，各项惠民新举措接踵而至，让民众的生活进一步改善，“幸福感”一词又在民众心中热了起来。幸福，已作为城市发展模式转型和关注民生幸福需求的重要风向标列入政府的责任清单。目前，我国100多个城市已经提出了建设“幸福城市”的口号。

伴随着城市的发展，人们的幸福感应该越来越强烈，因为人们享受到的优质资源越来越多。但事实并非如此，在城市发展的过程中，两者的天平常常倾斜。城市发展了，人们的幸福感却逐渐降低。显而易见的城市病蜂拥而至，交通拥堵、环境污染、上学难、就医难等，已经严重困扰城市居民的生活。“城市是一种心灵的状态，是一个独特风俗习惯、思想自由和情感丰富的实体。”著名的社会学家罗伯特·以斯拉·帕克说。对中国城市来说，给居民提供一个生活和工作的场所已非所求，城市有更为深远的追求：成为市民感知幸福的共同体。

城市发展和城市居民的幸福感，是城市并行不悖的发展宗旨和目标。城市具备一定的经济功能，人们才有幸福可言，而丧失了经济功能的城市，幸福只能纸上谈兵。然而过于追求城市的经济功能，忽视了城市的社会文化等生活功能，人们的幸福感就会受到伤害。这样的例子并不鲜见。

当一个国家中大部分人尚未解决温饱时，发展经济能提高国民幸福度；但经济发展到一定程度后，其关联度则会减弱。在中国最具幸福感城市调查活动持续开展的9年历程中，我们发现，城市管理者已经意识到经济发展和居民幸福协调发展的重要性，他们对居民幸福感的关注度日益上升，其视角已从单纯追求城市的经济功能转向城市居民的幸福感受度。

2015年是我国全面建设小康社会的第15个年头，为贯彻落实党的十八届三中全会精神，全面推进小康社会建设，集中展示中国城市在小康社会建设过程中的成就与经验，《瞭望东方周刊》联合中国市长协会《中国城市发展报告》继续主办“2015中国最具幸福感城市调查活动”。其目的是力图集中展示一批在全面建设小康社会过程中有突出贡献的幸福城市，并推广城市在小康社会建设过程中的成就和经验，为如期实现全面建成小康社会的目标提供现实的参考样本。

二、调查方法

此次调查活动采用公共调查（包含网络调查和微信公众号调查）、抽样调查、大数据采集和材料申报等四种方法进行。

其中，公共调查和抽样调查通过被调查者对其生活各方面具体指标的主观感受来获得生活具体幸福度，请被调查者在1到5中打分（1分最少，5分最高）。通过这种方式，测量了市民对于自己所在城市各个具体方面的感受，包括对于人情、赚钱机会、交通、生活便利、医疗卫生、教育、治安状况、环境等这些与生活息息相关的具体方面的幸福感。大数据采集通过与第三方的合作，在其数据库中采集与幸福感有关的行为数据，从而分析出幸福城市排名。材料申报由各城市自行申报。

（一）调查对象

中国社会科学院发布的2014中国城市综合竞争力百强城市：北京、上海、深圳、广州、天津、杭州、青岛、长沙、大连、佛山、苏州、无锡、沈阳、成都、南京、东莞、武汉、宁波、鄂尔多斯、济南、合肥、包头、常州、东营、厦门、福州、烟台、长春、重庆、中山、西安、南通、扬州、哈尔滨、大庆、南昌、珠海、徐州、郑州、石家庄、镇江、淄博、芜湖、呼和浩特、泰州、沧州、泉州、南宁、唐山、惠州、克拉玛依、舟山、温州、岳阳、昆明、株洲、马鞍山、鞍山、柳州、威海、日照、江门、营口、绍兴、嘉兴、廊坊、临沂、济宁、铜陵、泰安、漳州、常德、潍坊、湖州、秦皇岛、乌鲁木齐、盐城、湘潭、海口、湛江、太原、龙岩、连云港、莆田、淮安、吉林、三亚、银川、兰州、金华、贵阳、郴州。

本次报告集中研究综合排名前20位的城市，以期更客观地反映城市居民对于所居住城市的幸福感受。对中国城市来说，给居民提供一个生活和工作的场所已非所求，城市有更为深远的追求：成为市民感知幸福的共同体。

（二）调查时间

本次调查所属时间是“2015年8月1日0时”，调查的工作期限是“2015年8月1日至2015年9月30日”。其中，2015年8月1日至2015年8月30日为公共调查时间，2015年9月1日至2015年9月30日对公共调查排名前20位的城市进行抽样调查和大数据采集。

（三）评价体系

评价体系由《瞭望东方周刊》中国城市评价中心完成，评价中心通过9年来对城市幸福感的调查研究，从科学性、指导性和可操作性等多重角度进行考量，形成了一套完整的调查评价体系。

表 1　主观调查

序号	指标	指标释义
1	住房现状	受访者对当地住房现状感到的幸福程度
2	物价(含房价)	受访者对当地含房价的物价感到的幸福程度
3	交通状况	受访者对当地整体交通状况感到的幸福程度
4	气候	受访者对当地的气温及天气舒适度感到的幸福程度
5	医疗便利程度和质量	受访者对当地医疗的便利程度和质量感到的幸福程度
6	环境和污染程度	受访者对当地的空气、水质及道路干净程度等感到的幸福程度,对当地的绿化、山水等感到的幸福程度
7	治安	受访者对当地整体的治安状况感到的幸福程度
8	养老	受访者对养老状况感到的幸福程度
9	人情味	受访者对当地人情味浓厚感到的幸福程度
10	餐饮娱乐和文化、体育设施	受访者对当地文化体育设施等感到的幸福程度,对当地的餐饮设计以及娱乐设施的便利感到的幸福程度
11	生活节奏	受访者对当地的生活节奏感到的幸福程度
12	文明程度	受访者对当地居民整体文明程度感到的幸福程度
13	执法规范程度	受访者对执法文明程度感到的幸福程度
14	公共服务水平	受访者对公共服务质量感到的幸福程度
15	文化底蕴	受访者对当地的历史、传统等感到的幸福程度
16	购物便利性	受访者对购买各种生活相关产品的便利程度感到的幸福程度
17	赚钱机会	受访者对当地就业机会与赚钱机会感到的幸福程度
18	市民个人发展空间	受访者对个人发展感到的幸福程度
19	城市发展质量与速度	受访者对当地的发展和速度等感到的幸福程度
20	教育	受访者对当地学校质量、教学质量等感到的幸福程度
21	对外来人的包容度	受访者对外来人口感到的幸福程度
22	旅游度假	受访者旅游度假感到的幸福程度

表 2　大数据采集体系

序号	调查项目	样本数据
1	居民收入	人均住房面积; 人均汽车保有量; 物价收入比
2	生活品质	奢侈品订单量; 购物频次及时间; 智能家电购买量; 绿色有机食品购买量; 进口食品购买量; 书籍购买量; 文艺演出购票量

续表 2

序号	调查项目	样本数据
3	城市向往	昵称； 联系方式(手机、邮箱)； 居住地； 家乡； 常用地址(精确到区县)； 地址变更时间
4	旅游向往	城市被搜索的频次； 搜索人所在地； 长尾关键词； 旅游地产品网购量
5	就业	求职者性别； 年龄； 学历； 婚育状态； 招聘单位总数量； 职位总数量； 单位地址(精确到街)； 每个薪金阶层的岗位数量
6	生态环境	水过滤产品购买量； 污染检测产品(服务)购买量； 树苗花卉购买量； 空气过滤用品购买量
7	治安	网购防身用品的商品名称； 收货人性别； 年龄； 时间
8	诉讼咨询	民间借贷纠纷； 商品房销售纠纷； 车辆纠纷； 劳资纠纷； 离婚纠纷； 健康权纠纷
9	交通	拥堵路段名称； 高峰期拥堵里程； 易堵路段的拥堵频次； 施工路段及占用时间； 电子眼密度； 停车场数量及分布
10	教育	相邻地段，学区房与非学区房的单价； 留学类英语(托福、雅思等)的学习人数； 百度传课的用户量

注：大数据采集样本时间跨度为 2014 年 10 月至 2015 年 9 月。

小康社会标准：

一是人均国内生产总值超过 3 000 美元，这是建成全面小康社会的根本标志。

二是城镇居民人均可支配收入 1.8 万元。

三是农村居民家庭人均纯收入 8 000 元。

四是恩格尔系数低于 0.4。

五是城镇人均住房建筑面积 30 平方米。

六是城镇化率达到 50%。

七是居民家庭计算机普及率 20%。

八是大学入学率 20%。

九是每千人医生数 2.8 人。

十是城镇居民最低生活保障率 95% 以上。

（四）调查样本量

公共调查共回收问卷82 109 653份，其中有效问卷 79 400 185 份；抽样调查在 20 个城市共发放问卷 453 910 份，回收有效问卷 417 382 份。

大数据共采集有效样本5 396 728份。

（五）调查质量控制

本次调查活动的问卷合格率，即合格问卷数量占总回收问卷数量的比重，包括抽样调查、网络调查根据不同权重加权平均后为 96.67%，反映问卷可用程度较高，增强了本次调查的公信力。

三、样本结构及特征

（一）性别

从统计结果看，在 815 万参与调查的样本中，男性占了绝大多数，男性与女性的比例为 68:32，符合性别调查要求。

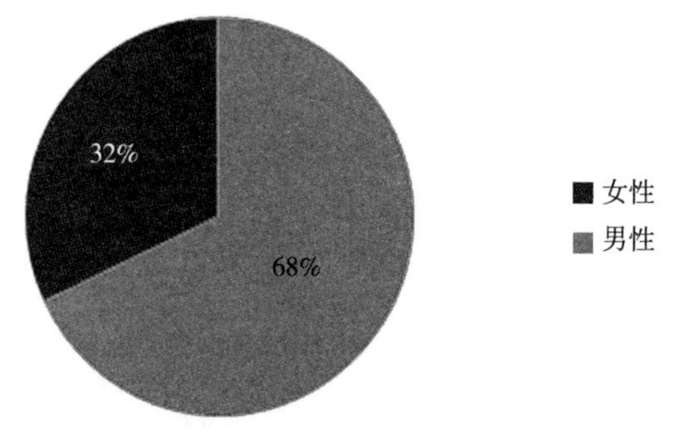

图 1　性别比例

（二）年龄

图 2 显示，被调查者年龄分布上，25～35 岁的人数达到 37%，36～45 岁的人数占

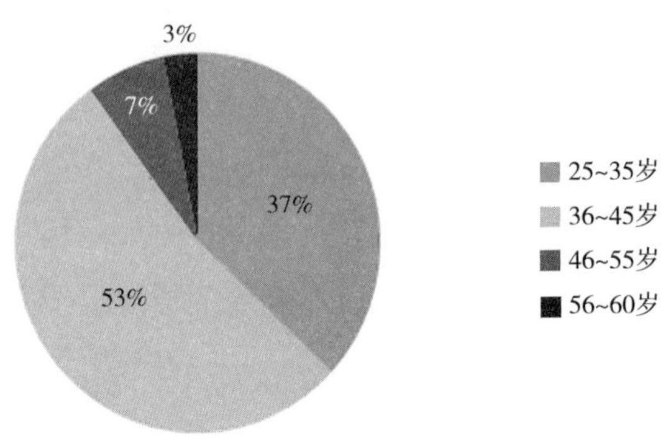

图2　年龄构成

53%，45~55岁的人数占比为7%，55岁以上的只有3%。

（三）学历

从学历分布来看，本科及以上的学历占了绝大多数，为83%，充分反映我国国民教育素质的水平不断提升。

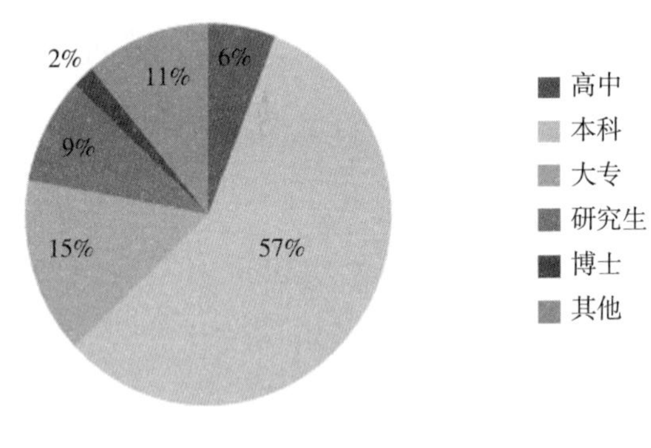

图3　学历

（四）职业

从职业分布来看，来自企业的被调查者比例最大，达到31%，党政机关、事业单位和

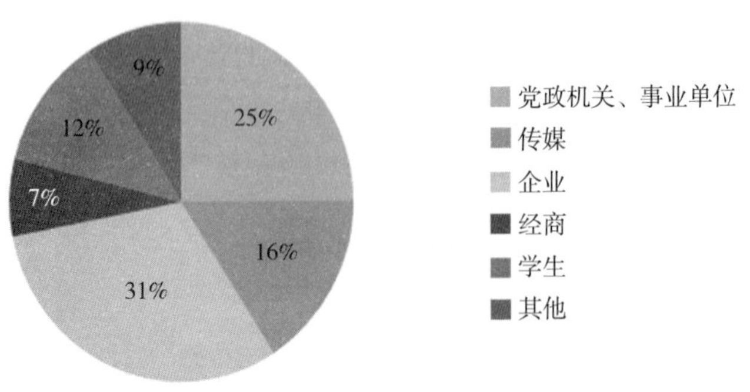

图4　职业

传媒的被调查者紧随其后，比例分别达到25%和16%，其他依次是经商、学生和其他人员。

（五）婚姻状况

从婚姻状态上看，参与调查的民众中，未婚的被调查者超过半数，为55%。

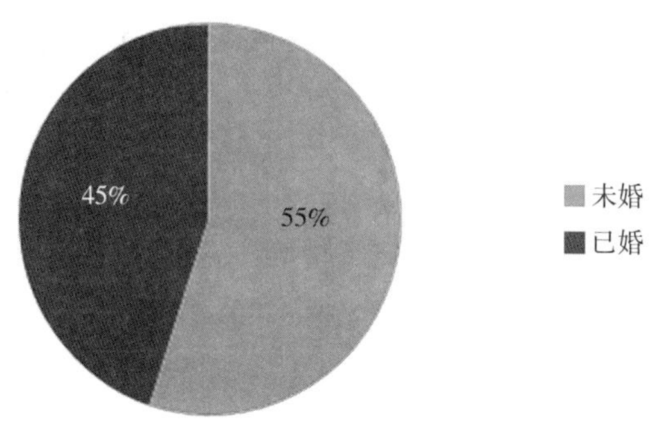

图5 婚姻状况

（六）居住年限

从居住时间上看，大部分受访者在城市中居住10年以上，充分体现了这次活动的公正性。

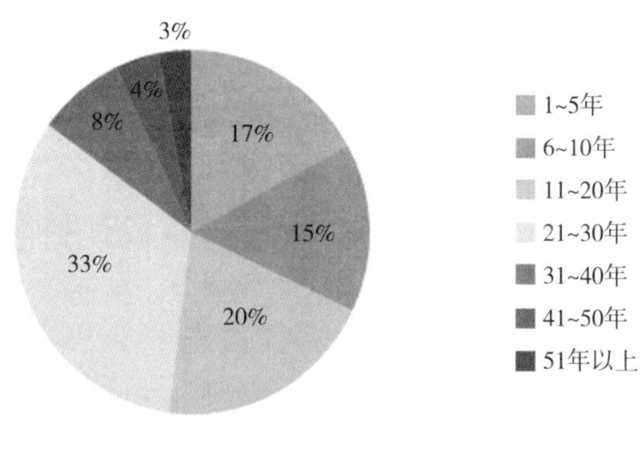

图6 居住年限

四、数据分析和结果

（一）2015中国最具幸福感城市调查总排名

根据公共调查（包含网络调查和微信公众号调查）、抽样调查、大数据采集和材料申报四部分数据的汇总，以及加权统计结果来看，被调查者认为最具幸福感城市前20位的依次是：成都、宁波、杭州、南京、西安、长春、长沙、苏州、上海、北京、深圳、厦门、重庆、珠海、佛山、无锡、南通、大连、绍兴、中山。

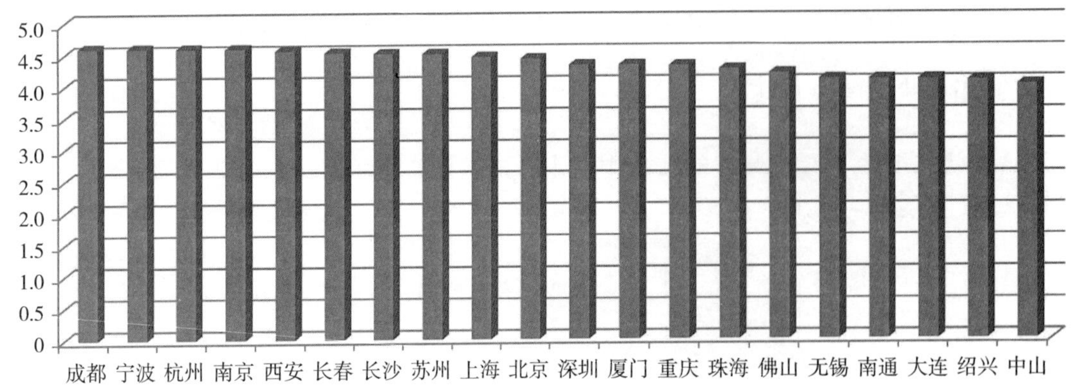

图 7　2015 中国最具幸福感城市调查总排名

（二）2015 中国最具幸福感城市调查分项排名

本次调查中，一个重要的部分是通过被调查者对“自身所在城市”城市幸福感受的各个方面进行打分，也就是说，本次调查中的数据体现得更多的是市民对所居住城市各个方面给他们带来的幸福感受。这些调查内容显然在相当程度上更加主观，特别是由于各地被调查者对自身所在城市形象的“期望值”不同，可能对不同城市之间衡量的标尺会发生一定程度的变化，甚至“变形”。但此种“变形”在客观材料申报和大数据采集环节中进行了较大程度的修正。

1. 被调查者对当地住房现状感到的幸福程度

近年来，由于中国的房地产市场的发展迅猛，住房问题已经随着房价的上涨变成百姓最为关心的话题，影响着广大人民群众的生活。住房问题既是经济问题，也是民生问题，因此百姓的关注度最高。调查数据表明，对于当地住房现状幸福感程度最高的城市前 10 位是成都、宁波、长春、杭州、西安、南京、长沙、苏州、绍兴、珠海（见图 8）。

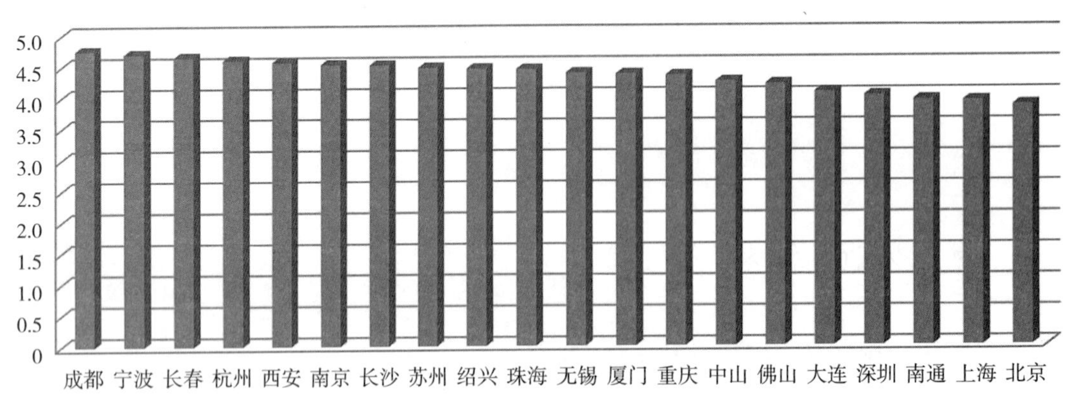

图 8　被调查者对当地住房现状感到的幸福程度

2. 被调查者对当地含房价的物价感到的幸福程度

物价与百姓的生活息息相关，上至房子车子，下至柴米油盐，百姓时时关注物价的变动，物价是幸福感直接体现的风向标。从图 9 可以看出，被调查者对当地物价感到幸福程度的城市，宁波位列第一，成都、杭州分列二、三位，紧接着是长沙、西安、长春、南京、苏州、中山、大连等。上海、北京等一线城市依旧在物价上不能给居民带来明显的幸福感。

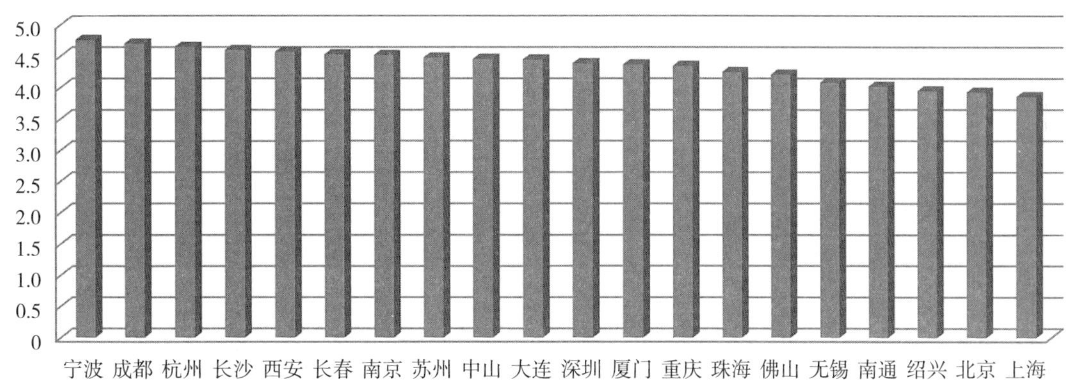

图 9　被调查者对当地含房价的物价感到的幸福程度

3. 被调查者对当地整体交通状况感到的幸福程度

随着城市经济的快速发展，人们生活水平显著提高，机动车保有量急剧上升，交通需求迅速增长，城市交通已经成为城市经济社会发展和人民生活水平提高的判断标准之一。调查数据表明，在对当地整体交通状况幸福感受上，成都、宁波、杭州名列三甲，长春、西安、南京、长沙、苏州、大连和珠海列居前十。一线城市虽然拥有较好的交通硬件，但是路况的拥堵仍然让居民无法感知到幸福的感觉。

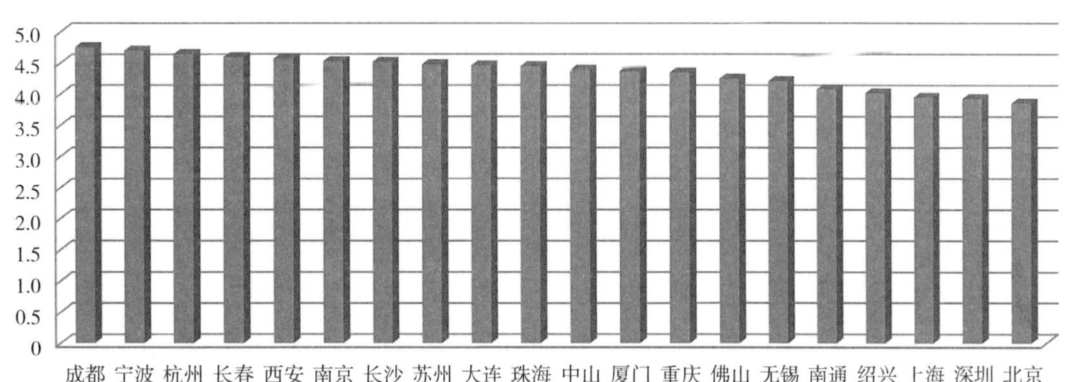

图 10　被调查者对当地整体交通状况感到的幸福程度

4. 被调查者对当地的气温及天气舒适度感到的幸福程度

在所有的气象要素中，气温是影响舒适度最直接的因素。从感觉上说，舒适度是人的主观认知和感受，标准因人而异，具有较强的主观性；从生理学角度分析，舒适度是人体机能在一定环境条件下保持正常运转时的一种状态，具有一定的客观性。因此，气温和天气舒适度从根本上反映人们对于当地气候的感受。图 11 表明，被调查者对当地的气温及天气舒适度感到的幸福程度排名前 10 位的城市是成都、宁波、杭州、南京、长春、西安、长沙、苏州、上海和绍兴。

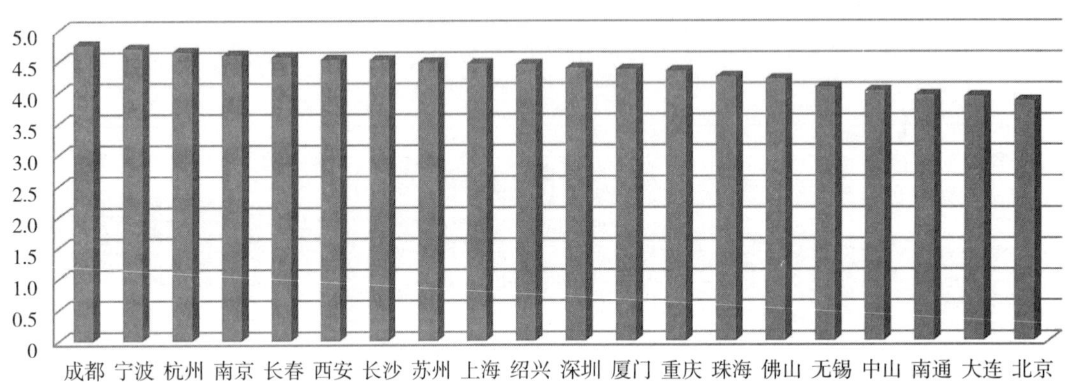

图 11 被调查者对当地的气温及天气舒适度感到的幸福程度

5. 被调查者对当地医疗的便利程度和质量感到的幸福程度

2015 年是进入医改的第六个年头，5 年的医改历程取得了一定的成效，比如，建立全民覆盖的医保网络，逐步健全基层医疗卫生体系和公共卫生服务体系，以及全面推开的基本药物制度等。2015 年也是全面深化公立医院改革的一年。这一年，100 个地级以上城市推行了公立医院综合改革试点。

城市居民对这些医改新政的感知度如何？他们如何评价自己所在城市的医疗服务，以及医疗的便利程度？图 12 显示，在该指标上，上海、北京和成都分列三甲，其次是南京、西安、长春、长沙、苏州、宁波和杭州。上海、北京拥有一流医疗设施和医护人员，得到了大多数被调查者的认可，其他城市也都是某一区域的城市代表，在该区域的医疗水平上具有一定的权威性。

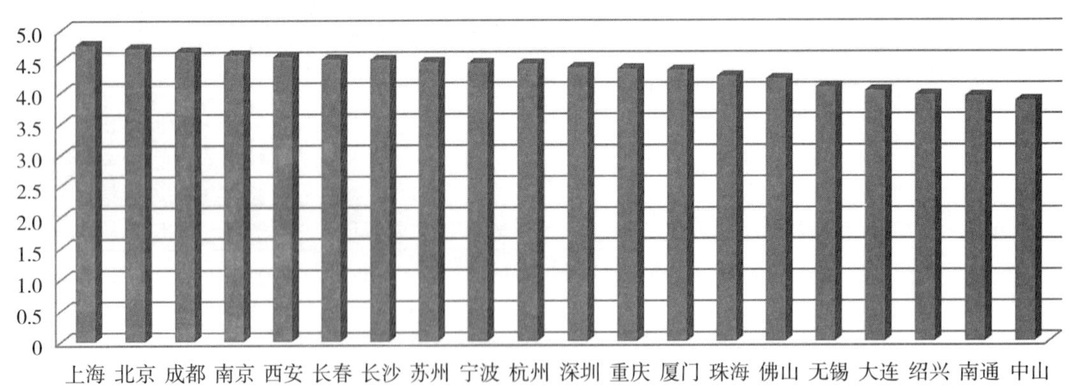

图 12 被调查者对当地医疗的便利程度和质量感到的幸福程度

6. 被调查者对当地的空气、水质及道路干净程度等感到的幸福程度，对当地的绿化、山水等感到的幸福程度

图 13 说明，对于当地空气、水质、道路干净程度以及绿化、山水等的幸福感受上，排名前 10 位的城市依次为杭州、宁波、成都、南京、西安、苏州、长春、长沙、上海和南通。

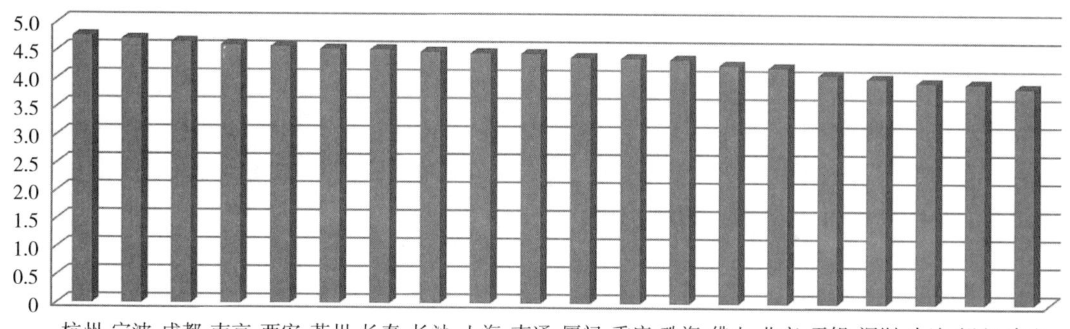

图 13 被调查者对当地的空气、水质及道路干净程度等感到的幸福程度，对当地的绿化、山水等感到的幸福程度

7. 被调查者对当地整体的治安状况感到的幸福程度

治安状况，一头连着千家万户，一头连着经济社会发展，是社会和谐发展的晴雨表。本次调查中，城市治安状况是其中的重要内容之一。图 14 说明，被调查者对于当地整体的治安状况感到幸福程度排名前 10 位的城市依次为北京、上海、成都、宁波、杭州、南京、长沙、苏州、西安和长春。

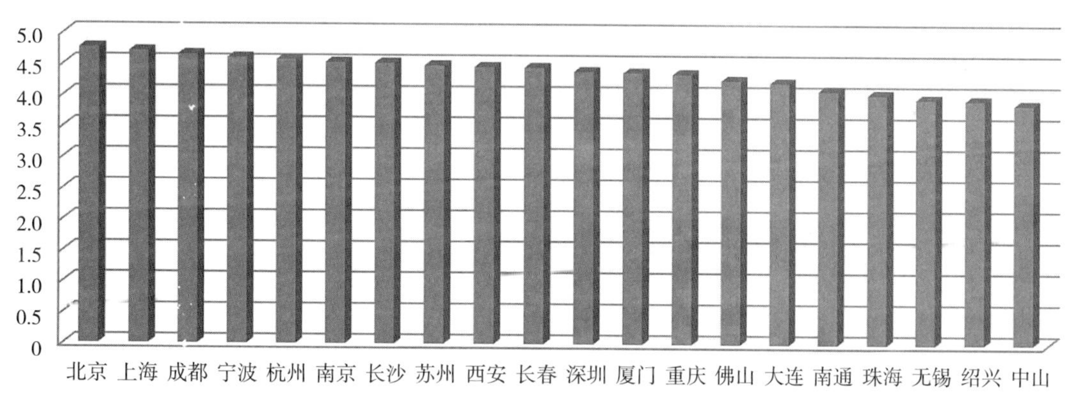

图 14 被调查者对当地整体的治安状况感到的幸福程度

8. 被调查者对养老状况感到的幸福程度

人口老龄化是当今世界各国普遍面临的一个重大社会问题，中国也不例外：中国老龄人口已经超过 2 亿人，预计到 2055 年，占总人口的比例将达 35%。人口老龄化问题将成为中国城市迫在眉睫的新挑战，养老问题成为人们最关注的焦点之一，也是考量一个城市发展是否协调发展的标准之一。被调查者对于养老状况感到幸福程度排名前 10 位的城市为杭州、南京、成都、宁波、西安、长春、珠海、苏州、佛山和长沙。

9. 被调查者对当地人情味浓厚感到的幸福程度

人情味源自人性之中最温情的一面，是人与人之间真挚情感的自然流露，是一种给人以爱与关怀的奇妙感觉，是一种由内而外感染他人的个性魅力，是一股可以温暖人心的精神力量。人情味是城市幸福感程度的重要体现因素之一。图 16 显示，人情味最浓厚的城市排名

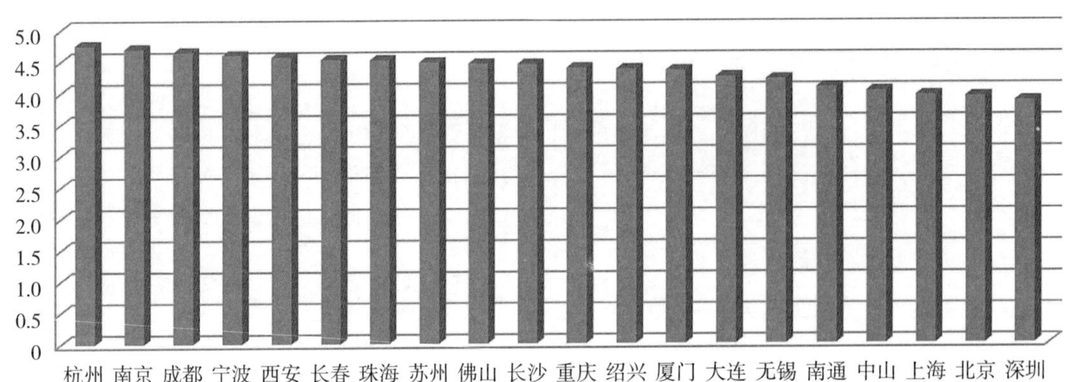

图 15 被调查者对养老状况感到的幸福程度

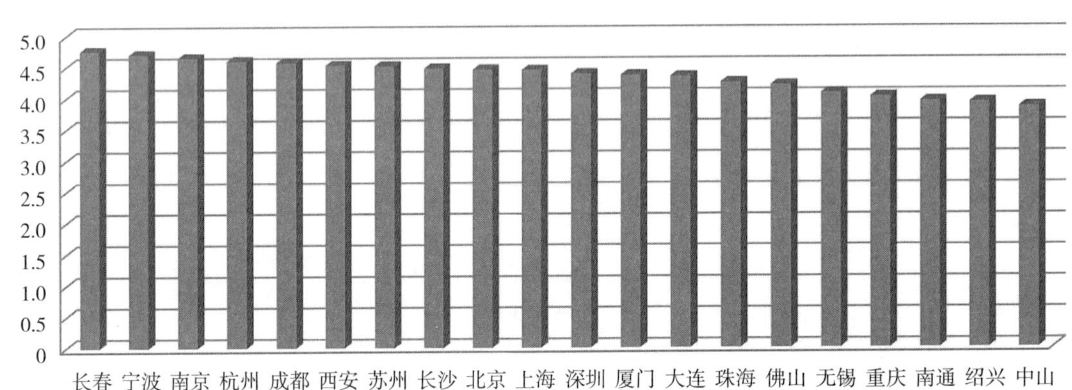

图 16 被调查者对当地人情味浓厚感到的幸福程度

前 10 位的是长春、宁波、南京、杭州、成都、西安、苏州、长沙、北京、上海。

10. 被调查者对当地文化体育设施等感到的幸福程度，对当地的餐饮设计以及娱乐设施的便利感到的幸福程度

调查中发现，随着居民生活水平的提高，对该项指标的关注度也相应增加。图 17 说明，被调查者对当地文化体育设施等感到的幸福程度，对当地的餐饮设计以及娱乐设施的便利感

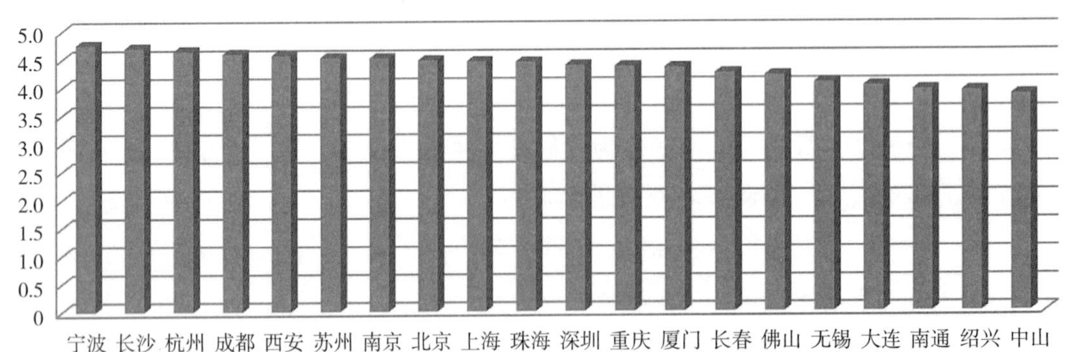

图 17 被调查者对当地文化体育设施等感到的幸福程度，对当地的餐饮设计以及娱乐设施的便利感到的幸福程度

到的幸福程度这一指标上，前 10 位城市依次为宁波、长沙、杭州、成都、西安、苏州、南京、北京、上海和珠海。

11. 被调查者对当地的生活节奏感到的幸福程度

生活节奏的快慢是百姓幸福感较明显的一个指标，现在越来越多的人崇尚慢节奏生活。图 18 为不同城市居民对其生活节奏幸福感排名前 10 位的城市，北上广等生活节奏较快的城市均未挤进前十，位列第一的是成都，紧随其后的是宁波、南京、杭州、西安、苏州、长春、长沙、大连和中山。

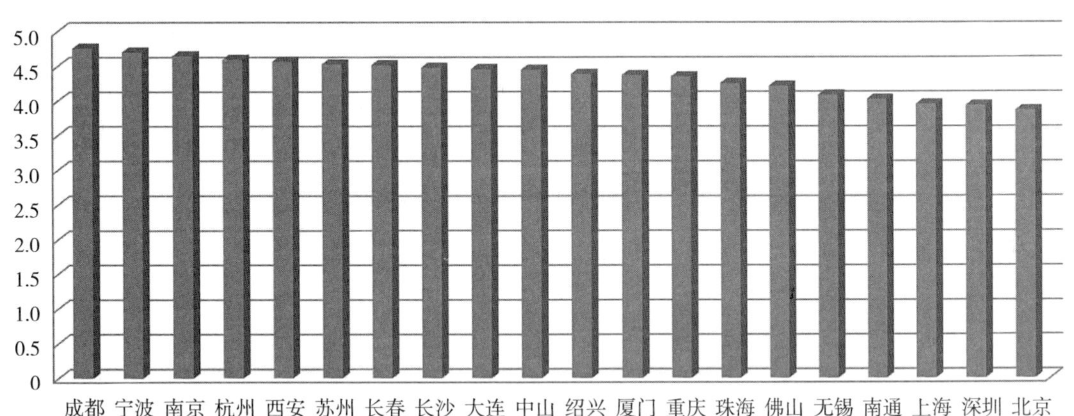

图 18　被调查者对当地的生活节奏感到的幸福程度

12. 被调查者对当地居民整体文明程度感到的幸福程度

城市居民的整体文明程度是城市文明度的缩影，代表了城市的发展水平。被调查者对当地居民整体文明成都感到幸福程度排名前 10 位的是成都、北京、杭州、南京、西安、宁波、上海、长沙、长春和苏州。

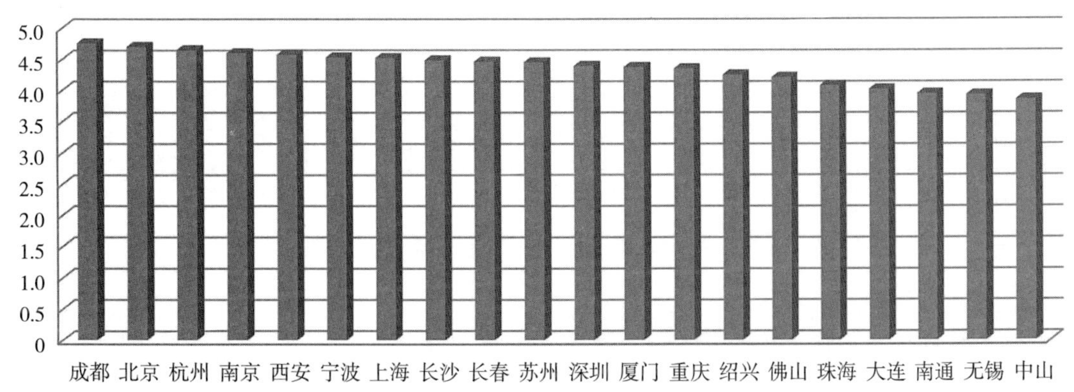

图 19　被调查者对当地居民整体文明程度感到的幸福程度

13. 被调查者对执法文明程度感到的幸福程度

文明执法是指执法人员以人为本，依照法律的规定和程序，运用法律规范办理各种案件，坚持教育与处罚相结合，坚持严格、公正、文明执法，目的是让不懂法者懂法，让懂法者自觉守法。图 20 显示，被调查者对执法文明程度感到的幸福程度排名前 10 位的城市是上海、南京、北京、西安、杭州、长春、长沙、苏州、成都和宁波。

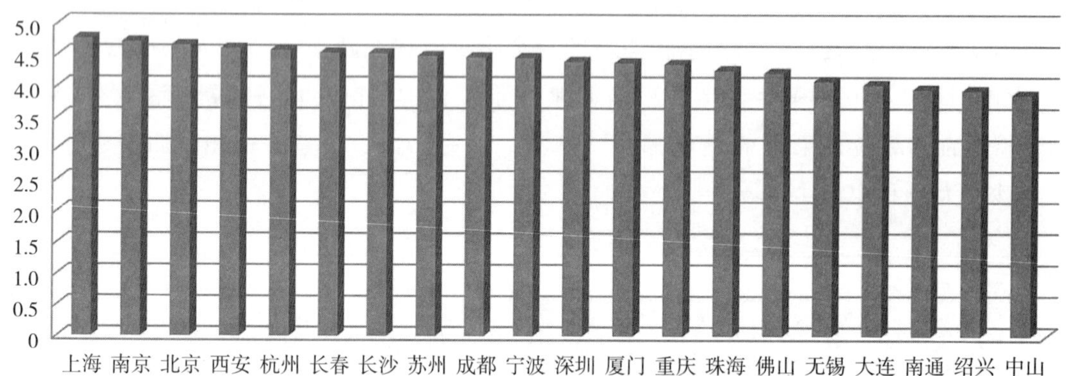

图 20 被调查者对执法文明程度感到的幸福程度

14. 被调查者对公共服务质量感到的幸福程度

公共服务是为满足社会公共需求、维护公共利益，由政府直接提供或由政府提供保障的公共产品和服务。改善公共服务是 21 世纪公共行政和政府改革的核心理念，也是我国建设服务型政府的主要内容，公共服务直接关系民生幸福。图 21 表明，被调查者对公共服务质量感到的幸福程度排名前 10 位的城市是上海、深圳、北京、成都、宁波、长沙、长春、苏州、西安和南京。

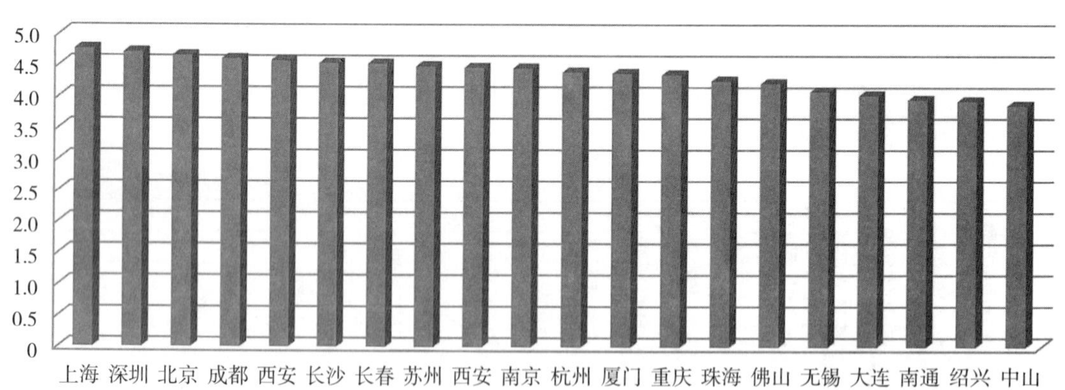

图 21 被调查者对公共服务质量感到的幸福程度

15. 被调查者对当地的历史、传统等感到的幸福程度

历史传统文化是城市的灵魂。一个城市的魅力不在于它有多少高楼大厦，而在于它的历史文化底蕴。城市从诞生之日起，就打上了各自历史传统文化和地域文化的烙印。那些保留至今不同时代、不同风格的建筑或古迹，以及具有浓郁地方和民族特色的工艺、戏剧、服装、民风、民俗等构成了现代城市发展的基础，为现代城市建设提供借鉴和启迪。图 22 显示，被调查者对当地的历史、传统等感到的幸福程度排名前 10 位的城市为南京、北京、西安、杭州、宁波、长春、成都、苏州、上海和长沙。

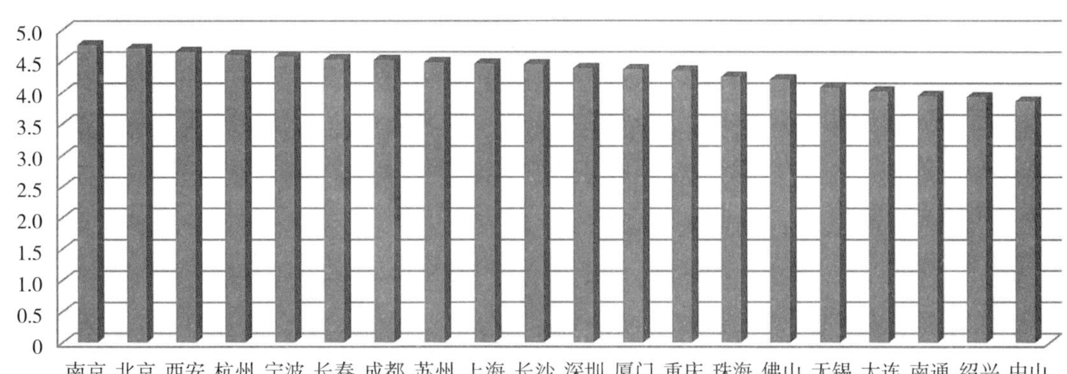

图 22　被调查者对当地的历史、传统等感到的幸福程度

16. 被调查者对购买各种生活相关产品的便利程度感到的幸福程度

随着社会经济的发展、技术的进步、竞争更为激烈的商业环境以及可选择活动的增多，市民购物对于便利的需求比以往任何时候都更强烈。图 23 显示，丰富的商户商品数量，便利的购物条件，高性价比的消费，都让其城市居民具有较高的幸福感。调查结果表明，被调查者对购买各种生活相关产品的便利程度感到的幸福程度排名前 10 位的城市是上海、成都、北京、杭州、西安、南京、长春、苏州、长沙和宁波。

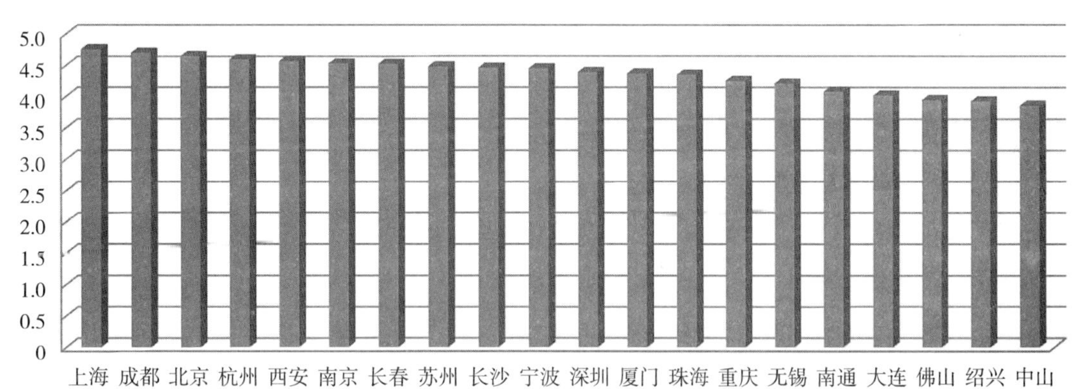

图 23　被调查者对购买各种生活相关产品的便利程度感到的幸福程度

17. 被调查者对当地就业机会与赚钱机会感到的幸福程度

就业机会与赚钱机会是被调查者普遍认可的幸福感集中体现的指标之一。就我国目前的居民生活水平，大部分被调查者的幸福感直接与经济挂钩，即与就业与赚钱机会挂钩。图 24 显示，在这一指标上，被调查者认可的就业机会与赚钱机会幸福程度最高的城市是上海和北京，其次是深圳、南京、西安、长春、长沙、苏州、成都、宁波。

18. 被调查者对个人发展感到的幸福程度

个人发展情况是被调查者选择生活城市的重要因素之一，该指标与赚钱机会有较高的相关性。图 25 说明，被调查者对个人发展感到的幸福程度排名前 10 位的城市是北京、上海、深圳、苏州、南京、西安、长沙、成都、杭州和宁波。

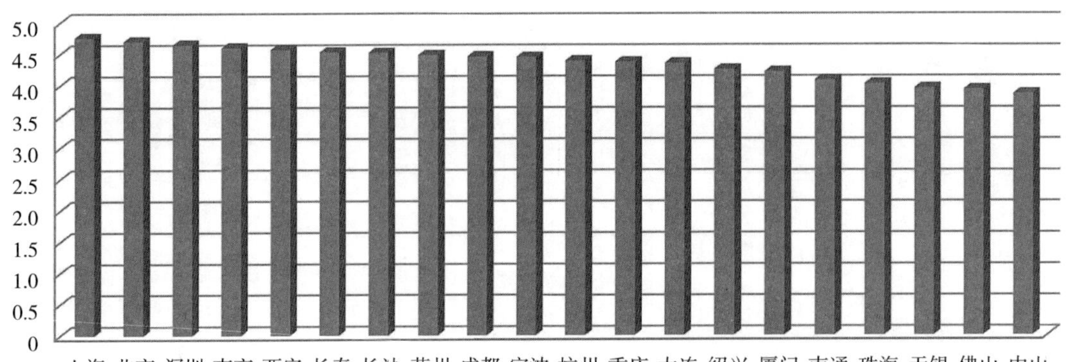

图 24　被调查者对当地就业机会与赚钱机会感到的幸福程度

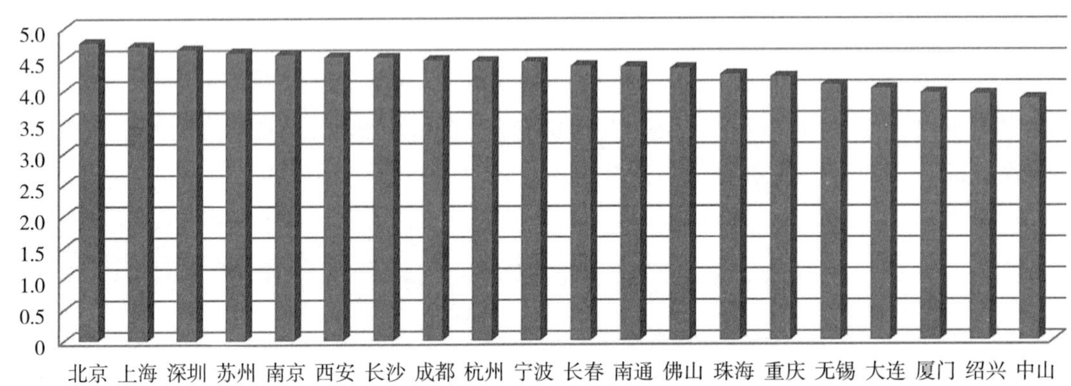

图 25　被调查者对个人发展感到的幸福程度

19. 被调查者对当地的发展和速度等感到的幸福程度

历次调查都显示，经济发展有助于增加幸福感，但人们的幸福感又在相当程度上取决于非财富因素。国外研究表明，当一个国家中大部分人尚未解决温饱时，发展经济能提高国民幸福度；但经济发展到一定程度会与幸福的关系减弱。图 26 显示，被调查者对当地的发展和速度等感到幸福程度排名前 10 位的城市是深圳、上海、北京、宁波、西安、南京、苏州、长沙、长春和杭州。

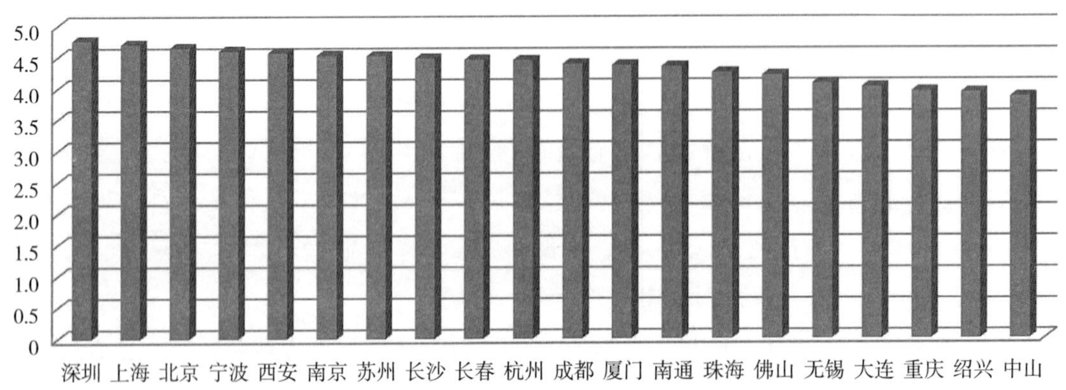

图 26　被调查者对当地的发展和速度等感到的幸福程度

20. 被调查者对当地学校质量、教学质量等感到的幸福程度

百年大计，教育为本。教育不仅仅是每个家庭、每个人成长发展的事，更是影响未来社会发展的大事，其作为社会发展过程中的刚性需求，一直肩负着重要的历史使命。一个人一生在教育上的投入非常巨大，而且是连贯性的，传承的，父辈投入在儿孙辈上的教育费用更是不计代价，为了子女的成才竭尽全力，倾其所有。对城市而言，能否提供较为均衡的教育资源，是衡量市民满意度的重要组成部分。被调查者普遍认为，对当地教育所感受到的幸福程度，是城市幸福度的重要体现指标。图 27 表明，被调查者对当地学校质量、教学质量感到的幸福程度排名前 10 位的城市是北京、上海、南京、杭州、长春、西安、长沙、苏州、宁波和成都。

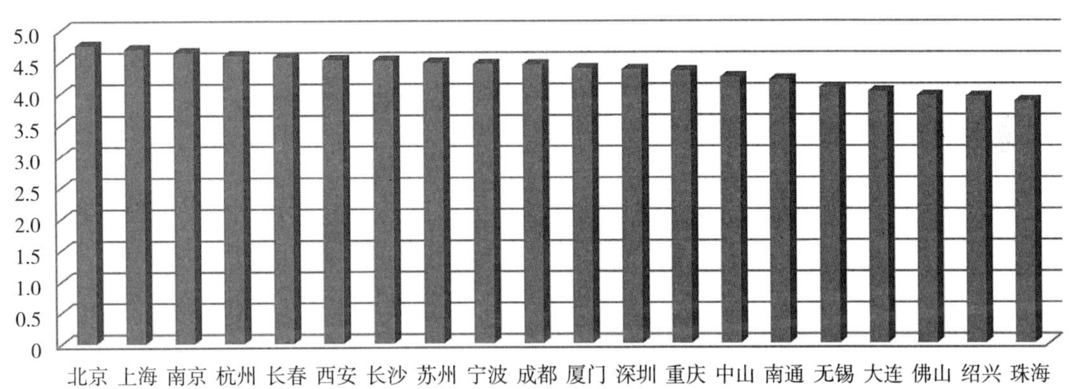

图 27 被调查者对当地学校质量、教学质量等感到的幸福程度

21. 被调查者对外来人口感到的幸福程度

改革开放以来，中国经济在飞速增长的同时也伴随着大规模的劳动力迁徙和流动，“孔雀东南飞”的迁徙路线和特征非常明显。外来人口大规模流向大城市和发达地区，为流入地经济发展做出了重要贡献。外来人口的幸福感，主要来自于城市的包容度和开放度。图 28 表明，宁波、成都、杭州、长春、西安、南京、北京、苏州、上海和长沙对该项指标具有较高的幸福感。

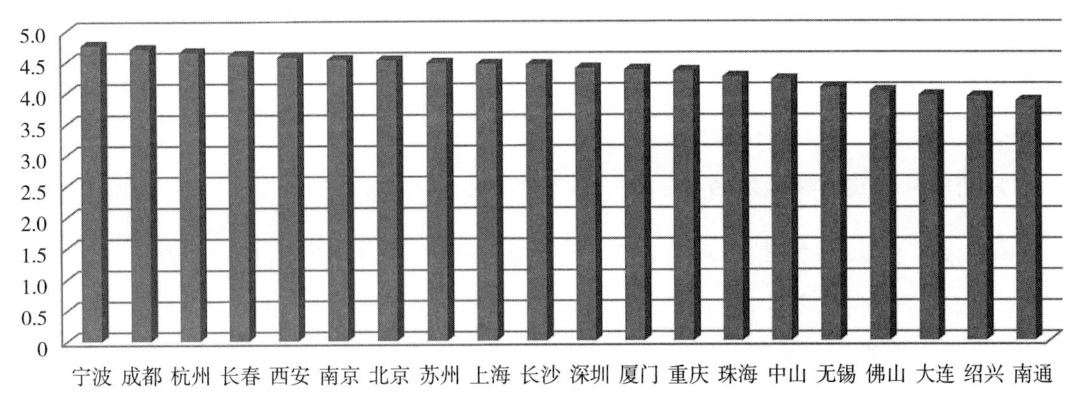

图 28 被调查者对外来人口感到的幸福程度

22. 被调查者对旅游度假感到的幸福程度

随着人们生活水平的提高，旅游度假已经成为大部分家庭每年计划表的一个固定选项，人们对于旅游度假的需求增强，也促进了旅游景区的日益兴盛和交通状况的改善。图 29 显示，在这一指标上杭州位居第一，苏州位居第二，北京、南京、西安、长春、宁波、长沙、上海、成都紧随其后。

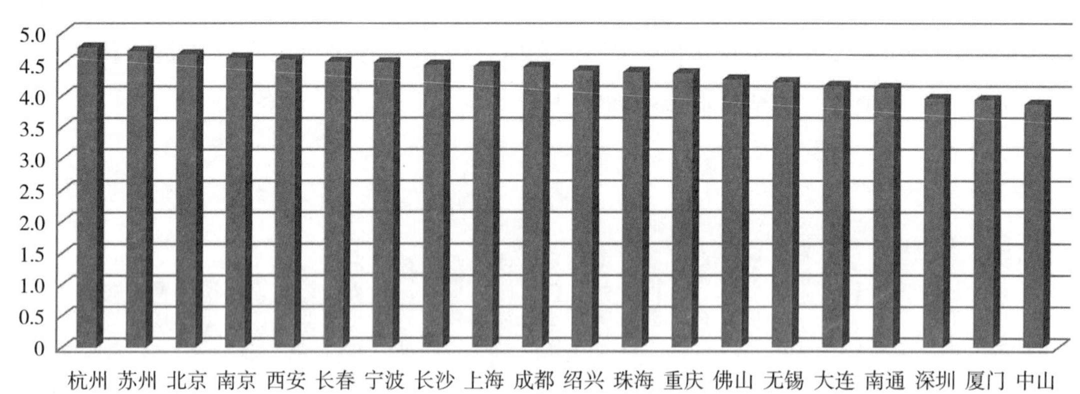

图 29 被调查者对旅游度假感到的幸福程度

（三）大数据采集对此次调查的意义

近年来，大数据如浪潮般席卷全球，并深度改变人们的生活、工作和思维方式。世界上越来越多的国家开始从战略层面认识大数据，在城市治理领域融入大数据思维和技术。2015 年 7 月 1 日，国务院办公厅发布的《关于运用大数据加强对市场主体服务和监管的若干意见》中明确提出，提高政府运用大数据的能力，推动政府向社会力量购买大数据资源和技术服务。第三方向政府提供的大数据资源和技术服务，将成为社会发展的主潮流。

通过对数据的整理与分析，城市管理者可预测民众的需求。提供大数据支持，可以及时、准确地反映城市的发展现状，为城市经济、社会发展提供决策依据，进而促进政府更加智能与高效的管理和服务。有利于打造平民政府、服务政府、开放政府，促进城市全面发展。

本次调查，对排名前 20 位的城市进行大数据采集，通过 10 项大指标、51 项小指标的数据分析，能够更客观地反映城市居民对于所居住城市的幸福感受。

（四）小康社会建设城市排名

小康社会是 20 世纪 70 年代末规划中国经济社会发展蓝图的战略构想。随着中国特色社会主义建设事业的深入，其内涵和意义不断地得到丰富和发展，在 20 世纪末基本实现“小康”的情况下，党的十六大报告明确提出了“全面建设小康社会”。党的十八大报告根据我国经济社会发展实际和新的阶段性特征，提出 2020 年全面建成小康社会。在习近平总书记提出的“四个全面”理论框架体系中，全面建成小康社会无疑是新时期党和国家各项工作的总目标，处于引领地位。全面建成小康社会注重的是经济、社会和公民素质的全面提升，可以增强中国人民对未来发展的信心，同时也让世界人民看到一个积极向上的中国形象。

排名前 20 位的城市已经率先达到小康社会的标准并具有示范作用。根据各城市发展情况，排名如图 30 所示。

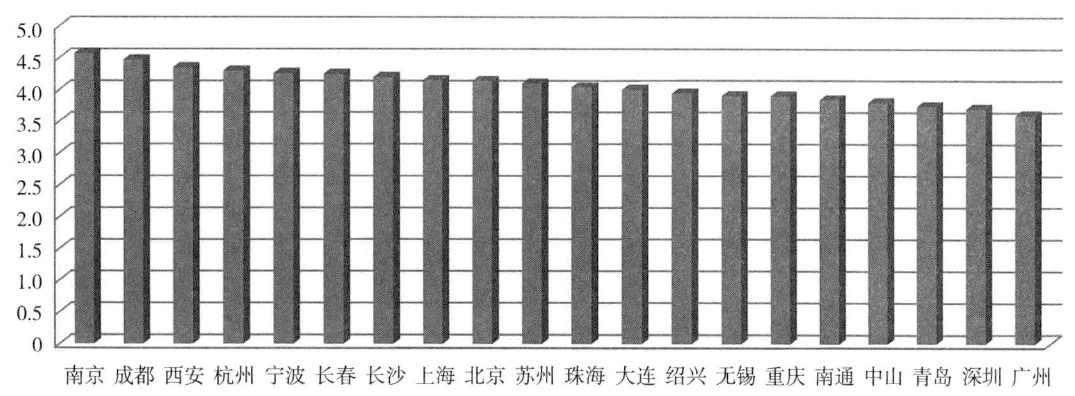

图 30 小康社会建设城市排名

五、结论

伴随着城市的发展，人们的幸福感应该越来越强烈，因为人们享受到的优质资源越来越多。但事实并非如此，两者的天平不容易平衡，有时候城市发展了，人们的幸福感反而降低。许多城市拥有一些共同的城市病：交通拥堵、环境污染、入托难、就医难等，已经严重困扰城市居民的生活。城市管理者对居民幸福感的持久关注，说明其视角从单纯追求经济功能，转向同时注重城市的生活功能。城市具备一定的经济功能，人们才有幸福可言，丧失了经济功能的城市，幸福只能是空中楼阁。然而，过于追求城市的经济功能，忽视城市的生活功能，人们的幸福感则会受到伤害。在现实生活中，一些城市的 GDP 等各项数据上去了，但是人们并没有从这些增长的数据中实现幸福感的提升，城市居民的生活质量和生活水准失去了应有的保障。

古希腊哲学家亚里士多德说过，人们来到城市，是为了生活，人们居住在城市，是为了生活得更好。中国最具幸福感城市调查活动迄今已举办 9 年，从中央到地方，从企业界到学术界，在干部和群众中都引起了强烈反响，全国千余家媒体给予了高度关注和报道，已成为中国最具影响力的城市调查活动。调查对于城市管理者在城市民生建设方面具有指导示范作用，对于提升中国城市形象，推动中国城市走向世界具有积极意义。

（作者：黄琳，《瞭望东方周刊》责任编辑；吴佳芯，中国最具幸福感城市调查活动组委会副秘书长）

成都：把民生工作做到群众心坎上

随着我国开始进入城镇化较快发展的中后期，亟须解决城市管理的“短板”问题，如管理理念落后、法律法规不健全、管理方式简单、服务意识不强、执法行为粗放等。

党的十八届三中、四中全会将理顺城市管理执法体制作为全面深化改革、全面推进依法治国的重要举措，提出了新要求，做出了新部署。2015 年 12 月 20 日至 21 日于北京召开的中央城市工作会议也强调，抓城市工作，一定要抓住城市管理和服务这个重点，不断完善城市管理和服务，彻底改变粗放型管理方式，让人民群众在城市生活得更方便、更舒心、更美好。

成都市委认真贯彻中央和四川省委部署，准确把握中央和四川省委对城市工作的新要求，努力提升城市建设管理科学化水平。重点在五个方面着力：一是以“四态合一”思路引领城市发展，切实做到形态美城、业态兴城、文态活城、生态优城。二是深入实施“立城优城”“统筹城乡”战略，加快推动城市空间由“圈层式”向“组团式”转变，构建以中心城区和天府新区为双核，以卫星城和区域中心城为支撑，以小城市、特色镇和农村新型社区为基础的“双核共兴、一城多市”的市域城镇体系。三是以“大开大合”气魄做强城市功能，跳出“盆地意识”，打破“西部宿命”，努力奠定成都在世界城市体系和国际分工格局中的地位。四是将“改革创新”精神贯穿于城市发展的各个领域和各个环节，不断增强城市发展的动力与活力。五是以“共建共享”原则凝聚城市主体，以共建促共享，以共享带共建，努力形成人人参与、人人尽力、人人享有的城市发展格局。

一、幸福“可触摸”，口碑方丰碑

由新华社《瞭望东方周刊》与中国市长协会《中国城市发展报告》共同主办的“2015中国最具幸福感城市调查活动”，成都蝉联“中国最具幸福感城市”第一名。这既是对成都城市功能品质的肯定，也是对成都城市建设管理的褒奖。中国城市评价中心、中国城市幸福感调查活动组委会领导用“实至名归”来评价成都获得的殊荣。

高度的评价，源于成都名副其实。继 2014 年成都市 GDP 突破万亿元大关后，2015 年，成都经济社会保持平稳较快发展，预计实现地区生产总值 1.08 万亿元左右，同比增长 8%左右，城镇和农村居民人均可支配收入分别增长 8.5%、10%，城镇和农村居民人均可支配收入比由2.16∶1缩小到1.9∶1。同时，成都市公共财政民生保障支出994亿元，增长11.1%，占一般公共预算支出67.2%，保障民生切实改善，社会事业全面进步。这座城市经济社会发展的同时，更是实实在在地为成都市民带来了“可以触摸”的幸福——从“六湖八湿地”① 一个个开门迎接市民，到地铁4号线建成通车，再到已经进入第四个年头的“北改”② 工程，还有继“北改”之后最大的民生工程“四改六治理”③，以及高举创新创业旗帜的“创业天府”计划。

坚持以人民为中心，是做好城市工作的出发点和落脚点。在成都这些可喜的变化和市民获得感背后，是成都市委、市政府贯彻落实省委重大要求，深入推进政府职能转变和治理创新，在城市工作中大力践行“三视三问”群众工作法——一是视市民为亲人，问需于民，把市民需求作为城市工作的决策源头和逻辑起点；二是视市民为老师，问计于民，主动邀请市民为城市工作出点子、当参谋；三是视市民为裁判，问效于民，把市民满意不满意、高兴不高兴作为检验工作的最终标准。

市民的口碑，是城市最好的丰碑。根据《成都市国民经济和社会发展第十三个五年规划纲要》，“建设幸福城市”正是成都站在新起点，坚持创新、协调、绿色、开放、共享五大发展理念，谋划新发展，实现新目标的重点工作，让全体市民过上更有获得感和幸福感、更有尊严的生活。

二、建立“大城市，细管理”的综合管理体系

2015年2月，位于成都市金河路57号的成都市城管局机关办公大楼下，工作人员将“成都市城市管理局”的牌匾摘下，挂上了“成都市城市管理委员会”的牌匾。一摘一挂间，完成了一次从“局”到“委”的转身。

---

① 六湖八湿地：也叫“六库八区”湖泊水系，成都环城生态区规划总规模187.15平方公里，其中“六库八区”是其核心内容。“六库”指锦城湖、江安湖水库、北湖水库、青龙湖水库、安靖湖水库、金沙湖水库。“八区”指水库周边和锦江区三圣片区、成华区龙潭片区布局的八片水生作物区。2015年年底，锦城湖、青龙湖一期、白鹭湾生态湿地、新都香城湿地一、二期、龙泉驿花田湿地、温江金沙湿地等7个湖泊湿地已建成。高新中和湿地、双流江安湿地、高新绿洲等项目仍在建设中。待成都环城生态区建设完毕后，每位市民乘公共交通30分钟即能享受到环城生态区内的山地、森林、湖泊和湿地。

② 北改：2012年，成都站在破除“城市二元结构”的高度，启动了“北改”这项最大的民生工程，提出用5年时间，还全市人民一个畅通城北、安居城北、宜人城北，通过改造城北片区老旧的城市形态和落后的生产力布局，改变“北乱”的旧患，让城市平衡发展。2015年年底，成都市“北改”累计改建道路196公里，关闭、搬迁、升级专业市场56家，完成21个棚户区改造，解放北路等一批梗阻多年的道路顺利打通，荷花池市场整治等一批老百姓热议多年的项目全面完成，北部城区正在加速蜕变。成都正按照“五年大变样”的目标倒排进度，提速推进基础建设、旧城改造、产业发展等工作，力争早日全面建成“四态合一”的新城北。

③ 四改六治理：2015年，成都启动“四改六治理”行动计划，这是继“北改”后，成都最大规模民生工程。“四改六治理”中的“四改”指棚户区、城中村、老旧院落、老旧市场改造，旨在改善居民生活环境；“六治理”指大气雾霾、河渠污染、交通秩序、市容市貌、违法建设、农村环境的治理，旨在提升城乡环境品质。“四改六治理”涵盖城市空间、产业、生态、管理和城乡形态多个方面，是一项内容丰富、涉及面广的系统工程。该项目将改造棚户区2 746万平方米、老旧院落1 134个、老旧批发市场127个、黑臭河流413条。

这不是简单的名称更替，简单背后颇有深意。成都作为西部特大中心城市和四川省首位城市，近年来，成都市的管理者积极推行“大城市，细管理”理念，坚持向细致要质量、向细节要形象、向细密要品质，城市管理切实加强，被评为中国最佳管理城市。正是在这样的理念和实践之下，成都致力于全面努力提升城市建设管理科学化水平，在全省乃至西部城镇体系和区域发展格局中充分发挥了带头、带动、引领、示范和辐射作用。

按照改革部署，“委”将承担起制定政策、规划、标准，以及监督执行、统筹协调等职责，也就是说，更名后的城市管理委员会，在之前执行、监管的职责基础上，新增了牵头建立城市管理综合协调和责任体系职能，负责城市管理领域的统筹协调、监督检查。

面对城市管理体制、机制、法规、力量、设施以及舆论等方面的矛盾和问题，被赋予城市管理重任的“新”机构——城管委，坚持以改革创新为统揽，既立足当前成都城管实际，又注重学习借鉴外地先进经验，梳理并确定72项改革创新项目和工作任务，成立深化城市管理领域改革领导小组，制定改革创新实施方案，形成了从组织构架到责任体系、从实施方案到保障措施等一套完整规范的工作布局。

对成都市锦江区水井坊的很多居民来说，2015年有很多令人欣喜的变化。“院落里的垃圾桶满了，打个电话给城管科工作人员，一会儿环卫公司就会有专人前来清理；路面出现状况，通知一声交通局，就能快速处理……”2015年2月，自从成立了城市管理社区服务站，处理城市管理的问题变得更加快捷、方便了。

破除城市管理的顽疾，必须充分发动和调动社会各界的广泛参与，形成共建共享治理成果的社会氛围。为了理顺区、街道、社区三级层面的关系，成都市城管委在建立决策、执行、监督三层体系的同时，在全市率先探索建立了水井坊社区、锦官驿社区2个城市管理社区服务站。

据社区相关负责人介绍，对于城市管理出现的问题，比如拾拣垃圾这些能及时处理的，服务站成员都会立即处理；不能处理的，如窨井盖遗失等，会立即上报解决。此外，服务站还广泛发动辖区商家共同参与城市管理，形成“共治共管”局面。“这改变了过去‘城市管理只归城管局负责’的片面认识，充分发动了社区一级参与城市管理的积极性和主动性。”

作为城市细管理的“示范区”，水井坊街道并不仅仅拥有城市管理社区服务站这一项“秘密武器”。为实现高效管理，水井坊街道还融合公安“天网”系统，建立起了街道综合信息指挥系统，实现了对主干街道及64个院落全天候网络监控。这样一来，城管队员就可以集中人力分布在各个背街小巷，管理力量平均密度达到每条街道8人，管理力量提高了2.7倍，帮助城市管理者及时发现各个问题，及时全面采集第一手信息。

“一旦街面发现问题，我们会立即指派距任务发生点最近的城管人员前往处理，实现突发事件快速、及时和有序地解决。”相关负责人说。那么，如何精确得知哪位城管队员距离远近呢？原来，每位城管队员都配备有GPS定位系统、执法记录仪等先进的执法装备。“可以实时采集城管协管员的GPS坐标，而城管队员在执法过程中也需要在记录仪上记录执法信息。”据介绍，这些数据都是他们考核城管队员的基础。

基于这套设备，水井坊街道已经建立起城市管理综合评价系统，客观评价结果与城管队员绩效考核挂钩，实现城管队员“网格化、系统化”的效能督查。这些系统，正是成都市城管委大力推行的“智慧城管”的生动案例。

城市管理社区服务站、街道综合信息指挥系统和城市管理综合评价系统，正是这些“小手段”，汇集成了一套“细管理”的组合拳。必须认识到的是，面对城市面积日益扩大、建设飞速发展、人口不断增加，精细化的管理才是打造宜居城市，让市民享受舒适生活的保障。

在精细化管理的基础上，按照“互联网 +”思维，成都还在2015年积极探索网格化的城市管理模式。通过在街道创建社区网格管理信息化指挥中心，构建大数据基础信息库，掌握社区院落动态管理情况，及时协调解决居民各种诉求。以成都市成华区为例，2015年，成华区将探索区域治理“大联动”作为深化社会治理创新的重要内容，加快构建“一个指挥系统、一套管理机制、一个服务平台、一张防范网络、一套服务体系”，推进指挥协调大统筹、社会服务大集中、管理资源大整合，建立健全集指挥、应急、排查等功能于一体的大数据应用中心、“大联动”管理网络平台体系，构建“区—街—社区”三级“大联动”中心与区公安指挥中心“双中心”管理体系，实现了行政管理资源的高效整合和社会治理效能的全面提升。

成都市城管委表示，将按照“大城市，细管理，严管理”和“天天归零”的要求，以“创新、协调、绿色、开放、共享”五大发展理念引领城市管理“五个新作为”，全力构建综合管理有机协调、法规标准健全配套、规划管理全域覆盖、基础要素保障有力、社会治理效能突出的城市综合管理体系，全面提升城市综合管理水平，努力实现“中西部第一、全国一流、国际领先”的城市管理奋斗目标。成都在奋力打造西部经济核心增长极、建设现代化国际化大都市进程中，城市管理转型升级向纵深推进，“大城市，细管理”的理念也贯彻到了城市管理的方方面面。市民在日常生活里，不仅感受到了成都的清爽有序，成都的城市品质也悄然得以提升。商务部中国国际经济合作学会副秘书长、新兴产业促进中心主任强宏说，成都全新的城市管理理念可以促进城市空间、产业、生态、管理和城乡形态多个方面快速发展，对城市居民生活水平提升、经济转型、结构平衡等促进很大。当前成都正处在城市化加速推进和城市品牌塑造提升的关键阶段，城市管理面临新的形势和挑战。推进城市建设管理转型升级，既是城市发展、时代进步的迫切要求，也是提升成都城市品质和魅力的必然选择。

城市管理水平的提高，与居住在城市中的每一个人都息息相关。过去取得的成绩，也必将鞭策成都进一步提升城市管理水平。《成都市国民经济和社会发展第十三个五年规划纲要》明确提出了“优化提升城市功能”的要求。未来五年的成都，要进一步提升城市发展品质，建立现代化城市综合管理体系，提升城市综合管理水平。中国城市经济学会副会长牛凤瑞认为，成都的“大城市，细管理”理念，是对现行城市管理体制、方式、方法的改进优化和提升，是对城市运行、发展各影响因子变化的精准预判和把握，是对管理细节、末端和管理第一线的精准规制和掌控，是确保城市稳定、健康、有序、高效运行的高水平管理。

三、建设市域和市区“半小时交通网”

2015年12月26日，成都地铁网络增添了一条新的“骨架”——4号线开始载客运营。地铁4号线一期全长约21公里，西起非遗博览园站，东至万年场站，东西向贯穿成都中心城区，是成都第三条穿城的地铁线路。

随着4号线的开通，成都地铁在原先以天府广场为中心、沿南北中轴线与东西交通“主动脉”为十字形支架的核心线路上，又增添了一条新的网线。作为第三条正式运营的地铁线路，4号线与也是在2015年开通运营的1号线南延线，正火热建设中的3号线和7号线等，进一步推进了成都地铁“连线成网”。成都地铁以每天几十万乘次的载客量，为广大乘客提供着快捷的出行服务，累计运送乘客总量已在2015年突破10亿人次。数据显示，乘着“交通先行”战略的东风，成都地铁在运和在建总里程已经达到了200多公里。目前，成都地铁营运里程达88公里，另有6条地铁线路正在抓紧推进。“十三五”期间，成都平均每年将开通地铁2条以上，累计建成投运地铁13条、总里程达到500公里。

除了地铁，成都在地面公交建设上取得的成果同样令人欣慰。在中心城区内，不管从什么地方出门，95.9%的市民都能在500米范围内找到一个公交站点；不管目的地在哪里，96%的市民最多只需要换乘一次就能到达；不管是早高峰还是晚高峰出行，都会发现不少路段公交车跑在专用道上，比私家车还快……

以快速公交为代表的城市公交的大力发展，使成都公交成了成都一张新的城市名片。于2013年开通的成都二环快速公交，使成都公交进入了快速时代。在2015年，成都公交集团进一步优化快速公交发车模式，高峰平均40秒一班，最密集时段25秒一班，成为全国之最。

此外，为了解决居民出行最后一公里的问题，成都大力开行免费乘坐的社区巴士。截至2015年年底，已有近100条社区公交穿行在成都的背街小巷，让成都公交“毛细血管”的微循环彻底畅通了起来。

交通先行，在于给城市提供一个畅通高效的交通运行网络，其最终落脚点在于“利城惠民”。打造便民交通圈，不仅需要构建成体系的公共交通网络，同样需要配套完善、秩序良好的交通环境。2015年，成都交委实施一系列民生工程，比如新建电子公交站牌300个，完成4个客运站的提升改造，开展出租车专项治理工作，启动机动车驾驶员培训公众服务平台等，在让老百姓感受到缓堵保畅工作带来变化的同时，也营造了更加良好的交通环境。

除此之外，为了从源头上解决电动自行车存在的超速、超大、超重问题，确保广大市民出行安全，成都市质监局会同市公安、工商、经信委、环保局于2014年底共同制定了《成都市电动自行车产品目录管理办法》，并于2015年初开始正式实施，电动自行车上牌、超标车三年后淘汰、限速15公里/小时、新车超速自动断电……保障了市民的出行安全。

在2015年实施的最大民生工程“四改六治理”中，为了规范交通秩序，成都市交委开展了一系列整治行动，包括交通硬件设施提升、交通治理模式创新和交通文明全民共建等。

为了缓解市民停车难的问题，还于寸土寸金的中心城区新增了数千个停车位，于四川大学华西校区和望江校区开建了三个大型地下停车场。同时，地铁 4 号线开通运营后，为了满足郊区居民驾私家车换乘地铁的需求，还将在部分地铁站设置 P + R 停车场。

2015 年，成都还完成了中心城区近 500 条道路的“整容”，在深入推进的“北改”工程中新改建道路 180 公里，同时红星路和老川藏路的“大手术”也进展有序。红星路改造已于 2016 年 1 月完成，老川藏路改造也将于 2016 年 4 月结束，改造后的红星路和老川藏路，将成为双向 8 车道的中心城区骨干道路。同时，成都还于 2015 年继续对城区内 62 条道路提高限速，提升了道路通行能力和通行效率。为推动成都市民绿色出行，成都市交管部门还实行了三种新能源汽车不限行的政策。

在 2015 年，成都继续大力实行“交通先行”战略，以地铁和公交为代表的密集公共交通网络进一步完善，一系列的道路大改造保证了道路资源利用效率的进一步提高，对电动自行车的综合整治保障了广大市民的出行安全，交通秩序整治行动也让成都的交通秩序越来越好，交通越来越文明。市域和市区两个“半小时交通网”基本成形。

北京大学城市与区域规划系主任吕斌认为，成都 2015 年的多项交通秩序治理举措，体现了相关部门精细化、智能化、智慧化的管理方式。城市发展，只是一味地修路是不行的，同时需要提高交通管理水平。根据道路的实际情况，适当提升道路的限速值，是从细微处入手，静态地解决出行问题，体现了成都管理的精细化。

四、提升生态环境治理

2015 年 11 月的一天，成都市市政工程设计研究院设计二所副所长游屹开车经过锦城大道旁的锦城湖畔时，停下了车子。接着，他走进公园南侧大门，围着 4 号湖步行了十余分钟，观察水质是否良好。作为锦城湖涉水工程的设计者，从 2013 年 5 月锦城湖建成开放至今，游屹只要经过锦城湖，都会停下来看看。

2012 年年初，成都启动“六湖八湿地”环城生态区的规划建设，打造“八十公里环城绿廊”。当时这个规划的背后，其实有一个令人尴尬的事实：向来以水资源丰富著称的成都，在主城区内，连一个湿地公园都没有。

对一个城市而言，湿地公园不仅能给市民提供亲水赏景的休闲去处，同时也会如城市之肺一般，让城市自如呼吸、永续发展。作为世界上第一个建在大都市中心的湿地公园，伦敦湿地中心距离白金汉宫仅有 25 分钟车程。湿地吸引了大量野生鸟类栖息，而大面积的水域和植被，使之可以有力调节城市地区小环境气候和空气质量。

正因如此，成都于当年启动了“六湖八湿地”环城生态区的规划建设。2013 年以来，“六湖八湿地”逐步进入了“丰收”阶段：2013 年建成开放了锦城湖、白鹭湾湿地，2014 年建成开放了新都区香城湿地一期、龙泉驿区花田湿地，2015 年建成开放了青龙湖一期、温江区金沙湿地、高新区中和湿地一期及二期、新都区香城湿地二期，2016 年将计划建成双流区江安湿地、全面建成高新区中和湿地和新都区香城湿地，启动龙泉驿青龙湿地、成华龙潭湿地、郫县安靖湿地等。

到现在为止，锦城湖已经晋升为成都人的夜跑胜地；相当于6个成都植物园大小的白鹭湾，是成都最大的水生动植物自然课堂；青龙湖吸引了3 500只以上的雁鸭类水鸟，成为成都平原最大水鸟越冬地，其中观察到了2只全球存量不足500只的青头潜鸭。

“六湖八湿地”的环城生态区是成都奋力打造宜人生态环境的一个剪影。不仅如此，近年来，成都围绕“两山两环、两网六片”[①]的市域生态格局，还加快龙泉山、龙门山和邛崃山系生态屏障建设，配套实施“百湖”工程，推进天然林保护、退耕还林工程，努力实现“山山见绿、川川见水”的生态建设目标。同时在中心城区，实施“三环六通道”绿化工程等重大民生绿化工程，建设社区绿地、街头绿地和邮票绿地。目前，城市绿地率达35.69%，全市自然保护区、风景名胜区和森林公园总面积达到3 773平方公里，全市森林覆盖率增至38.1%。

“我们将拿出最坚决的态度，坚持最严格的生态环境保护制度，尽最大努力推进生态建设和环境修复，努力让成都蓝天常在、绿水长流。”成都的管理者坚持把生态系统作为绿色的基础设施来打造，确立了“城区五百米见绿，有条件地区千米见水”的目标，在中心城区建成公园绿地89个、185公顷，在全市建成绿道2 007公里，成功创建国家级生态市。新华社用“水草相依、鸟鸣鱼游、万花掩映”描绘了成都生态发展的图景。环绕中心城区，一条绿水相融、功能复合的“生态绿肺”，像翡翠项链点缀城市之中，“出则田园，入则都市”的生态梦想就此实现。《凤凰周刊》对成都的印象是：纵观全球各大城市，能在高度城市化的进程中，同时近距离保留生态形态的，屈指可数。成都决定在寸土寸金的城区，保留下133平方公里的生态空间，为市民提供休闲场所，为城市提供绿肺空间，这不仅得益于卓越的眼光，更有本着对人民群众高度负责的态度。

韩国企业退休高管、周游世界后定居成都的“韩国大叔”郑尚文说，成都给我的感觉很好，自然环境优美，周边风景很棒，是中国最好的城市。四川大学社会发展与西部开发研究院杨明洪教授评价成都说，近年来越来越多的世界知名企业落户成都，一个关键因素就是“宜人”。“六湖八湿地”环城生态区有助于推进成都城市生态转型升级和保护，建成后势必进一步提升成都的宜商、宜居环境，属于在追求生态环境的基础上谋求经济发展。

五、建设优良人居环境

在成都市人民北路二段北站西三巷，有一幢三层红砖房，刘阿姨一家已经在里面居住了30余年。“住房条件差，还有不少老鼠、蟑螂，后来儿子娶了媳妇，房子不够住，只有租房子。”同刘阿姨一样的，还有83岁的杨敬书大爷，虽然住的不是红砖房，但住房条件也不好。“我们家4口人，1986年搬进了北站西一路6号，一直住到今天。房子近50平方米，以

---

① “两山两环、两网六片”市域生态格局规划：“两山”是龙门山和龙泉山生态屏障；“两环”是环城生态区和第二绕城高速路生态隔离带；“两网”是市域水网和绿道网；“六片”是六片防止城市连片发展的生态隔离区。

前倒还好，只有点小问题。现在年纪大了，我每天爬5层楼梯，很费力。”

刘阿姨和杨大爷居住的房屋均建于20世纪五六十年代，多为成都铁路局职工宿舍。房屋基础设施老化、配套落后，安全隐患等问题突出。居民们都希望能告别棚户区，期盼改造圆安居梦。

刘阿姨和杨大爷两家并非个案。伴随着城市功能的完善和城市品质的提升，一大批修建于几十年前的棚户区却越来越老旧，严重影响了生活于其中的人群的生活质量。2015年，成都市展开了声势浩大的民生工程“四改六治理”十大行动，其中包含了棚户区改造。在棚户区改造中，成都市严格按城市规划实施，坚持不以牺牲城市品质为代价，不盲目地追求投入产出平衡提高地块容积率，通过多种改造方式相结合，区分轻重缓急，对棚户区实施分类改造。

据《成都市棚户区改造专项工作方案》的规划，棚户区改造行动充分利用国家金融支持政策，加大财政投入，扩大融资规模，优先改造项目地块为绿地、公建配套用地，或者地块内现有房屋经鉴定为影响安全必须拆除的危房居住区及其他建筑物。各区（市）县政府统筹组织实施，积极推动其他类型的棚户区改造，计划到2017年完成棚户区改造10.36万户，改造面积1 946万平方米，争取在5年内基本消除棚户区。

除了棚户区改造，旨在改善成都生活环境的“四改六治理”行动还包括城中村改造、老旧院落改造、老旧市场改造、市容市貌治理、违法建设治理和农村环境治理等。

根据相关的专项工作方案，成都力求到2017年基本完成中心城区的城中村改造、五城区的老旧院落改造，并调迁改造三环路以内97家老旧市场，改善城市居住环境，提升城市形象，赋予城市新的容貌。在市容市貌治理和违法建设治理方面，到2017年，成都力求在五城区及高新区各建6座垃圾转运站并实现公共空间不新增违建。2015年，成都还完成了109个村庄的容貌整治先行试点。

当然，对2015年的成都来说，生活环境的改善不仅仅包括城市容貌和城市细节的美化，还包含了医疗、养老、教育、购物等直接关系民生的方方面面。

2015年，成都的城镇基本医疗保障覆盖率达到了98%，每万人拥有的医生数和医院床位分别达到了4.02人和90张，这一数字在全国的城市中处于领先水平。值得一提的是，2015年12月2日，成都在双流举办了“居民健康卡”首发仪式，逐步结束了“一院一卡”的时代，这意味着只要手持居民健康卡，成都市民可以到任何一家市级公立医疗机构完成预约挂号、诊间支付和出院结算等全过程。

同全国其他城市一样，面临着人口老龄化加剧的成都，在养老服务方面也频频“出手”。2015年起，成都政策扶持养老力度更大，安排养老服务业发展资金4亿元，专项用于推进养老服务业发展。对机构发展扶持政策力度同样加大，对新建并依法设立许可的社会化养老机构，属营利性的每张床位给予10 000元、属非营利性的每张床位给予12 000元的一次性建设补贴。值得一提的是，从7月份起，成都60岁以上低保老人均可申请养老补贴。同时，成都市还出台了《关于加快养老服务业创新发展的实施意见》，明确了养老服务业社会化、产业化的发展方向，而且明确将养老服务业发展纳入民生目标考核。到2015年年底，成都已经实现了养老服务设施城镇社区全覆盖，城镇基本养老保险覆盖率也达到了97%。

教育方面，在2015年，成都市的义务教育完成率达到了100%，高等教育毛入学率达到了84.55%，全市教育发展指数位居副省级城市第一。而对于占成都市总人口比例1/4的流动人口来说，2015年无疑也是值得开心的一年。2015年11月，成都市教育局印发了《关于做好2016年进城务工人员随迁子女接受义务教育工作的指导意见》，采取新举措进一步方便流动人口子女在成都接受义务教育，如往年进城务工人员为子女申请入学时须提交“申请人与其子女同一户籍的原籍户口簿”，2016年变更成了“申请人及其子女同一户籍的原籍户口簿或其他能够证明其法定监护关系的有效证明”。

2015年，成都市还大力完善公共文化服务，进一步推进文化惠民。在成都的21家公立图书馆，成都市民只需凭二代身份证便可借书，而且可在所有21家图书馆通借通还。在成都市高新区，启动了“一街一书屋”建设项目试点，以进一步满足居民精神文化需求。同时，成都市还进一步升级了已经启动一年多的公益电影进影院惠民活动，除了观看公益电影，市民还可以通过这项惠民活动同步观看最新上映的大片。

在购物方面，成都市在2015年出台了《成都建设具有国际影响力购物天堂行动计划》，标志着成都加快建设具有国际影响力购物天堂进入了全面实施阶段。随着《计划》的实施，一系列旨在提升成都投资贸易便利化水平，提升客货通达能力，加快国际化品牌引进培育，优化完善购物环境以及加强购物天堂建设氛围营造的行动也已全面展开。

值得一提的是，继2014年工商、质监部门宣布取消垂直管理后，成都市的县级市场监管部门2015年再次迎来了新一次机构改革。成都各个区（市）县将原有的工商局、质监局、食药监局撤销，组建市场监督管理局。这一改革旨在解决以往工商、质监和食药监局职能交叉、界限不清的问题，对市场秩序的监管形成“一竿子”到底的模式，从而更好、更迅捷地为成都市民服务，进一步提升成都生活品质。

统筹城乡，广袤农村是主战场。作为全国统筹城乡综合配套改革试验区、首批国家现代农业示范区、第二批全国农村改革试验区，成都是拥有上千万人口的大都市，具有典型的“大城市带大农村”的特色。如何缩小城乡的差距？怎样持续改变城乡的差距？成都开始了一场破解城乡二元化的探索试验。在成都的新村建设实践中，一个新模式的面目和轮廓日益清晰——“小规模、组团式、微田园、生态化”。“小组微生”的建设，不仅为成都的城市居民提供了一个领略田园风光的场景，也让千千万万农民享受了实惠，富裕了生活。

这种关于幸福的感悟，已在成都生活两年的国企员工徐健体会深刻。他说：“成都的生活环境很好，舒适度很高，衣食住行各方面都非常便捷。成都是一个包容性很强的城市，我准备在成都一直住下去，成家立业。”美国著名大厨里克·贝利斯也为在成都的幸福生活点赞：“现代化的成都迸发出的勃勃生机让我感到惊叹，亲眼见到成都时，才发现这是一个全新的世界，与香港、上海不同。生活环境特别安逸，我以后会常来。”

“人民对美好生活的向往就是我们的奋斗目标，必须始终饱含真挚感情，想群众之所想、急群众之所急，努力把民生工作做到群众的心坎上。”成都的城市管理者如是说。在2015年，成都坚持共享发展，不断增进民生福祉，坚持交通先行、立城优城等“五大兴市战略”，努力打造宜居生活环境。2015 年 12 月 20 日在北京举办的“2015 年第十届中国全面小康论坛”颁奖晚会上，成都更是荣获“2015 年中国全面建设小康突出贡献城市奖项”，并且总分排名第一。2015 年的成都，在公共服务均等化等方面成绩突出，交出了一份漂亮的“民生答卷”。

六、打造良好就业创业环境

2015 年 5 月 9 日，西南交大材料科学与工程学院特聘教授永远经历了一次大“意外”——当日，在西南交通大学举行的第四场“创业天府 · 菁蓉汇”活动上，他的“分子键裂型生物传感器”创业项目，被数十家“辣舌”投行 15 次追单，最终斩获 1.15 亿元意向投资。而在最初，永远教授的心理预期，仅仅是拿到近百万元创业投资，继续他的项目产业化。

这样的“意外”，实在情理之中。

2015 年，成都市委、市政府高度重视“大众创业、万众创新”。从 2 月 8 日“创业天府 · 菁蓉汇”城市创业品牌应运而生以来，从无到有，600 多家创业团队、2 万多名创业者参与其中，而与他们同行的，还有国内外 300 多家创投机构的追捧，资本市场的“活水”，源源不绝地在成都汇流。

“双创”时代，创业已从“小众”走向“大众”。而“创业天府 · 菁蓉汇”这个城市创业品牌，促进全球风投西进成都。永远教授的案例只是成都用活市场之手为创新创业清障搭台，让市场活力竞相迸发的一个缩影。

2015 年 2 月 8 日，成都举起“大众创业、万众创新”旗帜，启动成都“创业天府”行动，出台了《成都“创业天府”行动计划（2015－2025 年）》，鼓励青年大学生、科技人员、海归、蓉漂来蓉创业。

为进一步推进“一带一校”计划，2015 年 9 月，成都高新区管委会与电子科技大学签署战略合作协议，共建成都高新区国家自主创新示范区。围绕高校打造知识经济圈，构建贯通政产学研用的科技创新体系，这对于激发创新创造活力、培育创新性产业、推动高新技术产业发展有着重要意义。

2015 年 11 月 9 日，全国首个全球创新创业交易会——2015 成都全球创新创业交易会在蓉揭幕。30 个国家和地区、2 686 个创业项目参加交易、109 个全球项目实现交易总额 53.2 亿元……三天盛宴，在蓉凝聚成《全球创新创业成都共识》。

从校院地协同创新，到“创交会”，建设全国领先、国际知名的“创业之城、圆梦之都”，成都正探索深入实施创新驱动发展战略，聚集全球资源要素，打造直面全球的“双创”城市品牌。

成都努力推进“双创”的大动作，2015 年取得了卓越的成效，被评为“中国十大创业城市”“中国最具投资吸引力城市”和“中国最具发展潜力城市”。

林秀鸟自来。成都优良的创新创业环境，吸引了一大批优秀人才。打造“创业之城、圆梦之都”，绝不是成都市管理者“一厢情愿”地唱独角戏。依靠创新创业驱动新一轮发展，既是领命国家战略的必然，也是顺应成都可持续发展理念的必然逻辑。在这样的背景下，找准制约创新发展的“堵点”、创业谋事的“痛点”，激发市场活力，政府清障搭台，无疑能释放、引流市场源源动力与活水生态。

更加值得欣喜的是，2015 年 12 月举行的中共成都市委十二届六次全会审议通过了《中共成都市市委关于系统推进全面创新改革　加快建设具有国际影响力的区域创新创业中心的决定》。这不仅彰显了成都市委市政府将成都打造成具有国际影响力的区域创新创业中心的决心，也必将再次大大改善成都的就业创业环境，巩固就业这一“民生之本”。

2015 年，紧随“创业天府”行动计划的实施，成都大力推进包括商事制度改革等政策，简政放权、放管结合、优化服务，“简、放、优”的核心，就是处理好政府和市场的关系，使市场在资源配置中起决定性作用和更好地发挥政府作用，激发市场活力和社会的创造力。

2015 年，成都还把调结构作为发展的主攻方向，进一步提升了经济发展质效。主动对接“中国制造 2025”计划和“互联网＋”行动计划，前瞻编制了成都创造、服务业等一系列“2025”规划，并加快推动轨道交通、生物医药、电子信息等先进制造业发展，深入推进服务业核心城市建设，大力打造西部金融中心、世界软件名城、世界旅游目的地和国际购物天堂，积极发展都市现代农业，进一步加强了“三产融合、联动发展”的现代产业体系。

完善的现代产业体系、强大的投资吸引力和强劲的“双创”推动能力，2015 年的成都已经具备了国内领先的优越创业就业环境。“在未来 5 年和 10 年，成都就是中国的硅谷。”聚美优品 CEO 陈欧说不仅为自己代言，也为成都代言。

万达集团在成都的投资金额超过1 300亿元，使成都成为万达集团投资额度最大的城市。万达集团董事长王健林对成都有着非常深厚的感情。“这里是我的故乡。不论过去、现在还是将来，不管万达如何发展，我都不敢忘记我是四川人这一身份。我一直想为这里做更大的贡献。顶级的文化旅游、最好的国际医院项目、电商云基地都放在了成都，这都是转型之后万达最重要的产业，你说成都重要不？”

奥地利技术研究院创新部部长乔治·菲林格尔说，校地协同创新战略为成都构建了很好的“双创”环境，成都高校云集。这一点，与美国硅谷等地非常相似，正如斯坦福大学是硅谷的灵魂一样，做好高校、地方科技成果转化，让高校创新体系融入城市经济、产业之中，是成都最大的优势和竞争力。中国科技部火炬中心主任张志宏这样评价成都：成都再一次抓住了机遇。成都是一个充满魅力的城市，如果说过去成都给人留下的印象是美食、文化，那么今天，成都应该加上一个新的标签：创业之城、圆梦之都。

（作者：中共成都市委对外宣传办公室）

阜新：让转型发展成果惠及群众

阜新是全国典型的资源型城市，因煤而立、因煤而兴，是“一五”时期建设的国家重要能源基地之一。60多年来，累计生产原煤7亿多吨，发电3 000多亿千瓦时，为国家经济建设做出了重要贡献。

自20世纪80年代起，阜新煤炭资源逐渐枯竭，到2000年前后，全市陷入了“矿竭城衰”的境地。一是经济发展徘徊不前。“九五”时期全市地区生产总值增幅仅为2.1%，2000年增幅更降为0.2%。二是就业问题十分突出。全市下岗失业人员达15.6万人，城镇登记失业率居辽宁省之首。三是地方财政入不敷出。全市公共财政预算收入仅有4.2亿元，人均公共财政预算收入仅为辽宁省平均水平的34.5%，市本级和七个县区全部靠省补贴过日子。四是大量城乡群众处于贫困状态。城区有近四分之一人口的月收入低于最低生活保障线156元，农村有60%人口返贫；500多万平方米的集中连片工矿棚户区不具备基本生活条件。五是城市建设欠账和生态破坏严重。基础设施配套不全、功能缺失，采煤沉陷区面积达到100多平方公里。阜新全面告急，尖锐的矛盾一触即发。阜新发展中的问题，引起了党中央、国务院和辽宁省委、省政府的高度关注。2001年12月，时任国务院副总理李岚清、吴邦国召开办公会议，将阜新确定为首个资源型城市经济转型试点市。2008年，辽宁省委、省政府实施了“突破辽西北”战略，并明确将阜新作为重点地区。

转型试点14年来，在党中央、国务院和辽宁省省委、省政府的高度重视和大力支持下，阜新始终坚持以转型振兴为主线，突出经济发展、改革创新、生态建设、民生改善四大主题，经济社会实现了持续快速发展，取得了经济转型的阶段性成果。

——经济发展实力持续增强，2001年至2015年间，地区生产总值从70亿元增长到542.1亿元，年均增长12.6%；公共财政预算收入从4.54亿元增长到37.2亿元，年均增长16.2%；固定资产投资累计完成3 270.5亿元，年均增长25.2%。

——经济质量效益明显加强，二、三产业增速均高于经济增速，城乡居民收入增速均高于经济发展速度，人均财政收入由283元提高到1 945元，城镇和农村居民人均可支配收入分别达到22 662元、11 109元，年均增长12.6%、17.8%。农民收入从2008年开始超过全国平均水平。

——经济比重稳步上升，全市地区生产总值、公共财政预算收入占辽宁省的比重由转型之初的1.7%、1.4%上升到2.1%、2.2%，人均GDP占全省人均GDP比重由30.8%提高到

52%。

经济转型试点以来，阜新市按照国家老工业基地振兴和资源型城市转型的总体部署，始终将可持续发展作为重要战略，坚持以转型振兴为主线，以做大经济总量、做强财力、提高人民生活水平为根本，转方式、调结构、保生态、惠民生，积极探索具有阜新特色的转型振兴之路，走出了一条持续快速发展的新路子。

一、坚持把可持续发展作为最大民生，大力培育接续替代产业

转型以来，阜新市坚持培育接续替代产业、实现可持续发展作为重中之重来抓，一方面继续巩固扩大煤电等传统产业对全市经济的支撑作用，另一方面着力改变以煤炭为主导的单一产业结构，促进产业结构调整和优化，多元化产业格局已经形成。煤电产业占比持续下降，煤电产业占工业比重由56.9%降到32.3%，其中，煤炭占规模以上工业增加值比重由34.6%下降到17.9%，电力比重由22.3%下降到14.4%。新培育的支柱产业占比明显上升，装备制造业比重由3%提高到20.6%，农产品加工业比重由12.7%提高到24.7%。具体措施如下。

一是大力发展工业经济。依托产业优势和资源优势，逐步培育形成了液压、氟化工、皮革、板材家居、农产品加工、煤化工、铸造、新型能源、新型材料、玛瑙等产业集群，现有企业达到1107户。这些产业集群基地配套、环保设施、科技研发、检验检测、物流贸易等平台基本完备。通过井工矿提升等措施，稳定煤炭产量，全市年煤炭产量保持在千万吨左右；通过压小上大等措施，新增火电装机容量132.4万千瓦；新增新能源装机容量183万千瓦。

二是加速培育新兴产业。在现有产业集群的基础上，结合“十三五”规划编制，提出了“三四四”发展格局，改造提升液压装备、农产品加工、能源产业集群，发展壮大煤化工、氟化工、皮革、板材家居产业集群，着力培育新型建材、钛金属制品、新型电子信息、生物医药等战略性新兴产业。突出新兴产业的发展，使新兴产业逐步成为接续产业的重点。依托国家“双百工程”示范基地，发展新型建材产业；依托既有电子产业园，发展新型电子产业；依托原有企业技术基础，发展新型材料产业；依托天士力等龙头企业，发展生物医药产业；依托玛瑙行业，发展文化创意产业。

三是稳步推进现代农业。从2014年开始，统筹全市农业资源，在全市实施了沈阜200万亩现代农业示范区项目，重点发展粮油、果品、设施农业和畜牧业四大产业，建设优质果品、精品农业等七大示范区，截至2015年年底已建成126.9万亩，实现农业增加值111亿元，惠及农户70余万人，示范区内农民人均收入新增1.7万元。特别是阜新在连续两年大旱的情况下，示范区在抗旱抗灾方面发挥了重要作用，保证了农民持续增收。同时，全市花生种植面积260万亩，年产量60万吨，居辽宁省首位，阜蒙县成为全国花生第一大县；实施畜牧业强市战略，畜牧产业化水平居全省第二位，养殖小区达到3 100余个；节水滴灌面积达到197万亩。

四是着力做好服务业发展。围绕专业市场、温泉旅游、玛瑙等服务业发展，实施百个服务业项目攻坚战，狠抓服务业集聚区建设，目前省级现代服务业集聚区达到5个，海州中央集聚区规模实现百亿元，大商、兴隆、大润发、红星美凯龙、绿地、恒强等品牌项目入驻；温泉开发面积达到30万平方米，年接待能力50万人次；国家4A级景区2个；阜新银行晋升全国城市商业银行百强行列。

二、坚持把项目建设作为重要抓手，增强保障民生支出能力

阜新市委、市政府始终把招商合作放在突出位置，把重大项目紧紧抓在手上，坚持以存量稳增长、以增量调结构，全力做大总量、做强财力，既为当前稳增长、促就业作出贡献，又为长远调结构打下坚实基础。

一是推进了一批合资合作、产业升级项目。本地企业积极走出去，寻求合资合作，实现做强做大。徐工集团整车装备项目，一期除雪机械产品升级及扩大产能已经基本完成，并形成了年产1 300台除雪设备的生产能力。中国航天四川公司整体搬迁启动高端液压支架项目一期生产车间已全部建设完成。上海宝钢集成建筑基地，一期3万平方米厂房主体框架已完成。保利集团机器人项目正在推进中。阜新与新东北电气集团合资合作的封闭母线、光缆、电缆项目正在洽谈中。这些项目有利于提升产业层次，扩大产业规模，提高产业效益。

二是推进了一批优化布局、引领业态发展的项目。上海红星美凯龙投资的红星国际广场综合体项目开工建设，完成投资2亿元。大连万达广场项目2015年洽谈、签约，已经开工。香港豪德入驻阜新，商贸城项目投入使用，农产品市场项目即将开工建设。紫金财富广场一期即将竣工。亚欧建材城一期主体完工。兴隆CBD二期投入使用，三期已经启动。这些项目对于提升阜新市现代服务业水平具有积极作用，促进专业市场等商业布局得到进一步完善。

三是推进了一批提升区位优势、完善城市功能的项目。积极融入“一带一路”战略，作为中蒙俄经济走廊重要通道之一的巴新铁路正式运营，其延伸线项目正在全力加快前期工作。京沈客专阜新段拆迁工作在全省率先完成，确保了项目顺利实施，成为参与京津冀协同发展战略的重要对接点。彰城至通辽连接线拆迁提前完成，启动实施。这些项目的实施，为阜新融入“一带一路”、京津冀协同发展等重大战略提供了机会，创造了条件，进一步提升了阜新在区域中枢纽城市、节点城市的作用，对于阜新的长远发展具有十分重要的意义。

四是推进了一批技改扩能、转型升级项目。围绕市场前景好、产业基础优的地方现有企业，支持引导企业技改升级，推动远东铜业、大金重工、鲁花、双汇、上海富国、德尔、振隆、万达铸造、华禹冶金、伊利乳业、新希望六合等企业实施技术改造项目。这些项目的实施，对于企业快速做大规模、提升水平有着至关重要的作用。

五是推进了一批企业上市融资。继大金重工在深交所成功上市后，阜新德尔、天佐羊绒等企业成功实现上市。同时，全力推动阜新银行、振隆特产、田元实业、金谷实业等一批企业的上市融资步伐。

三、坚持城乡统筹，不遗余力打造宜居环境

阜新市委、市政府充分认识到，民生改善、生态建设不是一蹴而就的，在长期建设过程中，决不能贪图功绩，决不能劳民伤财，要坚持对经济发展与民生期待进行通盘考虑，城乡民生建设统筹推进，不断改善居住条件和环境。

阜新因煤而兴、因煤而建，转型之初，多数房屋都是20世纪六七十年代的劳工房，加上采煤沉陷造成部分房屋受损，矿工的居住条件和生活环境都极差。针对这种情况，阜新市重点抓了四件事。

一是全力推进棚户区改造。把棚改作为一项德政工程、民心工程来抓，并且与沉陷区治理相结合，与拓展产业发展空间相结合，与推进城镇化相结合。阜新棚改在辽宁省任务最重，面积最大，受益群众最多。从2005年至2015年年底，共改造拆迁棚户区851万平方米，新建住房1 179万平方米，棚户区居民户均居住面积由29.6平方米提高到52平方米，圆了近54万人的安居梦。在建成小区的同时，做到了基础设施到位、物业管理到位、公共配套到位。经过努力，全市集中连片棚户区、国有工矿棚户区基本改造完成，实现了居者有其屋的目标，居民的财产性收入大幅增加，居住面积和生活环境都大为改观，城市形象明显提升。

二是改造维修老旧住宅小区。连续实施了给排水、小区封闭、供热节能等改造工程，完善小区物业功能，2014－2015年连续改造105个老旧住宅小区。计划用3年时间基本完成全部老旧住宅小区的改造，形成功能齐备、干净明亮、管理有序的良好环境。

三是大力整治城市环境。连续两年开展了城市环境综合整治年活动，使城市管理更加规范有序，重点街路保洁、绿化、亮化水平实现提升。理顺下放城区环卫管理职责，加大环保工作投入力度，提高城区环保设施机械化水平。2016年，将进一步巩固治理成果，重点在城市管理上下功夫，完善网格化、属地化管理体制，着力打造整洁卫生、绿色宜居、规范有序的城市环境。

四是推进宜居乡村建设。以村容整洁为目标，以垃圾治理为重点，以健全管护长效机制为保障，改善农村环境，2016年，全市所有行政村的环境卫生将整治达标，逐步培育形成一批宜居示范村。

四、坚持绿色发展理念，全力以赴推进生态文明

良好的生态环境是最公平的公共产品，是最普惠的民生福祉。看什么样的天、望什么样的山、喝什么样的水、呼吸什么样的空气，已经成为人们关注的热点、议论的焦点。阜新市抓生态建设，在算经济账、生态账的同时，更看重道德账、良心账。

阜新受限于科尔沁沙地南缘地理位置、长期资源破坏性开采的产业结构及干旱少雨的气候特点等环境问题，生态基础十分脆弱，生态建设任务十分繁重。阜新市坚决做到不以环境

换发展，而是以青山碧水蓝天工程为载体，坚持综合整治理念，着力破解制约产业发展、影响人居的问题，相继启动实施完成了多项重点环境治理工程，阜新局部生态环境已发生重要扭转、明显改善。2015 年，阜新市坚持“巩固提升、突出重点、攻坚难点、坚持不懈”的原则，继续推进细河综合治理、海州露天矿综合治理、空气环境改善、污水处理厂建设运行、宜居乡村建设、绿化沙化治理、主城区空气整治的环境治理“6+1”工程。

一是在治水方面。阜新的母亲河——细河综合治理工程启动，5 条污染河流生态恢复工程、4 个生态示范点、3 个生态示范区全部完工，细河生态带新增 4 公里，建成伊吗图等湿地 19 处，对沿岸百余户生产企业进行整治治理，部分生态点已经呈现出水流清澈、仙鹤云集、鱼草丰美的动人景观，流域断面水质实现稳定达标，细河从一条散发臭味的水沟，变身成为清澈灵动的城市主要水体。同时重点抓节点工程建设、城市段提升、启动全流域综合治理，最终还“母亲河”以应有的尊严。污水处理厂在建项目进展顺利，建成的稳定运行，基本实现全市生活污水、工业废水处理全覆盖，日处理能力 29 万吨。依法封闭了 284 眼城区自备水源井，接管 77 处住宅供水二次加压泵房，达到涵养城市水源、保证城市供水需求和群众饮水安全的目标。

二是在治矿方面。重点实施海州露天矿综合治理工程。海州矿曾经是阜新人的骄傲，但是煤炭自燃、滑坡已经威胁到周边居民的安全，也是主城区烟尘的主要来源。2014 年年底工程全面启动，阜新市委、市政府共筹资 4 亿元，实现 4 户地方生产煤矿、阜矿集团海州矿及相关千余名矿工全部稳妥退出，回填废弃井 10 座、削坡平盘 200 万立方米，城市矿山环境治理短板基本实现了大幅弥补。2016 年将继续重点实施扬尘治理、生态绿化建设，彻底消除残煤自燃、滑坡危害地质危害。阜新市决心通过 5 年时间将烟尘弥漫的海州露天矿及周边地区变成树木茂盛、设施齐全、景色优美、宜居宜业的重要场所，提升城市南部宜居环境的生态品质。同时，实施高德矿矸石山综合治理工程，推广煤矸石、粉煤灰综合利用，年利用煤矸石 500 万吨、粉煤灰 300 万吨，大于新产出量。

三是在治气方面。针对社会普遍关注的雾霾问题，阜新相继完成发电公司、大鹰水泥等脱硫脱硝除尘工程 26 个；开展城区空气环境综合整治行动，集中整治露天煤场 155 家，逐步取消城区分散供暖锅炉；9 户主城区化工企业、铸造企业全部迁至产业园区。从推进城区煤炭销售企业集中经营、消除露天堆放造成煤尘的角度出发，启动煤炭物流园建设。全市 PM2.5、PM10 指标均优于省考核指标。2016 年将继续实施热电企业脱硫脱硝除尘工程，推进建成区集中高效供暖，开展主城区粉煤灰、煤矸石、露天储煤场、尾矿等综合清理整治专项行动。

四是在治沙方面。阜新位于辽宁省西北地区，阜新的治沙工作，不仅是为全市降低沙尘污染，更承担着为全省阻沙送雨的生态安全屏障作用。近年来，阜新相继启动实施了多项重大林业治理工程，大力推进辽西北边界防护林、退耕还林、防沙治沙等工程建设，构筑了一道宽 2 公里、长 322 公里的绿色生态屏障，在城市周边建设了一条长 100 公里、宽 500 米的环城防护林带，在 160 公里的高速公路两侧建成了绿化景观带。利用两年时间，完成 200 万亩经济林工程，全市森林覆盖率由 21.9% 提高到 32.5%。累计实施沙化治理 153 万亩，围栏封育1 686公里，全市25度以上坡耕地全部退出。城市绿化覆盖率达到42%。通过不懈的努力，做到每年都有新变化、新提升，最终让阜新人民看到蓝天白云，望见绿水青山，呼吸新鲜空气，享受优美景色，幸福指数持续攀升。

五、坚持把群众冷暖放在心上，千方百计提升各类保障

作为资源型城市，阜新的历史欠账比较多，就业、社保、城市建设等压力都非常大，阜新市委、市政府坚持以增进民生福祉为目的，加快发展社会事业，不断增加居民收入，促进社会公平正义与和谐进步，在国家和省的大力支持下，倾尽全力编织民生保障网。

一是把就业创业作为民生之本来抓。一方面，通过公益岗、技能培训等措施拓展就业渠道，全市累计实现实名制就业77.2万人，城镇登记失业率由转型前的7%下降到3.8%，“零就业家庭”动态为零，基本实现了劳者有其岗的目标。另一方面，鼓励全民创业，以创业带动就业，出台了9条政策支持大众创业、万众创新。全面落实“四个驱动”要求，出台了创新、改革、市场、开放驱动战略实施意见。

二是把社保体系作为关键之举来抓。坚持“全覆盖、保基本、多层次、可持续”的原则，初步建立覆盖城乡的社会保障体系，基本实现了人人享有基本社会保障。认真落实国家、省各项要求，建立了统一的城乡居民基本养老保险制度，城乡低保、农村五保、重点优抚对象生活补助标准年均提高10%以上，企业退休人员养老金实现了连续提标。启动城镇居民大病保险。新农合筹资标准每年每人达到500元。

三是把解决历史遗留问题作为稳定之基来抓。针对城市地下管网严重老化的情况，从2014年起开展地下管网攻坚行动，两年来累计改造新建供热、供水、供气管网370.4公里，基本完成了供水管网的改造。对城区街路、小街小巷进行维修改造，提高城区街路建设通行水平，基本消灭断头路，进一步提升通行能力、保洁水平。

四是把社会事业作为惠民之策来抓。先后建成了市第二人民医院、市图书馆、市体育馆、市中小学教育实践基地、市社会养老院改扩建工程、全科医生培训基地等一批公益项目。圆满完成万人坑死难矿工纪念馆维修保护工程。这些项目建成后，社会事业的硬件基本完备，布局更加合理，基本满足群众需求。这些工作就是一笔良心账、责任账，只要一件事一件事去抓，各类保障水平都会提升，人民的满意度也会越来越高。

六、坚持把体制机制创新作为重要突破口，激发内在发展活力

阜新主导产业伴随着国家经济体制转轨逐渐衰退，又因煤炭是最晚退出计划经济的行业之一，受计划经济影响较深，改革滞后。但阜新市奋起直追。

一是加大简政放权力度。2015年，调整行政职权420项，市级非行政许可审批事项全部取消，建立行政执法随机抽查制度，清理规范30项审批中介服务事项和46件政府文件。建设工程项目审批时限压缩至35个工作日。部门权责清单向社会公布。审批事项精简率达

78%。省级以上园区封闭运行，赋予新邱区、清河门区县级经济管理权限、国家高新技术产业园区市级经济管理权限，激发发展活力。

二是推进经济领域改革。正常生产经营的国有工业企业全部退出国有序列，商贸流通、粮食、公益性企业等转制面达到90%以上。坚持以民营为主推进转型，民营经济占全市经济比重由转型初的27%提高到67%，民营经济呈现出规模扩大、层次提升的良好局面，已成为阜新经济转型最具发展潜力的经济增长点和国民经济的重要支撑力量。建立完善了产业投资引导基金、养老风险基金和偿债准备金制度；积极推进国有资产集团化经营机制。

三是全方位扩大对外开放。坚持把开放放在工作首位，以招商引资为重点，推进对外开放向纵深领域扩展。不断创新招商方式，每年都组织近百批次“走出去”招商活动。紧紧把握发达地区产业转移、产业融合、产业布局的趋势，着力引进国内外知名企业和品牌。实施“融入战略”，加强沈阜互动发展，主动融入京津冀协同发展、“一带一路”等重大战略，着力融入蒙东经济区，形成了新的对外开放格局。转型以来，已有近百个知名品牌、央企和国内外500强企业落户。

四是大力推进科技进步和创新。积极培育和引进科技型企业，扶持企业技术创新，已建立市级工程技术研发中心33家、省级工程技术研发中心14家，拥有省级高新技术企业26户。与中国农业科学院、清华大学、浙江大学等20多家高校院所建立了科技合作关系，实施了一系列“产学研”合作，科技进步对经济增长贡献率由35%提高到58%，研发经费支出占GDP比重增长了163%。

七、坚持保根本兜底线，让弱势群体感受到温暖

阜新的经济总量全省最小，城乡居民双重困难，加之厂办大集体、破产矿安置等历史遗留问题，给阜新改善民生带来了巨大压力。怎么能让阜新的困难群众、弱势群体过得更好，是阜新市委、市政府始终放在心上、抓在手上的事情。我们一方面勒紧腰带千方百计节约其他开支，另一方面把有限的资金用在刀刃上，兜住底线、补齐短板。

一是兜住底线，保障生活。全市社会保障体系不断健全，14.7万名城乡低保群众生活保障费，按时提标、足额发放，做到应保尽保，保证这些人有衣穿、有饭吃、有房住，能够满足正常生活需求。

二是补齐短板，精准救助。进一步完善社会救助体系，健全和完善了以最低生活保障为基础，以专项救助为辅助，临时救助、慈善救助为补充的社会救助体系，大病救助覆盖面扩大、标准提高。注重发挥总工会、慈善总会、红十字、妇联、残联等社会团体作用，动员社会力量，对特殊困难人群进行“点对点”救助，不留保障死角，不让弱势群体吃苦受罪。

三是创新机制，精准扶贫。阜新市紧紧围绕国家扶贫改革试验区建设的机遇，创新农业生产经营体制机制、金融扶贫产品、社会扶贫模式和贫困监测机制等，做到了扶贫措施、项目资金、干部、机制到村到户。2015年阜新市以现代农业示范带、新一轮“集团帮村”和

驻村工作队为载体，创新“政银保”金融扶贫、互助式扶贫机制，实施精准扶贫，减少低收入贫困人口5.8万人。

坚决打赢脱贫攻坚战，全市目前共有贫困人口9.6万人，启动新一轮集团帮村，采取精准脱贫、精准服务，通过产业扶持、社保兜底、教育医疗救助、移民搬迁等措施，计划通过3年攻坚全部脱贫，2016年海州、细河、太平3个城区贫困人口全部脱贫，全年完成脱贫3.5万人任务，确保全市国标以下贫困人口2020年实现全部稳定脱贫。

八、坚持共享发展理念，全心全意回应群众期盼

日常工作中，阜新市坚持把群众所想、所盼作为工作的重点。受制于有限的财政实力，阜新市委、市政府在民生安排上，多做雪中送炭的民生实事，不搞锦上添花的民生工程，量力而行、尽力而为、逐项落实、逐项回应。

一是听民声。结合党的群众路线和三严三实专题教育，深入一线调研座谈，广泛征求到意见建议近200条。理顺五大系统管理体制，通过政府门户网站、民心网、行风热线等平台，广泛听取群众意见。整合118条投诉举报热线，开通市12345政府综合服务热线平台，率先完成省试点任务，群众诉求表达更加畅通，切实打通联系服务群众“最后一公里”。

二是应民盼。阜新市政府每年在政府工作报告中，都要筛选一批群众期盼、关注的热点难点问题作为实事，在2015年年初向全市人民做出承诺，年底兑现。几年来，已累计完成实事工程近200项，全都说到做到，与全市人民见面“对账”、全部兑现，切实解决群众的生活难点热点问题。

三是解民忧。认真落实信访责任制，建立了领导包案、信访接待等工作机制，突出抓好拖欠农民工工资、征地拆迁等信访问题，依法接访、耐心解答，做到事事有着落、件件有回音。几年来，阜新到省进京上访总量总体下降，始终在全省排位靠后，彻底摘掉了“全省最不稳定地区”的帽子。

经过10多年的转型，阜新广大干部群众积极探索，艰苦创业，逐步走出困境，夯实了发展基础，进入了经济加快发展的新阶段。特别是经济社会快速发展使困境中的阜新迎来了希望的曙光，使迷茫中的市民看到了希望，全市干部群众从转型前的那种焦虑、困惑里走出来，全市上下思想统一，信心坚定，政通人和，精神振奋，干劲充足。

2015年，中央审议通过的《关于全面振兴东北地区等老工业基地的若干意见》明确提出：到2020年，资源枯竭地区经济转型要取得显著成效。“十三五”时期，阜新转型发展进入新阶段，无论是转型振兴上的逐步积累，还是全面建成小康社会的客观需要，阜新经济发展、产业优化、改善民生等都到了体现效益、体现变化、体现成果的关键阶段，各行业各领域必将在“十三五”期内形成较大的经济效益、生态效益、民生效益和社会效益，确保到2020年转型振兴取得重大成果。

下一步，阜新市委市政府将紧紧围绕习近平总书记视察辽宁时提出的“积极探索资源枯竭型城市转型发展新路子，努力形成活力迸发的新增长区”的要求，以“五大发展理念”

为统领，以“四个着力”为指导，以“五个必须”为总要求，以“四个驱动”为动力，以“六个增长点”为抓手，继续高举经济转型试点市这面旗帜，以提高经济发展质量效益为中心，以做大经济总量、提高人民生活质量为目标，大力推进产业转型，争创经济转型示范市；大力推进城市转型，争创国家产城融合示范市；大力推进生态转型，打造环境更加宜居城市；大力推进社会转型，促进民生补短板、兜底线、保基本，推进阜新转型振兴迈出更加坚实的步伐，和全国人民一道步入全面小康社会。

（作者：阜新市人民政府）

长沙：板仓小镇的市民下乡试验

一、引言

开慧镇位于长沙县最北端，因革命烈士杨开慧得名。杨家世居隐储山下的板仓冲，故其父杨昌济被尊称为“板仓先生”。此地又有“板仓小镇”之名。小镇北接平江县，西连汨罗市，是长沙、平江、汨罗三县之交的边缘镇，面积 52.4 平方公里，距离长沙县城 38 公里，距省会长沙市约 59 公里，属于大都市区内的中远郊地带。由于距城区较远，基础设施薄弱，公共服务滞后，是产业结构单一、劳动力外流的农业乡镇。开慧镇属丘陵地形，因与都市区尚有距离，未被过度开发，所以生态环境保存完好。这里最大优势是“红色资源”——杨昌济（板仓先生）和杨开慧烈士故里、杨开慧与毛泽东的“初恋小镇”。这里有杨开慧烈士纪念馆，被定为国家 4A 级风景旅游区、红色旅游名胜。

长沙县委、县政府从开慧镇名人故里、旅游景区、距离县城远、工业配套不足、生态环境优越的特定条件出发，抓住这里的“红色资源”和“绿色资源”优势，在“南工北农”的整体布局之下制定开慧镇的发展思路：将开慧镇建设成一个重点发展文化创意、乡村旅游等产业的特色小镇，从而探索出一条不依赖于城市扩张而发展、可复制和推广的特色小镇发展路径。在文化旅游的战略定位、特色小镇政策支持、国际露营基地等项目引进、道路交通基础设施建设的同时，县委县政府认识到吸引高素质的市民下乡居住，成为这个特色小镇的常住居民，一定会对开慧镇的长期发展带来方方面面的促进。于是选择以土地管理创新破局，以“板仓小镇”的概念引领，推出了一个市民下乡的项目，是长沙县“敢为天下先”的市民下乡创新尝试。在为开慧镇发展引进下乡市民新资源的同时，也为打破城乡二元体制的土地结构做出了大胆的试验。

二、市民下乡的“非转农”户口指标

“市民下乡”这个目标，在当下的法律和制度环境下几乎是不可能办到的事。但是长沙县却在现有法律框架之下，经过一系列环环相扣的工作，最后将其变成合法的现实：第一，市民下乡要有处安身，这就要给每个下乡市民的家庭安排一块宅基地，而宅基地是农民特有的权益，因此第一步就是要创造条件让有意向下乡的市民取得农民身份；第二，“新村民”的户口要落在具体的行政村，这就需要征得村民自治组织的同意，这片土地上原住的农户如要拆迁，也就需要补偿安置；第三，新增的这块农村建设用地，其用地指标从哪里来？要通过另外地方复垦来“占补平衡”；第四，宅基地只有集中连片才可能修建水、电、路基础设施，这就需要向使用宅基地的“新村民”收取相应费用，交由专门的开发机构统一规划、开发建设；第五，“新村民”进入具体的行政村，按乡村组织制度要组成村民小组，但除了宅基地之外，不应享受村民在集体经济组织中的其他权益，这一点必须以法律认可的方式厘清；第六，既然是试验，就要做好失败的准备。试验的风险需要参与者共担，对于因政策掌握中的变数和执法裁量的不确定性，需要地方政府与下乡市民双方都做好对“不可抗力”的应对预案，并以契约方式明确下来。不管做这件事会遇到多少困难和麻烦，长沙县委、县政府看准了市民下乡是中国城市化中必须要迈出的一步，必须有人先行试验才知道这个过程会遇到什么问题。而且，他们经过充分的调研吃准了一条：如今城市居民只要是社保医保已经到位的前提下，择业自主，就业自由，户口的“非转农”已经不会对工作生活构成实际影响。这个项目一经提出，就会有人来“吃螃蟹”。

2009 年 7 月 18 日，长沙县委、县政府下发文件《关于鼓励板仓小镇建设的若干意见》（以下简称《意见》），提出为进一步鼓励和吸收城市资本与民间资本向板仓小镇集聚，把板仓小镇作为长株潭两型社会先行先试的试验区，将其打造为“中部名镇·红色板仓”和“新农村地标”。根据《意见》，板仓小镇规划区被确定为全县推行放宽城乡落户政策的试点区域，有条件的城镇居民可来此迁户定居；凡迁户定居者，经批准可享受当地村民建房待遇，同时需交纳一定的公共设施配套费。此外，在板仓小镇固定资产投资超过1 000万元的项目法人也可迁户定居，享受当地村民建房待遇。

城镇居民落户乡村并非全无政策支撑。早在 2008 年 11 月 23 日，长沙市公安局就曾下发《关于进一步放宽城乡落户政策的通知》（以下简称《通知》），提出进一步放宽长沙市城乡落户政策，使非农户口公民可通过未成年人投靠父母、夫妻投靠等方式落户农村。当然，亲属投靠方式涉及人群的范围有限，难以在人口结构、城乡互动上为乡村带来实质性改变。但这毕竟把市民下乡的户籍桎梏拉开一丝缝隙。那么，是否可以在长沙市公安局所发《通知》基础上再迈一步？这一步的跨度该如何掌握？

2010 年 6 月 10 日，长沙县在城乡一体化工作调研会议上将鼓励市民来长沙县迁户定居具体化，为了使这项具有牵一发动全身的试验高度可控，县委、县政府决定限制总量，在特定乡镇封闭运行：“允许金井镇和开慧镇各试点 100 户。”于是，由长沙县公安局牵头，国土局、开慧镇、金井镇共同研究制定出具体的城市居民下乡居住的实施细则。

（一）市民下乡居住点的选址、规划及管理

县委、县政府作为决策者提出思路，镇里作为执行者开始实施。板仓小镇市民下乡试验点的直接执行方、推动者，便是开慧镇城建投资有限公司。开慧镇城建投资有限公司成立于 2010 年 3 月，是经长沙县人民政府批准、开慧镇政府全资投入的企业，主要工作任务有二：

第一，筹集建设资金；第二，承担整个镇域范围内政府投资项目的实施和管理——板仓小镇市民下乡居住试点便是其全力推进、重点运作的项目。

2010年9月，板仓小镇市民下乡规划区项目正式启动。开慧镇城建投资有限公司公布规划设想后，由下辖各村自愿申报、推荐合适的试验点，开慧村、葛家山村等行政村认识到这个项目潜在的价值，都积极推荐了本村的地块。城建投经多方比较，本着交通相对便利、环境较好、住户较少、不占用基本农田等原则，选定了跨开慧村段老组、段冲组、蛇咀组三组的一个地块，面积约314亩。

这块土地大部分是林地，还有少量的一般农田，里面居住着9户人家。镇政府根据项目要求，将这些土地调整为集体建设用地，所占农田及林地秉持占补平衡的原则在他处补充；9户农民的宅基地则依据正常征地补偿标准给予划地安置，按照农户自身意愿，其中4户安置在本组的土地上，其余5户安置到了葛家山村的农民集中居住点。通过规划设计，这块土地被划分成94个地块。地块大小不一，大的有3亩多，小的1亩多；形状也并非四四方方的格子，而是依地势而定。

开慧镇城建投不仅统一规划地块、统一建设基础设施，而且统一处理规划区内的污水垃圾：污水管网早已提前建好，管道通到每家每户，将下乡市民的污水全部纳入管网中，集中排放到开慧镇污水处理厂；垃圾也是集中处理，开慧镇以服务外包方式同环保合作社合作，统一收集全镇垃圾。

在规划阶段，开慧镇就已开始设计下乡市民的社区管理形式。小区业主委员会尚未成立，城建投已选聘好前期物业服务企业以小区管理的形式介入前期物业管理；等业主全部入住、业主委员会成立后，将引进正式物业，同时收取一定数额的物业费。至于请哪一家物业公司、如何请，将由业主委员会决定。

（二）建房："统一规划，自己建设"

市民通过亲戚朋友、宣传网站等途径得知项目信息，有兴趣的就会前来看地、选地，并到城建投招商办了解用地的区域布置等基本情况、咨询价格。招商办已将规划提前做好，市民需要支付的费用从10多万到30多万不等。市民选地根据报名顺序排序，先报名者先选择。需要注意的是，下乡市民缴纳的费用并不是买卖地块的费用，而是为附着在地块上的基础设施（水、电、路等）付费，即基础设施配套费；地块不改变权属和用途，是农村集体建设用地提供给已迁转户口的下乡市民做宅基地，由县国土局颁发农村村民建房用地许可证。

市民对此确认并付费后，会拿到一张《板仓小镇迁农户口呈批表》，经公安局审批后将户口迁至开慧村。对于户口迁转，长沙县也设置了限制条件：所有的公职人员（公务员、事业单位人员）不允许迁转；未成年人和65岁以上的老年人也都不可以迁转。

户口迁转完毕就拿到了建房资格，房屋由开慧镇城建投"统一规划，自己建设"。"统一规划"，即城建投对建筑的面积、层高做出统一限定，以保证区域整体的协调性，根据规定，建筑高度不应超过12米，层数不应超过3层，占地面积不应超过170平方米；"自己建设"，即设计风格无明确限制，由市民自行设计建筑图纸，提供给城建投工程部，经审核通过后便可自行开建。

由于采取“统规自建”的项目建设方式，所以项目推进程度全看市民意愿及资金情况。如今，94个地块已全部有主，其中有10多户居民已建成入住、30多户宅院在建。

（三）选择：下乡市民的潜在价值

“昔孟母，择邻处。”选择迁户的市民就是选择未来与谁为邻——这是开慧镇政府的考虑。在项目建设中，城建投收取的配套费仅仅是打平规划建设投资，政府更关心的是下乡市民背后的专业、知识、人脉等社会资源。在项目初期设定板仓小镇吸引人群时，政府的期待受众便是城市高端人才。建房群体中文艺界、传媒界人士相对较多，主要来自湖南广电集团、湖南电影制片厂两个系统——这是开慧镇政府对下乡市民主动选择的结果。

开慧镇之所以更愿意引进文艺界、传媒界人士，与该镇发展定位是有关联的：开慧镇要走的并不是传统农业或工业发展之路，其大力推进的是乡村旅游、文化教育等产业。“板仓小镇”就是长沙县在开慧镇实施的建设项目，规划面积19.2平方公里的项目就是以田园文化理念为指导，具有湖湘文化特色、现代化农村气息、生态和环保相融、与县城星沙和长沙经开区互动的卫星镇，成为集商、旅、文化于一体的“田园城市”。通过板仓小镇的建设，打通农民进城和市民下乡的通道，从而实现城乡双向交流、资源共享。作为板仓小镇的重要组成部分，镇里希望市民下乡的平台吸引更多相关人才，利用人才背后的社会资源发展产业、扩大宣传。不负所望的是，来自文艺界、传媒界的下乡市民的确为当地带来了更多机遇。

产业发展需要大量地招商引资，下乡市民常介绍投资方与开慧镇洽谈。比如，由湖南广电集团投资的湖南卫视后勤影视基地已经谈成在建，该项目占地500亩，总投资3亿元，北至开明水库大堤、南抵毛家坳小学公路边沿，建成后将极大地推动开慧镇旅游产业的发展。该影视基地入驻开慧镇，正是由下乡市民促成的：为找到合适的影视基地建设点，项目工作人员考察了湖南省的很多地方，板仓小镇有下乡市民在广电集团担任高管，于是向相关人员推荐了开慧镇，列举出了这里的优势条件。基地项目负责人对该地进行考察了解、多方权衡后，最终敲定了开慧镇——在这个过程中，下乡市民起到了很好的牵线搭桥作用。

通过市民下乡项目与媒体建立良好关系也有利于开慧镇的对外推广、宣传。媒体关系的建立，使板仓小镇更易出现在活动、新闻报道中。有些媒体甚至会在活动中直接介绍：到开慧镇去看一看，那里做得很不错。由于开慧镇生态旅游产业成绩较突出，所以媒体做节目、出外景时很容易便想到这里，这是其他地方难以拥有的优势。通过电视播出、报纸宣传，开慧镇更易获得发展旅游产业所需的知名度——这也是下乡市民的潜在价值之一。

三、市民下乡的风险控制

（一）如何界定权益范围

市民迁转户口、下乡居住，目的不是成为农民，而是为了享受乡村清静、舒适的环境。

下乡市民与原住民身份背景、生活需求各不相同，应履行的义务、享有的权利也不尽相同。那么，该如何界定他们的权益范围，使同处一村的双方不会出现因界限不清而产生利益纠纷？

为使“新村民”的管理纳入当地体制，下乡市民所在区域通过民政区划成立了一个村民小组。该地块原本的地名叫“五子冲”，所以该村民小组叫作“五子冲村民小组”。“五子冲村民小组”是一个全新的集体经济组织，组员就是落户到这里的市民。小组虽受村委会管理，但是其权利和义务与一般的村民小组略有不同：

第一，小组成员暂时不参与村庄的政治生活，比如村委会选举等。虽然从法律层面讲，下乡市民已是该村村民，应当参加，但是因为他们并非土生土长的本地人，与原住民之间彼此了解不多，难以在短期内了解村庄内情，所以即使拥有选举权，恐也难以有效利用；下乡市民往往在他处有自己的本职工作，即使拥有被选举权、当选村主任等岗位，恐也难以全身心投入村内事务处理。特别是，目前下乡市民并未表现出参与乡村治理的强烈意愿，参与的可能性不大。未来该区域变为社区化管理形式，乐于公共事务的人们可以参与到业主委员会的工作中。

第二，下乡市民虽已转为农业户口，但是主要生活环境、工作地点仍在城市。他们已享受城镇社会保障体系，所以村庄中的新农合医疗保险、农村养老保险等社会保险都没有将他们纳入在内。

第三，该组组员也不享受314亩地之外耕地的承包权，但是在314亩地范围内，他们可以自己分配承包权——即，下乡市民只在这314亩地之内享有农民的权益。

由于下乡市民身份的特殊性，他们在入户板仓小镇时都已签订《板仓小镇集中居住项目业主承诺书》，承诺“入住板仓小镇后，仅享受与村民同等的建房待遇，并依法享有房屋的所有权”，除此之外，“主动放弃因为农业户口所享受的其他村民权利”——此举界定了下乡市民的权利范围，同时保证了其与原住村民之间不会产生利益纠葛。

（二）应对政策风险的途径

这项“步步走在法规之中、结果超出预料之外”的试验，毕竟是敢为人先的举措。下乡市民以迁转户口的方式到农村建房的过程中，同样也承担着相当的政策风险——如果将来政策生变，项目受到上级政府的相关部门不认可甚至查处，该怎么办？

市民之所以敢于下乡，是因为该试点项目由政府在推动，相对企业与个人，市民对政府的信任度更高：板仓小镇市民下乡试点是长沙县从本地发展需要实施的创新试点，“100户非转农户口指标”也是根据本地实际和上级相关规定精神，在总量控制、地点控制的前提下给出的。尽管这些做法都在现有法律法规的框架之内，而且要走通整个过程需要付出常人难以想象的很多努力，然而县级政府的先行先试无法保证省市、中央政府有关部门一定会认可、支持，也无法保证未来的产权就一帆风顺。例如，假如未来有更高一级政府再次征收这块土地从事其他项目建设，届时也只能按照当时的国家拆迁征地标准给予下乡市民以相应补偿。市民可自由选择通过夫妻投靠、买房、投资等方式将户口迁走，也可以选择继续保留；

只是对于保留而不迁出的户口，将只能采取货币安置办法，因为小组内已经没有宅基地来安置他们了。

所有报名迁户的市民完全了解这些政策风险，他们对此并无异议，入户板仓小镇之时便签订《板仓小镇集中居住项目招商协议》："由于国家政策变化等不可抗力因素发生，导致本协议无法实际履行的，本协议自动解除，双方互不追究违约责任。"

四、市民下乡的效果

（一）村民有了就近增收的机会

虽说板仓小镇市民下乡试点区内的314亩地是一个相对封闭的空间，这些"新村民"几乎不与村委会、原住民之间产生交集，但是随着下乡市民生活的日趋稳定、社交范围的日趋扩大，与原住民之间不可避免地产生了越来越多的联系，比如：

下乡市民虽然无法承包村里的耕地，但是可以流转其他村民承包的耕地，有些市民流转了周边小组村民的田地从事农业生产（种菜、养鱼等），在自己体验农村生活的同时，也使原住民得到了租金收入；下乡市民流转耕地的目的是"体验"，他们难以像当地农民那样每天为蔬菜浇水、施肥，所以就要聘请当地农民帮助他们打理庄稼和蔬菜。此外，下乡市民还需要人手帮助他们维护院落的花草树木小菜园，在回城期间需要有人帮助照看院落、打理住宅等，都会就近聘请原住村民来帮忙，雇佣关系使原住村民又可以获得一笔劳务收入。

板仓小镇所在地块并非高产出的沃土，其原本种植的林木并不是经济林，而是南方常见的灌木、乔木等；田地也是灌溉相对困难、产出较小的低产田——林与田都难产生经济效益，村民收入较少。下乡市民的到来增加了村民就地的收入来源，使村民得到了实惠。所以迄今为止，原住村民对下乡市民持接纳态度。

（二）城市文明带入乡村

作为长沙县城乡一体化建设体系中的重要组成部分，开慧镇市民下乡试点与发展文化产业、乡村旅游产业等举措同步进行，各民生项目的实施必然会对当地原有的生活方式产生影响。开慧镇虽为国家级风景旅游区，但在知名度尚未打开、基础设施尚未提升前，每年前来旅游的只有20万~30万人次。随着基础设施的完善、政府几年间不遗余力的打造，开慧镇越来越漂亮，吸引的游客越来越多。2014年，开慧镇游客人数超过120万，比以前增长了约100万。

外来人口的增加改变了当地村民的生活形态与思维方式：农民兴办的"民宿"从无到有，渐渐增加；眼界的开阔、服务意识的提高、经商思维的完善，使他们不再局限于从前的一亩三分田，他们将土地流转出去，放开手脚开店、经商。如今开慧镇的土地流转面积已达60%，腾出了多数村民的手脚，使他们可以自谋职业、自主创业——市民下乡直接间接地带来人们的思维盘活。

下乡市民自己设计建造、风格各异的房屋与当地民宅质量、形态都显著不同，在引导城市资本、信息下乡的同时，市民也将城市的建筑风貌与文化理念带到了乡村；开慧镇市民下乡试点在与文化、旅游产业同步推进的过程中，也在悄然改变着当地村民的生活方式、观念意识——无论生活形态、建筑风貌还是思想观念，下乡市民已在无意中将城市文明带入乡村。

城市化的过程也是城市文明下乡的过程，这一过程是人口集聚完成、多数城市已定型，甚至环境污染、交通压力、住房紧缺等诸多城市病已逐步显现时，自然而然延展出的“城市化后半部分”。对此，美国学者约翰·弗里德曼（J. Friedman）早有分析：城市化不仅包括人口和非农业活动在规模不同的城市环境的地域集中过程、非城市景观转化为城市景观的地域推进过程（城市化Ⅰ），还包括城市文明、城市生活方式和价值观在农村地域的扩散过程（城市化Ⅱ）——板仓小镇市民下乡试点令这一过程水到渠成。

（三）社会结构发生改变

“板仓小镇”并非简单、无序的郊区化蔓延。郊区是与城市接壤的乡村地带，在一定程度上仍属于城市扩张的范畴；而板仓小镇位置虽在大都市圈内，但距主城仍有一定距离，它的目标是成为一个相对独立的美丽小镇。要想建起一座真正意义上的小镇，仅靠数量有限的留守村民和来来往往的游客，而没有市民下乡，人口结构不发生改变，无论小城镇还是新农村的目标都是难以实现的。

开慧镇规划建设一个“板仓小镇”，吸引市民下乡增加常住人口数量、改变当地人口结构；乡村旅游带来流动的消费人群。两种力量推动着城乡人口对流、需求互补、功能耦合，真正实现了以城带乡、以工补农，并且逐步扭转着原住民的生活形态和思维方式。而城乡文化的交流融合，也在推动着社会结构的缓慢变革，板仓建起一座大都市圈内特色小镇的目标便有了实现可能。

板仓小镇是一个山清水秀的地方，且距主城区距离适当，市民周末便可驱车前往；类似的城郊乡村在全国相当普遍。同时，乡村旅游、乡村度假也已成为趋势。在城市化发展迅猛、边缘乡镇逐渐被中心城市吞噬的大背景下，板仓小镇的突围之路或许可为众多条件相近的郊区乡镇提供借鉴。

五、讨论

（一）真正的创新是基层自主选择

长沙县的市民下乡试验，显然不是为了贯彻上级指示，落实上位规划的行为，而是一项针对自身发展遇到的困境做出的自主创新。“我要做”还是“要我做”，其结果天壤之别。对于长沙县政府来说，自主决策过程没有外在的压力，压力完全来自内部，就是要全面地利弊权衡：在引导市民下乡的同时不侵害村民利益；促进发展的同时将风险控制在可承受范围内……所有措施的制定都是寻求各方平衡的结果。也正因此，长沙县充分尊重基层的自主性，尊重基层根据自身条件做出的选择。市民下乡的选址就是在开慧镇征求了不同村的意见，在村组自愿的基础上确定试点区域；试点开慧镇也是尊重了开慧镇的意愿，与板仓小镇一同获得“100户非转农户口指标”的还有区位条件类似的金井镇，然而金井镇的区位有别于开慧镇，发展战略是以“茶乡小镇”“乡村都市”为目标，并不急于在市民下乡上做出推进。因此这100个指标没有即时释放。随着互联网+有机农业、乡村旅游和乡村创客的聚集，未来金井镇也许会适时启动，打出这100张牌，这就全看基层政府审时度势的自主选择。

（二）一个行动胜过一打纲领

板仓小镇试验的结果是在开慧镇出现了一群“乡居的市民”。在城乡经济结构二元、管理制度二元的当下中国，这一打破城乡二元结构的举措可谓“石破天惊”：十七届三中全会以来，国家政策虽屡屡提及“形成以工促农、以城带乡、工农互惠、城乡一体的新型工农城乡关系”，然而各地实践还都只是城市资本、技术、产业的下乡，并没有涉及城市化主体——“人”的下乡。板仓小镇市民下乡以“100户非转农户口指标”破局，为了使项目全程不逾现行法律法规的界限，长沙县设置了一系列前置条件，将试验限制在特定空间（314亩地）、特定范畴（仅限宅基地），以双保险规避改革可能带来的风险。仿佛是在一个高压、恒温、无菌的环境下得出的少量珍贵的试验室成果。这一成果实现条件之复杂使其难以大面积推广，但是成果本身——市民下乡的实现，却实实在在地让人们看到了一个以往从未出现的社会现象：城市居民自主流动到乡村，带着资金、知识、建筑形式、生活方式来到乡村，与原住村民相互依靠、相互帮助，改变着乡村的人口结构，创造出乡村新的社区形态。

（三）超前、大胆而谨慎的探索

板仓小镇市民下乡试点可谓谨慎、大胆又超前：“谨慎”表现在对改革特定空间与范畴的限定；“大胆”表现在“100户非转农户口指标”的特批，放眼全国，尚无先例可循。其“超前”的表现也正在于此，长沙县有条件实践的事，国家的法律法规整体条件尚不允许，然而它代表了中国城市化的必然的发展方向——乡村不会永远被城市索取，它或借助城市的扩张而发展，或引入城市的资源独立发展。当他的一部分居民选择在乡村居住，并且将城市的资金、知识、生活方式甚至就业岗位带到乡村的时候，城乡之间就实现了平等全面的互动。长沙县的“先行先试”让我们看到，城郊乡村将城市资源整合进自身发展过程中的可能性。

六、展望未来

在英、美等国家，公民无“农业”与“非农”的户籍区别，所有国民享受公共服务的权利均等，“市民乡居”早已成为普遍现象；在中国，这个趋势亦将不可避免地到来，长沙县为这个迟早要到来的未来预设了一个试验室。

已经发现的问题包括：山区丘陵地带的农村宅基地并不是整齐的格子，而是因山就势，因水就形。本来就是“四荒地”，不值钱，宅基地可大可小，大小由之。在这样的地方建设乡居市民的居住区，居民宅院多占些路边地角如何管理？也有人提出疑义：乡居市民不少按“5+2”方式下乡居住，到了周一留下些垃圾回到城里，没有给当地留下什么。

展望未来，乡居市民们既是本地农村的社区成员，但又不是农村集体经济组织成员。因此，同一个行政村，会有两种不同的治理模式，一种是拥有集体经济的村民自治，一种是住房产权私有、不存在集体经济的居民自治加业主自治。前者由于是人民公社体制的遗产，未来将不断深化改革；而后者会不会成为中国农村一种新型的社区组织形式呢？还是简单地变成一块城市社会在乡村的“飞地”？这种新型的农村社区会遇到哪些治理的问题呢？乡居的市民在公共服务、公众参与方面会表现出与传统城乡社区哪些不同呢？显然，着眼于中国乡村未来的人们，一定会关注这个刚刚拉开大幕的社会试验。

（作者：李津逵，综合开发研究院（中国·深圳）理事、资深研究员；武凤珠，《城市化》杂志编辑）

南京：推动民生建设迈上新台阶

中共南京市第十三次党代会作出了建设幸福都市的重大战略部署，打造独具魅力的幸福都市成为南京全局工作的主旋律，并在全国副省级城市中率先建立了幸福都市考核评价指标体系。南京坚持以民生幸福为目标，以构建“保障和改善民生十大体系”为重点，以每年50件为民办实事项目为抓手，加快提升民生保障水平。在2014年进行的全省民生幸福建设监测统计测评中，南京民生发展水平指数位列全省第一；城乡居民收入达到42 568元和17 661元，分别列全省第二和第四；2015年上半年，全体居民人均可支配收入同比增长8.2%，农村居民人均可支配收入增长10.1%，快于城市居民2.1个百分点，较2011年启动居民收入倍增计划前有较大增长。人均养老床位数、企业退休人员月均基本养老金、最低生活保障标准等一批民生工作指标均位列全国全省前列。当前，南京市委提出要积极建设“经济强、百姓富、环境美、社会文明程度高”的新南京，中共南京市委、南京市人民政府出台《推动民生建设迈上新台阶行动计划》（宁委发〔2015〕29号），印发《〈2015年重点民生工作〉的通知》（宁委发〔2015〕27号），推动民生建设迈上新台阶。在南京“迈上新台阶，建设新南京”进程中，更加关注人的生活质量、发展潜能和幸福指数，实现幸福都市建设与“新南京”建设“并轨运行”。2015年10月，在新华社《瞭望东方周刊》联合中国市长协会《中国城市发展报告》共同主办的2015中国最具幸福感城市系列榜单中，南京荣获“最具幸福感城市”和“小康社会建设示范奖”双项荣誉称号，连续7年入选中国最具幸福感城市。南京在民生建设和幸福都市建设中形成了自身的经验和特色，其主要做法是：

一、着眼顶层设计和系统化思考，构建民生政策体系

初步构建纵向到底、横向到边、协调有序、执行有力的组织领导体系和工作网络。注重加强民生体系建设和制度安排，积极创新公共服务供给方式，连续出台一批重要民生政策，构建并不断完善具有南京特色的民生工作体系，初步形成南京推进民生建设的政策框架体系，提升了民生工作的法治化、规范化水平。

一是在全国较早成立了“幸福都市建设（民生工作）领导小组”，由市委、市政府主要领导挂帅负责，总体谋划、统筹协调和系统推进南京市幸福都市建设和民生发展的各项

工作。

二是出台了《城乡居民收入倍增实施意见》(宁委发〔2011〕43号),提出了“要在又好又快发展经济的同时,推进收入合理分配”。出台了《关于坚持民生为先,加强民生需求保障的意见》(宁委发〔2011〕50号),提出了“切实把实现民生幸福作为各项工作的根本,要完善保障和改善民生工作体系,强调以民生需求倒逼工作推进”。

三是出台了《保障和改善民生十大体系实施意见》(宁委发〔2012〕1号)。2012年1月,出台了《保障和改善民生十大体系实施意见》(宁委发〔2012〕1号),在省民生幸福“六大体系”的基础上做了进一步扩展,新增了公共安全体系、公共交通体系、公共文化体系、人口和家庭公共服务体系等四个体系(2013年又加入了优化和改善公共环境的相关内容),建立终身教育、就业服务、社会保障、基本医药卫生、住房保障、养老服务、公共安全、公共交通、公共文化、人口和家庭公共服务等具有南京特色的“保障和改善民生十大体系”,明确了建立完善民生十大体系的方法、路径和目标要求。近几年每年推进为民办50件实事项目,通过项目实施和年度计划,从群众最期盼的领域,从制约经济社会发展最突出的问题做起,强调以民生需求倒逼各项工作推进。

四是每年出台年度民生工作重点任务,将推进民生幸福工程和建设民生体系的任务落实到每个年度,循序渐进、有条不紊地开展工作(历年年度民生工作文件分别为:《2012年民生工作意见和2012年为民办实事项目》(宁委发〔2012〕6号)、《2013年民生工作五十项实事》(宁委发〔2013〕1号)、《2014年民生工作五十项实事》(宁委发〔2014〕12号)、《2015年重点民生工作》(宁委发〔2015〕27号)。

五是进一步出台推动民生建设迈上新台阶系列文件。2014年,南京市委、市政府相继出台了《关于加强和改进社会救助工作的意见》《关于开展城镇职工和居民大病保险工作实施意见》等系列政策,并相应调整幸福都市考核指标体系及办法,民生事业发展的动力活力明显增强。出台《深化街道和社区体制改革实施方案》,编制《关于加快智慧南京建设的意见》。2015年,南京市委、市政府出台《推动民生建设迈上新台阶行动计划》(宁委发〔2015〕29号),印发《2015年重点民生工作》的通知(宁委发〔2015〕27号),推动民生建设进一步改善。在建设方法上,也注重实现由平面化向立体化转变。改变“运动式”“战役式”等单一传统的建设模式,更加注重改革创新,突出问题导向,加快重点领域的社会体制改革,增强改革的系统性、整体性和协同性;更加注重手段创新,积极运用新媒体、新技术、新平台,开拓工作空间,提升治理能力与水平,形成立体多元的幸福都市建设模式。

二、着眼公平正义均衡,推动社会事业发展

一是加快教育现代化。学前教育普惠优质发展。实施了学前一年基本免费政策,建立了幼儿园生均公用经费制度。开展了“省学前教育改革发展示范区”创建工程,已有3个区创建成功。实施了幼儿园增量工程,全市新增幼儿园名额超过4.3万个。省优质幼儿园比例达66%。义务教育优质均衡发展。采取区域集团办学、优质学校办学联盟、就近兼并、跨

区域托管等方式，扩大优质教育资源，提升办学条件，重点推进农村小学标准化建设。职业教育创新发展。制定职业学校提升质量内涵的指标体系，在重点职校开辟就业创业实习基地，职教毕业生一次性就业率保持在97%以上，专业对口就业率84%以上，就业满意率92%以上。师资队伍整体素质得到新提高。启动实施“1130”优秀教育人才培养计划。探索建立“区管校用”制度，全市义务教育学校教师和校长流动累计2 642人。“十二五”以来，全市每年用于免费义务教育和各类助学的资金3.85亿元，向农村转移支付教育经费5亿元，先后开展三轮大规模的教育布局调整，撤并薄弱学校，增加新区学校布点，有效扩大了优质教育资源覆盖面，所有区被认定为“全国义务教育发展基本均衡区”。

二是加快医疗卫生事业发展。深化医疗卫生体制改革，推进医疗卫生资源均衡化、基本医疗卫生服务标准化、城乡医疗卫生服务一体化，加快实现基本医疗保障全覆盖。逐步提高城乡基本医疗保障标准。推进基本药物制度建设。推进卫生信息化建设，实现卫生信息资源共享。推进公立医院改革，建立科学规范的公立医院运行机制。截至2014年，全市每千人口医疗机构床位数达6.73张、每千人口执业（助理）医师数达3.33人、每千人口注册护士数达4.22人，接近中等发达国家水平。稳步推进基本公共卫生服务均等化。公共卫生服务范围拓展至十大类41项，基本公共卫生服务经费提高人均60元。加大医疗救助力度。低保对象政策范围内医疗救助比例达91%。年度救助封顶线提高到3万元。同时实现医疗救助与基本医保同步结算，医疗救助费用在基本医保报销的同时给予减免。积极推进智慧医疗建设。全市已有432家医疗卫生机构接入卫生专网，实现了自助发卡、自助挂号、自助缴费、自助打印等功能。优化卫生资源布局。加快主城区优质医疗资源向郊区延伸，推动市鼓楼医院、第一医院与六合、高淳、溧水、浦口四区政府的“院府合作”。探索新城医疗中心管理运行新模式，实行管办分开、所有权与经营权分离。健全以区县级医院为骨干、镇街卫生院和村卫生室为基础的农村医疗服务网络。

三是鼓励城乡居民就业创业。实施城乡一体的就业扶持政策，充分发挥政策引导效应。全面贯彻落实国家和省陆续出台的一系列新的就业促进政策，推动实施就业政策城乡一体化，实现全市各区在就业扶持政策上同城同策、同标同付。预计“十二五”期间，全市累计新增城镇就业人数100万人；实现再就业45万人；援助就业困难人员再就业6.5万人；农村劳动力转移就业31万人次；培育自主创业者7.3万人，创业带动就业50万人；城镇登记失业率控制在3%以内。创建“创业型城市”取得显著成果。坚持创业培训、创业服务、创业载体“三位一体”，努力营造鼓励支持创业的良好环境。打造全国大学生创业首选城市。“十二五”以来，全市发放创业小额担保贷款7.92亿元，培育大学生创业者1.33万人。2012年7月，南京市荣获国务院表彰的“全国创业先进城市”荣誉称号。加大就业困难群体帮扶力度。每年定期组织开展“就业援助月”“春风行动”等就业专项服务活动，促进失业人员、返乡农民工、高校毕业生等重点群体实现就业。保持城镇零就业家庭动态消零和当年南京籍困难家庭高校毕业生初次就业率达100%。提高劳动者就业能力，不断完善职业培训政策体系，进一步扩大培训补贴范围，提高培训补贴标准。健全职业培训工作机制，实施“分层分类”培训，围绕市场需求，实行“订单”式定向培训。“十二五”期间，累计开展各类职业培训141万人次，其中开展农村劳动力转移培训30万人次；新增高技能人才18万人，每万名劳动力中高技能人员数期末达到697人。

四是推动养老改革试点。作为全国第一批养老服务业综合改革示范市，养老服务网络实现居家、社区、机构“三位一体”。截至2014年年底，每千名老人拥有43张养老床位，提前三年完成省定目标，人均养老床位数保持全省第一，率先在国内形成医养融合的养老服务模式，并得到民政部推广。“医养融合”养老机构从25家增长10倍达258家，护理型床位达3.3万张。

三、着眼社会政策兜底，构建统一的社会保障体系

一是基本建立覆盖城乡的社会保障制度体系。“十二五”以来，全市社会保障体系已基本实现由城镇社会保障向统筹城乡社会保障、由城镇单位职工保障向城乡居民保障、由单一支柱向多层次保障体系的“三个转变”，基本形成了社会保障面向城乡居民及各种从业形态人员的全覆盖。建立城乡居民养老保险制度和被征地人员社会保障制度，将109万城乡居民和37.7万被征地人员纳入社会保险体系，建立老年生活困难补助人员一次性补缴纳入基本生活保障的政策通道；推进机关事业单位养老保险制度改革；实施机关事业单位公费医疗制度改革，将10余万机关事业单位职工全部纳入了职工医保；推进社会保险市级统筹，在完善养老保险市级统筹的同时，实现了全市失业、工伤、生育保险在制度政策、待遇发放、基金管理、业务经办方面的“四个统一”。

二是进一步扩大社会保险覆盖面。通过在全国、全省率先实施社会保险全民参保登记工作，为社会保险由“广覆盖”转向“全覆盖”提供数据支撑。“十二五”期间，预计全市各项社会保险参保将达到1 640万人次，较“十一五”末净增342万人次。城乡基本养老保险、基本医疗保险、失业保险的覆盖率均超过98%。

三是稳步提高社会保险待遇水平。建立了社会保险待遇的动态调整机制。企业退休人员月平均养老金由“十一五”末的1 672元提高至2 659元，位列全省第一；全市80万企业退休人员纳入社会化管理服务，享受“四走访、五慰问”和免费健康体检服务；失业保险金最高发放标准由960元/月提高到1 680元/月，最低发放标准由520元/月提高到910元/月；建立城乡居民大病保险制度，进一步提高重特大疾病保障水平；职工医保、居民医保、新农合制度范围内住院费用报销比例分别达到85%、75%和100%；工伤保险月人均伤残津贴水平达1 929元。低保政策实现城乡同标，成为继苏州之后全省第二个实现无区县差、无城乡差的低保同城同标城市。

四、补足社会建设短板，注重历史遗留问题化解

将民生改善作为深化改革和发展经济最终目标，在推进经济提升增效升级的同时，实现民生改善和经济发展共同进步。

一是统筹城市与乡村、江南与江北、主城与新区等公共服务布局，引导教育、医疗、文化等优质资源向新区、郊区和农村延伸，为城乡居民提供优质均衡的公共服务。

二是注重扶贫帮困，实行精准救助。加强政策扶持。“十二五”以来，南京市先后出台了《关于进一步扶持低收入农户增收的实施意见》《南京市 2013－2015 帮扶攻坚工程实施意见》《关于进一步提升村级“四有一责”建设水平的若干政策措施》和《“万名党员干部帮万家”活动实施方案》等系列政策文件，从农户、村社、镇街、郊区四个层面全方位、多领域扶贫，打出帮扶攻坚“组合拳”，有力地促进了郊区均衡协调和谐发展和农村弱势群体的增收致富。重点促进低收入农户增收脱贫。通过对低收入农户建档立卡进行动态监管、整村推进低收入农户增收、开展扶贫关怀活动等方式，实现整体脱贫率 80%。增强薄弱村集体经济综合实力。扶持 204 个村每村建设 5 000 平方米标房，帮助做好开发利用和后续管理，目前，全市 90% 以上的经济薄弱村已经实现脱贫。提升经济欠发达镇街发展能力，立足镇街各自特色编制帮促总体规划和分年度实施计划，推动帮促工作有力有效有序开展。统筹整合帮促资金，集中力量扶持每个镇街发展 2 ~ 3 个重点项目。支持欠发达镇街加快健全基本公共服务体系，促进发展环境提升。

三是注重历史遗留问题化解。历史遗留问题是信访老户、信访积案的重要根源，有关群体普遍诉求过高、行为激烈、容易反复。面对历史遗留的民生难题，南京市委市政府高度重视，通过改革创新和制度设计，建立了被征地人员社会保障办法，2011－2014 年共解决了 1983 年以来 57. 11 万被征地人员进城保障问题，真正实现了农民变市民；建立了企业退休职工“一次性奖励”金发放长效机制，为 1996 年以来 32. 21 万持证退休职工发放一次性奖励金；建立了稳步提高老知青、老军工等特殊群体的待遇水平机制，有效化解了社会矛盾，促进了社会和谐稳定。

五、顺应民生需求变化，探索民众参与和民生多主体供给模式

2014 年南京市全年实现地区生产总值 8 820. 75 亿元，按常住人口计，人均地区生产总值约为 10. 7 万元，全体居民人均可支配收入 37 283 元。2015 年上半年实现地区生产总值 4 523. 56亿元，全体居民人均可支配收入为 20 463 元，同比增长 8. 2%。根据发达国家发展经验，这一时期，一方面社会消费结构加快升级，由原来的吃穿为主的生存性消费向住、行、教育、养老、卫生、文化、旅游等发展性和享受性消费过渡，社会服务需求迅速增长并呈现出多层次、多元化和多样性的特点，另一方面公民诉求发生较大变化，人民群众对民生保障的法制化、均衡化、公平化、社会化的期盼更加迫切。当前，我国大多数民生建设与公共服务供给的决策都采用自上而下的模式，与政府层级结构相吻合。民生建设和公共服务需求的特点是地域性、差异性、多样性，在该模式下公共服务供给不充足、不丰富、不对路，居民的真实需求得不到发现和满足，以至于有一些决策部署和工作举措与民生需求相背离。南京长期形成的“主城强、郊区弱”的城市格局，以及外来人口流入大市的城市特质，使得南京有着复杂的社会成员组成结构，并伴生复杂、多元的公共服务需求。这进一步增加了

民生建设与公共服务供需对接的难度。民生需求与公共服务供给“政府派餐”而非“百姓点菜”的模式，往往导致“费力不讨好”的尴尬局面。

一是确立幸福都市建设多元参与理念。幸福都市建设涉及社会所有成员，需要在取得社会共识的基础上，将政府的积极性和社会的积极性有效结合。政府主要着力于各类环境建设和推进基本公共服务均等化、优质化，企业和社会组织履行应尽的社会责任，市民自觉承担社会义务，形成各尽所能、共建共享的幸福都市建设新格局。按照政府的作用是保基本，市场和社会的作用是形成市场化、多元化、社会化的公共服务供给机制的理念，南京积极推动公共服务主体由政府“单一”主体向政府、市场、社会“多元”主体转变。

二是培育壮大幸福都市建设主体。形成以社会组织为载体、城乡社区为平台、市民群众为主体的社会服务体系，强化社会自我调节、自我服务、自我管理功能。创新社会力量动员机制，完善文明创建、公益创投等制度化平台，整合社会资源，汇聚社会力量。发挥人民团体、村（居）自治组织、社会组织、经济组织等的社会动员作用，做好组织群众、引导群众、服务群众、维护群众合法权益等工作。突出文化引领，全面加强社会主义核心价值体系建设，挖掘南京文化的深厚底蕴和独特价值，培育奋发进取、理性平和、开放包容、知足常乐的社会心态，夯实幸福都市建设的德治基础。

三是发挥民众参与社会建设的基础作用。推动社区民主自治不断发展。鼓楼区工人新村的社区议事园、东井亭社区的居民民主听证会、阅江楼街道的社区自治协会、秦淮区瑞金新村的社区论坛、鼓楼区、玄武区等还有许多社区用群众自治的办法来填补物业管理的空白等，建立社区“当家人”民主直选制度，有力彰显了民主自治的特色和作用。注重发挥社会组织作用。南京市委在实施综合改革工程中，明确要求“发挥群团组织桥梁枢纽作用，南京市政府工作部门简政放权、向群团组织转移事务”，并颁布实施综合改革方案。全市探索实行了社区社会组织备案制，推进社区社会组织快速发展，是全国同类城市社区社会组织数量最多的城市。初步构建“社工 + 义工”的社会动员和服务联动模式。在队伍建设上，形成了一支职业化、专业化、公益化的社区工作者队伍。从 2007 年起，全市按每 300 户配 1 人的标准选配社区工作者，且每个社区不得少于 6 人。全市配置社工近万名，其中 6 个主城区平均每个社区的专职社工为 10 人，一个社区至少有 1 名大学生社工、一个社区有 1 名社会工作师或助理社会工作师。全市注册志愿者服务人数超百万人，这些社工和志愿者已成为南京市加强社会管理与创新的重要依靠力量。

六、注重民生建设投入，不断提高公共服务支出

南京市始终把民生投入作为公共财政支出重点，坚持新增财力首先用于民生改善，为保障改善民生提供了坚实支撑。财政支出结构逐步优化，全市城乡公共服务支出由 2011 年的 458 亿元，占一般公共预算支出的 68.8%，增加到 2014 年的 696.8 亿元，占一般公共预算支出的 75.6%，较 2011 年提高近 7 个百分点（见表 1），2014 年 139 项民生重点项目总投资额超过 700 亿元，有力保障了全市民生建设的顺利实施。2015 年 1-9 月，南京全市累计一

般预算支出703.6亿元，增长33.8%。其中，城乡公共服务支出554亿元，占一般公共预算支出比重为78.7%（含置换债及新增债支出），支出结构进一步优化。其中，教育支出90.2亿元，用于完善教育经费保障及扶困助学机制、加大学前教育和职业教育扶持、支持教育城乡统筹。社会保障和就业支出71亿元，用于提高企业职工基本养老金、城乡居民养老补贴标准、征地保障待遇、特殊群体社会保障待遇；完善社会救助、社会福利体系，落实积极就业政策等。医疗卫生与计划生育支出39.8亿元，用于提高城乡基本公共卫生服务项目补助标准、新农合和城镇居民医保筹资标准和保障水平。文化体育与传媒支出9.8亿元，用于推进文化、体育重点项目建设，完善公共文化、公共体育服务体系。

表1 “十二五”城乡公共服务财政支出情况

年份	2011	2012	2013	2014
公共财政预算支出(亿元)	666	770	851	921
城乡公共服务支出合计(亿元)	458	557	635	696
占财政支出比重(%)	68.8	72.3	74.6	75.6

七、顺应社会结构演化和社会矛盾凸显，推动社会治理创新

近年来，南京市在推进社会治理过程中，始终强化理念更新、系统设计、高位统筹，对服务、管理、自治、党建等各方面工作进行整体化布局。加快构建符合省会城市和特大型中心城市特点的整体治理模式，形成了一些具有南京特色的社会治理经验与做法。

一是不断加强社会协调治理。成立了城市治理委员会，调动和鼓励社会各类主体参与城市治理，长效机制基本建立。加大各类社会组织培育和发展，每万人拥有社会组织数量达到12.71个，居副省级城市之首，位居全国前列；每年制定政府购买公共服务目录，2014年推出10大类32子类131项公共服务购买目录，为全市人民提供更高质量、更为多样的公共服务。注册志愿者人数比例达到17.05%，较2012年上升2.05个百分点，人均慈善捐款（物）数由2012年的41.35次上升到2014年的151次。居民对社会诚信状况、社会公益状况满意度分别为84.44分和84.88分，较2012年分别提高6.91分和8.94分。2013年民政部发起了第三届“中国城市公益慈善指数”测评，南京在全国294个城市中位列第四，并蝉联“七星级慈善城市”称号。

二是坚持人性化管理。充分发挥“12345”政府服务呼叫中心功能，及时了解、处理群众反映的问题，使诉求表达更有效、反馈更及时，构建全天候、全方位、全覆盖的民意沟通机制和为民办实事平台。在社区普遍建立了“慈善超市”“爱心超市”和互助社，形成了覆盖全市的服务热线、遍布城乡的社区服务中心、普及社区的老人日间照料和文体活动室等民生设施。先后出台了《关于健全社会稳定风险评估和决策失误责任追究机制的实施意见》和《南京市人民政府议事决策规则》等政策文件，对涉及重大公共利益和与人民群众利益

密切相关的重大事项，通过听证会、座谈会、向社会公开征询意见等方式，充分听取社会各界的意见。凡涉及群众切身利益、需要群众广泛知晓的事项以及法律和上级国家行政机关规定需要公开的事项，均通过政府网站、政府公报、新闻发布会以及新闻媒体等方式，依法、及时、全面、准确地向社会公开。通过尊重群众的知情权、参与权，自下而上真正把老百姓的想法和建议收集上来，以此作为开展各项工作的依据，从而不断提升老百姓的幸福感和满意度。

三是加强食药品安全监管。着力完善集中统一食药品安全监管新体制，着力健全全程监管新制度，着力建立风险管理新机制，着力开创食药品安全监管新格局。“十二五”期间，南京市整合原市卫生、质监、工商、药监等部门食品和药品安全监管职能，对生产、流通、消费环节的食品安全和药品的安全性、有效性实施统一监督管理。整合原来的质量检验院、食品药品检验所检测等资源，组建新的食品药品检验研究院，提高食品药品安全检测力量。目前，全市共有登记取证食品生产经营单位 9.3 万家，食品、保健食品抽检覆盖主要食品品种 82%，合格率在 97% 以上。

四是不断改善社会公共安全。平安南京、法治南京建设取得新成效，安全生产、食品药品安全、信访维稳工作得到加强，2012－2014 年全市刑事案件发案呈负增长，分别为 －1%、－0.1%、－0.58%；亿元 GDP 生产安全事故死亡率分别为 0.08%、0.07% 和 0.06%；社会矛盾纠纷调处成功率分别为 94%、96.7% 和 95.59%。2014 年，公众安全感达 81.83 分，比 2012 年提高了 4.31 分，群众安全感达 93.4%，南京市再次荣获“全国社会管理综合治理优秀市”称号，社会保持和谐稳定。

八、开展街道、社区体制改革，推动基层社会治理创新

南京市在优化街道职能、完善街居体制、推进“街道中心化”等方面做了大量改革探索。这些改革极大整合了部门和行业服务资源，推进了公共服务管理的下沉，提升了服务的效率与便利度，得到国家和江苏省的肯定和推广。南京被评为全国和谐社区建设示范城市第一名；六个区被评为全国社区治理与服务创新试验区，数量位居全国第一；社区减负、街居体制改革相继被评为中国社区治理十大创新成果。

一是基层社会服务体制改革不断深化。推进公共服务工作重心下移，促进基层公共服务和民生建设职能回归。推进街道“去机关化”，取消了对玄武、秦淮、建邺、鼓楼 4 城区各街道经济指标的考核，促进社会管理和公共服务职能回归街道本位。推进社区去行政化改革，将社区的主要工作转移到为居民服务上，取消了社区 25 项工作任务、41 类评比、41 个机构、72 项台账，社区负担明显减轻。

二是坚持工作重心下移、工作力量下沉，推动管理服务触角向基层延伸，打牢基层工作基础，探索创新街道和基层社区的工作体系。建邺区按照“资源向下、民心向上、民主向前”的工作理念，率先在全市建立“一委一居一站一办”社区组织架构，让党务、居务、政务在社区分设共建，新的社区体制把人力、财力、物力更多投到基层，政府各项管理职

能、服务职能在社区得到有效承接。新的体制全面反映了管理、自治和服务三大功能，老百姓满意度、参与率明显提高，很多矛盾和问题都在基层得到解决。目前，“一委一居一站一办”模式已基本实现全市城乡社区全覆盖，这一做法被称为“建邺模式”已在全国推广。

三是探索网格化管理。栖霞区仙林街道“网格化”管理模式成效显著。自 2010 年 6 月以来，这个街道以社区为基本单位，把街道划分为 6 个一级网格，下辖 40 个二级网格、1144 个三级网格（驻街单位），以街镇干部、社区工作者、民警和社会志愿者等为责任主体，实行“人往格中去、事在网中办、制度为保障、督查求实效”的工作原则和运行机制，形成“多网合一、一网多格、一格多元、多元联动”格局，初步建立起责权利更加明晰的基层“网格化管理”长效机制。南京深入实施消防、车管、危管、外管、网管、物管“社区六进”工程，“平安南京”建设水平不断提高。2015 年，90% 以上的城市社区、80% 以上的农村社区达到省级和谐社区标准，国家和谐社区建设示范区数量居省会城市之首。

九、注重信息支撑，坚持标准化建设

近年来，南京顺应城市管理中心下移的大趋势，紧扣城市网格化管理和社区服务的模式创新，坚持以先进技术为引领，运用数字化、信息化现代技术手段，不断推动社会管理体制机制、方法载体、手段途径的改革创新，启动包括“智慧社区”“智慧城管”“智慧医疗”“数字管网”等一系列项目，推进城市管理标准化、智能化与信息化建设。加快推进并丰富信息化建设成果在城市管理方面的实际应用，按照“人地关联、人事关联、人时关联”要求，对人、地、物、事、组织等社会管理信息进行集中采集录入，建成区域社会管理基础数据库，为相关部门提供信息共享服务，实现区域内矛盾排查、来信来访、综治维稳、安全生产等数据信息“一网式”汇聚，采集、分析、交办、监督等功能“一体化”运行。依靠科技、依托网络，深入推进智能化技防“1136”工程建设，全力打造基于“云计算”的视频监控实战应用平台，构建“技防南京”整体格局。通过科技成果的不断运用，实现社会管理从粗放管理向科学管理转变、从低质运行向高效运行转变，全面提升社会管理服务效能和质量。社会管理的信息化建设进一步催生发展了社会建设的标准化建设，先后涌现出秦淮区、玄武区和谐社区标准化品牌以及市城管局的城市治理标准化典型。

（撰稿：周蜀秦，南京市社会科学院博士后、副研究员）

杭州：迈向法治化的综合考评和绩效管理

杭州是浙江省的省会，全市行政区域总面积16 596平方千米，常住人口有 884.4 万人，加上流动人口，超过1 000万人；以常住人口计算，2014 年杭州人均 GDP 超 10 万元，达103 757元，按照世界银行划分贫富程度标准，接近富裕国家的临界水平。

作为长三角南翼的中心城市，杭州处于中国改革开放的前沿，肩负着率先发展的历史使命，同时杭州也是一个生产资源禀赋相对匮乏的城市，如何通过政府创新来不断提升治理绩效，进而推动经济社会又好又快发展，始终是摆在杭州市政府面前的一项重大课题。与国内其他城市一样，杭州的政府绩效管理也走过了 20 多年的探索、发展历程。从 20 世纪 90 年代初开始实行机关目标责任制考核以来，杭州政府绩效管理经历了三次跨越：一是从机关目标责任制考核向满意不满意单位评选的跨越。2000 年，杭州在全国率先推出“满意单位和不满意单位”评选活动，以根治“门难进、脸难看、话难听、事难办”机关“四难”综合征，促进机关作风转变，由此迈出了让社会公众评议党政机关绩效的关键性一大步。二是从满意不满意单位评选向综合考评的跨越。2005 年，杭州市将目标责任制考核（目标考核）与满意评选活动（社会评价）结合，并增设领导考评，对市直单位实行全方位、多维度的综合考核评价，由此形成“三位一体”的杭州综合考评；2006 年 8 月，全国首家正局级常设绩效考评机构——杭州市综合考评委员会办公室正式成立，标志着杭州综合考评走向制度化、规范化、专业化；2008 年，杭州市对下辖 13 个区、县（市）实施综合考评，由此综合考评实现了全覆盖。三是从综合考评向绩效管理的跨越。2011 年 6 月，杭州市被列为全国政府绩效管理试点城市之一，杭州综合考评加快了向绩效管理转变的步伐，进一步优化指标体系，简化目标考核，创新社会评价，做实创新创优，规范各类考核，加快法治建设，在推进城市治理现代化进程中发挥更大作用。

一、杭州市政府绩效管理的基本架构

杭州市政府绩效管理是以综合考评为主载体，采用“3 + 1”的模式，分别从社会评价、目标考核、领导考评和创新创优四个维度，对市直单位和区、县（市）实施全方位、多维度、综合性的考核评价。

（一）市直单位综合考评

考评对象为116家市直党政机关和企事业单位。总分为100分，其中，社会评价占50分，主要是按比例随机抽取市民、企业、市党代表、市人大代表、市政协委员、专家学者等9个层面约1.5万名投票人员，以入户调查等方式，对各单位的“服务态度和工作效率，办事公正和廉洁自律，工作实效和社会影响”进行满意度评价；目标考核占45分，主要是对各单位年度绩效指标、工作目标以及领导班子党风廉政建设等专项目标进行考核；领导考评占5分，由党委、人大、政府、政协四套班子的负责人和法院、检察院两院院长对市直单位的总体工作实绩进行评价。创新创优由各单位自愿申报，经市考评办核验，组织专家分别进行远程专业评估和现场综合评估，对总分进入前30名的单位给予不同的加分。

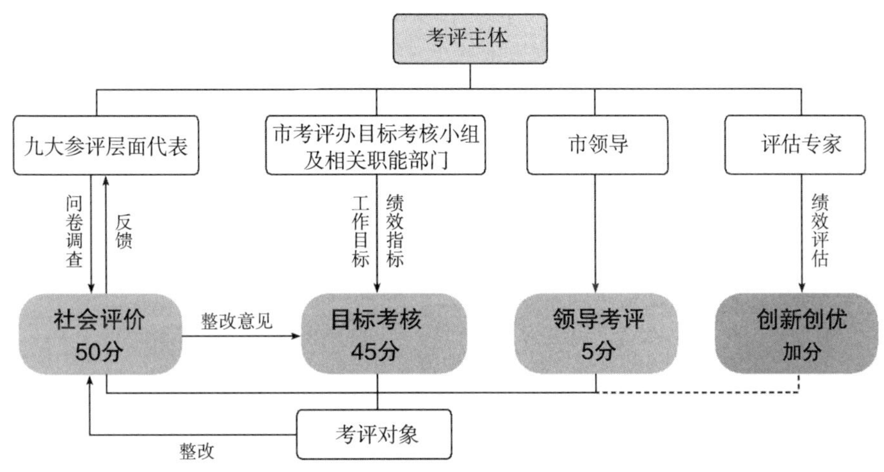

图1　杭州市直单位综合考评“3+1”模式示意图

表1　杭州市市直单位综合考核评价指标体系

<table>
<tr><th colspan="2">维度</th><th>分项指标</th><th>考核或评价指标内容</th><th>分值</th></tr>
<tr><td rowspan="11">目标考核</td><td rowspan="3">绩效指标</td><td>关键指标</td><td>市委、市政府确定的涉及本部门的相关国民经济和社会发展定量指标</td><td rowspan="11">45</td></tr>
<tr><td>职能指标</td><td>市直单位法定职责履行情况相关绩效指标</td></tr>
<tr><td>通用指标</td><td>适用于市直各单位的部分综合性绩效指标，包括依法行政、电子政务、行政效率和同报信息质量等指标</td></tr>
<tr><td rowspan="8">工作目标</td><td rowspan="5">重点工作目标</td><td>省委、省政府对杭州市的重点考核目标</td></tr>
<tr><td>市委、市政府确定的年度重点工作任务</td></tr>
<tr><td>市政府为民办实事项目</td></tr>
<tr><td>重点专项工作</td></tr>
<tr><td>跟踪督办社会评价意见整改目标</td></tr>
<tr><td>部门协作目标</td><td>由有关部门牵头、多部门协作配合的，事关全市、有明确年度目标任务、适于量化考核的阶段性工作目标，由若干专项组成</td></tr>
<tr><td>诉求回应目标</td><td>信访和“12345”办理、社会评价意见整改、效能投诉处理、公共服务窗口评价、建议提案办理</td></tr>
<tr><td>自身建设目标</td><td>领导班子建设、党风廉政建设、目标绩效管理（包括督查工作）、财政绩效评价、机构编制评估</td></tr>
</table>

续表 1

维度	分项指标	考核或评价指标内容	分值
领导考评	总体工作业绩	总体考评各单位完成工作目标和市委、市政府交办任务的情况	5
社会评价	专项社会评价	采用按事项评价的方法,即对市委、市政府部署的、由多部门协同推进的事关民生、有效高公众知晓度的年度重点工作任务,进行一事一评,再根据评价结果对工作关联单位予以赋分;公共服务窗口服务评价结果	50
	综合社会评价	服务态度和工作效率	
		办事公正和廉洁自律	
		工作实效和社会影响	
创新创优	创新目标	原创性创新:在全国、全省率先推行的具有改革性、创造性的工作理念、体制机制、方法手段等以及由此取得可持续运用的成果 继承性创新:(1)市直单位对原有的创新项目进行深化、完善、提升,并取得新的突破和成效。(2)整合利用自身或他人已有的工作平台和公共资源开展的开创性工作或拓展性应用,以及由此取得的新成果	"竞赛制和淘汰制"
	创优目标	综合性表彰奖励成果:在全国、全省范围内取得一流业绩,并获得国家部委以上或省委、省政府综合性表彰奖励的成果,或单位主要职能工作连续3年(次)以上(包括本年度)获省部级先进称号的项目(需提供相关表彰文件或奖牌) 提升服务质量项目:市直单位在增强履职能力、提高服务质量和绩效水平上取得的成果	
	克难攻坚目标	经济社会热点难点问题破解:针对当前杭州经济社会发展中面临的热点难点问题采取的有效对策措施,以及由此取得的新成果 机关绩效改进难题破解:针对影响机关绩效提升的老大难问题采取的有效对策措施,以及由此取得的新成果	
合计			100 +

(二)区、县(市)综合考评

考评对象为所辖的13个区、县(市)。在考评内容与权重设置上,目标考核占65%的权重,包括发展指标和工作目标两部分。发展指标按经济建设、社会管理和公共服务、发展潜力三大类设置了34项指标,占30%权重;工作目标着重考核年度工作任务和工作目标完

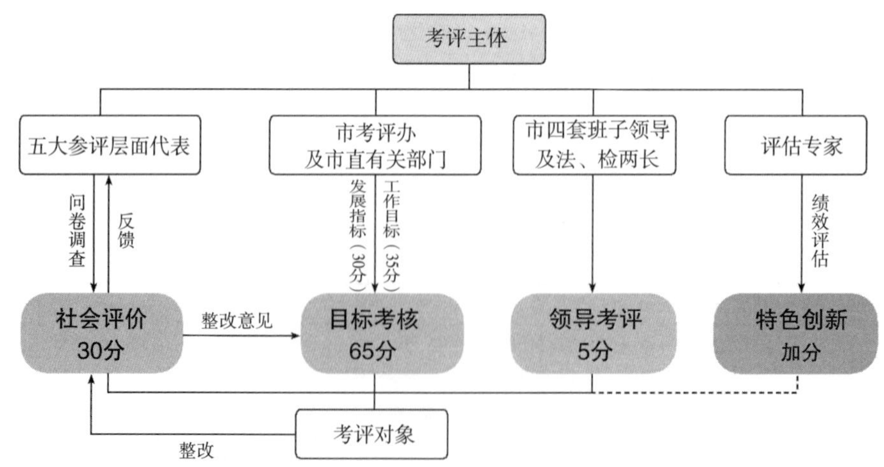

图2 杭州市区、县(市)综合考评"3+1"模式示意图

成情况，以及廉政建设、社会评价意见整改等情况，占35%权重。领导考评由市四套领导班子成员和市法、检两长对区、县（市）领导班子的领导力、执行力、协作力、创新力和总体工作业绩进行综合评定，占5%的权重。社会评价占30%的权重，主要由当地五个层面的代表对区、县（市）党委政府经济建设、社会管理、公共服务、依法行政等方面的工作业绩和社会效果进行满意度测评。特色创新作为加分项目，自愿申报，绩效评估。

表2　杭州市区、县（市）综合考核评价指标体系

考评维度	考核或评价指标内容		分值	分值合计
目标考核	发展指标	经济建设	30	30
		社会管理和公共服务		
		发展潜力		
	工作目标	重要工作目标，市委、市政府确定的涉及区、县（市）的重点目标任务，包括市委、市政府与各区、县（市）以签订责任状形式明确的一些工作任务，需要区，县（市）完成的年度重要工作，以及其他专项目标任务	20	35
		共性目标：各区、县（市）机关自身建设以及其他具有共性特征的工作目标任务，包括领导班子建设。党风廉政建设、机关效能建设、社会评价意见整改和目标组织管理等	15	
领导考评	综合评定各区、县（市）领导班子的领导力，执行力、协作力、创新力和总体工作业绩		5	5
社会评价	总体评价各区、县（市）党委和政府在经济建设、社会管理、公共服务、依法行政及自身建设等方面的工作业绩和社会效果		30	30
特色创新	对各区、县（市）在经济建设、社会管理，公共服务，政治民主、行政改革、党的建设等方面具有地方特色和推广价值的改革与创新举措实施绩效考核		5	5（加分）

表3　淳安县综合考评单列指标体系

类别		目标名称	分值及权重
发展指标	生态保护	环境质量综合评价指数	30
		镇村污水治理率	
		区域建设用地集约利用综合评价指数	
	生态经济	财政可用资金保障率	
		高新技术产业增加值增长率	
		服务业增加值增长率	
		全县景区化农民旅游产业收入占农村居民人均纯收入比重	
		社会消费品零售总额增长率	
		万元GDP综合能耗降低率	
	改善保障民生	社会保障支出占地方财政支出比重	
		城镇居民人均可支配收入增长率	
		农民人均纯收入增长率	
		社会治安秩序	

续表 3

类别	目标名称	分值及权重
重要工作目标	生态文明建设和“五水共治”工作	35
	生态功能示范区建设工作(国家良好湖泊建设工作)	
	城乡区域统筹发展(新农村建设)工作	
	“三改一拆”及无违建县创建工作	
	扩大有效投资及重点项目推进工作	
	领导班子建设	
	党风廉政建设	
	社会评价意见整改目标	
	信息督查与目标管理	
领导考评	综合评定县领导班子的领导力、执行力、协作力、创新力和总体工作业绩	5
社会评价	评价治安生态保护、社会管理、公共服务、依法行政及自身建设等方面的工作业绩和社会效果	30
特色创新	对淳安县在“美丽杭州”实验区建设中有关生态保护、生态经济建设、民生保障改善等方面具有地方特色和推广价值的改革与创新举措实施绩效考核	5 (加分)

二、杭州市政府绩效管理的主要特点

(一) 公民导向

一是在制度设计中充分体现社会公众的主体地位。在市直单位综合考评的组成中，社会评价占50%的比重，目标考核中也包含有社会评价意见整改结果的考核，如果考虑创新创优专家绩效评估的比重，社会公众在综合考评中所占的权重远超过50%。

二是形成了一个覆盖全市的公民参与网络。从初期的4个层面6 000余名参评代表到目前9个层面1.2万名参评代表。2007年度，外来务工人员作为市民代表参与社会评价；2010年度，提高了农村居民代表比例；2011年度，引入“社会组织代表”层面，具体包含三个子层面：社区居委会负责人、行业协会负责人、民办非企业单位负责人。所有的这些代表均从社会评价人员信息库中随机抽样而产生，他们既对政府部门工作进行独立评价，也提出各类改进意见和建议。

三是注重公众诉求回应机制的建设。在这一工作机制中，社会公众参与体现在3个层面上：第一层面是公众通过社会评价这一渠道，一方面行使评价权，另一方面也可以表达对政府部门改进工作的意见和建议；第二层面是公众有权利要求和监督政府机关根据社会评价意见进行认真整改，把评价意见落实为政府行动，2008年以来，我们每年都向社会公开发布由各部门制定的、总计近200项的年度社会评价意见整改目标；第三层面是社会公众对政府机关整改结果进行考核评价，从结果上进行监督，每年年底我们要对整改结果向社会进行公示，接受公众的再评价。这样就形成了“评价—整改—反馈—再评价—再整改—再反馈”，建立了对公众诉求的有效回应机制。

表4 杭州市直单位社会评价各层面代表及权重

	代表层面	样本量	
		数量	占比(%)
1	市党代表	315	2.67
2	市人大代表	267	2.27
3	市政协委员	278	2.36
4	区、县(市)领导代表(含四套领导班子成员)	330	2.80
5	区、县(市)机关代表(含各区县(市)部、委、办、局及街道(乡镇)党政(包括人大)负责人)	1 074	9.12
6	社会组织代表(含社区居委会、行业协会、民办非企业单位负责人)	1 000	8.49
7	社会监督代表(老干部、专家学者、省直机关、新闻媒体、绩效信息及市行风评议代表)	517	4.39
8	企业代表	2 000	16.98
9	市民代表(含城镇居民、农村居民、外来务工创业人员)	6 000	50.93
	合计	11 781	100

四是在结果运用中体现社会公众的意愿。最典型的就是推动了“破七难”工作的持续深入开展。

（二）注重绩效

一是健全绩效测评指标体系。与传统的目标考核相区别，在考核指标设置上，包涵了绩效测度和实现程度两个维度，也就是考核中不仅要看指标的完成情况，还要看指标完成的质量、效益、效果，包括服务对象的认可度、满意度。具体分为三类：第一类是满意度测评，每个单位在申报当年工作目标时，提出两项可以进行绩效测评的项目，由市考评办从中选定一项，组织服务对象进行满意度测评；第二类是挑战指标，即纵向与自身最优指标比，横向与该项指标发展领先的城市比，具有标杆意义；第三类是表彰奖励，即单位职能工作得到国家部委、主管部委的表彰奖励，也可作为绩效测度。

二是建立年度目标绩效改进工作机制。通过“数字考评”系统，及时跟踪目标完成进展情况并反馈绩效改进信息，实现工作目标动态跟踪的过程管理。确立以“发现存在问题，帮助查找差距，推动绩效改进，促进目标完成”为目标的日常抽查工作制度，形成常规检查与暗访、测评三种方式并用的检查工作机制。组建绩效信息员队伍、扩大绩效信息来源，定期编制《社情民意与绩效信息》周刊，建立“绩效信息库”，以《绩效改进通知书》形式向责任单位通报有关问题。

三是开展专项绩效评估。建立绩效评估专家库，充分发挥专家在绩效评估中的专业、中立、权威作用；选择公信力较高的专业中介机构，对社会聚焦的公共服务或重大政策进行专项评估。近年来我们相继就关系食品安全、教育、医疗、交通、就业、社会管理、城市建设等方面的工作进行了31项专项目标绩效测评，包含了政策措施、机制平台、公共服务、重点项目等各方面的评估内容。

四是探索绩效分析和治理诊断调查。坚持问题导向，针对综合考评中发现的一些带有共性的一些绩效问题，开展专题调研，会同相关部门和有关专家，进行治理诊断分析，向市委、市政府提出对策建议，督查相关部门提高绩效管理水平。

（三）引领创新

一是通过创新项目绩效考核的"激励机制"推进政府创新。创新创优绩效考核作为加分项目，得到被考评单位的高度重视。每年通过立项、评估的有近100个项目。为了确保创新的实际成效和可持续性，杭州市在立项、评估环节之外，还增设了跟踪环节，即对已完成绩效考核的创新项目定期进行跟踪。近年来，还相继增设了创优目标和克难攻坚目标，并鼓励多部门进行联合创新，以解决一些长期困扰的突出问题和深层次矛盾。2012年，杭州市编制《杭州市政府创新指南》，在经济建设、政治建设、文化建设、社会建设、生态文明建设、执政能力建设六个方面共确定了58个选题，供各部门在创新的过程中自主选择，引领政府的创新创优。

二是通过"评价—整改—反馈"的"压力机制"推进政府创新。通过广泛的公众参与，为更好地发现突出矛盾和深层次的问题提供了民意渠道，为引领政府创新提供了方向。通过社会评价意见整改，促进政府部门改革不合理的体制和机制问题，加快职能转变，引入外部监督的方式，检验了政府创新的成效。"评价—整改—反馈"工作机制通过外部评价和内部整改的"压力机制"推进了政府服务和管理创新，逐步构建回应公众诉求、创新公共治理、推动政府绩效持续改进的政府创新机制。

三、杭州市政府绩效管理的制度绩效

开展综合考评是杭州加强政府自身建设的一项制度创新，既具有一般的绩效管理工具价值，也具有鲜明的理念价值。在实践中，杭州市以"创一流业绩、让人民满意"为宗旨，坚持"让人民评判、让人民满意"的核心价值观，充分发挥综合考评的战略导向、公民导向、职责导向和创新导向，有效地把"开放、民主、责任、绩效"的价值理念融入制度设计和具体实践之中，力求使杭州综合考评和绩效管理成为一个"有思想"的工具。从制度绩效来看，杭州综合考评和政府绩效管理主要具有四大功效：

一是转变机关作风的"撒手锏"。通过社会评价，引导党政机关"眼睛向下"，更多地倾听老百姓的声音，认真总结经验、深刻查找问题、扎实改进工作，使政府工作人员的服务意识、责任意识明显增强，有效地将社会评价形成的外部压力转变为改进机关作风的内在动力，提升了机关效能，优化了发展软环境，从2006以来，社会公众对杭州市政府的满意度均保持在90%以上，综合考评已成为杭州市加强政府自身建设、提高行政效能的一项基本制度。

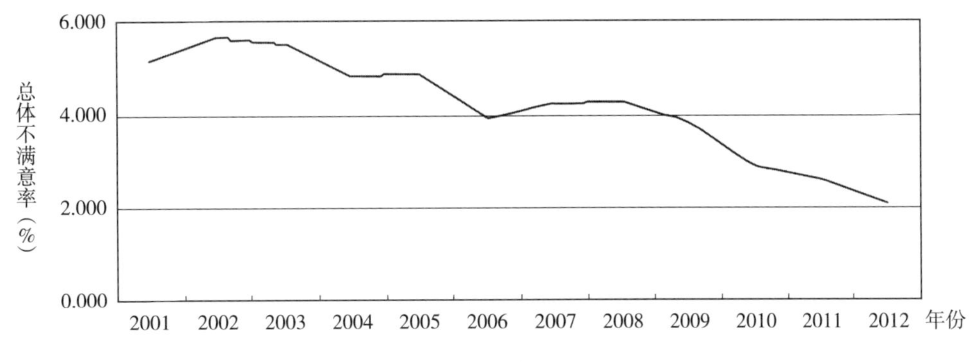

图 3　2001 年以来，人民群众对政府机关的总体不满意率连续多年呈下降趋势

二是破解民生问题的"指挥棒"。杭州综合考评完善的公民诉求回应机制和强大的发现功能，直接推动了政府责任机制的建立，促进了服务型政府建设。2003 年，通过对社会评价意见的梳理和分析，系统地梳理出人民群众关注的 7 个热点难点问题，即：困难群众生活就业难、看病难、上学难、住房难、行路难、停车难、办事难、清洁保洁难。杭州市委、市政府在此基础上将其上升为战略决策，制定长效机制，在全国率先提出了解决人民群众最关心、最直接、最现实的"七难"问题的工作目标，形成了"破七难"工作机制。经济社会的发展使得人民群众的关注点也有所转移，在 2006 年度社会评价意见的梳理中，发现人民群众对"食品药品安全"和"生态环境保护"新的"两难"关注度较高。杭州市委、市政府决定扩大"七难"的内涵，将它们纳入"破七难"范畴，形成了"7 + 2"的"破七难"新框架。2008 年，又将物价上涨、垄断行业服务等问题纳入"破七难"，形成"7 + X"新框架，进一步丰富"破七难"的内涵，有效地推动惠民为民工程建设，使民生问题不断得到改善。

三是引领创新创优的"方向标"。通过设置创新创优目标，实施绩效考核，鼓励市直单位和区、县（市）解放思想，开拓创新，积极探索新理念、新体制（机制）、新方法，着力解决本地本单位工作中遇到的突出矛盾和深层次问题。9 年来，共有 800 多项创新项目通过专家绩效评估，一系列的创新创优和特色创新项目不仅在政府管理创新、资源整合上取得突破性进展，同时创新的可持续性、可推广性，产生了显著的社会效益和经济效益。综合考评已经成为杭州市推进政府创新的重要平台。

四是促进科学发展的"助推器"。一方面，在考核中把党委政府的战略部署和重点工作，作为各单位指标设置的重要依据，进行科学量化、精准分解，确保目标落到实处；另一方面，在指标权重设置上切实体现了科学发展的要求，既要 GDP，又不唯 GDP；既重"显绩"，也重"潜绩"；既要"金山银山"，又要"绿水青山"；统筹处理好城乡发展、区域发展、经济社会发展、人与自然和谐发展之间关系，有效引导各地各单位创造经得起历史、人民和实践检验的实绩。

表5　杭州市"十二五"期间经济发展部分约束性考核指标完成情况

目标名称	十二五目标	2011 年目标	2012 年目标	2013 年目标	2014 年目标	责任部门
耕地保有量	22.1 万公顷	—	≥332.56 万亩	≥332.56 万亩	≥332.56 万亩	市国土资源局
单位 GDP 增长的新增建设用地消耗量		较"十一五"规划期间年均值降低 6%	下降率≥5%	下降率≥6%	下降率≥7%	市国土资源局
单位生产总值能耗	完成省下达指标	下降 3.1% 以上	下降 4.1% 以上	下降 4.8% 以上	下降 6.4%(提前完成十二五目标	市经信委
主要污染物排放(化学需氧量(COD)、氨氮(NH_3-N)、二氧化硫(SO_2)、氮氧化物(NOX)排放总量)	完成省下达指标	在 2010 年基础上削减 2.8%、2%、3%、2.6%	比上年削减 2.5%、2.5%、3.0%、3.0%	比上年削减 3%、4%、3%、4%	省里未下达	市环保局
林木蓄积量(万立方米)	4 650	比上年增 181	4 638	4 830	—	市林水局

四、持续深入推进政府绩效管理面临一些深层次矛盾

与国内很多地区一样，杭州市在政府绩效管理方面虽然进行了长期的实践探索，取得了较好成效，但要持续深入地推进政府绩效管理也面临许多新情况、新问题。从全国各地的情况看，更有一些带有普遍性的深层次矛盾，如果不能有效破解，将会影响政府绩效管理的深入开展。

（一）"政绩冲动"的困扰

经过 30 多年经济高速增长，传统的粗放式发展越来越难以为继，转型升级变得更加迫切。这在客观上要求政府加快职能转变，加大改革力度，进一步简政放权，创新治理方式，提高政府绩效。但在实际工作中，多年来唯 GDP 的发展模式和粗放型管理所形成的思想观念和施政行为，还很难适应绩效管理的要求。一些地方在开展政府绩效管理中，只是将传统的目标责任制考核进行简单移植，实际还停留在重数量轻质量、重速度轻效益、重当前轻长远、重显绩轻潜绩上，难以摆脱唯 GDP 的"政绩冲动"。尤其是在当前经济下行压力增大，保增长、保稳定的主题再次压倒调结构、促转型的现实下，发展方式的"路径依赖"某种程度上很容易使绩效管理沦为单纯追求 GDP 的"指挥棒"。加之以往"只算政治账不算经济账"这类行政观念的影响，也常常使绩效管理陷入进退两难的尴尬。政府绩效管理如何在围绕中心、服务大局"公转"的同时，能够遵循绩效管理的自身规律"自转"好，在促进科学发展、落实"四个全面"上发挥更加积极的导向助推作用，还需要我们进一步实践和把握。

（二）传统文化的制约

“绩效管理”是个舶来品，要在有着悠久历史文化传统的中国落地，还有一个文化碰撞和磨合的过程，比如中国传统文化中的愚民思想和“官本位”观念，至今仍有一定影响，造成社会公众的民主参与意识不强，参与渠道不畅，政务公开程度不够，行政主体与行政客体之间的“信息不对称”现象比较普遍，为客观评价政府组织的绩效带来困难。此外，由于中国传统文化形成的整体性、模糊性思维方式，与西方传统思维追求精确性、实证性有明显的区别，诚如黄仁宇先生指出的中国缺乏“数目字管理”的文化传统，也与绩效管理所要求的定量化、精细化、科学化存在一定排斥。目前在行政管理活动中，比较普遍的情况是，定性的评价多，定量的分析少，很多工作习惯于大而化之、“毛估估”，一些部门往往对绩效评估的一些方法运用难以适应，意见较多，甚至抵触。

（三）制度保障的缺失

从目前情况看，各地政府绩效管理工作尚未形成一种法制化的制度安排。这就使这项工作很容易随领导人的变动或其注意力的改变而变化。从国家治理体系来看，目前政府绩效管理机构和职能尚未统一纳入机构编制序列，缺乏“自上而下”的组织体系，各地负责政府绩效管理的组织机构不健全，大部分附属于不同的部门，机构设置及职责定位五花八门，形态各异。此外，部门之间职责边界不清也不利于政府绩效管理的开展。为协调跨部门事项而设置的大量临时协调机构，也使部门职能和责任进一步碎片化，本身又带来新的协调矛盾，造成协调机制的失灵，并形成对考核评比手段的过度依赖，导致各类考核和评比表彰过多过滥。

（四）技术手段的障碍

由于政府工作的特殊性，现实中很难找到相应的参照系进行对比评价，不同部门的工作性质和内容差异性相当大，很难形成统一的评价标准，给绩效评估制度设计带来相当大的难度。其次，社会评价中的信息不对称问题难以避免，一方面，评价代表对政府部门的职能划分和责任归属不清晰；另一方面，现代社会分工而形成的知识和信息上的局限加剧了评价过程中知识不对称和信息不对称的问题。从实践来看，目前社会公众的参与呈现多元化、分散化特征，社会组织的专业化参与相对缺乏，一定程度上影响了绩效评估的质量。此外，绩效评估结果也容易受社会聚焦点的影响，而这些聚焦点往往又是改革发展过程中的问题，解决起来需要较长时间或者在国家层面上取得改革突破，从而使评估结果容易产生一定的惯性。在互联网时代，如何运用手机互联网、大数据等技术手段来扩大多元主体的有效参与，也对我们提出了新的课题。

五、法治化是持续推进政府绩效管理的必由之路

尽管政府绩效管理在我国还刚刚起步，在推进过程中还会遇到许多矛盾和困难，但我们

完全有信心在全面深化改革、全面依法治国、努力实现国家治理体系和治理能力现代化的大背景下，顺势而为，大力推进政府绩效管理，并将其不断引向深入。

要持续深入地推进政府绩效管理，关键的一点就是要实现政府绩效管理的法治化。在这方面，杭州市经过各方努力，终于迈出了决定性的一步：2015 年 8 月 27 日，杭州市人大常委会审议通过《杭州市绩效管理条例》（以下简称《条例》），并于 9 月 25 日经浙江省人大常委会正式批准，《条例》业已颁布，于 2016 年 1 月 1 日起正式实施。这是杭州市运用法治思维和法治方式推进政府绩效管理的一个最新尝试。通过立法，使杭州市多年来行之有效的制度设计和实践经验法制化，将多元参与主体、参与方式和程序、结果运用、绩效问责等以地方性法规形式确立下来，实现了政府绩效管理“于法有据、依法管理”。

《条例》在法律制度设计与立法创新上，主要有以下方面：

一是界定了绩效管理的内涵。《条例》第二条明确，绩效管理是“根据本行政区域的发展目标和绩效责任单位履行的职责设定绩效目标，实施日常监控，并对目标的完成情况和实际效果进行综合考核评价，以达到绩效不断提升的全过程管理”。该条款是结合我们多年实践，对“绩效管理”进行了定义，并对绩效管理的依据、流程、方法和目的进行了法律上诠释。

二是确立了绩效管理机构的法律地位。《条例》第五条、第六条明确，由绩效管理委员会统一领导本行政区域的绩效管理工作，具体工作由绩效管理机构负责，机构编制、发展改革、监察、财政、人力资源和社会保障、审计、统计、政府法制等部门须按照各自职责，依法做好绩效管理工作。这些规定为绩效管理机构和相关部门开展绩效管理工作提供了有力的法律依据，实现了绩效管理机构“职责法定”。

三是明确了绩效管理的适用范围。《条例》第二条、第三十九条明确，绩效管理对象不仅覆盖市政府组成部门和区县政府及其组成部门、乡镇街道，还将其他依照公务员法管理的机构、组织，法律、法规授权的具有公共事务管理职责的组织，以及提供公共服务的企业（履行公共服务职责时）都纳入绩效管理范围。这样规定，也就是把党群部门以及承担公共服务职能的国有企事业单位都纳入进来，符合中国国情。

四是建立了绩效规划和绩效报告制度。建立绩效规划制度，有助于绩效责任单位保持正确的履职方向和施政行为的连续性，也有利于促进政府部门将当前工作与长远发展，业务工作与自身建设结合起来。《条例》第十条规定，“绩效责任单位应当根据本地区（行业）经济社会发展规划和本单位工作职能编制绩效管理规划，规划期限为五年”；第十一条对绩效规划的内容作了原则性要求。《条例》第二十三条还明确了建立绩效报告制度，即要求“绩效责任单位应当对照年度绩效目标，编制年度绩效自评报告”，促进各单位强化绩效理念，真正用绩效管理的方法来开展工作，以绩效标准来衡量工作质量。

五是确立了公众参与的主体地位。扩大多元主体参与，是政府绩效管理的发展方向。《条例》第十六条明确了多元主体在绩效管理中的地位和权利，特别是在绩效管理规划的编制，年度绩效目标的制定、调整、监督等过程中，享有充分的知情权、建议权、评价权；《条例》第二十六条还明确，在绩效管理全过程中必须注重吸收和应用的公众意见，强调群众满意度是检验政府绩效的重要标准。

六是规范了绩效沟通和绩效改进制度。《条例》突出了加强绩效沟通和绩效改进的理念，强调绩效管理责任主体与绩效管理组织者之间的互动，建立了绩效分析制度，明确绩效改进的内容、形式和要求，把绩效改进作为绩效管理的根本落脚点。《条例》第二十条明确，“绩效管理机构应当将日常管理中发现的问题及时告知绩效责任单位，绩效责任单位应当自收到告知单之日起十个工作日内做出情况说明，提出处理意见，反馈处理结果”；第三十一条明确，“绩效责任单位应当对绩效评估中反映的问题和社会评价意见进行分析，制定和落实整改措施。”

七是建立了专项绩效管理。《条例》第二十一条明确，“绩效管理机构应当会同绩效管理相关部门对本地区经济社会有重大影响、涉及公众利益、关系民生或者需要较大财政资金投入的事项实行专项绩效管理”。开展专项绩效管理是提升绩效管理全面性和科学性的重要举措，同时也为杭州市现有的综合考评和绩效管理工作了延展，预留了工作空间。

八是对第三方评估作了探索性规定。第三方评估具有相对的独立性、专业性和客观性。发展第三方评估，有助于促进绩效评估的规范化、科学化。《条例》第二十四条对此作了探索性规定，明确“绩效管理机构可以委托绩效评估专门机构、高等院校、科研院所、社会中介组织等第三方面机构对部分绩效目标开展专业测评”，为鼓励和引导第三方评估机构参与绩效评估，促进第三方评估规范发展提供了基础。

九是明确了绩效评估结果的综合运用。《条例》第三十二条明确“绩效管理结果作为政策调整、预算管理、编制管理、奖励惩戒、领导人员职务升降任免等方面的重要依据”，这不仅体现了绩效管理的导向和约束作用，也拓展了绩效管理在资源配置、干部管理等方面的作用。

十是建立了绩效问责制度。《条例》第三十五条、第三十六条、第三十七条规定，纳入绩效管理的单位及其工作人员，在工作过程中发生过错所应承担相应的责任，并对责任的种类以及问责的主体作了明确，强化了绩效管理的刚性。可以这么说，绩效管理立法也是杭州破解庸官懒政问题的重要举措之一，对进一步简政放权、提能增效、有效治理“为官不为”等现象将起到极大的推动作用。

十一是建立了权力机关监督绩效管理制度。《条例》第七条规定，“市和区、县（市）人民代表大会常务委员会每年上半年听取本级人民政府各部门上年度绩效管理工作情况的报告”。该条款进一步强化了政府绩效管理的重要性，并可以有效保证绩效管理工作的持续性和制度化。

（撰稿：伍彬，杭州市综合考评委员会办公室、杭州市绩效管理委员会办公室主任）

宁波：民生幸福的发展之路

一、序言

近年来，宁波按照“公平正义、共建共享”的理念和“保基本、抓重点、促均衡、提质量”的思路，推进经济转型升级，同步推动社会发展，不断提升公共服务水平，改革发展成果更加公平地惠及全体市民。

作为历史文化名城的宁波，文化是宁波的精、气、神。深厚的文化内涵为宁波插上经济腾飞的翅膀，成为宁波转型升级的助推器。

宁波大力实施“提升城乡品质、建设美丽宁波”行动计划，并出台了《关于实施“提升城乡品质，建设美丽宁波”行动计划的指导意见》，做精中心城区，做强县城功能，建设美丽乡村，努力把宁波打造成“山清水秀、天蓝地净、城美人和”的品质之城和宜居、宜业、宜商、宜游的现代化国际港口城市。在通往幸福的道路上，宁波深深感觉到：民生幸福，发展为要。

二、创建幸福城市的行动

2015 年 10 月 31 日，以“小康社会、幸福中国”为主题的“中国最具幸福感城市调查推选活动”获奖城市揭晓，东海之滨的港城宁波第七次入选“中国最具幸福感城市”。这项殊荣是全体宁波人民一直以来对幸福家园的认同和建设，这一荣誉属于生活和创业在宁波的每一位市民，是全体宁波人共同创造了宁波的美丽和幸福。

中心城区城中村改造、轨道交通快速发展、特色旅游蓬勃兴起，近年来，宁波以宜居、宜业、宜游等优势吸引着全国乃至全球人士的眼球，每个人都怀揣着对它未来发展的无限憧憬。

习近平总书记曾说，人民对美好生活的向往，就是我们的奋斗目标。经济社会的发展，就是要让每一个市民享有更加美好、更有品质、更有尊严的生活。作为长江三角洲南翼经济中心，宁波近年来按照“公平正义、共建共享”的理念和“保基本、抓重点、促均衡、提质量”的思路，推进经济转型升级，同步推动社会发展，不断提升公共服务水平，改革发展成果更加公平地惠及全体市民。

（一）历史名城，幸福源泉

宁波取自“海定则波宁”之意，简称“甬”，位于东海之滨，依山面海，地理条件优越，是长江三角洲南翼经济中心。宁波是一座美丽之城，兼具江南水乡和滨海城市特色，风光秀丽，景色宜人，名胜古迹众多。蒋氏故里溪口雪窦山是国家5A级风景名胜区，有千丈岩幽谷飞瀑，壁立千仞；东钱湖具有“西子风韵，太湖气魄”；古代水利建筑它山堰肇建于唐，阻咸蓄淡；松兰山一湾金沙，海天一碧；天明山南溪温泉，气候宜人；海防口岸招宝山，雄伟壮观；越窑遗址青瓷文明，熠熠生辉；天童寺列为天下禅寺五刹之一；阿育王寺藏有释迦牟尼真身舍利；保国寺大殿为现存江南最古老木结构建筑。

宁波又是一座文化名城，素有“文献名邦”的美誉。早在7000年前的新石器时代，就创造了河姆渡文化。宁波是浙东学术文化的发源地，历史上曾出过2400多位进士，当代更有100多位宁波籍两院院士活跃在学界、科技界，数量位居全国城市前列，2015年获得诺贝尔奖的屠呦呦就是宁波人。

宁波人文荟萃，儒商鼎盛。国内现存最古老的天一阁藏书楼，始建时间为亚洲最早；王守仁开创的“阳明学派”闻名于世；黄宗羲“浙东史学”影响深远；抗清英雄张苍水浩气长存；京剧麒派祖师周信芳，著名作家殷夫、柔石，书法泰斗沙孟海，国画大师潘天寿名闻全国；商界巨子包玉刚、邵逸夫、王宽诚、应昌期等享誉海内外。太空中有6颗以宁波籍人士命名的小行星在运行。

宁波还是一座著名的港城，历来是中外闻名的港埠。早在唐朝时就是中国与日本、朝鲜及东南亚国家通商的主要港口。近代以来，宁波为“五口通商”口岸之一。新中国成立特别是改革开放后，宁波港再次崛起，1984年成为中国首批进一步对外开放的沿海港口城市。

今天，历史文化名城宁波焕发新时期的勃勃生机，于2005年提炼出新时期“诚信、务实、开放、创新”的宁波精神，2009年提出“书藏古今，港通天下”的城市形象主题口号，并沿着这一精神和口号，带领宁波人民交出了一份“两高”的特殊答卷——2014年地区生产总值增速7.6%，全市居民人均可支配收入增速9.9%。其中城镇居民人均可支配收入增速9.2%；农村居民人均可支配收入增速11.0%。也就是说，城乡居民收入实际增速高于GDP增速，农村居民收入增速高于城镇居民收入增速。在经济增长放缓的2015年，宁波的“两个高于”是宁波转型发展、经济增长、质量和效益不断提高的一种信号，也是宁波促进民生发展、人民幸福的政策效应显现。

（二）民生福祉，保障幸福

城市发展无止境，幸福追求无极限。在通往幸福的道路上，宁波深深感觉到：民生幸福，发展为要。2014年实现人均地区生产总值1.6万美元，城镇居民人均可支配收入达44 155元，农村居民人均可支配收入达24 283元，连续多年居全国大城市前列；城乡居民收入更趋均衡，城乡居民收入之比缩小至1.82:1，远低于全国平均水平，差距之小在全国大城市中位居前列。2014 年，宁波港域货物吞吐量完成 2.97 亿吨，增长 7.6%，位居中国大陆港口第三位、世界港口第四位。集装箱吞吐量为1 870万标准箱，增长 11.5%，位居中国大陆港口第三位、世界港口第五位。

民生幸福，社保为本。宁波大力促进市民就业，近年来城镇登记失业率、高校毕业生就业率稳定在 1.9% 和 98% 左右；大力推进城乡居民养老保险、医疗保险和失业保险等各项制度的统筹并轨，实现城乡居民和外来务工人员社会保障同城同待遇。16 周岁以上应参保户籍人口参保率达到 91.5%，社保待遇持续提高。养老服务体系不断完善，残疾人共享小康政策全面覆盖。此外，宁波加强公共文化服务体系建设，构建形成了群众“15 分钟文化活动圈”，全市 11 个县（市）区均为浙江省文化先进县。

民生幸福，教育为先。据教育部有关研究报告，2014 年宁波教育公平指数在全国 15 个副省级城市中位居第一，教育现代化水平位居第四，11 个县（市）区全部通过全国义务教育发展基本均衡评估认定，26.43 万外来务工人员随迁子女中的 81.31% 在公办学校就读。

民生幸福，平安为基。宁波将社会安全稳定和谐视为民生幸福的根基，大力推进习总书记在浙江时倡导的“平安浙江”建设，连续 9 年获评浙江省“平安市”，人民群众的安全感稳步提升。

（三）开放包容，幸福基石

开放是海洋文明的鲜明特征，也构成了宁波这座城市的历史品格。宁波“向东是大海”，宁波帮素具“走天下”的不懈追求。宁波民谣唱道：“大海洋洋，忘掉爹娘。”“潮涌三江，送风远方。”“青春停泊遥远的他乡。”近海环境造就了历代宁波人开阔的视野和不断进取的精神，不少人不愿固守本乡，勇于闯荡天下，敢当“弄潮儿”，“足迹儿遍于国中”。孙中山先生曾称赞“宁波风气之开，在各省之先”。种子要在合适的土壤、阳光下才能发芽，改革开放让宁波人的开放品格、经济才干得到充分展现，宁波成为我国最为开放的城市之一，现在已拥有进口矿石中转、大型液体化工产品储存中转、国际集装箱远洋中转、大型煤炭储存中转，以及大型原油成品油储存中转“五大基地”，未来将进一步打造成为国际贸易物流港、东北亚航运中心深水枢纽港。

如今，在世界海图上，宁波已成为国际化知名大港。宁波从跻身沿海开放城市行列起步，一路走来，经济腾飞，港口跨越，地铁开通，长三角南翼交通枢纽与国际空港建成，世界名校引进，人民生活水平大幅提高。从海边渔村到东方大港再到世界强港，从浙东小城到著名都市。正如党的十八届五中全会所指出的，“开放是国家繁荣发展的必由之路”，宁波的小康巨变正是得益于改革开放的明证。

“港泊千国船，外贸达五洲。”开放，既是宁波港城的必备要素，更是宁波人通向幸福、走向世界的精神动力。宁波将进一步加快经济转型发展，充分发挥宁波世界级大港、国际贸易城市、享誉海内外的“宁波帮”、特色鲜明的现代产业、潜力巨大的海洋经济、充满活力的民营经济等优势，积极融入和服务国家“一带一路”、长江经济带、海洋经济战略，顺应“互联网+”趋势，大力推进“港口经济圈”与中国制造 2025、创业创新战略的深度融合，不断增强城市的综合实力和核心竞争力。

宁波人深知，要想实现宁波大建设、大发展，就要让“开放包容”化为自己的自觉行动，在经济、文化诸方面，特别是在地域认同上、在公共服务上、在对待外来人员上，树立一种更加开放的心态，确立博纳兼容、海纳百川的精神和气度，体现洋洋东方大港的胸襟，让更多来自世界各地的“帮宁波”人士，投身到宁波的又一轮大建设、大发展中来，最终实现全民幸福。

（四）便捷交通，品质提升

都说宁波是最具幸福感的城市，的确，这个海港之城的温润和轻缓，让很多人从心底里爱上她。如果要把这些幸福感具象化，便捷的交通，快捷的生活方式，应该是其中很重要的组成部分。2015 年 6 条地铁、4 条城际轻轨、10 条市区高架快速路、地下快速路和过江隧道获批建设或开工，形成了以民用航空、高速铁路、城市轨道交通、高速公路为骨架的综合交通体系，这无疑大大提升了宁波这座城市的生活品质。

2015 年 12 月底，铁路宁波枢纽货运北环线全线开通；2015 年 9 月，铁路宁波站枢纽全面启用；2012 年，杭甬客专建成并通车。过去 5 年，宁波铁路建设发生了前所未有的变化，宁波全面融入全国高铁网，形成了“南客北货”的格局。

“南客”即以铁路宁波站为枢纽的客运网络体系，该枢纽也是铁路总公司重点关注的全国 50 个铁路枢纽之一。在这个铁路网中，宁波通过甬台温铁路连接南线，结束了铁路末梢的历史，向北通过杭甬客专由杭州、上海接入全国高铁网。铁路客运量不断增加，客运到发量从“十一五”末期（2010 年）的 2 006 万人次增加到 2014 年的3 556.4万人次，增长 77.29%；2014 年日均发送旅客超 4 万人次，国庆、春节等高峰时段日均发送旅客 8 万人次，2015 年前 10 个月已完成铁路客运3 341.1万人次，预计全年可达到4 000万人次。

宁波铁路“南客北货、客货分流”的环形枢纽形成，机场三期工程也加快推进，完成投资 21.4 亿元。2015 年新辟公交线路 20 条，优化调整 48 条；年末有公交运营车辆7 445.8标台，运营线路 698 条，新增公交专用道 41.7 公里，全年共完成公交客运总量 6.9 亿人次，增长 7.5%。轨道交通 1 号线一期工程开通试运营，日均开行 243 列次，全线进站客流量1 387.51万人次，平均64 237人次/天，列车兑现率 100%、正点率 99.94%；2 号线一期工程全线基本实现“轨通”，1 号线二期工程年底车站主体结构全部完成，3 号线一期工程开工建设。新增公共自行车网点 200 个，新投放公共自行车 6 000 辆，全市共建成公共自行车网点 992 个，投放公共自行车21 035辆，办理租赁 IC 卡 32 万余张，累计租车量2 899.7万辆次。

（五）文化引擎，助推转型

文化赋予一座城市意义和光彩，提升一座城市的品质和内涵，更能为城市发展注入“强劲”的动力，成为一个城市发展内生力量的强劲“引擎”。作为历史文化名城的宁波，文化是宁波的精气神。深厚的文化内涵为宁波插上经济腾飞的翅膀，成为宁波转型升级的助推器。

2015年5月，宁波发布《宁波市文化产业发展三年行动计划（2015-2017）》：三年内，力争实现总投资超过1 000亿元，建成重点项目50个，培育形成20家以上实力雄厚、竞争力强的大型骨干企业集团，推动100家以上中小文化企业做大做强，文化产业上市公司力争达到8家，文化产业迎来井喷式发展。《关于推进文化产业加快发展的若干意见》同天出台，进一步明确宁波市文化产业转型提升发展的方向和重点。

按照三年行动计划，宁波将重点发展高端文化用品制造业、文化创意与设计服务业、文化演艺与影视制作业、文化休闲旅游业、现代工艺美术业、现代传媒、文化信息传输服务业、文化会展业等八大文化产业。重点打造宁波日报报业集团和宁波广播电视集团两大现代主流媒体集团。

为推动宁波市文化产业茁壮成长，三年内，宁波市除了大手笔投资兴建重点项目50项，还将新开工建设项目23项，推动建成宁波华强·中华复兴文化园等一批航母级文化产业项目。探索组建市文化投资控股有限公司、宁波文化产业投资基金，设立文化中小微企业信贷风险资金池，构建文化金融机构服务集群。

在文化产业园区建设上，宁波将着力打造国家级品牌园区、培育新增省级产业园区、改造新建特色专业园区。三年内，宁波市争取新增国家、省级文化产业园区2~3家，推动各县（市）区整合或新建市级重点文化产业园区1~2家，实现全覆盖。

“文化+”将在推动宁波市传统制造业转型升级中大放异彩。按照三年行动计划，宁波市将大力推动“文化+制造业”“文化+旅游”“文化+科技”“文化+金融”等融合发展，力争到2017年，新成功申报国家、省级工业设计中心22个，培育文化与科技融合示范企业、实施文化科技融合示范项目各50个。

宁波还将搭建文化“走出去”、文化招商、文化产业综合服务三大平台，同时拓展文化消费市场，谋划建设文化产业研究“智库”等人才支撑工程。

（六）公共服务，宜居宜业

在城市的高速发展过程中，优质的城市公共服务已成为决定城市发展、吸引优秀人才、人民生活满足的重要指标。近年来，宁波大力实施“提升城乡品质、建设美丽宁波”行动计划，并出台了《关于实施“提升城乡品质、建设美丽宁波”行动计划的指导意见》，做精中心城区、做强县城功能、建设美丽乡村，努力把宁波打造成“山清水秀、天蓝地净、城美人和”的品质之城和宜居、宜业、宜商、宜游的现代化国际港口城市。

“提升城乡品质，建设美丽宁波”被宁波人理解为“1+3”工程，即一个“山清水秀、天蓝地净、城美人和”品质之城的主要目标，中心城区品质提升、美丽县城（中心镇）品质提升、农村品质提升的三大工程。

中心城区品质提升以建设“人本之城、幸福之城”为目标，以一流的城市景观环境为发展依托，以一流的民生保障设施为基础支撑，以一流的城市功能品质为主攻方向。围绕“滨水、历史、文化”特色资源要素，宁波集中实施了核心景观、形象品质、文化特色、基础设施、民生服务、生态环境六大提升行动，并具化为384个项目，计划总投资1 849亿元，到2017年，把中心城区建设成为宜居、宜商、宜业、宜游的“四宜城市”，到2020年，把中心城区建设成为生态优良、环境优质、形象优秀、品质优越的“四优城市”。

美丽县城（中心镇）品质提升坚持“绿水青山就是金山银山”和尊重自然、保护自然、顺应自然的理念。815个项目将保证8个县（市）区到2017年实现核心城区空间优化美化提质，并在县城与重点新区及卫星城、中心镇之间实现美丽连线。基础设施品质提升与交通畅行、地域特色文化传承与合理开发、公共服务保障与活力城市提升也将同步实现，构建出集约高效的生产空间、宜居适度的生活空间、山清水秀的生态空间，建设现代化美丽县城。

农村品质提升目标以改善农村人居环境、提升农民群众生活质量为出发点和落脚点，提出了“洁化、序化、美化、长效化”要求。为此，宁波开展了农村环境卫生整治行动、农村生态环境建设行动、农村安居宜居美居行动、美丽乡村示范创建行动。两年后，宁波将建成100个试点村、30条美丽乡村风景线、30个美丽乡村示范镇乡（街道）、30个美丽乡村精品村。

进一步深化文明城市创建，大力弘扬“爱心宁波，尚德甬城”良好风尚，使尊道德、讲文明、重礼仪、守秩序成为人们的基本追求，让有爱心、讲奉献、乐助人、相友善成为宁波最美风景，真正把宁波建成全域化高水平文明之城。宁波市委市政府相信，只要一如既往地顺民意，解民忧，纾民困，促民生，就会让宁波人民生活得更加幸福，更有尊严。

（撰稿：蒋委根，宁波市文明办综合处处长；燕文慧，中国最具幸福感城市调查活动组委会副秘书长）

附录篇

附录 1

2015 年中国城市发展大事记

2015 年 1 月 1 日 全国首个省（自治区、直辖市）级单位统一编制实施的空间规划《宁夏回族自治区空间发展战略规划条例》开始施行。

2015 年 1 月 6 日 住房城乡建设部印发了《关于加快培育和发展住房租赁市场的指导意见》（建房〔2015〕4 号，以下简称《意见》）。《意见》明确提出，用 3 年时间，基本形成渠道多元、总量平衡、结构合理、服务规范、制度健全的住房租赁市场。

2015 年 1 月 9 日 四川省住房城乡建设厅发布《城市开发边界划定导则（试行）》，为四川省城市开发边界划定提供统一的原则和方法。

2015 年 1 月 10 日 国家旅游局印发《关于促进智慧旅游发展的指导意见》。

2015 年 1 月 15 日 全国国土资源工作会议在京召开。会议分析经济发展新常态下国土资源工作面临的形势任务，总结 2014 年工作情况，部署 2015 年重点工作。国土资源部部长姜大明指出，要找准稳增长与调结构的平衡点，坚持优化结构、有保有压。新常态下国土资源工作要五个“更加注重”：更加注重资源环境保护，更加注重提高耕地质量，更加注重资源节约集约，更加注重创新驱动，更加注重维护群众权益。

2015 年 1 月 19 日 财政部、住房城乡建设部、水利部下发通知，决定开展中央财政支持海绵城市建设试点工作。

2015 年 1 月 20 日 全国棚户区改造经验交流会在内蒙古自治区包头市召开。住房城乡建设部部长陈政高指出，棚改是重大民生问题、发展问题，把这项工作放到经济发展新常态中来审视，具有更为深远的重要意义。

2015 年 1 月 22 日 国务院办公厅发布关于引导农村产权流转交易市场健康发展的意见。

2015 年 1 月 26 日 世界银行发布报告称，中国珠江三角洲地区在 2010 年就已超过日本东京地区，成为全球最大城市片区。世界银行的报告借助卫星和地理空间信息分析等技术，评估了包括东北亚和东南亚在内的亚洲东部地区城市化进展。

2015 年 1 月 27 日 海绵城市建设国际研讨会暨中国海绵城市建设技术创新联盟成立大会在陕西西咸新区召开。海绵城市建设技术创新联盟是我国首个推进海绵城市建设的技术联盟，将以创新城市发展方式为主题，统筹协调相关资源，推动海绵城市建设理论和实践技术交流，研究推广新材料、新技术的应用，着力提升“海绵”型城市建设的相关技术及标准。

2015 年 1 月 30 日 住房城乡建设部在京组织召开《内蒙古自治区城镇体系规划》成果专家技术审查会,《内蒙古自治区城镇体系规划》原则上通过审查。

2015 年 2 月 1 日 中共中央、国务院发布了《关于加大改革创新力度加快农业现代化建设的若干意见》(以下简称《意见》)。《意见》指出,要稳步推进农村土地制度改革试点。

2015 年 2 月 3 日 由住房城乡建设部、科学技术部联合开展,委托中国城市科学研究会数字城市工程研究中心组织的智慧城市 2014 年度专项试点综合评审会、智慧城市 2014 年度试点现场答辩会在京召开。

2015 年 2 月 4 日 国家发展和改革委员会发布《国家新型城镇化综合试点总体实施方案》,确定在江苏、安徽两省和宁波等 62 个城市(镇)开展试点。此次试点的主要任务是:建立农业转移人口市民化成本分担机制;建立多元化可持续的城镇化投融资机制;改革完善农村宅基地制度;探索建立行政管理创新和行政成本降低的新型管理模式;综合推进体制机制改革创新。

2015 年 2 月 10 日 习近平总书记主持召开中央财经领导小组第九次会议,听取中央财经领导小组确定的新型城镇化规划等重大事项贯彻落实情况的汇报,审议研究京津冀协同发展规划纲要。习近平指出,疏解北京非首都功能、推进京津冀协同发展,是一个巨大的系统工程。目标要明确,通过疏解北京非首都功能,调整经济结构和空间结构,走出一条内涵集约发展的新路子,探索出一种人口经济密集地区优化开发的模式,促进区域协调发展,形成新增长极。

2015 年 2 月 13 日 住房城乡建设部公布了首批小城镇宜居小区示范名单。

2015 年 2 月 26 日 四川省委召开常委会议,审议通过《四川省新型城镇化规划(2014-2020 年)》。

2015 年 2 月 27 日 在中国社会科学院经济学部 2015 年经济形势座谈会上,发布了 2014 年以来关于新常态的三项重要研究成果:《论新常态》《引领新常态:若干重点领域改革探索》和《解读中国经济新常态——速度、结构与动力》,其中后两项成果为智库报告。

2015 年 2 月 27 日 交通运输部召开“2015 年完成民生 10 件实事”新闻发布会。包括完成高速公路电子不停车收费系统全国联网、在 20 个城市实现公交一卡通互联互通、国家高速公路断头路工程全部开工、建设 100 对高速公路示范服务区等。

2015 年 3 月 1 日 《不动产登记暂行条例》施行。不动产统一登记是转变政府职能、建立现代国家治理体系的一项基础性制度。

2015 年 3 月 1 日 《陕西省群众保护文物奖励办法》实施,依法对群众保护文物给予适当的精神鼓励和物质奖励。

2015 年 3 月 1 日 中国藏区首项生态建设立法——《青海省生态文明建设促进条例》(以下简称《条例》)开始施行。《条例》首次对青海省生态文明建设的责任主体、规划与建设、保护与治理、保障机制、监督检查、法律责任等内容做出明确规定。

2015 年 3 月 2 日 《中国省域竞争力蓝皮书》向社会公布。蓝皮书对 2012-2013 年中国内地31个省级行政区的经济综合竞争力进行综合排名。结果显示，2013年，江苏、广东、北京三省市继续蝉联全国31个省级行政区经济综合竞争力前三名。

2015年3月2日　北京市统计局、国家统计局北京调查总队发布2014年度人口抽样调查结果。2014年年末北京市常住人口为2151.6万人，比2014年增长1.7%，北京市人口发展呈现常住人口增量、增速保持“双下降”，常住外来人口“流动少”，出生人口逐年增加等特点。

2015年3月2日　国家发展和改革委员会发布《左右江革命老区振兴规划》，明确了未来10年左右江革命老区振兴的战略定位和发展目标，在基础设施建设、特色优势产业、城乡协调发展、生态文明建设等方面做出发展规划。

2015年3月2日　住房城乡建设部办公厅印发抗震防灾2015年工作要点。2015年，住房城乡建设部将继续以法规和标准体系建设为核心，以新建工程抗震设防为重点，推进农村危房改造和城市抗震防灾规划编制，推动城市抗震危房加固改造，强化震后应急制度建设，进一步提高工程抗震能力、城市抗震防灾能力和地震应急处置能力。

2015年3月2日　国家发展和改革委员会对住渝全国政协委员在2014年全国政协十二届二次会议上提交的《关于将渝东北生态涵养发展区和渝东南生态保护发展区纳入首批国家生态文明先行示范区的建议》的集体提案作出答复：已确定将包括重庆市渝东南武陵山区和渝东北三峡库区在内的57个地区，作为我国第一批开展生态文明建设先行示范区。这意味着，渝东北、渝东南区域生态建设已上升为国家战略。

2015年3月5日　国务院总理李克强作《2015年国务院政府工作报告》。

2015年3月5日　财政部、住房城乡建设部两部门联合下发通知，决定在城市供水、污水处理、垃圾处理、供热、供气、道路桥梁、公共交通基础设施、公共停车场、地下综合管廊等市政公用领域开展政府和社会资本合作（Public-Private Partnership）项目推介工作。

2015年3月5日　国家海洋局对外公布《2015年全国海洋生态环境保护工作要点》，明确在全国全面建立实施海洋生态红线制度，开展海洋资源环境承载能力监测预警试点，建立健全海洋生态损害赔偿制度和生态补偿制度，继续推进入海污染物总量控制制度试点。

2015年3月9日　习近平总书记在参加第十二届全国人民代表大会第三次会议吉林代表团审议时强调，东北老工业基地振兴发展，不能再唱工业“一柱擎天”、结构单一的“二人转”，要做好“加减乘除”。“加法多，其他少，亟待补课。”习近平总书记一针见血地指出了东北经济存在的问题。习近平强调，老工业基地要通过创新实现优化升级、脱胎换骨，进行深入改革创新，实现适应经济新常态的战略性调整。这一重要论述深入浅出、全面辩证地分析了东北老工业基地振兴发展的得与失，为新一轮东北振兴指明了前进方向。

2015年3月9日　上海智慧城市建设工作推进会召开。会议明确，2015年将围绕智慧城市建设新一轮三年行动计划明确的50个重点专项推进相关工作，加快以应用为核心的智慧城市建设。

2015年3月11日　住房城乡建设部、国家发展和改革委员会、财政部下发的《关于做好2015年农村危房改造工作的通知》提出，要逐步构建农民自筹为主、政府补助引导、银行信贷和社会捐助支持的多渠道农村危房改造资金投入机制。这是我国首次明确农民自筹为农村危房改造的主渠道。

2015年3月11日 全国绿化委员会办公室发布《2014年中国国土绿化状况公报》(以下简称《公报》)。《公报》显示,2014年我国城市人均公园绿地面积为12.64平方米,比2013年增加0.38平方米。

2015年3月15日 国务院总理李克强强调,在房地产调控过程中,要因地制宜、分城施策。李克强表示,中国城镇化进程在加快,中国房地产市场的需求是刚性的,中国政府鼓励居民自住性住房和改善性住房需求,保持房地产长期平稳健康发展。

2015年3月17日 博鳌亚洲论坛《亚洲竞争力2015年度报告》在京发布。报告显示,2014年,中国内地的综合竞争力在亚太地区37个经济体中排名较2013年度没有变化,排名第9位。排在前4位的依次是新加坡、中国香港、韩国和中国台湾。

2015年3月18日 国务院总理李克强主持召开国务院常务会议,明确《政府工作报告》的部门责任和分工,确保完成全年经济社会发展主要目标任务;部署推进农业可持续发展,加快农业现代化;确定改进口岸工作政策措施,促进扩大开放和外贸稳定发展。

2015年3月19日 住房城乡建设部公布新批准的国家城市湿地公园。包括山西省孝义市胜溪湖城市湿地公园、黑龙江省五大连池火山城市湿地公园、浙江省湖州市吴兴西山漾城市湿地公园、四川省阆中古城湿地公园。

2015年3月24日 中共中央政治局召开会议,审议通过《关于加快推进生态文明建设的意见》。审议通过广东、天津、福建自由贸易试验区总体方案、进一步深化上海自由贸易试验区改革开放方案。中共中央总书记习近平主持会议。

2015年3月25日 财政部公布2014年全国土地出让收支情况。2014年,我国经济发展进入新常态,固定资产投资增速放缓,土地市场呈现低迷状态,土地出让收支规模小幅增加。

2015年3月26日 国务院批复同意《长江中游城市群发展规划》。这是贯彻落实长江经济带重大国家战略的重要举措,也是《国家新型城镇化规划(2014-2020年)》出台后国家批复的第一个跨区域城市群规划,对于加快中部地区全面崛起、探索新型城镇化道路、促进区域一体化发展具有重大意义。

2015年3月27日 国家文物局在南京召开了海上丝绸之路保护和申遗工作会议。

2015年3月28日 博鳌亚洲论坛2015年年会在海南省博鳌开幕,国家主席习近平作主旨演讲。习近平称,中国经济发展进入新常态,正从高速增长转向中高速增长,从规模速度型粗放增长转向质量效率型集约增长,从要素投资驱动转向创新驱动。

2015年3月28日 经中国国务院授权,中国国家发展和改革委员会、外交部和商务部发布了《推动共建丝绸之路经济带和21世纪海上丝绸之路的愿景与行动》。

2015年3月30日 国土资源部办公厅、农业部办公厅联合下发《关于切实做好106个重点城市周边永久基本农田划定工作有关事项的通知》,在对106个重点城市周边未划为永久基本农田的现有耕地分布、面积、质量等别等进行分析评估的基础上,提出并下发了这些重点城市的永久基本农田划定初步任务，并细化、明确了推进划定工作的具体要求。

2015年3月30日　国家部委联合公布已取缔的高尔夫球场名单，包括北京、天津、河北、山西、内蒙古、辽宁、上海、江苏、浙江、安徽、福建、江西、山东、湖北、湖南、广东、广西、海南、四川、云南、贵州、陕西、宁夏23个省、自治区和直辖市的66座高尔夫球场。

2015年3月31日　广东省实施《珠三角规划纲要》领导小组召开会议，会议审议了《实施珠三角规划纲要2015年重点工作任务》和《2014年度省实施珠三角规划纲要考核方案》。

2015年4月1日　南通、淮安、盐城、泰州、宿迁的水生态文明城市建设试点实施方案已获得省政府批复。至此，江苏省9个国家级水生态文明城市建设方案全部获批，进入实施阶段。

2015年4月3日　住房城乡建设部和国家文物局公布第一批30个中国历史文化街区。

2015年4月7日　住房城乡建设部办公厅、科学技术部办公厅联合下发《关于公布国家智慧城市2014年度试点名单的通知》，确定北京市门头沟区等84个城市（区、县、镇）为国家智慧城市2014年度新增试点，河北省石家庄市正定县等13个城市（区、县）为扩大范围试点，航天恒星科技有限公司等单位承建的41个项目为国家智慧城市2014年度专项试点。通知同时就做好试点工作提出具体要求。

2015年4月8日　国务院批复同意设立湖南湘江新区。设立湖南湘江新区，是实施国家区域发展总体战略、贯彻落实《国务院关于依托黄金水道推动长江经济带发展的指导意见》（国发〔2014〕39号）的重要举措，有利于带动湖南省乃至长江中游地区经济社会发展，为促进中部地区崛起和长江经济带建设发挥更大作用。

2015年4月10日　财政部、住房城乡建设部、水利部公布2015年海绵城市建设试点城市名单。包括迁安、白城、镇江、嘉兴、池州、厦门、萍乡、济南、鹤壁、武汉、常德、南宁、重庆、遂宁、贵安新区和西咸新区16个城市。

2015年4月16日　国务院印发《水污染防治行动计划》，计划提出到2020年，全国水环境质量得到阶段性改善，污染严重水体较大幅度减少，饮用水安全保障水平持续提升，地下水超采得到严格控制，地下水污染加剧趋势得到初步遏制，近岸海域环境质量稳中趋好，京津冀、长三角、珠三角等区域水生态环境状况有所好转。

2015年4月16日　住房城乡建设部办公厅发布《关于加强风景名胜区安全管理工作的通知》，通知要求各风景名胜区管理机构全面排查安全隐患、合理限制游客容量、制定安全应急预案、落实安全工作责任制、做好信息上报工作。

2015年4月17日　国土资源部发布《国家土地督察公告》。国土资源部在核实土地违法违规问题，特别是乱占滥用耕地问题中，发现2 228件土地违法违规问题，涉及耕地12.24万亩。国土资源部已经向问题较为严重的陕西、甘肃、青海3个省政府发出整改意见书，促进依法依规审批土地。

2015年4月21日　国务院总理李克强主持召开国务院常务会议，通过《基础设施和公用事业特许经营管理办法》。

2015年4月22日 国土资源部公布《2014中国国土资源公报》(以下简称《公报》)。《公报》从土地资源、矿产资源、海洋资源、法治国土建设、国土资源领域改革、国土资源节约集约利用、地质调查、地质环境、科技与信息化、测绘地理信息服务10个方面，对2014年的国土资源工作进行了盘点。

2015年4月23日、25日 住房城乡建设部会同国家开发银行分别在长春、南宁召开全国棚改片区工作会。住房城乡建设部部长陈政高主持会议并提出总体要求：第一，各地要认清形势，统一思想，主动作为，不等不靠，千方百计完成今年棚改任务。第二，各地要加强与国家开发银行等相关金融机构做好项目对接，落实今年的棚改资金和新开工项目。第三，要探索多种融资渠道，拓展棚改资金来源。第四，要加大棚改货币化安置力度，提高货币化安置比例。第五，各地住房城乡建设部门要向当地党委政府主要负责人专题汇报棚改工作，争取更大的支持。

2015年4月23日 国家发展改革委员会、国土资源部、环境保护部、住房城乡建设部日前联合发布《关于促进国家级新区健康发展的指导意见》。

2015年4月24日 青海省启动可可西里申报世界自然遗产实地资源调查工作，将开展生物多样性、地理地质、水文气象、美学等方面的资源调查。

2015年4月25日 中共中央、国务院印发《关于加快推进生态文明建设的意见》。

2015年4月27-28日 住房城乡建设部、财政部、水利部在湖南省常德市组织召开全国海绵城市试点城市建设启动部署会。住房城乡建设部有关负责人强调，海绵城市建设的本质是通过转变城市规划建设理念修复城市自然生态本底，实现水环境改善、水资源承载能力提升、水安全保障能力加强等多重目标。

2015年4月29日 广东省住房和城乡建设厅在广州召开“三规合一”工作现场会，要求省、市、县各级政府和相关部门要明确责任、部门配合、上下联动，加快推进“三规合一”工作。

2015年4月30日 中共中央政治局召开会议，分析研究当前经济形势和经济工作，审议通过《京津冀协同发展规划纲要》等。

2015年4月30日 中共中央政治局就健全城乡发展一体化体制机制进行第二十二次集体学习。中共中央总书记习近平在主持学习时强调，加快推进城乡发展一体化，是党的十八大提出的战略任务，也是落实“四个全面”战略布局的必然要求。全面建成小康社会，最艰巨最繁重的任务在农村，特别是农村贫困地区。要继续推进新农村建设，使之与新型城镇化协调发展、互惠一体，形成双轮驱动。要坚持以改革为动力，不断破解城乡二元结构。要完善规划体制，通盘考虑城乡发展规划编制，一体设计，多规合一，切实解决规划上城乡脱节、重城市轻农村的问题。要完善农村基础设施建设机制，推进城乡基础设施互联互通、共建共享，创新农村基础设施和公共服务设施决策、投入、建设、运行管护机制，积极引导社会资本参与农村公益性基础设施建设。

2015年5月1日 《山东省南水北调条例》(以下简称《条例》)开始施行。该《条例》是中国首部南水北调地方法规，法规明确将水质保护列入县级以上人民政府考核内容。

2015年5月5日 国家发展改革委员会徐绍史主任主持召开全委“十三五”规划纲要编制工作领导小组和起草小组第一次全体会议，启动和部署“十三五”规划纲要编制工作，并作重要讲话。

2015年5月7日 国土资源部在国家发展改革委员会等部门联合举行的新闻发布会上透露，目前北京等14个城市开发边界划定试点工作已取得初步成效，相关原则、方法已基本确定。下一步，要在认真总结的基础上再扩大，争取划定全国600多个城市的开发边界并严格管理。划定城市开发边界有三重意义：一是促进城市转型发展，提高城镇化质量；二是有利于节约用地和保护耕地；三是通过划定城市开发边界，尽可能地把自然本底守住，把城市放在大自然当中，改善城市生态环境，推进生态文明建设。

2015年5月10日 国土资源部发布《关于取消国家地质公园规划审批等事项的公告》（以下简称《公告》）。《公告》明确，国土资源部将停止受理和审批国家地质公园规划。已审查通过的规划，修改完善后，按照相关程序发布实施。

2015年5月11日 历时3年编制的推荐性地方标准《城镇社区防灾减灾指南》日前在上海市“防灾减灾宣传周”活动启动仪式上首发，这是中国首个地方性防灾减灾建设标准，有望促进上海全市统筹协调区域防灾减灾能力建设，促进城乡社区防灾减灾标准化、规范化、专业化。

2015年5月13日 交通运输部公布《全国沿海邮轮港口布局规划方案》。

2015年5月14日 海南省人民政府与住房城乡建设部在海口共同举办《海南省总体规划》专家研讨会，住房城乡建设部部长陈政高、海南省省长刘赐贵出席会议并讲话。陈政高强调，要守住生态、风貌特色、城乡统筹发展三条底线，推动海南开启新的发展篇章。

2015年5月15日 上海市政府新闻办召开新闻发布会透露，《上海市城市更新实施办法》5月份正式实施。这标志着上海已经进入以存量开发为主的“内涵增长”时代。在目前上海建设规划用地规模“负增长”的前提要求下，“城市更新”将成为上海城市可持续发展的主要方式。

2015年5月16日 以“新常态，新应对”为主题的第四届“金经昌中国青年规划师创新论坛”在同济大学举办。此次论坛以“倡导规划实践的前沿探索、搭建规划创新的交流平台，彰显青年规划师的社会责任”。

2015年5月17日 国土资源部网站发布《关于下达〈2015年全国土地利用计划〉的通知》，要求各地区别对待、有保有压，合理安排建设用地计划指标，促进区域、城乡、产业协调发展。

2015年5月19日 中共中央政治局常委、国务院副总理张高丽出席在北京召开的京津冀及周边地区大气污染防治协作机制第四次会议并讲话。张高丽强调，要认真学习贯彻习近平总书记关于生态文明建设的重要讲话和指示精神，学习李克强总理重要指示要求，按照党中央、国务院决策部署，加强协作、联防联控，在推动京津冀协同发展中有效治理大气污染。

2015年5月20日 由上海市建筑学会与上海市创意产业协会共同主办的“上海市建筑艺术众创平台”正式启动，这意味着城市设计师进一步融入市场，上海首次出现了“互联网+”的城市设计运营模式。

2015年5月20日 住房城乡建设部召开全国住房城乡建设系统法治工作会议，旨在深入贯彻落实党的十八大和十八届三中、四中全会精神，全面推进住房城乡建设系统法治工作，加快法治政府建设步伐。

2015年5月21日 重庆市人民政府和四川省人民政府联合签署《关于加强两省市合作共筑成渝城市群工作备忘录》（以下简称《备忘录》），力争到2020年年底，将成渝经济区打造成为国家统筹城乡发展先行示范区，将成渝城市群建设成为国内领先、辐射带动西部地区经济发展的重要增长极。《备忘录》明确，重庆、成都两地未来将加强合作，推动交通、信息和市场一体化。

2015年5月21日 北京市统计局、国家统计局北京调查总队联合发布北京人口调查报告，首次披露了环线人口分布情况。数据显示，人口分布呈现由二、三环内向四环外聚集的特点，五环外常住人口达1097.9万人，占全市的51%。外来常住人口向外拓展聚集的特点更加突出，其中有65%的外来常住人口住在四环至六环间。此次人口抽样调查在北京市抽选3%的居民住户进行调查，涉及300个街道和乡镇、999个社区居（村）委会、1940个调查小区。

2015年5月22日 财政部、住房城乡建设部等6部门印发通知，鼓励地方运用PPP模式推进公共租赁住房投资建设和运营管理。

2015年5月25日 商务部等10部门联合印发《全国流通节点城市布局规划（2015-2020年)》，目的是加快构建全国骨干流通网络，努力提升流通节点城市功能，更好发挥流通产业的基础性和先导性作用，进一步释放消费潜力。

2015年5月26日 住房城乡建设部印发《城市地下综合管廊工程规划编制指引》的通知。以贯彻落实《国务院办公厅关于加强城市地下管线建设管理的指导意见》（国办发〔2014〕27号)，做好城市地下综合管廊工程规划建设工作。

2015年5月26日 住房城乡建设部公布2014年全国村庄规划、镇规划和县域乡村建设规划示范名单。

2015年5月27日 住房城乡建设部、国家发展改革委员会、财政部联合召开加强农村危房改造监管工作电视电话会议。会议强调，各地要进一步加大工作力度，建立起一个农民知晓政策、程序公开公正、资金直拨到户、档案信息完备、监督公开透明、处罚措施有力的运行和监管体系。

2015年5月28日 环境保护部在北京召开水污染防治工作座谈会，围绕贯彻党中央、国务院关于加强水污染防治工作的决策，部署、落实《水污染防治行动计划》，研究布置当前和今后一个时期的水环境治理工作。

2015年5月28日 北京将在雨洪利用、管网改造、节水器具推广、下凹式立交桥改造等方面全方位打造“海绵城市”，投入4亿元用于节水和水资源保护奖励补助，通过强化节水和扩大雨水、再生水利用，确保实现2015年全市总用水量控制目标。

2015年6月2日 四川省住房和城乡建设厅召开县域全域规划座谈会。会议明确，全省积极推进以县为单位的全域“多规合一”规划试点工作，都江堰市等8个县（市）已纳入第二批试点县名单，并将于2015年年底前完成规划编制工作。

2015年6月2日 国土资源部印发通知，正式启动“十三五”全国和省级土地整治规划编制工作。

2015年6月8日 住房城乡建设部向各地发出关于2015年美丽宜居小镇、美丽宜居村庄示范工作的通知。

2015年6月9日 国家发展改革委员会发布《推进关于建设长江经济带国家级转型升级示范开发区的实施意见》。

2015年6月15日 京津冀及周边地区大气污染联防联控国际研讨会在京召开。京津冀区域大气污染治理“路线图”，即《区域大气污染防治中长期规划》将于本月正式启动编制。该规划是我国首个“区域空气质量达标规划”。

2015年6月15日 《城市综合管廊投资估算指标》发布，由住房城乡建设部标准定额司、城市建设司组织部标准定额所、上海市政工程设计研究总院等单位联合编制完成。

2015年6月19日 住房城乡建设部、国土资源部和公安部发出通知，要求坚决制止异地迁建传统建筑，依法打击盗卖构件行为。

2015年6月23日 故宫博物院与中国建筑设计研究院建筑历史研究所合作编制的《故宫保护总体规划》发布。据故宫博物院院长单霁翔介绍，该规划是故宫博物院建院90周年来第一部以文化遗产价值整体保护为目标的专项保护管理规划，具有法律效力。

2015年6月24日 国务院总理李克强主持召开国务院常务会议，部署推进“互联网+”行动，促进形成经济发展新动能。会议通过《“互联网+”行动指导意见》。

2015年6月24日 为期两个月的2015年国家级风景名胜区执法检查启动，国家级风景名胜区执法检查将实现225处国家级风景名胜区全覆盖。

2015年6月25日 国务院发布《关于进一步做好城镇棚户区和城乡危房改造及配套基础设施建设有关工作的意见》。

2015年6月26日 住房城乡建设部研究印发《国家级风景名胜区总体规划大纲（暂行）》和《国家级风景名胜区总体规划编制要求（暂行）》。

2015年6月26日 我国已建立由国家发展改革委员会等25个部门组成的“促进智慧城市健康发展部际协调工作组”，依托该跨部门的智慧城市协调机制和监督考核机制，我国正在制订统一的智慧城市评价指标体系，以加强对智慧城市的指导和监督。

2015年6月26日 住房城乡建设部、中国气象局联合下发通知，明确提出，2015年汛期期间，北京、上海等城市将先行先试，率先建立信息共享、联合会商、联合发布的城市内涝联合预警工作机制和相关标准规范，为其他城市开展城市内涝风险预警工作提供示范。

2015年6月27日 国务院批复同意设立南京江北新区。

2015年6月28日 生态文明贵阳国际论坛2015年年会圆满闭幕，年会发布了《2015

贵阳共识》。

2015 年 6 月 30 日 国务院印发《关于进一步做好城镇棚户区和城乡危房改造及配套基础设施建设有关工作的意见》。

2015 年 6 月 30 日 住房城乡建设部成立全国老楼危楼安全排查整治工作领导小组。

2015 年 6 月 30 日 福建省选择漳州市、泉州市、莆田市、龙岩市等 12 个城市开展“多规合一”试点工作。

2015 年 7 月 1 日 全国首个地方性绿色建筑法规《江苏省绿色建筑发展条例》（以下简称《条例》）实施。该《条例》共七章 60 条。《条例》推行绿色建筑地方标准，并鼓励建设、购买、运营绿色建筑。

2015 年 7 月 3 日 2014 年城乡建设统计公报发布。

2015 年 7 月 3 日 上海社会科学院在沪发布《长三角城市环境绩效指数》，该报告“诊断”环境治理的薄弱环节，为长三角城市群未来的环境治理和合作指明方向。报告指出，5 年来长三角城市的资源环境效率不断提升，投入很大但成效不够显著，是我国建设生态文明亟须解决的难题之一。

2015 年 7 月 10－11 日 中共北京市委十一届七次全会召开。北京市委、市政府关于贯彻《京津冀协同发展规划纲要》的意见经市委全会审议通过。

2015 年 7 月 10 日 住房城乡建设部出台《海绵城市建设绩效评价与考核办法（试行)》，以科学、全面评价海绵城市建设成效。各地将依据试行办法中水生态、水环境、水资源等 6 个方面的指标，对海绵城市建设效果进行绩效评价与考核。

2015 年 7 月 12 日 天津市出台《天津市推进智慧城市建设行动计划（2015－2017 年)》提出，建设面向全市市民的智慧化服务平台，形成覆盖城乡的数字化社会服务体系。

2015 年 7 月 13 日 江苏省在全国率先出台指导意见推进海绵城市建设，明确总体思路及推进机制，并提出了具体要求。

2015 年 7 月 14 日 中共河北省第八届委员会第十一次全体（扩大）会议审议通过了《中共河北省委、河北省人民政府关于贯彻落实〈京津冀协同发展规划纲要〉的实施意见》。

2015 年 7 月 16 日 国务院批复同意设立云南勐腊（磨憨）重点开发开放试验区。

2015 年 7 月 21 日 住房城乡建设部、国家开发银行与吉林省人民政府在北京举行《全国城市综合管廊建设试点省合作框架协议》签字仪式。

2015 年 7 月 22 日 由中国城市科学研究会和广州市人民政府联合主办的“2015（第十届）城市发展与规划大会”在广州召开。本届大会的主题为“生态智慧·一带一路·绿色发展”。

2015 年 7 月 25 日 全国城市环卫保洁工作现场会在宁夏回族自治区中卫市召开。会上，住房城乡建设部部长陈政高要求，全国各个城市要行动起来，学习中卫市经验，清洁城市环境，创建美好家园。

2015 年 7 月 26 日 国务院办公厅发布《生态环境监测网络建设方案的通知》（以下简称《通知》)，《通知》指出，要加快推进生态环境监测网络建设，其中要求加强重要水体、水源地、源头区、水源涵养区等水质监测与预报预警。

2015 年 7 月 27 日　住房城乡建设部、国家旅游局公布了第三批全国特色景观旅游名镇名村示范名单。北京市门头沟区潭柘寺镇等 337 个镇上榜。

2015 年 7 月 27 日　四川省发展和改革委员会正式印发广安市、南部县、成都市温江区国家级中小城市综合改革试点实施方案。这是国家发展改革委批复全国中小城市综合改革试点以来，首批对外正式公布的实施方案。

2015 年 7 月 28 日　国务院总理李克强主持召开国务院常务会议，部署推进城市地下综合管廊建设，增加公共产品供给、提高新型城镇化质量等工作。

2015 年 7 月 29 日　国务院办公厅印发《关于同意在上海等 9 个城市开展国内贸易流通体制改革发展综合试点的复函》，同意在上海市、南京市、郑州市、广州市、成都市、厦门市、青岛市、黄石市和义乌市 9 个城市开展国内贸易流通体制改革发展综合试点。

2015 年 7 月 30 日　按照住房城乡建设部下发的《关于严格落实进一步治理违规私人会所实施方案的通知》要求，住房城乡建设部启动公园私人会所整治专项督察。

2015 年 7 月 31 日　《中国空气质量管理评估报告（2015）》（以下简称《报告》）发布。《报告》显示，过去一年各省（自治区、直辖市）PM2.5、PM10 等污染物年均浓度整体达标率仍较低。

2015 年 7 月　《江苏省城镇体系规划（2015－2030 年）》经国务院同意，获住房城乡建设部批复。规划到 2030 年，江苏省城镇化水平将达 80% 左右，城镇人口约 7200 万人，城乡建设用地总量得到有效控制。

2015 年 8 月 1 日　国务院印发《全国海洋主体功能区规划》。该规划是《全国主体功能区规划》的重要组成部分，是推进形成海洋主体功能区布局的基本依据，是海洋空间开发的基础性和约束性规划。

2015 年 8 月 3 日　国务院办公厅印发《关于推进城市地下综合管廊建设的指导意见》。

2015 年 8 月 3 日　国家发展改革委员会等七部委联合发布了《关于加强城市停车设施建设的指导意见》，旨在吸引社会资本、推进停车产业化、解决城市停车难等问题。

2015 年 8 月 10 日　住房城乡建设部、文化部、国家文物局、财政部、国土资源部、农业部、国家旅游局七部门联合发出通知，决定将北京市门头沟区大台街道千军台村等 491 个中国传统村落列入 2015 年中央财政支持范围。

2015 年 8 月 13 日　国务院下发《关于公布第二批国家级抗战纪念设施、遗址名录的通知》（以下简称《通知》），《通知》公布第二批 100 处国家级抗战纪念设施、遗址名录，并要求各地区、各有关部门要进一步加强抗战纪念设施、遗址的保护管理。

2015 年 8 月 18 日　中共中央总书记、国家主席、中央军委主席、中央全面深化改革领导小组组长习近平主持召开中央全面深化改革领导小组第十五次会议并发表重要讲话。习近平强调，2015 年以来，在 2014 年全面深化改革开局良好的基础上，各方面改革继续呈现蹄疾步稳、纵深推进的良好态势，在一些重要领域和关键环节取得新突破。各级党委和政府要增强改革定力、保持改革韧劲，加强思想引导，注重研究改革遇到的新情况新问题，锲而不舍、坚韧不拔，提高改革精确发力和精准落地能力，扎扎实实把改革举措落到实处。

2015 年 8 月 18 日 海南省住房城乡建设厅积极推进《海南省总体规划》编制工作，编制（修编）完成 157 个乡镇总体规划，基本实现村镇规划全覆盖。

2015 年 8 月 20 日 江苏省政府召开新闻发布会，宣布出台《江苏省人民政府关于落实国家“一带一路”战略部署建设沿东陇海线经济带的若干意见》。

2015 年 8 月 26 日 中国社科院发布的《中亚黄皮书：中亚国家发展报告（2015）》称，中亚国家将积极参加中国倡议的丝绸之路经济带建设。

2015 年 8 月 26 日 由中国科学院科技政策与管理科学研究所顾问牛文元主编、科学出版社出版的《2015 世界可持续发展年度报告》首发式在北京举行。该报告自 2012 年开始规划编纂，是中国第一份针对世界可持续发展科学与行动的专业研究报告。

2015 年 8 月 27 日 国内首个区域转型发展指数——“2014 年上海各区县转型发展指数”在沪发布。该指数由上海产业转型发展研究院历时一年编制完成。报告显示，浦东、静安、徐汇、虹口、黄浦排在综合指数前五位。

2015 年 8 月 31 日 国务院印发《促进大数据发展行动纲要》（以下简称《纲要》）。《纲要》指出，到 2018 年年底前建成国家政府数据统一开放平台，率先在信用、交通、医疗、卫生、就业、社保、地理、文化、教育、科技、资源、农业、环境、安监、金融、质量、统计、气象、海洋、企业登记监管等重要领域实现公共数据资源合理适度向社会开放。《纲要》部署了三方面主要任务：一要加快政府数据开放共享，推动资源整合，提升治理能力；二要推动产业创新发展，培育新兴业态，助力经济转型；三要强化安全保障，提高管理水平，促进健康发展。

2015 年 8 月 31 日 国家发展改革委员会就东北地区等老工业基地振兴工作举行发布会。截至 2015 年 7 月，根据国务院《关于近期支持东北振兴若干重大政策举措的意见》，由发展改革委员会牵头推进的 76 项重点任务中，有 15 项已进入常态化工作，20 项已经落实，30 项取得重大进展。139 个重大项目中，已经竣工在建 80 个，累计完成 5676 亿元。

2015 年 8 月 31 日 住房城乡建设部与广东省人民政府在广州举行部省共同推进城乡规划建设体制改革试点省建设领导小组第一次会议。会议通报了部省合作领导小组工作制度以及全省城乡规划大会战实施方案，审议落实部省《合作协议》行动计划，部署下阶段工作任务。

2015 年 8 月 31 日 国务院日前印发了《促进大数据发展行动纲要》（以下简称《纲要》）。《纲要》认为，坚持创新驱动发展，加快大数据部署，深化大数据应用，已成为稳增长、促改革、调结构、惠民生和推动政府治理能力现代化的内在需要和必然选择。

2015 年 9 月 1 日 住房城乡建设部印发《城市停车设施规划导则》，指导各地加快落实、规范推进城市停车设施规划编制工作，立足从规划源头上合理配置停车设施资源，有效引导交通需求，逐步缓解城市停车矛盾。另据了解，住房城乡建设部现已启动《城市停车设施建设指南》等文件制订工作。

2015 年 9 月 7 日 国务院批复同意设立云南滇中新区。

2015年9月8日 住房城乡建设部、工业和信息化部联合印发了《关于加强城市通信基础设施规划的通知》（建规〔2015〕132号），要求2016年年底前，所有大城市、特大城市应完成通信基础设施专项规划编制工作，其他城市应于2017年年底前完成专项规划编制工作。

2015年9月9日 国家发展改革委正式发布《国家级新区发展报告2015》（以下简称《报告》），系统总结梳理并向社会公开全国新区设立发展情况。《报告》总结了全国新区设立发展的历程、特点、成就和经验，梳理了2014年全国新区建设的主要进展，明确了2015年全国新区建设发展要切实把握发展环境、突出工作重点、创新体制机制、优化发展格局，着力建设成为引领经济发展新常态的新引擎、新时期深化改革创新的新载体、新形势下对外开放的新窗口、新格局下促进协调发展的新示范，在实现保持中高速增长和迈向中高端“双目标”上发挥重要引领作用。

2015年9月9日 国务院批复同意设立福州新区。

2015年9月10日 住房城乡建设部公布了第十四届全国优秀工程勘察设计奖获奖项目名单，包括侵华日军南京大屠杀遇难同胞纪念馆扩建工程在内的192个项目获奖，其中金质奖51项、银质奖141项。

2015年9月11日 由住房城乡建设部会同相关部门组织制订的《城市黑臭水体整治工作指南》正式公布。这是国家层面首次制定包括排查、识别、整治、效果评估与考核在内的城市黑臭水体整治长效机制。

2015年9月14日 住房城乡建设部发布《国家级风景名胜区规划编制审批办法》适用于国家级风景名胜区规划的编制和审批。办法自2015年12月1日起施行。

2015年9月14日 江苏省住房城乡建设厅发布《江苏省城市地下管线综合规划编制导则（试行）》，这是全国首部专门指导城市地下管线综合规划编制的地方性导则。加上之前出台的《江苏省城市地下管线探测技术规程》和《江苏省城市地下管线数据标准》，江苏省城市地下管线相关标准规范体系得到进一步完善。

2015年9月14日 河南省政府办公厅近日印发《河南省推进“三个一批人”城镇化实施方案》，切实推动一批具备条件、有意愿的农业转移人口及其他常住人口落户城镇，加快一批城中村和城镇棚户区改造，加快一批农村人口向城镇转移。

2015年9月15日 天津港爆炸事故周边区域规划初步方案公布，并对概念规划及周边环境配套设施建设计划征求意见。

2015年9月16日 铁道第三勘察设计集团有限公司发布《京津冀城际铁路网规划修编环境影响报告书》。京津冀三地未来将以城际铁路互联互通，城际铁路网以北京、天津、石家庄为核心形成“四纵四横一环线”，规划24条城际铁路线逐步建成，2050年全部建设完成。

2015年9月17日 在湖北省武汉市召开的湘鄂赣长江中游城市群住房城乡建设合作联席会上，湖北、湖南、江西三省共同签署《关于长江中游城市群住房城乡建设合作协议》，促进三省住房城乡建设领域深度合作。三省边界互临城市在编制城市总体规划中，将相互参加规划审查，进行实质性对接。协议执行期为2015年至2020年。

2015年9月19日 以“新常态：传承与变革”为主题的2015中国城市规划年会在贵阳开幕。

2015年9月21日 中共中央、国务院印发《生态文明体制改革总体方案》。该方案阐明了我国生态文明体制改革的指导思想、理念、原则、目标、实施保障等重要内容，提出要加快建立系统完整的生态文明制度体系，为我国生态文明领域改革做出了顶层设计。

2015年9月21日 第四届亚太地质公园网络研讨会在日本召开，经世界地质公园网络执行局审议和专家投票表决，中国甘肃敦煌和贵州织金洞被正式列入联合国教科文组织世界地质公园网络名录。

2015年9月22日 重庆市规划局举办“市民规划讲堂”活动，连续三天向市民重点介绍本市城乡总体规划深化成果和内容，听取市民的意见和建议，借以推动五大功能区域发展战略。

2015年9月24日 农业部公布中国最美休闲乡村名单，包括北京市密云县司马台村等120个村落。

2015年9月25日 由住房城乡建设部和湖北省人民政府共同主办的第十届中国（武汉）国际园林博览会在武汉开幕。

2015年9月27日 国务院批复同意《环渤海地区合作发展纲要》（以下简称《纲要》)。《纲要》提出，要把握实施“一带一路”、京津冀协同发展等国家重大战略的历史机遇，主动适应经济发展新常态，努力把环渤海地区建设成为我国经济增长和转型升级新引擎、区域协调发展体制创新和生态文明建设示范区、面向亚太地区的全方位开放合作门户。

2015年9月28日 《城市蓝皮书：中国城市发展报告No.8》(以下简称《报告》）在京发布。《报告》建议，明确城市规划的法律地位，在城市发展中坚持规划先行、依规建设，确保城市发展的长期性和稳定性。按照主体功能区划要求，推动城市发展由产城分离、职住失衡向产城融合、职住平衡转型，逐步改变目前城市发展中普遍出现的“圈地式”“摊大饼”“卧城”“鬼城”等现象。

2015年10月4日 国务院以国函〔2015〕160号文，对水利部《关于报请审批〈全国水土保持规划（2015-2030年)〉的请示》予以批复。

2015年10月9日 国务院办公厅印发《关于加快电动汽车充电基础设施建设的指导意见》，部署加快推进电动汽车充电基础设施建设工作。

2015年10月9日 住房城乡建设部副部长陆克华在国务院新闻办新闻发布厅举行的国务院政策例行吹风会上表示，中国计划3年内投资865亿元人民币，建设16个“海绵城市”试点，建设面积450多平方公里，在此基础上推出一批可复制、可推广的经验和模式。陆克华称，通过“海绵城市”建设，将70%的降雨就地消纳和利用，到2020年城市建成区20%以上的面积要达到目标要求，到2030年这一比例要提高到80%以上。针对资金来源，陆克华表示，将采取政府和社会资本合作（PPP）模式、政府购买服务、特许经营等方式，吸引社会资本参与“海绵城市”投资建设和经营管理。此外，还将支持符合条件的企业发行债券，用于“海绵城市”建设项目。

2015年10月10日　全国棚户区改造工作电视电话会议召开。李克强总理作重要批示：棚改寄托着千万住房困难家庭改善居住条件的希望，是推进以人为核心的新型城镇化的重要内容和抓手。各级政府要把棚改放在民生工作的突出位置，抓住“硬骨头”矢力攻坚，不断提升新型城镇化水平，为保障和改善民生、促进经济社会发展作出更大贡献。国务院副总理张高丽强调：统一思想，提高认识，加快推进棚户区改造工作。

2015年10月11日　国务院办公厅印发《国务院办公厅关于推进海绵城市建设的指导意见》，敲定推进海绵城市建设的“时间表”和“路线图”。

2015年10月11日　经海南省政府批准，海南省发展和改革委员会公布了海南省百个特色产业小镇名称及类型。《海南省百个特色产业小镇建设工作方案》强调，特色产业小镇建设重点在特色、关键是产业，形成一批带动力强、能助农增收的产业支撑，推动城乡一体化和就地城镇化，走出有海南特色的城镇化道路。

2015年10月12日　中共中央政治局召开会议，确定“十三五”期间将在原有四个区域板块基础上，增添“京津冀”“一带一路”“长江经济带”发展规划，打造“4+3”格局，连通四方城市群、城市带为主的区域发展线路图。

2015年10月12日　四川省委办公厅、省政府办公厅印发《四川省新村建设扶贫专项方案》，明确将以新村建设为综合载体，加快推进贫困户危房改造，同步提升扶贫新村公共服务和管理水平。到2020年，完成所有11 501个贫困村的新村建设。

2015年10月12日　河北省人民政府办公厅印发《河北省城镇棚户区改造货币化安置管理办法》，强调棚户区改造货币化安置要充分尊重棚户区改造居民的意愿，坚持以人为本，维护群众利益。

2015年10月13日　国务院批复同意《苏州工业园区开展开放创新综合试验总体方案》，并要求认真组织实施。

2015年10月14日　广东省住房城乡建设厅在广州召开省城乡规划建设遥感监测工作会议，贯彻落实省政府强化规划实施监管和执法监督的要求，部署规划建设遥感图斑核查处理工作。

2015年10月17日　国务院印发《关于全国水土保持规划（2015-2030年）的批复》，这是我国首部国家级水土保持规划。该规划明确治理目标：到2020年，基本建成水土流失综合防治体系，全国新增水土流失治理面积32万平方公里，年均减少土壤流失量8亿吨；到2030年，建成水土流失综合防治体系，全国新增水土流失治理面积94万平方公里，年均减少土壤流失量15亿吨。

2015年10月21日　国务院总理李克强主持召开国务院常务会议，通过《居住证暂行条例（草案）》，以法治助推新型城镇化。

2015年10月21日　山东省政府印发《加快推进城镇棚户区和城乡危房改造及配套基础设施建设的实施意见》，提出2015-2017年，全省改造城镇棚户区110万户以上，货币化安置比重达到50%以上，同步配套完善基础设施；改造农村危房20万户以上。

2015 年 10 月 23 日　住房城乡建设部海绵城市建设技术指导专家委员会成立大会在北京召开。包括城市给排水、城市规划、园林景观、环境工程、水文气象、道路建设以及投融资等产业发展领域的 37 名行业专家，接受了住房城乡建设部颁发的聘用证书，成为海绵城市建设技术指导专家委员会成员。

2015 年 10 月 26 日　海绵城市建设相关标准规范制订修订工作启动部署会召开，明确了综合标准《海绵城市建设工程技术规范》的编制工作进度以及《城市用地竖向规划规范》《城市排水工程规划规范》《建筑与小区雨水利用工程技术规范》等 11 项相关规范标准的修订工作。

2015 年 10 月 27 日　京津冀、珠三角、长三角三大地区战略环境评价项目启动，环境保护部环境影响评价专家咨询组同日宣布成立。

2015 年 10 月 27 日　陕西省政府在西咸新区召开全省城市地下综合管廊和海绵城市建设工作推进会。

2015 年 10 月 28 日　国土资源部印发《关于下达 2015 年城乡建设用地增减挂钩指标的通知》，明确 2015 年全国共安排城乡建设用地增减挂钩指标 90 万亩，要求各地落实好增减挂钩支持扶贫开发的政策措施。

2015 年 10 月 30 日　全国测绘地理信息应用成果和地图网上展览开通仪式在北京举行，标志着我国最新版（2015 版）基础地理信息数据库完成更新，并面向社会提供信息服务。

2015 年 10 月 30 日　山东省 11 部门出台意见，对城镇和国有工矿区 1995 年前建成的老旧住宅小区进行整治改造，五年内基本实现物业管理“全覆盖”。

2015 年 10 月 31 日　住房城乡建设部办公厅印发《关于切实加强住房城乡建设领域安全生产工作的紧急通知》，要求各地住房城乡建设主管部门及相关单位要严格落实安全生产责任制，加强建筑施工和房屋使用安全管理，确保城市运行安全。

2015 年 10 月 31 日　这天是第二届“世界城市日”。住房城乡建设部、上海市政府、联合国人居署在上海共同举办“2015 世界城市日论坛”。

2015 年 10 月 31 日　“2015 中国最具幸福感城市”系列榜单在京发布，“小康社会·幸福中国”成为今年新主题。经过活动组委会评审，成都、宁波、杭州、南京、西安、长春、长沙、苏州、上海、北京 10 座城市荣获“2015 中国最具幸福感城市”荣誉称号。

2015 年 11 月 1 日　江西出台《江西省改造约 270 万人居住的城镇棚户区和城中村实施方案》，江西省将从统筹编制改造规划、抓好房屋征收补偿等 6 个方面入手，充分利用财税、土地、融资等各类配套政策，确保完成 2013－2017 年 63.7 万户、2018－2020 年 18.6 万户的各类棚户区（危旧房）改造任务。

2015 年 11 月 2 日　中共中央办公厅、国务院办公厅印发《深化农村改革综合性实施方案》。方案指出农村改革是全面深化改革的重要内容，强调深化农村土地制度改革。

2015 年 11 月 3 日　《中共中央关于制定国民经济和社会发展第十三个五年规划的建议》（以下简称《建议》）发布。《建议》指出：“十二五”时期我国发展取得重大成就。我国经济总量稳居世界第二位，13 亿多人口的人均国内生产总值增至 7800 美元左右。第三产业增加值占国内生产总值比重超过第二产业，基础设施水平全面跃升，农业连续增产，常住人口城镇化率达到55%，一批重大科技成果达到世界先进水平。《建议》提出，“十三五”时期，各方面制度更加成熟更加定型。国家治理体系和治理能力现代化取得重大进展，各领域基础性制度体系基本形成。人民民主更加健全，法治政府基本建成，司法公信力明显提高。人权得到切实保障，产权得到有效保护。开放型经济新体制基本形成。

2015年11月3日　国家发展和改革委员会应对气候变化司副司长蒋兆理在武汉举行的C40可持续发展国际论坛上表示，我国在应对气候变化减少碳排放中，将对城市新建城区实施碳排放考核评估。城市“大拆大建”是不利于减少碳排放的重要因素。蒋兆理表示，我国将重点优化城镇体系和空间布局，对新建城区要进行碳排放考核评估。提高建筑质量，延长建筑使用寿命，加大现有建筑的节能低碳化改造力度，到2020年，绿色建筑要占新建建筑的50%以上。

2015年11月3日　住房城乡建设部、中央农村工作领导小组办公室、中央精神文明建设指导委员会办公室、国家发展改革委员会、财政部、环境保护部、农业部、商务部、全国爱国卫生运动委员会办公室、中华全国妇女联合会十部委联合出台《全面推进农村垃圾治理的指导意见》。该意见明确，以统筹城乡发展、造福农民群众为出发点，以实现农村垃圾的全面长效治理为目标，加大投入、健全机制、发动群众、科学施策，形成改善人居环境与提升乡风文明相互促进的良好局面，建设清洁卫生的宜居环境和农民群众安居乐业的美丽乡村。

2015年11月4日　上海市委、市政府举行撤销闸北区、静安区设立新的静安区工作大会。

2015年11月5日　第二次全国改善农村人居环境工作会议在广西壮族自治区桂林市召开，国务院副总理汪洋出席会议并讲话。

2015年11月6日　住房城乡建设部出台的《国家级风景名胜区管理评估和监督检查办法》规定，建立国家级风景名胜区黄牌警告和退出机制，实行濒危名单管理。

2015年11月9日　贵州省委、省政府印发了《生态文明体制改革实施方案》（以下简称《方案》）。《方案》要求，贵州省作为生态文明先行示范区，要根据中央的决策部署，努力在生态文明体制改革中走前列探新路，使贵州省经济社会发展建立在资源可支撑、环境能容纳、生态受保护的基础上，在加快经济社会发展的同时，守住良好生态环境，走出一条有别于东部、不同于西部其他省份的发展新路。

2015年11月11日　中共中央总书记、国家主席、中央军委主席、中央财经领导小组组长习近平主持召开中央财经领导小组第十一次会议，研究经济结构性改革和城市工作。习近平指出，做好城市工作，首先要认识、尊重、顺应城市发展规律，端正城市发展指导思想。要推进农民工市民化，加快提高户籍人口城镇化率；要增强城市宜居性，引导调控城市规模，优化城市空间布局，加强市政基础设施建设，保护历史文化遗产；要改革完善城市规划，改革规划管理体制；要改革城市管理体制，理顺各部门职责分工，提高城市管理水平，落实责任主体；要加强城市安全监管，建立专业化、职业化的救灾救援队伍。

2015 年 11 月 11 日 北京市园林绿化局、河北省林业厅组织召开了《2016 年京冀生态水源保护林合作项目实施方案》专家评审会并一致通过。

2015 年 11 月 11 日 国家发展改革委员会和住房城乡建设部联合发布通知，优化完善城市轨道交通建设规划审批程序。

2015 年 11 月 11 日 《地图管理条例》经国务院第 111 次常务会议通过，自 2016 年 1 月 1 日起施行。

2015 年 11 月 12 日 蜀道被联合国教科文组织世界遗产中心列入世界遗产预备名录，并被纳入申报世界自然与文化遗产提名地范围。

2015 年 11 月 16 日 环境保护部近日印发《关于加快推动生活方式绿色化的实施意见》。该意见明确，力争实现到 2020 年，生活方式绿色化的政策法规体系初步建立，公众绿色生活方式的习惯基本养成，最终全社会实现生活方式和消费模式向勤俭节约、绿色低碳、文明健康的方向转变。

2015 年 11 月 16 日 在贵州省黔东南苗族侗族自治州召开 2015 首届“中国传统村落·黔东南峰会”。

2015 年 11 月 17 日 《澳门特别行政区“五年发展规划”（2016－2020）基础方案》正式公布。这是澳门回归 16 年来首次公布中长期发展规划，该规划将与国家“十三五”规划同步落实并与之接轨。

2015 年 11 月 18 日 住房城乡建设部印发《城市轨道沿线地区规划设计导则》，进一步加强和改进城市轨道沿线地区规划设计工作，推进轨道交通与沿线地区地上与地下整体发展，促进轨道交通建设与城市发展相协调，提高轨道交通运营效益。

2015 年 11 月 18 日 住房城乡建设部公布了首批田园建筑优秀作品入选名单，河北省石家庄市平山县西柏坡乡霍家沟村华润希望小镇等 80 个乡村建筑入选。

2015 年 11 月 19 日 国土资源部部长、党组书记、国家土地总督察姜大明主持召开第 4 次部务会议，审议并原则通过《国家土地督察条例（草案送审稿)》。

2015 年 11 月 19 日 首份《大气污染防治行动计划（2013－2017）实施的投融资需求及影响》分析报告由中国清洁空气联盟秘书处发布。报告显示，我国大气污染防治行动计划实施的直接投资需求共计 1.84 万亿元，比之前预计的 1.7 万亿增加了 8%。

2015 年 11 月 19 日 河北省委、省政府日前出台的《关于加快推进生态文明建设的实施意见》提出，到 2020 年，资源节约型和环境友好型社会建设取得重大进展，京津冀生态环境支撑区初步建成，生态文明建设水平与全面建成小康社会目标基本适应。

2015 年 11 月 19 日 湖北省委办公厅、湖北省政府办公厅印发《关于深入推进农村社区建设试点工作的实施意见》，明确提出“十三五”期间，每年选择不低于总数 5% 的行政村开展农村社区建设试点。

2015 年 11 月 23 日 江西省推进新型城镇化领导小组办公室下发通知指出：为加大新型城镇化体制机制创新力度，探索具有江西特色的绿色城镇化发展的有效途径和模式，决定在全省开展新型城镇化综合试点工作。

2015年11月24日　住房城乡建设部印发《关于改革创新、全面有效推进乡村规划工作的指导意见》，从树立符合农村实际的乡村规划理念、着力推进县（市）域乡村建设规划编制、提高村庄规划的覆盖率和实用性、加强乡村规划管理工作、加强组织领导五个方面提出具体措施，改革创新，全面有效推进乡村规划工作，扭转上述不利局面，满足新农村建设需要。

2015年11月24日　《中国中小城市发展报告（2015）》（以下简称《报告》）绿皮书发布。《报告》显示，2015年我国广义中小城市经济总量达53.91万亿元，占全国经济总量的84.7%；中小城市科学发展指数为69.4，社会民生取得较大进步；中小城市“两型”指数为59.7，资源节约与生态环境水平提升明显。绿皮书同时发布2015年度中国中小城市综合实力百强县（区、镇）名单。

2015年11月24日　国家发展改革委员会、交通运输部联合印发《城镇化地区综合交通网规划》。该规划指出，中国城际交通结构不尽合理，城际铁路发展相对滞后，市域（郊）铁路规划建设基本空白，难以适应城镇化地区人口高度聚集、经济关联紧密、资源环境约束对交通的要求。该规划范围包括京津冀、长江三角洲、珠江三角洲、长江中游、成渝、海峡西岸、山东半岛、哈长、辽中南、中原、东陇海、关中—天水、北部湾、太原、滇中、黔中、呼包鄂榆、兰州—西宁、天山北坡、宁夏沿黄、藏中南，共计21个城镇化地区，涵盖215个城市。

2015年11月24日　江苏省印发《关于开展适宜养老住区建设试点示范工作的通知》，明确要围绕居住宜老，完善相关标准；围绕设施为老，加强配套建设；围绕活动便老，强化条件保障；围绕服务助老，鼓励各方参与；围绕和谐敬老，营造良好氛围。

2015年11月24日　北京市民政局、市规划委发布《北京市养老服务设施专项规划》。

2015年11月24日　住房城乡建设部印发《关于改革创新、全面有效推进乡村规划工作的指导意见》。该意见提出，应树立符合农村实际的乡村规划理念，应着力推进县（市）域乡村建设规划编制，应提高村庄规划的覆盖率和实用性，应加强乡村规划管理工作，应加强组织领导。

2015年11月24－25日　北京市委十一届八次全会召开，审议通过了《中共北京市委关于制定北京市国民经济和社会发展第十三个五年规划的建议（审议稿）》（以下简称《建议（审议稿）》）和《中国共产党北京市第十一届委员会第八次全体会议决议》。北京市市委书记郭金龙就《建议（审议稿）》中关于经济保持中高速增长、全国科技创新中心建设、全国文化中心建设、在通州建设市行政副中心、人口规模调控、缓解交通拥堵、加强水环境治理、推进服务业扩大开放综合试点、加快养老服务体系建设、全面做好2022年北京冬奥会筹备工作10个重点问题作说明。其中，在通州建设市行政副中心，基本出发点是疏解非首都功能。要按照2017年市属行政事业单位整体或部分迁入取得实质性进展的要求，科学规划，倒排工期，建设好增量，调整好存量，探索积累经验。

2015年11月25日　全国城市设计现场会暨全国城乡规划改革工作座谈会在深圳召开。住房城乡建设部副部长倪虹出席会议并讲话。会议认为，今后一个时期，我国城市发展将面临一次深刻的转型和变革。在这样的关键时期，城乡规划工作要坚持创新、协调、绿色、开放、共享“五大发展理念”，切实发挥好管长远、谋未来的作用，为推进城市转型发展、有效破解“城市病”和全面建成小康社会作出更大贡献。会议还专门研究了全力推进城市设计工作。

2015 年 11 月 26 日 长江经济带发展工作会议召开。国务院副总理张高丽在主持会议时强调，要强化规划引导，努力形成长江经济带发展规划纲要、专项规划、相关省市规划相互衔接、有机统一的规划体系，坚决防止重复建设和盲目开发。

2015 年 11 月 26 日 住房城乡建设部发布《世界自然遗产、自然与文化双遗产申报和保护管理办法（试行）》。该办法共 31 条内容，主要针对世界自然遗产申报、保护、规划、管理等方面的内容提出了明确要求。

2015 年 11 月 26 日 北京市政府办公厅发布《北京市城乡结合部建设三年行动计划(2015－2017 年)》。

2015 年 11 月 26 日 国家发展改革委员会、住房城乡建设部印发《关于城市地下综合管廊实行有偿使用制度的指导意见》，指导各地建立健全城市地下综合管廊有偿使用制度，形成合理收费机制，调动社会资本投入的积极性，促进城市地下综合管廊建设发展。

2015 年 11 月 28 日 贵州最大天然湖泊保护规划《贵州草海高原喀斯特湖泊生态保护与综合治理规划》获国家发展改革委员会批复同意。

2015 年 12 月 1 日 《黄山风景名胜区生态保护用水规划（2013－2025)》通过安徽省住房城乡建设厅审批，这是我国首个花岗岩山岳型景区生态保护用水规划。

2015 年 12 月 2 日 国务院常务会议决定，在 2020 年之前对燃煤电厂全面实施超低排放和节能改造，大幅降低发电煤耗和污染排放。

2015 年 12 月 3 日 中国社会科学院财经战略研究院发布《中国住房报告（2015－2016)》。报告指出，2015 年房地产市场的住房形势超出预期。一方面，投资增速呈俯冲式下降，对经济增长直接贡献几乎为零；另一方面，库存高企，去化压力增大，商品住房过剩，总库存高达 21 亿平方米，仅现房库存去化就需约 24 个月。

2015 年 12 月 6 日 国务院印发《关于加快实施自由贸易区战略的若干意见》。作为我国开启自贸区建设进程以来的首个战略性、综合性文件，该意见对我国自贸区建设做出了“顶层设计”，明确提出加快现有自由贸易区谈判进程，中长期形成全球自由贸易区网络。

2015 年 12 月 7 日 国务院副总理张高丽在京津冀协同发展工作推进会议上强调，要编制实施好京津冀“十三五”规划，通过科学合理总体布局，努力推动三地“一张图”规划、“一盘棋”建设、“一体化”发展。要抓紧出台控增量、疏存量政策，深入谋划和科学论证承接平台规划建设，有序疏解北京非首都功能。

2015 年 12 月 7 日 广西通过《关于制定国民经济和社会发展第十三个五年规划的建议》。提出未来 5 年，广西壮族自治区将积极稳妥推进新型城镇化，实施大县城战略，加快推进城乡基础设施建设，打造北部湾国家级沿海城市群。

2015 年 12 月 8 日 住房城乡建设部印发了《城市轨道沿线地区规划设计导则》。

2015年12月8日　国家发展改革委和交通运输部联合召开媒体通气会，发布《京津冀协同发展交通一体化规划》。该规划提出，扎实推进京津冀地区交通的网络化布局、智能化管理和一体化服务，到2020年基本形成多节点、网格状的区域交通网络。

2015年12月8日　国土资源部部长、党组书记、国家土地总督察姜大明主持召开第24次部长办公会，审议并原则通过《〈全国土地利用总体规划纲要（2006-2020年）〉调整方案》。

2015年12月10日　国土资源部、住房城乡建设部、国家旅游局联合发布《关于支持旅游业发展用地政策的意见》，从积极保障旅游业发展用地供应、明确旅游新业态政策、加强旅游用地服务监管三方面提出12条措施，全方位配合国家关于大力发展旅游业、促进旅游业改革发展的重大举措。

2015年12月10日　住房城乡建设部、国家开发银行下发通知，要求各地建立健全海绵城市建设项目储备制度，加大对海绵城市建设项目的信贷支持力度，建立高效顺畅的工作协调机制，推进开发性金融支持海绵城市建设。

2015年12月14日　中共中央政治局召开会议分析研究2016年经济工作，研究部署城市工作。会议强调，城镇化是现代化的必由之路，既是经济发展的结果，又是经济发展的动力。要坚持把“三农”工作作为全党工作重中之重，同时要更加重视做好城市工作。要认识、尊重、顺应城市发展规律，端正城市发展指导思想。要推进农民工市民化，加快提高户籍人口城镇化率。要增强城市宜居性，引导调控城市规模，优化城市空间布局，加强市政基础设施建设，保护历史文化遗产。要改革完善城市规划，准确把握城市规划定位，加强对规划实施情况的监督。要提高城市管理水平，落实城市管理主体责任，改革城市管理体制，理顺各部门职责分工，严格安全监管，健全城市应急体系。

2015年12月14日　工业和信息化部印发《工业和信息化部关于贯彻落实〈国务院关于积极推进“互联网+”行动的指导意见〉的行动计划（2015-2018年）》，提出到2018年，互联网与制造业融合进一步深化，制造业数字化、网络化、智能化水平显著提高，并推出旨在促进智能制造、下一代信息基础设施等产业发展的多个行动计划。

2015年12月16日　国务院以国函〔2015〕217号文，同意设立哈尔滨新区。要求把建设好哈尔滨新区作为推进“一带一路”建设、加快新一轮东北地区等老工业基地振兴的重要举措，积极扩大面向东北亚开放合作，探索老工业基地转型发展的新路径，为促进黑龙江经济发展和东北地区全面振兴发挥重要支撑作用。

2015年12月20日　《中华人民共和国澳门特别行政区行政区域图》开始施行。澳门特别行政区的行政区域界线包括陆地和海上两部分，海域面积明确为85平方公里。

2015年12月20-21日　中央城市工作会议在北京举行。习近平总书记在会上发表重要讲话，分析城市发展面临的形势，明确做好城市工作的指导思想、总体思路、重点任务。李克强总理在讲话中论述了当前城市工作的重点，提出了做好城市工作的具体部署，并作总结讲话。这是时隔37年后，“城市工作”再次上升到中央层面进行专门研究部署。会议决定实施六个主要任务：一是尊重城市发展规律。二是统筹空间、规模、产业三大结构，提高城市工作全局性。三是统筹规划、建设、管理三大环节，提高城市工作的系统性。四是统筹改革、科技、文化三大动力，提高城市发展持续性。五是统筹生产、生活、生态三大布局，提高城市发展的宜居性。六是统筹政府、社会、市民三大主体，提高各方推动城市发展的积极性。会议强调，做好城市工作，必须加强和改善党的领导。

2015 年 12 月 21 日 四川省政府办公厅下发严禁管廊外新建管线的实施意见，全面推进地下综合管廊建设。根据实施意见，各地将坚持“先规划、后建设”原则，组织相关部门和管廊使用单位编制地下综合管廊建设规划，严禁管廊外新建管线。

2015 年 12 月 22 日 住房城乡建设部与青海省人民政府在北京签署《共同推进青海省住房城乡建设事业健康发展合作协议》。

2015 年 12 月 23 日 李克强总理在国务院常务会议上表示，推进农村产业融合发展，不能再走过去“村村点火、户户冒烟”的老路，而要以新型城镇化和农业现代化协调并进作为重要载体。加快推进农业一、二、三产业融合发展，是从中国国情出发，加快发展现代农业、促进农业增效、农民增收和农村繁荣的重要举措。这一过程要与推进新型城镇化密切结合：农产品加工等产业要进入产业园区和城镇，推进“产城结合”的新型城镇化；反过来，大中城市的巨大市场，也能支撑农业现代化的健康发展。当前要抓住颁布居住证政策、深化户籍制度改革的契机，加快推动产城结合，促进新型城镇化与农业现代化协调发展，探索出一条农村产业融合发展的新路。

2015 年 12 月 24－25 日 中央农村工作会议在北京召开。会议全面贯彻落实党的十八大和十八届三中、四中、五中全会以及中央经济工作会议精神，总结“十二五”时期“三农”工作，分析当前农业农村形势，部署 2016 年和“十三五”时期农业农村工作。习近平强调，重农固本，是安民之基。“十二五”时期，我国农业农村发展成果丰硕，为我们赢得全局工作主动发挥了重要作用。同时，必须看到，我国农业农村发展面临的难题和挑战还有很多，任何时候都不能忽视和放松“三农”工作。“十三五”时期，必须坚持把解决好“三农”问题作为全党工作重中之重，牢固树立和切实贯彻创新、协调、绿色、开放、共享的发展理念，加大强农惠农富农力度，深入推进农村各项改革，破解“三农”难题、增强创新动力、厚植发展优势，积极推进农业现代化，扎实做好脱贫开发工作，提高社会主义新农村建设水平，让农业农村成为可以大有作为的广阔天地。

2015 年 12 月 26 日 上海交通大学城市科学研究院首次在沪发布的“2015 中国大都市发展指数报告”显示，中国大都市从总体发展上呈现为上扬态势，且在“经济新常态”的大背景下，中国大多数大都市已开始步入城市发展的稳定期。

2015 年 12 月 28 日 全国住房城乡建设工作会议在京召开。

2015 年 12 月 29 日 中国土地勘测规划院发布《全国城镇土地利用数据汇总成果分析报告》称，从 2009 年到 2014 年的 5 年间，中国城镇土地面积增加了 165 万公顷，增幅为 22.8%，年均增长 4.2%。

2015 年 12 月 30 日 中共中央政治局召开会议，审议通过《关于全面振兴东北地区等老工业基地的若干意见》。中共中央总书记习近平主持会议。

2015 年 12 月 30 日　《中共中央国务院关于深入推进城市执法体制改革改进城市管理工作的指导意见》印发，这是新中国成立以来中央层面首次对城市管理执法工作做出全面部署。

（作者：金晓春，中国城市规划设计研究院学术信息中心副主任）

附录 2

2015 年度中国城市规划相关政策法规索引

名　称	批号(文号)	发布机构	发布日期
国家发展改革委关于加强城市轨道交通规划建设管理的通知	发改基础〔2015〕49 号	发展改革委员会	2015-01-12
国务院办公厅关于推行环境污染第三方治理的意见	国办发〔2014〕69 号	国务院办公厅	2015-01-14
国务院办公厅关于印发《国务院关于促进旅游业改革发展的若干意见》任务分解表的通知	国办函〔2014〕121 号	国务院办公厅	2015-01-21
住房城乡建设部等部门关于加强村镇无障碍环境建设的指导意见	建标〔2015〕25 号	住房城乡建设部、民政部等	2015-02-04
国务院关于珠海市城市总体规划的批复	国函〔2015〕11 号	国务院	2015-02-06
住房城乡建设部关于公布第一批小城镇宜居小区示范名单的通知	建村〔2015〕29 号	住房城乡建设部	2015-02-13
国务院关于左右江革命老区振兴规划的批复	国函〔2015〕21 号	国务院	2015-02-16
住房城乡建设部 国家发展改革委 财政部关于做好 2015 年农村危房改造工作的通知	建村〔2015〕40 号	住房城乡建设部、发展改革委员会、财政部	2015-03-11
住房城乡建设部办公厅关于推荐城乡规划督察员候选人的通知	建办稽函〔2015〕171 号	住房城乡建设部	2015-03-13
国家发展改革委关于印发《东北城区老工业区搬迁改造专项实施办法》的通知	发改振兴〔2015〕493 号	发展改革委员会	2015-03-17
国土资源部办公厅关于实施《城镇土地分等定级规程》和《城镇土地估价规程》有关问题的通知	国土资厅发〔2015〕12 号	国土资源部办公厅	2015-03-18
住房城乡建设部关于公布国家城市湿地公园的通知	建城〔2015〕42 号	住房城乡建设部	2015-03-19
国务院关于宁波市城市总体规划的批复	国函〔2015〕50 号	国务院	2015-03-25
国土资源部 住房城乡建设部关于优化 2015 年住房及用地供应结构促进房地产市场平稳健康发展的通知	国土资发〔2015〕37 号	国土资源部、住房城乡建设部	2015-03-25
住房城乡建设部 国家文物局关于公布第一批中国历史文化街区的通知	建规〔2015〕51 号	住房城乡建设部、国家文物局	2015-04-03
国务院办公厅关于加强节能标准化工作的意见	国办发〔2015〕16 号	国务院办公厅	2015-04-04
国务院关于长江中游城市群发展规划的批复	国函〔2015〕62 号	国务院	2015-04-05
住房城乡建设部办公厅 科学技术部办公厅关于公布国家智慧城市 2014 年度试点名单的通知	建办科〔2015〕15 号	住房城乡建设部办公厅、科学技术部办公厅	2015-04-07

续表

名　称	批号(文号)	发布机构	发布日期
国家发展改革委关于印发《2015 年循环经济推进计划》的通知	发改环资〔2015〕769 号	发展改革委员会	2015-04-14
关于促进国家级新区健康发展的指导意见	发改地区〔2015〕778 号	国家发展改革委、国土资源部等	2015-04-15
国务院关于印发水污染防治行动计划的通知	国发〔2015〕17 号	国务院	2015-04-16
国务院关于印发中国(广东)自由贸易试验区总体方案的通知	国发〔2015〕18 号	国务院	2015-04-20
国务院关于印发进一步深化中国(上海)自由贸易试验区改革开放方案的通知	国发〔2015〕21 号	国务院	2015-04-20
国务院关于印发中国(福建)自由贸易试验区总体方案的通知	国发〔2015〕20 号	国务院	2015-04-20
关于印发生态保护与建设示范区名单的通知	发改农经〔2015〕822 号	发展改革委员会、科技部等	2015-04-23
国务院关于同意设立湖南湘江新区的批复	国函〔2015〕66 号	国务院	2015-04-25
国务院批转发展改革委关于 2015 年深化经济体制改革重点工作意见的通知	国发〔2015〕26 号	国务院	2015-05-18
国务院关于北京市服务业扩大开放综合试点总体方案的批复	国函〔2015〕81 号	国务院	2015-05-21
住房城乡建设部关于公布 2014 年全国村庄规划、镇规划和县域乡村建设规划示范名单的通知	建村函〔2015〕135 号	住房城乡建设部	2015-05-26
国务院关于大别山革命老区振兴发展规划的批复	国函〔2015〕91 号	国务院	2015-06-05
国务院关于全国基础测绘中长期规划纲要(2015—2030 年)的批复	国函〔2015〕92 号	国务院	2015-06-06
住房城乡建设部关于 2015 年美丽宜居小镇、美丽宜居村庄示范工作的通知	建村〔2015〕76 号	住房城乡建设部	2015-06-08
关于建设长江经济带国家级转型升级示范开发区的实施意见	发改外资〔2015〕1294 号	发展改革委员会	2015-06-09
国务院关于开展第三次全国农业普查的通知	国发〔2015〕34 号	国务院	2015-06-22
国务院关于修改《建设工程勘察设计管理条例》的决定	国令第 662 号	国务院	2015-06-23
国务院关于进一步做好城镇棚户区和城乡危房改造及配套基础设施建设有关工作的意见	国发〔2015〕37 号	国务院	2015-06-30
国务院关于同意设立南京江北新区的批复	国函〔2015〕103 号	国务院	2015-07-02
国务院关于积极推进“互联网+”行动的指导意见	国发〔2015〕40 号	国务院	2015-07-04
国家发展改革委关于印发《国家级区域规划管理暂行办法》的通知	发改地区〔2015〕1521 号	发展改革委员会	2015-07-04
国家发展改革委　国家能源局关于促进智能电网发展的指导意见	发改运行〔2015〕1518 号	发展改革委员会、国家能源局	2015-07-06
关于进一步鼓励和扩大社会资本投资建设铁路的实施意见	发改基础〔2015〕1610 号	发展改革委员会、财政部等	2015-07-10
住房城乡建设部　国家旅游局关于公布第三批全国特色景观旅游名镇名村示范名单的通知	建村〔2015〕106 号	住房城乡建设部、国家旅游局	2015-07-13

续表

名　称	批号(文号)	发布机构	发布日期
国务院关于兰州市城市总体规划的批复	国函〔2015〕109号	国务院	2015-07-20
国务院关于同意设立云南勐腊(磨憨)重点开发开放试验区的批复	国函〔2015〕112号	国务院	2015-07-23
国务院关于福州市城市总体规划的批复	国函〔2015〕125号	国务院	2015-08-03
关于请提供编制《节水型社会建设"十三五"规划》相关内容的通知	发改办环资〔2015〕2096号	发展改革委员会办公厅、水利部办公厅等	2015-08-07
国务院办公厅关于推进城市地下综合管廊建设的指导意见	国办发〔2015〕61号	国务院办公厅	2015-08-10
国务院办公厅关于进一步促进旅游投资和消费的若干意见	国办发〔2015〕62号	国务院办公厅	2015-08-11
国务院办公厅关于印发生态环境监测网络建设方案的通知	国办发〔2015〕56号	国务院办公厅	2015-08-12
国务院关于印发全国海洋主体功能区规划的通知	国发〔2015〕42号	国务院	2015-08-20
国家发展改革委关于加快配电网建设改造的指导意见	发改能源〔2015〕1899号	发展改革委员会	2015-08-20
国务院关于开展农村承包土地的经营权和农民住房财产权抵押贷款试点的指导意见	国发〔2015〕45号	国务院	2015-08-24
国务院关于公布第二批国家级抗战纪念设施、遗址名录的通知	国发〔2015〕47号	国务院	2015-08-24
住房城乡建设部办公厅关于开展2015年"世界城市日"活动及举办"2015世界城市日论坛"的通知	建办外函〔2015〕762号	住房城乡建设部	2015-08-24
住房城乡建设部　环境保护部关于印发城市黑臭水体整治工作指南的通知	建城〔2015〕130号	住房城乡建设部、环境保护部	2015-08-28
住房城乡建设部关于印发城市停车设施规划导则的通知	建城〔2015〕129号	住房城乡建设部	2015-09-01
国务院办公厅关于印发三网融合推广方案的通知	国办发〔2015〕65号	国务院办公厅	2015-09-04
国务院关于印发促进大数据发展行动纲要的通知	国发〔2015〕50号	国务院	2015-09-05
国务院关于同意设立福州新区的批复	国函〔2015〕137号	国务院	2015-09-09
住房城乡建设部村镇建设司关于征集中国传统村落数字博物馆设计方案的通知	建村建函〔2015〕91号	住房城乡建设部	2015-09-09
住房城乡建设部关于成立海绵城市建设技术指导专家委员会的通知	建科〔2015〕133号	住房城乡建设部	2015-09-11
国家级风景名胜区规划编制审批办法	住房和城乡建设部令第26号	住房城乡建设部	2015-09-14
国务院关于同意设立云南滇中新区的批复	国函〔2015〕141号	国务院	2015-09-15
国务院办公厅关于批准烟台市城市总体规划的通知	国办函〔2015〕92号	国务院办公厅	2015-09-16
关于开展循环经济示范城市(县)建设的通知	发改环资〔2015〕2154号	发展改革委员会、财政部等	2015-09-22
国务院关于环渤海地区合作发展纲要的批复	国函〔2015〕146号	国务院	2015-09-27
国务院办公厅关于批准安阳市城市总体规划的通知	国办函〔2015〕101号	国务院办公厅	2015-10-08
国务院办公厅关于加快电动汽车充电基础设施建设的指导意见	国办发〔2015〕73号	国务院办公厅	2015-10-09

续表

名　称	批号(文号)	发布机构	发布日期
国务院办公厅关于推进海绵城市建设的指导意见	国办发〔2015〕75号	国务院办公厅	2015-10-11
国务院关于苏州工业园区开展开放创新综合试验总体方案的批复	国函〔2015〕151号	国务院	2015-10-13
国务院办公厅关于推进海绵城市建设的指导意见	国办发〔2015〕75号	国务院办公厅	2015-10-16
国务院关于全国水土保持规划(2015—2030年)的批复	国函〔2015〕160号	国务院	2015-10-17
关于印发国家民用空间基础设施中长期发展规划(2015—2025年)的通知	发改高技〔2015〕2429号	发展改革委员会、财政部等	2015-10-26
国土资源部关于开展2015年度全国土地变更调查与遥感监测工作的通知	国土资发〔2015〕136号	国土部	2015-10-29
住房城乡建设部等部门关于全面推进农村垃圾治理的指导意见	建村〔2015〕170号	住房城乡建设部、中央农村工作领导小组办公室等	2015-11-03
国务院办公厅关于批准扬州市城市总体规划的通知	国办函〔2015〕132号	国务院办公厅	2015-11-06
国务院办公厅关于促进农村电子商务加快发展的指导意见	国办发〔2015〕78号	国务院办公厅	2015-11-09
关于公布第二批国家新型城镇化综合试点地区名单的通知	发改规划〔2015〕2665号	发展改革委员会、中央编办等	2015-11-16
国务院关于呼和浩特市城市总体规划的批复	国函〔2015〕194号	国务院	2015-11-17
国务院办公厅关于印发编制自然资源资产负债表试点方案的通知	国办发〔2015〕82号	国务院办公厅	2015-11-17
关于举办3S技术在城市规划设计管理中的应用培训班(二期)的通知	建科综函〔2015〕151号	住房城乡建设部	2015-11-17
住房城乡建设部关于印发城市轨道沿线地区规划设计导则的通知	建规函〔2015〕276号	住房城乡建设部	2015-11-18
住房城乡建设部关于改革创新、全面有效推进乡村规划工作的指导意见	建村〔2015〕187号	住房城乡建设部	2015-11-24
国家发展改革委　交通运输部关于印发《城镇化地区综合交通网规划》的通知	发改基础〔2015〕2706号	发展改革委员会、交通运输部	2015-11-24
国务院办公厅关于调整河北昌黎黄金海岸等6处国家级自然保护区的通知	国办函〔2015〕138号	国务院办公厅	2015-11-25
国土资源部　住房和城乡建设部　国家旅游局关于支持旅游业发展用地政策的意见	国土资规〔2015〕10号	国土资源部、住房城乡建设部	2015-11-25
住房城乡建设部关于印发世界自然遗产、自然与文化双遗产申报和保护管理办法(试行)的通知	建城〔2015〕190号	住房城乡建设部	2015-11-26
关于举办"智慧城市规划建设管理培训班"的通知	建科研函〔2015〕156号	住房城乡建设部	2015-11-26
国务院关于成都市城市总体规划的批复	国函〔2015〕199号	国务院	2015-12-04
住房城乡建设部　国家开发银行关于推进开发性金融支持海绵城市建设的通知	建城〔2015〕208号	住房城乡建设部、国家开发银行	2015-12-10
国务院关于加快实施自由贸易区战略的若干意见	国发〔2015〕69号	国务院	2015-12-17
国务院关于西宁市城市总体规划的批复	国函〔2015〕214号	国务院	2015-12-18
国务院关于同意设立哈尔滨新区的批复	国函〔2015〕217号	国务院	2015-12-22

(作者:金晓春,中国城市规划设计研究院学术信息中心副主任)

中国城市基本数据(2013年)

城市名称	Name of cities	行政级别 Administrative level	行政区域土地面积(平方公里) Total land area of city's administrative region(sq. km)	年末总人口(万人) Total population at year-end (10 000 persons)	六普常住人口(万人) Total residents of the Sixth National Population Census (10 000 persons)	建成区面积(平方公里) Area of built-up district (sq. km)	地区生产总值(万元) Gross regional product (10 000 yuan)	人均地区生产总值(元) Per capita gross regional product(yuan)	用水普及率(%) Water coverage rate(%)	污水处理率(%) Wastewater treatment rate(%)	人均公园绿地面积(平方米) Per capita public green space(sq. m)	生活垃圾处理率(%) Domestic garbage treatment rate(%)
北京市	Beijing	直辖市	16 411	1 316. 3	1 961. 24	1 306	195 005 600	93 213	100. 00	84. 60	15. 70	99. 30
天津市	Tianjin	直辖市	11 917	1 004. 0	1 293. 87	736	143 701 600	99 607	100. 00	90. 03	10. 97	96. 80
河北省	Hebei											
石家庄市	Shijiazhuang	地级市	15 848	1 003. 2	1 016. 38	217	48 636 583	46 574	100. 00	94. 46	15. 05	100. 00
唐山市	Tangshan	地级市	13 472	738. 7	757. 73	249	61 212 139	79 617	100. 00	94. 81	15. 05	100. 00
秦皇岛市	Qinhuangdao	地级市	7 802	292. 7	298. 76	97	11 687 549	38 530	100. 00	95. 01	20. 58	100. 00
邯郸市	Handan	地级市	12 065	994. 0	917. 47	121	30 615 043	32 899	100. 00	97. 52	18. 10	100. 00
邢台市	Xingtai	地级市	12 433	762. 9	710. 41	79	16 045 756	22 277	100. 00	90. 60	11. 65	100. 00
保定市	Baoding	地级市	20 900	1 163. 9	1 119. 44	144	29 043 115	25 513	100. 00	96. 50	10. 35	100. 00
张家口市	Zhangjiakou	地级市	36 873	466. 9	434. 55	86	13 169 971	29 997	100. 00	91. 98	12. 33	87. 00
承德市	Chengde	地级市	39 735	378. 1	347. 32	114	12 720 917	36 235	100. 00	95. 38	24. 19	99. 29
沧州市	Cangzhou	地级市	14 053	754. 3	713. 41	64	30 129 850	41 406	100. 00	100. 00	10. 60	96. 27
廊坊市	Langfang	地级市	6 382	422. 4	435. 88	65	19 431 340	43 628	100. 00	87. 66	13. 16	95. 50
衡水市	Hengshui	地级市	8 825	447. 5	434. 08	46	10 702 335	24 330	100. 00	79. 64	12. 21	100. 00
辛集市	Xinji	县级市	951	63. 5	61. 59	29	3 635 419	57 251	89. 03	94. 39	9. 13	90. 91
藁城市	Gaocheng	县级市	836	81. 6	77. 51	18	4 748 770	58 196	96. 79	98. 29	10. 20	97. 99
晋州市	Jinzhou	县级市	619	55. 3	53. 77	15	2 291 967	41 446	100. 00	95. 84	9. 62	100. 00

续表

城市名称 Name of cities		行政级别 Admini-strative level	行政区域土地面积（平方公里）Total land area of city's administrative region(sq. km)	年末总人口（万人）Total population at year-enc (10 000 persons)	六普常住人口（万人）Total residents of the Sixth National Population Census (10 000 persons)	建成区面积（平方公里）Area of built-up district (sq. km)	地区生产总值（万元）Gross regional product (10 000 yuan)	人均地区生产总值（元）Per capita gross regional product(yuan)	用水普及率（%）Water coverage rate(%)	污水处理率（%）Wastewater treatment rate(%)	人均公园绿地面积（平方米）Per capita public green space(sq. m)	生活垃圾处理率（%）Domestic garbage treatment rate(%)
新乐市	Xinle	县级市	525	51.0	48.77	13	1 721 801	33 761	100.00	95.01	8.02	100.00
鹿泉市	Luquan	县级市	603	40.4	43.29	19	3 200 581	79 222	100.00	97.05	10.50	100.00
遵化市	Zunhua	县级市	1 509	74.7	73.70	25	5 634 245	75 425	100.00	91.13	11.59	100.00
迁安市	Qian'an	县级市	1 227	74.4	72.82	37	10 051 327	135 098	100.00	100.00	19.02	100.00
武安市	Wu'an	县级市	1 806	81.1	81.90	32	5 950 141	73 368	100.00	95.74	15.20	100.00
南宫市	Nangong	县级市	861	49.0	46.90	16	857 198	17 494	100.00	92.08	11.49	98.89
沙河市	Shahe	县级市	859	43.5	49.84	16	2 175 408	50 009	100.00	86.01	13.63	100.00
涿州市	Zhuozhou	县级市	751	65.8	60.35	32	2 236 476	33 989	100.00	97.25	10.64	82.01
定州市	Dingzhou	县级市	1 283	123.4	116.52	36	2 537 115	20 560	100.00	93.09	9.06	100.00
安国市	Anguo	县级市	486	41.9	37.03	13	971 641	23 190	100.00	90.07	10.20	99.73
高碑店市	Gaobeidian	县级市	618	57.1	64.03	17	1 252 733	21 939	100.00	99.59	8.36	98.94
泊头市	Botou	县级市	1 009	62.2	58.43	20	1 735 234	27 898	100.00	100.00	8.52	100.00
任丘市	Renqiu	县级市	1 012	86.7	82.25	44	5 645 505	65 115	100.00	98.03	8.22	100.00
黄骅市	Huanghua	县级市	1 545	46.6	54.85	30	2 522 216	54 125	100.00	98.13	11.81	100.00
河间市	Hejian	县级市	1 333	84.9	81.03	21	2 516 368	29 639	100.00	100.00	12.73	100.00
霸州市	Bazhou	县级市	802	63.0	62.30	18	3 462 583	54 962	100.00	96.99	12.89	95.45
三河市	Sanhe	县级市	634	59.8	65.20	19	4 588 213	76 726	100.00	94.28	10.37	35.08
冀州市	Jizhou	县级市	878	34.8	36.20	18	814 807	23 414	100.00	100.00	14.74	100.00
深州市	Shenzhou	县级市	1 245	57.3	56.61	19	1 256 335	21 926	100.00	89.04	8.23	99.02
山西省	Shanxi											
太原市	Taiyuan	地级市	6 977	367.5	420.16	320	24 128 724	56 547	100.00	85.00	12.52	100.00
大同市	Datong	地级市	14 127	337.5	331.81	108	9 674 311	28 741	100.00	83.21	8.16	90.60
阳泉市	Yangquan	地级市	4 570	132.7	136.85	54	6 118 094	44 251	100.00	89.83	9.49	88.98

续表

城市名称	Name of cities	行政级别 Administrative level	行政区域土地面积(平方公里) Total land area of city's administrative region(sq. km)	年末总人口(万人) Total population at year-end (10 000 persons)	六普常住人口(万人) Total residents of the Sixth National Population Census (10 000 persons)	建成区面积(平方公里) Area of built-up district (sq. km)	地区生产总值(万元) Gross regional product (10 000 yuan)	人均地区生产总值(元) Per capita gross regional product(yuan)	用水普及率(%) Water coverage rate(%)	污水处理率(%) Wastewater treatment rate(%)	人均公园绿地面积(平方米) Per capita public green space(sq. m)	生活垃圾处理率(%) Domestic garbage treatment rate(%)
长治市	Changzhi	地级市	13 896	338. 6	333. 46	59	13 337 207	39 474	97. 20	92. 57	10. 02	100. 00
晋城市	Jincheng	地级市	9 425	219. 3	227. 91	44	10 319 143	44 940	99. 08	95. 00	12. 77	100. 00
朔州市	Shuozhou	地级市	10 674	174. 4	171. 49	42	10 264 012	59 003	99. 06	97. 72	10. 71	100. 00
晋中市	Jinzhong	地级市	16 392	330. 5	324. 94	53	10 222 281	31 015	100. 00	96. 50	12. 62	75. 30
运城市	Yuncheng	地级市	14 181	522. 4	513. 48	52	11 401 151	21 887	94. 00	92. 00	10. 02	95. 00
忻州市	Xinzhou	地级市	25 117	311. 4	306. 75	32	6 547 321	21 074	94. 03	95. 00	12. 86	
临汾市	Linfen	地级市	20 275	427. 2	431. 66	54	12 239 045	27 949	93. 01	90. 86	13. 29	100. 00
吕梁市	Lvliang	地级市	21 239	393. 9	372. 71	24	12 286 015	32 484	95. 02	90. 93	12. 43	100. 00
古交市	Gujiao	县级市	1 584	22. 2	20. 51	17	275 119	12 393	100. 00	87. 26	7. 58	94. 38
潞城市	Lucheng	县级市	630	22. 9	22. 69	8	894 390	39 056	98. 24	90. 78	9. 00	100. 00
高平市	Gaoping	县级市	946	48. 2	48. 49	18	2 335 259	48 449	99. 09	86. 23	13. 02	100. 00
介休市	Jiexiu	县级市	744	41. 8	40. 65	18	1 491 194	35 674	100. 00	94. 93	9. 35	85. 00
永济市	Yongji	县级市	1 208	44. 4	44. 47	23	1 271 847	28 645	99. 01	86. 40	13. 16	65. 00
河津市	Hejin	县级市	593	40. 6	39. 55	29	1 955 801	48 172	90. 91	86. 10	15. 00	81. 00
原平市	Yuanping	县级市	2 571	49. 7	49. 12	11	1 180 690	23 756	99. 91	93. 07	4. 43	100. 00
侯马市	Houma	县级市	221	24. 0	24. 00	20	831 831	34 660	99. 29	91. 59	10. 58	100. 00
霍州市	Huozhou	县级市	764	30. 5	28. 29	15	855 717	28 056	98. 07	80. 03	9. 21	
孝义市	Xiaoyi	县级市	938	49. 0	46. 88	23	4 123 487	84 153	86. 67	81. 61	11. 86	100. 00
汾阳市	Fenyang	县级市	1 175	42. 6	41. 62	16	1 099 236	25 804	91. 68	68. 85	6. 88	24. 66
内蒙古自治区	Inner Mongolia											
呼和浩特市	Huhhot	地级市	17 186	234. 0	286. 66	230	27 103 900	91 107	98. 35	80. 74	15. 01	98. 74
包头市	Baotou	地级市	27 768	225. 0	265. 04	186	35 030 200	127 434	99. 44	85. 62	12. 74	95. 13
乌海市	Wuhai	地级市	1 754	55. 3	53. 29	63	5 701 293	103 519	97. 84	93. 01	12. 24	87. 16

续表

城市名称 Name of cities		行政级别 Admini-strative level	行政区域土地面积（平方公里）Total land area of city's administrative region(sq. km)	年末总人口（万人）Total population at year-end (10 000 persons)	六普常住人口（万人）Total residents of the Sixth National Population Census (10 000 persons)	建成区面积（平方公里）Area of built-up district (sq. km)	地区生产总值（万元）Gross regional product (10 000 yuan)	人均地区生产总值（元）Per capita gross regional product(yuan)	用水普及率（%）Water coverage rate(%)	污水处理率（%）Wastewater treatment rate(%)	人均公园绿地面积（平方米）Per capita public green space(sq. m)	生活垃圾处理率（%）Domestic garbage treatment rate(%)
赤峰市	Chifeng	地级市	90 021	464.3	434.12	104	16 861 549	39 125	95.20	88.05	16.18	100.00
通辽市	Tongliao	地级市	59 535	321.2	313.92	76	17 818 000	56 943	94.49	99.44	15.83	82.00
鄂尔多斯市	Ordos	地级市	86 752	154.3	194.07	113	39 558 982	196 728	99.29	98.14	29.87	95.10
呼伦贝尔市	Hulunbeier	地级市	252 777	253.2	254.93	114	14 305 520	56 470	94.49	93.86	21.51	63.94
巴彦淖尔市	Bayannur	地级市	64 413	183.2	166.99	42	8 348 900	49 996	95.50	93.96	16.39	97.50
乌兰察布市	Ulanqab	地级市	54 500	283.3	214.36	57	8 337 947	39 213	97.00	98.48	35.02	98.06
霍林郭勒市	Huolinguole	县级市	585	8.2	10.22	24	3 205 715	390 941	94.20	98.08	9.95	85.00
满洲里市	Manzhouli	县级市	732	17.0	24.95	27	1 949 719	114 689	98.92	84.10	12.87	90.91
牙克石市	Yakeshi	县级市	27 590	35.1	36.63	19	2 120 248	60 406	91.60	84.51	12.90	83.13
扎兰屯市	Zhalantun	县级市	16 800	42.2	35.22	19	1 656 746	39 259	93.25	86.25	13.96	97.00
额尔古纳市	Eerguna	县级市	28 958	8.3	11.04	10	409 188	49 300	84.27	83.33	14.04	84.96
根河市	Genhe	县级市	19 659	15.3	7.67	18	376 482	24 607	90.82	85.29	13.07	97.54
丰镇市	Fengzhen	县级市	2 704	33.8	24.56	25	1 325 694	39 222	95.01	90.71	29.64	91.16
乌兰浩特市	Wulanhaote	县级市	2 728	32.4	32.71	39	1 361 940	42 035	85.58	85.71	16.41	96.00
阿尔山市	Aershan	县级市	7 409	4.9	6.83	10	138 167	28 197	18.57	28.57	39.57	94.29
二连浩特市	Erlianhaote	县级市	4 013	2.7	7.42	27	790 402	292 741	100.00	93.59	17.19	100.00
锡林浩特市	Xilinhaote	县级市	14 780	17.9	24.59	41	2 064 748	115 349	93.44	75.05	16.02	100.00
辽宁省	Liaoning											
沈阳市	Shenyang	副省级市	12 980	727.1	810.62	455	71 585 745	86 850	100.00	95.00	12.39	100.00
大连市	Dalian	副省级市	12 574	591.5	669.04	396	76 507 861	110 600	100.00	95.96	11.22	100.00
鞍山市	Anshan	地级市	9 255	349.8	364.59	167	26 232 539	74 939	100.00	87.09	11.20	100.00
抚顺市	Fushun	地级市	11 272	218.0	213.81	134	13 404 459	63 922	98.63	75.00	10.36	100.00
本溪市	Benxi	地级市	8 411	152.3	170.95	109	11 936 598	69 118	97.89	94.42	10.26	99.95

续表

城市名称 Name of cities		行政级别 Administrative level	行政区域土地面积(平方公里) Total land area of city's administrative region(sq. km)	年末总人口(万人) Total population at year-end (10 000 persons)	六普常住人口(万人) Total residents of the Sixth National Population Census (10 000 persons)	建成区面积(平方公里) Area of built-up district (sq. km)	地区生产总值(万元) Gross regional product (10 000 yuan)	人均地区生产总值(元) Per capita gross regional product(yuan)	用水普及率(%) Water coverage rate(%)	污水处理率(%) Wastewater treatment rate(%)	人均公园绿地面积(平方米) Per capita public green space(sq. m)	生活垃圾处理率(%) Domestic garbage treatment rate(%)
丹东市	Dandong	地级市	15 290	239. 7	244. 47	53	11 072 964	46 206	100. 00	89. 42	10. 99	100. 00
锦州市	Jinzhou	地级市	10 047	305. 9	312. 65	77	13 449 310	43 497	100. 00	84. 35	12. 83	100. 00
营口市	Yingkou	地级市	5 242	232. 5	242. 85	110	15 131 145	61 937	97. 17	100. 00	10. 15	100. 00
阜新市	Fuxin	地级市	10 355	191. 1	181. 93	77	6 151 240	34 259	98. 77	51. 12	12. 09	99. 55
辽阳市	Liaoyang	地级市	4 736	180. 0	185. 88	104	10 799 909	58 236	100. 00	100. 00	9. 54	100. 00
盘锦市	Panjin	地级市	4 065	129. 0	139. 25	70	13 510 562	94 052	100. 00	100. 00	11. 63	100. 00
铁岭市	Tieling	地级市	12 985	301. 9	271. 77	38	10 312 722	34 143	97. 70	100. 00	11. 95	100. 00
朝阳市	Chaoyang	地级市	19 698	339. 5	304. 46	59	10 028 603	33 591	98. 84	77. 84	8. 87	100. 00
葫芦岛市	Huludao	地级市	10 414	279. 9	262. 35	76	7 751 057	29 973	100. 00	85. 64	14. 95	100. 00
新民市	Xinmin	县级市	3 297	68. 7	65. 78	25	4 516 339	65 740	92. 43	100. 00	8. 45	100. 00
瓦房店市	Wafangdian	县级市	3 643	100. 0	94. 22	35	10 559 408	105 594	100. 00	96. 04	13. 43	100. 00
普兰店市	Pulandian	县级市	3 375	92. 7	74. 12	36	7 823 705	84 398	97. 39	25. 57	8. 93	100. 00
庄河市	Zhuanghe	县级市	4 114	90. 2	84. 13	41	8 184 716	90 740	99. 82	92. 83	12. 80	100. 00
海城市	Haicheng	县级市	2 563	109. 4	129. 39	36	8 775 709	80 217	87. 18	97. 35	5. 60	97. 36
东港市	Donggang	县级市	2 399	60. 8	62. 75	32	5 115 706	84 140	100. 00	61. 39	8. 71	100. 00
凤城市	Fengcheng	县级市	5 515	57. 3	54. 39	21	4 560 756	79 594	86. 35	86. 01	8. 90	86. 00
凌海市	Linghai	县级市	2 585	52. 3	50. 81	21	2 656 900	50 801	100. 00	100. 00	9. 73	100. 00
北镇市	Beizhen	县级市	1 694	51. 9	51. 49	15	1 461 930	28 168	78. 22	98. 25	3. 15	100. 00
盖州市	Gaizhou	县级市	2 946	70. 4	69. 16	29	2 303 096	32 714	90. 26	90. 05	5. 70	100. 00
大石桥市	Dashiqiao	县级市	1 598	70. 4	70. 49	35	5 141 337	73 030	98. 46	92. 17	8. 31	100. 00
灯塔市	Dengta	县级市	1 166	44. 5	49. 61	13	2 550 638	57 318	95. 95	100. 00	11. 33	100. 00
调兵山市	Diaobingshan	县级市	262	23. 8	24. 14	19	1 801 050	75 674	99. 06	100. 00	9. 03	100. 00
开原市	Kaiyuan	县级市	2 838	58. 3	54. 56	24	3 300 858	56 618	100. 00	100. 00	11. 09	100. 00

续表

城市名称 Name of cities		行政级别 Admini-strative level	行政区域土地面积（平方公里）Total land area of city's administrative region（sq. km）	年末总人口（万人）Total population at year－end（10 000 persons）	六普常住人口（万人）Total residents of the Sixth National Population Census（10 000 persons）	建成区面积（平方公里）Area of built－up district（sq. km）	地区生产总值（万元）Gross regional product（10 000 yuan）	人均地区生产总值（元）Per capita gross regional product（yuan）	用水普及率（%）Water coverage rate（%）	污水处理率（%）Wastewater treatment rate（%）	人均公园绿地面积（平方米）Per capita public green space（sq. m）	生活垃圾处理率（%）Domestic garbage treatment rate（%）
北票市	Beipiao	县级市	4 469	56.0	49.62	18	2 305 298	41 166	96.67	95.22	7.44	
凌源市	Lingyuan	县级市	3 282	64.5	57.07	25	1 960 534	30 396	95.75	100.00	8.17	78.90
兴城市	Xingcheng	县级市	2 119	54.3	54.62	30	1 489 194	27 425	100.00	60.39	11.41	100.00
吉林省	Jilin											
长春市	Changchun	副省级市	20 604	752.7	767.44	452	50 031 808	66 286	99.46	81.43	13.90	99.66
吉林市	Jilin	地级市	27 205	429.1	441.32	173	26 174 061	60 877	98.20	94.05	11.94	100.00
四平市	Siping	地级市	14 080	328.4	338.52	54	12 103 434	36 292	75.20	75.06	9.28	96.00
辽源市	Liaoyuan	地级市	5 140	121.9	117.62	46	7 003 010	57 421	97.25	96.13	7.53	100.00
通化市	Tonghua	地级市	15 608	222.3	232.44	50	10 034 500	44 909	91.69	92.41	11.49	97.45
白山市	Baishan	地级市	17 485	127.1	129.61	47	6 736 447	52 831	82.31	62.86	10.05	99.83
松原市	Songyuan	地级市	21 090	283.0	288.01	48	16 504 848	57 639	95.46	95.79	17.34	95.75
白城市	Baicheng	地级市	25 745	199.1	203.24	42	6 923 486	34 411	98.09	62.09	7.90	95.60
九台市	Jiutai	县级市	3 375	81.8	61.17	24	3 643 377	44 540	95.54	96.02	7.69	97.50
榆树市	Yushu	县级市	4 712	127.6	116.06	40	3 671 842	28 776	76.50	99.89	4.64	100.00
德惠市	Dehui	县级市	3 435	93.1	74.84	31	3 601 061	38 679	93.20	49.17	13.87	95.97
蛟河市	Jiaohe	县级市	6 364	44.0	44.72	19	2 120 505	48 193	73.48	68.82	13.79	100.00
桦甸市	Huadian	县级市	6 625	44.8	44.48	20	3 033 852	67 720	99.26	85.11	16.90	100.00
舒兰市	Shulan	县级市	4 557	65.0	64.57	25	2 007 092	30 878	74.62	70.85	11.92	100.00
磐石市	Panshi	县级市	3 867	53.4	50.58	17	2 933 445	54 933	80.00	82.05	6.43	88.33
公主岭市	Gongzhuling	县级市	4 140	107.0	109.29	33	3 850 512	35 986	99.58	88.40	6.04	95.98
双辽市	Shuangliao	县级市	3 121	39.0	42.07	21	1 920 921	49 254	84.24	91.72	6.55	100.00
梅河口市	Meihekou	县级市	2 174	61.0	61.52	24	2 900 003	47 541	98.04	70.27	10.56	100.00
集安市	Ji'an	县级市	3 342	21.9	23.23	14	917 389	41 890	87.84	99.78	9.79	100.00

续表

城市名称 Name of cities		行政级别 Administrative level	行政区域土地面积(平方公里) Total land area of city's administrative region(sq. km)	年末总人口(万人) Total population at year - end (10 000 persons)	六普常住人口(万人) Total residents of the Sixth National Population Census (10 000 persons)	建成区面积(平方公里) Area of built - up district (sq. km)	地区生产总值(万元) Gross regional product (10 000 yuan)	人均地区生产总值(元) Per capita gross regional product(yuan)	用水普及率(%) Water coverage rate(%)	污水处理率(%) Wastewater treatment rate(%)	人均公园绿地面积(平方米) Per capita public green space(sq. m)	生活垃圾处理率(%) Domestic garbage treatment rate(%)
临江市	Linjiang	县级市	3 008	16.8	17.50	9	951 428	56 633	94.96	98.50	21.03	100.00
扶余市	Fuyu	县级市	4 654	75.5	71.90	10	3 481 587	46 114	71.29	95.29	5.81	72.91
洮南市	Taonan	县级市	5 031	43.4	43.21	23	1 271 102	29 288	100.00	87.23	8.90	100.00
大安市	Da'an	县级市	4 879	40.0	43.10	15	1 319 005	32 975	90.22	96.62	10.16	100.00
延吉市	Yanji	县级市	1 748	53.0	56.30	35	3 054 781	57 637	98.88	90.55	9.97	98.57
图们市	Tumen	县级市	1 142	12.2	13.45	10	429 930	35 240	68.42	76.84	10.64	99.85
敦化市	Dunhua	县级市	11 957	47.4	48.35	31	1 700 500	35 876	95.85	87.60	21.72	100.00
珲春市	Hunchun	县级市	5 161	26.4	24.18	18	1 400 000	53 030	82.17	48.58	8.62	78.85
龙井市	Longjing	县级市	2 208	17.4	17.72	10	384 382	22 091	97.56	93.65	12.71	100.00
和龙市	Helong	县级市	5 069	18.5	18.95	13	566 085	30 599	94.54	63.16	5.17	100.00
黑龙江省	Heilongjiang											
哈尔滨市	Harbin	副省级市	53 068	995.2	1 063.60	391	50 170 491	50 498	100.00	90.47	10.52	87.29
齐齐哈尔市	Qiqihar	地级市	42 469	557.0	536.70	140	12 303 980	23 396	98.75	73.60	10.02	50.43
鸡西市	Jixi	地级市	22 531	186.6	186.22	79	5 709 117	30 653	98.45	34.58	10.75	84.74
鹤岗市	Hegang	地级市	14 657	107.8	105.87	66	3 200 142	29 594	86.37	45.42	14.97	
双鸭山市	Shuangyashan	地级市	23 209	149.8	146.26	58	5 551 063	36 983	100.00	42.62	14.78	81.11
大庆市	Daqing	地级市	21 522	282.6	290.45	241	41 814 993	148 209	93.37	96.60	14.50	90.03
伊春市	Yichun	地级市	32 759	123.2	114.81	165	2 844 921	22 911	74.95	37.21	20.51	1.99
佳木斯市	Jiamusi	地级市	32 704	242.1	255.21	97	7 921 480	31 613	96.29	66.92	14.02	92.11
七台河市	Qitaihe	地级市	6 221	92.0	92.05	68	2 409 883	26 148	96.03	51.20	11.99	100.00
牡丹江市	Mudanjiang	地级市	38 405	259.0	279.87	78	12 160 742	43 682	96.07	41.88	10.69	100.00
黑河市	Heihe	地级市	68 240	171.5	167.39	19	3 896 462	22 654	94.01	90.01	14.62	100.00
绥化市	Suihua	地级市	34 873	556.2	541.82	35	11 838 630	20 903	94.28	100.00	9.04	78.36

续表

城市名称 Name of cities		行政级别 Administrative level	行政区域土地面积（平方公里） Total land area of city's administrative region (sq. km)	年末总人口（万人） Total population at year - enc (10 000 persons)	六普常住人口（万人） Total residents of the Sixth National Population Census (10 000 persons)	建成区面积（平方公里） Area of built - up district (sq. km)	地区生产总值（万元） Gross regional product (10 000 yuan)	人均地区生产总值（元） Per capita gross regional product (yuan)	用水普及率（%） Water coverage rate (%)	污水处理率（%） Wastewater treatment rate (%)	人均公园绿地面积（平方米） Per capita public green space (sq. m)	生活垃圾处理率（%） Domestic garbage treatment rate (%)
双城市	Shuangcheng	县级市	3 112	82.1	82.56	30	4 289 158	52 243	95.68	90.28	11.83	
尚志市	Shangzhi	县级市	8 891	61.3	58.54	18	2 507 779	40 910	98.82	92.00	11.39	100.00
五常市	Wuchang	县级市	7 512	101.0	88.12	25	3 211 712	31 799	97.73	46.88	14.02	
讷河市	Nehe	县级市	6 660	73.1	62.59	11	1 104 643	15 111	93.50	100.00	12.50	100.00
虎林市	Hulin	县级市	9 334	15.8	31.79	11	648 234	41 027	100.00	90.91	14.99	100.00
密山市	Mishan	县级市	7 731	35.4	40.75	22	1 007 513	28 461	98.81	100.00	12.30	100.00
铁力市	Tieli	县级市	6 443	37.9	34.94	17	774 798	20 443	89.93	88.16	14.42	83.33
同江市	Tongjiang	县级市	6 229	11.1	17.98	10	380 292	34 261	80.81	100.00	15.44	
富锦市	Fujin	县级市	8 224	39.0	43.72	16	1 546 512	39 654	100.00	100.00	7.59	100.00
绥芬河市	Suifenhe	县级市	422	6.9	13.23	27	1 234 353	178 892	73.97	100.00	9.13	
海林市	Hailin	县级市	8 711	39.4	40.09	14	1 712 784	43 472	99.60	100.00	13.83	100.00
宁安市	Ning'an	县级市	7 891	43.4	43.75	11	1 734 339	39 962	100.00	100.00	13.20	100.00
穆棱市	Muling	县级市	6 212	29.2	29.33	11	1 654 039	56 645	95.17	100.00	13.90	
北安市	Bei'an	县级市	7 194	39.1	43.64	21	700 081	17 905	88.87	97.50	10.28	
五大连池市	Wudalianchi	县级市	9 874	36.1	32.64	6	477 793	13 235	83.67	98.21	8.76	3.28
安达市	Anda	县级市	3 586	47.8	47.28	25	3 788 024	79 247	94.26	99.90	3.77	100.00
肇东市	Zhaodong	县级市	3 905	92.4	90.31	34	4 978 081	53 875	94.25	100.00	13.07	
海伦市	Hailun	县级市	4 667	79.3	76.94	21	1 081 365	13 636	94.93	100.00	5.60	
上海市	Shanghai	直辖市	6 340	1 432.3	2 301.92	999	216 021 200	90 092	100.00	87.12	7.10	90.58
江苏省	Jiangsu											
南京市	Nanjing	副省级市	6 587	643.1	800.37	713	80 117 800	98 011	99.98	94.22	14.55	100.00
无锡市	Wuxi	地级市	4 627	472.2	637.44	325	80 701 800	124 640	100.00	96.12	14.71	100.00
徐州市	Xuzhou	地级市	11 259	1 006.9	857.72	276	44 358 243	51 714	99.44	91.50	16.31	100.00

续表

城市名称 Name of cities		行政级别 Admini-strative level	行政区域土地面积(平方公里) Total land area of city's administrative region(sq. km)	年末总人口(万人) Total population at year - end (10 000 persons)	六普常住人口(万人) Total residents of the Sixth National Population Census (10 000 persons)	建成区面积(平方公里) Area of built - up district (sq. km)	地区生产总值(万元) Gross regional product (10 000 yuan)	人均地区生产总值(元) Per capita gross regional product(yuan)	用水普及率(%) Water coverage rate(%)	污水处理率(%) Wastewater treatment rate(%)	人均公园绿地面积(平方米) Per capita public green space(sq. m)	生活垃圾处理率(%) Domestic garbage treatment rate(%)
常州市	Changzhou	地级市	4 372	365. 9	459. 24	186	43 609 347	92 995	100. 00	94. 42	12. 83	99. 99
苏州市	Suzhou	地级市	8 488	653. 8	1 045. 99	441	130 157 000	123 209	100. 00	95. 49	15. 14	100. 00
南通市	Nantong	地级市	8 001	766. 5	728. 36	172	50 388 916	69 049	100. 00	91. 80	14. 30	100. 00
连云港市	Lianyungang	地级市	7 615	520. 2	439. 35	150	17 854 217	40 416	100. 00	83. 81	14. 10	100. 00
淮安市	Huai'an	地级市	10 072	553. 0	480. 17	140	21 558 600	44 774	98. 60	79. 50	12. 99	79. 34
盐城市	Yancheng	地级市	16 972	823. 8	726. 22	96	34 755 000	48 150	100. 00	86. 03	12. 04	100. 00
扬州市	Yangzhou	地级市	6 591	459. 8	446. 01	132	32 520 078	72 775	100. 00	93. 05	17. 33	100. 00
镇江市	Zhenjiang	地级市	3 847	271. 8	311. 41	128	29 272 800	92 627	100. 00	92. 61	17. 80	100. 00
泰州市	Taizhou	地级市	5 787	507. 8	461. 89	96	30 069 100	64 917	100. 00	89. 44	9. 28	100. 00
宿迁市	Suqian	地级市	8 524	572. 1	471. 92	75	17 062 756	35 484	100. 00	90. 07	13. 01	100. 00
江阴市	Jiangyin	县级市	987	121. 7	159. 51	55	27 060 600	222 355	100. 00	93. 82	14. 60	100. 00
宜兴市	Yixing	县级市	1 997	107. 9	123. 55	75	11 902 300	110 309	100. 00	87. 95	15. 82	100. 00
新沂市	Xinyi	县级市	1 571	109. 7	92. 06	34	4 122 200	37 577	85. 63	75. 54	8. 39	95. 88
邳州市	Pizhou	县级市	2 088	183. 0	145. 80	43	5 991 400	32 740	97. 75	62. 99	11. 83	100. 00
溧阳市	Liyang	县级市	1 535	79. 0	74. 95	26	6 372 000	80 658	100. 00	93. 81	12. 03	100. 00
金坛市	Jintan	县级市	976	55. 2	55. 20	22	4 061 200	73 572	100. 00	90. 02	12. 10	100. 00
常熟市	Changshu	县级市	1 276	106. 7	151. 05	98	19 803 100	185 596	100. 00	91. 21	19. 44	100. 00
张家港市	Zhangjiagang	县级市	990	91. 5	124. 68	68	21 453 100	234 460	100. 00	92. 02	14. 06	100. 00
昆山市	Kunshan	县级市	932	75. 3	164. 49	72	29 200 800	387 793	100. 00	94. 06	14. 95	100. 00
太仓市	Taicang	县级市	823	47. 5	71. 19	48	10 022 800	211 006	100. 00	91. 52	13. 57	100. 00
启东市	Qidong	县级市	1 208	112. 4	97. 25	24	6 583 100	58 569	100. 00	81. 80	10. 20	100. 00
如皋市	Rugao	县级市	1 492	143. 2	126. 71	31	6 570 100	45 881	100. 00	86. 62	11. 53	100. 00
海门市	Haimen	县级市	939	100. 1	90. 76	24	7 400 100	73 927	100. 00	86. 24	10. 26	100. 00

续表

城市名称 Name of cities		行政级别 Admini-strative level	行政区域土地面积(平方公里) Total land area of city's administrative region(sq. km)	年末总人口(万人) Total population at year-end (10 000 persons)	六普常住人口(万人) Total residents of the Sixth National Population Census (10 000 persons)	建成区面积(平方公里) Area of built-up district (sq. km)	地区生产总值(万元) Gross regional product (10 000 yuan)	人均地区生产总值(元) Per capita gross regional product(yuan)	用水普及率(%) Water coverage rate(%)	污水处理率(%) Wastewater treatment rate(%)	人均公园绿地面积(平方米) Per capita public green space(sq. m)	生活垃圾处理率(%) Domestic garbage treatment rate(%)
东台市	Dongtai	县级市	3 221	113. 6	99. 03	35	5 640 900	49 656	100. 00	81. 71	12. 60	100. 00
大丰市	Dafeng	县级市	3 059	72. 5	70. 67	27	4 435 200	61 175	100. 00	80. 64	10. 14	100. 00
仪征市	Yizheng	县级市	902	56. 4	56. 40	39	4 101 600	72 723	100. 00	89. 57	9. 56	100. 00
高邮市	Gaoyou	县级市	1 922	81. 8	74. 47	25	3 815 000	46 638	100. 00	83. 63	9. 99	100. 00
丹阳市	Danyang	县级市	1 047	81. 3	96. 07	26	9 251 500	113 795	100. 00	85. 43	9. 71	100. 00
扬中市	Yangzhong	县级市	331	28. 2	33. 50	13	3 951 000	140 106	100. 00	90. 98	10. 48	100. 00
句容市	Jurong	县级市	1 387	58. 9	61. 77	24	3 856 500	65 475	100. 00	85. 78	11. 45	100. 00
兴化市	Xinghua	县级市	2 395	157. 8	125. 35	36	5 758 400	36 492	100. 00	87. 53	13. 15	100. 00
靖江市	Jingjiang	县级市	656	66. 8	68. 44	34	6 704 300	100 364	100. 00	85. 39	11. 13	100. 00
泰兴市	Taixing	县级市	1 170	120. 0	107. 39	25	6 106 100	50 884	100. 00	88. 77	9. 40	100. 00
浙江省	Zhejiang											
杭州市	Hangzhou	副省级市	16 596	706. 6	870. 04	462	83 435 193	94 566	100. 00	95. 50	15. 13	100. 00
宁波市	Ningbo	副省级市	9 816	580. 2	760. 57	295	71 288 672	93 176	100. 00	90. 32	10. 58	100. 00
温州市	Wenzhou	地级市	11 784	807. 2	912. 21	205	40 038 617	43 632	100. 00	88. 30	11. 32	100. 00
嘉兴市	Jiaxing	地级市	3 915	345. 9	450. 17	93	31 476 636	69 164	100. 00	90. 38	13. 50	100. 00
湖州市	Huzhou	地级市	5 824	262. 5	289. 35	92	18 031 501	61 953	100. 00	91. 01	16. 51	100. 00
绍兴市	Shaoxing	地级市	8 279	441. 7	491. 22	197	39 672 887	80 212	100. 00	88. 26	13. 38	100. 00
金华市	Jinhua	地级市	10 942	473. 4	536. 16	77	29 587 771	62 688	97. 73	89. 01	11. 61	98. 73
衢州市	Quzhou	地级市	8 845	254. 2	212. 27	67	10 565 716	41 676	100. 00	88. 23	14. 11	100. 00
舟山市	Zhoushan	地级市	1 455	97. 3	112. 13	60	9 308 493	81 582	99. 89	86. 21	13. 34	100. 00
台州市	Taizhou	地级市	9 411	594. 0	596. 88	116	31 533 369	52 368	100. 00	89. 09	11. 60	100. 00
丽水市	Lishui	地级市	17 308	263. 9	211. 70	33	9 830 769	46 383	100. 00	87. 50	10. 76	100. 00
建德市	Jiande	县级市	2 364	50. 9	43. 08	9	2 716 954	53 378	100. 00	87. 41	11. 62	100. 00

续表

城市名称 Name of cities		行政级别 Admini-strative level	行政区域土地面积(平方公里) Total land area of city's administrative region(sq. km)	年末总人口(万人) Total population at year-end (10 000 persons)	六普常住人口(万人) Total residents of the Sixth National Population Census (10 000 persons)	建成区面积(平方公里) Area of built-up district (sq. km)	地区生产总值(万元) Gross regional product (10 000 yuan)	人均地区生产总值(元) Per capita gross regional product(yuan)	用水普及率(%) Water coverage rate(%)	污水处理率(%) Wastewater treatment rate(%)	人均公园绿地面积(平方米) Per capita public green space(sq. m)	生活垃圾处理率(%) Domestic garbage treatment rate(%)
富阳市	Fuyang	县级市	1 808	65. 9	71. 77	25	5 713 954	86 706	100. 00	85. 46	8. 61	100. 00
临安市	Lin'an	县级市	3 124	52. 7	56. 67	15	4 092 264	77 652	100. 00	90. 07	9. 29	100. 00
余姚市	Yuyao	县级市	1 527	83. 5	101. 07	49	7 496 274	89 776	100. 00	85. 02	10. 27	95. 00
慈溪市	Cixi	县级市	1 361	104. 4	146. 24	43	10 310 947	98 764	100. 00	85. 00	13. 01	100. 00
奉化市	Fenghua	县级市	1 268	48. 4	49. 17	19	2 903 589	59 992	100. 00	85. 15	12. 03	100. 00
瑞安市	Rui'an	县级市	1 271	122. 3	142. 47	23	6 359 498	51 999	100. 00	87. 99	11. 78	100. 00
乐清市	Leqing	县级市	1 174	127. 8	138. 93	20	6 579 239	51 481	100. 00	44. 54	6. 70	85. 94
海宁市	Haining	县级市	668	66. 9	80. 70	35	6 336 483	94 716	100. 00	90. 00	14. 58	100. 00
平湖市	Pinghu	县级市	537	49. 0	67. 18	19	4 613 064	94 144	100. 00	89. 74	12. 48	100. 00
桐乡市	Tongxiang	县级市	727	68. 3	81. 58	39	5 734 665	83 963	100. 00	90. 02	14. 80	100. 00
诸暨市	Zhuji	县级市	2 311	107. 7	115. 79	38	9 008 773	83 647	100. 00	85. 10	11. 06	100. 00
嵊州市	Shengzhou	县级市	1 790	73. 4	67. 98	41	3 963 787	54 003	100. 00	79. 56	10. 74	100. 00
兰溪市	Lanxi	县级市	1 312	66. 7	56. 05	34	2 512 945	37 675	100. 00	82. 02	9. 63	100. 00
义乌市	Yiwu	县级市	1 105	76. 0	123. 40	101	8 828 716	116 167	100. 00	89. 01	11. 02	100. 00
东阳市	Dongyang	县级市	1 747	83. 1	80. 44	37	4 039 146	48 606	100. 00	85. 03	9. 79	100. 00
永康市	Yongkang	县级市	1 047	58. 5	72. 35	35	4 225 621	72 233	100. 00	82. 11	9. 55	95. 03
江山市	Jiangshan	县级市	2 019	60. 7	46. 79	16	2 352 485	38 756	100. 00	85. 95	11. 32	100. 00
温岭市	Wenling	县级市	836	121. 1	136. 68	33	7 482 779	61 790	100. 00	89. 22	11. 90	100. 00
临海市	Linhai	县级市	2 171	118. 5	102. 88	41	4 204 419	35 480	100. 00	88. 72	12. 78	100. 00
龙泉市	Longquan	县级市	3 059	28. 9	23. 46	14	958 870	33 179	100. 00	85. 47	12. 81	100. 00
安徽省	Anhui											
合肥市	Hefei	地级市	11 445	711. 5	570. 25	393	46 729 100	61 555	99. 78	98. 80	11. 76	100. 00
芜湖市	Wuhu	地级市	5 988	384. 5	226. 31	155	20 995 271	54 676	100. 00	93. 99	13. 80	96. 20

续表

城市名称 Name of cities		行政级别 Admini-strative level	行政区域土地面积（平方公里）Total land area of city's administrative region (sq. km)	年末总人口（万人）Total population at year-end (10 000 persons)	六普常住人口（万人）Total residents of the Sixth National Population Census (10 000 persons)	建成区面积（平方公里）Area of built-up district (sq. km)	地区生产总值（万元）Gross regional product (10 000 yuan)	人均地区生产总值（元）Per capita gross regional product (yuan)	用水普及率（%）Water coverage rate (%)	污水处理率（%）Wastewater treatment rate (%)	人均公园绿地面积（平方米）Per capita public green space (sq. m)	生活垃圾处理率（%）Domestic garbage treatment rate (%)
蚌埠市	Bengbu	地级市	5 952	366. 6	316. 45	119	10 078 541	31 482	100. 00	99. 95	11. 16	100. 00
淮南市	Huainan	地级市	2 584	243. 3	233. 39	106	8 193 895	34 897	99. 17	98. 18	12. 00	98. 13
马鞍山市	Maanshan	地级市	4 049	228. 4	136. 63	89	12 928 032	58 733	100. 00	97. 36	15. 71	97. 50
淮北市	Huaibei	地级市	2 741	214. 5	211. 43	80	7 036 634	32 996	99. 03	97. 68	14. 86	100. 00
铜陵市	Tongling	地级市	1 201	74. 2	72. 40	69	6 806 000	92 599	100. 00	85. 51	14. 34	100. 00
安庆市	Anqing	地级市	15 318	621. 7	531. 14	81	14 182 282	26 596	100. 00	97. 91	11. 93	98. 16
黄山市	Huangshan	地级市	9 807	147. 4	135. 90	60	4 702 965	34 721	98. 69	91. 36	14. 96	100. 00
滁州市	Chuzhou	地级市	13 516	449. 5	393. 79	83	10 861 431	27 474	99. 87	95. 28	13. 24	100. 00
阜阳市	Fuyang	地级市	9 776	1 053. 2	759. 99	98	10 624 758	13 839	92. 76	90. 01	10. 01	94. 00
宿州市	Suzhou	地级市	9 787	641. 9	535. 29	70	10 143 289	18 768	99. 96	99. 10	11. 73	98. 70
六安市	Lu'an	地级市	18 011	716. 7	561. 17	70	10 103 100	17 828	99. 49	91. 14	14. 06	100. 00
亳州市	Bozhou	地级市	8 374	632. 9	485. 07	49	7 910 950	16 071	91. 22	96. 91	11. 50	100. 00
池州市	Chizhou	地级市	8 272	161. 9	140. 25	37	4 622 452	32 541	99. 01	91. 38	17. 08	99. 91
宣城市	Xuancheng	地级市	12 453	280. 2	253. 29	49	8 428 049	32 928	99. 11	87. 20	12. 54	100. 00
巢湖市	Chaohu	县级市	2 046	88. 0	78. 07	47	2 352 983	26 738	95. 03	86. 99	12. 36	100. 00
桐城市	Tongcheng	县级市	1 546	75. 9	66. 45	26	2 001 458	26 370	93. 15	84. 85	8. 64	100. 00
天长市	Tianchang	县级市	1 751	63. 0	60. 28	29	2 372 544	37 659	86. 22	99. 93	14. 79	100. 00
明光市	Mingguang	县级市	2 335	64. 0	53. 27	25	1 024 263	16 004	90. 72	97. 06	4. 84	95. 27
界首市	Jieshou	县级市	667	79. 9	56. 20	18	1 125 725	14 089	85. 86	93. 65	4. 60	96. 76
宁国市	Ningguo	县级市	2 487	39. 0	37. 69	26	2 039 633	52 298	98. 00	97. 23	11. 46	100. 00
福建省	Fujian											
福州市	Fuzhou	地级市	13 066	655. 5	711. 54	248	46 784 951	64 045	99. 99	86. 37	12. 84	98. 97
厦门市	Xiamen	副省级市	1 573	196. 8	353. 13	282	30 181 565	81 572	100. 00	91. 62	11. 47	99. 20

续表

城市名称 Name of cities		行政级别 Administrative level	行政区域土地面积(平方公里) Total land area of city's administrative region(sq. km)	年末总人口(万人) Total population at year-end (10 000 persons)	六普常住人口(万人) Total residents of the Sixth National Population Census (10 000 persons)	建成区面积(平方公里) Area of built-up district (sq. km)	地区生产总值(万元) Gross regional product (10 000 yuan)	人均地区生产总值(元) Per capita gross regional product(yuan)	用水普及率(%) Water coverage rate(%)	污水处理率(%) Wastewater treatment rate(%)	人均公园绿地面积(平方米) Per capita public green space(sq. m)	生活垃圾处理率(%) Domestic garbage treatment rate(%)
莆田市	Putian	地级市	4 131	334. 2	277. 85	55	13 428 623	47 619	99. 64	85. 51	12. 72	99. 10
三明市	Sanming	地级市	22 965	278. 5	250. 34	34	14 775 868	58 986	99. 87	84. 70	12. 82	97. 85
泉州市	Quanzhou	地级市	11 015	703. 5	812. 85	205	52 180 021	62 679	98. 84	87. 20	13. 90	99. 21
漳州市	Zhangzhou	地级市	12 554	489. 5	481. 00	59	22 360 244	45 494	99. 78	89. 03	13. 59	99. 06
南平市	Nanping	地级市	26 280	316. 0	264. 55	28	11 058 215	42 127	100. 00	88. 97	13. 75	99. 00
龙岩市	Longyan	地级市	19 063	302. 6	255. 95	45	14 798 988	57 472	99. 61	89. 36	12. 05	99. 09
宁德市	Ningde	地级市	13 452	347. 2	282. 20	25	12 387 205	43 617	99. 16	86. 98	13. 94	91. 01
福清市	Fuqing	县级市	1 518	131. 9	123. 48	44	6 671 851	50 583	99. 94	86. 26	12. 28	98. 92
长乐市	Changle	县级市	664	70. 4	68. 26	22	4 845 667	68 830	99. 50	80. 00	16. 90	90. 50
永安市	Yong'an	县级市	2 931	33. 0	34. 70	23	2 699 889	81 815	98. 11	85. 53	10. 09	97. 98
石狮市	Shishi	县级市	160	32. 2	63. 67	30	5 709 125	177 302	99. 97	86. 00	12. 89	98. 97
晋江市	Jinjiang	县级市	650	109. 0	198. 64	38	13 637 774	125 117	99. 34	86. 21	10. 24	98. 85
南安市	Nan'an	县级市	1 985	154. 4	141. 85	31	7 096 127	45 959	92. 59	81. 20	10. 25	98. 95
龙海市	Longhai	县级市	1 316	84. 0	87. 78	19	5 199 643	61 901	98. 81	80. 51	14. 99	98. 41
邵武市	Shaowu	县级市	2 859	30. 7	27. 51	18	1 641 971	53 484	100. 00	88. 42	15. 45	96. 11
武夷山市	Wuyishan	县级市	2 814	23. 5	23. 36	9	1 098 287	46 736	96. 99	85. 98	14. 16	100. 00
建瓯市	Jian'ou	县级市	4 233	54. 5	45. 22	13	1 583 867	29 062	98. 47	66. 91	11. 30	100. 00
建阳市	Jianyang	县级市	3 379	34. 8	28. 94	11	1 250 202	35 925	99. 25	85. 86	16. 00	100. 00
漳平市	Zhangping	县级市	2 976	28. 8	24. 02	10	1 547 409	53 729	96. 52	81. 49	14. 97	98. 20
福安市	Fu'an	县级市	1 880	66. 3	56. 36	13	3 069 108	46 291	99. 12	81. 47	11. 75	90. 50
福鼎市	Fuding	县级市	1 530	59. 0	52. 95	19	2 481 179	42 054	98. 99	83. 75	10. 63	90. 60
江西省	Jiangxi											
南昌市	Nanchang	地级市	7 402	510. 1	504. 26	250	33 360 265	64 678	98. 85	90. 97	12. 04	99. 99

续表

城市名称 Name of cities		行政级别 Administrative level	行政区域土地面积（平方公里）Total land area of city's administrative region(sq. km)	年末总人口（万人）Total population at year-end (10 000 persons)	六普常住人口（万人）Total residents of the Sixth National Population Census (10 000 persons)	建成区面积（平方公里）Area of built-up district (sq. km)	地区生产总值（万元）Gross regional product (10 000 yuan)	人均地区生产总值（元）Per capita gross regional product(yuan)	用水普及率（%）Water coverage rate(%)	污水处理率（%）Wastewater treatment rate(%)	人均公园绿地面积（平方米）Per capita public green space(sq. m)	生活垃圾处理率（%）Domestic garbage treatment rate(%)
景德镇市	Jingdezhen	地级市	5 261	166. 3	158. 75	79	6 802 847	42 130	99. 80	71. 34	14. 92	100. 00
萍乡市	Pingxiang	地级市	3 831	193. 6	185. 45	51	7 983 294	42 515	100. 00	82. 99	10. 73	100. 00
九江市	Jiujiang	地级市	19 078	508. 1	472. 88	100	16 017 317	33 500	100. 00	99. 43	17. 23	100. 00
新余市	Xinyu	地级市	3 178	121. 5	113. 89	72	8 450 692	73 275	100. 00	100. 00	18. 18	100. 00
鹰潭市	Yingtan	地级市	3 560	124. 7	112. 52	33	5 534 700	48 542	96. 73	93. 78	14. 27	100. 00
赣州市	Ganzhou	地级市	39 379	928. 5	836. 84	95	16 733 140	19 768	99. 78	46. 37	12. 23	100. 00
吉安市	Ji'an	地级市	25 283	509. 1	481. 03	50	11 239 013	23 521	93. 15	90. 87	16. 97	100. 00
宜春市	Yichun	地级市	18 669	578. 1	541. 96	65	13 870 708	25 352	95. 18	93. 15	14. 99	100. 00
抚州市	Fuzhou	地级市	18 799	419. 6	391. 23	56	9 406 413	23 780	99. 08	91. 12	16. 64	100. 00
上饶市	Shangrao	地级市	22 791	759. 7	657. 97	48	14 013 134	21 061	99. 72	90. 32	14. 31	100. 00
乐平市	Leping	县级市	1 974	92. 2	81. 04	19	2 384 353	25 861	98. 58	78. 42	17. 71	100. 00
瑞昌市	Ruichang	县级市	1 423	46. 0	41. 90	19	1 259 752	27 386	100. 00	95. 63	12. 47	100. 00
共青城市	Gongqingcheng	县级市	308	7. 0		14	672 513	96 073	76. 09	94. 38	25. 18	100. 00
贵溪市	Guixi	县级市	2 493	62. 8	55. 85	29	3 147 421	50 118	97. 26	41. 86	11. 93	100. 00
瑞金市	Ruijin	县级市	2 448	67. 8	61. 89	25	1 010 897	14 910	91. 80	58. 39	13. 95	100. 00
南康市	Nankang	县级市	1 740	83. 3	78. 76	30	1 372 921	16 482	99. 40	55. 85	13. 21	100. 00
井冈山市	Jinggangshan	县级市	1 276	16. 4	15. 23	9	492 838	30 051	83. 33	90. 05	48. 81	100. 00
丰城市	Fengcheng	县级市	2 845	141. 8	133. 64	46	3 408 687	24 039	91. 04	72. 54	12. 31	100. 00
樟树市	Zhangshu	县级市	1 289	59. 3	55. 51	26	2 667 382	44 981	87. 23	69. 64	12. 37	100. 00
高安市	Gao'an	县级市	2 429	85. 4	81. 16	26	1 664 737	19 493	99. 83	10. 63	13. 89	100. 00
德兴市	Dexing	县级市	2 082	33. 0	29. 32	11	975 500	29 561	99. 07	75. 10	18. 11	100. 00
山东省	Shandong											
济南市	Jinan	副省级市	8 177	613. 3	681. 40	372	52 301 948	74 993	100. 00	98. 79	10. 35	94. 82

续表

城市名称 Name of cities		行政级别 Administrative level	行政区域土地面积(平方公里) Total land area of city's administrative region(sq. km)	年末总人口(万人) Total population at year-end (10 000 persons)	六普常住人口(万人) Total residents of the Sixth National Population Census (10 000 persons)	建成区面积(平方公里) Area of built-up district (sq. km)	地区生产总值(万元) Gross regional product (10 000 yuan)	人均地区生产总值(元) Per capita gross regional product(yuan)	用水普及率(%) Water coverage rate(%)	污水处理率(%) Wastewater treatment rate(%)	人均公园绿地面积(平方米) Per capita public green space(sq. m)	生活垃圾处理率(%) Domestic garbage treatment rate(%)
青岛市	Qingdao	副省级市	11 282	773. 7	871. 51	470	80 066 000	89 797	100. 00	94. 38	14. 58	100. 00
淄博市	Zibo	地级市	5 965	425. 3	453. 06	251	38 012 400	82 889	100. 00	95. 10	15. 79	100. 00
枣庄市	Zaozhuang	地级市	4 563	396. 0	372. 91	146	18 306 300	48 346	99. 26	93. 14	14. 58	100. 00
东营市	Dongying	地级市	8 243	187. 0	203. 53	113	32 502 000	156 356	100. 00	93. 78	20. 90	100. 00
烟台市	Yantai	地级市	13 852	651. 2	696. 82	276	56 138 700	80 358	100. 00	95. 24	23. 45	100. 00
潍坊市	Weifang	地级市	16 143	882. 9	908. 62	171	44 207 000	47 943	100. 00	93. 15	17. 74	100. 00
济宁市	Jining	地级市	11 311	847. 8	808. 19	176	35 015 400	42 796	100. 00	93. 58	13. 68	100. 00
泰安市	Tai'an	地级市	7 762	558. 8	549. 42	121	27 907 000	50 296	100. 00	94. 43	19. 88	100. 00
威海市	Weihai	地级市	5 786	253. 8	280. 48	142	25 496 900	91 010	100. 00	93. 90	25. 18	100. 00
日照市	Rizhao	地级市	5 359	290. 1	280. 10	97	15 001 600	52 778	100. 00	94. 13	22. 33	100. 00
莱芜市	Laiwu	地级市	2 246	126. 5	129. 85	120	6 534 800	49 390	100. 00	94. 28	18. 96	100. 00
临沂市	Linyi	地级市	17 191	1 090. 4	1 003. 94	195	33 368 100	32 902	100. 00	94. 06	18. 90	100. 00
德州市	Dezhou	地级市	10 356	578. 8	556. 82	128	24 605 900	43 542	100. 00	94. 97	24. 48	100. 00
聊城市	Liaocheng	地级市	8 984	597. 5	578. 99	74	23 658 700	40 083	99. 11	94. 62	13. 05	100. 00
滨州市	Binzhou	地级市	9 660	381. 6	374. 85	83	21 557 271	56 770	100. 00	91. 14	18. 68	100. 00
菏泽市	Heze	地级市	12 239	957. 5	828. 77	90	20 500 100	24 542	98. 19	89. 57	11. 76	100. 00
章丘市	Zhangqiu	县级市	1 855	101. 9	106. 42	42	7 552 384	74 116	100. 00	85. 09	16. 80	100. 00
胶州市	Jiaozhou	县级市	1 324	81. 6	84. 31	49	8 367 300	102 540	100. 00	96. 84	12. 14	100. 00
即墨市	Jimo	县级市	1 780	113. 8	117. 72	57	8 781 605	77 167	100. 00	96. 12	12. 42	100. 00
平度市	Pingdu	县级市	3 176	138. 1	135. 74	54	7 901 066	57 213	100. 00	94. 52	10. 44	100. 00
莱西市	Laixi	县级市	1 568	73. 8	75. 02	32	5 949 143	80 612	100. 00	97. 00	14. 56	100. 00
滕州市	Tengzhou	县级市	1 495	169. 3	160. 37	51	9 026 354	53 316	99. 97	93. 42	13. 54	100. 00
龙口市	Longkou	县级市	901	63. 5	68. 83	41	9 352 321	147 281	99. 97	97. 00	14. 94	100. 00

续表

城市名称 Name of cities		行政级别 Admini-strative level	行政区域土地面积（平方公里）Total land area of city's administrative region(sq. km)	年末总人口（万人）Total population at year-end (10 000 persons)	六普常住人口（万人）Total residents of the Sixth National Population Census (10 000 persons)	建成区面积（平方公里）Area of built-up district (sq. km)	地区生产总值（万元）Gross regional product (10 000 yuan)	人均地区生产总值（元）Per capita gross regional product(yuan)	用水普及率（%）Water coverage rate(%)	污水处理率（%）Wastewater treatment rate(%)	人均公园绿地面积（平方米）Per capita public green space(sq. m)	生活垃圾处理率（%）Domestic garbage treatment rate(%)
莱阳市	Laiyang	县级市	1 732	86.6	87.86	42	3 031 711	35 008	99.75	96.99	13.80	100.00
莱州市	Laizhou	县级市	1 928	85.4	88.39	41	6 426 583	75 253	100.00	97.01	14.60	100.00
蓬莱市	Penglai	县级市	1 129	44.9	45.11	26	4 575 547	101 905	94.10	95.70	14.03	100.00
招远市	Zhaoyuan	县级市	1 432	56.7	56.62	31	6 047 971	106 666	100.00	90.06	17.49	100.00
栖霞市	Qixia	县级市	2 016	58.8	58.96	17	2 210 767	37 598	98.72	97.01	12.50	100.00
海阳市	Haiyang	县级市	1 909	66.0	63.87	34	3 025 800	45 845	99.61	88.81	14.71	100.00
青州市	Qingzhou	县级市	1 569	92.5	94.04	49	5 042 686	54 516	100.00	97.02	25.50	100.00
诸城市	Zhucheng	县级市	2 151	109.1	108.62	47	6 427 183	58 911	100.00	97.01	23.56	100.00
寿光市	Shouguang	县级市	1 990	105.8	113.95	39	7 012 793	66 283	100.00	97.00	23.46	100.00
安丘市	Anqiu	县级市	1 712	95.3	92.69	40	2 479 398	26 017	100.00	96.99	26.87	100.00
高密市	Gaomi	县级市	1 527	87.9	89.56	49	5 013 619	57 038	100.00	97.00	23.82	100.00
昌邑市	Changyi	县级市	1 628	58.3	60.35	25	3 265 043	56 004	100.00	97.00	20.93	100.00
曲阜市	Qufu	县级市	815	63.5	64.05	27	3 316 635	52 230	100.00	95.19	15.00	100.00
邹城市	Zoucheng	县级市	1 616	116.0	111.67	41	7 315 800	63 067	100.00	92.35	14.46	100.00
新泰市	Xintai	县级市	1 934	138.7	131.59	67	7 650 000	55 155	100.00	96.23	20.28	100.00
肥城市	Feicheng	县级市	1 277	98.7	94.66	32	6 744 631	68 335	100.00	97.02	20.85	100.00
文登市	Wendeng	县级市	1 829	64.3	67.36	45	6 350 774	98 768	100.00	97.01	22.65	100.00
荣成市	Rongcheng	县级市	1 526	66.9	71.44	47	8 785 911	131 329	100.00	97.01	22.76	100.00
乳山市	Rushan	县级市	1 665	56.4	57.25	32	3 997 649	70 880	100.00	93.96	18.31	100.00
乐陵市	Leling	县级市	1 173	70.0	65.24	33	2 136 368	30 520	99.82	90.35	11.18	100.00
禹城市	Yucheng	县级市	992	52.7	49.00	31	2 335 377	44 315	97.86	96.98	15.66	100.00
临清市	Linqing	县级市	950	76.3	71.96	26	3 358 000	44 010	99.64	94.54	12.96	100.00
河南省	Henan											
郑州市	Zhengzhou	地级市	7 446	919.1	862.71	383	62 019 000	68 070	100.00	95.86	6.65	89.72

续表

城市名称 Name of cities		行政级别 Admini-strative level	行政区域土地面积(平方公里) Total land area of city's administrative region(sq. km)	年末总人口(万人) Total population at year - end (10 000 persons)	六普常住人口(万人) Total residents of the Sixth National Population Census (10 000 persons)	建成区面积(平方公里) Area of built - up district (sq. km)	地区生产总值(万元) Gross regional product (10 000 yuan)	人均地区生产总值(元) Per capita gross regional product(yuan)	用水普及率(%) Water coverage rate(%)	污水处理率(%) Wastewater treatment rate(%)	人均公园绿地面积(平方米) Per capita public green space(sq. m)	生活垃圾处理率(%) Domestic garbage treatment rate(%)
开封市	Kaifeng	地级市	6 444	553. 1	467. 65	113	13 635 447	29 327	97. 58	73. 39	8. 98	68. 38
洛阳市	Luoyang	地级市	15 236	692. 3	654. 99	192	31 407 596	47 569	98. 83	98. 57	7. 39	83. 72
平顶山市	Pingdingshan	地级市	7 904	537. 5	490. 47	73	15 568 788	31 521	96. 91	89. 99	10. 25	92. 10
安阳市	Anyang	地级市	7 352	602. 0	517. 32	110	16 836 494	33 100	100. 00	97. 71	9. 75	100. 00
鹤壁市	Hebi	地级市	2 182	165. 9	156. 92	64	6 221 183	37 493	93. 65	83. 01	14. 39	92. 50
新乡市	Xinxiang	地级市	8 552	625. 0	570. 82	110	17 660 960	31 138	99. 08	90. 00	10. 20	100. 00
焦作市	Jiaozuo	地级市	4 071	367. 8	354. 01	108	17 073 608	48 545	99. 83	87. 30	10. 08	97. 32
濮阳市	Puyang	地级市	4 136	417. 3	359. 87	50	11 304 789	31 483	91. 49	89. 08	13. 36	90. 96
许昌市	Xuchang	地级市	4 996	499. 0	430. 75	92	18 775 574	44 298	96. 85	96. 97	10. 40	96. 29
漯河市	Luohe	地级市	2 617	274. 2	254. 43	61	8 615 355	33 568	91. 45	95. 03	14. 78	100. 00
三门峡市	Sanmenxia	地级市	10 496	226. 8	223. 40	30	11 920 868	53 299	98. 05	92. 68	14. 65	87. 39
南阳市	Nanyang	地级市	26 509	1 171. 0	1 026. 37	149	24 992 201	24 697	68. 55	92. 65	17. 30	68. 25
商丘市	Shangqiu	地级市	10 704	942. 6	736. 30	62	15 382 197	21 073	61. 92	86. 62	6. 05	84. 87
信阳市	Xinyang	地级市	18 915	859. 8	610. 91	84	15 811 632	24 762	96. 21	96. 91	14. 14	92. 73
周口市	Zhoukou	地级市	11 961	1 130. 8	895. 38	63	17 906 548	20 359	95. 80	80. 04	10. 36	92. 09
驻马店市	Zhumadian	地级市	15 083	896. 0	723. 12	69	15 420 210	22 296	81. 64	92. 06	10. 05	91. 89
巩义市	Gongyi	县级市	1 041	82. 8	80. 79	28	5 812 240	70 196	97. 01	49. 50	12. 98	100. 00
荥阳市	Xingyang	县级市	943	67. 0	61. 38	23	5 200 436	77 618	91. 80	96. 28	11. 20	98. 51
新密市	Xinmi	县级市	1 001	88. 0	79. 73	23	5 598 318	63 617	90. 85	84. 98	13. 24	100. 00
新郑市	Xinzheng	县级市	887	67. 0	75. 81	30	6 064 742	90 519	64. 26	85. 25	7. 95	100. 00
登封市	Dengfeng	县级市	1 217	71. 0	66. 86	22	4 509 039	63 508	74. 09	91. 94	9. 12	92. 03
偃师市	Yanshi	县级市	668	60. 0	66. 67	18	3 569 317	59 489	95. 18	92. 00	9. 12	100. 00
舞钢市	Wugang	县级市	641	33. 7	31. 38	16	1 019 214	30 244	97. 14	84. 27	11. 94	99. 98

续表

城市名称 Name of cities		行政级别 Admini-strative level	行政区域土地面积（平方公里）Total land area of city's administrative region (sq. km)	年末总人口（万人）Total population at year – end (10 000 persons)	六普常住人口（万人）Total residents of the Sixth National Population Census (10 000 persons)	建成区面积（平方公里）Area of built – up district (sq. km)	地区生产总值（万元）Gross regional product (10 000 yuan)	人均地区生产总值（元）Per capita gross regional product (yuan)	用水普及率（%）Water coverage rate (%)	污水处理率（%）Wastewater treatment rate (%)	人均公园绿地面积（平方米）Per capita public green space (sq. m)	生活垃圾处理率（%）Domestic garbage treatment rate (%)
汝州市	Ruzhou	县级市	1 573	106.5	92.79	33	3 316 636	31 142	49.92	97.24	8.17	98.82
林州市	Linzhou	县级市	2 046	109.2	78.97	22	4 241 275	38 840	92.84	70.60	10.54	100.00
卫辉市	Weihui	县级市	859	52.0	49.57	20	1 064 233	20 466	99.14	100.00	7.99	100.00
辉县市	Huixian	县级市	2 007	84.8	74.04	22	2 895 949	34 150	96.18	92.03	6.98	100.00
沁阳市	Qinyang	县级市	624	47.8	44.77	20	3 299 309	69 023	93.38	80.19	8.40	93.10
孟州市	Mengzhou	县级市	542	38.1	36.71	15	2 458 415	64 525	96.30	97.47	10.00	93.18
禹州市	Yuzhou	县级市	1 461	129.3	113.19	43	4 522 527	34 977	90.92	99.70	8.10	74.55
长葛市	Changge	县级市	650	77.5	68.71	25	4 108 512	53 013	86.28	98.45	14.88	97.60
义马市	Yima	县级市	112	16.4	14.48	18	1 617 805	98 647	89.65	9.53	11.14	68.42
灵宝市	Lingbao	县级市	3 011	74.8	72.10	21	4 686 371	62 652	95.21	81.44	10.27	98.23
邓州市	Dengzhou	县级市	2 369	175.4	146.82	32	3 070 589	17 506	70.01	88.04	5.71	91.14
永城市	Yongcheng	县级市	2 006	152.8	124.04	35	4 024 390	26 338	80.12	94.81	11.38	91.07
项城市	Xiangcheng	县级市	1 083	133.8	100.37	30	2 213 923	16 547	99.40	90.73	10.53	95.19
济源市	Jiyuan	县级市	1 894	69.6	67.58	43	4 601 336	66 111	99.93	96.22	12.03	100.00
湖北省	Hubei											
武汉市	Wuhan	副省级市	8 494	822.1	978.54	534	90 512 700	89 000	100.00	95.40	10.54	100.00
黄石市	Huangshi	地级市	4 583	262.3	242.93	88	11 420 300	46 750	100.00	92.40	12.37	100.00
十堰市	Shiyan	地级市	23 680	346.7	334.08	72	10 805 900	32 094	96.40	92.41	11.37	100.00
宜昌市	Yichang	地级市	21 084	400.1	405.97	153	28 180 700	68 846	100.00	91.00	14.15	91.57
襄阳市	Xiangyang	地级市	19 728	595.1	550.03	157	28 140 200	50 512	99.06	91.18	13.86	99.42
鄂州市	Ezhou	地级市	1 596	109.8	104.87	60	6 309 400	59 791	100.00	88.69	14.94	100.00
荆门市	Jingmen	地级市	12 404	300.8	287.37	54	12 026 100	41 668	100.00	85.58	10.00	100.00
孝感市	Xiaogan	地级市	8 910	527.4	481.45	62	12 389 300	25 582	97.03	95.00	11.56	100.00

续表

城市名称 Name of cities		行政级别 Admini-strative level	行政区域土地面积(平方公里) Total land area of city's administrative region(sq. km)	年末总人口(万人) Total population at year - end (10 000 persons)	六普常住人口(万人) Total residents of the Sixth National Population Census (10 000 persons)	建成区面积(平方公里) Area of built - up district (sq. km)	地区生产总值(万元) Gross regional product (10 000 yuan)	人均地区生产总值(元) Per capita gross regional product(yuan)	用水普及率(%) Water coverage rate(%)	污水处理率(%) Wastewater treatment rate(%)	人均公园绿地面积(平方米) Per capita public green space(sq. m)	生活垃圾处理率(%) Domestic garbage treatment rate(%)
荆州市	Jingzhou	地级市	14 099	661. 0	569. 17	72	13 349 300	23 259	99. 02	90. 17	10. 44	100. 00
黄冈市	Huanggang	地级市	17 457	750. 2	616. 21	47	13 325 500	21 314	98. 28	97. 05	13. 09	99. 45
咸宁市	Xianning	地级市	10 027	300. 5	246. 26	72	8 721 100	35 166	91. 51	90. 93	12. 46	100. 00
随州市	Suizhou	地级市	9 636	257. 6	216. 22	45	6 619 400	30 377	93. 09	90. 27	9. 09	95. 52
大冶市	Daye	县级市	1 566	96. 2	90. 97	27	4 559 200	47 393	97. 72	94. 41	5. 30	
丹江口市	Danjiangkou	县级市	3 121	46. 1	44. 38	28	1 507 151	32 693	82. 93	99. 48	8. 68	100. 00
宜都市	Yidu	县级市	1 357	39. 7	38. 46	24	4 028 225	101 467	100. 00	95. 75	13. 38	95. 84
当阳市	Dangyang	县级市	2 159	48. 4	46. 83	20	3 521 672	72 762	97. 80	86. 94	9. 08	100. 00
枝江市	Zhijiang	县级市	1 314	49. 1	49. 60	19	3 419 527	69 644	93. 28	90. 91	8. 71	100. 00
老河口市	Laohekou	县级市	1 032	53. 2	47. 15	27	2 401 709	45 145	100. 00	91. 85	9. 38	95. 69
枣阳市	Zaoyang	县级市	3 277	112. 6	100. 47	38	4 254 331	37 783	100. 00	89. 09	12. 73	100. 00
宜城市	Yicheng	县级市	2 115	56. 8	51. 25	25	2 324 551	40 925	96. 26	84. 00	9. 89	93. 02
钟祥市	Zhongxiang	县级市	4 488	106. 3	102. 25	23	3 323 700	31 267	100. 00	90. 40	11. 42	100. 00
应城市	Yingcheng	县级市	1 103	66. 6	59. 38	24	2 015 176	30 258	92. 16	79. 32	8. 68	95. 24
安陆市	Anlu	县级市	1 355	62. 8	56. 86	20	1 447 867	23 055	92. 54	50. 00	8. 73	100. 00
汉川市	Hanchuan	县级市	1 659	112. 3	101. 55	26	3 447 097	30 695	95. 42	85. 40	6. 20	50. 93
石首市	Shishou	县级市	1 406	66. 6	57. 70	23	1 219 092	18 305	99. 93	93. 05	9. 12	100. 00
洪湖市	Honghu	县级市	2 519	93. 5	81. 94	40	1 634 795	17 484	93. 37	85. 40	12. 47	100. 00
松滋市	Songzi	县级市	2 177	84. 8	76. 59	15	1 792 936	21 143	99. 06	75. 07	10. 78	100. 00
麻城市	Macheng	县级市	3 747	117. 8	84. 91	25	2 018 507	17 135	98. 67	81. 86	9. 38	95. 17
武穴市	Wuxue	县级市	1 246	80. 8	64. 42	29	2 012 511	24 907	98. 18	95. 98	10. 47	98. 15
赤壁市	Chibi	县级市	1 723	52. 8	47. 84	26	2 847 600	53 932	97. 96	83. 00	9. 51	82. 00
广水市	Guangshui	县级市	2 647	94. 7	75. 59	30	2 109 823	22 279	96. 73	62. 24	10. 86	99. 52

续表

城市名称 Name of cities		行政级别 Admini-strative level	行政区域土地面积(平方公里) Total land area of city's administrative region(sq. km)	年末总人口(万人) Total population at year - end (10 000 persons)	六普常住人口(万人) Total residents of the Sixth National Population Census (10 000 persons)	建成区面积(平方公里) Area of built - up district (sq. km)	地区生产总值(万元) Gross regional product (10 000 yuan)	人均地区生产总值(元) Per capita gross regional product(yuan)	用水普及率(%) Water coverage rate(%)	污水处理率(%) Wastewater treatment rate(%)	人均公园绿地面积(平方米) Per capita public green space(sq. m)	生活垃圾处理率(%) Domestic garbage treatment rate(%)
恩施市	Enshi	县级市	3 972	81.4	74.96	33	1 414 951	17 383	93.97	93.02	9.83	100.00
利川市	Lichuan	县级市	4 607	92.4	65.41	18	820 094	8 875	81.24	48.87	6.24	100.00
仙桃市	Xiantao	县级市	2 538	156.1	117.51	43	5 043 585	32 310	100.00	88.15	9.15	100.00
潜江市	Qianjiang	县级市	2 004	103.8	94.63	50	4 927 000	47 466	100.00	85.17	10.02	100.00
天门市	Tianmen	县级市	2 622	163.9	141.89	30	3 651 900	22 281	100.00	86.78	12.70	100.00
湖南省	Hunan											
长沙市	Changsha	地级市	11 816	662.8	704.10	326	71 531 346	99 570	100.00	96.54	9.20	100.00
株洲市	Zhuzhou	地级市	11 262	399.6	385.71	133	19 494 317	49 723	100.00	90.92	10.84	100.00
湘潭市	Xiangtan	地级市	5 008	289.9	275.22	79	14 430 649	51 717	97.69	87.85	9.02	100.00
衡阳市	Hengyang	地级市	15 303	785.9	714.83	159	21 694 404	30 030	95.07	75.58	7.75	100.00
邵阳市	Shaoyang	地级市	20 830	808.3	707.17	56	11 300 386	15 727	94.40	81.18	8.54	95.40
岳阳市	Yueyang	地级市	14 858	560.0	547.61	88	24 355 050	43 953	100.00	88.95	9.23	100.00
常德市	Changde	地级市	18 177	607.2	571.46	86	22 649 358	39 169	95.97	90.31	14.25	100.00
张家界市	Zhangjiajie	地级市	9 516	170.9	147.81	33	3 656 506	24 259	96.86	80.74	9.95	100.00
益阳市	Yiyang	地级市	12 320	480.0	430.79	67	11 231 297	25 773	82.58	82.53	7.93	100.00
郴州市	Chenzhou	地级市	19 342	512.1	458.35	72	16 855 232	36 256	96.63	90.24	11.06	100.00
永州市	Yongzhou	地级市	22 260	622.6	519.43	60	11 754 466	22 210	99.08	81.29	8.10	100.00
怀化市	Huaihua	地级市	27 573	515.0	474.17	61	11 176 674	23 285	97.42	83.44	7.74	91.67
娄底市	Loudi	地级市	8 117	438.6	378.46	46	11 181 729	29 249	99.79	80.33	9.60	100.00
浏阳市	Liuyang	县级市	4 997	144.0	127.95	38	9 242 905	64 187	98.36	100.00	4.89	100.00
醴陵市	Liling	县级市	2 157	106.6	94.74	29	4 421 034	41 473	100.00	82.49	7.24	100.00
湘乡市	Xiangxiang	县级市	1 967	92.1	78.82	20	2 656 934	28 848	96.35	95.05	8.39	89.68
韶山市	Shaoshan	县级市	247	11.9	8.60	5	575 618	48 371	97.69	65.47	9.77	100.00

续表

城市名称 Name of cities		行政级别 Administrative level	行政区域土地面积(平方公里) Total land area of city's administrative region(sq. km)	年末总人口(万人) Total population at year-end (10 000 persons)	六普常住人口(万人) Total residents of the Sixth National Population Census (10 000 persons)	建成区面积(平方公里) Area of built-up district (sq. km)	地区生产总值(万元) Gross regional product (10 000 yuan)	人均地区生产总值(元) Per capita gross regional product(yuan)	用水普及率(%) Water coverage rate(%)	污水处理率(%) Wastewater treatment rate(%)	人均公园绿地面积(平方米) Per capita public green space(sq. m)	生活垃圾处理率(%) Domestic garbage treatment rate(%)
耒阳市	Leiyang	县级市	2 656	139. 3	115. 16	42	3 214 008	23 073	93. 59	81. 03	7. 02	100. 00
常宁市	Changning	县级市	2 064	92. 9	81. 04	16	2 216 755	23 862	93. 02	53. 22	5. 86	41. 03
武冈市	Wugang	县级市	1 549	83. 0	73. 49	16	954 211	11 497	94. 69	72. 47	8. 99	100. 00
汨罗市	Miluo	县级市	1 780	75. 0	69. 21	17	3 289 940	43 866	97. 91	83. 19	7. 60	100. 00
临湘市	Linxiang	县级市	1 754	52. 6	49. 83	16	1 790 214	34 034	96. 34	79. 69	8. 71	100. 00
津市市	Jinshi	县级市	557	27. 0	25. 09	15	969 690	35 914	97. 89	92. 95	7. 43	92. 45
沅江市	Yuanjiang	县级市	2 020	74. 3	66. 63	15	1 951 252	26 262	96. 86	63. 60	4. 46	100. 00
资兴市	Zixing	县级市	2 747	37. 5	33. 73	21	2 473 685	65 965	93. 37	66. 33	10. 22	100. 00
洪江市	Hongjiang	县级市	2 289	49. 8	47. 80	7	823 873	16 544	91. 24	89. 44	14. 88	100. 00
冷水江市	Lengshuijiang	县级市	439	36. 7	32. 71	22	2 364 075	64 416	98. 91	92. 37	12. 06	100. 00
涟源市	Lianyuan	县级市	1 912	115. 6	99. 55	15	2 068 079	17 890	92. 94	93. 19	2. 12	100. 00
吉首市	Jishou	县级市	1 058	30. 5	30. 21	29	1 041 179	34 137	86. 98	91. 26	9. 60	100. 00
广东省	Guangdong											
广州市	Guangzhou	副省级市	7 434	832. 3	1 270. 19	1024	154 201 434	119 695	99. 71	91. 38	19. 92	87. 05
韶关市	Shaoguan	地级市	18 412	328. 0	282. 62	92	10 100 737	35 100	96. 50	81. 46	12. 14	98. 14
深圳市	Shenzhen	副省级市	1 997	310. 5	1 035. 84	871	145 002 302	136 947	100. 00	96. 22	16. 70	98. 36
珠海市	Zhuhai	地级市	1 658	108. 6	156. 25	124	16 623 757	104 786	99. 66	88. 52	18. 50	100. 00
汕头市	Shantou	地级市	2 064	540. 0	538. 93	247	15 659 049	28 661	92. 51	91. 95	13. 90	80. 62
佛山市	Foshan	地级市	3 798	381. 6	719. 74	157	70 101 725	96 310	100. 00	94. 28	12. 13	99. 35
江门市	Jiangmen	地级市	9 505	393. 0	445. 07	158	20 001 764	44 546	97. 70	88. 85	17. 35	100. 00
湛江市	Zhanjiang	地级市	13 261	804. 2	699. 48	108	20 600 069	28 859	97. 55	89. 96	12. 93	100. 00
茂名市	Maoming	地级市	11 426	757. 7	581. 75	103	21 601 686	36 063	99. 84	86. 70	12. 58	93. 81
肇庆市	Zhaoqing	地级市	14 891	429. 8	391. 65	95	16 600 720	41 479	99. 96	94. 10	21. 67	98. 73

续表

城市名称 Name of cities		行政级别 Admini-strative level	行政区域土地面积（平方公里）Total land area of city's administrative region(sq. km)	年末总人口（万人）Total population at year-end (10 000 persons)	六普常住人口（万人）Total residents of the Sixth National Population Census (10 000 persons)	建成区面积（平方公里）Area of built-up district (sq. km)	地区生产总值（万元）Gross regional product (10 000 yuan)	人均地区生产总值（元）Per capita gross regional product(yuan)	用水普及率（%）Water coverage rate(%)	污水处理率（%）Wastewater treatment rate(%)	人均公园绿地面积（平方米）Per capita public green space(sq. m)	生活垃圾处理率（%）Domestic garbage treatment rate(%)
惠州市	Huizhou	地级市	11 343	343.4	459.84	237	26 783 541	57 144	97.53	97.03	16.80	88.16
梅州市	Meizhou	地级市	15 865	525.0	423.85	50	8 000 148	18 603	96.49	79.99	12.83	100.00
汕尾市	Shanwei	地级市	4 865	352.5	293.55	16	6 717 548	22 560	93.44	86.01	13.21	80.00
河源市	Heyuan	地级市	15 654	361.0	295.02	32	6 803 296	22 499	100.00	89.39	12.36	100.00
阳江市	Yangjiang	地级市	7 956	285.1	242.17	49	10 398 362	42 017	100.00	81.81	11.51	100.00
清远市	Qingyuan	地级市	19 036	409.8	369.84	88	10 930 403	28 928	98.79	83.81	15.94	100.00
东莞市	Dongguan	地级市	2 460	188.9	822.02	112	54 900 207	66 109	100.00	95.20	16.71	100.00
中山市	Zhongshan	地级市	1 784	154.1	312.13	106	26 389 329	83 393	100.00	90.70	17.41	100.00
潮州市	Chaozhou	地级市	3 146	267.2	266.95	42	7 803 423	28 837	100.00	86.27	13.08	100.00
揭阳市	Jieyang	地级市	5 266	682.7	588.43	109	16 053 517	26 866	72.49	74.08	8.39	93.00
云浮市	Yunfu	地级市	7 785	290.3	236.72	71	6 022 990	24 863	99.72	87.27	11.61	100.00
增城市	Zengcheng	县级市	1 616	85.0	103.71	38	9 894 494	116 406	100.00	99.99	17.90	48.91
从化市	Conghua	县级市	1 975	60.2	59.34	19	2 841 460	47 200	90.85	55.57	14.80	100.00
乐昌市	Lechang	县级市	2 421	51.5	39.78	16	953 802	18 520	95.09	67.11	10.70	100.00
南雄市	Nanxiong	县级市	2 326	47.8	31.62	12	1 007 886	21 085	86.36	76.36	10.91	49.49
台山市	Taishan	县级市	3 285	98.5	94.11	28	3 134 068	31 818	94.94	89.23	13.75	100.00
开平市	Kaiping	县级市	1 659	68.5	69.92	50	2 602 329	37 990	91.34	80.04		100.00
鹤山市	Heshan	县级市	1 083	36.6	49.49	25	2 175 886	59 450	100.00	86.36	13.13	100.00
恩平市	Enping	县级市	1 698	50.0	49.28	33	1 332 464	26 649	95.97	79.60	15.04	100.00
廉江市	Lianjiang	县级市	2 867	175.5	144.31	26	3 055 674	17 411	88.11	55.04	29.34	100.00
雷州市	Leizhou	县级市	3 662	172.3	142.77	28	2 009 854	11 665	80.36	92.68	7.79	100.00
吴川市	Wuchuan	县级市	876	115.9	92.73	19	1 758 671	15 174	87.61	61.71	12.88	98.50
高州市	Gaozhou	县级市	3 276	172.5	128.87	33	4 088 661	23 702	100.00	92.69	11.60	100.00

续表

城市名称 Name of cities		行政级别 Admini-strative level	行政区域土地面积(平方公里) Total land area of city's administrative region(sq. km)	年末总人口(万人) Total population at year - end (10 000 persons)	六普常住人口(万人) Total residents of the Sixth National Population Census (10 000 persons)	建成区面积(平方公里) Area of built - up district (sq. km)	地区生产总值(万元) Gross regional product (10 000 yuan)	人均地区生产总值(元) Per capita gross regional product(yuan)	用水普及率(%) Water coverage rate(%)	污水处理率(%) Wastewater treatment rate(%)	人均公园绿地面积(平方米) Per capita public green space(sq. m)	生活垃圾处理率(%) Domestic garbage treatment rate(%)
化州市	Huazhou	县级市	2 357	165. 9	117. 88	30	3 553 475	21 419	100. 00	75. 97	4. 21	100. 00
信宜市	Xinyi	县级市	3 081	139. 6	91. 37	24	3 289 409	23 563	100. 00	87. 26	8. 73	
高要市	Gaoyao	县级市	2 186	79. 1	75. 31	21	3 460 829	43 753	91. 30	81. 58	18. 52	100. 00
四会市	Sihui	县级市	1 262	44. 7	54. 29	26	4 572 248	102 287	93. 70	80. 71	8. 95	86. 89
兴宁市	Xingning	县级市	2 104	119. 0	96. 29	24	1 324 355	11 129	92. 42	48. 96	11. 55	100. 00
陆丰市	Lufeng	县级市	1 541	185. 2	135. 83	20	2 011 779	10 863	91. 58	66. 03	7. 82	
阳春市	Yangchun	县级市	4 054	121. 0	84. 95	20	3 030 186	25 043	98. 54	79. 80	10. 37	
英德市	Yingde	县级市	5 634	109. 4	94. 20	26	2 001 425	18 295	99. 46	96. 11	18. 22	100. 00
连州市	Lianzhou	县级市	2 668	51. 4	36. 76	14	1 091 304	21 232	84. 57	94. 54	13. 96	100. 00
普宁市	Puning	县级市	1 635	241. 6	205. 56	55	5 047 625	20 892	95. 96	62. 98	4. 03	
罗定市	Luoding	县级市	2 327	124. 6	95. 90	43	1 341 424	10 766	98. 96	87. 27	11. 61	100. 00
广西壮族自治区	Guangxi											
南宁市	Nanning	地级市	22 244	724. 4	665. 87	283	28 035 444	38 994	96. 81	81. 21	13. 74	100. 00
柳州市	Liuzhou	地级市	18 597	372. 4	375. 87	178	20 100 543	52 342	97. 93	91. 00	13. 16	100. 00
桂林市	Guilin	地级市	27 850	521. 8	474. 80	67	16 579 048	34 114	88. 13	92. 27	10. 28	100. 00
梧州市	Wuzhou	地级市	12 588	336. 2	288. 22	39	9 917 096	33 710	95. 70	87. 50	8. 50	100. 00
北海市	Beihai	地级市	3 337	169. 4	153. 93	71	7 349 971	46 560	99. 73	83. 48	10. 85	100. 00
防城港市	Fangchenggang	地级市	6 238	93. 0	86. 69	35	5 251 470	58 810	100. 00	70. 51	8. 12	95. 00
钦州市	Qinzhou	地级市	10 895	396. 5	307. 97	87	7 537 500	23 957	97. 25	87. 96	7. 52	91. 18
贵港市	Guigang	地级市	10 602	538. 2	411. 88	69	7 420 091	17 652	100. 00	89. 36	13. 20	98. 50
玉林市	Yulin	地级市	12 824	700. 9	548. 74	67	11 984 584	21 349	100. 00	99. 10	9. 58	100. 00
百色市	Baise	地级市	36 202	411. 7	346. 68	37	8 038 711	22 762	100. 00	55. 13	9. 54	100. 00
贺州市	Hezhou	地级市	11 753	233. 6	195. 41	31	4 238 481	21 260	70. 60	67. 34	12. 14	100. 00

续表

城市名称 Name of cities		行政级别 Admini-strative level	行政区域土地面积（平方公里）Total land area of city's administrative region（sq. km）	年末总人口（万人）Total population at year－end（10 000 persons）	六普常住人口（万人）Total residents of the Sixth National Population Census（10 000 persons）	建成区面积（平方公里）Area of built－up district（sq. km）	地区生产总值（万元）Gross regional product（10 000 yuan）	人均地区生产总值（元）Per capita gross regional product（yuan）	用水普及率（%）Water coverage rate（%）	污水处理率（%）Wastewater treatment rate（%）	人均公园绿地面积（平方米）Per capita public green space（sq. m）	生活垃圾处理率（%）Domestic garbage treatment rate（%）
河池市	Hechi	地级市	33 476	413.7	336.93	21	5 286 188	15 440	98.12	89.08	6.63	100.00
来宾市	Laibin	地级市	13 409	255.6	209.97	37	5 155 700	24 069	96.84	82.33	10.26	100.00
崇左市	Chongzuo	地级市	17 331	246.5	199.43	26	5 846 288	28 886	72.28	50.71	8.60	61.56
岑溪市	Cenxi	县级市	2 770	92.6	77.21	16	2 034 859	21 975	98.77	80.82	16.85	100.00
东兴市	Dongxing	县级市	589	13.9	14.47	10	728 683	52 423	99.36	83.79	10.50	86.70
桂平市	Guiping	县级市	4 071	195.0	149.69	28	2 477 796	12 707	99.49	83.96	5.66	99.80
北流市	Beiliu	县级市	2 452	145.1	113.22	22	2 323 588	16 014	100.00	98.22	10.26	100.00
宜州市	Yizhou	县级市	3 857	64.6	55.86	14	942 753	14 594	100.00	83.70	10.73	100.00
合山市	Heshan	县级市	366	13.7	11.45	7	337 700	24 650	100.00	81.01	7.89	86.39
凭祥市	Pingxiang	县级市	645	11.1	11.22	10	403 998	36 396	99.08	70.44	8.77	86.69
海南省	Hainan											
海口市	Haikou	地级市	2 305	163.2	204.62	124	9 046 355	42 317	99.68	89.00	12.55	100.00
三亚市	Sanya	地级市	1 919	57.7	68.54	47	3 734 888	64 989	99.01	77.71	16.15	100.00
三沙市	Sansha	地级市	13	0.1		0.25						
五指山市	Wuzhishan	县级市	1 131	11.2	10.41	10	183 031	16 342	96.49	60.75	7.37	100.00
琼海市	Qionghai	县级市	1 710	50.7	48.32	25	1 626 056	32 072	91.81	47.48	14.95	99.79
儋州市	Danzhou	县级市	3 394	98.7	93.24	32	1 947 202	19 728	100.00	32.68	9.88	100.00
文昌市	Wenchang	县级市	2 485	59.7	53.74	16	1 738 040	29 113	99.36	50.00	6.00	100.00
万宁市	Wanning	县级市	1 884	63.4	54.56	10	1 468 466	23 162	95.08	95.06	14.89	98.25
东方市	Dongfang	县级市	2 256	45.9	40.83	17	1 239 433	27 003	93.68	29.40	10.53	99.90
重庆市	Chongqing	直辖市	82 374	3 358.4	2 884.62	1 115	126 566 900	42 795	96.25	93.95	18.04	99.43
四川省	Sichuan											
成都市	Chengdu	副省级市	12 133	1 188.0	1 404.76	529	91 088 904	63 977	98.33	89.01	13.44	100.00

续表

城市名称 Name of cities		行政级别 Admini-strative level	行政区域土地面积(平方公里) Total land area of city's administrative region(sq. km)	年末总人口(万人) Total population at year-end (10 000 persons)	六普常住人口(万人) Total residents of the Sixth National Population Census (10 000 persons)	建成区面积(平方公里) Area of built-up district (sq. km)	地区生产总值(万元) Gross regional product (10 000 yuan)	人均地区生产总值(元) Per capita gross regional product(yuan)	用水普及率(%) Water coverage rate(%)	污水处理率(%) Wastewater treatment rate(%)	人均公园绿地面积(平方米) Per capita public green space(sq. m)	生活垃圾处理率(%) Domestic garbage treatment rate(%)
自贡市	Zigong	地级市	4 381	329. 7	267. 89	106	10 016 028	36 746	69. 15	90. 55	10. 43	92. 00
攀枝花市	Panzhihua	地级市	7 401	112. 0	121. 41	69	8 008 832	65 001	92. 94	81. 45	9. 29	97. 62
泸州市	Luzhou	地级市	12 236	508. 4	421. 84	109	11 404 815	26 848	90. 82	84. 04	9. 02	100. 00
德阳市	Deyang	地级市	5 910	392. 0	361. 58	70	13 959 445	39 573	97. 91	89. 99	10. 00	100. 00
绵阳市	Mianyang	地级市	20 248	547. 4	461. 39	110	14 551 243	29 575	99. 06	91. 86	9. 12	100. 00
广元市	Guangyuan	地级市	16 311	310. 2	248. 41	50	5 187 500	20 443	92. 32	81. 14	11. 71	82. 99
遂宁市	Suining	地级市	5 325	379. 4	325. 26	76	7 366 143	22 517	82. 24	93. 29	8. 22	93. 73
内江市	Neijiang	地级市	5 385	426. 8	370. 28	58	10 693 429	28 735	85. 81	85. 11	8. 60	65. 91
乐山市	Leshan	地级市	12 723	356. 0	323. 58	68	11 347 900	34 863	96. 05	81. 45	8. 87	99. 74
南充市	Nanchong	地级市	12 477	759. 0	627. 86	109	13 285 528	21 059	97. 17	83. 57	10. 05	87. 06
眉山市	Meishan	地级市	7 140	352. 2	295. 05	45	8 600 424	28 934	95. 57	86. 91	11. 53	100. 00
宜宾市	Yibin	地级市	13 271	550. 4	447. 19	94	13 428 937	30 093	96. 65	87. 96	13. 90	96. 57
广安市	Guang'an	地级市	6 341	470. 4	320. 55	47	8 351 436	25 933	91. 85	92. 82	18. 20	92. 60
达州市	Dazhou	地级市	16 588	687. 6	546. 81	37	12 454 149	22 632	73. 18	39. 79	14. 18	86. 35
雅安市	Ya'an	地级市	15 046	157. 0	150. 73	29	4 179 698	27 317	99. 46	62. 88	9. 63	97. 58
巴中市	Bazhong	地级市	12 293	390. 2	328. 31	28	4 159 422	12 556	94. 29	82. 25	13. 86	97. 79
资阳市	Ziyang	地级市	7 960	507. 3	366. 51	43	10 923 616	30 514	94. 89	90. 36	9. 11	100. 00
都江堰市	Dujiangyan	县级市	1 208	61. 6	65. 80	34	2 298 590	37 315	89. 00	94. 27	10. 06	100. 00
彭州市	Pengzhou	县级市	1 421	80. 6	76. 29	21	2 356 851	29 241	68. 17	81. 47	9. 08	89. 09
邛崃市	Qionglai	县级市	1 376	65. 7	61. 28	21	1 654 313	25 180	82. 96	78. 27	10. 90	93. 00
崇州市	Chongzhou	县级市	1 088	66. 8	66. 11	29	1 834 032	27 456	97. 03	49. 03	13. 10	96. 00
广汉市	Guanghan	县级市	548	60. 7	59. 11	49	2 749 759	45 301	86. 34	23. 03	7. 74	98. 97
什邡市	Shifang	县级市	820	43. 8	41. 28	13	2 070 608	47 274	78. 71	82. 65	10. 09	99. 78

续表

城市名称 Name of cities		行政级别 Admini-strative level	行政区域土地面积（平方公里）Total land area of city's administrative region(sq. km)	年末总人口（万人）Total population at year－end (10 000 persons)	六普常住人口（万人）Total residents of the Sixth National Population Census (10 000 persons)	建成区面积（平方公里）Area of built－up district (sq. km)	地区生产总值（万元）Gross regional product (10 000 yuan)	人均地区生产总值（元）Per capita gross regional product(yuan)	用水普及率（%）Water coverage rate(%)	污水处理率（%）Wastewater treatment rate(%)	人均公园绿地面积（平方米）Per capita public green space(sq. m)	生活垃圾处理率（%）Domestic garbage treatment rate(%)
绵竹市	Mianzhu	县级市	1 246	50.7	47.79	14	1 859 629	36 679	92.84	90.36	10.89	100.00
江油市	Jiangyou	县级市	2 720	88.9	76.21	35	2 687 070	30 226	93.33	83.20	9.90	100.00
峨眉山市	Emeishan	县级市	1 181	43.4	43.71	19	1 791 771	41 285	88.80	93.97	12.82	100.00
阆中市	Langzhong	县级市	1 875	87.7	72.89	27	1 527 965	17 423	96.92	81.55	9.54	85.15
华蓥市	Huaying	县级市	464	36.2	27.84	13	1 108 352	30 617	99.11	35.29	8.75	78.87
万源市	Wanyuan	县级市	4 051	59.9	40.76	11	1 083 782	18 093	64.77		24.65	100.00
简阳市	Jianyang	县级市	2 213	148.6	107.12	26	3 447 817	23 202	98.83	66.78	7.99	100.00
西昌市	Xichang	县级市	2 657	64.6	71.24	37	3 735 410	57 824	80.74	69.76	10.99	100.00
贵州省	Guizhou											
贵阳市	Guiyang	地级市	8 034	379.1	432.26	299	20 854 252	46 479	94.43	95.01	15.47	95.43
六盘水市	Liupanshui	地级市	9 914	325.4	285.13	39	8 821 100	30 770	79.06	98.66	3.00	100.00
遵义市	Zunyi	地级市	30 762	778.5	612.71	86	15 846 700	25 852	98.68	88.72	13.10	100.00
安顺市	Anshun	地级市	9 267	285.6	229.76	41	4 291 600	18 725	95.91	92.73	2.39	70.28
毕节市	Bijie	地级市	26 853	870.6	653.75	39	10 419 300	15 953	91.98	92.10	19.96	98.83
铜仁市	Tongren	地级市	18 003	429.2	309.32	43	5 352 236	17 270	79.48	95.84	2.64	91.07
清镇市	Qingzhen	县级市	1 492	50.4	46.78	16	1 750 128	34 725	86.45	100.00	5.94	100.00
赤水市	Chishui	县级市	1 852	31.0	23.71	10	596 582	19 245	76.03	88.20	4.97	87.72
仁怀市	Renhuai	县级市	1 788	69.0	54.65	14	3 844 631	55 719	99.77	95.16	1.58	100.00
兴义市	Xingyi	县级市	2 943	83.4	78.31	38	2 378 023	28 513	91.90	83.18	8.04	100.00
凯里市	Kaili	县级市	1 306	48.7	47.90	67	1 480 875	30 408	91.94	98.90	14.84	90.55
都匀市	Duyun	县级市	2 305	48.1	44.37	24	1 268 310	26 368	100.00	100.00	8.25	95.44
福泉市	Fuquan	县级市	1 692	32.7	28.39	10	922 405	28 208	92.39	71.04	8.04	100.00
云南省	Yunnan											
昆明市	Kunming	地级市	21 012	546.8	643.22	397	34 153 115	52 094	99.11	98.00	9.92	97.88

续表

城市名称 Name of cities		行政级别 Administrative level	行政区域土地面积(平方公里) Total land area of city's administrative region(sq. km)	年末总人口(万人) Total population at year - end (10 000 persons)	六普常住人口(万人) Total residents of the Sixth National Population Census (10 000 persons)	建成区面积(平方公里) Area of built - up district (sq. km)	地区生产总值(万元) Gross regional product (10 000 yuan)	人均地区生产总值(元) Per capita gross regional product(yuan)	用水普及率(%) Water coverage rate(%)	污水处理率(%) Wastewater treatment rate(%)	人均公园绿地面积(平方米) Per capita public green space(sq. m)	生活垃圾处理率(%) Domestic garbage treatment rate(%)
曲靖市	Qujing	地级市	28 905	641. 9	585. 51	66	15 839 411	26 599	99. 01	90. 45	9. 02	100. 00
玉溪市	Yuxi	地级市	15 285	214. 7	230. 35	36	11 024 677	47 215	98. 67	80. 00	8. 34	100. 00
保山市	Baoshan	地级市	19 637	256. 9	250. 65	27	4 497 419	17 657	90. 61	88. 02	7. 08	99. 00
昭通市	Zhaotong	地级市	22 440	586. 5	521. 35	37	6 347 027	11 933	97. 48	91. 70	5. 77	100. 00
丽江市	Lijiang	地级市	21 219	120. 1	124. 48	23	2 488 114	19 661	100. 00	95. 91	31. 03	100. 00
普洱市	Pu'er	地级市	45 385	258. 4	254. 29	25	4 253 855	16 491	98. 20	81. 34	10. 59	96. 74
临沧市	Lincang	地级市	23 620	236. 4	242. 95	18	4 160 951	16 839	87. 05	90. 00	10. 38	97. 39
安宁市	Anning	县级市	1 301	26. 9	34. 13	26	2 306 785	85 754	93. 73	88. 50	15. 10	99. 90
宣威市	Xuanwei	县级市	6 053	151. 8	130. 29	35	2 376 301	15 654	99. 10	85. 03	9. 53	100. 00
楚雄市	Chuxiong	县级市	4 512	51. 7	58. 86	40	2 436 426	47 126	99. 37	88. 89	14. 91	100. 00
个旧市	Gejiu	县级市	1 587	39. 2	45. 98	13	1 760 264	44 905	90. 82	88. 46	10. 40	100. 00
开远市	Kaiyuan	县级市	1 950	28. 3	32. 27	20	1 324 928	46 817	96. 89	86. 99	11. 42	95. 89
蒙自市	Mengzi	县级市	2 228	38. 8	41. 72	31	1 182 902	30 487	98. 43	83. 00	8. 26	100. 00
弥勒市	Mile	县级市	4 004	53. 2	53. 97		2 272 710	42 720				
文山市	Wenshan	县级市	2 977	47. 5	48. 15	32	1 580 951	33 283	100. 00	50. 00	9. 21	100. 00
景洪市	Jinghong	县级市	6 867	41. 3	51. 99	27	1 447 804	35 056	100. 00	80. 72	16. 21	100. 00
大理市	Dali	县级市	1 815	61. 3	65. 20	39	2 873 274	46 872	95. 00	93. 65	9. 37	92. 67
瑞丽市	Ruili	县级市	1 020	13. 1	18. 06	25	471 246	35 973	100. 00	46. 79	19. 72	82. 45
芒市	Mangshi	县级市	2 987	37. 8	38. 99	18	724 426	19 165	100. 00	83. 27	14. 14	100. 00
西藏自治区	Tibet											
拉萨市	Lasa	地级市	29 518	60. 1	55. 94	66	3 048 700	51 663	97. 28	0. 08	3. 51	
日喀则市	Rikaze	县级市	3 875	11. 7	12. 04	27	461 016	39 403	95. 34		36. 60	71. 78
陕西省	Shaanxi											
西安市	Xi'an	副省级市	10 097	806. 9	846. 78	424	48 841 300	56 988	100. 00	91. 50	11. 20	99. 86

续表

城市名称 Name of cities		行政级别 Admini-strative level	行政区域土地面积（平方公里）Total land area of city's administrative region(sq. km)	年末总人口（万人）Total population at year - end (10 000 persons)	六普常住人口（万人）Total residents of the Sixth National Population Census (10 000 persons)	建成区面积（平方公里）Area of built - up district (sq. km)	地区生产总值（万元）Gross regional product (10 000 yuan)	人均地区生产总值（元）Per capita gross regional product(yuan)	用水普及率（%）Water coverage rate(%)	污水处理率（%）Wastewater treatment rate(%)	人均公园绿地面积（平方米）Per capita public green space(sq. m)	生活垃圾处理率(%) Domestic garbage treatment rate(%)
铜川市	Tongchuan	地级市	3 937	85.6	83.44	44	3 219 750	38 248	94.80	89.26	11.41	88.30
宝鸡市	Baoji	地级市	18 117	385.6	371.67	98	15 459 100	41 327	100.00	93.52	12.25	100.00
咸阳市	Xianyang	地级市	10 189	533.2	509.60	88	18 603 870	37 695	92.42	82.71	15.03	93.35
渭南市	Weinan	地级市	13 134	569.8	528.61	71	13 490 070	25 327	99.32	83.18	12.20	75.83
延安市	Yan'an	地级市	37 037	237.8	218.70	36	13 541 350	61 493	87.90	89.19	9.79	88.77
汉中市	Hanzhong	地级市	27 285	386.2	341.62	34	8 817 300	25 769	81.00	90.28	14.81	84.00
榆林市	Yulin	地级市	43 578	377.0	335.14	70	28 467 500	84 634	93.68	84.06	10.55	91.32
安康市	Ankang	地级市	23 536	308.3	262.99	39	6 045 520	22 938	90.17	85.78	11.10	100.00
商洛市	Shangluo	地级市	19 292	250.6	234.17	25	5 108 800	21 795	90.45	94.74	9.43	100.00
兴平市	Xingping	县级市	508	61.8	54.16	21	1 762 241	28 515	98.58	74.22	13.05	86.33
韩城市	Hancheng	县级市	1 621	40.5	39.12	18	2 815 294	69 513	99.88	72.32	8.73	90.33
华阴市	Huayin	县级市	817	27.0	25.81	18	736 175	27 266	91.96	79.07	8.30	91.13
甘肃省	Gansu											
兰州市	Lanzhou	地级市	13 086	368.6	361.62	207	17 762 823	48 852	95.07	76.65	10.46	100.00
嘉峪关市	Jiayuguan	地级市	2 935	20.0	23.19	68	2 262 175	96 335	100.00	85.64	14.78	100.00
金昌市	Jinchang	地级市	8 896	46.9	46.41	39	2 520 357	53 854	100.00	100.00	17.67	100.00
白银市	Baiyin	地级市	21 158	177.0	170.88	60	4 633 061	27 004	100.00	67.52	9.17	92.58
天水市	Tianshui	地级市	14 277	378.0	326.25	46	4 543 365	13 820	80.67	83.19	6.89	100.00
武威市	Wuwei	地级市	33 238	188.5	181.51	31	3 811 838	21 057	91.02	99.09	14.94	98.98
张掖市	Zhangye	地级市	41 924	131.3	119.95	63	3 359 718	27 788	100.00	87.04	71.15	100.00
平凉市	Pingliang	地级市	11 170	231.9	206.80	38	3 410 775	16 364	99.83	95.25	8.10	99.73
酒泉市	Jiuquan	地级市	193 974	110.8	109.59	48	6 419 382	58 088	100.00	94.36	9.76	100.00
庆阳市	Qingyang	地级市	27 119	264.1	221.12	25	6 053 667	27 261	98.67	90.22	6.45	92.31

续表

城市名称 Name of cities		行政级别 Administrative level	行政区域土地面积(平方公里) Total land area of city's administrative region(sq. km)	年末总人口(万人) Total population at year-end (10 000 persons)	六普常住人口(万人) Total residents of the Sixth National Population Census (10 000 persons)	建成区面积(平方公里) Area of built-up district (sq. km)	地区生产总值(万元) Gross regional product (10 000 yuan)	人均地区生产总值(元) Per capita gross regional product(yuan)	用水普及率(%) Water coverage rate(%)	污水处理率(%) Wastewater treatment rate(%)	人均公园绿地面积(平方米) Per capita public green space(sq. m)	生活垃圾处理率(%) Domestic garbage treatment rate(%)
定西市	Dingxi	地级市	20 330	300.1	269.86	23	2 522 182	9 106	95.99	90.65	10.58	98.00
陇南市	Longnan	地级市	27 839	282.8	256.77	14	2 495 000	9 699	69.29	97.40	1.44	100.00
玉门市	Yumen	县级市	13 496	16.1	15.98	24	1 351 491	83 944	100.00	73.01	10.11	100.00
敦煌市	Dunhuang	县级市	31 200	14.3	18.60	15	911 783	63 761	100.00	97.99	12.59	100.00
临夏市	Linxia	县级市	89	24.8	27.45	22	443 209	17 871	86.10	89.39	2.94	99.02
合作市	Hezuo	县级市	2 291	9.2	9.03	10	254 960	27 713	80.94	99.21	5.76	85.19
青海省	Qinghai											
西宁市	Xining	地级市	7 649	226.8	220.87	85	9 785 314	43 346	99.99	71.40	10.97	92.67
海东市	Haidong	地级市	13 390	170.5	139.68	37	3 370 087	23 552	99.59	69.23	4.69	93.10
格尔木市	Golmud	县级市	119 200	13.3	21.52	34	3 188 835	239 762	100.00	56.30	5.72	98.17
德令哈市	Delingha	县级市	27 800	7.6	7.82	17	496 429	65 320	98.25	31.51	7.02	97.14
玉树市	Yushu	县级市	15 400	10.8	12.04	14	100 489	9 305	85.03	53.70	5.10	94.51
宁夏回族自治区	Ningxia											
银川市	Yinchuan	地级市	9 025	172.6	199.31	149	12 890 199	62 437	98.94	99.40	16.80	87.56
石嘴山市	Shizuishan	地级市	5 310	76.6	72.55	103	4 464 393	59 474	100.00	94.40	22.21	94.00
吴忠市	Wuzhong	地级市	16 757	143.7	127.38	48	3 519 276	26 622	91.32	90.05	21.00	98.88
固原市	Guyuan	地级市	13 047	154.2	122.82	39	1 829 501	14 587	95.91	60.47	8.71	93.42
中卫市	Zhongwei	地级市	17 448	121.5	108.08	38	2 868 250	25 700	77.37	100.00	18.66	100.00
灵武市	Lingwu	县级市	4 539	24.6	26.17	12	2 867 388	116 560	98.35	93.02	19.38	100.00
青铜峡市	Qingtongxia	县级市	2 525	28.2	26.47	32	1 321 185	46 851	98.96	85.87	17.26	88.54
新疆维吾尔自治区	Xinjiang											
乌鲁木齐市	Urumqi	地级市	13 788	262.9	311.26	391	22 028 545	64 695	99.95	84.81	10.05	92.04
克拉玛依市	Karamay	地级市	7 735	37.9	39.10	64	8 531 091	149 127	100.00	93.87	10.20	100.00

续表

城市名称 Name of cities		行政级别 Administrative level	行政区域土地面积(平方公里) Total land area of city's administrative region(sq. km)	年末总人口(万人) Total population at year-end (10 000 persons)	六普常住人口(万人) Total residents of the Sixth National Population Census (10 000 persons)	建成区面积(平方公里) Area of built-up district (sq. km)	地区生产总值(万元) Gross regional product (10 000 yuan)	人均地区生产总值(元) Per capita gross regional product(yuan)	用水普及率(%) Water coverage rate(%)	污水处理率(%) Wastewater treatment rate(%)	人均公园绿地面积(平方米) Per capita public green space(sq. m)	生活垃圾处理率(%) Domestic garbage treatment rate(%)
吐鲁番市	Turpan	县级市	13 650	28. 2	27. 34	21	696 221	24 689	98. 65	64. 29	14. 80	89. 23
哈密市	Hami	县级市	85 587	42. 6	47. 22	36	2 627 458	61 677	100. 00	86. 59	8. 55	98. 84
昌吉市	Changji	县级市	8 215	36. 8	42. 63	54	2 933 915	79 726	99. 39	95. 89	10. 37	95. 00
阜康市	Fukang	县级市	8 529	16. 9	16. 50	20	1 293 697	76 550	98. 90	99. 76	13. 75	95. 08
博乐市	Bole	县级市	7 790	27. 1	23. 56	20	798 300	29 458	98. 98	98. 14	10. 15	75. 52
库尔勒市	Korla	县级市	7 267	46. 9	54. 93	70	6 502 476	138 646	99. 89	95. 62	11. 73	95. 57
阿克苏市	Akesu	县级市	15 033	50. 9	53. 57	47	1 438 134	28 254	87. 85	97. 14	10. 45	91. 90
阿图什市	Atus	县级市	16 151	26. 0	24. 04	8	334 676	12 872	100. 00	75. 10	1. 73	93. 33
喀什市	Kashi	县级市	791	53. 1	50. 66	56	1 609 018	30 302	100. 00	100. 00	11. 11	89. 48
和田市	Hetian	县级市	510	33. 2	32. 23	29	465 904	14 033	97. 30	84. 99	7. 37	91. 67
伊宁市	Yining	县级市	761	53. 6	51. 51	37	1 636 964	30 540	99. 94	80. 07	9. 50	98. 00
奎屯市	Kuitun	县级市	1 110	15. 7	16. 63	25	1 264 458	80 539	91. 50	68. 88	7. 88	98. 00
塔城市	Tacheng	县级市	4 353	15. 5	16. 10	14	667 701	43 077	93. 60	87. 60	13. 26	95. 59
乌苏市	Wusu	县级市	13 729	23. 0	29. 89	19	1 430 169	62 181	90. 36	78. 08	6. 22	98. 63
阿勒泰市	Aletai	县级市	11 481	19. 7	19. 01	26	519 316	26 361	96. 23	100. 00	18. 09	97. 07
石河子市	Shihezi	县级市	457	35. 5	38. 01	37	2 550 000	71 831	100. 00	88. 56	10. 70	100. 00
阿拉尔市	Alar	县级市	5 264	22. 0	15. 86	27	1 499 317	68 151	85. 60	50. 28	9. 10	92. 00
图木舒克市	Tumushuke	县级市	1 927	13. 5	13. 57	13	481 730	35 684	74. 45	49. 30	10. 09	
五家渠市	Wujiaqu	县级市	710	12. 0	9. 64	14	699 558	58 297	100. 00	89. 87	11. 32	95. 89
北屯市	Beitun	县级市	911	5. 0	7. 63	20	191 806	38 361	82. 75	99. 25	1. 22	97. 16
阿拉山口市	Alashankou	县级市	1 204	1. 0		11			80. 31	80. 00	16. 58	85. 00
铁门关市	Tiemenguan	县级市	590	3. 6		8			89. 60	74. 00		69. 10

一、数据来源（Data Resources）

1. 行政级别（Administrative level）

2. 行政区域土地面积（Total land area of city's administrative region）

3. 年末总人口（Total population at year-end）

4. 建成区面积（Area of built-up district）

5. 地区生产总值（Gross regional product）

6. 人均地区生产总值（Per capita gross regional product）

以上数据来源：国家统计局城市社会经济调查司．中国城市统计年鉴（2014）［M］．北京：中国统计出版社，2014.

（注：该年鉴未发表2013年全国368个县级市的人均地区生产总值，本数据根据地区生产总值除以年末总人口得到。2004年1月6日国家统计局发布《关于改进和规范地区GDP核算的通知》（国统字〔2004〕4号），要求各省、区、市统一使用常住人口计算人均GDP。本统计得到的县级市人均地区生产总值并不一定确切反映城市的实际情况。）

7. 污水处理率（Wastewater treatment rate）

8. 生活垃圾处理率（Domestic garbage treatment rate）

9. 用水普及率（Water coverage rate）

10. 人均公园绿地面积（Per capita public green space）

以上数据来源：中华人民共和国住房和城乡建设部．中国城市建设统计年鉴（2013年）［M］．北京：中国计划出版社，2014.

二、指标解释（Data Illumination）

1. 行政级别：按行政级别分组，全国658个城市分为：4个直辖市，15个副省级城市，271个地级市，368个县级市。

——《中国城市统计年鉴（2014）》第3页

2. 行政区域土地面积：指在辖区内的全部陆地面积和水域面积。包括耕地、荒山、荒地、山林、草原、滩涂、道路和建筑物占地等陆地面积，以及河流、湖泊、水库等水域面积。

——《中国城市统计年鉴（2014）》第465页

3. 年末总人口：是指本市本年12月31日24时的人口总数，为公安部门的户籍人口数。

——《中国城市统计年鉴（2014）》第465页

4. 六普常住人口：以2010年11月1日零时为标准时点进行的第六次全国人口普查中的常住人口，包括居住在本乡镇街道、户口在本乡镇街道或户口待定的人；居住在本乡镇街道、离开户口登记地所在的乡镇街道半年以上的人；户口在本乡镇街道、外出不满半年或在境外工作学习的人。不包括常住在省内的境外人员。

——《第六次全国人口普查数据公报》

5. 建成区面积：指实际已成片开发建设、市政公用设施和公共设施基本具备的区域。

——《中国城市统计年鉴（2014）》第465页

6. 人均地区生产总值：指按市场价格计算的一个地区所有常住单位在一定时期内生产活动的最终成果。

——《中国城市统计年鉴（2014）》第465页

7. 用水普及率：指报告期末城区内用水人口与总人口的比率。计算公式为：

用水普及率 = 城区用水人口/（城区人口 + 城区暂住人口）×100%

——《中国城市建设统计年鉴（2013年）》第633页

8. 污水处理率：指报告期内污水处理总量与污水排放总量的比率。计算公式：

污水处理率 = 污水处理总量/污水排放总量 × 100%

——《中国城市建设统计年鉴（2013年）》第633页

9. 人均公园绿地面积：指报告期末城区内平均每人拥有的公园绿地面积。计算公式：

人均公园绿地面积 = 城区公园绿地面积/（城区人口 + 城区暂住人口）

——《中国城市建设统计年鉴（2013年）》第634页

10. 生活垃圾处理率：指报告期内生活垃圾处理量与生活垃圾产生量的比率。计算公式：

生活垃圾处理率 = 生活垃圾处理量/生活垃圾产生量 × 100%

——《中国城市建设统计年鉴（2013年）》第634页

注：

1. 2013年1月24日，民政部发布《民政部关于同意吉林省撤销扶余县设立扶余市的批复》（民函〔2013〕28号），经国务院批准，撤销扶余县，设立县级扶余市。在本次“2013年中国城市基本数据”的统计工作中，以原扶余县的六普常住人口作为扶余市的六普常住人口。

2. 2013年2月8日，国务院发布《国务院关于同意青海省撤销海东地区设立地级海东市的批复》（国函〔2013〕23号），撤销海东地区和乐都县，设立地级海东市。原乐都县的常住人口为原海东地区统计的一部分，故在本次“2013年中国城市基本数据”的统计工作中，以原海东地区的六普常住人口作为海东市的六普常住人口。

3. 2013年7月3日，民政部发布《民政部关于同意青海省撤销玉树县设立县级玉树市的批复》（民函〔2013〕219号），经国务院批准，撤销玉树县，设立县级玉树市。在本次“2013年中国城市基本数据”的统计工作中，以原玉树县的六普常住人口作为玉树市的六普常住人口。

4. 2013年1月24日，民政部发布《民政部关于同意云南省撤销弥勒县设立弥勒市的批复》（民函〔2013〕29号），经国务院批准，撤销弥勒县，设立县级弥勒市。在本次“2013年中国城市基本数据”的统计工作中，以原弥勒县的六普常住人口作为弥勒市的六普常住人口。

5. 2012年12月17日，国务院发布《国务院关于同意江苏省调整泰州市部分行政区划的批复》（国函〔2012〕208号），撤销县级姜堰市，设立泰州市姜堰区。原县级姜堰市的六普常住人口为泰州市统计的一部分，故在本次“2013年中国城市基本数据”的统计工作中，不再重复计数泰州市的这一部分人口。

6. 2013年10月18日，国务院发布《国务院关于同意浙江省调整绍兴市部分行政区划的批复》（国函〔2013〕112号），撤销县级上虞市，设立绍兴市上虞区。原县级上虞市的六普常住人口为绍兴市统计的一部分，故在本次“2013年中国城市基本数据”的统计工作中，不再重复计数绍兴市的这一部分人口。

7. 2013年10月18日，国务院发布《国务院关于同意山东省调整济宁市部分行政区划的批复》（国函〔2013〕115号），撤销县级兖州市，设立济宁市兖州区。原县级兖州市的六普常住人口为济宁市统计的一部分，故在本次“2013年中国城市基本数据”的统计工作中，不再重复计数济宁市的这一部分人口。

8. 2012年12月17日，国务院发布《国务院关于同意新疆维吾尔自治区设立县级阿拉山口市的批复》（国函〔2012〕205号），设立县级阿拉山口市；2012年12月17日，国务院发布《国务院关于同意新疆维吾尔自治区设立县级铁门关市的批复》（国函〔2012〕206号），设立县级铁门关市。《中国城市统计年鉴（2014）》未统计阿拉山口市和铁门关市数据；二者的行政区域土地面积和年末总人口取自《中国城市建设统计年鉴（2013）》

9. 《中国城市统计年鉴（2014）》未统计以下城市的建成区面积：上海市，海南省三沙市，贵州省贵阳市，以及全部县级市。在本次“2013年中国城市基本数据”的统计工作中，上述数据取自《中国城市建设统计年鉴（2013年）》。

10. 《中国城市统计年鉴（2014）》未统计新疆维吾尔自治区博乐市的地区生产总值。在本次“2013年中国城市基本数据”的统计工作中，上述数据取自《博乐市2013年国民经济和社会发展统计公报》。

11. 目前，由于各城市户籍改革步伐进展不一，一些地区已经把暂住人口完全纳入当地人口管理范畴，而另一些地区则仍维持原来的户籍人口管理办法，把暂住人口排除在外，导致各城市总人口概念差异较大。因此，本统计中的总人口及在此基础上计算出的各项人均指标均采用所引资料中的定义，可能与其他渠道统计数据存在出入，仅供参考。

（数据收集整理：毛其智，清华大学教授，国际欧亚科学院院士；胡若函，清华大学建筑学院博士研究生）

附录4

2014年中国人居环境范例奖获奖名单

根据《关于印发〈中国人居环境奖评价指标体系（试行）〉和〈中国人居环境范例奖评选主题及内容〉的通知》（建城〔2010〕120号）和《住房城乡建设部办公厅关于做好2014年中国人居环境奖和中国人居环境范例奖申报工作的通知》（建办城函〔2013〕653号）精神，住房和城乡建设部组织专家对各地推荐的申报项目进行评审并经社会公示，决定授予“北京市朝阳循环经济产业园项目”等54个项目2014年中国人居环境范例奖。

2014年中国人居环境范例奖获奖名单如下：

1. 北京市朝阳循环经济产业园项目
2. 天津市供热改革和建筑节能泰达示范项目
3. 河北省张家口市山体绿化建设项目
4. 山西省晋城市白马寺沉陷区生态综合整治工程
5. 内蒙古自治区赤峰市喀喇沁旗锦山镇小城镇建设项目
6. 内蒙古自治区兴安盟乌兰浩特市成吉思汗公园维修改造项目
7. 辽宁省沈阳市于洪新城旧城改造项目
8. 上海市徐汇区历史文化风貌整体保护工程
9. 上海市长宁区城市网格化管理项目
10. 上海市静安区旧住房综合改造工程
11. 上海市普陀区长风老工业区转型生态商务区建设项目
12. 江苏省村庄环境整治苏南实践项目
13. 江苏省徐州市云龙湖风景名胜区生态景观修复工程
14. 江苏省常州市数字化城市管理项目
15. 江苏省常熟市虞山镇历史文化遗产保护项目
16. 江苏省太仓市沙溪镇特色小城镇建设项目
17. 浙江省杭州市公租房日常管理服务体系建设项目
18. 浙江省杭州市市区道路分类保洁管理项目
19. 浙江省德清县下渚湖湿地风景区资源保护项目
20. 浙江省龙泉市溪头村新农村建设项目

21. 安徽省合肥市滨湖湿地生态修复和公园建设项目
22. 安徽省合芜蚌实验区科技创新公共服务和应用技术研发中心可再生能源建筑应用项目
23. 安徽省潜山县官庄村美好乡村规划建设项目
24. 福建省漳州市郊野公园龙文段项目
25. 福建省长泰县上蔡村村庄环境综合整治项目
26. 江西省赣州市中心城区章江水环境治理暨健身绿道建设项目
27. 山东省济南市保障房人居环境建设项目
28. 山东省潍坊市虞河上游湿地综合整治工程
29. 山东省日照市沙墩河绿道工程
30. 山东省菏泽市数字化城市综合管理项目
31. 山东省寿光市城市绿荫系统建设项目
32. 河南省许昌市数字化城市管理项目
33. 河南省三门峡市迎宾花园保障性住房建设项目
34. 湖南省长沙市洋湖生态新城建设项目
35. 湖南省长沙市梅溪湖生态公园建设项目
36. 湖南省湘潭市盘龙新农村建设示范项目
37. 广东省广州市轨道交通 5 号线首期工程滘口至文冲段工程
38. 广东省广州市第一资源热力电厂二分厂城市固废物环境教育项目
39. 广东省深圳市盐田区餐厨垃圾处理项目
40. 广东省惠州市金山河水清岸绿工程
41. 重庆市云阳县龙脊岭生态文化长廊建设项目
42. 四川省北川新县城灾后重建工程
43. 贵州省盘县古银杏风景名胜区妥乐景区保护与治理项目
44. 云南省昆明市保障性住房信息系统平台建设项目
45. 云南省红河州蒙自市空气环境治理项目
46. 云南省红河州弥勒市西三镇可邑村特色民居保护建设项目
47. 甘肃省临泽县大沙河流域综合治理工程
48. 宁夏回族自治区中卫市商住小区水源热泵供热建筑应用项目
49. 宁夏回族自治区青铜峡市库区湿地生态保护建设项目
50. 新疆维吾尔自治区乌鲁木齐市煤改气工程
51. 新疆维吾尔自治区乌鲁木齐市紫美雅和项目建筑节能与利用工程
52. 新疆维吾尔自治区昌吉市公园绿地建设项目
53. 新疆维吾尔自治区库尔勒市旧城改造项目
54. 新疆维吾尔自治区克拉玛依市白碱滩区数字化城市管理项目

（数据收集整理：毛其智，清华大学教授，国际欧亚科学院院士；胡若函，清华大学建筑学院博士研究生）

附录 5

2015 年中国人居环境奖获奖名单

经有关省、自治区、直辖市住房城乡建设主管部门推荐、专家评审和社会公示，并报中国人居环境奖工作领导小组批准，住房和城乡建设部决定授予江苏省常州市、江苏省宿迁市、河南省济源市 2015 年中国人居环境奖，授予上海市嘉定区新城核心区生态系统规划建设等 31 个项目 2015 年中国人居环境范例奖。

2015 年中国人居环境奖获奖名单如下：

（一）综合奖

1. 江苏省常州市
2. 江苏省宿迁市
3. 河南省济源市

（二）范例奖

1. 上海市嘉定区新城核心区生态系统规划建设项目
2. 上海市徐汇区滨江工业旧址改建公共开放空间项目
3. 江苏省南京市滨江带建设工程
4. 江苏省南京市高淳区桠溪国际慢城建设项目
5. 江苏省徐州市九里湖采煤塌陷区生态修复项目
6. 江苏省太仓市浏河镇特色小城镇建设项目
7. 浙江省海宁市住房保障体系建设项目
8. 浙江省宁波市粪便无害化处理及资源化利用项目
9. 浙江省绍兴市供水管网漏损控制项目
10. 浙江省绍兴市规范建筑泥浆管理利用项目
11. 浙江省湖州市三大综合性公园建设项目
12. 浙江省龙泉市“中国青瓷小镇”建设项目
13. 浙江省仙居县永安溪绿道建设项目

14. 福建省漳州市西环城路景观整治提升暨绿道建设工程
15. 山东省济南市山体生态修复暨山体公园建设项目
16. 山东省青岛市高实馨城公共租赁住房项目
17. 山东省青岛市环卫物流园建设项目
18. 山东省济宁市农村环境综合整治项目
19. 河南省洛阳市数字化城市管理系统建设项目
20. 河南省信阳市平桥区五里店办事处郝堂村新农村建设项目
21. 湖北省荆门市数字化城市管理项目
22. 广东省珠海市横琴新区综合管廊建设项目
23. 广东省珠海市香洲区社区体育公园规划建设项目
24. 重庆市巫溪县大宁古城旧城改造项目
25. 四川省宜宾市全域数字化城市管理项目
26. 四川省郫县沱江河综合整治项目
27. 云南省昆明市城市公园雨水处理及资源化利用项目
28. 云南省昆明市中心城区综合交通体系规划项目
29. 云南省昆明市数字化城市管理模式创新项目
30. 新疆维吾尔自治区泽普县生态保护及城市绿化项目
31. 内蒙古自治区呼和浩特市成吉思汗公园生态节约型景观治理项目

（数据收集整理：毛其智，清华大学教授，国际欧亚科学院院士；胡若函，清华大学建筑学院博士研究生）

附录6

中国历史文化名街名录（第一批）

为了更好地保护我国优秀历史文化遗存，完善历史文化遗产保护体系，进一步做好历史文化街区保护工作，按照《住房城乡建设部、国家文物局关于开展中国历史文化街区认定工作的通知》（建规〔2014〕28号），在各地推荐的基础上，经专家评审和主管部门审核，住房城乡建设部、国家文物局决定公布北京市皇城历史文化街区等30个街区为第一批中国历史文化街区。

第一批中国历史文化街区名单

1. 北京市皇城历史文化街区
2. 北京市大栅栏历史文化街区
3. 北京市东四三条至八条历史文化街区
4. 天津市五大道历史文化街区
5. 吉林省长春市第一汽车制造厂历史文化街区
6. 黑龙江省齐齐哈尔市昂昂溪区罗西亚大街历史文化街区
7. 上海市外滩历史文化街区
8. 江苏省南京市梅园新村历史文化街区
9. 江苏省南京市颐和路历史文化街区
10. 江苏省苏州市平江历史文化街区
11. 江苏省苏州市山塘街历史文化街区
12. 江苏省扬州市南河下历史文化街区
13. 浙江省杭州市中山中路历史文化街区
14. 浙江省龙泉市西街历史文化街区
15. 浙江省兰溪市天福山历史文化街区
16. 浙江省绍兴市蕺山（书圣故里）历史文化街区
17. 安徽省黄山市屯溪区屯溪老街历史文化街区
18. 福建省福州市三坊七巷历史文化街区
19. 福建省泉州市中山路历史文化街区

20. 福建省厦门市鼓浪屿历史文化街区
21. 福建省漳州市台湾路—香港路历史文化街区
22. 湖北省武汉市江汉路及中山大道历史文化街区
23. 湖南省永州市柳子街历史文化街区
24. 广东省中山市孙文西历史文化街区
25. 广西壮族自治区北海市珠海路—沙脊街—中山路历史文化街区
26. 重庆市沙坪坝区磁器口历史文化街区
27. 四川省阆中市华光楼历史文化街区
28. 云南省石屏县古城区历史文化街区
29. 新疆维吾尔自治区库车县热斯坦历史文化街区
30. 新疆维吾尔自治区伊宁市前进街历史文化街区

（数据整理：廖远涛，广州市城市规划勘测设计研究院城市与建筑设计所副所长，高级工程师；雷轩，广州市城市规划勘测设计研究院）

附录 7

国家城市湿地公园名录

国家城市湿地公园，是指利用纳入城市绿地系统规划的适宜作为公园的天然湿地类型，通过合理的保护利用，形成保护、科普、休闲等功能于一体的公园。住房和城乡建设部于2015 年 3 月公布了第十一批 4 个国家城市湿地公园名单。至此，国家城市湿地公园总数达到 52 处，详细名单如下：

第一批国家城市湿地公园（2005 年 2 月）1 个

山东省荣成市桑沟湾国家城市湿地公园

第二批国家城市湿地公园（2005 年 6 月）9 个

北京市海淀区翠湖国家城市湿地公园
河北省唐山市南湖国家城市湿地公园
江苏省无锡市长广溪国家城市湿地公园
江苏省常熟市尚湖国家城市湿地公园
浙江省绍兴市镜湖国家城市湿地公园
山东省东营市明月湖国家城市湿地公园
山东省东平县稻屯洼国家城市湿地公园
湖南省常德市西洞庭湖青山湖国家城市湿地公园
安徽省淮北市南湖国家城市湿地公园

第三批国家城市湿地公园（2007 年 2 月）12 个

江苏省常熟市沙家浜国家城市湿地公园
浙江省临海市三江国家城市湿地公园
宁夏回族自治区银川市宝湖国家城市湿地公园
河南省三门峡市天鹅湖国家城市湿地公园

黑龙江省讷河市雨亭国家城市湿地公园
河北省保定市涞源县拒马源国家城市湿地公园
山东省临沂市滨河国家城市湿地公园
山东省海阳市小孩儿口国家城市湿地公园
山东省安丘市大汶河国家城市湿地公园
山东省沾化县徒骇河国家城市湿地公园
安徽省淮南市十涧湖国家城市湿地公园
湖北省武汉市金银湖国家城市湿地公园

第四批国家城市湿地公园（2007 年 6 月）4 个

江苏省南京绿水湾国家城市湿地公园
山东省临沂市双月湖国家城市湿地公园
山西省长治市长治国家城市湿地公园
河南省南阳市白河国家城市湿地公园

第五批国家城市湿地公园（2008 年 7 月）4 个

吉林省镇赉县南湖国家城市湿地公园
江苏省昆山市国家城市湿地公园
江西省新余市孔目江国家城市湿地公园
广东省湛江市绿塘河国家城市湿地公园

第六批国家城市湿地公园（2009 年 12 月）7 个

浙江省台州市鉴洋湖国家城市湿地公园
河南省平顶山市平西湖国家城市湿地公园
河南省平顶山市白鹭洲国家城市湿地公园
贵州省贵阳市花溪国家城市湿地公园
甘肃省张掖市城北国家城市湿地公园
辽宁省铁岭市莲花湖国家城市湿地公园
黑龙江省哈尔滨市群力国家城市湿地公园

第七批国家城市湿地公园（2011 年 1 月）3 个

江苏省南京固城湖国家城市湿地公园

山东省昌邑市潍水风情国家城市湿地公园
福建省厦门市杏林湾国家城市湿地公园

第八批国家城市湿地公园（2012年8月）2个

新疆生产建设兵团农六师五家渠市青格达湖国家城市湿地公园
山东省寿光市滨河国家城市湿地公园

第九批国家城市湿地公园（2012年11月）2个

贵州省贵阳红枫湖—百花湖国家城市湿地公园
甘肃省张掖高台黑河国家城市湿地公园

第十批国家城市湿地公园（2013年12月）4个

重庆市璧山县观音塘国家城市湿地公园
内蒙古自治区额尔古纳国家城市湿地公园
浙江省嘉兴市石臼漾国家城市湿地公园
广东省东莞市国家城市湿地公园

第十一批国家城市湿地公园（2015年3月）4个

山西省孝义市胜溪湖国家城市湿地公园
黑龙江省五大连池火山国家城市湿地公园
浙江省湖州市吴兴西山漾国家城市湿地公园
四川省阆中古城国家城市湿地公园

（数据整理：廖远涛，广州市城市规划勘测设计研究院城市与建筑设计所副所长，高级工程师；雷轩，广州市城市规划勘测设计研究院）

附录8

全国特色景观旅游名镇名村名单

按照《住房城乡建设部办公厅关于做好2013年全国特色景观旅游名镇名村示范工作的通知》（建办村函〔2013〕313号）要求，在各地推荐的基础上，经组织专家评审，住房城乡建设部、国家旅游局于2015年7月评选出第三批全国特色景观旅游名镇名村示范，详细名单如下：

一、北京市（6个）

门头沟区潭柘寺镇、房山区韩村河镇、昌平区南口镇、怀柔区九渡河镇、密云县古北口镇、延庆县千家店镇

二、天津市（11个）

津南区小站镇、宁河县七里海镇、蓟县官庄镇、蓟县下营镇、西青区辛口镇水高庄村、西青区精武镇小南河村、北辰区双街镇沙庄村、静海县双塘镇西双塘村、蓟县下营镇常州村、蓟县下营镇郭家沟村、蓟县穿芳峪镇毛家峪村

三、河北省（11个）

唐山市滦县滦州镇、唐山市滦县响嘡镇、唐山市滦县王店子镇、张家口市张北县张北镇、廊坊市霸州市胜芳镇、衡水市武强县周窝镇、唐山市滦县滦州镇滦州古城、秦皇岛市昌黎县十里铺乡西山场村、邢台市邢台县路罗镇英谈村、邢台市内丘县南寨乡神头村、保定市易县西陵镇凤凰台村

四、山西省（1个）

忻州市原平市崞阳镇

五、内蒙古自治区（32 个）

呼和浩特市清水河县城关镇、赤峰市喀喇沁旗美林镇、赤峰市喀喇沁旗王爷府镇、赤峰市宁城县黑里河镇、通辽市科尔沁左翼中旗花吐古拉镇、通辽市科尔沁左翼后旗阿古拉镇、通辽市库伦旗库伦镇、鄂尔多斯市准格尔旗龙口镇、鄂尔多斯市准格尔旗布尔陶亥苏木、鄂尔多斯市鄂托克前旗上海庙镇、鄂尔多斯市鄂托克前旗城川镇、鄂尔多斯市鄂托克旗乌兰镇、鄂尔多斯市乌审旗无定河镇、呼伦贝尔市阿荣旗那吉镇、呼伦贝尔市陈巴尔虎旗巴彦库仁镇、呼伦贝尔市扎兰屯市成吉思汗镇、呼伦贝尔市扎兰屯市柴河镇、呼伦贝尔市额尔古纳市莫尔道嘎镇、呼伦贝尔市额尔古纳市黑山头镇、呼伦贝尔市额尔古纳市蒙兀室韦苏木、呼伦贝尔市额尔古纳市恩和俄罗斯族民族乡、呼伦贝尔市额尔古纳市奇乾乡、呼伦贝尔市根河市敖鲁古雅鄂温克族乡、乌兰察布市察哈尔右翼中旗科布尔镇、乌兰察布市四子王旗乌兰花镇、阿拉善盟阿拉善右旗巴丹吉林镇、阿拉善盟额济纳旗达来呼布镇、赤峰市松山区城子乡瓦房村、赤峰市敖汉旗四道湾子镇白斯朗营子村、鄂尔多斯市准格尔旗纳日松镇松树墕村、鄂尔多斯市准格尔旗十二连城乡兴胜店村、呼伦贝尔市阿荣旗新发朝鲜民族乡东光村

六、辽宁省（10 个）

大连市长海县广鹿乡、大连市普兰店市安波镇、鞍山市海城市牛庄镇、丹东市宽甸满族自治县青山沟镇、丹东市东港市孤山镇、盘锦市大洼县赵圈河镇、本溪市本溪满族自治县东营坊乡东营坊村、丹东市凤城市凤山街道大梨树村、盘锦市大洼县西安镇上口子村、葫芦岛市建昌县石佛乡灰窑子村

七、吉林省（11 个）

长春市南关区玉潭镇、长春市双阳区山河镇、长春市九台市土们岭镇、吉林市龙潭区乌拉街满族镇、四平市伊通满族自治县伊通镇、通化市辉南县庆阳镇、白山市浑江区三道沟镇、延边朝鲜族自治州图们市月晴镇、白山市长白朝鲜族自治县十四道沟镇望天鹅新村、白山市长白朝鲜族自治县马鹿沟镇果园村、延边朝鲜族自治州安图县万宝镇红旗村

八、黑龙江省（7 个）

哈尔滨市尚志市帽儿山镇、鹤岗市萝北县名山镇、牡丹江市东宁县三岔口镇、牡丹江市东宁县道河镇、绥化市绥棱县四海店镇、齐齐哈尔市梅里斯达斡尔族区雅尔塞镇哈拉新村、齐齐哈尔市甘南县兴十四镇兴十四村

九、上海市（4个）

嘉定区南翔镇、金山区廊下镇中华村、金山区山阳镇金山嘴渔村、崇明县陈家镇瀛东村

十、江苏省（10个）

南京市六合区竹镇镇、无锡市惠山区阳山镇、苏州市吴江区震泽镇、苏州市常熟市梅李镇、苏州市太仓市沙溪镇、淮安市淮阴区码头镇、南京市高淳区桠溪镇蓝溪村、苏州市常熟市碧溪街道李袁村、南通市通州区五接镇开沙村、镇江市句容市天王镇戴庄村

十一、浙江省（18个）

宁波市鄞州区龙观乡、宁波市象山县石浦镇、嘉兴市嘉善县西塘镇、湖州市德清县新市镇、绍兴市新昌县镜岭镇、绍兴市诸暨市山下湖镇、衢州市江山市廿八都镇、台州市仙居县白塔镇、宁波市镇海区澥浦镇十七房村、宁波市余姚市大岚镇柿林村、温州市永嘉县岩头镇苍坡村、温州市永嘉县岩坦镇屿北村、嘉兴市秀洲区王店镇建林村、湖州市南浔区和孚镇荻港村、绍兴市诸暨市东白湖镇斯宅村、金华市磐安县盘峰乡榉溪村、衢州市柯城区七里乡大头村、台州市天台县街头镇后岸村

十二、安徽省（18个）

马鞍山市当涂县太白镇、安庆市枞阳县浮山镇、安庆市潜山县天柱山镇、安庆市宿松县趾凤乡、黄山市歙县雄村乡、阜阳市颍上县八里河镇、六安市金寨县天堂寨镇、宣城市泾县桃花潭镇、合肥市巢湖市黄麓镇洪疃村、淮北市烈山区烈山镇榴园村、安庆市潜山县官庄镇官庄村、黄山市黄山区甘棠镇庄里村、黄山市黟县宏村镇卢村、滁州市凤阳县小溪河镇小岗村、宿州市萧县白土镇费村、池州市贵池区梅村镇霄坑村、宣城市绩溪县上庄镇上庄村、宣城市宁国市云梯畲族乡千秋畲族村

十三、福建省（9个）

福州市永泰县嵩口镇、泉州市惠安县崇武镇、龙岩市上杭县才溪镇、宁德市福安市晓阳镇、宁德市福鼎市嵛山镇、福州市长乐市航城街道琴江村、三明市尤溪县洋中镇桂峰村、泉州市晋江市金井镇围头村、龙岩市武平县城厢镇云礤村

十四、江西省（8个）

南昌市湾里区太平镇、宜春市靖安县宝峰镇、赣州市南康区坪市乡谭邦村、赣州市赣县湖江镇夏浒村、赣州市赣县白鹭乡白鹭村、赣州市宁都县田埠乡东龙村、赣州市石城县琴江镇大畲村、上饶市婺源县江湾镇篁岭村

十五、山东省（14个）

济南市历城区柳埠镇、枣庄市山亭区店子镇、枣庄市山亭区北庄镇、潍坊市青州市庙子镇、潍坊市安丘市辉渠镇、济宁市微山县南阳镇、济宁市邹城市峄山镇、泰安市岱岳区满庄镇、泰安市东平县银山镇、威海市乳山市海阳所镇、日照市五莲县松柏镇、临沂市沂水县院东头镇、菏泽市单县浮岗镇、烟台市栖霞市桃村镇国路夼村

十六、河南省（16个）

郑州市登封县告成镇、洛阳市栾川县石庙镇、洛阳市汝阳县付店镇、平顶山市郏县姚庄回族乡、平顶山市舞钢市尹集镇、安阳市林州市石板岩乡、焦作市修武县岸上乡、南阳市南召县乔瑞镇、南阳市方城县二郎庙乡、信阳市新县田铺乡、济源市五龙口镇、驻马店市驿城区蚁蜂镇、洛阳市栾川县石庙镇杨树坪村、洛阳市栾川县栾川乡养子沟村、信阳市平桥区五里店街道郝堂村、信阳市罗山县涩港镇灵山村

十七、湖北省（14个）

宜昌市五峰土家族自治县长乐坪镇、鄂州市梁子湖区梁子镇、荆门市钟祥市客店镇、孝感市大悟县宣化店镇、黄冈市罗田区九资河镇、咸宁市赤壁市赤壁镇、随州市随县长岗镇、神农架林区大九湖镇、宜昌市兴山县水月寺镇高岚村、孝感市安陆市王义贞镇钱冲村、荆州市荆州区川店镇张新场村、咸宁市嘉鱼县官桥镇官桥村、随州市曾都区三里岗镇吉祥寺村、恩施土家族苗族自治州建始县花坪镇小西湖村

十八、湖南省（13个）

长沙市望城区铜官镇、长沙市宁乡县花明楼镇、长沙市浏阳市大围山镇、湘潭市湘乡市壶天镇、邵阳市城步苗族自治县南山镇、郴州市汝城县热水镇、郴州市资兴市黄草镇、长沙市望城区白箬铺镇光明村、长沙市长沙县白沙镇双冲村、邵阳市邵东县堡面前乡大羊村、岳阳市岳阳县张谷英镇张谷英村、常德市石门县罗坪乡长梯隘村、益阳市安化县江南镇高城村

十九、广东省（15个）

广州市增城区派潭镇、汕头市潮阳区海门镇、佛山市南海区西樵镇、梅州市大埔县百侯镇、梅州市丰顺县八乡山镇、东莞市清溪镇、广州市番禺区石楼镇大岭村、珠海市香洲区万山镇万山村、佛山市南海区西樵镇上金瓯松塘村、江门市新会区会城镇新会陈皮村（茶坑村）、江门市开平市塘口镇自力村、惠州市博罗县龙华镇旭日村、河源市和平县林寨镇林寨古村（兴井村）、清远市连南瑶族自治县三排镇南岗古排、云浮市郁南县连滩镇兰寨村

二十、广西壮族自治区（11个）

河池市宜州市刘三姐乡、崇左市大新县硕龙镇、柳州市融水苗族自治县香粉乡雨卜村、桂林市兴安县华江瑶族乡高寨村、桂林市灌阳县新圩乡小龙村、桂林市恭城瑶族自治县平安乡社山村、梧州市岑溪市南渡镇吉太社区三江口自然村、防城港市港口区企沙镇簕山村、百色市乐业县同乐镇火卖村、来宾市武宣县东乡镇下莲塘村、来宾市金秀瑶族自治县长垌乡古占民俗旅游村

二十一、海南省（5个）

琼海市中原镇、琼海市博鳌镇、琼海市潭门镇、保亭黎族苗族自治县三道镇什进村、琼中黎族苗族自治县红毛镇什寒村

二十二、重庆市（12个）

万州区甘宁镇、涪陵区武陵山乡、九龙坡区白市驿镇、綦江区黑山镇、巴南区东温泉镇、长寿区长寿湖镇、武隆县仙女山镇、万州区太安镇凤凰村、綦江区永新镇石坪村、渝北区统景镇印盒村、巫溪县文峰镇红池村、彭水苗族土家族自治县绍庆街道阿依河村

二十三、四川省（9个）

泸州市纳溪区天仙镇、泸州市古蔺县太平镇、德阳市绵竹市九龙镇、广元市剑阁县剑门关镇、内江市隆昌县云顶镇、南充市西充县青龙乡、乐山市沐川县沐溪镇三溪村、眉山市丹棱县顺龙乡幸福村、阿坝藏族羌族自治州小金县沃日乡官寨村

二十四、贵州省（18个）

贵阳市花溪区青岩镇、六盘水市盘县城关镇、安顺市西秀区旧州镇、安顺市平坝县天龙镇、毕节市大方县普底彝族苗族白族乡、毕节市威宁彝族回族苗族自治县板底乡、黔西南布依族苗族自治州普安县龙吟镇、黔东南苗族侗族自治州黄平县旧州镇、六盘水市盘县石桥镇妥乐村、六盘水市盘县四格彝族乡坡上村、毕节市威宁彝族回族苗族自治县石门乡石门坎村、铜仁市碧江区漾头镇九龙村、铜仁市江口县太平镇云舍村、铜仁市松桃苗族自治县乌罗镇桃花源村、黔东南苗族侗族自治州从江县丙妹镇岜沙村、黔南布依族苗族自治州三都水族自治县三合镇姑鲁村、黔南布依族苗族自治州三都水族自治县都江镇怎雷村、黔南布依族苗族自治州三都水族自治县九阡镇水各村

二十五、云南省（9个）

丽江市玉龙纳西族自治县石鼓镇、普洱市镇沅彝族哈尼族拉祜族自治县九甲镇、楚雄彝族自治州大姚县石羊镇、红河哈尼族彝族自治州红河县迤萨镇、普洱市宁洱哈尼族彝族自治县同心镇那柯里村、临沧市沧源佤族自治县勐角傣族彝族拉祜族乡翁丁村、文山壮族苗族自治州广南县坝美镇者歪村委会坝美村小组、大理白族自治州宾川县平川镇朱苦拉村、大理白族自治州鹤庆县草海镇新华村

二十六、西藏自治区（1个）

拉萨市尼木县吞巴乡吞达村

二十七、陕西省（6个）

咸阳市永寿县永平镇、咸阳市彬县太峪镇、咸阳市武功县武功镇、榆林市绥德县名州镇、安康市岚皋县花里镇、安康市旬阳县蜀河镇

二十八、甘肃省（9个）

兰州市皋兰县什川镇、武威市天祝藏族自治县天堂镇、平凉市崆峒区崆峒镇、平凉市华亭县西华镇、平凉市庄浪县韩店镇、酒泉市肃州区果园乡、酒泉市瓜州县锁阳城镇、酒泉市敦煌市月牙泉镇、平凉市灵台县独店镇张鳌坡村

二十九、青海省（9个）

西宁市大通回族土族自治县桥头镇、海东市互助土族自治县加定镇、海北藏族自治州祁连县八宝镇、海南藏族自治州贵德县河阴镇、西宁市湟源县东峡乡下脖项村、海东市循化撒拉族自治县街子镇三兰巴海村、黄南藏族自治州尖扎县坎布拉镇直岗拉卡村、果洛藏族自治州班玛县灯塔乡班前村、玉树藏族自治州称多县拉布乡拉司通村

三十、宁夏回族自治区（11个）

银川市兴庆区掌政镇、银川市西夏区镇北堡镇、吴忠市青铜峡市青铜峡镇、吴忠市青铜峡市峡口镇、固原市泾源县泾河源镇、固原市泾源县六盘山镇、中卫市沙坡头区迎水桥镇、吴忠市利通区东塔寺乡穆民新村、固原市隆德县城关镇杨店村、中卫市沙坡头区迎水桥镇北长滩村、中卫市沙坡头区香山乡南长滩村

三十一、新疆维吾尔自治区（3个）

昌吉州木垒县西吉尔镇、阿勒泰地区布尔津县冲乎尔镇、阿勒泰地区布尔津县禾木哈纳斯蒙古民族乡禾木村

三十二、新疆生产建设兵团（6个）

第五师84团托里镇、第八师石河子市150团西古城镇、第十师北屯市187团丰庆镇、第十二师西山农场烽火台小镇、第六师五家渠市103团蔡家湖镇、第十三师黄田农场庙尔沟镇

（数据整理：廖远涛，广州市城市规划勘测设计研究院城市与建筑设计所副所长，高级工程师；雷轩，广州市城市规划勘测设计研究院）

编后语

2015 年，是中华民族走向复兴的历史征程中不寻常的一年，是大有作为的一年。

2015 年，中共十八届五中全会针对中国经济转型时期面临的种种问题，提出了“创新、协调、绿色、开放、共享”这五大重要发展理念。

2015 年，面对错综复杂的国际形势和不断加大的国内外经济下行压力，经过全国人民共同努力，“十二五”规划圆满收官，“一带一路”建设取得实质性进展，亚洲基础设施投资银行正式成立，丝路基金投入运营，人民币纳入国际货币基金组织特别提款权货币篮子，中国经济增长继续居于世界前列。

2015 年 12 月，中央城市工作会议在北京举行。会议指出，城市工作是一个系统工程。做好城市工作，要顺应城市工作新形势、改革发展新要求、人民群众新期待，坚持以人民为中心的发展思想，坚持人民城市为人民。这是我们做好城市工作的出发点和落脚点。会议要求，城市工作要把创造优良人居环境作为中心目标，努力把城市建设成为人与人、人与自然和谐共处的美丽家园。

《中国城市发展报告（2015 年卷）》面世了。它记录了上述不寻常一年在城市发展中的轨迹，反映了城市发展中的成就和尚需进一步解决的短板，为读者了解我国一年来城市发展的全貌提供了可靠的信息。《中国城市发展报告（2015 年卷）》在结构上延续了原有的框架，包含综论篇、论坛篇、观察篇、专题篇、案例篇和附录篇六部分。约请了全国人大常委会原副委员长、国际欧亚科学院执行院长、国际欧亚科学院中国科学中心主席蒋正华院士和住房和城乡建设部部长、中国市长协会执行会长陈政高先生分别为本卷撰写了序言一和序言二。

综论篇包括 7 篇文章，对 2015 年中国城市发展作了全面综述（中、英文），回顾了本年度城市发展的 10 大事件，并就城市交通建设、城市基础设施、城市信息化和智慧城市建设进展等主题作了年度发展状况的综述。

论坛篇约请清华大学吴良镛院士、住建部原副部长仇保兴教授等就城乡规划、智慧城市、城市幸福感和城市服务业发展等问题发表了具有指导性的论述和评论。

观察篇含有6篇文章，围绕社会舆情观察、海绵城市、珠三角城市群的产业转型变革、产业发展空间布局态势，海南省海澄文一体化的保障机制，以及建筑能效公示对降低能耗的作用等专题，专家们从不同角度观察，提出了问题和改进的建议。

专题篇紧扣年度城市发展的热点，特别是在新常态下，城市的创新发展模式、空间格局、发展趋势与途径等作了多方论述，并就城市发展中目前亟待解决的养老服务、户籍制度等作了专题分析。

案例篇以城市发展惠及民生为主题，选择了成都、阜新、长沙板仓小镇、南京、杭州和宁波等为例，从管理服务、民生建设、法治化考评、发展成果共享等多角度，考察公众生活得到的实惠，以及它们对公众生活幸福感的影响效果。

附录篇从三方面反映年度城市发展的实绩：一方面是年度城市规划发展大事记和政策法规的颁布与实施；另一方面是城市的基本数据，这是认识城市一个最根本的依据；再一方面是有关城市人居环境、历史文化街区、湿地公园和特色景观游名镇名村名录，它显示了城市绿色发展与人居环境优化的进步。

2015年是国际欧亚科学院中国科学中心和中国市长协会携手合作编制出版《中国城市发展报告》的第11年。前10年（2005－2014年），我们紧密合作，认真做好年度性的《报告》，忠实反映了我国城市发展的历程，为读者提供了一份十分有用的城市发展变化的记录，从而赢得了读者的信任与赞誉。在第二个十年开始的时候，我们将更加努力探索创新，把《中国城市发展报告》办成为国家、社会和公众生活在城市发展方面不可或缺的年度性报告，并大力促进国际与地区的交流，共同发展。

《中国城市发展报告》信息源多，涉及面广，并受人员能力的限制，疏漏之处在所难免。恳请城市的领导、专家学者、各界读者不吝赐教，帮助我们改进提高。

戴　逢

2016年4月

（作者：戴逢，国际欧亚科学院中国科学中心城市科学部副主任，国际欧亚科学院院士）